Covers HTML 4 and Dynamic HTML

Everything You Need to Create
Professional-Looking Web Pages

HTML
Publishing
on the Internet

Second Edition

CD-ROM

D1314707

ALL PLATFORMS

Brent Heslop
David Holzgang

CORIOLIS
VENTANA

The Coriolis Group, Inc.
An International Thomson Publishing Company
14455 N. Hayden Road, Suite 220
Scottsdale, AZ 85260

602/483-0192
FAX 602/483-0193
http://www.coriolis.com

Library of Congress Cataloging-in-Publication Data
Heslop, Brent D.
HTML publishing on the Internet / Brent Heslop. – 2nd ed.
p. cm.
Rev. ed. of : HTML publishing on the Internet for Macintosh, 1995
   and HTML publishing on the Internet for Windows, 1995
ISBN 1-56604-625-4
1. Hypertext systems. 2. HTML (Document markup language)
I. Heslop, Brent D. HTML publishing on the Internet for Macintosh.
II. Heslop, Brent D. HTML publishing on the Internet for Windows.
III. Holzgang, David.
IV. Title
QA76.76.H94H48 1997
005.7'2—dc21   97-13769
                                                   CIP

Printed in the United States of America
10 9 8 7 6 5 4 3 2 1

President
Michael E. Moran

Associate Publisher
Robert Kern

Editorial Operations Manager
Kerry L. B. Foster

Production Manager
Jaimie Livingston

Brand Manager
Jamie Jaeger Fiocco

Art Director
Marcia Webb

Creative Services Manager
Diane Lennox

Acquisitions Editor
Neweleen Trebnik

Project Editor
Jennifer H. Mario

Development Editor
Linda Orlando

Copy Editor
Judy Flynn

CD-ROM Specialist
Ginny Phelps

Technical Reviewer
Russ Mullen

Desktop Publishers
Scott Hosa
Kristin Miller

Proofreaders
Alicia Farris
Jessica Ryan

Indexer
Dick Evans

Interior Designer
Patrick Berry

Cover Illustrator
Lisa Gill

About the Authors

Brent D. Heslop has co-authored more than 15 books on a wide range of computer topics. He teaches classes on HTML and interactive World Wide Web programming for the University of California, Santa Cruz and also teaches corporate seminars. He is a partner in Bookware, a technical communications firm with offices on the East and West coasts. Brent has written for numerous computer-related magazines, such as *PC Magazine* and *NetGuide*. He lives in Mountain View, California, with his lovely wife Kim and their devoted dog Cassius.

David A. Holzgang is a recognized authority on automated text and document handling and printing in distributed systems. He is the author of many leading books on programming, desktop publishing, and graphics. David is the founder and managing general partner of the Cheshire Group, which is a software development and consulting organization. The Cheshire Group specializes in graphics and graphics programming and has developed programs and presentation material in both the IBM and Macintosh environments. He lives and works in the San Francisco Bay area.

Acknowledgments

No one person can tackle as fast changing a topic as publishing on the Internet. Numerous people supplied us with valuable information for which we are extremely grateful. First and foremost we want to thank Bob Kern at Ventana Communications and our agent, Matt Wagner, at Waterside Productions for helping make this second edition a reality. A few people we want to thank in particular for their research and contributions to this book are Alan Trow-Poole for applying his masterful hand at many of the graphics used in this book. Alan owns and operates Lichfield Graphics (http://www.lichfieldgraphics.com), a Graphics design firm in San Jose, California. Alan spent countless hours creating the graphics used for this book and for the Web site that accompanies this book. Always enthusiastic and helpful, he also acted as our graphics guru providing valuable input for Chapter 6, "Getting Graphic With Images," and Chapter 7, "Editing & Optimizing Images." We are also greatly indebted to Stuart Harris, Gayle Kidder, Allen Wyke, and Stephanie Cottrell. Allen helped us with Chapter 9, "Getting Interactive With Forms, CGI & Perl." Stuart Harris and Gayle Kidder helped write Chapter 11, "Interactive Pages & Scripting," and wrote Chapter 12, "Dynamic HTML." Stephanie helped us complete this project by updating Chapter 13, "Web Servers at Your Service" and the Resource Guide. We would also like to thank Frank Mullin of IMagic in Santa Monica (http://www.prestidigitator.com) for his expert help in preparing the chapter on Multimedia. We also want to thank Dawn Merry, David Angell, and Jan Weingarten for their help and comments about the book's content.

Essential to writing a book on publishing on the Internet is an Internet connection. We are in debt to Rich White and Best Internet Communications for letting us use their services to test the examples in this book and publish the Authors Web site (http://www.authors.com) that is constantly being updated to support the readers of this book. We also want to thank Larry Sherman at Best for his technical support during this project.

Many thanks to Ginny Phelps at Ventana Communications, who was instrumental in setting up the Companion CD-ROM, and all the companies and individuals that let us include their software on the Companion CD-ROM. There are a few companies we would like to thank in particular. We were overjoyed that O'Reilly and Associates let us include the WebSite server. We are grateful to Tammy Wing at Image Club Graphics, Inc., Roger Bloxberg at Nova Development, and Adam Flick at PhotoDisk for letting us include some impressive clip art and digital photos. On the subject of graphics we are also indebted to Jonathan Ort at JASC for letting us include Paint Shop Pro, a powerful graphics editor. Jon was a fountain of information on working with graphics on the Web. Thanks to Todd Wilson for letting us include his Map

This program, which is sure to save users time creating image maps. Thanks to Chris Craig for letting us include his GoldWave sound editor. Thanks also to Rebecca Michals for letting us include Adobe Acrobat Reader. We also want to express our thanks to Dan Baumbach at Canyon Software for letting us use his company for some of the examples in this book and letting us include Drag And File, Drag And Zip, and Drag And View.

Numerous other companies gave us information and products related to Internet publishing. In particular we would like to thank Michelle Seibel at Intel for letting us use the Intel Smart Video Recorder Pro for the video editing chapter. There are a few people that we would like to thank at Adobe: Peter Card for his help with Adobe Photoshop and Premiere, Jill Nakashima for Adobe Illustrator, and Rebecca Michals for her help with Adobe Acrobat products. We want to extend our gratitude to McLean Public Relations, specifically Jill Ryan for help with Ulead Systems PhotoImpact and Media Studio Pro. Thanks to Terri Campbell at MetaCreations for Painter and RayDream Studio 5. Doug Frohman at Digital Frontiers was extremely helpful by supplying us with updated versions of the impressive HVS JPEG and HVS color Photoshop plug-ins. At Auto F/X we want to thank Shayne Jolie for sending us WebVise Totality. Thanks also to Suzanne Porta and Steve Cherneff at Macromedia for Director and Flash and their valuable input.

Additionally we want to thank Scott Hosa, Caroline McKenzie, and Kristin Miller at Ventana who worked on the production of this book. We want to thank Jennifer Mario, Judy Flynn, Russ Mullen, and Linda Orlando, our editors, who offered valuable insight and guidance to help improve this book. Jennifer went beyond the call of duty in order to help us keep the book as up-to-date as possible by making numerous last-minute changes. Last but not least, we want to thank our wives Kim Merry and Shirley Grant for supporting us through this entire project.

Contents

Introduction

Everyone wants to get published on the Internet, and why not? Publishing on the Internet is one of the most important and exciting happenings in computing since the launching of the PC revolution back in the early '80s. This book focuses on the most effective and by far the most popular Internet publishing method, publishing on the World Wide Web using HTML and HTTP.

Who Needs This Book?

Any person interested in how to publish pages on the World Wide Web will find the answers in this guide. Even if you don't want to create the pages yourself, this book offers helpful information as to what you need to do to have someone publish Web pages for you. Knowing how Web publishing works can save you time and money. Many services charge over $100 an hour to create Web pages. So if you're interested in creating a presence for yourself or your company on the Internet, this book will step you through the entire Web publishing process.

This book is written for the new user as well as the seasoned Web surfer. If you are already familiar with HTML, you'll find that it includes numerous Web design tips, powerful Web publishing tools, and a valuable HTML reference. If you're not familiar with the Web, the first part of the book gives a concise introduction to the Web and hypermedia publishing.

What's Inside?

The book is divided into fourteen chapters and four appendices. The following gives a brief description of the main topics covered in each of the chapters and the appendices.

Chapter 1, "The World Wide Web & Hypermedia Publishing," introduces you to Internet jargon and provides a broad overview of publishing on the Internet.

Chapter 2, "Designing & Structuring Your Web Site," provides a short introduction to structuring and designing effective hypertext documents.

Chapter 3, "Creating & Editing HTML Documents," is a hands-on guide to creating a home page, the cornerstone of your Web site. It also introduces you to the many possibilities for creating and formatting text using HTML.

Chapter 4, "The Art of Linking," shows you how to exploit the power of links to publish complex Web documents and connect to files and other Web documents around the world.

Chapter 5, "Tables, Columns & Frames," teaches you how to present tabular data using tables. It also shows how you can use tables, columns, and frames to lay out text on a page.

Chapter 6, "Getting Graphic With Images," explains the fundamental image file formats and shows you how to include and align images.

Chapter 7, "Editing & Optimizing Images," introduces image editors and optimization tools and shows you essential image editing concepts and techniques for creating and optimizing images. It also shows you how to create animated images and image maps.

Chapter 8, "Style Sheets," explains how to use cascading style sheets to modify the formatting of your pages. It shows you how you can use style sheets to specify margins, indents, fonts, and control background images for all the pages at a site by modifying a single file.

Chapter 9, "Getting Interactive With Forms, CGI & Perl," gives step-by-step instructions for creating forms and using the Common Gateway Interface to publish interactive documents.

Chapter 10, "Adding Scintillating Sound & Vivid Video," takes a look at publishing multimedia files, both sound and video, on the Internet.

Chapter 11, "Interactive Pages & Scripting," explains the difference between Web-related programming languages and shows you how to add Java applets, JavaScript programs, and VRML worlds to your pages. The chapter also gives you a crash course in JavaScript and shares examples of some common JavaScript programs.

Chapter 12, "Dynamic HTML," explains the difference between Microsoft and Netscape's document object model (DOM). It shows how, using scripting languages with a DOM, you can precisely position and layer page elements and control how page elements interact with users. It also covers Netscape's dynamic fonts and Microsoft's font embedding technologies.

Chapter 13, "Web Servers at Your Service," explains the different Web publishing alternatives, including using a service provider, server service, or setting up a Web server and publishing Web documents from your own PC.

Chapter 14, "XML & Metadata: The Future of Web Publishing," explains how the Extensible Markup Language (XML) will change Web publishing by letting you create your own document type definition (DTD) and create your own custom tags. It also takes a look at how metadata can be used to identify the content of your Web pages.

In the appendices you'll find an annotated HTML and cascading style sheet reference section that includes HTML tags, extensions to HTML, and a listing of commonly used styles. Each HTML tag and style sheet entry includes the standard syntax and cross-references to similar or associated HTML tags and extensions. Also included is a descriptive listing of the contents on the CD-ROM accompanying this book and a comprehensive resource listing of Internet publishing-related programs and periodicals.

About This Book's Companion Site

Many of the examples in this book are available online at the Authors site at http://www.authors.com. The Authors site includes numerous HTML and interactive World Wide Web programming tutorials to aid in your understanding of HTML authoring, programming, and publishing on the World Wide Web. It also provides you with links to the resources and utilities you need to accomplish these tasks. So you can just click on the hypertext reference to jump directly to the Web publishing topic or resource in which you are interested.

Keeping up with Web publishing is a never-ending task. The Authors site is continually being updated to augment the material in this book. As this book went to press, HTML 4.0 and cascading style sheets were still in the review process. We highly recommend that you check the Authors site for updates to these emerging standards and other new Web publishing related topics.

What You Need

Other than an Internet connection, this book includes all you need to get started publishing on the World Wide Web. The Companion CD-ROM includes several of the Web-related applications and Web publishing tools. See Appendix A, "About the Companion CD-ROM," for a complete listing of the CD's contents.

As we mentioned, at the rate things are changing on the Internet, it's nearly impossible to provide information that is 100 percent up-to-date. If you find something we've missed or if you have any comments about this book, we would appreciate hearing from you. Please send us e-mail at either of the following addresses:

Brent Heslop
bheslop@bookware.com

David Holzgang
cheshire@sonic.net

chapter 1

The World Wide Web & Hypermedia Publishing

In today's fast-moving, competitive, global business environment, it is crucial for current information to be available to the consumer who needs it. Just as Johannes Gutenberg's invention of the printing press advanced the economy and commerce, politics, society, literature, and ideological changes that marked the beginning of the Renaissance, the World Wide Web is changing the publishing world by making it possible for anyone to publish information to people around the world.

The World Wide Web is growing at an astounding rate, bringing together hypertext, multimedia, and global networking to usher in the next generation of publishing. The Web lets you quickly publish marketing, customer service, and research information from a central location. The Web is also a great forum for personal expression and sharing ideas and topics of interest with others around the world. This chapter introduces the World Wide Web, explains how Web publishing works, and gives an overview of Web publishing options.

What Is the World Wide Web?

Tim Berners-Lee started the World Wide Web project in 1989 at the CERN high-energy physics laboratory. The goal of the project was to find a way to share research and ideas with other employees and researchers scattered around the world. In its initial proposal, the Web was called "a hypertext project." *Hypertext* is a term coined by Ted Nelson back in the '60s that refers to text containing connections to other documents; the reader can click a word or phrase to get additional information about a related topic. *Hypermedia* is a broader term for documents that include information in multimedia formats, such as sound and video.

Technically speaking, the World Wide Web refers to the abstract cyberspace of information. The Internet typically refers to the physical side of the network—that is, the hardware consisting of cables and computers. The foundation of the Internet and the World Wide Web is the use of *protocols*, the language and rules by which the computers communicate. For example, Transmission Control Protocol/Internet Protocol (TCP/IP), the underlying protocol of the Internet, is a set of networking protocols that lets different types of computers communicate. The World Wide Web does not just use one type of protocol. Like a puzzle, the Web connects several protocols together, including File Transfer Protocol (FTP), Telnet, Wide Area Information Servers (WAIS), and more. Figure 1-1 shows the protocols that are used to share information. Because the World Wide Web uses the standard Internet protocols to transmit files and documents, *the Web* is often used as a synonym for *the Internet*, referring to the collective network of computers as well as the body of information.

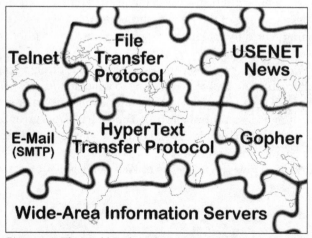

Figure 1-1: The World Wide Web includes several Internet protocols, including FTP, Telnet, WAIS, and more.

Demographics of the Web

The release of the Mosaic Web browser, a Web client used to request and receive information from a Web server, by the National Center for Supercomputing Applications (NCSA) in November 1992 marked the beginning of the Web's popularity. At the beginning of 1993, there were only 130 sites that provided content for the World Wide Web; less than half a year after the introduction of Mosaic, there were over 10,000 servers. And the growth continues! In January 1997, the Netcraft Web Server Survey found more than 646,000 servers attached to the World Wide Web. In October 1997, the same survey found 1,466,906 servers; a growth rate of over 227 percent in 10 months.

Using a survey-based approach, in October 1995 Matrix Information and Directory Services (MIDS) and Texas Internet Consulting (TIC) sent their third demographic questionnaire by electronic mail to most of the domains representing organizations on the Internet and received responses from over 1,000 organizations. From the results of the survey they estimated that there are "39 million users of electronic mail as of October 1995" and "26.4 million users of 10.1 million computers that can access information by interactive TCP/IP services such as Web (HTTP) servers or FTP."

▼ Who's Counting?

There are multiple sources of information about the current size and composition of the Web. A good place to start is CyberAtlas (http://www.cyberatlas.com), which provides a wide variety of marketing and demographic statistics on the Web, including summaries of results from major surveys.

Besides CyberAtlas, we've used three resources for this short summary of the current status of the Web. The Netcraft Web Server Survey (http://www.netcraft.co.uk/Survey/) provides a look at servers around the world on a monthly basis. Matrix Information and Directory Services (http://www.mids.org) publishes a wide variety of information about the composition, content, and users of the Internet and other networks. Finally, Matthew Gray of MIT provides a good source of historical data in his Web Growth and Internet Growth summaries (http://www.mit.edu/people/mkgray/net/).

How Web Publishing Works

Web publishing works on the client/server model. A *Web server* is a program running on a computer that is set up to serve documents to other computers that send requests for the documents. A *Web client*, also commonly called a *browser*, is a program that lets the user request documents from a server. The server operates only when a document is requested by a client. The client requests the document; the request opens a connection to the server; upon receiving the request, the server sends the document and closes the connection. Closing the connection after each request is an efficient way to share documents because each transaction requires only a small amount of the server's resources. For example, a Windows NT or Macintosh server can serve up Web documents to over 200 clients connected at one time. Figure 1-2 shows an example of the client/server process of requesting and delivering Web documents.

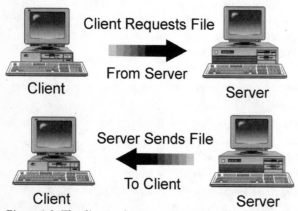

Figure 1-2: The client and server connection.

▼ **Browsers & User Agents**

When you read official Web documents, or when you read the more technical articles about the Web, you may come across the term *user agent*, abbreviated UA. A user agent is any form of client software used with World Wide Web documents. Normally, of course, this will be a browser, but the Web was designed from the beginning to accommodate other types of software as well. For the sight-impaired, for example, the user agent software might be a program that reads back the pages found on the Web. The term *user agent*, then, is a way to describe such client software without suggesting that it must display pages.

What Is a Web Browser?

A Web browser connects to a computer specified by a network address, called a *Uniform Resource Locator* (URL). The browser (via the user) sends a request to that computer's Web server for a *Web document*, and the server responds by sending the requested Web document to the user's computer. A Web document is written in *HyperText Markup Language* (HTML) and can contain text and any other media (pictures, sounds, animations, or movies) referenced by a *hypertext link*. A Web document lets the reader click on a hypertext word or phrase to access files or to display other HTML documents. These hypertext links between files and documents from servers around the world make the system work as if it were one huge web of information.

The best-known browsers are the Microsoft Internet Explorer family of browsers and the Netscape Communications family of Netscape Navigator browsers for UNIX, Windows, Macintosh OS/2, and Amiga computers. There are also a variety of other browsers available, many based on improvements and modifications to the original NCSA Mosaic family of browsers. In addition, text-based browsers, such as Lynx and Emacs-W3, are available for terminals such as the VT100, which cannot display graphics.

The appearance of a document will vary from one browser to the next according to the document structure, the capabilities of each system, and the user's preferences. Because there are different browsers, it's important to write and publish documents that will look good on any browser and not just the specific browser you have access to. Later in this chapter we'll discuss some of the important issues that you must take into account if you want your pages to look good in multiple browsers.

What Is a URL?

Web browsers allow you to specify a Uniform Resource Locator (URL) and connect to a document or resource. When you click on a hypertext link in a Web document, you are actually sending a request to open a URL. It's possible to represent nearly any file or service on the Internet with a URL. A Web browser can also act as an FTP, Gopher, and Telnet client. Hypertext links then can be made not only to other Web documents and media, but also to other network services. You can access different resources by using different types of URLs. Figure 1-3 shows the structure of a URL.

Figure 1-3: The structure of a URL.

Notice that the first part of the URL (before the slashes) specifies the method of access. The second part is typically the address of the computer where the data or service is located. Further parts may specify the names of files, the port to connect to, or the text to search for in a database. Table 1-1 lists some of the most common examples of URLs for accessing different resources.

Resource	URL
HTTP	http://home.netscape.com/
FTP	ftp://ftp.microsoft.com/
Gopher	gopher://gopher.micro.umn.edu:70/
Telnet	telnet://rs.internic.net
Usenet news	news:comp.infosystems.www.announce

Table 1-1: URLs for Internet resources.

What Is an HTTP Server?

The language Web clients and servers use to communicate with each other is called *HyperText Transfer Protocol* (HTTP). All Web clients and servers must be able to "speak" HTTP in order to send and receive hypermedia documents. The success of the Web is due partly to HTTP's ability to handle multiple application protocols that allow users access to many Internet protocols, such as anonymous FTP, Gopher, and WAIS data servers. HTTP also supports the retrieval and display of text, graphics, and animation, and the playback of sound. Because HTTP is the foundation for most Web transactions, Web servers are often called HTTP servers.

Although HTTP servers are primarily run on the UNIX platform, they are available for many platforms and environments, including Windows, Windows NT, Macintosh, VM, and VMS. The domination of the Internet by UNIX servers is likely to change slowly as other fast, secure, and robust operating systems are introduced for other platforms.

Which operating system and Web server you use to publish your Web documents depends largely on the operating system or systems that your Internet Service Provider (ISP) will support, your requirements for reliability, the number of users you want to support, and your familiarity with the operation of the system. If you want to make your documents available to all the users on the Internet, you'll need to publish your Web documents on a multitasking operating system that can handle more than one user at a time. Chapter 13, "Web Servers at Your Service," explains how to use a full-time connection offered by an ISP or a server service to publish Web documents. It also gives advice on setting up your own HTTP server to publish Web documents using any of the popular server packages.

Almost all HTTP transactions are transparent to the person reading your documents. The person typically sees only the requested HTML document in the browser window. The only time a user will see anything of the HTTP protocol is when, for example, the server cannot access a requested document and the user sees an HTTP error message. The next section takes a look at the HTML side of the Web publishing coin by exploring its history, the different versions of HTML, and extensions to HTML.

The HTML Standard & Extensions

The standard language the Web uses for creating and recognizing hypermedia documents is HTML. Until the advent of Mosaic, the Internet was a multi-platform environment that made interchanging documents somewhat difficult. A special language called Standard Generalized Markup Language (SGML) was invented as a solution to the problems of sharing documents. SGML focuses on the structural elements in a document, so the recipient of information is freed from the layout choices of the author. For example, you may want headings and paragraph text to appear in a larger size font than the author specified. SGML documents let you change display and print options for best presentation on your system without losing the essential layout that the author provided.

HTML was derived from SGML as a simple nonproprietary delivery format for hypertext. Like SGML, HTML provides a common method of authoring and format conversion. HTML is fairly new and the language itself is easy to master. Web documents are typically written in HTML and the document files are usually named with the extension .html or .htm. These HTML documents are nothing more than standard ASCII files with formatting codes, commonly called *tags*, that contain information about layout, such as text styles, document titles, paragraphs, lists, and hypertext links.

The Four Versions of HTML & HTML Extensions _____

HTML is called a *markup language*. The description of the markup language is called a *Document Type Definition*, or DTD. The current HTML DTD supports basic hypermedia document creation and layout. There are four versions of HTML DTDs. HTML 1.0 was created primarily with specifications for creating hypertext links. It was replaced by HTML 2.0, the standard ratified by the Internet Engineering Task Force (IETF). The IETF is an open, international community of professionals dedicated to protocol engineering and development of the Internet. HTML 2.0 specifications define features that let users display inline images and use interactive forms.

Version 3.0 did not incorporate many of the latest HTML tags that were being created by browser vendors. Version 3.0—also called HTML+—consisted of so many additions to HTML that the standard could not be ratified. In June 1995, version 3.0 expired, and by May 1996, a draft for version 3.2 emerged to include only the most popular extensions to HTML.

The current approved version of HTML is version 3.2, which incorporates many of the HTML extensions, enhancements that have been developed by Netscape, Microsoft, and others. In particular, HTML 3.2 adds tags that support widely deployed features, such as tables, applets, and text flow around images, while providing full backward compatibility with the existing HTML 2.0 standard. The next section takes a look at HTML and the HTML 3.2 standard.

The Web moves fast, and most Web authors are always looking for new possibilities. As a result, the World Wide Web Consortium is already working on HTML 4.0. The specification for HTML 4.0 is currently being reviewed. This is a much-expanded version of HTML that incorporates many new features, including new features to handle multiple languages and features to improve access for the handicapped. It also includes most of the extensions that have been put in place by the most popular browsers. Of these, the most important is Cascading Style Sheets. Because the specification is still in draft and is not yet fully implemented by any popular browser, it isn't possible to give working examples of all the new tags and features. However, we will cover style sheets and other 4.0 tags where the current generation of browsers supports them. We have also noted in the text where the new tags will have an impact on your HTML coding; for example, where there are new tags that supercede old ones.

▼ The Last Word on HTML

The World Wide Web Consortium, commonly referred to as W3C, was founded in 1994 to develop common protocols for the evolution of the World Wide Web. The current HTML 3.2 Reference Specification is available from the W3C in ASCII text format at http://www.w3.org/pub/WWW/TR/PR-html32-961105.

A complete reference for all the HTML 3.2 tags and many current HTML extensions is provided in "bare bones" text format by Kevin Werbach at http://werbach.com/barebones/.

A list of all Netscape extensions to HTML, showing which version of Netscape introduced each tag, is provided at http://developer.netscape.com/library/documentation/htmlguid/index.htm. Note, however, that many of the extensions created by Netscape for early versions of their browser are included in the HTML 3.2 specification.

A complete reference to HTML, including all the Microsoft extensions, is available at http://www.microsoft.com/workshop/author/newhtml/. This reference, however, does not indicate which tags and attributes are specifically Microsoft's and which are standard HTML. If you use this document, use the HTML 3.2 Reference Specification as a cross-reference to ensure that your HTML will work on most platforms and with most browsers.

Finally, the new HTML 4.0 draft specification is available from the W3C at http://www.w3.org/TR/WD-html40-970917/.

Elements of HTML

When you compare HTML documents to those created with word processors and desktop publishing programs, you can see that HTML is a fairly limited formatting language. HTML includes markup elements for headers, paragraphs, various types of character formatting, inline images, hypertext links, lists, preformatted text, and a simple search facility. What HTML doesn't do is let you specify margins, indents, tabs, and exact placement of images and text. These major formatting omissions are being addressed by the addition of Cascading Style Sheets, a feature that is not a part of the 3.2 standard.

As of this writing, HTML 3.2 has just received its final approval, and most browsers already support HTML 3.2 features, such as tables, for example. HTML 3.2 also supports inclusion of small Java programs called *applets* and script languages such as Netscape's JavaScript or Microsoft's version called

JScript. For instance, by adding a Java applet or a script to an HTML page, you can add a variety of programmed actions, such as animating a display, changing the page in response to movement of a cursor, and so on. More layout and formatting options, such as text flow around floating images, styles, figures, and tables, are being added. HTML 3.2 additionally allows arbitrary nesting of the various kinds of lists, and list items can now include horizontal rules. HTML 3.2 also adds additional tags for Web information-searching programs. And many browsers now support some of the new HTML 4.0 tags, like Cascading Style Sheets.

The Fallacy of HTML Programming

Note that HTML is a markup language, not a programming language. Many people incorrectly say that they are "programming" in HTML when they are marking up pages for display. The HTML markup language has no statements that allow you to change the sequence of action or execution, which are essential to a programming language. The idea of a program is that the computer takes different actions depending on some external set of information—which may be user actions, like mouse clicks or menu selections, or may be data supplied by some external source. In any case, an HTML page cannot change based on user actions without adding some form of programming language, such as Java or JavaScript, to the HTML markup tags.

The Netscape/Microsoft Browser Battle

The client/server model that the Web uses for presentation of information is very powerful. As the Internet expands, many observers feel that it will become the next major focus of application development and information distribution, rivaling the original impact of the personal computer on how we all work and play. The availability of information over a worldwide, platform-independent network radically changes how software will work in the future. The client/server interaction allows information to be organized, distributed, and presented in new and exciting ways. As a result, new software applications may replace or radically modify existing work patterns.

Netscape Communications, whose Netscape Navigator browser is the dominant browser on the World Wide Web, has continued to press forward with these ideas. Netscape has moved quickly and repeatedly to extend and enhance its browser to allow developers and users to get the maximum advantage from this new technology. As a result, Netscape Navigator is the browser standard that most Web developers use as a benchmark for how their documents will look and act on the Web. Netscape has moved to position the Internet at the heart of every computer user's daily work.

This obviously represents a real challenge to existing software companies. Microsoft, as the dominant software purveyor for personal computers, has responded to the challenge of the Internet by making major changes in its software development approach and operating system strategy. As part of this response, Microsoft has developed a browser, called Internet Explorer, that rivals Navigator in both features and ease of use. Starting from nothing, Internet Explorer has become a strong second in the browser marketplace.

As the old joke goes, there's good news and bad news for Web developers and users in this rivalry. The bad news is that you need to work at keeping up with the latest features and advances in Web technology, which come along with remarkable frequency and often cause major changes in how pages are laid out and displayed. The good news, however, is that this rivalry produces constant improvements in browser technology and expands use of the Web. As a result, your ability as a designer to present what you want in an efficient and useful way to an increasingly large and sophisticated audience grows better with each new release. In addition, the W3C, the committee for establishing Web standards, and other interested but noncommercial participants help keep the rivals open and aboveboard in handling these changes.

Netscape Navigator & Netscape Communicator

Although Microsoft's Internet Explorer is catching up fast, Netscape's browsers are the most widely used on the World Wide Web. One authoritative source for browser statistics is BrowserWatch (http://browserwatch. iworld.com/). Recent (December 1996) BrowserWatch statistics show that 50.5 percent of all browsers are Netscape browsers, 37.9 percent are some version of Microsoft's Internet Explorer, and the remaining 11.6 percent are browsers developed by other manufacturers. It isn't surprising that Netscape holds the dominant position in browser use. Netscape's chief technology officer, Marc Andreessen, was a primary developer of the original NCSA Mosaic browser before moving on to found Netscape. From the beginning, Netscape has been a major force in expanding the Web. Netscape continues to pioneer Web technology on both client and server computing platforms by adding new HTML tags, by enhancing client- and server-related programming and scripting languages, by developing multiple technology partnerships with other computer firms, and by participation in W3C committees.

From its inception, Netscape has been firmly committed to open standards and expanding the Web. Netscape clearly hopes to position the Web—and the company's browser and server technology—at the center of the personal computer user's experience. Netscape Communicator 4.0 is a collection of software that includes the latest version of the Netscape Navigator browser. The overall product name change, from Navigator to Communicator, indicates how Netscape views the changing role of its software in the user's world.

The new Communicator package—which includes a new version of the Navigator browser as well as other communication modules—has many improvements and additional features. Following are a few of the most prominent:

- New floating toolbars, including a custom toolbar, that allow easy access to working components of the browser.

- Improved bookmark management, including multiple bookmark files and the ability to add items directly to bookmark folders.

- Full support for HTML 3.2 tags.

- Advanced HTML extensions that allow layering of text and graphics and precise placement of elements on the page.

- Support for Cascading Style Sheets.

- Enhanced e-mail capabilities that include support for additional types of mail protocols.

- A new real-time conferencing tool that allows you to share information with another user, including moving both browsers to the same page at the same time.

TIP *The exact distribution and use of browsers is subject to a lot of hype and confusion. Unlike the statistics on servers and domain names cited earlier, statistics on browser use are simply generated by a site counting the different types of browsers that access that site. Clearly this can be subject to distortion and even, in some cases, to manipulation. If you're concerned about these numbers, you might want to read BrowserWatch's explanation of how its statistics are generated (http://browserwatch.iworld.com/stats/stats.html).*

Microsoft Internet Explorer

Microsoft has been working hard to catch up to and overtake Netscape Navigator's number-one position in the browser market. With the introduction of Internet Explorer 3.0, Microsoft showed its strength in the first notable battle of the browser war. Internet Explorer 3.0 met Netscape Navigator 3.0

head-on, matching each of Navigator's main features and adding a few of its own. Because of Microsoft's large bankroll behind its Internet onslaught against Netscape, Microsoft is giving Internet Explorer away for free. Netscape Communicator sells for less than $60.

Most notably, Microsoft beat Netscape to the punch by being the first to add support for Cascading Style Sheets, a formidable blow. Microsoft gained ground by this forward-looking action, inducing numerous users to experiment with or switch to Internet Explorer. Adding support for Cascading Style Sheets before Netscape did made even Microsoft's most severe critics sit up and take notice. With Cascading Style Sheets, you can have numerous HTML documents linked to a style sheet so that by changing the style sheet, you can change your entire Web site. Cascading Style Sheets give you typographic formatting controls that have previously been unavailable, such as setting margins, specifying fonts, and formatting for specific HTML markup elements. Microsoft Internet Explorer also ships with Web fonts to let you tap into the typographic formatting power of style sheets.

Part of the success of Netscape Navigator over Internet Explorer has been due to the numerous sites that have been optimized for Netscape Navigator plug-ins and JavaScript. A *plug-in* is an application that is set up to run from a browser. Plug-ins let you view files in the browser window that you would otherwise need a stand-alone program to run; you can display Adobe Acrobat documents or play RealAudio sound and QuickTime video files. Microsoft attacked the massive support for Navigator plug-ins, Java applets, and JavaScript by not only adding support for plug-ins, Java, and JScript (Microsoft's version of JavaScript), but also by supplementing them with ActiveX, a technology that lets you embed executable programs (called *controls*) in a Web page. Microsoft is addressing the security issues of running ActiveX controls by using digital signing.

Another area where Microsoft has lagged behind Netscape is in providing versions of Internet Explorer for platforms other than Windows. This oversight is changing fast: Microsoft released a Macintosh version of Internet Explorer that received a number of favorable reviews and announced a UNIX version of Internet Explorer that is slated for release in 1998.

The next salvo in the browser war is Microsoft's Internet Explorer 4.0, which shipped in the second half of 1997. The latest version also acts as an update to the Windows 95 desktop. The most notable addition to Internet Explorer 4.0 is the integration of broadcast capabilities through a feature called the Active Desktop. The Active Desktop lets you add any HTML component, such as Web pages, Java applets, ActiveX controls, floating frames, and images, to your desktop. Active themes are customized information that you want to receive from live feeds over the Internet. Say, for example, you want to follow a sports theme. Your desktop can connect to an Internet server that downloads sports-related information weekly, daily, or even continuously. Unlike "broadcasting," active themes only deliver the news and information you specify. Live feeds can appear on the desktop and display information that is updated daily, hourly, or continuously. You can choose to update different feeds at different intervals. For example, you can receive headline news once a day, sports scores once an hour, and stock reports continuously. PointCast, Marimba, and other Web broadcasting companies make it possible to integrate live feeds with Internet Explorer. For example, if you install Internet Explorer 4.0 and run PointCast, you can embed the feed so that it appears as the desktop background or in a floating window. Figure 1-4 shows a live feed from C | Net in a floating window.

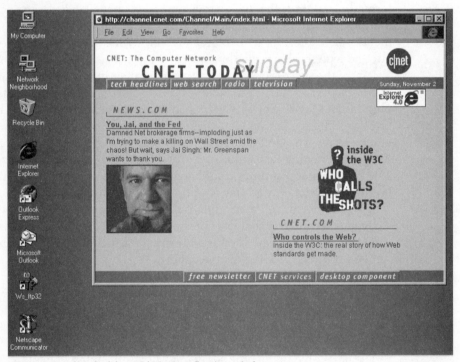

Figure 1-4: A live feed from C | Net in a floating window.

As you'd expect, Internet Explorer 4.0 ties itself into the Windows operating system, and you can use Internet Explorer in a new mode called Web View to access the desktop, Windows Explorer (file manager), or the Control Panel. Web View gives you a unified view of the Internet, your local system, and your entire network. Web View mode includes forward and backward buttons that let you navigate your hard disks much as you navigate Web sites. Other interface changes include Hover Select, which presents a new mode for working with files and icons. With Hover Select, you select a file or icon by simply moving the mouse over it, so you can start the program or open the file by single-clicking on the icon or filename.

Finally, the new IE 4.0 adds support for what Microsoft is calling *Dynamic HTML*. This is a new technique that combines several of the existing Internet Explorer features, such as ActiveX and VBScript, to allow you to add interactivity, animation, and other features to your Web pages. Dynamic HTML extends standard HTML tags by adding a set of addressable, object-oriented features to page elements to allow scripts or programs to change styles and attributes or even to replace existing elements with new ones as the reader views the page. Other additions in the Dynamic HTML extensions include multimedia and database features.

▼ The Various Faces of Dynamic HTML

Different folks mean different things when they talk about Dynamic HTML, and you need to be sure that you understand what each author or speaker means when using that term.

In its simplest form, Dynamic HTML means creating HTML pages on a server on request rather than serving pages that already exist. This technique is often used for displaying information from a database, generating catalog pages, or responding to queries. Chapter 9 explains how to create pages based on user input.

Dynamic HTML can also mean creating different pages for different viewers based on the type of browser or some other variable. This technique requires using some form of scripting language in your documents. You will learn about scripting in Chapter 11.

Finally, Dynamic HTML can mean creating or updating interactive Web pages without requiring the client to reconnect to the server. This definition also includes the ability to layer and position elements on the page, change fonts and styles, and update table data on the fly at the speed of the local computer. This includes all the other forms of dynamic pages and is what Microsoft means when it discusses Dynamic HTML in IE 4.0. With this final form of Dynamic HTML, the major issues are what tools are required to create and view the pages and how stable these tools are. We will look at some of these issues in "The Future of Web Publishing" later in this chapter.

Helper Applications & Plug-ins

One advancement Netscape brought to the browser competition is the use of auxiliary programs that allow a browser to display or otherwise use a wide variety of data types. For example, this technology allows you to hear audio played through your computer from Web sites that have audio files. Even if the browser itself can't interpret the type of information being presented, it can use an auxiliary program to understand and display the data. This approach is so useful that both Netscape and Microsoft now use it in their browsers; moreover, most of these programs will work with either browser.

Basically, these helpers come in two forms: separate applications or plug-ins (which are extensions to the browser itself). The browser determines which files it can handle and which require auxiliary support by checking the Multi-purpose Internet Mail Extension (MIME) type, which is identified by the file extension of the file being loaded by the browser. For example, a file extension of .htm or .html indicates an HTML document, while an extension of .gif or .jpg indicates an image, and so on. Most common formats, with extensions such as .html, .gif, and .jpg, are handled by the browser itself. However, for Adobe Acrobat portable documents (.pdf), for instance, the browser requires the additional help of the Acrobat Reader application or the Acrobat plug-in.

Acrobat offers a good example of the differences between plug-ins, which extend the browser itself, and auxiliary applications. For versions of Acrobat before 3.0, the Acrobat reader was an auxiliary application. When the browser encountered a file with the MIME type PDF—a .pdf file extension—it would download the Acrobat file to the system's hard disk and then launch the Acrobat Reader application to display the downloaded file. Obviously, this required that you had the Reader application on your system and enough system resources—memory, disk space, and so on—to allow it to run. More subtly, it also required that the complete file be downloaded before you ever got to see even one page of data. For a large file, this might mean a substantial wait, only to discover after reading the first page that this wasn't the document you actually wanted.

With Acrobat 3.0, however, the Reader is supplied as a plug-in to the browser. Now when you click on a link to a PDF file, the plug-in loads into the browser and displays the file as it loads from the server. This improves the display in two ways. First, the file is displayed page by page as you read it rather than being completely loaded before you can see even the first page. Second, the PDF document is displayed within your browser window, rather than in another application, so that the process of looking at the document is seamlessly integrated with the overall process of viewing Web information. Figure 1-5 shows an Acrobat document displayed by the Acrobat plug-in inside a Netscape Navigator browser. As you can see, the Acrobat plug-in buttons appear along with the standard Navigator navigational buttons.

Figure 1-5: How Acrobat functions as a plug-in to display PDF documents in your browser.

There is a wide variety of auxiliary applications and plug-ins, and these resources are becoming more prevalent every day. To find the most recent auxiliaries for a browser, visit the Web site for the browser's creator and look for supporting applications. Then you can review the types of data that each application supports and decide which ones you'd like to add to your system.

Publishing for Multiple Platforms & Browsers

HTML markup generally allows the browser a lot of leeway in how a document is presented. As a result, how a browser implements the various features of HTML makes a substantial difference in how a document will look on your screen. Different browsers may choose to represent standard HTML in different ways. In addition, each major browser has markup extensions that allow a page designer to customize a page to get special effects that may not be available in other browsers.

Although the World Wide Web is by design platform-independent, the fact is that what platform the browser is running on presents some important and sometimes frustrating limits on how pages are displayed. HTML was designed so that browsers could take platform limitations into account and still display a page more or less as the author intended. Nevertheless, some HTML commands don't translate from platform to platform very well. For example, Windows and Macintosh platforms both have standard font-handling mechanisms and standard fonts that are provided by the operating system; basic UNIX, on the other hand, does not, although many windowing systems that run on top of UNIX do provide font-handling mechanisms. As a result, some HTML format commands for setting and using specific fonts may give unexpected results when using a browser on a UNIX platform.

Another issue is that different browsers, and even different versions of the same browser, may display certain HTML tags differently. This is particularly a concern if you're using advanced HTML tags or tags that are HTML extensions created for a single browser. For example, the display of the TABLE tag has varied quite a bit from one browser to another. Whenever you choose to use advanced HTML tags, such as the TABLE or STYLE tag, you should be especially cautious and test your pages well before you publish them.

Finally, you need to remember that even all computers running the same operating system don't have the same resources. For example, a Windows machine may vary from a Pentium II with a 24-inch SVGA monitor and a large graphics cache to a simple 386 with a 12-inch VGA monitor and no cache. Similarly, a Macintosh might be a 133 MHz PowerMac with an 18-inch monitor running "millions of colors" to an SE/30 with its small, black-and-white screen. Obviously, what the browser can do on these systems varies enormously. So, if you want to reach a wide audience, you need to keep these types of variations in mind as you create your Web site.

Basically, there are three platforms in widespread use: Apple Macintosh, Microsoft Windows, and UNIX, in all its various flavors. And, of course, each of these systems comes in several versions. Thus, recalling our earlier discussion of browsers, you can see that a serious Web developer needs to take into account several possible combinations of browser software (the Internet Explorer and the Netscape Navigator browsers) and each of the three platforms.

Controlling Layout in Web Documents

As HTML expands, it includes more and more features that allow a page designer to control how pages look on a viewer's browser. Designers can also use advanced tools to create active, innovative Web pages. In this section, we'll get a quick overview of some of the current options for controlling presentation of information in Web documents.

The options for creating precise layouts on the Web are still evolving, but there are essentially two types of layout issues that designers contend with. The first is how to control the placement of graphics and text precisely on a Web page. The second is how to add interaction and intelligence to the pages.

These two problems can be handled in different ways, depending on your audience, your budget, and your team's expertise.

Generally speaking, there are three approaches that you can use to solve these problems. First, you can use some of the advanced HTML tags and extensions for page layout and display. Second, you can use one of the available scripting options to make your pages lay out the way you want and interact with the viewer for improved presentation. Third, you can use a program or applet to generate and display the page. These approaches are not mutually exclusive; you can mix and match to meet your own site's requirements.

Controlling Layout With HTML Tags

You can use a variety of advanced HTML tags to improve the placement and display of elements on your pages. As discussed earlier, when using such tags you need to be aware of which browsers support the tags and how the tags will be interpreted by the browser.

One advanced HTML tag is the TABLE tag, which allows you to lay a page out in a table format. At first glance, it might not seem to you that this tag is used for layout. However, because of its wide acceptance, this is probably the most commonly used tag for controlling placement of text and images on a page. The tag is used to create a table for all or part of a page, and then images and text are placed in the table cells to control how the page displays. You'll see exactly how to do this in Chapter 5, "Tables, Columns & Frames," when we discuss advanced HTML tags and layout.

Using JavaScript & JScript

The most common scripting language on the Web is JavaScript. JavaScript was created by Netscape to allow development and presentation of interactive Web pages. At about the same time that Netscape was developing its scripting language—then called LiveScript—Sun Microsystems was developing the Java language. When Java was announced, Netscape incorporated several Java ideas into its scripting language and renamed it JavaScript. JavaScript has become so pervasive that Microsoft, which had at first supported only its VBScript language (derived from Microsoft's Visual Basic), has added support for a variant of JavaScript called JScript.

JavaScript allows you to create small procedures and processes that run when certain events happen or when the user takes certain actions in a Web page. Unlike Java, which is a full-fledged programming language—with all of a programming language's power, but also with its complexity and pitfalls—JavaScript is simpler and easier to work with.

Java vs. JavaScript

If you're a programming type and want to know how Java and JavaScript differ, here's a brief rundown of the major differences between these two languages:

- JavaScript is embedded in the HTML page where it is run; Java applets are executed by the page but not embedded in it.

- JavaScript is purely interpreted; Java applets are compiled into a platform-independent byte-code format before being interpreted in the browser.

- JavaScript uses loosely typed, nondeclared variable data types; Java uses strongly typed, declared variables for data.

- JavaScript is object based; Java is object oriented. This means that JavaScript uses built-in, extensible objects but does not support classes and inheritance, which are the essential hallmarks of an object-oriented language.

- JavaScript checks object references only at run time, using dynamic binding; Java objects must exist at compile time and use static binding.

Using Microsoft's VBScript & ActiveX

Microsoft has created tools that compete with JavaScript and Java: VBScript and ActiveX. VBScript is a scripting language, similar to JavaScript, that can be embedded into HTML pages. It is based on Microsoft's popular Visual Basic language and is intended to be easier for someone who understands Visual Basic to use. ActiveX is an extension of Microsoft's OLE (Object Linking & Embedding) technology, which allows applications to share data and processing interactively. Together, these two technologies allow a Web page to work with other, non-Web-based applications—so long as these other applications understand OLE and ActiveX, which pretty much means that the other applications must be Windows based.

As might be expected, VBScript and ActiveX are based on proprietary Microsoft technologies. Because this was so clearly a serious drawback, Microsoft has recently announced that it will make VBScript an open standard and will turn over control of ActiveX to an independent standards group. Even with this opening, however, VBScript and ActiveX have only limited utility. At present, only the most recent version of Microsoft's Internet Explorer has any support for these tools, and that's still limited and unreliable. Since the support of these tools is dependent upon the browser, and since Microsoft has been slow in supporting platforms and operating systems other than Windows, it's probably wisest to avoid these tools and techniques in your Web pages. To the best of our knowledge, there's nothing relating to the Web that they allow you to do that cannot be done in other, more Web-friendly ways. However, if you're sure that all your clients are running Windows 95 or Windows NT, and you have some need to integrate your Web pages into other Windows applications, then you may wish to investigate these tools.

Using Java

Java is a fully functional, object-oriented language that is designed to work across the Web and be executed on multiple platforms. Java was created by Sun Microsystems as a cross-platform programming language that could be used successfully on the World Wide Web. Applications developed in most programming languages are restricted to a single platform since the commands of the language must be compiled into a series of instructions, called *machine code,* that are understood only on that platform. Java, on the other hand, is compiled into a special byte-code format, which is then interpreted by the browser to run with the operating system in which the browser is running. The Java byte-code structure is designed to make this process fast and transparent to the user.

Java programs are called *applets* and make use of a set of existing processes that allow a Java applet to perform a variety of standard tasks. Java allows a programmer to create a wide variety of applets, such as games, interactive displays, and more. However, this power comes at a price: Java is complex and requires a real programmer to create and test a Java applet. In addition, because Java applets have full program functionality, there are serious concerns about security and privacy with Java. Over time, however, we can expect to see Java becoming more and more prevalent as these problems are addressed and answered. Java represents a powerful and useful tool to expand the Web into a real online community.

Authoring & Publishing Tools

There are a variety of tools to help you create and publish Web documents, and most of them are available—at least in demonstration versions—over the Web itself. In addition, you can find relatively unbiased reviews of tools, along with comments (and often newsgroups) that will help you find out not only what tools you need, but how to get the most out of them. Typical tools cover the areas of image creation and control, HTML document creation and management, and a variety of auxiliary applications (compression, audio support, and so on), as described earlier.

Finding What You Need

The easiest way to find the tools that will suit you is to look on the Web itself. You can do this by using one of the several excellent search engines that are available. The search sites, such as Yahoo, AltaVista, Excite, HotBot, and Lycos, allow you to search through almost the entire Web for specific information. These search sites use one or both of two separate methods to find data anywhere on the Web: text indexing and site reviews. The text-indexing method looks at all the text in all the documents posted on a Web site and catalogs the important words—not including words like *the* and *and*—into a searchable database. When you perform the search, you're presented with a series of hyperlinks to sites that contain the word or words that you requested, ranked by how frequently the words occur. AltaVista is a good example of this type of search. Figure 1-6 shows you the AltaVista main page (http://www.altavista.digital.com).

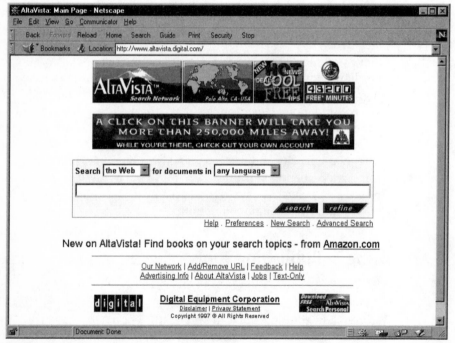

Figure 1-6: AltaVista allows you to search for text strings anywhere on the Web.

The site-review method uses personal reviews to classify sites by their content. This allows you to easily find sites dedicated to specific subjects and issues without being overwhelmed by a large number of sites that mention the topic in passing but have no real relevance to your interests. Yahoo is the original search site using this method and still one of the best. Figure 1-7 shows the Yahoo main page (http://www.yahoo.com/).

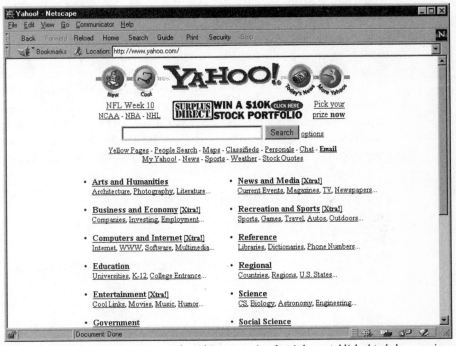

Figure 1-7: Yahoo allows you to search within categories that it has established to help organize information.

As you can see by comparing the two figures, the Yahoo site displays a set of topics that you can use to organize your search, while the AltaVista site has a direct search that can be pointed to all of the Web or limited to Usenet newsgroups only. Both search methods are useful and, most importantly, are complementary, not competing.

When you use search sites, you should remember that there are various ways to control your searches to limit the number of responses to those directly relevant to your interests. For example, both AltaVista and Yahoo have advanced search capabilities that allow you to add Boolean conjunctions

(AND, NOT, OR) to help define how your search is conducted. To use these tools, look for Advanced Search or Options links. They usually take you to an advanced search page that will both allow you to enter such search criteria and give you some help on query structure.

Accessing Information in Archived Files

Typically, tools that you find on the Web will be stored in some form of archive file. An archive is a single file that acts as a container, holding one or more files or folders. Usually the files in an archive are compressed so they take less room to store and take less time to transmit over networks and modems. Unless the archive is *self-extracting* (.sea on the Macintosh and .exe on the PC), you'll need a separate utility to decompress and access the files in an archive.

There are many compression formats used on the Web, reflecting the variety of platforms available. Table 1-2 is a listing of the more common compression formats. When you're looking for software on the Web, be sure to select your application in a format that you can decompress and install.

Format	Extension	Platform
AppleLink Package	.pkg	Macintosh
ARC	.arc	UNIX
gzip (GNU Zip)	.gz	UNIX
MacBinary	.hqx	Macintosh
StuffIt	.sit	Macintosh
TAR	.tar	UNIX
UNIX Compress	.Z or .z	UNIX
UUcode	.uu	UNIX
ZIP	.zip	DOS or Windows

Table 1-2: Compression formats.

Although there are many types of compression formats, you can usually find one or two tools that will handle all of them at once. For Windows, the WinZip and Drag And Zip programs decompress all of these formats except some of the Macintosh ones (.sit and .pkg), but you generally won't want Mac-format files for your PC anyway. WinZip is a product of Nico Mak Computing (http://www.winzip.com/), and Drag And Zip is from Canyon Software (http://www.canyonsw.com/). For the Macintosh, the StuffIt Expander, with DropStuff Enhancer, automatically handles all of these formats. The StuffIt family of compression utilities is available from Aladdin Systems (http://www.aladdinsys.com/).

Web Publishing Options

In order to publish a Web document, you need to make sure that it's located on a server that is constantly available. Paying for a full-time connection is costly and publishing documents at modem speed is an unrealistic way to handle traffic. But relax, you don't have to have a Web server with a full-time connection in order to publish on the Internet.

Many service providers include special options for publishing Web documents as a part of their service or for a small fee. How much it costs to publish a Web document depends on the service you're using and what you want to publish. Costs can range from $10 a month for a simple home page to thousands of dollars a month for an interactive storefront. You also don't have to create a Web document entirely on your own. Once you have an idea of what you want, there are many server services and Web design services that will gladly take your concept and work with you to turn it into a Web site—for a price. Appendix C lists server services and Web design services that can help you publish Web documents.

Web publishing can be broken down into three categories: single-page brochure, information center, and virtual storefront. The main page that most users connect to is called a *home page*. The following are among the types of documents that can be published on the Web: advertisements, brochures, databases, demos, newsletters, press releases, customer support/FAQs (Frequently Asked Questions), interactive storefronts, and magazines.

The Future of Web Publishing

As fast as the Web is growing, there are a number of new developments you may want to keep an eye on. The largest of these developments address the issues of additional formatting and styles for Web documents and adding greater interactivity to Web processing. The following sections look at each of these issues and where they're headed.

Extended Styles for Web Documents

Originally, the World Wide Web was intended as a tool to allow scientists located all over the world to share information and to work collaboratively on projects. As such, the design of HTML and the Web in general was intended to allow each user and browser to format documents in a way that was appropriate to the platform and hardware available without too much concern for exactly how that was done. This meant that pages would look different on different browsers, no matter what the page's creator did.

However, as the Web has expanded and become more consumer oriented, page designers have wanted more precise control over the layout and display of pages no matter what browser or platform is being used. Basically, the Web is in the process of changing from a medium of scientific content to one of consumer content, and so the pages presented are becoming more and more like magazine ads or even television spots.

This difference in viewpoint has created a certain tension between the Web's creators and the larger design community that creates most of the major Web sites. The W3C, where these questions are resolved, has been a continuing forum where both parties can present their views. Overall, this has been good for Web development; we have not lost the flexibility of the original design in the rush for the consumer marketplace.

As a result, HTML is becoming a more flexible and precise tool. The introduction of tags like TABLE to display tabular data and STYLE to handle style sheets is an example of this growth. HTML 4.0 adds more such tags, allowing the designer more control over the exact placement of page elements, such as images and text. There are several major changes on the horizon. First, the issue of how to implement and use style sheets is not yet completely resolved. Microsoft has championed the use of Cascading Style Sheets (CSS1), while Netscape is plugging for a superset of this specification, JavaScript-enabled style sheets (JSSS), which would allow a designer to automate substitutions within the style sheets themselves. The W3C is discussing both of these proposals. Second, new tags are being proposed that will allow designers to control overlapping of page elements and even, under some circumstances, to precisely place elements on the display, using X-, Y-, and Z-coordinates.

Besides placement of page elements, use of color has been another major problem that designers have dealt with in Web graphics. One of the constant complaints of Web designers is that colors that looked great on their systems turn muddy and patchy when viewed on another platform or another system with different color settings or fewer color resources. Chapters 6, "Getting Graphic With Images," and 7, "Editing & Optimizing Images," will discuss how you can avoid some of these problems. However, we can expect that the

Web will have more precise and more flexible methods of handling colors in the future. Recently, Microsoft and Hewlett-Packard have jointly proposed a new standard for handling colors, along with some HTML extensions that would help to eliminate these problems.

Downloadable Fonts

Both Microsoft and Netscape are adding downloadable font support to their browsers (Internet Explorer and Navigator). Netscape is working in conjunction with Bitstream to use TrueDoc technology for embedding fonts in Web pages. Dynamic fonts let you incorporate a font in a document so it is downloaded just like an image is downloaded. A standard set of fonts is installed with Netscape Communicator, so the same fonts will be available on all three major platforms (Windows, Macintosh, and UNIX). The files are also referred to as PFR files (Portable Font Resource). Netscape has several examples of dynamic fonts available at http://home.netscape.com/comprod/products/communicator/fonts/. For more information on Bitstream's TrueDoc technology, visit http://www.bitstream.com/.

Microsoft and Adobe are currently working on the OpenType font specification. This new font specification lets you send a cross-platform, cross-browser typeface along with a page so the page is rendered the same regardless of the platform or browser. The transmission time could be even faster than sending an image, since only the necessary characters would be sent (instead of the entire font), and the characters would be sent in a compressed format. You can get more information on the OpenType standard at http://www.adobe.com/type/opentype.html.

As expected, the World Wide Web Consortium is also scouting the font frontier for solutions through its Font Working Group. The W3C's manifesto on fonts, along with numerous links to sites related to working with fonts on the Web, is available at http://www.w3.org/pub/WWW/Fonts/.

Push vs. Pull

One of the most interesting changes happening in Web publishing is the change from *pull* to *push* publishing. The original concept of the Web was that visitors would come to a site, select the information that they wanted, and then leave. If the site was interesting and well designed, they would return over time to find out what new and useful or entertaining information had been added to the site. This is the pull concept: that visitors "pull" the site's information to come to them.

The push concept doesn't require the visitor to return—or, possibly, to even come the first time. The original push concept was born with PointCast, a news network that uses the Internet to deliver news and allows you to select a variety of information that you wish to see on a regular basis. PointCast collects the information you want from a variety of Web sites, packages it with some additional advertising materials, and sends it to you. In this way, the information that you want is "pushed" to you rather than you having to go find and retrieve it. The push model is particularly useful for information such as stock prices, weather, sports scores, and so on, which change on a regular basis, but it can be applied in some ways to any type of information.

Say you're a doctor and you wish to follow the latest information on medical imaging, and suppose there are various Web sites that contain information about your subject. Using the current pull model, you would bookmark these sites and visit them on some regular or irregular basis. However, if the sites were smart, you could simply register with each site, telling them what information you wanted to track. Then, as the sites make changes, they could inform your browser of these changes; you could then review at your leisure. This is the push model of Web publishing, and as you can see, it will potentially have a wide impact on how the Web is structured and used.

Both Microsoft and Netscape have embraced this idea and are preparing both client and server software to support it. This change will also affect how Web sites are designed and how they are funded. The push model corresponds much more closely to existing broadcasting in that a single body of information is, essentially, broadcast to a group of subscribers.

Personalizing Web Pages

There are already a number of ways to add interactive elements to your Web pages: CGI programs; various scripting languages, such as JavaScript and VBScript; the Java language itself; and even HTML-based techniques. And interactive pages, especially those providing personalized Web content, will become even more popular in the future. As a result, the HTML language will need a standard and simplified method for handling all these approaches. The new OBJECT tag is proposed as a method for handling a wide variety of embedded options within one standard HTML tag. We can expect to see additional use of this tag (and perhaps other, related tags) in the future as Web pages become more customized.

Moving On

With a possible audience of millions, the Web is becoming the new frontier of publishing. After browsing Web sites, you're bound to wonder how you can get started publishing your own Web documents. This book will guide you through the process, providing hands-on examples you can easily modify to match your own publishing needs.

In order to publish on the Internet, you'll first want to take a look at the types of tools you have to work with. Although HTML is a fairly easy language to master, creating effective HTML documents can be a difficult process. How you design your pages and organize your site makes a big difference in whether your site is useful and attractive to Web visitors. The next chapter gives you an overview of how to create compelling and informative documents for the Web.

chapter 2
Designing & Structuring Your Web Site

At first glance, publishing on the World Wide Web may appear to be fairly easy. So easy, in fact, that the temptation exists to slap some words on a page, toss in your favorite hyperlinks, throw in a few images, and put your creation on the Web for the world to see. Unfortunately, many Web authors have taken this approach by constructing documents that show little consideration for the reader.

The Web is dynamic and brings new complexities and benefits to the world of publishing. Hypertext, multimedia, and interactivity all make designing and structuring information dramatically different than designing and structuring static printed pages. Creating a Web site encompasses many different areas of expertise, including design, writing, graphic arts, and programming. Key to the success of your Web site is determining what information to present and how to present it effectively.

This chapter helps bring efficiency and elegance to your documents by addressing the special design needs and structural possibilities presented by the new publishing paradigm of the Web. It also offers some tried-and-true design principles from the world of "paper publishing" that apply to Web documents as well.

Linear vs. Hypermedia Documents

Typically, when you pick up a book, you flip it open to the first page and start reading. Perhaps you look at the table of contents to see what's there, and you skip around, awkwardly, by going to a particular chapter and skimming it until you find the reference or thought that aroused your interest in the first place. The author has structured the information in a way that best presents the point he or she is trying to make, and you have little say in the way the author feels you should absorb information. This kind of a publication is called *linear*. You start at point A and go to point B, and so on. If the writer feels you should learn about birds before bees are discussed, that's the way it is going to be.

If the process of gathering honey has captured your interest and you want to learn a bit about it before continuing on with the book, you have to wait until the author is ready to present this information. You could shuffle through the book or check the index to find references to the process. It is also possible, but not probable, that you could go to the library and get another book that discussed the honey-gathering process in detail to find the information you want. If you want to learn about something, you want it now. You don't want to have to wade through a lot of text that has little or no bearing on what you want to learn about.

That brings us to *hypermedia*. On the Web, nonlinear publications are the rule. Nonlinear publishing taps the power of the computer and the client/server model to let a reader follow almost any tangent (if the author provides the pathways, that is). In the previous example, if you wanted to learn about acquiring honey, and the path to that information had been presented in a Web document, you could simply position your cursor on the hypertext link, click, and be transported to the beekeeping home page of the entomology department at a local university, or wherever the relevant information happened to be. When you got your fill of information on honey and wanted to go back and learn something about birds, another click could zip you back from whence you came. Figure 2-1 shows an example of linear and nonlinear information.

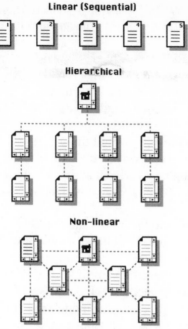

Figure 2-1: Linear information and nonlinear information.

Structuring Your Web Site

Creating an architecture for the information you want to get across is not a trivial matter. You need to define a goal and then create an architecture that lends itself to delivering the message yet allows for change. You will want to plan and design a Web site so that you can present information in digestible chunks. The following sections will help you structure and organize your site by helping you define your goals, map the main pages, and divide information into palatable chunks while creating categories for content that can be easily revised and updated.

Defining Your Goals

To help you begin structuring your site, ask yourself, "What is the goal of my Web site?" No matter what type of site you want to present, you should be able to summarize the main point you want to get across, or at least express what you want to offer your visitors. Even if you intend to create the site for pure escapist entertainment, it's important to define that as the goal you want to achieve. Once you have defined the goal, then you can structure your Web pages to help get your message across.

Before you create an outline, you need to articulate the document's goals, or purpose. A document that simply provides information can be successful by just including pointers to Web sites that have the information your reader wants to see. A corporate page, on the other hand, needs to provide a message of what the company is offering or trying to accomplish.

It may sound simplistic, but the most important thing you have to do is decide what you want to do. And the best way to define this is to ask yourself, "When a reader has finished reading my work, what do I want him or her to know?" Everything else you do will be judged by this standard. Keep focused and don't lose sight of your goal.

Throughout this book we will refer to the online site that acts as a companion to this book. You can find the Authors site at http://www.authors.com/. The bottom-line goal for the Authors site is to help readers understand HTML tags and illustrate the possibilities of interactive World Wide Web programming. Don't think that because this model is related to Web publishing that Web pages have to focus on the Web or computer products; the model could just as easily apply to a company like Acme Uniforms that sells sports uniforms.

Mapping Your Site

The best way to initiate a structure is to create a top-level outline for your site. An outline helps you create a structured home page document and determines the links you need to create to other local documents or sites elsewhere on the Web, or even within your own document. Make the home page the front door to your document so visitors can move to other pages from the home page. The following outline of the home page uses a real-world example from the Authors Web site that is used to teach HTML publishing and interactive World Wide Web programming:

I. Home Page: The Authors Site Home Page
   A. About Authors
   B. What's New
   C. HTML
   D. Interactive World Wide Web Programming
   E. Resources
   F. UCSC Projects and Handouts
   G. Feedback

"Chunking" Information

The next decision you must make when creating a Web document is how to structure the information in subsequent pages to meet the goal of your site. Web documents most often contain a series of linked elements presenting one idea or action at a time. The term "chunking" is used in hypertext to describe dividing information into small units. If, for example, one part of your document included a customer survey or a large collection of links to software, this would be a stand-alone element accessed by a link from other pages in your document.

Keeping this one-at-a-time approach in mind helps readers digest information and helps you impose a structure to your document. The next problem we need to consider is how to tie these documents together in a coherent way. Before you create any pages, it's a good idea to sketch out the structure of *all* your Web pages. Figure 2-2 shows the structure of the Authors site Web pages. These pages may also be visited directly from links that other authors have added to their documents at sites anywhere in the world. The following shows the next level of structuring information to be presented in subsequent pages:

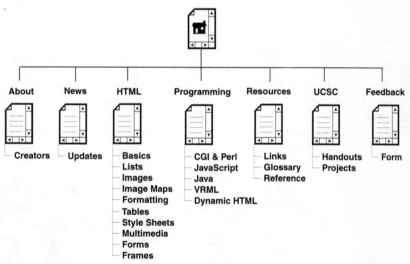

Figure 2-2: It's a good idea to sketch out Web documents and links before creating your Web document.

A. What's New
  1. Updates to the Authors site
B. HTML
  1. Basic tags
  2. List
  3. Links
  4. Images
  5. Image maps
  6. Advanced formatting
  7. Tables and columns
  8. Cascading Style Sheets
  9. Multimedia
  10. Forms
  11. Frames
C. Interactive World Wide Web Programming
  1. CGI and Perl
  2. JavaScript
  3. Java
  4. VRML
  5. Dynamic HTML
D. Resources
  1. Links to utilities and other related sites
  2. Web publishing glossary
  3. HTML reference
E. UCSC Extension
  1. Handouts
  2. Sample projects
F. Feedback
  1. Visitor feedback form

The depth of content is another major issue. The beauty of publishing on the Web is the ability to link elements within (and outside of) your document. Keep your pages short, concise, and dedicated to one issue or topic. Include branches that lead to pages containing other ideas or issues. This type of structure makes your pages easy to maintain as well as aesthetically pleasing and easy to use. If all information about a topic is included in a known place, you have to update it only once. This structure also allows you to refer to one page, like an Order Form or Feedback page, over and over from various places within the document.

Interface Design & Navigation

A Web site isn't just a source of information or a marketing tool, it's also a navigational tool. By creating a Web site, you are also creating a user interface for navigating through your site. Web sites can use clickable images along with hypertext links to help readers navigate the site. Some well-designed sites use a theme to help users navigate the site (such as a restaurant style menu, a signpost, a radio dial, a TV remote control, a map, and so on). Other sites use graphics as standard navigational controls, such as menu bars, buttons, and icons.

Using intuitive images is important. A good interface uses metaphor, shape, and color to help readers navigate the site. Ask yourself, "Are the navigation options obvious and are my navigational cues and feedback consistent?" Navigational cues comfort readers by letting them easily identify where they are and where they have been. For example, you may want to use a specific background color for an icon to indicate it has been selected. You want to avoid using the same color for a different icon on another page. The HTML page at the Authors site uses tabs and buttons that the reader can click on to jump to other pages at the site. Figure 2-3 shows the navigational tabs and buttons at the Authors site. Notice that the button for the current page has a different color background to identify to the reader which page he or she is viewing.

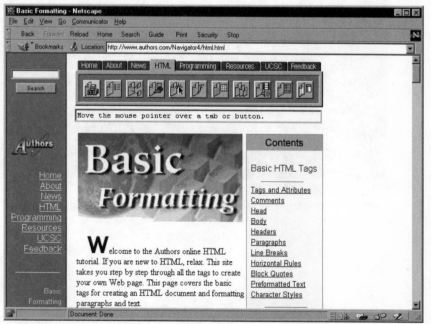

Figure 2-3: The Authors site navigation bar includes visual cues as to the reader's location.

Be aware that if you use buttons or icons, it is difficult to make sure that your icons are universally understood. Consider using a text label or adding a status line to help your readers navigate. When *Wired* first designed their Web site, many readers were left trying to decipher the obscure graphics used as navigational icons.

Presenting interesting and intuitive images can help pull readers to different sections of your Web site. For example, when the Web design team at Sun changed the images on the navigational buttons at their site, they recorded a 48-percent increase in activity. A nice example of a site that uses a metaphor throughout the publication as a navigational aid is the periodic table navigation icons at *Fine Magazine* (http://www.finemagazine.com/). Figure 2-4 shows the *Fine Magazine* home page.

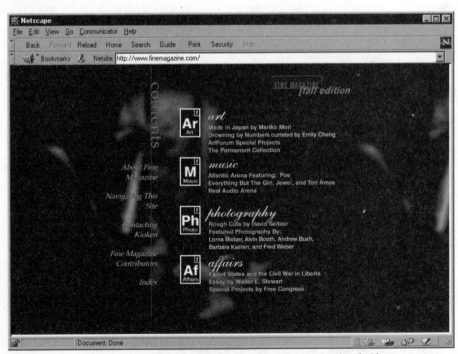

Figure 2-4: Fine Magazine *uses a periodic table metaphor as a navigational aid.*

> **TIP** *The Yale Center for Advanced Instructional Media (C/AIM) has created an excellent manual of style that discusses interface and page design in World Wide Web systems. The manual is available online at http://info.med.yale.edu/caim/manual/contents.html.*
>
> *Another excellent manual of style for creating Web sites is the Sun Microsystems Guide to Web Style. The manual is available at http://www.sun.com/styleguide/.*

Defining & Capturing Your Audience

The key to creating an effective site is defining your audience. By defining your audience, you can match the structure, tone, and style of the site to the message you want to convey. The image you want to portray should be driven by the audience you want to attract. For example, match.com is a dating service on the Web. Because research has shown that the Web is dominated by male users, it was already likely that men would visit the site. Therefore, match.com created their site to attract women. Figure 2-5 shows the match.com home page. You can visit match.com at http://www.match.com.

Figure 2-5: Match.com developed their site to attract women.

A considerable amount of thought should be devoted to defining the characteristics of your target audience. If you make your message too simple, or too complex, you will either insult or bore many of the people who visit your site. You are safe in assuming that anyone accessing your work through the Web is literate and a possessor of sufficient resources to get onto the Web in the first place. You are certainly sure that any reader has a curious bent of mind. This definition, however, includes the 14-year-old hacker as well as the 40-year-old rocket scientist.

The trick, then, becomes how to structure your presentation and language to appeal to your ideal audience. Most of this selection process is accomplished by the style of writing you choose. For example, including puns, word games, and hyperbole or adding too lighthearted a style could affect your credibility, causing others to view your site as a frivolous pastime rather than a serious professional effort. This isn't to say you can't create a fun Web page; just be sure your writing style doesn't distract from its goal. The main *National Geographic* page is a good example of a site that includes graphics that cater to people who are interested in travel and geography, young and old alike. Figure 2-6 shows the main *National Geographic* page. You can visit the page at http://www.nationalgeographic.com/main.html.

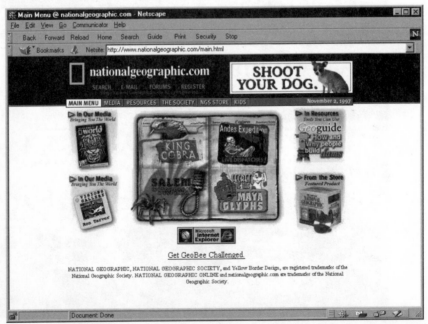

Figure 2-6: The main page at nationalgeographic.com is a good example of presenting a site to appeal to young and old alike.

Developing a Consistent Look & Feel

Because readers will be jumping into, out of, or around in your Web pages, it is highly desirable to develop a look that will carry throughout the pages. A consistent look accomplishes several purposes. First, especially for commercial pages, readers should constantly be aware of who you are, and one good way to achieve this is through consistent visual cues—a logo on each page, for example. Second, and of equal importance, lack of consistency presents a scattered, unprofessional image you don't want to broadcast. Even if you're publishing an anarchistic newsletter, readers are more likely to keep reading when they are presented with a consistent structure and design.

The look of your presentation is very important. Consider how you look at your "snail" or postal mail. There are some publications you get that you know by sight. They could have a logo, a color, an envelope, or almost any unique identifier. You immediately know that this is a publication you want to read (or toss). You want your Web document to be read. Many of the same things that attract you to a mailed document can be used to make your Web publication stand out, too. The visual appeal of a page, the amount of white space, the depth of content, and the ease of access all must be thought through.

Ask yourself how you can make your pages artistically pleasing given the limitations of your authoring tools. Can you stand back from the page when it is displayed in a browser and feel welcome? Everyone senses the artistic page on one level or another, however, and often this element above all others has an almost subconscious effect on how a reader perceives you and your organization.

TIP *If you're not an artistic type, seek out someone who is and have that person review your work. Several individuals and companies exist that provide Web design services. If you're interested in contacting a Web design service, check out Appendix C for a list of some Web design service companies.*

Internet Underground Music Archive (IUMA) is a good example of a site that uses a theme to present a consistent look and feel—in this case, a '50s theme. IUMA is a site featuring musicians who aren't in the mainstream of the music industry. Figure 2-7 shows a page from the IUMA site. You can visit IUMA at http://www.iuma.com/.

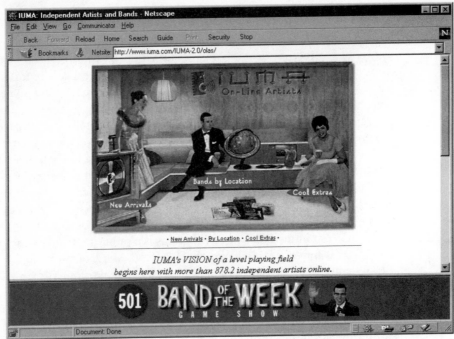

Figure 2-7: IUMA uses a '50s theme to present a consistent look and feel.

Another consideration is the size and placement of your navigational graphics. The amount of text on the screen at any given time should not be out of proportion to the size and placement of graphic elements. Don't clutter your page with too much text and too many links. A page that contains a lot of text and links is often called a *gray page*. Not only do gray pages make you feel intimidated by the amount of information they appear to contain, they look cluttered and unappealing.

Determining Your Navigational Links

Once the Web documents have been outlined, you're ready to consider how you will link the various parts together. The actual process of linking will be covered in Chapter 4, but you need to decide what you want to link early in the design process.

A navigational design technique that is becoming more and more prevalent on the Web is what Web designer David Siegel calls an *entry tunnel*. Siegel compares these entry tunnels to taking the reader on a little ride before entering the heart of the site. An entry tunnel might be a random image, a special graphic effect, a trivia game, a sweepstakes page, or a simple joke. The purpose of adding an entry tunnel is to build anticipation. An entry tunnel can also be used to address any requirements that the site might impose on the reader. Figure 2-8 shows an entry tunnel to the Yale Manual of Web Style that displays a random image and informs the reader that the page requires using a JavaScript-enabled browser. The entry tunnel to the Yale Center for Advanced Instructional Media's (C/AIM) WWW style manual is http://info.med.yale.edu/caim/manual/.

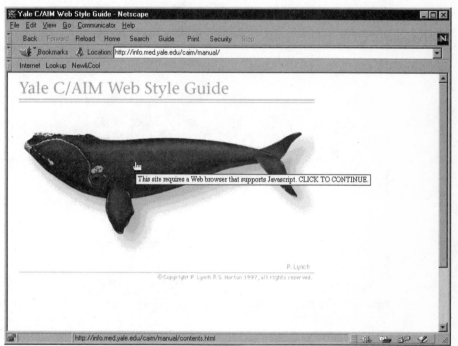

Figure 2-8: The entry tunnel to the Yale Center for Advanced Instructional Media's (C/AIM) WWW style manual.

Be aware that the very nature of the Web allows visitors to enter in places other than the uppermost level. Readers can jump to a specific Web page by following a link that someone else established and find themselves on a page that is far removed from any introductory material. For this reason, one of your initial design considerations is to provide the visitors with an easy way to get to your home page if they wish. This can be accomplished by providing a hyperlink to your home page on all of your Web pages. By creating a hyperlink to the home page, you can help people easily find the points of interest by the links established in the directing document (the home page). In addition to providing links to your home page, you may also want to include links for readers to visit or return to other pages within the document. Figure 2-9 shows a site map of the Hanson/Dodge site.

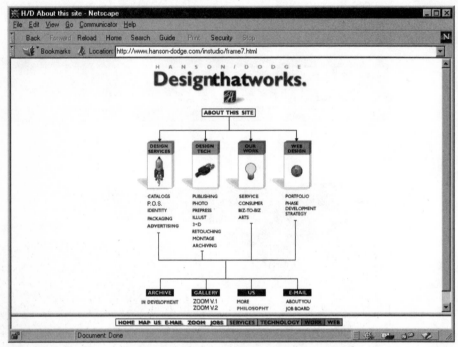

Figure 2-9: The Hanson/Dodge site includes a site map so readers can easily move to any page.

Balancing Access & System Performance

It is also important to keep in mind the equipment that will be used to view your site—there are many different hardware/software configurations and capabilities out there. Some machines don't display graphics at all, so you want to write for both graphic- and text-based Web browsers. Keep in mind that there are also many different Web browsers: Netscape Navigator and Communicator, Microsoft Internet Explorer, Lynx (a text-based browser), and so on. Each browser may display your presentation differently.

There has been a long-standing tradition of Web publishers to include information about the browser that was used when creating the document. This is really important if you use a feature that isn't supported by other browsers. For example, if you create a page using Netscape Communicator's new layer features, the page should include a message that states, "Use Netscape Communicator to view this document at its highest quality." Depending on the type of features you want to use to present your message, you might want to consider creating links only to other pages designed specifically for a particular browser or plug-in. Additionally, if people have to download and set up a plug-in or use a particular browser, you need to inform them and make it easy for them to get the plug-in. Otherwise you risk losing your reader. An excellent site that addresses the needs of its readers is Enigma3.com. The first page displays a flickering candle and a request that the reader use Netscape Navigator or Explorer 3.0 and Shockwave. Figure 2-10 shows Enigma3's opening page. You can visit Enigma3 at http://www.Enigma3.com/.

Figure 2-10: Enigma3 informs the reader of the site's requirements before entering.

Most instances of readers bailing out of a site are caused by overtaxing their bandwidth. Consider the constraints placed on a reader by his or her hardware. It is also important, and prudent, to consider the limitations that your readers may have due to the version of browser and equipment they are using, such as a 28,800 bps modem or a high-speed ISDN connection. The majority of people browsing the Web are connected with modems. Make your presentation simple enough to be adequately viewed using a modem, or create both high- and low-bandwidth pages and let the reader choose between the two. Adjacency cleverly uses a light-switch metaphor to let readers choose between a high- and low-bandwidth version of Madison Gas and Electric's Web site, as shown in Figure 2-11.

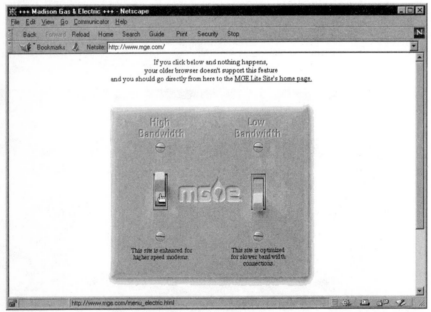

Figure 2-11: Adjacency uses a light-switch metaphor to let readers choose between a high- and low-bandwidth version of Madison Gas and Electric's Web site.

Besides the differing browser types and bandwidth constraints, consider the many types of screens that will be used and test your pages using the lowest common denominator. It is all too common to create a site for a browser at SVGA 800 x 600 with 16 million colors that is difficult to read by individuals viewing the page using computers in 640 x 480 mode with a 256-color display mode, such as a notebook. If you take into account the lower-resolution screen, you can create pages that will look good on both computers.

If your pages contain large graphics, the process of downloading the graphic to the reader's browser can take so much time that the reader becomes impatient and unreceptive to your message. If you want to include graphics (and you should), keep them small. You can offer the option of viewing a more complex version of the graphic by linking the smaller (thumbnail) version of it to the larger one. You don't want the reader choosing the option of not loading graphics just because you have overloaded your page with large graphics. The Adobe home page consists of an optimized image that fits in a 640 x 480 window and displays correctly in high-resolution screens as well. Figure 2-12 shows Adobe's home page.

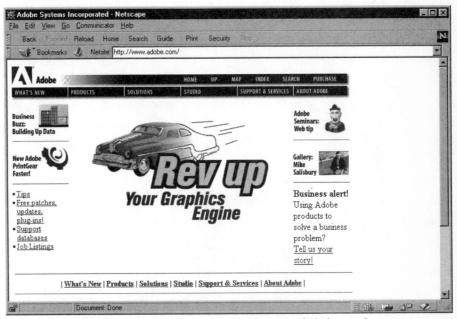

Figure 2-12: Adobe's home page was designed to display correctly in low- and high-resolution screens.

Individual Web Page Design Tips

Up to this point, we've talked about the collection of pages that, when assembled, make up your Web presence. Our consideration has also been directed toward the "big picture" design. Now it's time to examine the process of constructing and designing individual pages. Each individual page in your document should contain certain elements: identity, look, links, and information.

Structuring and designing individual Web documents is not a simple job. Be prepared to make changes. It's a good strategy to plan it as if the home page will be the first page read. If you include a link on every page of your document that takes the reader to the home page, it really doesn't matter where the reader starts reading. The following sections list and describe design issues you'll want to keep in mind when creating Web documents.

Design Tips for Your Home Page

Before creating your home page, decide what you want to do. If you don't know where you're going with your document, you will never get there. It is really difficult to keep yourself focused when you are writing any document, and the more structure you can bring to the process, the better the results.

A good design idea is to use your home page or a secondary page as a table of contents for the rest of your documents. Figure 2-13 shows the home page for the Authors Web site. Notice that the page displays the Authors logo, an image map to the Web site's contents on the right side of the page, and corresponding hyperlinks at the bottom of the page. The links act as a table of contents that allows readers to further refine what they want to read. Adding both text-based and graphic design elements makes navigating the site easy for any visitor.

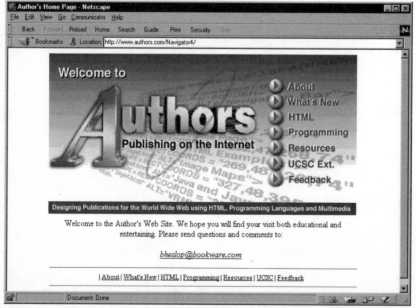

Figure 2-13: A well-designed page includes an image map and text-based links.

Another aspect of good design is to show sensitivity to all viewers. For example, you may want to present your home page with links to pages in different formats: one for users who can handle large graphics and another for those who use text browsers. If you are going to include browser-specific features, it's also a good idea to give users a link to take them to a version of the document that has been created for the browser.

Design Tips for Subsequent Pages

The following are some general guidelines for creating subsequent Web pages:

- *Include only one or two topics per page.* Your readers came to this page expecting to see what they had selected on your home page, and little else. If you're going to include large Web documents, such as a brochure or an online book, it is helpful to create a table of contents or present the information as a document in the Adobe Acrobat portable document format so that the reader can download the file and read the document offline.

- *Consider presenting text in your pages by using style sheets with wide margins or by using tables.* At normal reading distances, the eye's span of movement is about 3 inches wide. One of the basic tenets of typography is to present passages of text in printed columns no wider than the reader's comfortable eye span. Wider lines of text require the reader to move his or her head slightly or strain the eye muscles to track the lines of text. Most Web pages are close to twice as wide as the reader's eye span, so extra effort is required to scan through the lines of text. Figure 2-14 shows a page at the *Salon Magazine*'s Web site presented using text in tables to increase readability by eliminating long lines of text. You can visit *Salon Magazine*'s Web site at http://www.salonmagazine.com/.

- *Identify yourself or your company.* It is quite common to include company-oriented information, such as a logo, your name and contact information (such as an e-mail address), the date the site was last revised, and copyright information, in the footer of the page. It's your turn on stage; take advantage of it.

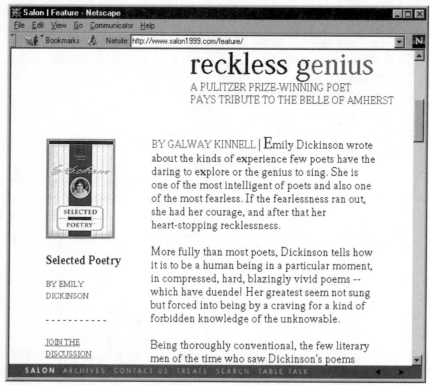

Figure 2-14: Using tables or margins (with style sheets) lets you present shorter lines of text to reduce eyestrain.

- *Keep it simple.* A person reads a page on a computer screen at about 25 percent the speed that the person reads a printed page. Therefore, an important design consideration is to avoid overwhelming the reader. Pages that contain massive amounts of text are typically not read. A good rule of thumb is never to have more than 50 percent of the screen covered with anything. When you are viewing your page, step back from the monitor so you can't read any of the text and look to see if the appearance of the gray (text-filled) areas and the rest of the screen is pleasing to the eye.

- *Vary the text styles.* Break down your information in such a way that you can use different levels of headings when appropriate. Each level displays differently and gives your document eye-appeal. When called for, include text attributes that emphasize key points.

■ *Include a graphic or two.* Graphics are a great way to provide interest and style to your page. You will learn how to link images in Chapter 6. Use graphics as design elements to break up text or lend a little variety to your presentation. Keep inline graphics small (in bytes) and simple (in colors). They'll load faster.

■ *Give people a reason to return to your site.* Many Web sites are one-shot wonders. Add value to your site to entice readers back by adding a tutorial, a column, reviews, comics, tips, or links to interesting sites or software. C|NET's BUILDER.COM page is updated on a regular basis, providing readers with excellent articles featuring tips and techniques about Web publishing. Figure 2-15 shows C|NET's BUILDER.COM site; you can visit it at http://www.cnet.com/Content/Builder/.

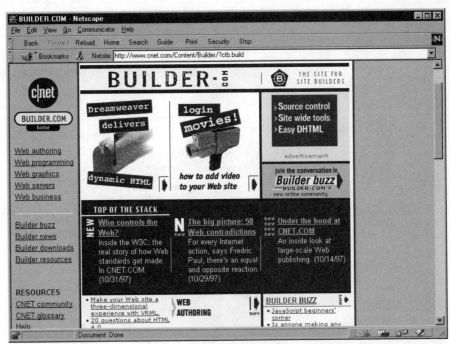

Figure 2-15: C|NET's BUILDER.COM page is updated on a regular basis and provides current information about Web publishing techniques to draw readers back.

■ *Include a logo or some information that identifies yourself on each page.* Remember that a reader does not necessarily use the front door (or your home page) to get into your document. You can use a simple logo or some text that is linked to your home page or another page where information about you can be found. Many sites use an embossed logo as a tiled background image. Your purpose is to get your name and message out. You don't want readers scratching their heads wondering who you are.

■ *Use headings sparingly to structure your document.* Don't use a heading just to change fonts. Just because there are six levels of headings doesn't mean you should use them all. In fact, you should really only use up to four headings. If you have more than four headings, go back and divide your page into additional pages with fewer headings.

■ *Include a Feedback or Comments page so your site is interactive.* One of the main benefits of the Web is that it lets you interact with your reader. If you don't include a way for your readers to communicate, you are losing one of the major advantages of the Web. Vivid Studio's site includes an e-mail list and a search facility along with a Feedback link so readers visiting the site can interact. Figure 2-16 shows the Vivid Studio page. You can visit the Vivid Studio home page at http://www.vivid.com.

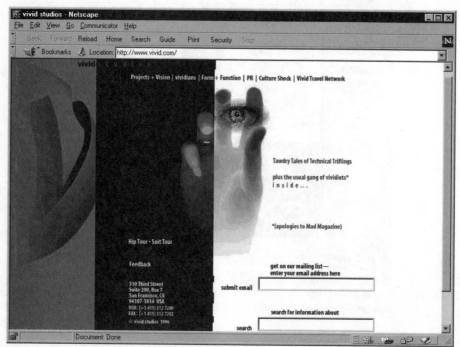

Figure 2-16: Vivid Studio's site includes options for an e-mail list and a search facility along with a Feedback link to interact with readers.

■ *Provide pathways for your readers that lead directly to important pages.* For example, include links to your home page, or an order form if you have one, and a link to go directly to a Feedback or Comments page. If you are presenting a tutorial or presentation, provide navigational aids—links— to go forward and backward so the reader can see what came before the current page in your presentation or go to the next logical page.

■ *Know your audience.* Design pages that will be pleasing to view on a "low- end" computer system so you don't alienate your readers. Structure your language, vocabulary, and syntax to the audience you want to address. This kind of structure can serve as a gatekeeper, welcoming in those you want and excluding those you don't. If you have high-quality graphics you want to include (pictures of your product, for example), consider creating a thumbnail of each image or linking those pictures to a page that individuals with slower modems can skip if they wish.

■ *Use white space wisely.* Use graphics and white space as design elements to break up your page. Using tables or style sheets, you can create mar- gins to make your pages more readable.

■ *Keep your design simple and intuitive.* Allow linked documents to provide more in-depth information and keep all of your pages as simple and uncluttered as you can. There is no limit to the number of pages you can create. Keep the information presented highly focused on your goals. If you think a reader may want to go off on a tangent, provide a link in- stead of placing the extra verbiage on the current page.

■ *Be consistent.* It is easy to view each document as a separate work, and in a sense you should do just that. Remember, though, that your readers will jump from page to page within your document. Try to develop your own style for text, graphics, and other design elements and carry it through the entire publication. People remember the look and feel of your publications, and a consistent approach will gain you recognition much more quickly than an inconsistent one.

■ *Know your writing and artistic skills and get feedback.* Publishing documents is a blend of art and craft. A publishing house employs designers, artists, and page layout professionals in addition to the editors, marketers, and accountants. If you're publishing Web pages on your own, ask other people for their opinions about your finished document.

■ *Test your links to make sure they work and are up-to-date.* A link that displays a message informing the reader that the page has moved to a new loca- tion sends a message to the reader that you have not checked your own pages. All too often, authors use links to sites that have changed. It is frustrating to surf the Internet and encounter a dead link or a link to a site in which the URL has changed. You should check your links and plan to recheck them regularly. Otherwise you're sending a message to the reader that not only is the link dead, but the information you are presenting is also out-of-date.

■ *Test your page with other browsers.* If possible, check your page using a browser on other platforms, such as UNIX and the Macintosh. Test your pages using a character-based browser, or at least test your page without graphics.

Moving On

We've covered a lot in this chapter. Much of it will be reinforced as you continue reading and using Web authoring tools. Take the time to determine the goal of your site and design your Web pages to meet that goal—it will save you time in the long run. An efficient structure and a consistent, visually appealing design improves the chances that people will return to your site. Designing a well-structured site is only the first step, though; it's time to begin learning how to use HTML. The next chapter explains how to get started using HTML to create your own documents for publishing on the World Wide Web.

chapter 3

Creating & Editing HTML Documents

There are a few ways you can start creating a Web document. You can begin with a template and modify it to meet your needs, or you can download and modify the source code of an existing Web document off the Internet. Web browsers, such as Netscape Navigator and Internet Explorer, let you both display a window containing the HTML codes and text used to create documents on the Web and save the HTML codes and text to a file. The problem with this method is that it is amazing how many Web documents break the basic rules of HTML. Just because you're viewing a home page for a large company is no guarantee that the page is created correctly.

This chapter takes a different approach to creating Web documents. It discusses the basic elements used to create a simple page and presents valid elements and procedures you can follow to construct your own HTML documents. References are made throughout this chapter to other areas in this book where you can obtain more detailed information about many of these subjects. To help you create correct Web pages, we'll focus in this chapter on inserting basic elements and verifying your documents.

Getting Started With HTML

As mentioned in Chapter 1, the elements that specify how to display text are collectively called *markup*. Markup is the use of codes that tell the Web browser how to display your text. The document is composed of text that takes its cues from the markup.

Using markup is a lot like using parentheses in algebra or entering a formula into a spreadsheet. Instead of parentheses, HTML markup uses codes within angle brackets. Markup typically consists of a beginning code (commonly referred to as a *tag*) that specifies the effect and an ending tag that includes a forward slash to identify the end of the markup. Every tag begins with a left angle bracket (<) and ends with a right angle bracket (>), with the name of the tag in between. End tags have a slash (/) between the left angle bracket and the name of the tag. For example <TITLE> signifies the beginning and </TITLE> marks the end of the title tag. Each tag has a name that corresponds with the tag; for example, <TITLE> </TITLE> specifies the title tag.

When text or data appears within a beginning and ending tag, the entire set of tags is called a *container*. Containers always require an end tag, which defines where the effect of the tag ends. For example, the text between the beginning <TITLE> tag and the end </TITLE> tag will all be the title of the document. Without the end tag, the browser wouldn't know where the title text stopped. However, tags that are not containers, like the <META> tag described later in this chapter, do not have an end tag. Many tags also have additional elements, called *attributes*, which are included after the tag name but before the ending right angle bracket (>) character. Attributes never appear in end tags.

Not all tags demand a closing markup, and not all tags must contain text. Tags that don't contain text and don't permit an end tag are sometimes referred to as *empty tags*. Some tags let you define attributes specific to the type of tag. For example, by using an attribute, you can define where text is placed next to an image or define alternative text to accommodate viewers that are unable to handle images.

Documents that follow an SGML specification exactly, such as HTML 3.2, are called *conforming* documents. Generally, any HTML editor or validation software will expect that your documents are conforming, and good practice suggests that you attempt to make all your Web pages conforming documents. This will ensure that they will parse correctly on all types of browsers and will give you the best assurance that they will continue to display properly as the HTML standard grows over time.

Options for Creating HTML Documents _____

You can create a document and mark it up with HTML tags using any word processing program or text editor you want. HTML documents are by design plain text and all HTML tags can be entered as plain text elements. The only point you need to be careful about is that you save your document as plain text; most word processing programs, like Microsoft Word, WordPerfect, or Lotus AmiPro have a Save As option that allows you to set the type of the document to plain text. On the other hand, every computer system that we are familiar with has a plain text editor included in the system software: vi on UNIX; SimpleText on the Macintosh, and Notepad or Write on Windows. All of these programs read and write only plain text. So the easiest way to create an HTML document is to use the most basic editor you have and create the text (with tags).

This is the easiest way to create an HTML document for your Web site, in that it requires no additional investment in new software on your part and you are probably already familiar with the text editor from other uses. This approach, however, is not usually the easiest in the sense of making it simple to ensure that your HTML tags are used or entered correctly. Because many people would like to have some help in entering and using HTML tags, there are various HTML editing software packages available for your use. Most of them will add several important features over and above providing basic text editing. First of all, they usually help you create and use tags correctly, ensuring, for example, that ending tags are correctly provided for tags that require them. Some editors, like Adobe's PageMill, go so far as to hide the actual HTML tags from you unless you ask to see them. Second, they offer intelligent tools, like spell-checking, that understand the HTML tags and will ignore them when appropriate. Finally, they often will help you enter images and other graphic elements onto the page, either by using a drag-and-drop technique or by allowing you to browse your storage media for the exact image you want to insert.

Another advantage to using standard text editing software, especially editors that were created for programming, like WinEdit and BBEdit, is that you can use them to indent your HTML text. Indentation is useful to help you match tags and to help you see how the page is structured from a markup standpoint. As we progress through the examples in this chapter, you will see how indentation can be used to help you avoid common HTML coding errors.

Is it WYSIWYG?

HTML editors often also boast that they provide *WYSIWYG* (What You See Is What You Get) editing. Don't be fooled. No HTML editor can provide actual WYSIWYG editing because HTML itself doesn't always render in the same way.

As you read in Chapter 1, differences in browsers, in platforms, in displays, in installed helper and auxiliary applications, and in the user's choices for browser setup will all affect how the page is displayed on the Web. At best, all an HTML editor can do is show you how the page will look on *your* system with *your* browser settings; at worst, the editor will emulate one of the standard browsers—and not necessarily the one you're using, either. In some ways, this attempt at WYSIWYG display is actually misleading and may cause unwary or novice Web developers to assume that they actually know how a page will look when it's published.

For this reason, many advanced Web developers prefer to use simpler tools for creating pages and then to preview the pages using one or more browsers. This is very easy to do and provides a constant reminder that what you see is unlikely to be what the user sees unless you take special efforts to ensure it.

If you choose to use a text editor or an HTML editor that doesn't automatically insert tags, it's helpful to know that markup tags are not case sensitive; for example <title>, <TITLE>, and <Title> all can be used for the title tag.

TIP *Because you don't know which browser will be used to view your documents, you should attempt to create conforming documents and to follow all the rules in the HTML language as closely as possible. Currently, some HTML editors and templates let you get away with ignoring some elements or omitting certain tags and still produce a readable document. Keep in mind, however, that anyone can easily download your source code. If you don't follow HTML formatting rules, others may make judgments about you and your company from the quality of your documents. Furthermore, as HTML evolves, you may discover that your pages don't display correctly on the latest versions of some browsers.*

Basic Document Structure

Every HTML document must start with the markup tag <HTML>. The initial <HTML> tag informs the browser what kind of document it's looking at so it can be displayed properly. This becomes more important as other documents, such as SGML documents for Panorama and other non-HTML browsers, start being used. The end tag </HTML> instructs the browser that the document is complete. It's included as the last tag in your document.

An HTML document is divided internally into two sections, the head section (delimited by the <HEAD> </HEAD> tags) and the body section (delimited by the <BODY> </BODY> tags). Each section may contain other useful tags. Within the head section is the <TITLE> tag, which is the only tag absolutely required in an HTML document, and the <DOCTYPE> tag (discussed later), which is required for a conforming document to define what standard the document follows. Following this logic, the following code represents the absolute minimum conforming document:

```
<!DOCTYPE HTML PUBLIC "-//W3C//DTD HTML 3.2 Final//EN">
<HTML>
<HEAD>
<TITLE>A Sample Document Title</TITLE>
</HEAD>
</HTML>
```

Note, however, that this document won't actually display any text on your browser; to do that, it would have to have a body section as well, along with some text or images and so on. Nothing contained in the head section actually displays on your browser except the title. Therefore, for this document, the only evidence that it exists will be the title that appears at the top of the browser window.

Adding Comments

HTML allows you to enter comments into your documents. As the name implies, information embedded within a comment is not used by the browser for display but is still part of the HTML markup of the document. Typically, comments are used to describe the parts of a document or to insert information that you wish to note for reference when you work with the document.

You include comments in an HTML document by inserting a comment declaration. A comment declaration consists of the characters <! followed by zero or more sets of comment text, followed by the delimiter character >. Each comment text starts with -- and includes all text up to and including the next occurrence of --. In a comment declaration, white space characters—spaces, tabs, newlines, and carriage returns—are allowed after each comment but not before the first comment. In other words, the comment must begin with <!-- followed by some text, a comment delimiter --, and possibly additional comments; the comment is terminated by a >. The entire comment declaration is ignored by the browser. The following is an example of a simple comment:

```
<!-- Make sure BKGND color is white -->
```

A more extensive comment might look like this, which incorporates two sets of comment text within one declaration:

```
<!-- Make sure BKGND color is white --
   -- and that the FONT is set correctly -->
```

Since you can include white space characters within comment declarations and since a newline or carriage return is simply a type of white space character, you can correctly create multiple line comments. However, because some Web browsers balk at multiple line comments, it is best to keep comments to a single line or use a comment declaration for each line you want to add.

The DOCTYPE Tag

When you are creating an HTML document that conforms to the current HTML 3.2 standard, you should start the document with this DOCTYPE declaration:

```
<!DOCTYPE HTML PUBLIC "-//W3C//DTD HTML 3.2 Final//EN">
```

Every conforming HTML 3.2 document must start with this <!DOCTYPE> declaration, which is needed to distinguish HTML 3.2 documents from other versions of HTML. As you will read in Chapter 14, "XML & Metadata: The Future of Web Publishing," this tag will also allow your document to be parsed by XML engines without any further coding changes.

The HEAD Tags

Immediately following the <HTML> tag in a conforming document is a tag called <HEAD>. The <HEAD> tag allows the HTTP server software to discover information about the document. The <HEAD> tag begins the head section of the document, which is terminated by the </HEAD> tag. As you read earlier, there is no displayable content between the <HEAD> tags except the document's title.

The TITLE Tag

The next item that is included is a document title. This is the only tag that is absolutely required in a document. The title of a document, contrary to what you would expect, doesn't appear at the top of your document. Every HTML 3.2 document must have exactly one TITLE element in the document's HEAD section. This tag provides a title that is displayed in a browser's window title bar. The title is also used for index information by Web searching programs such as Web spiders and robots. Any valid character data can be inserted in the title. As a result, accented characters and other special characters such as & and < can be used just as they would be used in the body of the document, as described in "Adding Special Characters" later in this chapter. Additional markup is not permitted in the TITLE element.

TIP *The <TITLE> tag is a container tag: That is, the text for the tag is contained between the beginning <TITLE> tag and the ending </TITLE> tag. All container tags must have ending tags associated with them.*

To create a title, type a title for your sample document between the beginning and ending <TITLE> tags. Keep the title short yet descriptive. A descriptive title is important because many browsers will use this title if the reader saves your page as a bookmark or hotlist item. When you display this document in a browser, the contents of the title element will be displayed in the window's title bar. It is possible that the title will display in some browsers on a Document Title line. The following is a sample of how to use the <TITLE> tags:

```
<TITLE>Authors Home Page</TITLE>
```

The META Tag

The META tag can be used to include name/value pairs describing properties of the document, such as author, expiration date, a list of key words, and so on. The NAME attribute specifies the property name while the CONTENT attribute specifies the property value, as shown in the following example:

```
<META NAME="Author" CONTENT="Brent Heslop,David Holzgang">
```

In this case, the <META> tag is being used to tell who the author of a page is. There is also an HTTP-EQUIV attribute that you can use in place of the NAME attribute. This allows you to insert information that will be sent to any browser that requests the page. You can use this attribute to set an expiration date for a page, as shown in the following code example:

```
<META HTTP-EQUIV="Expires" CONTENT="31 December 1997 00:00:00 GMT">
```

This code will send a header message that tells a browser the page expires on the date and time shown. It's up to the browser how it uses this information; typically, a browser might use this information to delete the page from any existing cache and to reload the page.

In addition, the <META> tag is often used to insert information that is used within a Web site for document control or indexing. As such, when you see <META> tags in documents, you may not understand what purpose they serve; in these cases, the NAME and CONTENT values will be set by the site for internal use.

Other HEAD Tags

Besides <TITLE> and <META>, there are other tags that can appear in the head of a document. Here is a short list of these tags and what they stand for. For more information on all the heading tags, see Appendix B, "An HTML & Style Sheet Reference."

- ISINDEX provides for simple keyword searches; used in conjunction with the PROMPT attribute.

- BASE defines a base URL for resolving relative URLs.

- LINK is used to define relationships with other documents.

- SCRIPT, at present, is simply a placeholder for a future tag for use with scripting languages. See "HTML 4.0 Extensions" later in this chapter for examples of how they are used in current browsers.

- STYLE, at present, is simply a placeholder for a future tag for use with style sheets. See "HTML 4.0 Extensions" later in this chapter for examples of how they are used in current browsers.

The BODY Tags

The main part of your document is the body, contained within the BODY element. Except for the ending </HTML> tag, everything from here on is a body element, including headings, paragraphs, special characters, lists, images, hyperlinks, and so on. The following sections explain how to identify the beginning and the contents of the body of your Web page.

BODY Tag Attributes

In HTML 3.2, the <BODY> tag includes attributes that allow you to control the display of the background and foreground colors of the browser's window. You can specify the color of the background or you can tile an image in the background. Keep in mind that not all browsers can display background and foreground colors, so people using a different browser may not see the background color or the background tiled image and the foreground colors you specify. The following sections explain how to include these background and foreground extensions in your Web pages.

TIP *You can request the display attributes, but you can't be sure that the page is displayed the way you requested. Viewers can set their browsers to ignore your color selections and use their own if they choose to. So never assume that you have control over the final display of your pages.*

Specifying Colors

You can set colors in your HTML code in two ways. The most basic way is to give the color as three separate values, one value for each of the primary display colors, red, green, and blue (RGB). Colors are given in the RGB color space as two-digit hexadecimal numbers, thus allowing 256 possible settings for each color component. For example, BGCOLOR="#80FF00" sets the red component to 128 (half of the maximum, or most intense, color), the green component to 255 (the maximum), and the blue component to 0 (the minimum value, representing no blue at all); the resulting color approximates a neon green. This method allows you complete flexibility in setting colors, but there is some cost in figuring out what values you need to use in order to get the color you want.

The second way to specify colors is by using one of 16 widely understood color names defined in the HTML 3.2 specification. For example, you can set the background color to maroon by using BGCOLOR="maroon." These colors were originally picked as being the standard 16 colors supported with the Windows VGA palette. Table 3-1 shows you the color names and their equivalent RGB values in hexadecimal.

Black = "#000000"	Green = "#008000"
Silver = "#C0C0C0"	Lime = "#00FF00"
Gray = "#808080"	Olive = "#808000"
White = "#FFFFFF"	Yellow = "#FFFF00"
Maroon = "#800000"	Navy = "#000080"
Red = "#FF0000"	Blue = "#0000FF"
Purple = "#800080"	Teal = "#008080"
Fuchsia = "#FF00FF"	Aqua = "#00FFFF"

Table 3-1: Color names and their equivalent RGB values.

Note that individual browsers may recognize and support more than these 16 colors; Netscape, for example, recognizes 140 color names. However, if you want to ensure that your color is recognized by the widest possible number of browsers, you should use the hexadecimal representation for the color since all browsers that support color can use these settings.

TIP

This book's Companion CD-ROM contains a color-picker application that will help you with the task of specifying colors. The JavaScript Color Picker is a JavaScript-based application that allows you to select background, text, and link colors directly and insert the code into your page. You can also check Appendix B for a complete listing of hexadecimal color listings.

If you want to set your own colors, you can use your graphics program to display any color that you want and determine what the RGB values for that color are. Then use any scientific calculator to convert the decimal RGB values into hexadecimal. However, remember that colors display differently on different systems, so your viewer may not see the exact same color you have selected.

Specifying the Background Color

BGCOLOR is added as a BODY attribute to specify an overall background color for the browser's window. The syntax for specifying the background color is:

```
<BODY BGCOLOR="#rrggbb">
Body text
</BODY>
```

or:

```
<BODY BGCOLOR="color">
Body text
</BODY>
```

You must enter the red, green, blue color settings (rrggbb) in hexadecimal format or select one of the color names from Table 3-1 in the previous section.

Using an Image for the Background

The specifications for HTML 3.2 add the BACKGROUND attribute to the <BODY> tag. The BACKGROUND attribute lets you specify a URL pointing to an image that is tiled to form a background for your browser's window. The syntax for using the BACKGROUND attribute is:

```
<BODY BACKGROUND="path/image.gif">
Body text
</BODY>
```

The URL can point to an image at any location, including another site. The specified image is tiled across the browser's display by repeating the image horizontally and vertically to fill the window. Then the content of the page, including text and graphics, is displayed over the background image.

TIP   *Note, however, that if you use an image that is not on your site as a background, the image may move or be changed without your knowledge. For example, Netscape posted a number of background images on its site for a long time, but they are now gone. If you had used one of these images as a background, you would now have a broken link. The best way to use images as a background is to create it yourself or download it to your own site so that you can always ensure that the image will be available.*

Changing the Foreground: Text & Links

In addition to changing the background colors, you can also specify the color of text and links in a Web page by setting attributes in the <BODY> tag. The TEXT attribute lets you specify the color of text other than links in your Web page. The syntax for the TEXT attribute is:

```
<BODY TEXT="#rrggbb">
Body Text
</BODY>
```

or:

```
<BODY TEXT="color">
Body Text
</BODY>
```

As you read earlier, you must enter the red, green, blue color settings (rrggbb) in hexadecimal format or select one of the color names from Table 3-1 in the previous section.

Three attributes let you specify the color of links: LINK, VLINK, and ALINK. LINK refers to the links as they first appear on the page. The default color for links is blue. The *V* in VLINK stands for *visited*. VLINK changes the color of links that the user has chosen. The default color for visited links is purple. The *A* in ALINK stands for *active*. ALINK changes the color at the moment when the hyperlink is chosen. The default for active links is red. The following is an example that includes a navy blue color for the background, white for text, yellow for links, medium gray for visited links, and fuchsia for active links:

```
<BODY BGCOLOR="navy" TEXT="white" LINK="yellow" VLINK="#A0A0A0"
ALINK="#FF00FF">
Body Text
</BODY>
```

Readability Considerations

If you do change the background color or add a background image, or if you change the color of the text for the display, be sure that the result is clearly visible. Obviously, using black text on a dark background or using yellow text on a white background results in pages that are hard to read. But not all of these types of errors are quite that obvious. The intensity of colors varies from platform to platform and from one display to another. Make sure that any combinations you use are clearly contrasting since you can't be sure that the viewer's colors are exactly the same as the ones you see on your system. It's safest to stick with black text on a white or light background—your viewers will appreciate it!

Organizing Your Document

Like any well-organized document, it's a good idea to start with a heading. There are six possible heading tags, <H1> through <H6>. Each tag works just like a heading style in a word processing document or levels in an outline, providing structure and division in your document. The type style and size of the heading changes depending on how the individual browser that is displaying your document is configured. The following is a sample heading:

```
<H2>Introduction</H2>
```

Even though you can use up to six different levels of headings, it is best to stick to only four. Many browsers are not set up to display higher-level heads with font and character attributes that differ enough from each other to make them noticeable. Keep your headings structured like any outline. For example, you wouldn't put a lower-level heading before a higher-level heading in an outline. The same holds true for HTML headings.

Even though most browsers display heading tags with different font styles—larger or smaller text, in bold or italic, and so on—you should not use the head tags to change fonts or styles. Use them for headings and nothing else. One of the most common mistakes that beginning HTML authors make is to use heading tags to set font size or style; a particularly common error is to use <H5> or <H6> tags to force small size text. The exact representation of a heading depends on the browser, and the purpose of a heading is to create structure. If you want to control the font size or style, use one of the other tags, like <FONT> or <BOLD> (discussed later in this section), which will make the changes you want directly, without introducing potentially confusing structural elements.

On the other hand, once you have created a heading, don't make the opposite mistake of inserting format tags into the heading. For example, there's no need to set type size or style in a heading, and doing so may lead to very unpleasant page displays since the browser will try to combine its internal settings for a particular heading with your style commands.

TIP   *Don't try to combine the heading and title tags for the first level of a document. For example, <H1><TITLE>Author's Home Page </TITLE></H1> is incorrect. The <TITLE> tag should appear only inside the <HEAD> tags at the start of the document.*

Inserting Inline Graphic Images

Most Web documents contain inline graphics. This section contains an example of a logo added as an inline graphic. For this example, the logo is kept on your local drive in the same directory or folder that the source HTML document is kept.

In its simplest terms, a local inline graphic can be included in a document using raw HTML by including its source after the IMG markup in the form <IMG SRC= "path/filename.type">, where the .type extension is one of the standard image file types, such as .gif or .jpg. If you need to specify a path to the image file, you should use forward slashes, even if you are working on a Windows system where paths are usually specified with backslashes. The browser will correctly translate the forward slashes in the IMG path into backslashes if required. If you are storing the HTML document in the same directory as the graphic file, you can omit the path. For example, the raw HTML entry for an inline image without a path may appear as:

```
<IMG SRC="logo.jpg">
```

This adds the logo to the document and displays it at the point in the document where the <IMG> tag is placed. By default, text is aligned with the bottom of the image, but not all browsers follow this standard. You can use the ALIGN attribute to specify that the text should be aligned at the top, bottom, or middle of an inline graphic. Table 3-2 shows you a list of the common alignment options for images in relation to any surrounding text.

Attribute	Description
<ALIGN="left">	Aligns the image with the left margin. Subsequent text will flow along the image's right side.
<ALIGN="right">	Aligns the image with the right margin. Subsequent text will flow along the image's left side.
<ALIGN="top">	Aligns the top of the image with the top of the tallest item in the current text line.
<ALIGN="bottom">	Aligns the bottom of the image with the baseline of the current text line. Note that this alignment rule is slightly different than ALIGN="top" in that the text baseline is the line that runs under the text and that some characters, like 'g' and 'y', will extend below the baseline. This is the default alignment.
<ALIGN="middle">	Aligns the middle of the image with the baseline of the current text line.

Table 3-2: Alignment attributes for images.

Not all browsers can display graphic images, and all browsers provide options to allow the user to disable image display if they wish—which makes pages display much faster. To make sure that others viewing your page are not left in the dark, use the ALT attribute of the <IMG> tag to specify text to display in place of the image. For example, using the text "Welcome to the Authors Home Page" for the alternate text results in HTML code that appears as:

```
<IMG SRC="logo.jpg" ALT="Welcome to the Authors Home Page">
```

Specifying text in the ALT attribute field lets a person viewing the page from a text-based browser, such as Lynx on a VT100 terminal, see the words "Welcome to the Authors Home Page" at the location of the logo. In addition, the latest browser versions from Netscape and Microsoft display the ALT text in the status line at the bottom of the browser.

Note that not all images need to have an ALT attribute. If you use an image as a simple graphic or placement element, such as a fancy bullet or as a replacement for a horizontal rule, you don't need, and probably shouldn't have, an ALT attribute. The point to keep in mind here is that the ALT attribute is an alternative to the image; if the image isn't essential to the navigation or understanding of the page, you should consider whether you need an ALT attribute with the tag.

TIP *There are many other attributes for the <IMG> tag that you will want to use. A complete discussion of creating and using both inline and external graphics is the subject of Chapter 6.*

Using the Paragraph Tag & Its Attributes

Unlike in typical word processor documents, line wraps in your document have no effect on how the HTML document displays in a browser. Pressing Enter may add line spaces to your HTML document, but the lines will not appear when displayed in a browser. Multiple spaces are also ignored. All spaces and multiple returns are collapsed to a single space. In order to specify a paragraph, you use the standard opening and closing paragraph tags (<P> and </P>). The paragraph tag ends the current line and automatically inserts additional spacing prior to the start of the next line.

Although the paragraph tag is a container tag, it does not strictly require an ending tag since the browser can always figure out where the paragraph ends. However, good practice recommends that you use the end tag. This is partially to make HTML more compatible with SGML, but more importantly, it opens the way to include attribute information for the paragraph, such as centering or justification. The following is the HTML source code for the single paragraph of text for the Authors home page:

```
<P>Welcome to the Authors Web Site. We hope you will find your visit both
educational and entertaining.</P>
```

The <P> tag has an associated ALIGN attribute that allows you to align the paragraph text on the left or right margins or to center the text. For example, you can use the following code to center the paragraph text shown earlier:

```
<P ALIGN="center">Welcome to the Authors Web Site. We hope you will find
your visit both educational and entertaining.</P>
```

A Simple HTML Page

At this point we can show you a basic HTML page. Here is the code for a page that simply displays a logo image and some text and uses the points you have just read about:

```
<!DOCTYPE HTML PUBLIC "-//W3C//DTD HTML 3.2 Final//EN">
<HTML>
<HEAD>
<META NAME="Author" CONTENT="Brent Heslop,David Holzgang">
<TITLE>Authors Home Page</TITLE>
</HEAD>
<!-- MAKE SURE BKGND COLOR IS WHITE -->
<BODY BGCOLOR="white">
<IMG SRC="logo.jpg" ALT="Welcome to Authors Home Page">
<H2>Authors Home Page</H2>
<P>Welcome to the Authors Web Site. We hope you will find your visit both
educational and entertaining.</P>
</BODY>
</HTML>
```

Figure 3-1 shows you this very simple page.

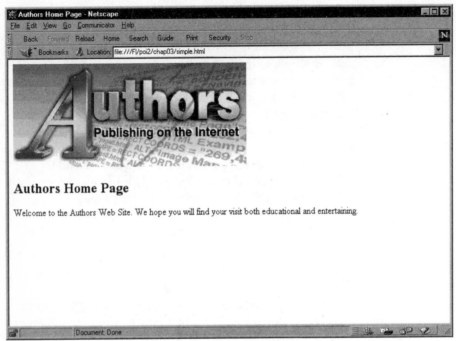

Figure 3-1: A simple HTML page showing an image and some text.

Using Horizontal Rules

The horizontal rule element is another way to divide your document into sections. The default rule is a shaded line that, when viewed with a gray background, looks like an inset 3D bar drawn across the width of the page. You may see some impressive horizontal rules in Web pages. Many people use inline graphic images in place of horizontal rules. You insert a horizontal rule into your document by using the <HR> tag. Since a horizontal rule is not a container, it does not have an end tag.

In HTML 3.2 there are four attributes to the horizontal rule to let you specify the thickness, width, alignment, and shading of horizontal rules. For example, you could specify a rule that is a line 18 pixels thick, appears centered, and is 50 percent of the width of the document. Table 3-3 shows you the attributes that allow you to describe how the horizontal rule should look. Figure 3-2 shows you examples of different horizontal rule settings.

Attribute	Description
<HR SIZE="*n*">	Specifies the thickness of the horizontal rule in pixels. The "*n*" stands for the number of pixels.
<HR WIDTH="*n*">	Specifies an exact width in pixels or a relative width measured in percentage of document width. The "*n*" stands for a number of pixels; if followed by a "%" sign, it indicates the percent of document width.
<HR ALIGN="*alignment*">	Specifies the alignment of the rule. The three choices are LEFT (left aligned), RIGHT (right aligned), or CENTER (centered). By default, the rule is centered.
<HR NOSHADE>	Specifies that you do not want any shading of your horizontal rule.
<HR COLOR="#*rrggbb*">	Specifies a color for your horizontal rule. Uses the same techniques for setting color described under the BGCOLOR attribute for the <BODY> tag. *This attribute is a Microsoft extension, so it will only work with Microsoft Internet Explorer.*

Table 3-3: Attributes for horizontal rules.

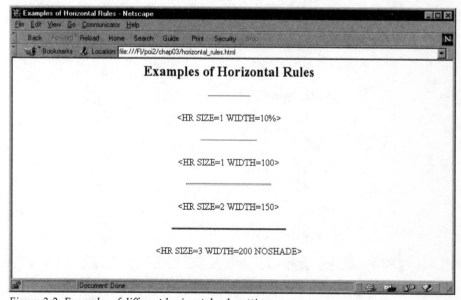

Figure 3-2: Examples of different horizontal rule settings.

TIP

Just because something looks great in your browser doesn't mean it will look great when viewed in other browsers. Many Web designers overuse graphic elements like the horizontal rule. A good rule of thumb is to use a horizontal rule only where you would put one on a paper document.

Using Lists

There are three basic types of lists you can use in an HTML document: unordered lists, ordered lists, and definition lists. An *unordered* list is simply a bulleted list. An *ordered* list is a numbered list. A *definition* list is also called a *glossary* list. Definition lists let you create two columns, one for terms and one for the description of the term. Figure 3-3 shows you examples of how each type of list is typically displayed.

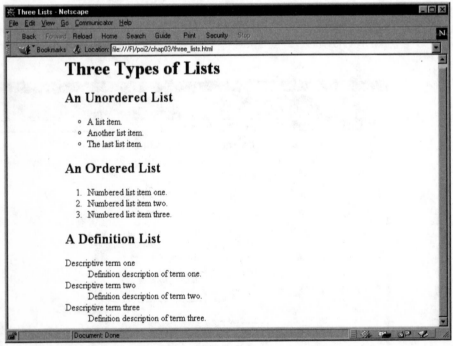

Figure 3-3: Examples of the three types of HTML lists.

In addition to these three basic types of lists, HTML defines two others: directory lists and menu lists. These are both unordered lists but were meant to be rendered in a slightly different format. A *directory* list is a list of short items (less than 24 characters) meant to be rendered without bullets in multiple columns. A *menu* list is a similar list of short items meant to be rendered in a single column. These tags date from early in the HTML standard; however, most browsers don't make any distinction between these two types of lists and ordinary unordered lists. For that reason, we don't recommend that you use these tags.

Because basic lists are so common in HTML documents, we'll briefly cover each of these three types of lists in this chapter. Of the three types, however, the unordered (bulleted) list is the most common.

Unordered (Bulleted) Lists

You create an unordered list by using the <UL> tag. This tag requires an end tag. The unordered list uses the list item tag <LI> to indicate each separate list entry. This tag appears before the text used to denote the list item; the ending </LI> tag is optional. The browser determines what character to use for a bullet. A DOS browser, for example, may use an asterisk or a dash. The following is an example of the unordered list shown in Figure 3-3:

```
<H2>An Unordered List</H2>
<UL>
    <LI>A list item.
    <LI>Another list item.
    <LI>The last list item.
</UL>
```

Normally, list items are displayed as single-spaced lines. However, you can combine the paragraph tag to create a double-spaced effect around list items, as shown in the following example:

```
<H2>A Single-spaced and Double-spaced List</H2>
<P>This is a standard, single-spaced, unordered list</P>
<UL>
<LI>Check out the 32-bit version of Drag And File.
<LI>View any file with Drag And View Gold.
<LI>The new version of Drag And Zip includes Zip View, which lets you
decompress files from any Web browser.
</UL>
<P>Here is a double-spaced unordered list<P>
<UL>
<LI><P>Check out the 32-bit version of Drag And File.</P>
<LI><P>View any file with Drag And View Gold.</P>
<LI><P>The new version of Drag And Zip includes Zip View, which lets you
decompress files from any Web browser.</P>
</UL>
```

This would appear similar to Figure 3-4 in your document.

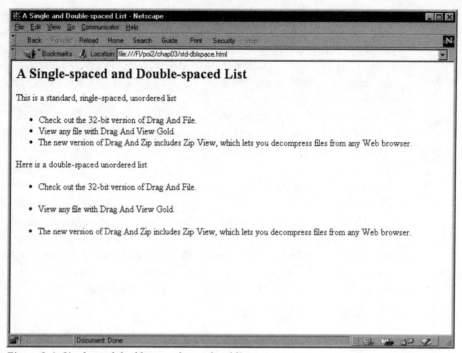

Figure 3-4: Single- and double-spaced unordered lists.

A common mistake is to embed a heading within a list to make the list font larger. Doing so will lead to unpredictable results. It may look fine on your screen, but it will most likely cause problems when viewed with other browsers.

The <UL> tag and its associated <LI> tag have an associated TYPE attribute that allows you to specify the type of bullet used for display. If you wish to set your list to use circles, for example, you would code:

```
<UL TYPE="circle">
```

You may choose "disc," "square," or "circle"; "disc" is the normal default. Adding the attribute to the <UL> tag sets the type of bullet for the entire list. Adding the attribute to the <LI> tag sets the type of bullet for that individual list item and, usually, for all subsequent items as well. It is up to the browser how it displays each of these bullets; however, you can generally be confident that each will display differently.

The <UL> tag also has a COMPACT attribute. This is used to request that the browser render the list in a more compact style; however, for many browsers, this has no obvious effect.

Ordered (Numbered) Lists

You create an ordered or numbered list by using the <OL> tag. This tag requires an end tag. Like the unordered list, the ordered list uses the list item tag <LI> to indicate each separate list entry. This tag appears before the text used to denote the list item; the ending </LI> tag is optional.

When the page is displayed, the browser will automatically insert the numbers for each list item. This is convenient because it eliminates numbering errors. The following is an example of an ordered list:

```
<H2>An Ordered List</H2>
<OL>
    <LI>Numbered list item one.
    <LI>Numbered list item two.
    <LI>Numbered list item three.
</OL>
```

This code would appear onscreen as shown earlier in Figure 3-3.

The <OL> tag and its associated <LI> tag have an associated TYPE attribute that allows you to specify the type of numbers used for display. Table 3-4 shows you the values of the TYPE attribute that can be used with the <OL> tag to format all the list items in a list or can be used with individual <LI> tags to selectively format list items.

Value	Description
<OLTYPE="1"> <LITYPE="1">	Uses Arabic numerals for the list or list item.
<OLTYPE="I"> <LITYPE="I">	Uses capital Roman numerals for the list or list item.
<OLTYPE="i"> <LITYPE="i">	Uses lowercase Roman numerals for the list or list item.
<OLTYPE="A"> <LITYPE="A">	Uses capital letters for the list or list item.
<OLTYPE="a"> <LITYPE="a">	Uses lowercase letters for the list or list item.

Table 3-4: Type attributes for ordered lists.

The <OL> tag also has a START attribute that allows you to specify the starting value used for the list. The value for START is always a number, even if you have set the list to use Roman or alphabetic numbering; the browser will convert the sequence number to the correct display value. And, like the

<UL> tag, there is also a COMPACT attribute. This requests that the browser render the list in a more compact style; however, for many browsers, this has no obvious effect.

In addition to the TYPE attribute, LI entries for an ordered list can have a VALUE attribute, which specifies the sequence number for the list item. Like its unordered counterpart, setting the VALUE or TYPE for a list item generally affects all subsequent items in the list. Using the various attributes together, you can create a variety of useful and easily understood lists in your documents.

Definition Lists

You create a definition list by using the <DL> tag. This tag requires an end tag. The definition list tags are used to construct a glossary-like entry. A definition list contains two elements: a definition title, <DT>, and its related list entry. Each definition list entry is preceded by the markup definition description <DD>. Like the <LI> tag, these tags do not require end tags. The definition title can only include text; however, definition descriptions can include additional HTML elements such as paragraphs, tables, or other list items. The following is an example of a definition list:

```
<H2>A Definition List</H2>
<DL>
   <DT>Descriptive term one
     <DD>Definition description of term one.
   <DT> Descriptive term two
     <DD> Definition description of term two.
   <DT>Descriptive term three
     <DD> Definition description of term three.
</DL>
```

This code would appear onscreen as shown earlier in Figure 3-3.

Combining Lists

You can also combine lists within one another and combine list types. For example, you can use two ordered lists and a definition list to create an outline as shown in the following code, which also combines Roman numerals with lowercase letters. This code appears onscreen as shown in Figure 3-5:

```
<H2>Outline Example</H2>
<P>Here is a combination of list types used to create an outline.</P>
<OL>
<LI TYPE="I" VALUE="1">Topic One
<DL>
<DT>
     <OL TYPE="a">
```

```
        <LI>sub-topic 1
        <LI>sub-topic 2
    </OL>
</DL>
<LI TYPE="I" VALUE="2">Topic Two
<DL>
<DT>
    <OL TYPE="a">
        <LI>sub-topic 1
        <LI>sub-topic 2
    </OL>
</DL>
<LI TYPE="I" VALUE="3">Topic Three
<DL>
<DT>
    <OL TYPE="a">
        <LI>sub-topic 1
        <LI>sub-topic 2
    </OL>
</DL>
</OL>
```

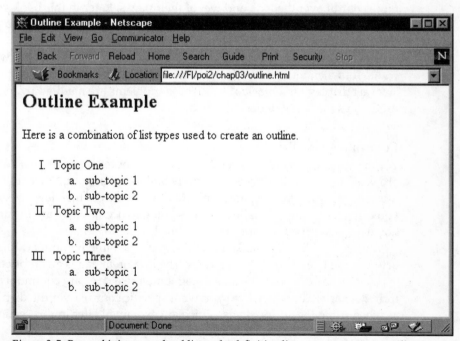

Figure 3-5: By combining an ordered list and a definition list, you can create an outline.

There are a few points worth noting in this code. First, you can see that we have indented the HTML code here to make the tags easier to follow. This helps to avoid problems with missed end tags and incorrect tag use. Second, note that we used the definition list <DL> tag without using both of the subsequent item tags; instead, only the <DT> tag was used to force the items over a small amount. Using a definition list to move items over and align text under items is a common way to create lists that look more like the standard ones you would create on paper.

Adding White Space

By now you can see a striking difference between how HTML documents are written and how documents are created with a word processor. Instead of focusing on a physical description of a page's margins, fonts, and formatting, the tag structure of HTML focuses on the content of a document and what the various parts of a document mean. The original focus of HTML markup is on the classification and content of a paragraph or group of words instead of the look of the displayed or printed page, and this is still a major issue in the Web community. However, as time goes on and more demands are made to make pages look exciting, new tags and methods have arisen to allow designers more control over the look and feel of their pages. Later in this book you will read all about how to control the look and feel of your pages using advanced tags like <TABLE> and <STYLE> (Chapters 5 and 8).

One basic stylistic requirement is to be able to force lines to break when you want, not when the browser feels it's ready. Another is the ability to predefine an exact display for a block of text. These problems are handled by the very useful tags that we will describe next.

Controlling Line Breaks

When the page you create is rendered on a computer screen with a Web browser, the size of the screen is entirely beyond your control. Generally, the browser itself flows your paragraphs to fit the width of the view screen, so you can never tell where a line break is going to occur. There are instances, however, where you'll want to force a line break.

You can use the line-break tag, <BR>, to break a line without adding a space between the lines as the <P> tag does. The line-break tag is an empty element and therefore does not have an end tag. Line-break tags are commonly used to format a variety of data where you want specific control over the display, such as when using the address tags, which are explained later in this section.

The <BR> tag takes one attribute, CLEAR. The CLEAR attribute can be used to move down past floating images on either margin. <BR CLEAR=LEFT> moves down past floating images on the left margin, <BR CLEAR=RIGHT> does the same for floating images on the right margin, while <BR CLEAR=ALL> does the same for such images on both left and right margins. Figure 3-6 shows you an example of how you can use the <BR CLEAR=LEFT> to move text down below an image.

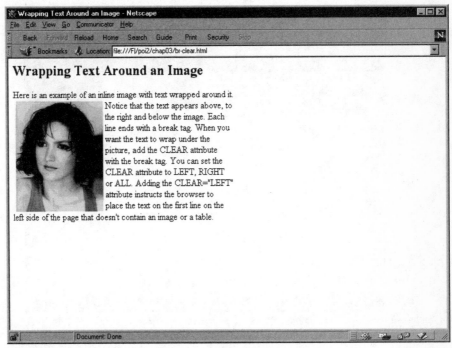

Figure 3-6: Using the CLEAR attribute with the <BR> tag.

Displaying Preformatted Paragraphs

If you want to create a block of text on a page and be sure that the style of text will not change when rendered by a Web browser, use the preformatted text element. This shows up as the <PRE> tag in HTML text. When rendering this tag, Web browsers use a fixed-width font, like Courier, and break lines exactly where they are broken in your source document. Preformatted text is useful when you want to create a computer listing or a simple table (we'll cover using HTML tags for more complex tables later). For example, the following code describes a simple table in HTML using the <PRE> tag:

```
<PRE>
<STRONG>Conversion Table</STRONG>

Country          Currency       Value in US $

France           Franc          5.54
Germany          Mark           1.64
Great Britain    Pound          0.62
Italy            Lira           1616
Spain            Peseta         139
</PRE>
```

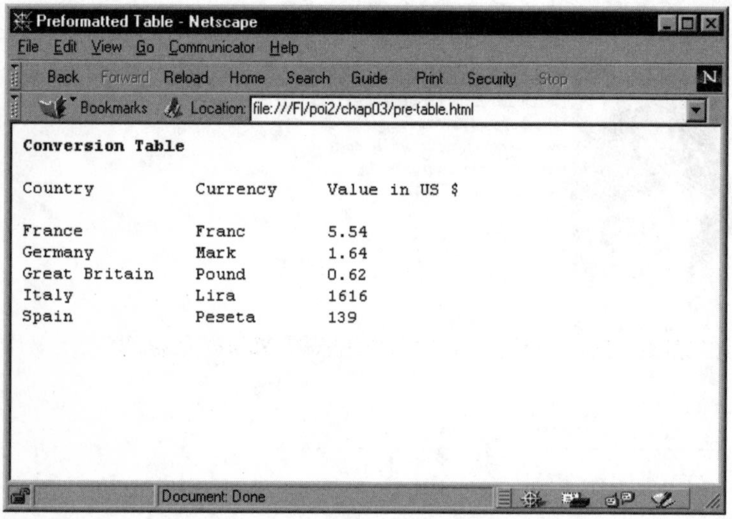

Figure 3-7: Using the <PRE> tag to generate a simple table.

This displays as shown in Figure 3-7. Note that you can use character styles, like strong and bold, within the PRE text, but you add spacing by simply entering carriage returns; tags like <BR> don't work inside a <PRE> tag.

You can also use the <PRE> tag to insert a text file like a Usenet news article or to add white space to a document. As you see in Figure 3-7, any white space you add between the opening <PRE> and the closing </PRE> tags displays when viewed in a browser. When you use the <PRE> tag, you can add character styles and links, but not paragraph elements such as headings. Keep your text lines between 60 to 80 characters when using the <PRE> tag. If you exceed 80 characters, it's likely that the text will not display correctly since most screens are only 80 characters wide and the browser will not break lines of text within the <PRE> tags.

Adding an Address

The <ADDRESS> tag, as the name implies, is used to identify a block of text that contains an address. The <ADDRESS> tag is similar to the <P> tag in that it represents a set of distinctive text that is usually separated from text before and after it by a standard paragraph break. However, the <ADDRESS> tag requires an end tag. As with most HTML tags, the address is rendered in a distinctive fashion by Web browsers. Although different browsers choose different styles, typically the address will appear in italics. As mentioned earlier, the <ADDRESS> tag is frequently used with the <BR> tag to separate each line of the address. Here is an example of how to code the <ADDRESS> tag:

```
<H2>Contact Information</H2>
<ADDRESS>
The Coriolis Group<BR>
14455 N. Hayden Road, Suite 220<BR>
Scottsdale, AZ  85260<BR>
Tel: (602) 483-0192<BR>
Fax: (602) 483-0193
</ADDRESS>
```

This would be rendered as shown in Figure 3-8. Note that, like a <P> tag and unlike the <PRE> tag, you can use formatting tags in an address.

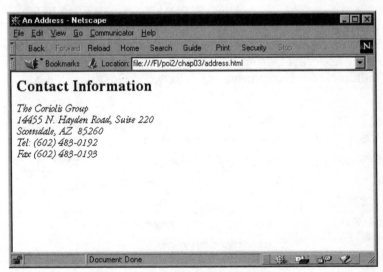

Figure 3-8: An address style rendered by Netscape Navigator.

Formatting Characters

You may want to control some elements of text layout within a paragraph as well. There are some tags that give explicit directions about rendering text, such as bold or italic, while others are focused on the *logical* meaning instead of the *physical* rendering.

Using Logical Styles to Format Characters

Logical styles tell the browser what kind of text to present and leave the rendering decisions to the browser. In general, you should use a logical representation instead of the physical representation whenever you don't have a strong design reason to do otherwise. Logical style tags are preferred over physical tags because logical styles allow for more intelligent handling of text. Logical styles also give users more flexibility, allowing anyone to set up their browser however they see fit. Finally, logical styles can be rendered in non-print forms, such as reading text for vision-impaired users. The biggest limitation to logical styles is that you often find instances that have no corresponding logical style. Suffice it to say that the use of logical styles versus physical styles is a subject of great contention within the Web community.

There are two common forms of logical emphasis used on an HTML page, <EM> for emphasis and <STRONG> for strong emphasis. Typically, the <EM> tag is rendered as *italic*, and the <STRONG> is rendered as **bold**.

Table 3-5 is a list of the logical styles and how they are used. Note that Table 3-5 lists the opening tag but you also need to end each formatting markup with the respective closing tag for the style. For example: <EM>This appears in italics</EM>. This appears in <STRONG>bold</STRONG>.

Tag	Used For
<EM>	Basic emphasis; typically rendered in an italic font.
<STRONG>	Strong emphasis; typically rendered in a bold font.
<DFN>	Defining instance of the enclosed term.
<CODE>	Extracts from program code.
<SAMP>	Sample output from programs, scripts, etc.
<KBD>	Text to be typed by the user.
<VAR>	Variables or arguments to commands.
<CITE>	Citations or references to other sources.

Table 3-5: Logical style tags.

Using Physical Styles to Format Characters

The second category of styles for formatting characters is *physical styles*. Physical styles give an explicit direction to a Web browser about how to render a character. There are several physical styles, including bold, italic, underline, strikethrough, and fixed-width fonts. The physical styles also include subscript and superscript and give you some control over font size, which we will discuss further in the next section.

Unlike the paragraph formatting tags, both the logical and the physical character formatting tags do *not* cause a line break, and you can use multiple styles in the same sentence. Character formatting tags always *surround* the text that is to appear formatted; for example, bold text would start with <B> and end with </B>. Browsers will do their best to respect multiple nested character formatting tags as well; most browsers will accept and display correctly the following:

```
<P>You can insert <I>multiple nested <B>character formatting</B> tags</I> in a sentence.</P>
```

However, you must take care to nest tags correctly. For example:

```
<P>You can insert <I>multiple nested <B>character formatting</I> tags</B> in a sentence.</P>
```

would be an error and would not display properly since the bold and italic tags overlap.

Table 3-6 is a list of the physical styles and how they are rendered.

Tag	Renders As
<B>	Bold
<I>	Italic
<TT>	Teletype or monospaced font
<U>	Underline
<STRIKE>	Strikethrough
<SUB>	Subscript
<SUP>	Superscript
<BIG>	Larger font
<SMALL>	Smaller font

Table 3-6: Physical style tags.

Setting Font Size in Text

The <BIG> and <SMALL> tags are a fairly coarse method for setting font sizes. HTML 3.2 has a more effective and more controlled method, which is using the <FONT> and <BASEFONT> tags.

The <FONT> tag requires an end tag and has two attributes: SIZE and COLOR. The COLOR attribute specifies the color of the enclosed text using the same technique as the BGCOLOR attribute that you read about earlier.

The SIZE attribute is a little more complicated. The idea is that the font being displayed on the viewer's browser is being displayed at some specific point size the viewer has set. This is taken as the base font size for adjustment purposes. The <FONT> tag provides for seven levels of font size, from 1 to 7. By default, the current size of the text being displayed by the browser is considered to be SIZE=3. You may specify alternative sizes for the enclosed text by using either absolute values, from 1 to 7, or relative values, specified by + and –. Using these methods, the two following lines of HTML generate the same display, shown in Figure 3-9:

```
<H2>Changing Font Sizes Using Absolute Values</H2>
<P>Set font size to<FONT SIZE=2> absolute two</FONT> and then set font size
to<FONT SIZE=6> absolute six</FONT> and now back to normal size.</P>
<H2>Changing Font Sizes Using Relative Values</H2>
<P>Set font size to<FONT SIZE=-1> two using a --1 setting</FONT> and then
set font size <FONT SIZE=+3>to six using a +3 setting</FONT> and now back to
normal size.</P>
```

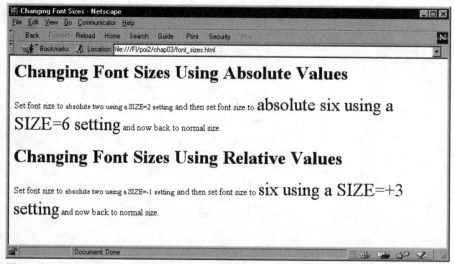

Figure 3-9: Using the <FONT> tag to control font size in your documents.

The <BASEFONT> tag, as you might expect, is used to set the base font size for all text following the tag. Unlike the <FONT> tag, <BASEFONT> is an empty tag so the end tag is forbidden. Like the <FONT> tag, the SIZE attribute is an integer value ranging from 1 to 7. The base font size applies to the normal and preformatted text but not to headings, except where they are modified using the <FONT> tag with a relative font size.

TIP *Some authors have incorrectly used the <BASEFONT> tag to set intermediate font sizes within the document. They do this by adding an end tag, </BASEFONT>, and then resetting the <BASEFONT> with a new tag. This is both incorrect and unnecessary. As noted, the <BASEFONT> tag is an empty tag and should never have an end tag. Furthermore, once you have set the base font, you should control any further font size changes by using the <FONT> tag. You can always use <FONT> with a specific SIZE value to get the size that you want. You should never use more than one <BASEFONT> tag in a document.*

You can use the <FONT> tag along with some of the other text tags to create some useful effects. For example the following two lines of code use standard HTML markup to show a chemical symbol and a trademark name:

```
<H2>Examples of using the Font tag Subscript and Superscript to add a
chemical symbol and the Trademark symbol. </H2>

<P>The presence of water (H<FONT SIZE=1><SUB>2</SUB></FONT>O) is an
essential element of life on our planet.</P>
<P>PhotoDeluxe<SUP><FONT SIZE=1>TM</FONT></SUP> is an easy and inexpensive
photo modification package from Adobe.</P>
```

This would be rendered as shown in Figure 3-10. Note that you can specify the tags in any order as long as you terminate them in the reverse order.

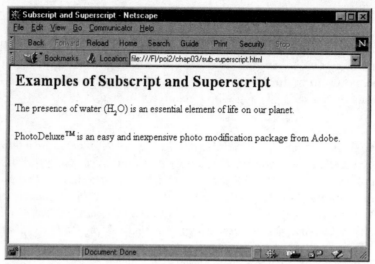

Figure 3-10: You can use the <FONT> tag along with some of the other text tags to create some useful effects.

Specifying a Font

Both Netscape and Microsoft have implemented an additional attribute (called FACE) in the <FONT> tag that allows you to specify what font you want used for rendering the enclosed text. Although this is a very useful and desirable feature, it has already been superceded by the new Cascading Style Sheets, which allow you to set many design and display features of your documents, including selecting fonts, in a simple and elegant way. You will learn all about using style sheets in your HTML documents later in Chapter 8. In addition, the style sheet specification is a fully developed and supported extension to HTML, while the FACE attribute is not. If you need to set the font for your Web documents, we recommend that you use the new <STYLE> tag or its variants to do so and avoid the FACE attribute.

Adding Special Characters

HTML lets you include a large number of "special" characters that can be displayed by a browser but are not normally found on a U.S. keyboard. The word *special* is in quotes because for many writers of HTML pages, these characters are simply part of the alphabet; however, because of the limitations of the original definition of the 7-bit character set, we are now forced to take special measures to create these characters. In HTML parlance, these special characters are called *character entities*. Most of these characters are accented characters, symbols such as currency marks, and characters that have special meaning to the HTML language, such as the double quotation mark ("), the greater than (>) and less than signs (<), and the ampersand (&).

The special characters of HTML include all accented characters plus special punctuation and currency marks. HTML uses a special escape code to identify characters that have special meaning to HTML. An *escape code* refers to a character that is used to identify to a program that the character or characters following it represent a control or special character. The escape code begins with an ampersand (&) and ends with a semicolon. With HTML, you can enter special characters in one of two ways:

■ Begin with the escape code, followed by a special mnemonic keyword, followed by the semicolon; for example, © inserts the copyright symbol in your text.

■ Begin with the escape code, followed by a pound sign and a number representing the character, followed by the semicolon; for example, © enters the same copyright symbol in your text.

A complete list of these special characters, including both keywords and numeric values, can be found in Appendix B, "An HTML & Style Sheet Reference." Using these methods, the two following lines of HTML generate the same display, which is shown in Figure 3-11:

```
<H2>Adding Special Characters Using Names</H2>
<P>You can code &quot;special&quot; characters in two ways: using names or
numbers. The special characters include characters like &eacute; and
&Eacute; as well as symbols like &copy;. But the most common special
characters are ones like &amp;, &gt;, &lt;, and &quot; which are used in
HTML coding and so cannot be used in ordinary text.</P>
<H2>Adding Special Characters Using Numbers</H2>
<P>You can code &#34;special&#34; characters in two ways: using names or
numbers. The special characters include characters like &#233; and &#201; as
well as symbols like &#169;. But the most common special characters are ones
like &#38;, &#62;, &#60;, and &#34; which are used in HTML coding and so
cannot be used in ordinary text.</P>
```

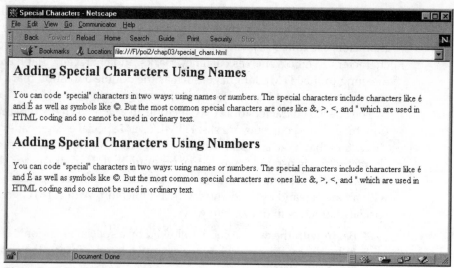

Figure 3-11: Displaying special characters in your documents.

There are a few special characters that you should take particular note of: the non-breaking space, the copyright symbol, and the registered trademark symbol. The *non-breaking space* (or) allows you to enter one or more spaces into a standard HTML document and ensure that the browser will not compress that space into any surrounding white space characters and will not break a line of text at that space. The copyright and registered trademark symbols are often required for legal protection. Note that the standard trademark symbol is not included in the special characters because it can be created with standard HTML markup (see "Setting Font Size in Text" earlier in this chapter).

▼ A Multilingual Web

One common use of special character codes in documents is to add accented characters to display non-English language text. To enhance the "World Wide" aspect of the Web, the next version of HTML, 4.0, has taken special care to provide better ways of handling multiple languages in documents. This will ultimately create a more truly multilingual and international Web environment.

The new language attributes are LANG and its associated direction attribute, DIR. These new attributes may be applied to most tags that are containers; in

➡

particular, they can be applied to the <BODY> tag and related content tags such as <P> within the body section. For example, you can set the language attribute within the body of a document like this:

```
<BODY LANG="en-US">
```

The language attribute takes a single value, which should be a language code that identifies a natural language spoken, written, or otherwise conveyed by human beings for communication of information to other human beings. Computer languages are explicitly excluded from these codes.

Language codes consist of a primary code and an optional series of subcodes; in the example above, the primary code is en for English and the secondary code is US to indicate the U.S. variant of the English language. RFC1766 (available at ftp://ds.internic.net/rfc/rfc1766.txt) gives the list of language codes available for HTML documents.

Not all languages read in the same direction—for example, while English reads from right to left, Hebrew and Arabic read from left to right. To handle this problem, HTML 4.0 provides an additional direction attribute, DIR (not to be confused with the <DIR> tag). This attribute tells the browser what direction the named language should be read in. The two allowed values are RTL for reading right to left and LTR for reading left to right. This attribute is particularly useful if you have embedded text within your page that reads in different directions; English text embedded within a page in Hebrew, for example.

Using Divisions

The division tag, <DIV>, can be used to break your document into a structure of hierarchical divisions. The <DIV> tag is a container for text or other elements and that means that it must have an end tag. The division tag will end a paragraph if inserted after a <P> tag, even if there is no end paragraph tag in front of it. Unlike the paragraph tag, however, a division tag causes text to display on a new line but does not cause spacing in front of and behind the text. For example, the following will display on successive lines in the display:

```
<DIV>This is an example of the &lt;DIV&gt; tag. All this text is within one
DIV section with no specific alignment requested.</DIV>
<DIV>This is a continuation of the text in a new DIV section with no
alignment.</DIV>
```

The <DIV> tag has an associated ALIGN attribute that allows you to align the division's text on the left or right margins or to center the text. For example, the following code provides the various alignments as shown in Figure 3-12:

```
<H2>A Left-aligned Division</H2>
<DIV ALIGN="left">This is an example of the &lt;DIV&gt; tag. All this text
is within one DIV section aligned left.</DIV>
<DIV>This is a continuation of the text in a new DIV section with no
alignment.</DIV>
<H2>A Centered Division</H2>
<DIV ALIGN="center">This is an example of the &lt;DIV&gt; tag. All this text
is within one DIV section aligned center. This is extended to show how the
centering works for a single DIV section.</DIV>
<DIV>This is a continuation of the text in a new DIV section with no
alignment.</DIV>
<H2>A Right-aligned Division</H2>
<DIV ALIGN="right">This is an example of the &lt;DIV&gt; tag. All this text
is within one DIV section aligned right.</DIV>
```

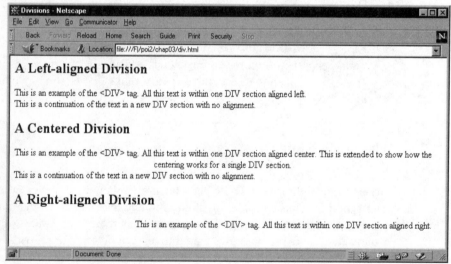

Figure 3-12: Examples of alignment for the <DIV> tag.

Note in Figure 3-12 that the new <DIV> tags without specific alignment default to ALIGN="left" setting.

HTML 4.0 Extensions

Although we have occasionally shown attributes for tags that are limited to one or another of the browsers, all of the tags described so far in this chapter are part of the HTML 3.2 standard. However, in this section we will look at a few tags that have been proposed as part of the HTML 4.0 standard and implemented by Netscape and Microsoft. Use these extensions with care because a page created to look great on the Netscape or Microsoft browser may look positively dreadful on another browser until all the browsers support 4.0.

Theoretically, a browser should ignore any markup elements or attributes that it doesn't understand; unfortunately, not all of them do so. You should always check your work with an assortment of browsers to make sure the rendering is acceptable on all of them.

Client-Pull Using the <META> Tag

You read earlier about using the <META> tag to embed additional information into your HTML pages. One use of this tag is to allow a browser to "pull" information from the server by loading successive pages. This depends on having the browser interpret the tag and take the correct action. Fortunately, both Netscape's and Microsoft's browsers already understand and support this tag.

To make client-pull work, you must use specific attributes in the <META> tag. The following shows two simple pages that call one another in an endless loop:

```
<HTML>
<HEAD>
<META HTTP-EQUIV="REFRESH" CONTENT="5; URL=file:///MacaoHD/page2.html">
<TITLE>Load Second Document</TITLE>
</HEAD>
<BODY>
<P>After five seconds have elapsed, the document
"page2.html" will be loaded.
</BODY>
</HTML>

<HTML>
<HEAD>
<META HTTP-EQUIV="REFRESH" CONTENT="5; URL=file:///MacaoHD/page1.html">
<TITLE>Load First Document</TITLE>
</HEAD>
<BODY>
<P>After five seconds have elapsed, the document
"page1.html" will be loaded.
</BODY>
</HTML>
```

This technique requires that you set the two attributes HTTP-EQUIV and CONTENT, as shown in the code. Setting the HTTP-EQUIV attribute to "REFRESH" causes the document to be reloaded. The CONTENT attribute contains a number, which specifies the number of seconds to wait before the reload occurs. The optional URL element within the CONTENT attribute gives the URL of the page to be loaded; if no URL is given, the current document is reloaded.

TIP

According to the HTML 4.0 specification, you can also use the NAME attribute (NAME="REFRESH") instead of the HTTP-EQUIV="REFRESH" attribute to generate the reload action. (See Netscape's tag reference at http:// developer.netscape.com/library/documentation/htmlguid/ and the HTML 4.0 specification at http://www.w3.org/TR/WD-html40-970917/.) However, with the current generation of browsers, using the NAME attribute won't work; you must use the HTTP-EQUIV attribute to generate the header required for the reloading.

Common Extensions

There are two very important extensions to HTML that have been implemented by both Netscape and Microsoft, but in slightly different ways. These are the <SCRIPT> tag and the <STYLE> tag. Both of these tags are defined in HTML 4.0.

The <SCRIPT> tag allows you to embed scripting commands into your HTML pages. If the browser understands the scripting language you have selected, you can get it to perform various functions. The <SCRIPT> tag is a container tag and contains the scripting commands that should be executed. It takes three possible attributes: LANGUAGE, TYPE, and SRC. However, only one attribute, LANGUAGE, which specifies the scripting language included within the tag, is currently supported. At present, the Netscape browser only understands the JavaScript scripting language. Microsoft's Internet Explorer understands JavaScript, JScript, and VBScript, a proprietary scripting language used by Microsoft's applications. You will learn more about scripting later in Chapter 11, "Creating Interactive Pages With Scripts & Objects."

The <STYLE> tag represents a new effort to allow specific design layout on a Web page without losing the benefits of cross-platform and multiple-user environments. The <STYLE> tag is a container and contains a variety of layout information for the browser. It has three defined attributes: TITLE, MEDIA, and TYPE. However, only TYPE and TITLE are currently supported. You will learn all about using style sheets in your HTML documents later in Chapter 8.

Validating Your Web Document

One simple but important final step you should take is to validate your document before publishing it. Validation ensures that your HTML code meets the HTML specifications and that there are no broken links or missing elements in the document.

There are three basic methods of validation. First, you may be using an HTML editor, like SoftQuad's HoTMetaL Pro, that will perform validation for you. Second, you may have a stand-alone program, like Spyglass HTML validator, that will perform a validation for you. Finally, you can use a Web-based, real-time application program, like Doctor HTML, to validate your document. If you have validate built into your HTML editor, this is the easiest and, probably, the best way to validate your documents. However, if you don't, the following two sections discuss the other alternatives.

Validation Software

One way to validate your HTML documents is to use a validation application. There is a variety of validation applications, covering every standard platform and operating system. Each application works somewhat differently, and each one has different requirements. As you might expect, the best way to find a satisfactory validation application is on the Web itself. See the tip for some recommendations on where you can start your search.

Real-Time Web Validation

There is one unique option that you have for validating your Web documents—using a real-time validation site to inspect a page or pages that you designate and to provide instant feedback on what's right and wrong along with the location of any errors. Some sites, like Doctor HTML, also provide spell-checking—after removing the HTML codes from the text of the document—and estimates of how long it will take to download your page.

All of these sites use a similar technique. You enter a URL and the site will download the page and evaluate the HTML code. Generally, the validator site then provides a display that highlights any questionable tags and gives you their location by line number on the page. You can often also get a display of the HTML code with line numbers so that you can immediately see what the problem might be.

One of the best sites for real-time validation is Doctor HTML (located at http://www2.imagiware.com/RxHTML/), which provides an extensive check of how a page is tagged. Figure 3-13 shows you a typical summary output of our Author's Web site from Doctor HTML.

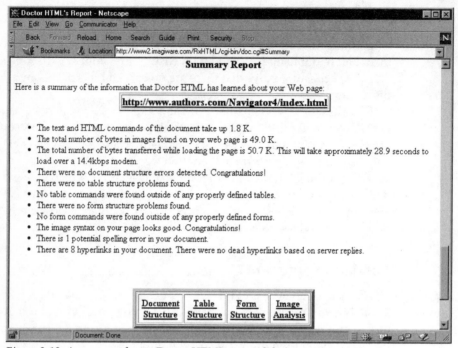

Figure 3-13: A summary from a Doctor HTML page validation report.

TIP

As always, there are many sources on the Web itself for more information on validation. The Web Design Group keeps a great list of validators, among other useful information. You can check their recommendations at http://www.htmlhelp.com/links/validators.htm. Another good list of validators is provided by Khoral Research Inc. at http://www.khoral.com/staff/neilb/weblint/validation.html. Last, but never least, Yahoo also provides an excellent list of validation software and real-time validation sites at http://www.yahoo.com/Computers_and_Internet/Software/Data_Formats/HTML/Validation_Checkers/.

Publishing Your Web Document

When you get ready to publish your work on the Internet, you'll need to replace all the local references with URLs that point to your system as the network sees it. For example, during development, a local reference might be:

```
hyperlink file:///c:/mydoc/support/page1.htm
```

but the network reference might be:

```
http://www.mycompany.com/info/mydoc/support/page1.htm
```

If all of your local references are going to change in a uniform way, you can ease this transition by setting a <BASE> tag in the HEAD section of the document. During development, the <BASE> tag would read:

```
<BASE HREF="file:///c:/mydoc/support/">
```

but when you publish it, you would change that to:

```
<BASE HREF="http://www.mycompany.com/info/mydoc/support/">
```

This would redirect all the references within the document to point to the new location.

When you use paths to set where your documents and images—and any other elements on the page—are located, you make use of some standard path elements. In particular, you can include paths in your page as absolute paths, like "http://www.mycompany.com/info/mydoc/support/image.gif" or you can use a relative path, which might look like "support/image.gif." Generally, the relative path method will work best for most references and requires the least modification when you go to publish the page. Which method you use, however, depends on several factors. You will read a complete discussion of these issues in Chapter 4, "The Art of Linking."

Moving On

You can create professional-looking pages with the text elements you've learned about in this chapter. But to really capture your audience, you'll want to be able to both link your pages together using hypertext links and mix text with images. The next chapter reveals how to effectively add links to the text components you have learned about in this chapter to create even more effective and more powerful Web pages. Then, in Chapters 6 and 7, you will learn all about creating and using images in your documents.

chapter 4

The Art of Linking

The last chapter took you through HTML basic training, showing you how to create a Web page. This chapter shows you how to create more exciting, interactive Web pages by including hypertext links to HTML documents and files. In addition to text-based links, this chapter explains how you can create links using images. For example, if you're creating a Web site for your business, you may want to use your company logo as a link to your home page.

There are three types of links you can create: intra-system links, inter-system links, and intra-page links. *Intra-system* links link to other pages or files on the current server; *inter-system* links link to a page or file on another server; and *intra-page* links link to another place in the current page. Well-designed Web pages make use of all three types of links to produce easy-to-use, easy-to-read Web documents and to link to other related sites and resources on the Web.

Whether you want to include a link to a document or file residing on the current server, to a document or file on another server, or to a section of the current page, you use the anchor tag to create the link. The next sections explain how to use the anchor tag.

The Anchor Tag

As we just stated, the anchor tag lets you create a link. A typical anchor tag for an inter-system link looks similar to the following:

```
<A HREF="http://www.acme.com/products.html"> Acme Products</A>
```

The opening <A> tag includes the hypertext reference (HREF) that specifies the place you're linking to, that is, the destination URL or the name of a file. In this case, the destination is the URL http://www.acme.com/products.html.

Notice that this links to a file named products.html. Between the opening <A> and closing </A> tags is the text that will be highlighted on the page as the *link text*, in this case, "Acme Products." Figure 4-1 identifies the parts of an anchor tag that point to a remote file.

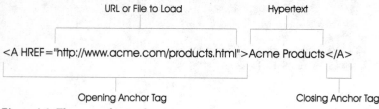

Figure 4-1: The parts of an anchor tag.

Creating a Link to a Local Page or File

When you're authoring for the Web, you keep individual pages as short as is practical. This means you will wind up with a lot of intra-system links to individual pages. The following example steps you through the process of creating two pages that point to each other with links. Figure 4-2 shows the results of these two pages.

1. In a text or HTML editor, type the following tags to create the first page that includes a link to page2.html:

```
<HTML>
<HEAD>
   <TITLE>Link Sample Page 1</TITLE>
</HEAD>
<BODY>
<H1>Link Sample Page 1</H1>
<P>
This is a reference to <A HREF="page2.html">page two</A>.
</P>
</BODY>
</HTML>
```

2. Save the file as page1.html.

3. In the HTML editor, create a new HTML document that contains the following. This creates a page titled Link Sample Page 2 that includes a link to page1.html:

```
<HTML>
<HEAD>
    <TITLE>Link Sample Page 2</TITLE>
</HEAD>
<BODY>
<H1>Link Sample Page 2</H1>
<P>
This is a reference to <A HREF="page1.html">page one</A>.
</P>
</BODY>
</HTML>
```

4. Save the file as page2.html.

5. To test your sample link pages, open either page with File | Open Page, File | Open, or the equivalent command in your Web browser. When you click on the hypertext, you are transported to the page referenced as the hypertext reference in the anchor tag.

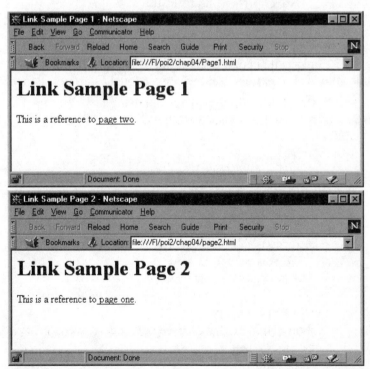

Figure 4-2: How page1.html and page2.html appear in the Netscape Navigator browser.

The links you include to pages at your site need to be clearly organized and easily accessible. For example, you may want to add a list of links to the bottom of your home page. It is important that you present links that match the structure of your site. The following text-based navigation links follow the structure set up in Chapter 2 and build on the sample HTML page presented in the previous chapter. The Web documents that need links are as follows:

- About links to about.html, which explains the purpose of the Authors Web site. It also supplies information on various methods of support, including phone numbers and e-mail addresses.

- What's New? links to news.html, which contains information about updates to the site.

- HTML links to html.html. The HTML page includes a listing of HTML tags and examples.

- Programming links to prog.html, a page containing links to helpful pages about interactive World Wide Web programming including CGI and Perl, JavaScript, Java, and VRML.

- Resources links to resources.html, which includes numerous links to helpful Web publishing tutorials and utility programs.

- UCSC links to a page that present links to Web projects created by the talented HTML students at the University of California, Santa Cruz Extension.

- Feedback links to feedback.html, which includes a comments-and-suggestions form.

```
<P ALIGN="CENTER">
[
<A HREF="about.html">About</A>
<A HREF="news.html">What's New?</A> |
<A HREF="html.html">HTML</A> |
<A HREF="prog.html">Programming</A> |
<A HREF="resources.html">Resources</A> |
<A HREF="ucsc.html">UCSC</A> |
<A HREF="feedback.html">Feedback</A> |
]
</P>
```

Figure 4-3 shows how these text-based navigation links appear when viewed in Netscape Navigator.

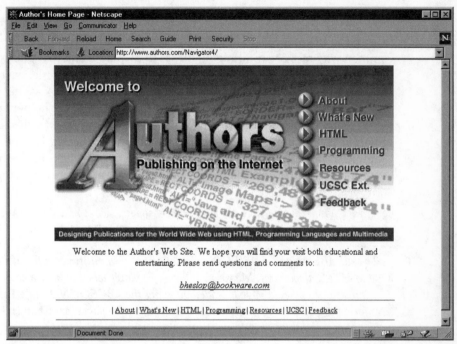

Figure 4-3: Sample text-based navigation links.

The Importance of Local Links

As a rule, you should always include a link from every HTML page back to your home page. From your home page you can create links to other pages or to other interesting places on the Web. It's also important if you are presenting information in a linear manner, such as a structured tutorial, to use links that assist readers navigating through your pages in both forward and backward directions.

Imagine for a moment you've navigated through the Web to a particularly interesting page. You add it to your bookmark list for future reference. Several days later, you call up the bookmark to look at that page again. Now you may wish to look at other pages on the same site, but unfortunately there are no links on the page you are viewing. At this point, you are effectively "lost in hyperspace," with little or no idea how to move around to other pages on the same server.

Linking to Local Files

In addition to linking to local HTML pages, you can also link to a local file. A common way to share multimedia files is to display a link that points to the file. When a reader clicks on the hypertext that points to the file, the browser will either begin downloading the file or display a dialog box asking the reader how he or she wants to handle the file. If a plug-in or helper application is set up to handle the file type, clicking on the hypertext will start the plug-in or helper application and load the file automatically. The following example shows a link to a sound file. When the person clicks on the hypertext, "sound file," the browser displays its audio player and begins playing the audio file:

```
Here is a link that points to a <A HREF="speech.au">sound file</A>.
```

TIP *The <EMBED> and <OBJECT> tags let you have a multimedia file display inside your HTML document. Microsoft Internet Explorer lets you have a sound file play automatically when a page is loaded by using the <BGSOUND> tag. For more information on adding multimedia files to your Web pages, see Chapter 10.*

Absolute & Relative Paths

When you link to a file at your site, you need to use only the filename as the HREF attribute setting. You don't need a full URL prefix. This is allowed because your browser uses the HREF as a relative path. That is, if you opened the first file with File | Open Page, File | Open, or the equivalent browser command, the browser assumes that all HREFs that do not have a prefix specified, such as http://www.authors.com/, are located in the same relative directory as the first file you opened. This is a handy feature, since you can move both files to another directory and the links will still work. The following shows a link that uses a relative path:

```
<A HREF="page2.html">page one</A>
```

If you look at the "jump destination" in the status line of your browser (typically found at the bottom of the browser), you'll see the complete path to the file; for example:

```
file:///d|/html/page2.html
```

The file URL is used to reference files contained on your local disk. Once you publish your document, the file URL is replaced with the HTTP URL of your site. For example, after copying the page1.html and page2.html files to the directory storing your public HTML documents and moving the mouse pointer on the page 2 hyperlink text, you'll see in the status line that the URL is added before the filename automatically. Using the relative filename page2.html as the hypertext reference (HREF="page2.html"), the status bar displays the full URL in a format that is similar to the following:

```
http://www.authors.com/page2.html
```

Use relative filenames instead of full or file URLs. You never need to use a drive name when referencing an HTML document or file in a link. If you want to reference a file in your Web page, simply put it in the same directory as your HTML documents or create a subdirectory and reference the subdirectory in your URL.

When you reference a subdirectory, don't preface the subdirectory with a forward slash. This indicates starting at the top or root of the file system. Instead, you want to use the relative directory path. For example, if you store all your press releases in a subdirectory named news and you wanted to link to the file named rel-1097.html, you reference the file in the subdirectory as:

```
<A HREF="news/rel-1097.html">
```

Adding Special Characters

To reference some documents and files, you may need to use a special character in the URL or filename. For example, with the Macintosh, it is common practice to include spaces in filenames. In order to use the space character, you would need to use an escape code, which is indicated by a percent sign (%) and a two-character hexadecimal symbol from the ISO-Latin-1 character set. An *escape code* refers to a character that is used to identify to a program that the character or characters following it represent a control or special character. For example, the hexadecimal equivalent for the space is 20, so to add a space, you would add %20, as shown in the following example:

```
<A HREF=http://www.authors.com/special%20characters.html>Special
Characters</A>
```

Table 4-1 lists some of the most common special character escape codes. Appendix B includes a complete listing of the hexadecimal equivalents for all the characters in the ISO-Latin-1 character set.

If you surround a URL or path and filename with quote marks in the HREF attribute setting, you can include spaces that are a part of a filename. However, if you omit the quotes, the link most likely will not work.

TIP

To make your pages easy to reference, make sure your file and directory names use only alphanumeric characters, a dash (-), an underscore (_), or a period (.). A plus sign (+) and a dollar sign ($) are also legal but are rarely used in filenames. If you use any other character, anyone trying to link to your site will need to use an escape code to add the special character.

ASCII Value	Special Character	Escape Code
09	Tab	%09
32	Space	%20
35	Number sign (#)	%23
37	Percent sign (%)	%25
38	Ampersand (&)	%26
39	Apostrophe (')	%27
63	Question mark (?)	%3f
64	At symbol (@)	%40

Table 4-1: Escape codes for special characters.

Creating a Link to Another Site

The most powerful type of link allows you to create a link from your page to any page on the Web. Remember that since this is an actual inter-system link, you'll need to be connected to the Internet for it to work.

To help you understand inter-system links, the following examples take a look at each part of an anchor tag. After the opening anchor tag (<A), you need to add the HREF attribute followed by the protocol you want to use. In most cases this will be the http:// prefix followed by the host address of the site. If you want to connect to the site and open the default HTML document, usually index.htm or index.html, you can simply end the URL with a forward slash. For example, to specify the URL for the Authors Web site, enter:

```
<A HREF="http://www.authors.com/">
```

If you want to open a specific HTML document or link to a specific file, also enter the path and the name of the HTML document or file to be opened on the remote system:

```
<A HREF="http://www.authors.com/links.html">
```

In order for the person reading your page to be able to activate your link, you need to add the hypertext that you want the person to click on and add the closing anchor tag. Typically the hypertext appears underlined in blue on the page:

```
<A HREF="http://www.authors.com/">The Authors Web Site</A>
```

TIP | *Be careful to check the link on a regular basis. Because you generally don't control the location of the destination page you are linking to, it's possible that the link may change. It is also possible that the network or host system you're linking to may be down at various times, making your link inoperative.*

Creating a Link Within a Page

Sometimes presenting a short page isn't practical or desirable. For example, you may have a long product price list or a FAQ (Frequently Asked Questions) list you may want to keep together so people can easily print it out. When you have long pages, it's convenient to provide links between sections of the same page. This is done with intra-page links. There are a couple of unique steps for creating intra-page links; specifically, establishing names or labels for the jump-to destinations in the page. Labels in pages are also created with the anchor tag, using the NAME attribute of the anchor tag to create the label.

TIP | *In order for a link within a page to work, you need to include enough text so the link points to a section that isn't on the screen at the same time as the hyperlink text.*

The following example steps you through the process of creating a link within a page (remember all the examples are included on the Companion CD-ROM, so you don't have to type in all the text):

1. Move the insertion point and enter the text you want to use as the starting (source) hyperlink text.

   As the HREF attribute setting, enter a pound sign (#) and a label name that describes the section to which you want the person to move. In this example we used the label #contact. This link is sometimes called the *source* link, and the link that it points to is called the *target* link. After adding the label name, add the hypertext that the reader clicks onto to move to the destination (target) link and add the closing anchor tag </A>:

```
<HTML>
<HEAD>
   <TITLE>About Authors</TITLE>
</HEAD>
<BODY>
<H1>About the Authors Web Site</H1>

<P>
This site is designed to help anyone learn about HTML and interactive
World Wide Web programming.
</P>

<P>
If you would like to contact us, you can jump directly to the section
with information about
<A HREF="#contact">contacting the Authors</A>.
</P>
   . . .
```

2. Move the insertion point to the destination you want to let your reader jump to in your document. To create a target link, you use the anchor tag with the NAME attribute instead of the HREF attribute. Omitting the pound sign (#), enter the text you used as the label name in step one for the NAME attribute setting. When you create a target link, which is where you want the reader to end up, you don't need hyperlink text, so you can add the closing anchor tag directly after the opening anchor tag. The following is an example of a destination (target) link:

```
   . . .
<A NAME="contact"></A>
<H2>Contacting the Authors</H2>
<P>We are committed to creating useful and productive Web sites. To
help you make full use of HTML and World Wide Web and interactive
programming, we will gladly do our best to answer your questions. You
can contact us by phone at</P>
<PRE>
   Phone           (415) 967-0559
   Fax             (415) 967-8283
</PRE>
<P>If you would like to contact us via e-mail, send a message to one of
the following e-mail addresses/P>
<ADDRESS>
Brent Heslop bheslop@bookware.com
David Holzgang cheshire@sonic.net
</ADDRESS>
</BODY>
</HTML>
```

3. Save your file.

4. To test the intra-page links, open the document with File | Open Page, File | Open, or the equivalent command in your Web browser. When you click on the hypertext, you are transported to the section containing the target link.

In the preceding example, the destination for the specified jump appears as a label named "contact" in the same page. The pound sign prefix in the HREF attribute (HREF="#contact") indicates that the jump is internal to this page; the jump takes the reader to the place in the document with the label "contact."

Anchor tags can be used for creating hypertext jumps and creating labels at the same time if you use both HREF and NAME attributes. Also, you can combine inter-page jumps with jumps to specific labels so that you can jump from a particular point in one page to a particular point in another page. To jump to a target link located in a different page, simply preface the label name with the name of the HTML document containing the target link. For example, suppose the following source link was contained in a page named graphics.html:

```
<A HREF="resources.html#graphics">Image Editors</A>
```

When a reader clicks on this link's hypertext, the resources.html document is opened displaying the section containing the target link:

```
<A NAME="graphics"></A>
```

Creating a Link With an Image

Images that appear in your page are referred to as *inline* images. Inline images can also be used as links. To create a link using an image, replace the link text with the <IMG> tag to specify the image. Remember that if you're using an image as a link, be sure to include the <IMG> tag's ALT attribute to let readers using text-based browsers know what type of image you're displaying.

TIP *By default, a blue border appears around a linked image. You can remove the blue border by adding the BORDER="0" attribute to the <IMG> tag.*

The following is an example of an image link that uses the company logo as a link to the Web site's home page:

```
<A HREF="index.html"><IMG SRC="logo.gif" ALT="Logo" BORDER="0"></A>
```

Navigation bars are usually created with image maps. However, you can also create a navigation bar with individual linked images. The following example shows a series of images used as navigation icons:

```
<P>
<A HREF="index.html"><IMG SRC="images/home.gif" ALT="Home" BORDER="0"></A>
<A HREF="about_us.html"><IMG SRC="images/about_us.gif" ALT="About"
BORDER="0"></A>
<A HREF="news.html"><IMG SRC="images/news.gif" ALT="News" BORDER="0"></A>
<A HREF="order.html"><IMG SRC="images/order.gif" ALT="Order Form"
BORDER="0"></A>
<A HREF="links.html"><IMG SRC="images/links.gif" ALT="Links" BORDER="0"></A>
<A HREF="feedback.html"><IMG SRC="images/feedback.gif" ALT="Feedback Form"
BORDER="0"></A>
</P>
```

Figure 4-4 shows the result of using the previous example of linked images.

Figure 4-4: Linked images let you create a simple navigation bar.

Inline images are usually small in size. Creating a link using an image lets you present a *thumbnail*, a small version of an image, that links to a larger high-resolution image. If you want to present a large version of an image, create a thumbnail that links to the larger image rather than slow down your page by adding a large high-resolution image. Clicking on the thumbnail displays the image as an *external image* so it appears by itself in the browser window. These are the tags used to create a link from a thumbnail:

```
<A HREF="globe.jpg"><IMG SRC="globe.gif" ALT="World Globe" BORDER="0"></A>
```

TIP *Be careful not to include a space before the opening or after the closing <IMG> tags. Otherwise a blue line appears where you have added spaces.*

Figure 4-5 shows an example of a photo album displaying small thumbnails that each link to an external image.

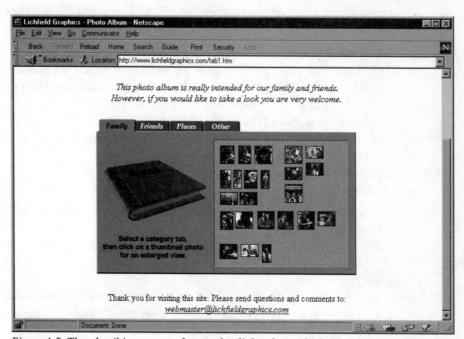

Figure 4-5: Thumbnail images are often used to link to larger, higher-resolution versions of the images.

Creating Links to Different Types of URLs _____

As you learned in Chapter 1, you can use different types of URLs to connect to different protocols. You can also use different protocols to create links. For example, using FTP, you can link directly to files residing at an FTP site. The following sections list examples of links created using protocols other than HTTP. We have identified optional parts of a protocol in square brackets, [ ]. Items in the square brackets need to be specified only when necessary.

TIP | *Always use lowercase letters to specify the protocol in a link.*

Using FTP URLs _____

The File Transfer Protocol, FTP, is the most popular way to deliver text or binary files over the Internet. Most FTP sites are anonymous FTP sites that let anyone log in using the login name *anonymous* and a non-restrictive password such as *guest* or an e-mail address. An FTP URL appears in the following format:

```
ftp://hostname[:port]/[path]/[filename]
```

It is rare that you need to specify a port number when connecting to an FTP site. The default FTP port is port 21. However, if you are making a link to a specific port, you will need to add the port number.

Most anonymous FTP sites use a directory named pub for storing public files. The following is a link that moves the reader directly to the pub directory at Netscape's FTP site:

```
<P>Here is a link that goes directly to
<A HREF="ftp://ftp.netscape.com/pub/">Netscape's FTP site</A>.</P>
```

You can connect to a non-anonymous FTP site by specifying a URL using the following format:

```
ftp://[username:password@]hostname [:port]/[path]/[filename]
```

TIP | *Although it is possible to add a link to a non-anonymous FTP site, it is not a good idea to link to an FTP site that is password-protected. Doing so makes the password available for anyone viewing your HTML source.*

Just as you can link to a local file, you can also make the link point to a specific file at an FTP site. For example, you could add the path and filename to the previous example's link to point to the Windows version of the Netscape Communicator file at Netscape's FTP site to let a person directly download the file, as shown here:

```
Here is a link that points to the <A HREF="ftp://ftp.netscape.com/pub/
communicator/4.0/windows/c32e40.exe">Windows version of Netscape
Communicator file</A> at Netscape's FTP site.
```

Using Gopher URLs

The Gopher protocol lets you connect to a Gopher site and transfer several different types of files. The easiest way to connect to a Gopher site is to link to the top level of the site. A Gopher URL appears in the following format:

```
gopher://hostname[:port]/[gophertype][selector]
```

The following example connects to the top level of the home of the first Gopher site at the University of Minnesota:

```
<A HREF="gopher.tc.umn.edu/">University of Minnesota's Gopher site</A>
```

Gopher servers typically reside on port number 70; however, it is possible that it could be on another port. If the port is different from the default, you will need to add the port number. For example, the Gopher server on the University of California, Santa Barbara's host machine, ucsbuxa.ucsb.edu, is on port 3001 instead of port 70, so the corresponding URL is:

```
<A HREF="gopher://ucsbuxa.ucsb.edu:3001/">InfoSurf</A>
```

Sometimes you'll see another number following the port address. This number is the gophertype. The *gophertype* is a single number or letter that identifies the type of file or server. Table 4-2 lists the most common gophertypes. After the hostname, port number, and the gophertype, the Gopher server can specify a selector. The *selector* is one or more characters that give the path to a particular area of a Gopher server. The path to a file in a Gopher URL can consist of keywords, escaped hexadecimal equivalents for the space, a tab and other special characters, and cryptic numeric codes. The following shows a Gopher URL with a gophertype and a selector.

```
<A HREF="gopher://gopher.ucsc.edu:70/11/">UCSC InfoSlug</A>
```

The first *1* in the *11* is the directory gophertype, and the second *1* is the selector. As you can see, linking to a specific Gopher document or file can be a little tricky. The easiest way to link to a Gopher document is to follow the links to the document and then copy and paste the URL as the HREF attribute setting.

Gophertype	File or Server
0	Text file
1	Directory
2	CSO phone-book server
3	Error
4	BinHex (.hqx) Macintosh file
5	DOS binary archive
6	UNIX uuencoded file
7	Index-Search server
8	Telnet session
9	Binary file
g	GIF format graphics file
T	tn3270 session
I	Image file

Table 4-2: Gophertypes.

Using News URLs

Usenet news URLs let you refer to a newsgroup. The Network News Transfer Protocol (NNTP) server specified in the browser's preferences responds to the request. A news URL appears in the following format:

`news:newsgroup`

Notice that the news URL doesn't include the double forward slashes that you use with the http:// and ftp:// URLs. A news URL opens the browser's newsreader with the current newsgroup selected. The following is an example of a link to the comp.infosystems.www.authoring.html newsgroup:

```
<A HREF="news:comp.infosystems.www.authoring.html">
comp.infosystems.www.authoring.html newsgroup</A>
```

If you want to display a specific newsgroup article, you would add the message-ID to the news URL. The message-ID is the unique ID of the posted news article. This is usually a long string of alphanumeric characters used internally by the news server. Newsgroup articles frequently change or expire and are deleted. If you want to make sure the article is available, copy the article and save it as an HTML document; then create a link to the file rather than to the news article itself.

TIP *In order for a person to link to a newsgroup or article, his or her browser must be set up in the preferences section to work with an NNTP (Network News Transfer Protocol) server.*

Using Mailto URLs

To let your readers communicate with you via e-mail, add *mailto:* and your e-mail address as the anchor tag's HREF attribute setting. A mailto URL appears in the following format:

```
mailto:username@hostname
```

As in the news URL, you don't include forward slashes after the colon. If the person has set up the mail (Simple Mail Transfer Protocol) server and an e-mail program for his or her browser, clicking on the link using mailto displays the e-mail Composition window with the To field addressed to the e-mail address you specified. Figure 4-6 shows the results of clicking on a link using mailto, as shown in the following example:

```
<P>Please send questions and comments to:
<ADDRESS>
<A HREF="mailto:bheslop@bookware.com">bheslop@bookware.com</A>
</ADDRESS>
</P>
```

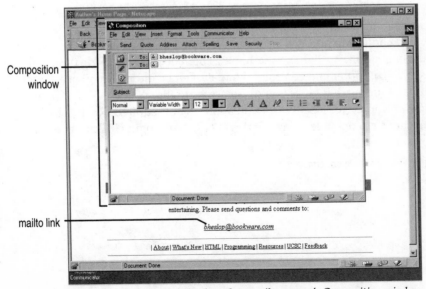

Figure 4-6: A mailto link displays the e-mail program's Composition window.

TIP | *Be careful! Some e-mail addresses contain the percent sign (%). You need to use the escape sequence for the percent sign, which is %25.*

TIP | *Not all browsers support the mailto URL scheme. To make sure your readers can still send you e-mail, it is a good idea to use your e-mail address as the hyperlink text.*

Using Telnet & Rlogin URLs

The *Telnet* protocol is a general, bidirectional, communications facility that lets you log in to other computers or use an interactive service on a remote host. In order for a Telnet link to work, the reader must have specified a Telnet application. When the reader clicks on a link pointing to a Telnet server, a Telnet terminal window appears and opens the Telnet session. A Telnet URL appears in the following format:

```
telnet://hostname[:port]
```

You do not need to specify a port number if you want to connect to the default Telnet port, which is port 23. However, if you are making a link to a specific port, you will need to add the port number. The following is a link to the National Basketball Schedule Service provided by the University of Colorado at Boulder:

```
<A HREF="telnet://culine.colorado.edu:859/">NBA schedule service</A>
```

Clicking on the hypertext causes the browser to open a Telnet terminal window and connect to port 859 on the host culine.colorado.edu.

Rlogin is similar to Telnet. Like Telnet, rlogin allows you to log directly on to the server computer and control it remotely. Telnet and rlogin open a Telnet terminal window that gives you direct access to the specified host. The reader will be prompted for a password unless one is not required. Remote login connections are possible using the rlogin URL. An rlogin URL appears in the following format:

```
rlogin://username@hostname
```

Using Links Effectively

The following is a list of tips to help you use links effectively when you're creating your Web pages:

- Place punctuation after the closing anchor tag (</A>). Also, make sure you do not include any spaces before or after the link text. If you insert a punctuation mark or add a space, the punctuation mark or space will appear underlined.

- Give readers a way to visit or return to your home page. Every subsequent page should include a link back to the home page.

- Don't use the phrase "click here." This not only insults the intelligence of your reader, but it is a nondescriptive way of presenting information.

- Include tables of contents, indexes, or cross-reference links for long Web documents. You want readers to be able to go directly to the page or section that contains the information they want. If you need to present a long document, such as documentation or a manual, consider using a portable document format such as Adobe Acrobat for the file and including a link to it.

- Don't use too many links. Numerous links can make your pages difficult to read.

- Use thumbnails for large images. This lets readers decide which images they want to view in a larger size.

- Include the size of the file in the text if you include links to a large file such as an image, sound, or video file. This gives users some idea of how long it will take to download the file.

- Make sure readers using text-based browsers can navigate your site. If you add an image as a link, also add a text-based link to the page. This is also important if you include links using image maps (clickable images). Creating image maps is covered in Chapter 6, "Getting Graphic With Images."

- Test your links to other Web pages. Many Web publishers have the best intentions when publishing a Web page but don't take the time to ensure that the links work and are up-to-date. The next section lists validation utilities that test both local and remote links.

Verifying Links

One of the most common and aggravating situations on the Web is encountering links that are outdated or links that just don't work. Before you publish your Web document, use a Web validation utility or service such as Doctor HTML to test your links. You can check just the links using Doctor HTML by clicking on the Verify Hyperlinks check box in the report form, as shown in Figure 4-7. Doctor HTML is free. If you don't have a Web site that can be reached by Doctor HTML, you can select, copy (Ctrl-C), and paste (Ctrl-V) your text and Doctor HTML will verify that your links work. The URL for Doctor HTML is http://www2.imagiware.com/RxHTML/.

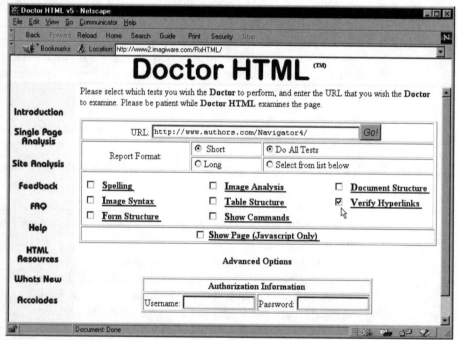

Figure 4-7: Doctor HTML includes an option to verify links.

If you are using Windows, an excellent validation program is the InfoLink Link Checker, which is available in both a shareware and freeware version. InfoLink Link Checker is impressive. The interface is intuitive and link checking is very fast. The results are displayed in the InfoLink browser in HTML format. InfoLink allows the user to have control over what links to verify and how to display the results. You can even verify links of multiple pages at the same time by using the Page List feature. Both the shareware and freeware versions are included on the Companion CD-ROM. Figure 4-8 shows the InfoLink Link Checker program. You can check for the latest version of the InfoLink Link Checker at http://www.biggbyte.com/.

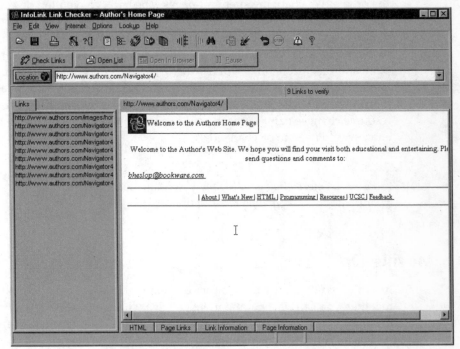

Figure 4-8: The Windows InfoLink Link Checker is an excellent tool for verifying links.

UNIX users can use missinglink (ml), which is a Perl shareware program that validates links. The missinglink program searches through HTML files and checks each hyperlink to make sure the file it references really does exist. It can check links to files on the server, links that point to files on other HTTP servers, and links within image maps. The program will report any problems it finds to the user. The missinglink program is also on the Companion CD-ROM. You can check for new versions of the missing link program at http:// www.rsol.com/ml/.

The Future of Links & URLs

Web sites and pages are frequently deleted, renamed, or moved. Because no single entity owns or runs the Internet, it is impossible to keep track of all Web sites and let readers know about the changes. The Universal Resource Name (URN) convention, a new naming scheme that is still in the works, addresses the problem of changing sites and pages. The URN convention doesn't rely on specific hostnames. Instead it relies on a name server system similar to domain name servers set up to identify Web resources by a unique ID name assigned to them. The idea is that instead of referring to a specific machine, directory path, and file, future links will use the URN convention to refer to a unique ID name. When a link is attempted, the computer will access a lookup table that in turn translates the name into the specific address information. This way, if a resource changes names or is moved to another location, only the lookup table entry would need to be changed.

TIP *For more information on URL and URN addressing, check out the following URL: http://www.w3.org/pub/WWW/Addressing/.*

Moving On

Now that you've learned the basics of creating HTML pages and linking them together, you can start getting more creative with the content of the pages. In Chapter 5, you'll learn about the many possibilities for using tables and frames for formatting your pages.

chapter 5

Tables, Columns & Frames

Once you have begun presenting pages on the Web, you are likely to run into certain limitations in basic HTML fairly quickly. As time has passed, HTML has advanced to include more sophisticated elements that allow a page designer more control over the presentation of text or images on a page. Three of the most common elements that are used for advanced presentation are tables, multiple columns, and frames. Tables allow you to present both images and text in a conventional tabular format; however, with a little ingenuity, HTML tables can also be used to control presentation on your Web pages in ways that don't initially seem to have any relationship to a table layout at all. Multicolumn text is another useful tool; the same table tags and attributes allow you to use this staple of printed presentation as a part of your Web documents as well. In addition to providing you with the ability to use tables to create columns, Netscape has introduced an HTML extension to create snaking, newspaper-style columns. Netscape and Microsoft have both implemented an additional layout element, frames, which allow you to partition the user's browser display into separate areas and display different pages in each area.

This chapter introduces you to all of these advanced HTML features for controlling your page layout. First it explains how to use tables to present data in a tabular format and lay out pages. Next it illustrates ways to present information using multiple columns. Finally, it shows how you can create and manipulate frames to display your data in some useful and creative ways.

Creating Tables

One of the simplest and clearest ways to present many types of complex data is to use a table. Properly designed and used, tables allow the reader to see many relationships within a set of data in a clear and intuitive way. In this section, you will see how to create basic tables in HTML and how to adjust table presentation so that you can get the presentation effects that you want.

TIP *If you find creating tables from scratch a little daunting, you can easily use one of the standard HTML editors, like Netscape Composer, Microsoft FrontPage, HoTMetaL Pro, or Adobe PageMill, to create a simple table. All the HTML editing tools have support for simple tables and allow you to create them by simply specifying the number of rows and columns you want and then setting the associated table information. However, you generally cannot use these tools to create advanced tables or tables that will be used for layout purposes.*

Creating a Simple Table

A table is defined by the <TABLE> tag; since <TABLE> is a container, it requires an ending tag </TABLE>. So the actual table data is contained between the two tags. A table consists of a series of cells arranged in rows and columns. For an HTML table, you define each row and then the columns of cells within the row. The first tag used to create a table is the <TR> tag, which defines a single row. Within each row, the columns are formed from a series of table heading and table data cells.

Each cell contains table data, defined by the <TD> tag, or table headings, defined by the <TH> tag. The only difference between these tags is how the contents of the cell are displayed; generally, table headings are centered and rendered in bold font, while table data is rendered in a standard font. None of the interior table tags, <TR>, <TD>, or <TH>, requires an ending tag; however, for ease of reading and improved comprehension, we recommend that you use the ending tags, as shown in the following example. Figure 5-1 shows the results of the code in Listing 5-1.

Listing 5-1

```
<TABLE>
   <TR>
       <TH>Table Header (Row 1 Column 1)</TH>
       <TH>Table Header (Row 1 Column 2)</TH>
```

```
    </TR>
    <TR>
        <TD>Table Data (Row 2 Column 1)</TD>
        <TD>Table Data (Row 2 Column 2)</TD>
    </TR>
</TABLE>
```

Note that we have used indentation here to show the relationship of the various code elements. This can be important when working with tables, since tables can be nested inside one another and since it may not always be easy to tell without some help where one row ends and the next begins.

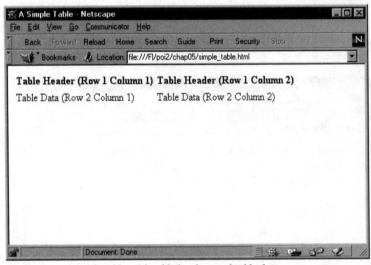

Figure 5-1: A simple table with table headers and table data.

Adding a Caption & Borders

The example in Figure 5-1 is fine as a basic table, but it lacks some elements that you would normally use in presenting information in a table. For example, most tables have some type of title, or caption, to tell the viewer what the table represents. In addition, tables often have borders around them to make them stand out from the surrounding text. HTML includes the <CAPTION> and <BORDER> tags that allow you to add these features to your tables. Listing 5-2 adds the BORDER attribute to the <TABLE> tag and adds a caption in italics at the bottom of the table.

Listing 5-2

```
<TABLE BORDER=2>
<CAPTION ALIGN="BOTTOM"><EM>A table with a border and a caption</EM></
CAPTION>
<TR>
   <TH>Table Header (Row 1 Column 1)</TH>
   <TH>Table Header (Row 1 Column 2)</TH>
</TR>
<TR>
   <TD>Table Data (Row 2 Column 1)</TD>
   <TD>Table Data (Row 2 Column 2)</TD>
</TR>
</TABLE>
```

The added HTML code is shown in bold for clarity. The results of these enhancements are shown in Figure 5-2.

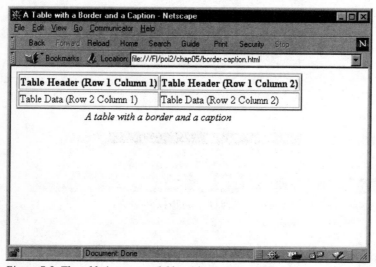

Figure 5-2: The table is more readable with a caption and borders.

Setting the BORDER attribute to 2 places a 2-pixel border around all the cells of the table. The number to which the attribute is set defines the width of the border in pixels. By default, the border is applied around the table and all the cells as well; however, as you will see later, you can control the interior borders by using another attribute, CELLSPACING.

The <CAPTION> tag defines a caption or title for the table. It requires an end tag. The <CAPTION> tag has only one attribute, ALIGN, which can be set to TOP or BOTTOM to define where the table title should be displayed. By default, the caption text is centered and aligned at the top of the table. Notice here that the attribute is set to ALIGN="BOTTOM," which causes the title to be displayed at the bottom of the table even though the actual caption text is defined at the beginning of the table. Note that you can use text tags, like <STRONG> and <EM>, within a <CAPTION>.

Controlling the Width & Height of a Table

Tables are automatically resized when the reader changes the size of his or her browser window. You can specify the width and height of the entire table by adding the WIDTH and HEIGHT attributes to the <TABLE> tag. The WIDTH attribute can be set to a number of pixels or as a percentage. For example, to specify a table that is 100 pixels wide, add WIDTH=100 to the <TABLE> tag. To specify a table that is the size of the current browser window, add WIDTH=100% to the <TABLE> tag.

To make the table display as small as possible, set a width smaller than the size of the text. However, specifying WIDTH=0 displays the table as though you didn't add the WIDTH attribute. Figure 5-3 shows a table without a WIDTH setting and a table with a WIDTH=1.

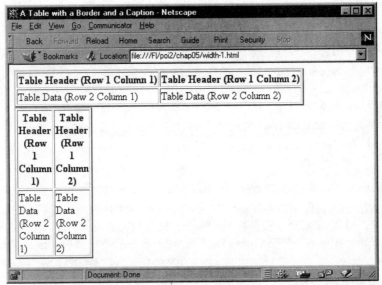

Figure 5-3: A table without the WIDTH attribute (top) and a table with the WIDTH set to a size smaller than the contents of the table cell (bottom).

TIP *To use a table to force a page layout, set the WIDTH so the table can be displayed without scrolling (for readers using laptops and low-resolution display screens). For example, to ensure the contents of your table can be read by the largest number of readers, set your table to a width of 440 pixels or less.*

Specifying the Width & Height of a Table Cell

In addition to specifying the width of an entire table, you can similarly specify the width and height of a table heading or table data cell. To specify the width of the individual cell, you add the WIDTH attribute to a table heading tag, TH, or a table data tag, TD. The WIDTH attribute can be set to a number of pixels or as a percentage. For example, adding WIDTH=50 to a <TD> tag specifies that the cell is 50 pixels wide. Adding the WIDTH=50% attribute setting to the <TD> tag would specify that the table cell be 50 percent the size of the table's width.

Note that although the WIDTH attribute only applies to the individual cell, by expanding a cell, you automatically influence all the other cells in the column since the browser automatically sizes all the cells in the column to match the largest cell.

To specify a minimum height for a table heading or table data cell, add the HEIGHT attribute to the <TD> or <TH> tag. By specifying the height for one cell, all the cells in the row are changed. If you don't specify the HEIGHT attribute or if a cell's contents, such as an image, have a greater height than specified, the cells are set to the height of the size of the largest cell.

Aligning Tables & Data in Table Cells

To align the entire table on the page, use the opening <DIV> tag and the alignment setting before the beginning <TABLE> tag, and use the closing <DIV> tag after the ending <TABLE> tag. For example, to center a table, you would enter:

```
<DIV ALIGN=CENTER>
<TABLE>
Table rows and cells…
</TABLE>
</DIV>
```

Alternatively, you can use the <CENTER></CENTER> tags in place of the <DIV ALIGN=CENTER> tag to center the table, as shown in the following example (the <CENTER> tag is an older tag, introduced before HTML 3.2; because it has become common practice to use the <CENTER> tag, it has been added to the HTML 3.2 standard).

```
<CENTER>
<TABLE>
Table rows and cells…
</TABLE>
</CENTER>
```

Using the <DIV> tag, you can use the ALIGN="RIGHT" setting to position the table on the right side of a page. By default, tables are left aligned.

Data in table cells can be aligned horizontally, vertically, or both horizontally and vertically. Table data cells are left aligned within the cell by default. As we mentioned previously, table headings are centered by default. The ALIGN attribute specifies the horizontal alignment. The available settings are LEFT, CENTER, and RIGHT. You can apply the horizontal text alignment to a specific cell or to a whole row at a time. For example, to right-align the data in every cell in a row, you would add the ALIGN attribute as follows:

```
<TR ALIGN="RIGHT">
```

To right-align the data in a single table data cell, you would add the ALIGN attribute to the <TD> tag, as shown here:

```
<TD ALIGN="RIGHT">
```

Microsoft Internet Explorer lets you use the VALIGN attribute with the <TABLE> tag to align all table data vertically. To align data vertically within a row or cell for both Netscape Navigator and Internet Explorer browsers, you need to use the VALIGN attribute in the table row or table heading tags and in the table data tags. The VALIGN attribute settings include TOP, MIDDLE, and BOTTOM. For example, the code in Listing 5-3 aligns the column headings of the table at the tops of the cells; it also horizontally centers all the table cell's contents. Figure 5-4 shows the results for this code, which aligns items in cells horizontally and vertically.

Listing 5-3

```
<TABLE WIDTH="80%" HEIGHT="80%" BORDER>
<TR>
<TD></TD>
<TH><FONT SIZE=+1>Left</FONT></TH>
<TH><FONT SIZE=+1>Center</FONT></TH>
<TH><FONT SIZE=+1>Right</FONT></TH>
</TR>

<TR>
<TH><FONT SIZE=+1>Top</FONT></TH>
<TD ALIGN=LEFT VALIGN=TOP><IMG SRC=" top_left.gif" HEIGHT=55 WIDTH=58></TD>
```

```
<TD ALIGN=CENTER VALIGN=TOP><IMG SRC=" top_center.gif" HEIGHT=55 WIDTH=58></
TD>
<TD ALIGN=RIGHT VALIGN=TOP><IMG SRC="top_right.gif" HEIGHT=55 WIDTH=58></TD>
</TR>

<TR>
<TH><FONT SIZE=+1>Middle</FONT></TH>
<TD ALIGN=LEFT VALIGN=MIDDLE><IMG SRC="middle_left.gif" HEIGHT=55
WIDTH=58></TD>
<TD ALIGN=CENTER VALIGN=MIDDLE><IMG SRC="middle _center.gif" HEIGHT=55
WIDTH=58></TD>
<TD ALIGN=RIGHT VALIGN=MIDDLE><IMG SRC="middle _right.gif" HEIGHT=55
WIDTH=58></TD>
</TR>

<TR>
<TH><FONT SIZE=+1>Bottom</FONT></TH>
<TD ALIGN=LEFT VALIGN=BOTTOM><IMG SRC="bottom_left.gif" HEIGHT=55
WIDTH=58></TD>
<TD ALIGN=CENTER VALIGN=BOTTOM><IMG SRC="bottom_center.gif" HEIGHT=55
WIDTH=58></TD>
<TD ALIGN=RIGHT VALIGN=BOTTOM><IMG SRC="bottom_right.gif" HEIGHT=36
WIDTH=36></TD>
</TR>
</TABLE>
```

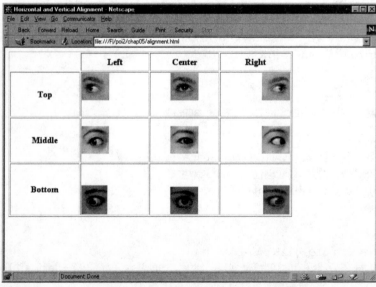

Figure 5-4: Table data can be aligned horizontally and vertically.

While you can align data inside individual cells, you can't align data between cells. For example, you can't vertically align the decimal points in a column of numbers unless you use a monospaced font.

Adding Background Colors to Table Cells _____

The BGCOLOR attribute that is used to set the color of the cells in the last column of the table is an HTML extension and not part of the HTML 3.2 standard. However, it is an extension that is supported by both Microsoft and Netscape, so you can use it with reasonable confidence that it will work in most browsers.

Be aware that changing the background color to a dark color may make the text in the cell unreadable, but you can always change the font to a light color so the text can be easily read. Figure 5-5 shows the results of the code in Listing 5-4, which specifies table headers with a black background and white text and table data cells with a yellow background.

Listing 5-4

```
<TABLE BORDER="2"HEIGHT=80% WIDTH=80%>
<TR>
   <TH BGCOLOR="#000000"><FONT COLOR="#FFFFFF"> Table Header<BR> (Row 1
Column 1)</FONT></TH>
   <TH BGCOLOR="#000000"><FONT COLOR="#FFFFFF">Table Header<BR> (Row 1
Column 2)</FONT></TH>
</TR>
<TR>
   <TD BGCOLOR=#FFFF00" ALIGN="CENTER"> Table Data<BR> (Row 2 Column 1)</TD>
   <TD BGCOLOR="#FFFF00" ALIGN="CENTER"> Table Data<BR> (Row 2 Column 2)</
TD>
</TR>
</TABLE>
```

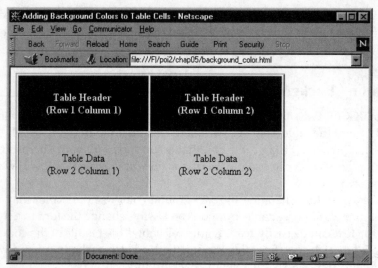

Figure 5-5: Table headers and table data cells with background colors.

Controlling the Appearance of Blank Cells

In some cases, you may want a cell to appear blank. Inserting <TD></TD> tags without text creates a cell, but the border doesn't appear since there is no text in the cell. This can make a report look a little odd, especially if adjoining cells are blank. To ensure that a border appears around a cell, insert a single nonbreaking space character ( ) or a <BR> tag. Figure 5-6 shows the results of Listing 5-5, which includes two tables; one has empty table data cells, and the other has nonbreaking spaces in each of the table cells to create a border around empty table data cells.

Listing 5-5

```
<TABLE BORDER="2">
<CAPTION ALIGN="BOTTOM"><EM>A table with empty cells</EM></CAPTION>
<TR>
    <TD></TD>
    <TH>Table Header (Row 1 Column 2)</TH>
    <TH>Table Header (Row 1 Column 3)</TH>
</TR>
<TR>
    <TH>Table Header (Row 2 Column 1)</TH>
    <TD></TD>
    <TD></TD>
```

```
</TR>
<TR>
   <TH>Table Header (Row 3 Column 1)</TH>
   <TD></TD>
   <TD></TD>
</TR>
</TABLE>
<BR>
<TABLE BORDER="2">
<CAPTION ALIGN="BOTTOM"><EM>A table with nonbreaking spaces in empty cells</
EM></CAPTION>
<TR>
   <TD> </TD>
   <TH>Table Header (Row 1 Column 2)</TH>
   <TH>Table Header (Row 1 Column 3)</TH>
</TR>
<TR>
   <TH>Table Header (Row 2 Column 1)</TH>
   <TD> </TD>
   <TD> </TD>
</TR>
<TR>
   <TH>Table Header (Row 3 Column 1)</TH>
   <TD> </TD>
   <TD> </TD>
</TR>
</TABLE>
```

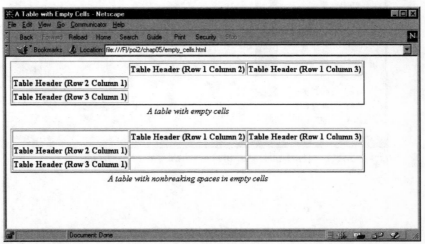

Figure 5-6: Adding a nonbreaking space to an empty table cell displays a border around the empty table cell.

It is essential to add a nonbreaking space when you are working with background colors since the color of the background will not show unless there is something in the cell. Any white space character, like a normal space, will be ignored by the browser. However, nonbreaking spaces and line breaks are characters that must be displayed by the browser. So using the nonbreaking space or the line break (
 tag) allows us to show the border even though nothing is apparent in the cell.

The table in Figure 5-7 presents the 16 named colors defined in HTML 3.2; it shows the color name, the hexadecimal color equivalent, and the color itself. Notice that the last cell in each row is made up of a cell containing only a nonbreaking space ( ) so the table cell will appear in the background color specified. The code shown in Listing 5-6 produces the table shown in Figure 5-7.

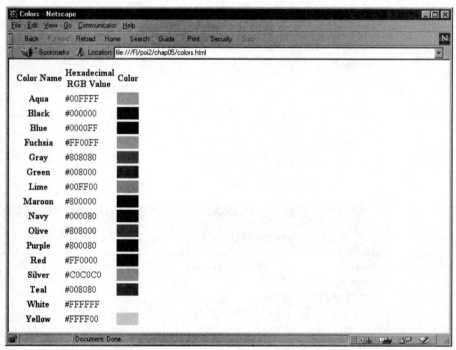

Figure 5-7: An HTML table showing color values and their names.

Listing 5-6

```
<TABLE>
<TR>
    <TH>Color Name</TH>
    <TH>Hexadecimal<BR>RGB Value</TH>
    <TH>Color</TH>
</TR>
<TR>
    <TH>Aqua</TH>
    <TD> #00FFFF </TD>
    <TD BGCOLOR="aqua"> </TD>
</TR>
<TR>
    <TH>Black</TH>
    <TD> #000000 </TD>
    <TD BGCOLOR="black"> </TD>
</TR>
<TR>
    <TH>Blue</TH>
    <TD> #0000FF </TD>
    <TD BGCOLOR="blue"> </TD>
</TR>
<TR>
    <TH>Fuchsia</TH>
    <TD> #FF00FF </TD>
    <TD BGCOLOR="fuschia"> </TD>
</TR>
<TR>
    <TH>Gray</TH>
    <TD> #808080 </TD>
    <TD BGCOLOR="gray"> </TD>
</TR>
<TR>
    <TH>Green</TH>
    <TD> #008000 </TD>
    <TD BGCOLOR="green"> </TD>
</TR>
<TR>
    <TH>Lime</TH>
    <TD> #00FF00 </TD>
    <TD BGCOLOR="lime"> </TD>
</TR>
```

```
<TR>
   <TH>Maroon</TH>
   <TD> #800000 </TD>
   <TD BGCOLOR="maroon"> </TD>
</TR>
<TR>
   <TH>Navy</TH>
   <TD> #000080 </TD>
   <TD BGCOLOR="navy"> </TD>
</TR>
<TR>
   <TH>Olive</TH>
   <TD> #808000 </TD>
   <TD BGCOLOR="olive"> </TD>
</TR>
<TR>
   <TH>Purple</TH>
   <TD> #800080 </TD>
   <TD BGCOLOR="purple"> </TD>
</TR>
<TR>
   <TH>Red</TH>
   <TD> #FF0000 </TD>
   <TD BGCOLOR="red"> </TD>
</TR>
<TR>
   <TH>Silver</TH>
   <TD> #C0C0C0 </TD>
   <TD BGCOLOR="silver"> </TD>
</TR>
<TR>
   <TH>Teal</TH>
   <TD> #008080 </TD>
   <TD BGCOLOR="teal"> </TD>
</TR>
<TR>
   <TH>White</TH>
   <TD> #FFFFFF </TD>
   <TD BGCOLOR="white"> </TD>
</TR>
<TR>
   <TH>Yellow</TH>
   <TD> #FFFF00 </TD>
   <TD BGCOLOR="yellow"> </TD>
</TR>
</TABLE>
```

The table in Figure 5-7 itself contains 17 rows, one for each color and one at the top for a set of column headings. Each row consists of 3 cells: the color name, the hexadecimal color value, and the color itself, which is used to paint the cell background.

Notice that in the top header row, the middle caption has been forced into two lines by using a <BR> tag. This allows the table to be smaller than it would otherwise be since, by default, the overall size of any column is set by the longest row. Since all the other elements in this column are of a fixed size, breaking the heading allows the column to fit the overall data better.

Adjusting Cell Borders & Spacing

The table still doesn't look quite the way we would like it to look. So far, we've let the browser use the default cell to control all the table sizing and placement. However, you can control the amount of space that appears between cells and the amount of space that appears surrounding the data in a cell by using the CELLSPACING and CELLPADDING attributes. Listing 5-7 shows the CELLPADDING attribute added to the <TABLE> tag. Setting the CELLPADDING to 4 expands the area around the data elements in the table by 4 pixels in each direction. This makes the layout easier to read. The results of the following code, which includes the CELLPADDING attribute, are shown in Figure 5-8.

Listing 5-7

```
<TABLE BORDER="2" CELLPADDING="4">
<TR>
   <TH>Color Name</TH>
   <TH>Hexadecimal<BR>RGB Value</TH>
   <TH WIDTH="70">Color</TH>
</TR>
```

Adding the CELLSPACING attribute to the <TABLE> tag adjusts the amount of space between table cells. This changes the size of the borders around the table data cells. Of course, to see the size of the borders change, you need to use the BORDERS attribute along with the CELLSPACING attribute. For example, the following code shows the CELLSPACING attribute set to 2 pixels. (Figure 5-9 shows the results of changing the previous example to include a CELLSPACING=4.)

```
<TABLE BORDER="2" " CELLSPACING="4">
```

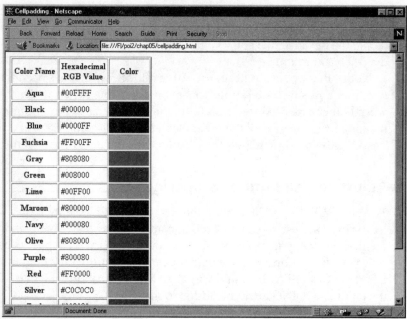

Figure 5-8: To control the amount of space surrounding data in a cell, add the CELLPADDING attribute to the <TABLE> tag.

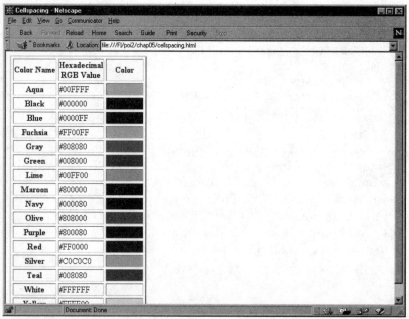

Figure 5-9: To control the amount of space between table cells, add the CELLSPACING attribute to the <TABLE> tag.

Spanning a Cell Across Rows & Columns _____

Tables frequently include table cells that span multiple rows or columns. To lay out complicated pages with tables, it is essential to span rows and columns. Adding the ROWSPAN attribute to the <TH> or <TD> tag forces the cell to span the number of rows specified. Adding the COLSPAN attribute spans the number of columns specified. The following listing shows a simple table that includes a table cell that spans two columns and another cell that spans two rows. Figure 5-10 shows the results of Listing 5-8.

Listing 5-8

```
<TABLE BORDER>
<TR>
    <TH COLSPAN=2></TH>
    <TH>Western Region</TH>
</TR>
    <TR ALIGN=CENTER>
    <TH ROWSPAN=2>This Year's<BR>Sales</TH>
    <TH>First Half</TH>
    <TD ALIGN=RIGHT>1,000,000.00</TD>
</TR>
<TR ALIGN=CENTER>
    <TH>Second Half</TH>
    <TD ALIGN=RIGHT>2,000,000.00</TD>
</TR>
<TR ALIGN=CENTER>
    <TH ROWSPAN=2>Last Year's<BR>Sales</TH>
    <TH>First Half</TH>
    <TD ALIGN=RIGHT>100.00</TD>
</TR>
<TR ALIGN=CENTER>
    <TH>Second Half</TH>
    <TD ALIGN=RIGHT>200.00</TD>
</TR>
</TABLE>
```

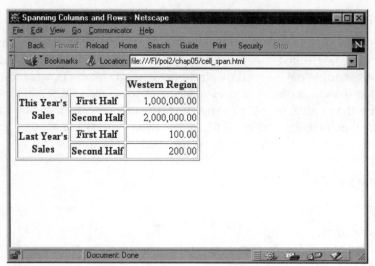

Figure 5-10: The COLSPAN and ROWSPAN attributes let you have a cell span a column or a row.

Nesting Tables

You can nest one or more tables within another table. By placing a table within a cell of another table, you can achieve an effect that you can't accomplish using a table cell by itself. For example, you may want to group elements together or you may want to control the amount of space between a cell with a background color and adjacent cells. Another reason you may want to nest tables is to have a border appear around a single cell or portion of a table, but not the whole table. One big advantage of nesting tables is that it lets you control how a group of form elements, such as radio buttons and check boxes, appear on a page. Figure 5-11 shows an example of using nested tables to create margins and include headers with a background.

Anatomy of an Advanced Table

Not all tables need to be quite so simple. A quick look through any print document will show you that there are many ways to use tables for presenting data. Figure 5-12 shows you another, more complex use of table information.

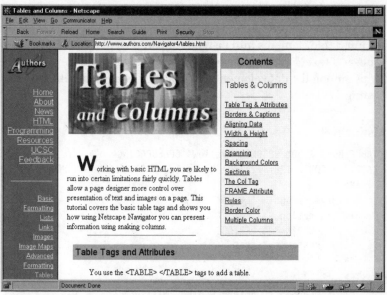

Figure 5-11. Nesting tables gives you more possibilities for laying out and positioning.

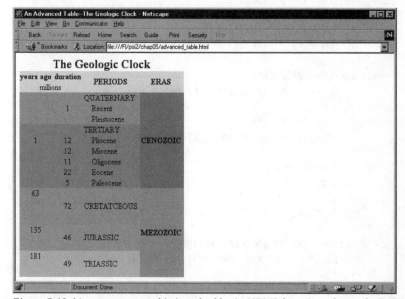

Figure 5-12: You can create sophisticated tables in HTML by using advanced <TABLE> tag attributes.

This table uses several traditional techniques to make the data more accessible. First of all, there are no borders to the table, and color is used to unify various table elements into visual groups. Also, placement of data within the table and text elements, like bold, are used to help the viewer see the relationships among the data elements. The table was created with the code shown in Listing 5-9.

Listing 5-9

```
<TABLE BORDER="0" BGCOLOR="yellow" CELLSPACING="0">
<CAPTION><FONT SIZE="+2"><B>The Geologic Clock</B> </FONT></CAPTION>
    <TR>
        <TH>years ago
        <TH>duration
        <TH ROWSPAN="2">PERIODS
        <TH ROWSPAN="2">ERAS
    </TR>
    <TR>
        <TD COLSPAN="2" ALIGN="CENTER">millions
    </TR>
    <TR ALIGN="CENTER" BGCOLOR="#B0B0FF">
        <TD ROWSPAN="3"> 
        <TD ROWSPAN="3">1
        <TD ALIGN="LEFT">QUATERNARY
        <TD ROWSPAN="9" VALIGN="CENTER" BGCOLOR="#80A0FF"> <B>CENOZOIC</B>
    </TR>
    <TR BGCOLOR="#B0B0FF">
        <TD>    Recent
    </TR>
    <TR BGCOLOR="#B0B0FF">
        <TD>    Pleistocene
    </TR>
    <TR BGCOLOR="#B0A0FF">
        <TD> 
        <TD> 
        <TD>TERTIARY
    </TR>
    <TR ALIGN="CENTER" BGCOLOR="#B0A0FF">
        <TD VALIGN="TOP" ROWSPAN="5">1
        <TD>12
        <TD ALIGN="LEFT">    Pliocene
    </TR>
```

```
<TR BGCOLOR="#B0A0FF">
    <TD ALIGN="CENTER">12
    <TD>    Miocene
</TR>
<TR BGCOLOR="#B0A0FF">
    <TD ALIGN="CENTER">11
    <TD>    Oligocene
</TR>
<TR BGCOLOR="#B0A0FF">
    <TD ALIGN="CENTER">22
    <TD>    Eocene
</TR>
<TR BGCOLOR="#B0A0FF">
    <TD ALIGN="CENTER">5
    <TD>    Paleocene
</TR>
<!-- Each 10 pixels in height represents ~10 Million years -->
<TR ALIGN="CENTER" BGCOLOR="#FFA0C0">
    <TD HEIGHT="70" VALIGN="TOP">63
    <TD HEIGHT="70" VALIGN="CENTER">72
    <TD HEIGHT="70" VALIGN="CENTER" ALIGN="LEFT">CRETATCEOUS
    <TD ROWSPAN="3" VALIGN="CENTER" BGCOLOR="#FFA0A0"> <B>MEZOZOIC</B>
</TR>
<TR ALIGN="CENTER" BGCOLOR="#FFA0E0">
    <TD HEIGHT="50" VALIGN="TOP">135
    <TD HEIGHT="50" VALIGN="CENTER">46
    <TD HEIGHT="50" VALIGN="CENTER" ALIGN="LEFT">JURASSIC
</TR>
<TR ALIGN="CENTER" BGCOLOR="#FFC0FF">
    <TD HEIGHT="50" VALIGN="TOP">181
    <TD HEIGHT="50" VALIGN="CENTER">49
    <TD HEIGHT="50" VALIGN="CENTER" ALIGN="LEFT">TRIASSIC
</TR>
</TABLE>
```

Although it doesn't look like it at first glance, this table is 14 rows by 4 columns. By using some of the advanced table controls, you can make a sophisticated table by combining rows and columns as required to present your data. The most obvious effect here is the combination of various rows and columns to create visual groups. To do this, you use the COLSPAN and ROWSPAN attributes to force a data element to occupy more than one cell.

For example, these lines of code from the table make the text "millions" occupy two columns instead of the normal one, and they make the table headings "PERIODS" and "ERAS" occupy two rows instead of one:

```
<TR>
    <TH>years ago
    <TH>duration
    <TH ROWSPAN="2">PERIODS
    <TH ROWSPAN="2">ERAS
</TR>
<TR>
    <TD COLSPAN="2" ALIGN="CENTER">millions
</TR>
```

As you would expect, the numbers after the ROWSPAN and COLSPAN attributes specify the number of rows or columns that the given element should span. Notice that, even though this code represents two rows and four columns of data, there aren't four sets of tags in the second row. In the first row, two <TH> tags, one for "PERIODS" and one for "ERAS," are specified as filling two rows; since they take up this space, you can't have any tags in the next row for these columns. In the second row, the <TD> tag for "millions" takes up two columns, so you don't need an additional tag for the second column here. As a result, you have eight cells defined by five tags, since three of the tags each take up one additional cell. Also note that, since the "millions" data takes up two columns, we've used the ALIGN="CENTER" attribute to force the text into the middle of the two combined cells.

The next three row definitions show you more about how you can space your table:

```
<TR ALIGN="CENTER" BGCOLOR="#B0B0FF">
    <TD ROWSPAN="3"> 
    <TD ROWSPAN="3">1
    <TD ALIGN="LEFT">QUATERNARY
    <TD ROWSPAN="9" VALIGN="CENTER" BGCOLOR="#80A0FF"><B>CENOZOIC</B>
</TR>
<TR BGCOLOR="#B0B0FF">
    <TD>    Recent
</TR>
<TR BGCOLOR="#B0B0FF">
    <TD>    Pleistocene
</TR>
```

The center alignment and color assignment on the first row shown here applies to all the data elements in the row unless they are overridden by a matching attribute for a specific cell. So, for example, all the cells of the row have the same background color except the last cell, "CENOZOIC," which specifies an alternate color for the background, and text in all the cells is horizontally centered except the third cell, "QUATERNARY," which specifies that the text is to be aligned left. Since the last cell spans nine rows, we also used the vertical alignment attribute, VALIGN, to center the text vertically as well as horizontally.

Each of the next two rows contains only one tag, since the first row fills up all but one cell in these rows by using the ROWSPAN attribute. In each case, the text for the cells is aligned left—the default alignment—and nonbreaking spaces are used to indent the headings under the text in the top row. Notice that you cannot use ordinary spaces for this because the browser will ignore them for layout purposes.

For a final example of layout, let's look at the last three rows of the table, as shown in the following code fragment:

```
<!-- Each 10 pixels in height represents ~10 Million years -->
<TR ALIGN="CENTER" BGCOLOR="#FFA0C0">
    <TD HEIGHT="70" VALIGN="TOP">63
    <TD HEIGHT="70" VALIGN="CENTER">72
    <TD HEIGHT="70" VALIGN="CENTER" ALIGN="LEFT">CRETATCEOUS
    <TD ROWSPAN="3" VALIGN="CENTER" BGCOLOR="#FFA0A0"><B>MEZOZOIC</B>
</TR>
<TR ALIGN="CENTER" BGCOLOR="#FFA0E0">
    <TD HEIGHT="50" VALIGN="TOP">135
    <TD HEIGHT="50" VALIGN="CENTER">46
    <TD HEIGHT="50" VALIGN="CENTER" ALIGN="LEFT">JURASSIC
</TR>
<TR ALIGN="CENTER" BGCOLOR="#FFC0FF">
    <TD HEIGHT="50" VALIGN="TOP">181
    <TD HEIGHT="50" VALIGN="CENTER">49
    <TD HEIGHT="50" VALIGN="CENTER" ALIGN="LEFT">TRIASSIC
</TR>
```

As the comment indicates, the intention here is to size the cells of these rows in rough proportion to the amount of time each represents. To do so, we used another useful attribute, HEIGHT, which is set in pixels. This forces the cells of the table to be a specific height unless this height set conflicts with the height required for other cells in the same row. It works in a way that is similar to how the WIDTH attribute you saw in the earlier example works. Although it is not strictly required, we did set the height for each cell individually here; as you read earlier, you could simply set the first cell and the browser will force the rest of the row to the same height. However, for ease of understanding and modification, we felt that this was a clearer approach. The vertical alignment attribute is used to position the "years ago" column value at the top of its cell, while the remainder of the text is placed in the center of the cell both horizontally and vertically.

This table is a good example of how you can use table tags to make your Web presentation just as compelling and interesting as a printed document even before you add unique interactive and multimedia elements that go beyond print.

Advanced Table Tags & Attributes

This section presents some less common table tags and attributes for controlling sections of a table, displaying table and cell rules and borders, and grouping columns. These table tags and attributes currently work with Microsoft Internet Explorer only, but they are in fact a part of the recommended table specification in HTML 4.0. So don't think that because the tag or attribute works only with Internet Explorer, it is a Microsoft extension. Although Netscape does not currently support these table tags and attributes, it's likely that it will support them in the future because they are a part of the table specification.

Defining Table Sections

HTML 4.0 gives you greater control over sections of a table by including the THEAD, TBODY, and TFOOT tags. You can use the TBODY, THEAD, and TFOOT tags when displaying long tables to ensure that page headers and footers appear on the printed pages. The <THEAD></THEAD> tags are used to specify the head section of the table. The <TBODY></TBODY> tags are used to specify the body section of the table and are similar to the <BODY> element of an HTML document. The <TFOOT></TFOOT> tags are used to specify the footer section of the table.

The benefit of using these tags isn't evident by inserting the tags by themselves. To see how they work, you need to use them in conjunction with the FRAME and RULE attributes and the <COL> and <COLGROUP> tags, all of which are explained in the following sections.

Controlling Table Borders & Cell Rules

HTML 4.0 lets you control outer table borders, called frames, and inner cell borders, called rules, by adding the FRAME and RULES attributes. The FRAME attribute specifies the sides of the table frame to display. The value of the FRAME attribute specifies the way frames appear around tables. For Internet Explorer, you can use the TABLE's BORDER attribute along with the FRAME and RULES attributes to create frame borders for portions of a document. In order to use the FRAME and RULES attributes, the BORDER attribute must be specified. Table 5-1 shows value settings you can use with the FRAME attribute. Figure 5-13 shows Microsoft Internet Explorer displaying the results of Listing 5-10, which creates a table using the FRAME attribute with the VOID setting.

Listing 5-10

```
<TABLE CELLPADDING="5" BORDER="4" FRAME="VOID">
<CAPTION ALIGN="TOP"><STRONG>Names of Days</STRONG></CAPTION>
<TR>
      <TH ALIGN="CENTER">English</TH>
      <TH ALIGN="CENTER">Latin</TH>
      <TH ALIGN="CENTER">Saxon</TH>
</TR>
<TR>
      <TD ALIGN="CENTER">Sunday</TD>
      <TD ALIGN="CENTER">Dies Solis (Sun)</TD>
      <TD ALIGN="CENTER">Sun's Day</TD>
</TR>
<TR>
      <TD ALIGN="CENTER">Monday</TD>
      <TD ALIGN="CENTER">Dies Lunae (Moon)</TD>
      <TD ALIGN="CENTER">Moon's Day</TD>
</TR>
      <TD ALIGN="CENTER">Tuesday</TD>
      <TD ALIGN="CENTER">Dies Martis (Mars)</TD>
      <TD ALIGN="CENTER">Tiw's Day</TD>
</TR>
      <TD ALIGN="CENTER">Wednesday</TD>
      <TD ALIGN="CENTER">Dies Mercurii (Mercury)</TD>
      <TD ALIGN="CENTER">Woden's Day</TD>
</TR>
      <TD ALIGN="CENTER">Thursday</TD>
      <TD ALIGN="CENTER">Dies Jovis (Jupiter)</TD>
      <TD ALIGN="CENTER">Thor's Day</TD>
</TR>
      <TD ALIGN="CENTER">Friday</TD>
      <TD ALIGN="CENTER">Dies Veneris (Venus)</TD>
      <TD ALIGN="CENTER">Frigg's Day</TD>
</TR>
      <TD ALIGN="CENTER">Saturday</TD>
      <TD ALIGN="CENTER">Dies Saturni (Saturn)</TD>
      <TD ALIGN="CENTER">Saterne's Day</TD>
</TR>
</TABLE>
```

Value	Description
ABOVE	Displays an external border at the top of the table.
BELOW	Displays an external border at the bottom of the table.
BOX	Displays borders on all sides of a table to create a box around the table.
HSIDES	Displays external borders at the horizontal sides, the top, and the bottom of the table.
LHS	Displays external borders on the left-hand side of a table.
RHS	Displays external borders on the right-hand side of a table.
VOID	Removes all existing external borders.
VSIDES	Displays external borders on the left and right sides of a table.

Table 5-1: The value settings you can use with the FRAME attribute.

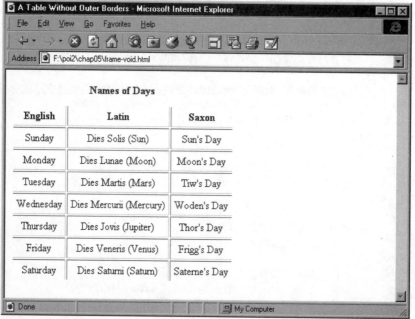

Figure 5-13: Adding the FRAME="VOID" attribute to the <TABLE> tag creates a table without outer borders.

The RULES attribute specifies where to display internal table borders. In order to use the RULES attribute in a table, the BORDER element must also be included. For example, to display rules for the rows in a table, you would add the RULES="ROWS" attribute to the <TABLE> tag as follows:

```
<TABLE CELLPADDING="5" BORDER="4" RULES="ROWS">
```

To display rules for the columns in a table, you would add the RULES="COLS" attribute to the table tag as follows:

```
<TABLE CELLPADDING="5" BORDER="4" RULES="COLS">
```

Table 5-2 lists and describes the value settings you can use with the RULES attribute. Figure 5-14 shows an example of two tables, one that uses the RULES attribute with the ROWS setting and another that uses the RULES attribute with the COLS setting.

Value	Description
ALL	Displays internal rules between every row and column in a table.
BASIC	Displays a horizontal rule between the TBODY, THEAD, and TFOOT sections of a table.
COLS	Displays a horizontal rule between all the columns in a table.
NONE	Removes all internal rules.
ROWS	Displays horizontal rules between all the rows in a table.

Table 5-2: The value settings for the RULES attribute.

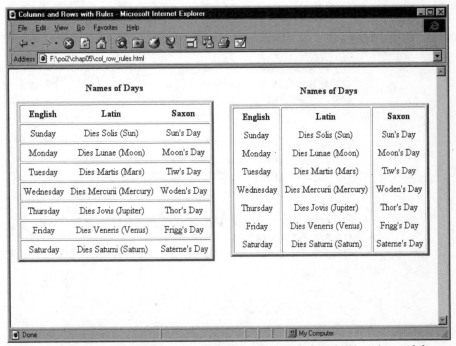

Figure 5-14: The table on the left uses the RULES attribute with the ROWS setting, and the one on the right using the RULES attribute with COLS setting.

If you use the TBODY, THEAD, and TFOOT tags, you can use the RULES="GROUPS" setting to automatically display rules between each section. Figure 5-15 shows the table created by the code in Listing 5-11, which includes the RULES="GROUPS" attribute along with the TBODY, THEAD, and TFOOT tags.

Listing 5-11

```
<TABLE BORDER RULES="GROUPS" WIDTH="100%">
<THEAD>
<TR>
        <TH COLSPAN="3">Solar System Orbits<SUP>*</SUP></TH>
 </TR>
</THEAD>
<TBODY>
<TR>
        <TH ALIGN="CENTER">Planet</TH>
        <TH ALIGN="CENTER">Year(s)</TH>
        <TH ALIGN="CENTER">Days</TH>
</TR>
<TR>
        <TD ALIGN="CENTER">Pluto</TD>
        <TD ALIGN="CENTER">247</TD>
        <TD ALIGN="CENTER">256</TD>
</TR>
<TR>
        <TD ALIGN="CENTER">Neptune</TD>
        <TD ALIGN="CENTER">164</TD>
        <TD ALIGN="CENTER">298</TD>
</TR>
<TR>
        <TD ALIGN="CENTER">Uranus</TD>
        <TD ALIGN="CENTER">84</TD>
        <TD ALIGN="CENTER">4</TD>
</TR>
<TR>
        <TD ALIGN="CENTER">Saturn</TD>
        <TD ALIGN="CENTER">29</TD>
        <TD ALIGN="CENTER">168</TD>
</TR>
```

```
<TR>
      <TD ALIGN="CENTER">Jupiter</TD>
      <TD ALIGN="CENTER">11</TD>
      <TD ALIGN="CENTER">314</TD>
</TR>
<TR>
      <TD ALIGN="CENTER">Mars</TD>
      <TD ALIGN="CENTER">1</TD>
      <TD ALIGN="CENTER">322</TD>
</TR>
<TR>
      <TD ALIGN="CENTER">Earth</TD>
      <TD ALIGN="CENTER">1</TD>
      <TD ALIGN="CENTER">365</TD>
</TR>
<TR>
      <TD ALIGN="CENTER">Venus</TD>
      <TD ALIGN="CENTER"> </TD>
      <TD ALIGN="CENTER">225</TD>
</TR>
<TR>
      <TD ALIGN="CENTER">Mercury</TD>
      <TD ALIGN="CENTER"> </TD>
      <TD ALIGN="CENTER">88</TD>
</TR>
</TBODY>
<TFOOT>
<TR>
      <TD COLSPAN="3" ALIGN="CENTER"><EM><SUP>*</SUP>Period of orbit around
the Sun in Earth years/days</EM></TD>
</TR>
</TFOOT>
</TABLE>
```

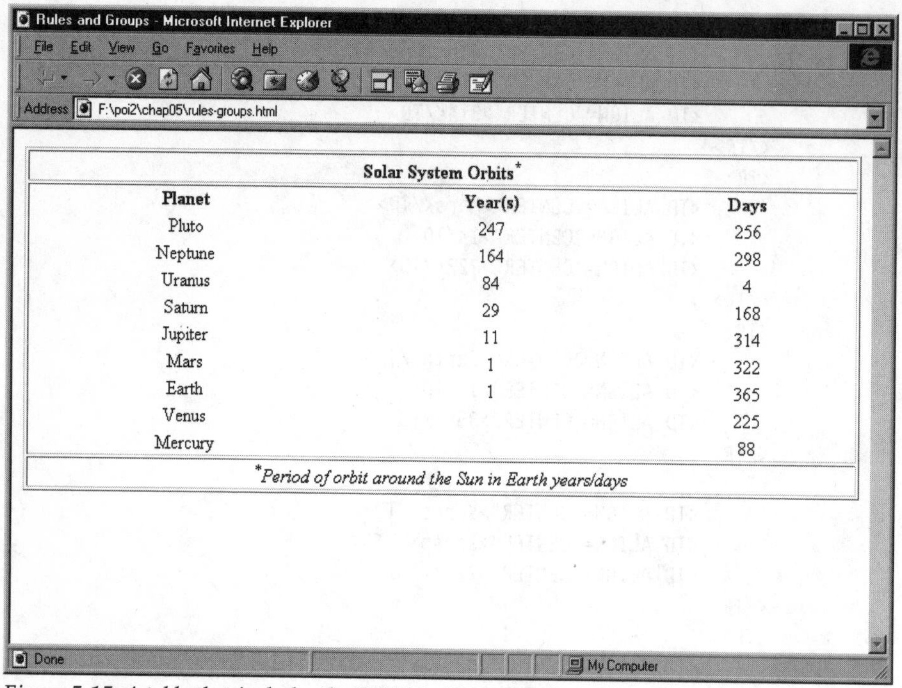

Figure 5-15: A table that includes the RULES="GROUPS" attribute along with the TBODY, THEAD, and TFOOT tags.

Defining & Aligning Columns

Notice that the previous example includes center alignment settings for each table data cell (<TD ALIGN="CENTER">). Using the <COL> tag, you can specify the alignment for an entire column. If you add an ALIGN attribute to a table data cell <TD>, the data cell attribute setting takes precedence over the <COL> alignment setting. Listing 5-12 shows columns aligned using the <COL> tag. Figure 5-16 shows the table created by the code shown in Listing 5-12.

Listing 5-12

```
<TABLE BORDER RULES="GROUPS" WIDTH="100%">
<COL ALIGN="LEFT">
<COL ALIGN="CENTER">
<COL ALIGN="RIGHT">
<THEAD>
```

```
<TR>
        <TH COLSPAN="3">Solar System Orbits<SUP>*</SUP></TH>
 </TR>
</THEAD>
<TBODY>
<TR>
        <TH>Planet</TH>
        <TH>Year(s)</TH>
        <TH>Days</TH>
</TR>
<TR>
        <TD>Pluto</TD>
        <TD>247</TD>
        <TD>256</TD>
</TR>
<TR>
        <TD>Neptune</TD>
        <TD>164</TD>
        <TD>298</TD>
</TR>
<TR>
        <TD>Uranus</TD>
        <TD>84</TD>
        <TD>4</TD>
</TR>
<TR>
        <TD>Saturn</TD>
        <TD>29</TD>
        <TD>168</TD>
</TR>
<TR>
        <TD>Jupiter</TD>
        <TD>11</TD>
        <TD>314</TD>
</TR>
<TR>
        <TD>Mars</TD>
        <TD>1</TD>
        <TD>322</TD>
</TR>
<TR>
        <TD>Earth</TD>
        <TD>1</TD>
        <TD>365</TD>
</TR>
```

```
<TR>
      <TD>Venus</TD>
      <TD> </TD>
      <TD>225</TD>
</TR>
<TR>
      <TD>Mercury</TD>
      <TD> </TD>
      <TD>88</TD>
</TR>
</TBODY>
<TFOOT>
<TR>
      <TD COLSPAN="3" ALIGN="CENTER"><EM><SUP>*</SUP>Period of orbit around
the Sun in Earth years/days</EM></TD>
</TR>
</TFOOT>
</TABLE>
```

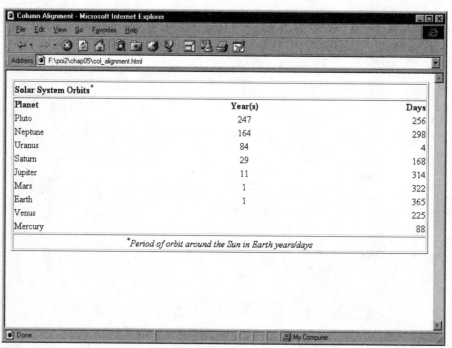

Figure 5-16: A table with columns aligned using the <COL> tag.

Grouping Columns _____

You can group columns together by adding the <COLGROUP> tag before
the <COL> tags you want grouped together. You don't need a closing
<COLGROUP> tag. Simply add another <COLGROUP> tag before the next
set of <COL> tags. The following example creates two column groups and
aligns the columns to the left and right side. Figure 5-17 shows the results of
Listing 5-13. Notice that the RULES="GROUPS" setting displays a single
line between the two column groups.

Listing 5-13

```
<TABLE BORDER RULES="GROUPS" WIDTH="80%">
<CAPTION><FONT FACE="ARIAL,HELVETICA" SIZE="4">Highest Mountains in the
World<FONT></CAPTION>
<COLGROUP>
    <COL ALIGN="LEFT">
    <COL ALIGN="RIGHT">
<COLGROUP>
    <COL ALIGN="LEFT">
    <COL ALIGN="RIGHT">
<THEAD>
<TR>
        <TH ALIGN="LEFT">Mountain</TH>
        <TH ALIGN="RIGHT">Country</TH>
        <TH ALIGN="LEFT">Feet</TH>
        <TH ALIGN="RIGHT">Meters</TH>
</TR>
<TBODY>
<TR>
        <TD>Everest</TD>
        <TD>Nepal/Tibet</TD>
        <TD>29,022</TD>
        <TD>8,846</TD>
</TR>
<TR>
        <TD>K2</TD>
        <TD>Kashmir/China</TD>
        <TD>28,250</TD>
        <TD>8,611</TD>
</TR>
<TR>
        <TD>Kanchenjunga</TD>
        <TD>Nepal/Sikkim</TD>
        <TD>28,208</TD>
        <TD>8,598</TD>
</TR>
```

```
<TR>
      <TD>Lhotse</TD>
      <TD>Nepal/Tibet</TD>
      <TD>27,890</TD>
      <TD>8,501</TD>
</TR>
<TR>
      <TD>Makalu I</TD>
      <TD>Nepal/Tibet</TD>
      <TD>27,790</TD>
      <TD>8,470</TD>
</TR>
<TFOOT>
<TR>
    <TD COLSPAN="4" ALIGN="LEFT"><SUP>*</SUP><FONT SIZE="2">Mount Everest is
also known as Chomolungma.</FONT><BR>
<SUP>**</SUP><FONT SIZE="2">K2 is also known as Chogori and Godwin-Austen
(after Lieutenant Henry Haversham Godwin-Austen, who first surveyed the
mountain in 1865).</FONT></TD>
</TR>
</TABLE>
```

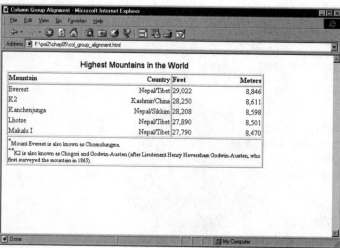

Figure 5-17: Two column groups with columns aligned to the left and right side in each group.

Adding Background Images to a Table

Internet Explorer supports the use of the BACKGROUND attribute with the <TABLE>, <TH>, and <TD> elements to add background images. If the image is used in the <TH> or <TD> element, it is tiled behind the particular data cell.

You can make a single image appear in the background of a single cell by making the height and width of the cell the same height as the image. Figure 5-18 shows a background image added to a table with white text displaying on top of the image, the code for which is shown in Listing 5-14.

Listing 5-14

```
<DIV ALIGN=CENTER>
    <TABLE>
      <TR>
        <TD HEIGHT="400" WIDTH="100"></TD>
        <TD HEIGHT="400" WIDTH="336" BACKGROUND="images/tv.jpg"
ALIGN="CENTER" VALIGN="TOP">
          <P ALIGN="CENTER"><FONT FACE="Verdana" SIZE="6"
COLOR="#FFFFFF"><BR>
            The Medium<BR>is the<BR>Message</FONT></P>
          <P><FONT FACE="Verdana" SIZE="2" COLOR=#FFFFFF>Marshall McLuhan</
FONT></P>
        </TD>
        <TD HEIGHT="400" WIDTH="100"></TD>
      </TR>
    </TABLE>
</DIV>
```

Figure 5-18: A background image added to a table.

Unlike the attributes discussed earlier, this attribute is not part of the HTML 4.0 specification. It is an extension, but it is supported by both Microsoft Internet Explorer and Netscape Navigator 4.

Creating Color 3D Table Borders

Internet Explorer also supports using BORDERCOLOR, BORDERCOLORDARK, and BORDERCOLORLIGHT attributes to control the border colors of a table. BORDERCOLOR specifies the color of a table's border. The value of the BORDERCOLORDARK attribute specifies the color of the shaded edge of a 3D table border. The value of the BORDERCOLORLIGHT attribute specifies the color of the side of a 3D border that is not shaded. A color can be specified as a color name or as a hexadecimal value. This example creates a red border with the BORDERCOLORDARK attribute and a pink border with the BORDERCOLORLIGHT attribute:

```
<TABLE BORDER="5" BORDERCOLORDARK="#CC3333" BORDERCOLORLIGHT="#FFCCCC">
```

Unlike the attributes discussed earlier, these attributes are not part of the HTML 4.0 specification. They are extensions that are only supported by Microsoft Internet Explorer.

Laying Out Web Pages With Tables

Once you start working on a Web page layout, chances are you will quickly come to the realization that you can't do everything you'd like. HTML tags do not always allow you to position and specify elements on your page exactly the way you want—indeed, part of the purpose of HTML is to avoid such specific layout issues. The biggest examples of this are that basic HTML tags don't allow you to position text in a specific location on the page and they don't allow you much control over white space around your page. Control over placement of page elements and over white space is an important element in the designer's tool kit in all other media. As such, once the Web became a commercial success, it was inevitable that ways to control these elements for Web presentation would become desirable. Once the need was recognized, creative designers adapted existing HTML tags to allow this type of control.

One method of controlling placement is to lay out a page as a table, using the table as a kind of layout grid rather than using it for presenting data in tabular format as you saw in the preceding sections of this chapter. This process uses the <TABLE> tags and attributes to insert margins and other forms of white space and allows you to control, at least to some extent, how the text and graphic elements are positioned on the page.

A better way to do these types of layout is to use style sheets, which are designed to allow you to control placement of text and graphics precisely. However, only the newest versions of browsers support style sheets, so it's often necessary to use alternative methods like tables to provide layout that can be viewed by the largest possible audience. Before doing layout with tables on new pages, you should seriously consider whether using style sheets might not provide better layout and easier maintenance for your site.

A Simple Layout Grid

Using tables to lay out pages can get very complex in a hurry. However, let's look at a simplified example so you can see how this might work. One common reason to use this type of layout is to place navigational elements like links on one margin of the page so they are easily seen. Listing 5-15 shows you a simple page layout with the anchor tags along one side of the page for easy and obvious reference. Figure 5-19 shows the page created by the code in Listing 5-15.

Listing 5-15

```
<HTML>
<HEAD>
<TITLE>
Authors Information Page
</TITLE>
</HEAD>

<BODY BGCOLOR="white">
<TABLE BORDER="0" CELLPADDING="0" CELLSPACING="0" WIDTH="100%">
<TR>
   <TD ALIGN="CENTER" COLSPAN="4"><FONT SIZE="6" FACE="Verdana, Helvetica,
sans-serif">The Information Page</FONT></TD>
</TR>
<TR>
   <TD WIDTH="20%"> </TD>
   <TD WIDTH="1%">  </TD>
   <TD WIDTH="5%">  </TD>
   <TD HEIGHT="30"> </TD>
</TR>
<TR>
   <TD>Information</TD>
   <TD BGCOLOR="yellow"> </TD>
   <TD> </TD>
```

```
    <TD ROWSPAN="8"><P>This site is an online work in progress that shows
interactive World Wide Web authoring and programming examples. It is
designed to supplement the book <EM>HTML Publishing on the Internet Second
Edition</EM> written by Brent Heslop and David Holzgang and published by The
Coriolis Group.</P>
    <P>You can see what examples have been added since the book was first
published by clicking on one of the links in the left column. If you would
like help on something related to Web publishing, please use the feedback
link in the left column. We really do appreciate any comments or suggestions
you may have to make this a better site.</P>
    <P> </P>
    <P> </P>
    </TD>
    </TR>
    <TR>
        <TD><A HREF="new.html">What's New</A></TD>
        <TD BGCOLOR="yellow"> </TD>
        <TD> </TD>
        <TD> </TD>
    </TR>
    <TR>
        <TD><A HREF="html.html">HTML</A></TD>
        <TD BGCOLOR="yellow"> </TD>
        <TD>  </TD>
        <TD>  </TD>
    </TR>
    <TR>
        <TD><A HREF="prog.html">Programming</A></TD>
        <TD BGCOLOR="yellow"> </TD>
        <TD> </TD>
        <TD>  </TD>
    </TR>
    <TR>
        <TD><A HREF="resource.html">Resources</A></TD>
        <TD BGCOLOR="yellow"> </TD>
        <TD> </TD>
        <TD> </TD>
    </TR>
    <TR>
        <TD><A HREF="feedback.html">Feedback</A></TD>
        <TD BGCOLOR="yellow"> </TD>
        <TD> </TD>
        <TD>  </TD>
    </TR>
```

```
<TR>
   <TD> </TD>
   <TD BGCOLOR="yellow"> </TD>
   <TD> </TD>
   <TD> </TD>
</TR>
<TR>
   <TD> </TD>
   <TD BGCOLOR="yellow"> </TD>
   <TD> </TD>
   <TD> </TD>
</TR>
</TABLE>
</BODY>
</HTML>
```

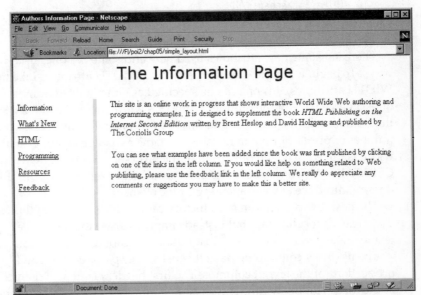

Figure 5-19: You can use table tags to lay out pages like this.

This table layout is very simple. The page is laid out in a grid of four columns, where the first column is used for the navigational anchors. The second column is used as a color bar separation between the anchors and the text, the third column functions as a spacing device, and the fourth column contains the text. Much of the table uses tags and attributes that you are already famil-iar with from the earlier examples. Notice again the use of indentation to show the table layout, and notice that we have removed the ending tags for the table data elements. This was done simply to save space and to illustrate that pres-ence or absence of these tags has no effect on the presentation.

The most important part of the layout is in the definition and the top two rows, as shown in this code:

```
<TABLE BORDER="0" CELLPADDING="0" CELLSPACING="0" WIDTH="100%">
<TR>
    <TD ALIGN="CENTER" COLSPAN="4" ><FONT SIZE=6>The Information Page</
FONT></TD>
</TR>
<TR>
    <TD WIDTH="20%"> </TD>
    <TD WIDTH="1"> </TD>
    <TD WIDTH="5%"> </TD>
    <TD HEIGHT="30"> </TD>
</TR>
```

There are some new attributes used here and some old ones used in new ways. To begin with, the <TABLE> tag has a WIDTH attribute. Like most WIDTH attributes, this one can be specified as either a fixed number of pixels or as a percentage of the browser window's width; here, the percent sign after the number tells the browser that this is a percentage value and not a specific number of pixels. Since you're using the table as a page layout grid, the table's width is forced to be the full width of the browser's window. BORDER, CELLPADDING, and CELLSPACING are all set to zero so that the table doesn't introduce any extraneous graphic elements.

The next row presents an introductory caption for the page. In this case, we don't use the heading tags but instead simply increase the size of the caption text to make it more prominent. In addition, the caption spans all four columns.

The next row contains no data; it is used as a spacer element and to set the proportions of the layout columns. The first header element is set to 20 percent of the total window width. The second column is set to 1 pixel, and the third column is set to 5 percent. This holds the colored line and the text spacing constant no matter what size the browser's window is set to. The final cell in this row defines the text column. This will take up the remainder of the width of the window. The height of the cell is set to 30 pixels to move the remaining rows down, away from the caption text. By changing the height value, you can increase or decrease the space between the caption and the subsequent text.

The next row, shown in the following code fragment, contains some important features:

```
<TR>
    <TD>Information</TD>
    <TD BGCOLOR="yellow"> </TD>
    <TD> </TD>
    <TD ROWSPAN="8"><P>This site is an online work in progress that shows
interactive World Wide Web authoring and programming examples. It is
designed to supplement the book <EM>HTML Publishing on the Internet Second
Edition</EM> written by Brent Heslop and David Holzgang and published by The
Coriolis Group.</P>
<P>You can see what examples have been added since the book was first
published by clicking on one of the links in the left column. If you would
like help on something related to Web publishing, please use the feedback
link in the left column. We really do appreciate any comments or suggestions
you may have to make this a better site.</P>
<P> </P>
<P> </P>
    </TD>
</TR>
```

This row of the table defines the first navigational element, "Information Page." Since that is the current page, there is no active link on this element, and its different color in the page display will alert users that they are already on this page. The second and third columns are just as you would expect; they create the color bar and the spacing for the text. The last column, however, is quite interesting. Here the table cell consists of a full paragraph of text, which is much larger than any other cell in this row.

To get the table layout to look correct, then, you need to get this larger cell to span the remaining rows of the table—in this case, eight rows. This allows the text to flow down the right column to match the navigational elements on the left.

The remainder of the rows consists of the navigational links, all anchors from this point on, and the color bar and spacing elements. There are two additional rows at the bottom of the table that have no navigational elements. These are here to extend the color bar somewhat below the text and navigational links, and they also help keep the layout together if the browser window is very small or narrow.

This last point may not be easy to visualize. Figure 5-20 shows you the same page displayed in a narrow browser window.

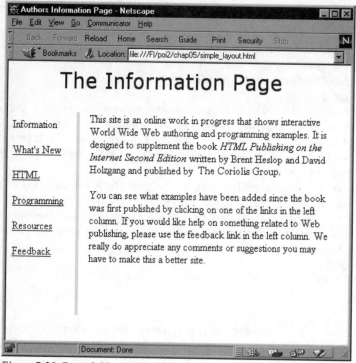

Figure 5-20: Pages laid out with a table will alter to fit the size of the display.

Because the display is now much narrower than it was in Figure 5-19, you can see that the spacing of the navigational elements on the left has spread out. This is required because the text cell now flows further down the page and the remaining cells must expand to match it. Here's where the extra cells come in handy. They also expand and thus preserve to some degree the page layout and spacing you wanted.

Creating Multiple Columns

You can use these same techniques—table layout and cell controls—to create multiple-column documents. Listing 5-16 shows you some code that lays out two parallel columns of text on a page along with an image and some intensive spacing for type control. The table lays out the page shown in Figure 5-21.

Listing 5-16

```
<!DOCTYPE HTML PUBLIC "-//W3C//DTD HTML 3.2 Final//EN">
<HTML>
<HEAD>
<TITLE>The Authors Online Companion</TITLE>
</HEAD>
<BODY BGCOLOR="#FFFFFF">
<TABLE BORDER="0" CELLPADDING="0" CELLSPACING="0">
<TR>
   <TH WIDTH="175" HEIGHT="50"> </TH>
   <TH WIDTH="328"> </TH>
   <TH WIDTH="97"> </TH>
</TR>
<TR>
   <TD WIDTH="175" ALIGN="LEFT" VALIGN="TOP">
      <P ALIGN="CENTER">
         <SPACER TYPE="VERTICAL" SIZE="6">
         <FONT FACE="Verdana, Arial, Helvetica" SIZE="5">
         Welcome <BR>
         to the<BR>
         <FONT COLOR="RED">Authors</FONT><BR>
         Online<BR>
         Companion</FONT>
      </P>
      <P ALIGN="CENTER">
         <FONT FACE="Verdana, Arial, Helvetica" SIZE="1">
         This page was designed
         <SPACER TYPE="VERTICAL" SIZE="6">
         to be displayed using
         <SPACER TYPE="VERTICAL" SIZE="6">
         Netscape Navigator.
      </P>
      <P ALIGN="CENTER">
         <FONT FACE="Verdana, Arial, Helvetica" SIZE="1">
         If you don't have the latest
         <SPACER TYPE="VERTICAL" SIZE="6">
         version, you can download <SPACER TYPE="VERTICAL" SIZE="6">
         <A HREF="ftp://ftp.netscape.com/pub/">Navigator 4.0</A>
         <SPACER TYPE="VERTICAL" SIZE="6">
         directly from Netscape's
         <SPACER TYPE="VERTICAL" SIZE="6">
         FTP site.
```

```
</FONT>
    </P>
    <!--The tag below was added to act as a spacer GIF to enforce the
width of col 1-->
    <P><SPACER TYPE="HORIZONTAL" SIZE="175"> </P>
  </TD>
  <TD BGCOLOR="#F7F7FF" ALIGN="LEFT" VALIGN="CENTER">
    <!--This image defines the width of col 2 -->
    <IMG SRC="images/aoc.gif" WIDTH="328" HEIGHT="150">
    <P>
       <SPACER TYPE="HORIZONTAL" SIZE="35">
       The following is an online work in progress
       <SPACER TYPE="VERTICAL" SIZE="10">
       <SPACER TYPE="HORIZONTAL" SIZE="20">
       that shows Web authoring and programming
       <SPACER TYPE="VERTICAL" SIZE="10">
       <SPACER TYPE="HORIZONTAL" SIZE="20">
       examples. It is designed to supplement the
       <SPACER TYPE="VERTICAL" SIZE="10">
       <SPACER TYPE="HORIZONTAL" SIZE="20">
       book <EM>HTML Publishing on the Internet
       <SPACER TYPE="VERTICAL" SIZE="10">
       <SPACER TYPE="HORIZONTAL" SIZE="20">
       Second Edition</EM> published by The Coriolis Group.
       <SPACER TYPE="VERTICAL" SIZE="10">
       <SPACER TYPE="HORIZONTAL" SIZE="20">
       To <A HREF=page2.html>continue</A> click on the carriage return
handle.
    </P>
  </TD>
  <TD>
    <P><SPACER TYPE="HORIZONTAL" SIZE="97"> </P>
  </TD>
</TR>
<TR>
<TD COLSPAN=3><IMG SRC="images/typewrtr.jpg" WIDTH="600" HEIGHT="160">
</TABLE>
</BODY>
</HTML>
```

Figure 5-21: You can use table layout to create multiple columns of text.

Let's look at the code for this page. The table is defined so that is has no borders or cell spacing and takes up the full width of the display. This is the same technique you saw in the earlier layout example.

This table layout actually consists of three rows and three columns. The first row of the table sets the column widths and, by setting the height, also acts as a spacer for the top of the page. The second row contains all the data for the page. The first column contains a general introduction to the page and some links to allow viewers to access browser software in order to view the page correctly. This column finishes with a small spacer element to ensure that the column width is set correctly; testing with multiple browsers and platforms showed that sometimes the column width was lost or set incorrectly. The second column consists of an image at the top followed by a paragraph of text. Note that the background color is set to make the table cell look like paper coming out of the typewriter image at the bottom of the table. The third column sets a right margin for the page; the column is intentionally left blank here, but it could be used for other text or graphics. The last row is used to display the typewriter image.

The following code is typical of what is used on this page:

```
<TD WIDTH="175" ALIGN="LEFT" VALIGN="TOP">
    <P ALIGN="CENTER">
        <SPACER TYPE="VERTICAL" SIZE="6">
        <FONT FACE="Verdana, Arial, Helvetica" SIZE="5">
        Welcome <BR>
        to the<BR>
        <FONT COLOR="RED">Authors</FONT><BR>
        Online<BR>
        Companion</FONT>
    </P>
    <P ALIGN="CENTER">
        <FONT FACE="Verdana, Arial, Helvetica" SIZE="1">
        This page was designed
        <SPACER TYPE="VERTICAL" SIZE="6">
        to be displayed using
        <SPACER TYPE="VERTICAL" SIZE="6">
        Netscape Navigator.
    </P>
```

This is a part of the code that defines the first cell in the second row. The text is centered in the cell and aligned at the top. This paragraph includes a new tag, <SPACER>, which is a Netscape extension to HTML. As the name implies, the <SPACER> tag provides a nonimaging space of any dimension for your page layout. The <SPACER> tag has a TYPE attribute that sets how the space is to be applied. Table 5-3 shows you the attributes for the <SPACER> tag.

The first paragraph in the cell sets a large font size (SIZE="5") for the entire paragraph. Then it breaks the text into four lines, using a <BR> tag, and sets the central line of text to red.

TIP

To make the page display in browsers that don't support the <SPACER> tag, you can use the IMG tag and a transparent pixel image. By specifying the HEIGHT and WIDTH attributes, you can specify the amount of space that would have been added by the <SPACER> tag. Chapter 7 goes into more detail about creating and using transparent pixel images.

Attribute	Description
<SPACER TYPE="*type*">	Specifies the type of space to insert. Valid entries are:
	VERTICAL Inserts spacing between lines.
	HORIZONTAL Inserts spacing between words.
	BLOCK Inserts a rectangular block of space.
<SPACER SIZE="*n*">	Valid with types VERTICAL and HORIZONTAL, and specifies the size of the space inserted in pixels.
<SPACER WIDTH="*n*">	Valid only with type BLOCK, and specifies the width of the spacing rectangle in pixels.
<SPACER HEIGHT="*n*">	Valid only with type BLOCK, and specifies the height of the spacing rectangle in pixels.
<SPACER ALIGN="*alignment*">	Valid only with type BLOCK, and specifies the alignment of the spacing rectangle. Valid choices are:
	LEFT Aligns a spacing rectangle with the left margin.
	RIGHT Aligns a spacing rectangle with the right margin.
	TOP Aligns the top of a spacing rectangle with the top of the tallest item in the current line.
	ABSMIDDLE Aligns the middle of a spacing rectangle with the middle of the text in the current line.
	ABSBOTTOM Aligns the bottom of a spacing rectangle with the bottom of the lowest item in the current line.
	TEXTTOP Aligns the top of a spacing rectangle with the top of the tallest text in the current line.
	MIDDLE Aligns the middle of a spacing rectangle with the baseline of the text in the current line.
	BASELINE Aligns the bottom of a spacing rectangle with the baseline of the text in the current line.
	BOTTOM The same as BASELINE.

Table 5-3: Attributes for the <SPACER> tag.

Here we use the <SPACER> tag to insert vertical spacing between lines. This is the equivalent of leading in ordinary typography. In other parts of this page, you will see the <SPACER> tag used to insert horizontal spacing as well. This creates a more polished, professional, and typeset look to the page.

TIP

This is a simplified version of a page at the Authors Web site. The original uses additional tags and attributes that result in an even more polished page that truly looks typeset. You can see the original at http://www.authors.com/authors.htm.

Creating Resizable Vertical & Horizontal Rules

One of the most clever tricks in HTML publishing is resizing a transparent GIF to create blank space. You can use a transparent pixel and specify a background color in a cell to create horizontal and vertical rules that act as resizable horizontal rules and column separators. Figure 5-22 is created by the code shown in Listing 5-17; it shows how the line separators (the cells with a background color) automatically change as the table is resized when a reader changes the size of the window.

Listing 5-17

```
<HTML>
<HEAD>
<TITLE>Resizable Vertical and Horizontal Rules</title>
</HEAD>
<BODY>
<DIV ALIGN="CENTER">
<TABLE BORDER="0" CELLPADDING="0" CELLSPACING="10">
<TR>
    <TD COLSPAN="5" BGCOLOR="#000000"><IMG SRC="dot_clear.gif" WIDTH="1"
HEIGHT="1"></TD>
</TR>
<TR>
    <TD VALIGN="TOP"><P ALIGN="LEFT"> When you resize the window the vertical
and horizontal rules separating each section will automatically be
resized.</P>
    </TD>
    <TD VALIGN="TOP" BGCOLOR="#000000"><IMG SRC="CLEARDOT.GIF" WIDTH="1"
HEIGHT="1"></TD>
    <TD VALIGN="TOP"><P ALIGN="LEFT"> When you resize the window the vertical
and horizontal rules separating each section will automatically be resized.
</P>
    </TD>
    <TD VALIGN="TOP" BGCOLOR="#000000"><IMG SRC="CLEARDOT.GIF" WIDTH="1"
HEIGHT="1"></TD>
```

```
    <TD VALIGN="TOP"><P ALIGN="LEFT">When you resize the window the vertical
and horizontal rules separating each section will automatically be resized.
</P>
    </TD>
</TR>
<TR>
  <TD COLSPAN="5" BGCOLOR="#000000"><IMG SRC="dot_clear.gif" WIDTH="1"
HEIGHT="1"></TD>
</TR>
</TABLE>
</DIV>
</BODY>
</HTML>
```

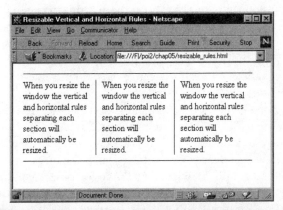

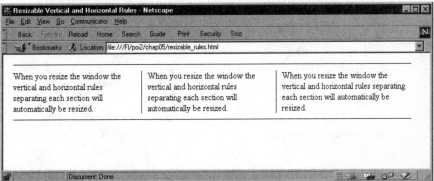

Figure 5-22: You present text with resizable horizontal and vertical rules by specifying a background color for a cell containing a transparent GIF.

Table Differences in Browsers

When you begin to do fancy layouts like these last two examples, you also begin to get into the areas where differences between browsers becomes critical. Look again at the code in Listing 5-16 for the last part of the first cell in the second row:

```
    <!--The tag below was added to act as a spacer GIF to enforce the
width of col 1-->
    <P><SPACER TYPE="HORIZONTAL" SIZE="206"> </P></TD>
    </TD>
```

Here is a good example of the type of problem you may encounter when you start to use advanced features like tables for layout. When we tested the page with several versions of browsers and on different platforms, we saw that we couldn't always rely on the settings in the first row—which are intended to establish the spacing of the columns—to make the first column as wide as we wanted. We inserted this last paragraph simply to enforce the WIDTH setting that was used previously. Logically, this shouldn't be necessary; practically, it is. It's because of problems like this that you need to check your code with several browsers.

Besides encountering spacing problems, you may find that handling margins with tables in different browsers can be difficult. For example, if you use a table to add a background color to a left or right column of the browser, a margin will appear between the edge of the browser and the table. Microsoft includes a couple of extensions that overcome the margin setting when you're aligning tables, ALIGN="BLEEDLEFT" or ALIGN="BLEEDRIGHT." The BLEEDLEFT and BLEEDRIGHT settings are not defined in HTML 4.0; however, the problem of controlling margins has been addressed with Cascading Style Sheets. If the browser understands the BLEEDLEFT and BLEEDRIGHT attribute, it forces the table all the way to the left or right of the display, ignoring any margins. Since any browser that doesn't understand this will use the default value of ALIGN="LEFT" or ALIGN="RIGHT," using this alignment doesn't cost anything and may be helpful.

In addition, you should know that many older versions of popular browsers do not support tables, or don't support them correctly. When that happens with a table full of data, the result is difficult to read and may not be very clear. However, if you're using the table as a page layout—with multiple text columns and images—the result will be a disaster, and probably not readable at all. If you rely on certain browser features and attributes, as we do here, you should always let the viewer know that and, if possible, provide a link to the browser or browsers that will display your design properly.

As we mentioned earlier, one way to avoid some of these problems is to use a real image as a spacing element. In that case, you would insert a transparent

GIF file wherever the <SPACER> tag is used, setting the WIDTH and HEIGHT attributes to create the spacing you want. This has the advantage of being more browser independent. On the other hand, it has the disadvantage that you now have multiple images on your page, which will require more communication between the viewer's browser and your server.

Creating Snaking Columns

Netscape added the <MULTICOL> tag as an extension to HTML to display text in a multicolumn text layout. You must have Netscape Navigator 3.0 or higher to view a multicolumn page correctly. The multicolumn text appears as snaking newspaper columns. The <MULTICOL> tag is used with COLS, GUTTER, and WIDTH attributes to control the number of columns, the space between the columns, and the width of individual columns, respectively. This example of multicolumn text shows four columns with a GUTTER="20" setting. This sets the gutter width to 20 pixels. The default is 10 pixels. The width of this set of columns is 600 pixels. You can also set these values to a percentage. Figure 5-23 shows an example of multiple column text created using the <MULTICOL> tag. The code is as follows:

```
<MULTICOL COLS="3" GUTTER="20" WIDTH="600">
Text to appear in columns...
</MULTICOL>
```

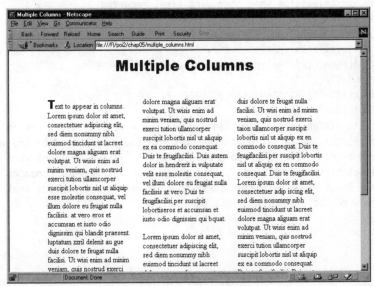

Figure 5-23: An example of text in multiple columns.

If you don't include the WIDTH attribute, the columns extend across the width of the browser window. The Netscape browser calculates the size of the equal length columns by using a page break algorithm based on the total length of the text contained in the columns. Preformatted tags take precedence over the column settings. Therefore, you should be careful when you use the PRE tag to present preformatted text in multiple columns. If a long line of preformatted text does not break within a column, it overwrites text in the next column.

You can nest <MULTICOL> tags so you have multiple columns within one another. The following code shows two columns, with the first column containing two nested columns. Figure 5-24 shows the results of the code shown in Listing 5-18.

Listing 5-18

```
<HTML>
<HEAD>
<TITLE>Original Radio and Television News Articles</TITLE>
</HEAD>
<BODY>
<DIV ALIGN="CENTER">
<H2>Original Articles on the Invention of Radio and Television</H2>
<MULTICOL COLS="2" GUTTER="20" WIDTH="640">
   <P ALIGN="LEFT"><BR>
   The following are articles that were written about the invention of
radio and television when they were first reported.
   </P>
<MULTICOL COLS="2" GUTTER="12">
   <H3>Television</H3>
   <P ALIGN="LEFT">Belin Shows Tele-vision</P>
   <FONT SIZE="2">
   <P ALIGN="RIGHT">December 2, 1922</P>
   <P ALIGN="LEFT">
"Tele-vision or 'long-distance sight' by wireless, had a preliminary
experimental demonstration at the Sorbonne today by Edward Belin, inventor
of the transmission of photo-graphs by wire. Flashes of light were directed
on a selenium element, which, through another instrument, produced sound
waves. These waves were then taken up by a wireless apparatus that
reproduced the flashes of light on a mirror.
```

```
    </P>
    <P ALIGN="LEFT">
"This was offered as proof that the general principle of projecting a
stationary scene had been solved."
    </P>
    </FONT>
    <H3>Radio</H3>
    <P ALIGN="LEFT">Topics of the Times</P>
    <FONT SIZE="2">
    <P ALIGN="RIGHT">May 26, 1897</P>
    <P ALIGN="LEFT"> "English electricians, particularly those connected with
the army and navy, are much interested in the Marconi system of telegraphy
without wires. Some remarkable work has already been done with this machine,
and improvements being made are expected to add many miles to the two or
three over which it is already effective.
    </P>
    <P ALIGN="LEFT">
The system, it is thought, will be of especial use to the commanders of
fleets at sea by enabling them to communicate with their other vessels
without the use of visible signals."
    </P>
    </FONT>
</MULTICOL>
    <P ALIGN="LEFT">
Although the article credits Edward Belin, as being the inventor of "the
transmission of photo-graphs by wire," Vladimir Zworykin is the person who
is most often credited for the invention of the television. He developed the
iconoscope which is a scanning tube for the television camera and kinescope,
a cathode-ray picture tube.
    </P>
    <P ALIGN="LEFT">
The article on the invention of the radio was written in 1897. Marconi
had sent long-wave signals over a distance more than a mile in 195 and
received the first transatlantic wireless signals in 1901. Marconi was
awarded the Nobel Prize in Physics in 1909. He shared the Nobel Prize along
with Karl Braun.
    </P>
</MULTICOL>
</DIV>
</BODY>
</HTML>
```

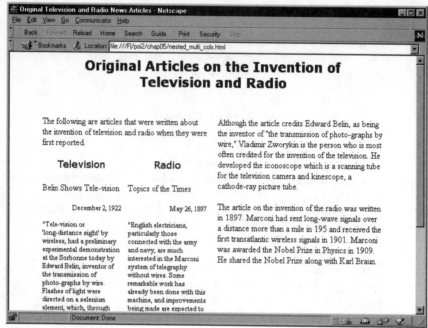

Figure 5-24: An example of nested multiple columns.

Designing With Frames

Another way to achieve an effect similar to the table layouts you saw in the preceding sections is to create several independent areas, called frames, within the browser display. A *frame* is an individual, independently scrolling region of a Web page. You can use each frame to show various elements of the overall page layout that you have created. You do this by using two complementary tags: <FRAMESET> and <FRAME>. The <FRAMESET> tag defines a group of frames that display in one browser window. The <FRAME> tag defines each individual frame in an associated <FRAMESET>. Each frame can be defined with unique features and characteristics using the <FRAME> tag's attributes.

Presenting Pages in Frames

Frames allow you to set up pages in a variety of formats; the advantage is that the data in each frame is independent of any other frames. This means that you can use one frame for a table of contents or a navigation bar and always keep it available for the viewer. If you worked with the table layouts in the preceding sections, you may have noticed that this is one serious drawback to using table layout for navigation elements, as you saw in the first example. If the page being presented had required scrolling, then the navigation elements on the left side of the layout would have scrolled out of sight with the top of the page. With frames, you can avoid this problem.

To show you how this works, let's re-create the earlier example presented in Figure 5-19 using frames rather than a table-based layout. The results of the changes are shown in Figure 5-25.

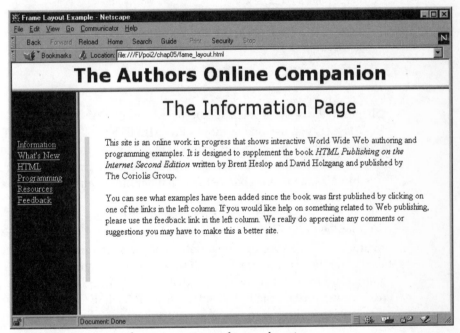

Figure 5-25: You can use frames to create complex page layouts.

For this example, you set up three frames: one across the top of the page for the caption, one down the left side of the page for the navigational elements, and one containing the body text. To do that, you need to set up four HTML files: one each for the content of the three frames and one master file that creates the framed page. The code for the master page is quite short and looks like Listing 5-19.

Listing 5-19

```
<HTML>
<HEAD>
<TITLE>Frame Layout Example</TITLE>
</HEAD>

<FRAMESET ROWS="50,*">
<FRAME SRC="title.html" MARGINWIDTH="15" MARGINHEIGHT="0" SCROLLING="NO"
NORESIZE>

  <FRAMESET COLS="15%,85%">
      <FRAME SRC="navbar.html">
      <FRAME SRC="info.html" NAME="text_frame">
  </FRAMESET>

</FRAMESET>
</HTML>
```

Pages that display frames do not include a <BODY> tag. In place of the <BODY> tag, you use one or more <FRAMESET> tags. The <FRAMESET> tags specify the subdocuments that will make up the frames on the page. In this case, the document consists of three subordinate frames: a title, named "title.html"; a navigation bar, named "navbar.html"; and the text for the home page, contained in "home.html."

The <FRAMESET> tag has two important attributes: ROWS and COLS. As you might expect, they set the number of rows and columns in the framed document. ROWS specifies the numbers of rows for each frame. COLS specifies the number of columns for each frame in the document. For example, to create columns, you use the COLS attribute, <FRAMESET COLS="n">. To create rows, you use the ROWS attribute, <FRAMESET ROWS="n">, where n represents the width of the columns or the height of the rows.

Defining Column Width & Row Height

As is true of many of the size specifications in HTML, the width of a column or height of a row may be specified in pixels or percentages. For example, this code creates three frame rows:

```
<FRAMESET ROWS="50%, 30%, 20%">
```

The first row takes up 50 percent of the window, the second takes up 30 percent, and the last 20 percent. An asterisk (*) may be used to indicate that the corresponding frame should receive all the remaining space. For example, this code creates two frame columns:

```
<FRAMESET COLS="200,*">
```

The first column has a width of 200 pixels; the second takes up the remaining part of the screen. You can also use asterisks to evenly distribute the space. For example, this code specifies that the frames display as three equal rows:

```
<FRAMESET ROWS="*, *, *">
```

In this case, you see that the first <FRAMESET> tag creates a document with two rows. The first row is 50 pixels high; the second takes all the remaining space in the frame. Within the first <FRAMESET> is a second one, which defines the second row of the frame. This is itself a <FRAMESET> that consists of two columns, the first of which is 15 percent of the screen width, while the second takes the remaining 85 percent.

Creating Individual Frames

Once you have defined the structure, you need to add the individual frame references. In order for a document to appear in a frame, you need to use the SRC attribute to refer to the source document you want to be displayed in this frame. In addition, if you want to use the frame to display multiple documents, you need to add the NAME attribute, as shown here:

```
<FRAME SRC="navbar.html">
<FRAME SRC="info.html" NAME="text_frame">
```

These two lines of code show you a basic frame that will display the navigation bar page and the adjacent frame, which will begin by displaying the home page and then may display other pages, depending on which link is selected in the navigation bar.

The <FRAME> tag has additional attributes, as shown in the definition of the frame that creates the title in the top row of the page:

```
<FRAME SRC="title.html" MARGINWIDTH="15" MARGINHEIGHT="0" SCROLLING=NO
NORESIZE>
```

This frame is a little more complex. Since the frame holds the caption for the page, you set some additional attributes to establish margins, to suppress scrolling in the frame no matter what the size of the browser window, and to prevent the user from resizing the frame. Table 5-4 shows a list of the attributes that are used here.

Attribute	Description
MARGINHEIGHT="*n*"	Controls the margin height for the frame, in pixels.
MARGINWIDTH="*n*"	Controls the margin width for the frame, in pixels.
NAME="*name*"	Provides a target name for the frame.
NORESIZE	Prevents the user from resizing the frame.
SCROLLING="YES"|"NO"|"AUTO"	Creates or suppresses scrolling in a frame. The AUTO selection allows the browser to enable scrolling if the contents of the frame require it and not otherwise; this is the default setting.

Table 5-4: Attributes for the <FRAME> tag.

Creating the Target Pages

Once you have set up the master page, you need to define the target pages that will populate the frames on the master. Listing 5-20 shows you the title information.

Listing 5-20

```
<HTML>
<HEAD>
<TITLE>Authors Online Companion</TITLE>
</HEAD>
<BODY BGCOLOR="white">
<DIV ALIGN="CENTER">
<P><FONT SIZE="6" FACE="Verdana, Helvetica, sans-serif"><STRONG>The Authors
Online Companion</STRONG></FONT></P>
</DIV>
</BODY>
</HTML>
```

By now, this code should be fairly clear to you. The <DIV> tag is used to set the title in the center of the frame, and a large type is used to make it prominent.

Listing 5-21 shows you the navigational bar.

Listing 5-21

```
<HTML>
<HEAD>
<TITLE>
Navigation Links
</TITLE>
</HEAD>
```

```
<BODY BGCOLOR="blue" LINK="white" VLINK="yellow">
<P>
<SPACER TYPE="VERTICAL" SIZE="70">
    <A HREF="info.html" TARGET="text_frame">Information</A><BR>
    <A HREF="new.html" TARGET="text_frame">What's New</A><BR>
    <A HREF="html.html" TARGET="text_frame">HTML</A><BR>
    <A HREF="prog.html" TARGET="text_frame">Programming</A><BR>
    <A HREF="resource.html" TARGET="text_frame">Resources</A><BR>
    <A HREF="feedback.html" TARGET="text_frame">Feedback</A><BR>
</BODY>
</HTML>
```

This code is a little more complex. The basic layout is quite clear: You use the <SPACER> tag to position the first item in the list, and then you have a list of anchors. The new item here is the TARGET attribute. This attribute, if present, names the frame where the page referenced by the anchor link is to be displayed. If you don't enter this, the page linked to is displayed in the current frame. In this case, of course, you want to keep the current frame as the navigational links and display any related information in the main text frame, which you named "text_frame" when you defined the frame earlier in Listing 5-19.

In contrast to the rest of the page, the background in this frame is set to blue, and the links are shown in white if they have not been visited and yellow if they have.

Finally, you need to define the text page, "info.html." The code for this page is shown in Listing 5-22.

Listing 5-22

```
<HTML>
<HEAD>
<TITLE>
Authors Information Page
</TITLE>
</HEAD>

<BODY BGCOLOR="white">
<TABLE BORDER="0" CELLPADDING="0" CELLSPACING="0" WIDTH="100%">
<TR>
    <TD ALIGN="CENTER" COLSPAN="4"><FONT SIZE="6" FACE="Verdana, Helvetica,
sans-serif">The Information Page</FONT></TD>
</TR>
<TR>
    <TD WIDTH="1%">  </TD>
    <TD WIDTH="5%">  </TD>
    <TD HEIGHT="30"> </TD>
```

```
</TR>
<TR>
<TD BGCOLOR="yellow"> </TD>
   <TD> </TD>
   <TD ROWSPAN="8"><P>This site is an online work in progress that shows
interactive World Wide Web authoring and programming examples. It is
designed to supplement the book <EM>HTML Publishing on the Internet Second
Edition</EM> written by Brent Heslop and David Holzgang and published by The
Coriolis Group.</P>
<P>You can see what examples have been added since the book was first
published by clicking on one of the links in the left column. If you would
like help on something related to Web publishing, please use the feedback
link in the left column. We really do appreciate any comments or suggestions
you may have to make this a better site.</P>
<P> </P>
<P> </P>
</TD>
</TR>
<TR>
<TD BGCOLOR="yellow"> </TD>
   <TD> </TD>
   <TD> </TD>
</TR>
<TR>
<TD BGCOLOR="yellow"> </TD>
   <TD>  </TD>
   <TD>  </TD>
</TR>
<TR>
<TD BGCOLOR="yellow"> </TD>
   <TD> </TD>
   <TD>  </TD>
</TR>
<TR>
<TD BGCOLOR="yellow"> </TD>
   <TD> </TD>
   <TD> </TD>
</TR>
<TR>
<TD BGCOLOR="yellow"> </TD>
   <TD> </TD>
   <TD>  </TD>
</TR>
<TR>
```

```
<TD BGCOLOR="yellow"> </TD>
   <TD> </TD>
   <TD> </TD>
</TR>
<TR>
<TD BGCOLOR="yellow"> </TD>
   <TD> </TD>
   <TD> </TD>
</TR>
</TABLE>
</BODY>
</HTML>
```

This looks very much like the code you saw earlier in Listing 5-15, where you created the original table layout. Frames do not allow tricks like the vertical colored stripe, so to keep that visual metaphor, this page continues to use a table to create the stripe and the associated spacing; the previous navigational links, which are now incorporated into the navigational frame shown in Listing 5-21, have been removed from the page.

Targeted Windows

You can always name your frames in the top-level <FRAMESET> to allow you to display items in any frame. In addition, you have two reserved names that you can use to place your new information, even if you haven't named the frame. The first reserved name is TARGET="blank." This sends the linked page to a new, empty browser window. As a result, the original browser window will remain open with the same information displayed, and a new browser window will open displaying the new information. This is essentially the same as choosing New Web Browser from the File menu in Netscape Navigator.

The second reserved name is TARGET="_top." This causes the linked page to completely replace all frames in the frame window—in effect, replacing the original document defined by the <FRAMESET> tag. This can be particularly useful when you wish to exit the frame environment or send the viewer to another site that doesn't use frames.

Inline Frames

You can also add inline, or floating, frames to a page. With inline frames, you can embed one Web page inside another. Inline frames are not added with the <FRAMESET> tag. Instead you use the <IFRAME> tag. Like an <IMG> tag, you can add an <IFRAME> tag anywhere in a document. You use the SRC attribute to specify which document you want to appear in the inline frame. You also need to add the WIDTH and HEIGHT to specify how big you want the inline frame to be. The <IFRAME> tag can accept any of the attributes used with the <FRAME> tag, such as MARGINHEIGHT MARGINWIDTH, SCROLLING, NAME, and so on. You can also use the ALIGN attribute to align the floating frame to the left or right side of the browser window. Figure 5-26 shows the results of the example code shown in Listing 5-23, which uses <IFRAME> tags to display the Microsoft home page and the Netscape home page side by side, each in an inline frame. At present, inline frames are supported only in Microsoft Internet Explorer.

Listing 5-23

```
<HTML>
<HEAD>
<TITLE>Inline Frames</TITLE>
</HEAD>
<BODY>
<P>
<FONT SIZE=4>Microsoft's Site</FONT>
<IFRAME SRC="http://home.microsoft.com/" NAME="Microsoft" WIDTH="250"
HEIGHT="250" SCROLLING="YES" FRAMEBORDER="1" NORESIZE MARGINWIDTH="5"
MARGINHEIGHT="0" HSPACE="5">
    <FRAME SRC="http://www.microsoft.com/" NAME="Microsoft" WIDTH="250"
HEIGHT="250" SCROLLING="YES" FRAMEBORDER="1" MARGINWIDTH="5"
MARGINHEIGHT="0" NORESIZE>
</IFRAME>
<FONT SIZE=4>Netscape's Site</FONT>
<IFRAME SRC="http://home.netscape.com/" NAME="NS" WIDTH="250" HEIGHT="250"
SCROLLING="YES" FRAMEBORDER="1" NORESIZE MARGINWIDTH="5" HSPACE="5"
MARGINHEIGHT="0">
    <FRAME SRC="http://home.netscape.com/" NAME="Netscape" WIDTH="350"
HEIGHT="250" SCROLLING="YES" FRAMEBORDER="1" MARGINWIDTH="5"
MARGINHEIGHT="0" NORESIZE>
</IFRAME>

</P>
</BODY>
</HTML>
```

If you click on a link in a page in an inline frame, the browser will display the page inside the frame. You can even use the Back button to return to the previous page. Although you can display pages at other sites, pages are designed to display in full windows, so inline frames are typically used to display smaller documents designed for the frame.

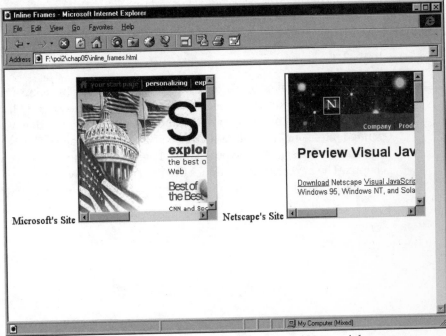

Figure 5-26: Inline frames displaying Microsoft's home page and Netscape's home page.

Controlling Frames With Scripts

HTML 4.0 provides a variety of scripting mechanisms to help you make active pages. JavaScript, which is the most popular, is a scripting language that was developed by Netscape and has been widely adopted. At present, most browsers, including current versions of Netscape's and Microsoft's browsers, support JavaScript applets embedded in HTML code. Besides the standard JavaScript, frame documents support some special JavaScript effects. Table 5-5 shows you a list of the special attributes you can set in a <FRAMESET> tag to take advantage of JavaScript functions. You will learn about adding JavaScript code to your pages in Chapter 11, "Interactive Pages & Scripting."

Attribute	Description
ONLOAD="loadJScode"	Specifies the script function to execute when the frameset is loaded into the frame
ONUNLOAD="unloadJScode"	Specifies the script function to execute when the frameset is unloaded (exited).

Table 5-5: Scripting extensions for use with <FRAMESET>.

Moving On

This chapter has taken you into new territory. You began by using a table to display data on your page, which is an extension of the use of HTML tags you have been reading about from the beginning of this book. But then you expanded into using the table as a layout mechanism for pages. This is a whole new realm of design and layout that we haven't really investigated until this chapter. The next chapter continues this advance by showing you how to use graphic images to create even more effective and more powerful Web pages.

## chapter 6

Getting Graphic With Images

No matter how impressive your message, people respond to images. The reader's eye is naturally drawn to a picture before text and the choice and quality of the images you use will largely determine whether someone will take the time to read your Web page or pass it by. Much of the Web's success is due, in part, to its ability to include graphic images. Cliché as it may sound, a picture is worth a thousand words. Because of the importance of images in Internet publishing, it's important to take the time to master the tags and options for including graphics.

This chapter covers Web graphic file formats and points out the benefits and problems these file formats present to a Web publisher. It also covers adding existing images to a Web page and changing background and text colors and explains how to use an image for a background or page border. The next chapter explains how to use image editors and utilities to create and modify image files.

Web Graphic Fundamentals

In order to begin working with graphic images, it's helpful to know what choices you have and some fundamental terms, such as pixels and palettes. The two graphic file formats supported by most Web browsers are GIF and JPEG. It's easy to set up browsers to load applications that will display other formats, such as tagged image file format (TIFF) and Encapsulated PostScript (EPS), but Web documents can only display files in the GIF and JPEG format. The following sections give you a quick overview of graphic terms and point out the differences between the GIF and JPEG file formats.

Understanding Pixels & Bit-Depth

A *pixel* is the smallest measurement of part of an image. The *pixel-depth*, or *bit-depth*, refers to a measurement of the number of bits of stored information per pixel. In other words, each pixel is assigned a numeric value to represent a color. The greater the bit-depth, the more colors you have available. Table 6-1 shows the number of colors available for different bit-depths.

Bit-Depth	Number of Colors
1	2
2	4
3	8
4	16
5	32
6	64
7	128
8	256
16	65,536
24	16.7 million
32	16.7 million plus a 256 level grayscale mask

Table 6-1: Bit-depth and number of colors.

Resolution & Screen Space

Computer screens are quite different from the printed page. The size of a typical monitor is only 640 X 480 pixels (less if you consider the space the browser requires), which is much smaller than an average printed page. In addition the average resolution of a computer display is 72 dpi (dots per inch). In contrast, the most basic printer available today is capable of 300–1400 dpi or more. A typical photograph is 2000 dpi or higher. Figure 6-1 compares the typical resolutions for photographs, laser printers, and computer screens.

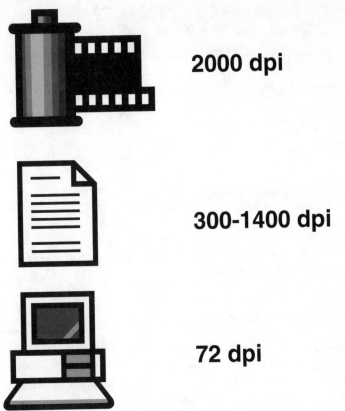

2000 dpi

300-1400 dpi

72 dpi

Figure 6-1: A comparison of dots per inch for film, printers, and computer screens.

When you are creating pages, consider the amount of space that will be needed to display your images and text on a 640 X 480 monitor. Actually you don't have a full 640 X 480 pixels if you want the page displayed in the browser window. Figure 6-2 shows the amount of space you can safely use.

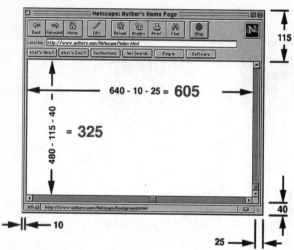

Figure 6-2: The amount of space that is available depends on the resolution of the monitor the person is using to view your page.

The Web-Safe Color Palette

A *color palette*, sometimes called a color look-up table (CLUT) or a *swatch*, is a mathematical table that defines the colors of pixels. Each displayed pixel has a value that matches one of the indexed locations in a palette. An image that uses a palette is sometimes called an indexed color image.

Linda Weinman was the first person to point out that there are 216 colors that are common to the browsers and operating systems of different computers. If you use any other color outside of the common 216-color palette, the browser will either convert the color to the closest color it can find in the palette or it will dither (add colors to try to match the color). Dithering is covered in more detail in the next chapter.

Say you created some artwork using a set of colored crayons, like the picture and crayons shown in Figure 6-3. If you wanted someone to be able to re-create the picture at another location, you would need to make sure that the person copied your artwork using the same make of colored crayons and the same size and type of paper. The resulting copy would look very similar if not exactly like your original. The online equivalent of using the same colored crayons and paper is the *browser-safe palette*. If you only use colors from this palette, the colors will appear consistent on most browsers and computers.

Figure 6-3: Using the browser-safe palette, you can be sure that images display on different operating systems and computer screens.

If you want to use a color for text or a background, it is helpful to know which colors are browser-safe colors. Browser-safe colors can be represented by RGB values, percentages of each color, or hexadecimal code. RGB stands for red, green, and blue. Monitors display images by emitting red, green, and blue light. Table 6-2 shows the RGB, hexadecimal triplets, and percentages for choosing a browser-safe color. When you specify a color, you typically use a pound sign and the hexadecimal red, green, and blue values. Using style sheets, you can specify a color with the RGB decimal values or as percentages.

RGB	Hex	Percentage
0	00	0
51	33	20
102	66	40
153	99	60
204	CC	80
255	FF	100

Table 6-2: Browser-safe colors.

You can use this table to make sure that you are using a browser-safe color for a background or text. The next chapter explains where to download the browser-safe palette and how to use the browser-safe palette in a graphic editor to display and specify a particular color.

Interlaced Images

An interlaced image can be progressively displayed. When an interlaced file is downloaded, it appears with a venetian blind or sparkling effect. Interlaced files let the user begin viewing the rest of the document while the image is downloading. Different file formats have different methods of interlacing. Figure 6-4 shows the process of displaying an interlaced file in the Graphics Interchange Format (GIF).

Figure 6-4: An interlaced image displays portions of the picture as the image downloads, so it seems to display faster than a non-interlaced file.

The GIF Format

The most common type of image file format on the Web is Graphics Interchange Format (GIF), pronounced jif, according to its creator. The GIF format was created by CompuServe to provide a way to quickly exchange graphic image files over phone lines. GIF files are stored in a compressed format so that the download time is minimal. A major benefit of GIF files is that they can be displayed on UNIX, Mac, and Windows platforms.

GIF files have a color-depth of 8 bits per pixel for a total of 256 colors. Therefore, GIF files use a color palette with up to 256 colors. These colors can be 256 colors out of millions of possibilities. Only one combination of 256 colors can be used at one time. Windows itself reserves 20 colors for displaying windows. If you use a palette of 256 colors for one image and another color palette that includes additional colors for another image, the screen may flash strange colors while Windows creates a new palette and the old colors change to the new palette.

Using more than 256 colors can also cause distorted images. The colors are allocated as they are requested until all 256 colors are used. Any additional graphics displayed onscreen can only use colors that are already allocated unless a new palette is used. This is why some images may appear fine at the beginning of a Web page and subsequent images appear distorted. For example, if your page has two images that use more than 256 colors, when the browser displaying your page runs out of colors, the remaining colors will not be created. Instead, the colors closest to those already allocated will be used, which can distort your image.

The best way to keep from having images distort when displayed is to use the same palette for all images appearing on the same page. Graphic editors let you remap, optimize, and customize palettes, which is covered in the next chapter.

▼ The GIF LZW Controversy

In December 1994, a controversy arose concerning the GIF file format. The controversy started because CompuServe and Unisys, the two companies that own the rights to the GIF file format, decided to start charging developers for products that include GIF support. Until this announcement, the GIF format was treated as a public-domain standard—although it really wasn't. The GIF file format uses LZW compression. LZW comes from the names Lempel, Ziv, and Welch. Lempel and Ziv were mathematicians who were originators of several compression schemes. Welch later added his input to Lempel and Ziv's compression algorithm. Unisys, a large networking and information management company, owns the patent for LZW and is requiring licensing for all software developers (*not* end users) using the LZW compression. CompuServe Information Services has provided an optional licensing agreement that CompuServe-related software developers can enter into instead of dealing with Unisys directly. Software developers whose software is not "primarily for use with the CompuServe Information Service" will have to obtain a license from Unisys. CompuServe is licensing the usage of LZW in GIF products for 1.5 percent of the selling cost of the product. Of the 1.5 percent, 1 percent goes to Unisys. Unfortunately this has caused a lot of confusion and has been a stumbling block to many software vendors.

When to Use the GIF Format

Because GIF images include up to 256 colors, it is the file format for line art and large areas of flat-color, geometric images. If you have text you want to display as an image, use the GIF format.

There are two types of GIF file formats: GIF89a and GIF87a. GIF89a includes a transparency index that causes the background color of the display to remain unchanged for the color indexed as transparent. If you want to have an image appear to float on the page, you will want to use the GIF89a format. Another option when using a GIF file is that you can save large files as interlaced so they appear to load faster on the page. Unique to the GIF87a format is the capability to store multiple images in a single file to display as animation. If you want to use an image to display animation, you have to use the GIF87a format.

The JPEG Format

The Joint Photographic Experts Group (JPEG) file format supports 24-bit color, which gives you up to 16.7 million colors. With JPEG images, you don't have to worry about palettes. Actually, JPEG refers to a compression scheme, not a file format, but just about everyone refers to JPEG as a file format. A file format that is closely associated with JPEG files is the JFIF (or JPEF) format.

The JPEG compression algorithm is referred to as *lossy*, meaning that some data is lost. JPEG identifies and ignores pixels that are not essential to the overall quality of the image, such as a large area of a single color. Typically, the absence of subtracted information is not noticeable. Once an image is compressed using JPEG, it loses some information, so the image may appear indistinguishable from the original JPEG file and will be much smaller. Another advantage of JPEG is that it's supported in PostScript Level 2. PostScript has long been a standard on the Internet. When a JPEG compressed image is sent to a PostScript Level 2 printer, the file is first sent to the printer and then it is decompressed.

The JPEG file format doesn't support interlacing, but another format called Progressive JPEG does. Progressive JPEG has higher compression rates and works with Netscape Navigator and Internet Explorer. The only real drawback to using the Progressive JPEG format is that some older browsers may not be able to display them.

When to Use the JPEG File Format

The human face consists of thousands of skin-tone colors that are not easily matched using the 256 colors found in a GIF palette. The JPEG format is much more suitable for high-resolution photographs and organic images. Organic images are images that contain numerous irregularities and soft edges rather than straight lines. For example, a landscape of a mountain range would be a good example of an organic image. The more irregular patterns, or noise, in an image, the more suited it is for JPEG. If you know that your audience is using Netscape Navigator or Internet Explorer, use the Progressive JPEG format.

Many graphic editors, such as Adobe Photoshop, let you choose a quality setting for the compression. High quality is less compressed, with a ratio of about 5:1 to 15:1. JPEG images are automatically decompressed when they are loaded in the browser. JPEG reduces image files to about 10 percent of their original size or smaller.

The PNG Format

There is a new format called PNG (Portable Network Graphics); however, it is currently only supported by Microsoft Internet Explorer. If you are using Netscape Navigator, you can obtain plug-ins that let you display PNG as inline images. The PNG format has an impressive list of features that are likely to make it the graphics choice of the future. The following lists the main benefits of using the PNG format:

- PNG supports images with different bit-depths, including full color (24 bit), thousands (16 bit), and 256 (8-bit indexed) images.

- PNG uses a compression technology called *deflation* that is used in many freeware programs. It was developed to be a free and open standard.

- PNG format has a full-color, non-lossy image compression, which makes files smaller and quicker to load.

- The Adam 7 interlacing scheme that PNG uses improves the illusion that images load quickly.

- Gamma correction is unique to the PNG format. The term *Gamma* refers to the brightness of an image. Images created on computers with screens that use Gamma correction, such as an Apple Macintosh, Sun, or SGI, will look dark on a PC monitor. An PNG image's brightness is automatically corrected to display consistently for differing types of monitors regardless of the computer used to create the image.

- The PNG format supports alpha channels, also called *masks*, to define varying levels of transparency. This lets you create transparent images with fading edges, such as a vignette. Figure 6-5 shows an image with differing levels of transparency.

Figure 6-5: An image with differing levels of transparency.

You can find out more about the PNG specification at http://www.wco.com/ ~png, at Thomas Boutell's Web site at http://sunsite.unc.edu/boutell/png.html, and at http://www.quest.jpl.nasa.gov/PNG/.

When to Use the PNG Format

Unless you are checking and displaying separate pages for readers who are using the Internet Explorer 4.0 browser, it isn't recommended that you use PNG files. PNG support is scheduled to be included in the next release of Netscape Navigator. Still, readers using older browsers will be out of luck and a broken image will display instead of the PNG image file.

If you are on an intranet that uses only Internet Explorer or you are creating pages that are specifically for IE 4, you should use PNG files rather than GIF or JPEG for the following types of images:

- Full-color images you want saved in a lossless format.
- Images with one or more levels of transparency.
- Line art images or images that contain type.
- Flat-color images.
- Organic and geometric images that consist of smooth edges and areas of sharp contrast, such as text on a photograph.

If you want to start using PNG files that will be viewed with Netscape Navigator 4, you will need to use the <EMBED> tag to add the image. The person viewing the page will need to have a PNG plug-in, such as the PNG Live plug-in available for Windows 95/NT and Power Macintosh from Siegel and Gale at http://codelab.siegelgale.com/solutions.

Acquiring Image Files

Images can give your Web pages a polished, professional look, thereby making a strong statement about you and your company. The biggest hurdle in creating a Web page, however, is acquiring and editing images to add to your page. If you are creating a Web site for your business, you may want to hire a desktop publisher to scan or create pictures. Even if you have the graphic tools, there's a long learning curve for becoming a graphic artist.

In order to add an inline image, you'll need to create a GIF image (which requires a bitmap editing program such as Adobe Photoshop or Paint Shop Pro), have access to an existing GIF image, or use a scanner to acquire an image.

TIP *If you want to present a Web page for your business, consider using digitized photos rather than illustrations. Readers tend to show more trust in photographic images than in illustrations.*

Images & Copyrights

Publishing on the Web carries with it the same restrictions traditional publishing does. You're still subject to copyright and trademark laws. Be careful of what you use in your document. Many files are available that break copyright restrictions; just because they're available at a site doesn't mean you have the legal right to publish them in your document.

If you would like more information on copyrights, Thomson & Thomson, a trademark and copyright research firm that provides some helpful resources on copyrights, is located at http://www.thomson.com/thomthom/resmain.html. A copyright FAQ is also available at http://www.cis.ohio-state.edu/hypertext/faq/usenet/Copyright-FAQ/top.html. You can also check the U.S. Copyright Office, a department of the Library of Congress, at gopher://marvel.loc.gov/11/copyright.

Professional Clip Art & Photo Images

Commercial clip art and photo images are everywhere. Clip art and photos seem to be the most popular add-on for most graphics and multimedia programs. Many packages include samples from different clip-art and photo vendors. CorelDRAW! 8, for example, includes 22,000 clip-art images and symbols and 100 high-resolution photos. If that isn't enough, and believe it or not, it isn't, Corel also sells additional clip art and a photo library of another 200,000 photo images. Be aware, however, that the quality of clip art and photos can vary dramatically. Just because it's a commercial product doesn't mean that it belongs in the professional-quality category. The following are some of the best companies we've found that sell professional-quality clip art and photo images.

Image Club is one company that has always stood out as a leader in the professional-quality clip-art category. Image Club also offers affordable professional photo images. Adobe acquired Image Club in 1995. You can check out Image Club's home page at http://www.adobe.com/imageclub.

PhotoDisk images are without a doubt the best in the business. You can order a starter kit for under $40 that includes hundreds of low-resolution samples. PhotoDisk also distributes CMCD's images. CMCD is an offshoot of Clemont Mok's design firm. A trend in photo images is to use single everyday objects as metaphors. You can check out CMCD's latest releases of everyday objects at http://www.cmdesigns.com.

MetaPhotos, previously named KPT Power Photos, are available from MetaCreations. The images come in a series of over 30 volumes. Each series sells for under $50. These high-resolution images are drum-scanned with built-in channels, so you can easily specify transparent backgrounds to the image.

Keep in mind that there is not one standard format for clip-art and photo files. Image Club's graphics are in EPS and TIF format. PhotoDisk ships images in JPEG and TIF format and CMCD ships photos in Kodak's PhotoCD format. The Companion CD-ROM contains image samples from Image Club, PhotoDisk, and CMCD.

TIP *Don't mix different types of graphic images. Black-and-white illustrations, color photos, and clip art all have definite looks and moods. Choose images carefully so that the images complement your document's message. Using black-and-white illustrations and color photos on the same page may leave readers with a mixed message, which is likely to leave them cold.*

Scanning Images & Digital Cameras

A common Web publishing scenario is to take an existing photo or image and add it to your page. Your business, for example, may have a logo that you want to use at the top of your home page. If you're creating a personal home page, you may want to include a mug shot of yourself. One way to acquire the image is to scan an existing photo or picture. Keep in mind that scanning images that you didn't create, such as a photo from a magazine or other publication, is infringing on someone's copyright. It's much safer to take your own photos, create your own images, or purchase royalty-free images. Scanners have come down in price dramatically. If you plan on using a scanner to add color photos or images, make sure the scanner can save color files at 300 dpi and a color depth of 24 bits. If you scan in an image to create an inline image, it is best to edit the image at a high resolution even though inline images are not published at a high resolution. Scanned images frequently need a little editing. Most scanners come bundled with image editing and Optical Character Recognition (OCR) software, which is a great bargain. If you only need to scan a few images, most copy centers and service bureaus will scan your logo and pictures for a small fee. If you plan to have your own Web site, you might want to consider purchasing a color flatbed scanner. You can easily find an excellent scanner for Web publishing for under $300.

Free Images at Web Sites

There are thousands of GIF files on the Internet. Several sites on the Web include free images you can use to create your Web documents. You can get collections of decorative elements, such as bullets, icons, and line drawings, that enhance the appearance of your Web document. You simply download the files to your system. Because GIF images are internally compressed, you don't need a decompression program. The viewer or paint program you display the image with will automatically decompress the GIF file. If you want to get collections of clip art, they may be stored in PKZip format. To help you expand compressed files, check out the version of Drag And Zip included on the Companion CD-ROM. Drag And Zip works with browsers to decompress PKZip files on the fly. Table 6-3 lists some sites that include graphic images, including bullets, icons, and lines.

URL	Contents
http://www.yahoo.com/yahoo/computers/multimedia/pictures	A great inventory of picture files.
http://www.yahoo.com/Computers/World_Wide_Web/Programming/ Icons/	A huge listing of icons and clip-art links.
http://www.idb.hist.no/~geirme/gizmos/gizmo.html	GIF images, icons, buttons, bullets, and lines plus links to other resource archives.
http://inls.ucsd.edu/y/OhBoy/icons.html	GIF images, icons, bullets, and lines.
http://ns2.rutgers.edu/doc-images/small_buttons/	Standard GIF icons.
http://white.nosc.mil/images.html	Space, travel, medical, and other images plus links to other resource sites.
http://www-ns.rutgers.edu/doc-images/icons/	Standard GIF bullets.
http://www.cit.gu.edu.au/~anthony/icons/	Standard GIF icons.
http://www.cs.yale.edu/HTML/YALE/CS/HyPlans/loosemore-sandra/clipart.html	Pointers to archives filled with clip art.
http://www.cli.di.unipi.it/iconbrowser/icons.html	A large collection of icons.

Table 6-3: URLs for image collections.

Including Inline Images

An inline image is an image that is displayed in the Web page. As we mentioned in Chapter 3, the IMG tag <IMG> is used to insert graphic image files:

```
<IMG SRC="graphicsfile.gif">
```

There is no limit to the number of inline images you can use in a document.

If you want to use a PNG file, remember that you need to use the <EMBED> tag, as shown in the following example:

```
<EMBED SRC="imagefile.png"WIDTH="125" HEIGHT="125">
```

Providing Alternative Text for an Image

Not everyone can view or chooses to view inline images. It's possible that some people who have slow modem connections turn off inline images to get information faster. To address people accessing your page using a text-based browser such as Lynx, be sure to include alternative text to clue them in to what they can't see. To add alternative text, set the ALT attribute for the <IMG> tag to the text you want to appear if the image isn't displayed. This text appears while the image is loading, and once the image is loaded, the alternative text displays when the reader moves the mouse pointer on the image, as shown in Figure 6-6.

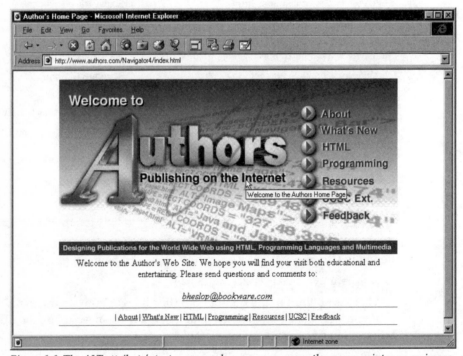

Figure 6-6: The ALT attribute's text appears when a person moves the mouse pointer on an image.

Specifying the Width & Height of an Image

The WIDTH and HEIGHT attributes for the <IMG> tag help speed up display of the document. When the browser encounters a new Web page, it has to create an area called a *bounding box* for loading each image. Including the

WIDTH and HEIGHT attributes saves the browser the time needed to calculate the size of the image. If a Web browser doesn't support the WIDTH and HEIGHT attributes, it ignores them. If you specify the wrong size for an image, it will be scaled to fit in the dimensions you specified.

TIP *Don't use the WIDTH and HEIGHT attributes to scale your image. This will slow down the display of your page. If you want the image to appear in a different size, use an image editor to resize the image. Resizing images is covered the next chapter.*

You can find the width and height of your images using Netscape Navigator or a graphic editor. Using Netscape Navigator 4, you can choose File | Load and select All Files from the File Types list to display the image. If the image is showing in a page, you can right-click on the image and choose View | Image. The height and width appear in the title bar, as shown in Figure 6-7. Paint Shop Pro lists the width and height of the image along with the number of colors in the first panel of the status bar. Add the Width and Height settings to specify the width and height in pixels of the image. The HTML tag will be similar to the following:

```
<IMG SRC=imagefile.gif WIDTH="125" HEIGHT="125">
```

Figure 6-7: In Netscape Navigator, the height and width of an image are displayed in the title bar.

Fading in High-Resolution Images From Low-Resolution Images

LOWSRC is a Netscape attribute extension to the <IMG> tag. By adding the LOWSRC attribute to the <IMG SRC> tag, you can specify a low-resolution version of an image to load first and then load a higher-resolution version of the same image. The LOWSRC attribute instructs Netscape to load the specified image on its first pass through the document. When all of the images are displayed in full, Netscape performs another pass and loads the image specified by the <IMG SRC> tag. The high-resolution image you specify as the IMG SRC fades in, replacing the low-resolution graphic. Browsers that don't recognize the LOWSRC attribute load the image specified by IMG SRC. You can include both GIF and JPEG images using this method. The following shows an example of an <IMG> tag that includes the LOWSRC attribute. Figure 6-8 shows a browser displaying the low-resolution image specified by the LOWSRC attribute. Figure 6-9 shows the browser displaying an HTML document that includes the high-resolution image specified by the SRC attribute.

```
<IMG SRC="high-res.jpg" LOWSRC="low-res.gif">
```

Figure 6-8: A browser displaying the low-resolution image with the LOWSRC attribute.

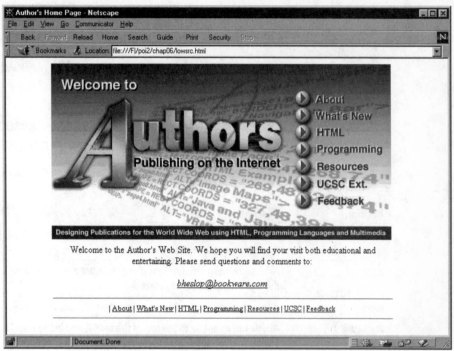

Figure 6-9: A browser displaying the high-resolution image after loading the image specified by the LOWSRC attribute.

Positioning Inline Images

Several Netscape extensions have been added to help you align text and images. The "left" and "right" settings are two powerful attribute additions that let you align images that can float in margins. The rest of the align options correct what Marc Andreessen thought were "horrible errors" he made when first implementing the <IMG> tag.

The raw HTML syntax for the alignment attribute is <IMG ALIGN="*postion*">. Table 6-4 explains the different alignment options and Figure 6-10 shows a document displaying images with different alignment attribute settings.

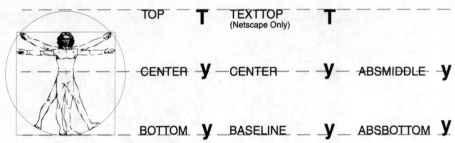

Figure 6-10: A document displaying images with different alignment attribute settings.

Position	Description
left	Aligns the image in the left margin. Subsequent text will wrap around the right-hand side of that image.
right	Aligns the image in the right margin. Subsequent text wraps around the right-hand side of that image.
top	Aligns the image with the top of the tallest item on the line.
texttop	Aligns the image with the top of the tallest text in the line. The texttop attribute is usually the same as the top attribute.
middle	Aligns the image so the baseline of the current line appears aligned with the middle of the image.
absmiddle	Aligns the middle of the current line with the middle of the image.
baseline	Aligns the bottom of the image with the baseline of the current line.
bottom	Aligns the bottom of the image with the baseline of the current line. This is the same as baseline.
absbottom	Aligns the bottom of the image with the bottom of the current line.

Table 6-4: Position attributes for images.

Adding Space Around an Image

Two attributes let you add space around an image: <IMG VSPACE="*n*" and HSPACE="*n*">. The VSPACE attribute sets the vertical space above and below the image. The HSPACE attribute sets the horizontal space to the left and right of the image. Without these commands, images press up against the text wrapped around the image.

As we mentioned in Chapter 3, Netscape added a CLEAR attribute to the <BR> tag to help you better place images. The CLEAR attribute has three settings: left, right, and all. CLEAR="left" breaks the line, and moves vertically down until you have a clear left margin. CLEAR="right" breaks the line and moves vertically down until you have a clear right margin. CLEAR="all" moves down until both margins are clear of images.

The Transparent Pixel

A popular method of spacing images is using a transparent GIF. The best way to create a spacer is to create a transparent GIF that is a pixel high and wide. You can download a transparent pixel image from the FTP site ftp://ftp.authors.com/clear_dot.gif. Once you have the transparent pixel image, you can use the height and width to adjust for the size of the space you want to add. For example, the following lets you indent a line of text 30 pixels:

```
<IMG SRC="image_dot_clear.gif" HEIGHT="1" WIDTH="30">
```

Adding a Border to an Image

A border can help accent an image, drawing the reader's eye to a graphic. The BORDER attribute lets you control the thickness of the border framing an image. In most cases, you don't really want to set a border for images that are also part of anchors. This can confuse people because they are used to having a colored border indicate that an image is an anchor.

To display a border around an image, add the BORDER attribute to the <IMG> tag and set the BORDER attribute to the number of pixels you want to define as a border to your image. The syntax for adding a border is <IMG BORDER="*n*">, where *n* is the width in pixels of the border. Another way to add a border to an image is to display the image in a table cell and set the BORDER attribute of the <TABLE> tag to create a border with dimensions. Figure 6-11 shows an image with a three-pixel border and an image in a table cell with the BORDER attribute set to 10 pixels.

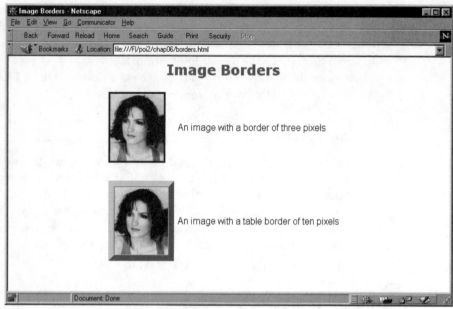

Figure 6-11: An image with a 3-pixel border and an image in a table with a 10-pixel border.

Saving Bandwidth by Using Thumbnails

As we mentioned in the Chapter 4, any inline image can be used as a hyperlink to another file. When you insert an image tag in the hypertext part of the anchor, a border is automatically displayed around the outside of the image. The following example displays an image named orderdsk.gif as a hyperlink:

```
<A HREF="order.html"><IMG SRC="orderdsk.gif"></A>
```

Clicking on the image lets the user jump to an HTML document named order.html. Figure 6-12 shows a thumbnail image that displays a larger version of the image.

Say you have a large 24-bit graphic you want to show off. Don't include the large JPEG as an inline image. Instead, present a thumbnail that links to the image in a larger size. Clicking on the inline image hyperlink automatically opens the larger JPEG image file. Figure 6-13 shows the results of clicking on the thumbnail to display the larger file to which it points. To create a thumbnail image that is linked to a larger image, use the Anchor tag. The following is a raw HTML example of a GIF thumbnail file named thumbnail.jpg linked to display a file named large.jpg:

```
<A>HREF="large.jpg"><IMG SRC="thumbnail.jpg"></A>
```

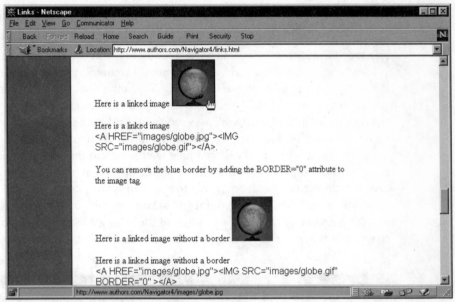

Figure 6-12: A thumbnail of an image in a Web page.

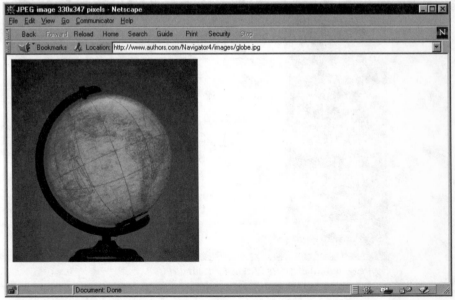

Figure 6-13: The larger linked image of the globe.

Using an Image as a Horizontal Rule or an Accent

Horizontal rules are effective for visually breaking up your Web page. To enhance the separators in your Web documents, you can use colored lines or colored bars as horizontal rules. They are not created by using the <HR> tag but instead are graphic inline images. Using inline images as horizontal rules is a great way to add color and pizzazz to your document. It is easy to go overboard with rules. In most cases, you will find that a simple colored horizontal rule will make your page more appealing than gaudy rules. Choosing a simple colored horizontal rule is a nice way to accent the image colors in your document. If you want to take a more subtle approach, use a simple decorative accent rather than a horizontal rule to break up your pages. Figure 6-14 shows an inline image used as horizontal rules. You can pick up graphic files of horizontal rules by checking out some of the sites we listed earlier in this chapter, or you can make your own as explained the next chapter.

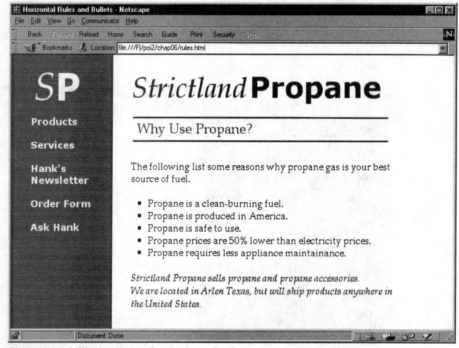

Figure 6-14: Inline images used as horizontal rules.

TIP *Avoid using animated horizontal rules that distract the reader from the text on the page. A rule is supposed to help divide up the page, not be the main attraction.*

Using an Image as Bullets in a List

Besides using graphics for horizontal rules, you can also use them as bullets to create unnumbered lists. Many of the sites containing images that were listed earlier in this chapter used icons and images to replace bullets in lists. Figure 6-15 shows an example of using an image instead of a standard bullet to present a bulleted list. The following lines show how to create a list of hyperlinks using the <DL> and <DD> tags and how to use an image as a bullet instead of using the standard unordered list (<UL> and <LI>) tag's bullets:

```
<DL>
<DD><IMG ALT="*" src="images/red_ball.gif" ALIGN="TOP">Propane is a clean-
burning fuel.
<DD><IMG ALT="*" src="images/red_ball.gif" ALIGN="TOP">Propane is produced
in America.
<DD><IMG ALT="*" src="images/red_ball.gif" ALIGN="TOP">Propane is safe to
use.
<DD><IMG ALT="*" src="images/red_ball.gif" ALIGN="TOP">Propane prices are
50% lower than electricity prices.
<DD><IMG ALT="*" src="images/red_ball.gif" ALIGN="TOP">Propane requires less
appliance maintenance.
</DL>
```

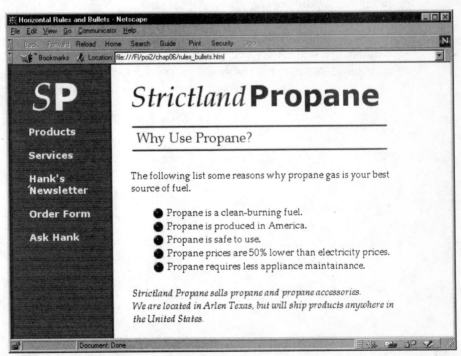

Figure 6-15: Customized bullets in a list.

Changing the Background & Foreground Colors

The <BODY> tag lets you add attributes to control the display of the background and foreground colors of the browser window. You can specify the color of the background or you can tile an image in the background, which is similar to using an image in the Windows Wallpaper feature that you can set using the Desktop icon found in the Control panel. Not all browsers can display background and foreground colors, so people using an older browser may not see the background color or the background tiled image and the foreground colors you specify. The following sections explain how to change the background and foreground colors in your Web pages.

Choosing Web-Safe Colors

In order to specify a color, you need to choose a color and convert the RGB (red, green, blue) decimal settings to hexadecimal RGB triplet. As we mentioned earlier, if you use more than 256 colors, images will not display correctly. If you are concerned that your page contains images that use too many colors, stick with the standard Windows palette colors. This lessens the possibility that you will use a color that will affect the display of your inline graphics. You can see a table of the browser-safe colors, shown in Figure 6-16, at http://www.authors.com/browser_safe.html.

It is possible to use color names for certain colors. Be aware that it is safer to use the hexadecimal RGB triplets rather than color names. Table 6-5 lists the hexadecimal settings for over a hundred color names. *Color names do not include spaces.* Note that the table separates each red, green, blue setting with a comma, but *you do not include commas* when specifying a color.

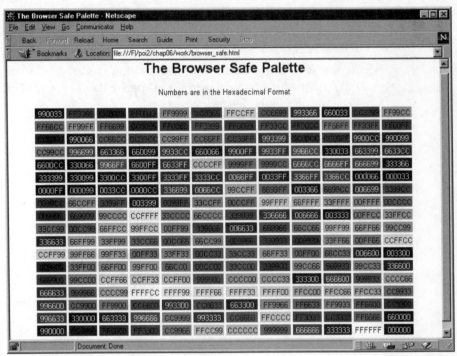

Figure 6-16: A table of the browser-safe colors.

Most graphic editors display colors as RGB decimal values. Converting a decimal RGB color setting to hexadecimal is simple. Using Windows, click on the Start menu and choose Programs | Accessories | Calculator. To use the calculator to convert decimal RGB settings to hexadecimal:

1. Click the Start button in the taskbar and choose Calculator from the Accessories menu. The Calculator window appears.

2. Choose View | Scientific.

3. Enter the decimal setting for the red, green, or blue color you want to display as hexadecimal. For example, the color hot pink has the RGB settings Red=255, Green=204, Blue=153, so first you would enter 255.

4. Click the Hex radio button and the hexadecimal equivalent appears. If you entered 255, for example, the hexadecimal number FF appears. Write the number down and click the Decimal radio button.

5. Repeat steps 3 and 4 for the additional blue and green settings. You can then use the hexadecimal settings to specify the foreground or background color in the following sections.

Color Name	Hexadecimal RGB settings
Aqua	00,FF,FF
Aquamarine	7F,FF,D4
Medium Aquamarine	66,CD,AA
Azure	F0,FF,FF
Beige	F5,F5,DC
Bisque	FF,E4,C4
Black	**00,00,00**
Blanched Almond	FF,EB,CD
Blue	**00,00,FF**
Dark Blue	00,00,8B
Light Blue	AD,D8,E6
Medium Blue	00,00,CD
Alice Blue	F0,F8,FF
Cadet Blue	5F,9E,A0
Cornflower Blue	64,95,ED
Dodger Blue	1E,90,FF
Midnight Blue	19,19,70
Navy	00,00,80
Powder Blue	B0,E0,E6
Royal Blue	41,69,E1
Slate Blue	6A,5A,CD
Dark Slate Blue	48,3D,8B
Medium Slate Blue	7B,68,EE
Sky Blue	87,CE,EB
Deep Sky Blue	00,BF,FF

Light Sky Blue	87,CE,FA
Steel Blue	46,82,B4
Light Steel Blue	B0,C4,DE
Blue Violet	8A,2B,E2
Brown	A5,2A,2A
Rosy Brown	BC,8F,8F
Saddle Brown	8B,45,13
Sandy Brown	F4,A4,60
Burly Wood	DE,B8,87
Chartreuse	7F,FF,00
Chocolate	D2,69,1E
Coral	FF,7F,50
Light Coral	F0,80,80
Cornsilk	FF,F8,DC
Crimson	DC,14,3C
Cyan	**00,FF,FF**
Light Cyan	E0,FF,FF
Dark Cyan	00,8B,8B
Firebrick	B2,22,22
Fuchsia	**FF,00,FF**
Gainsboro	DC,DC,DC
Gold	FF,D7,00
Goldenrod	DA,A5,20
Dark Goldenrod	B8,86,0B
Light Goldenrod Yellow	FA,FA,D2
Pale Goldenrod	EE,E8,AA

Gray	80,80,80
Dark Gray	A9,A9,A9
Dim Gray	69,69,69
Light Gray	D3,D3,D3
Silver	C0,C0,C0
Slate Gray	70,80,90
Dark Slate Gray	2F,4F,4F
Light Slate Gray	77,88,99
Green	00,80,00
Dark Green	00,64,00
Light Green	90,EE,90
Pale Green	98,FB,98
Forest Green	22,8B,22
Lawn Green	7C,FC,00
Lime	**00,FF,00**
Lime Green	32,CD,32
Dark Olive Green	55,6B,2F
Seagreen	2E,8B,57
Dark Seagreen	8F,BC,8B
Light Seagreen	20,B2,AA
Medium Seagreen	3C,B3,71
Medium Spring Green	00,FA,9A
Spring Green	00,FF,7F
Green Yellow	AD,FF,2F
Honeydew	F0,FF,F0
Indigo	4B,00,82
Ivory	FF,FF,F0
Khaki	F0,E6,8C
Dark Kahki	BD,B7,6B

Lavender	E6,E6,FA
Lavender Blush	FF,F0,F5
Lemon Chiffon	FF,FA,CD
Linen	FA,F0,E6
Magenta	**FF,00,FF**
Dark Magenta	8B,00,8B
Maroon	80,00,00
Mint Cream	F5,FF,FA
Misty Rose	FF,E4,E1
Moccasin	FF,E4,B5
Old Lace	FD,F5,E6
Olive	80,80,00
Olive Drab	6B,8E,23
Orange	FF,A5,00
Dark Orange	FF,8C,00
Orange Red	FF,45,00
Orchid	DA,70,D6
Dark Orchid	99,32,CC
Medium Orchid	BA,55,D3
Papaya Whip	FF,EF,D5
Peachpuff	FF,DA,B9
Peru	CD,85,3F
Pink	FF,C0,CB
Deep Pink	FF,14,93
Light Pink	FF,B6,C1
Hot Pink	FF,69,B4

Plum	DD,A0,DD
Purple	80,00,80
Medium Purple	93,70,DB
Red	**FF,00,00**
Dark Red	8B,00,00
Indian Red	CD,5C,5C
Salmon	FA,80,72
Light Salmon	FF,A0,7A
Dark Salmon	E9,96,7A
Seashell	FF,F5,EE
Sienna	A0,52,2D
Snow	FF,FA,FA
Tan	D2,B4,8C
Teal	00,80,80
Thistle	D8,BF,D8
Tomato	FF,63,47
Turquoise	40,E0,D0
Dark Turquoise	00,CE,D1
Medium Turquoise	48,D1,CC
Pale Turquoise	AF,EE,EE
Violet	EE,82,EE
Dark Violet	94,00,D3
Medium Violet Red	C7,15,85
Pale Violet Red	DB,70,93
Wheat	F5,DE,B3

White	FF,FF,FF
Antique White	FA,EB,D7
Floral White	FF,FA,F0
Ghost White	F8,F8,FF
Navajo White	FF,DE,AD
White Smoke	F5,F5,F5
Yellow	**FF,FF,00**
Light Yellow	FF,FF,E0
Yellow Green	9A,CD,32
Bold indicates a browser-safe color.	

Table 6-5: Hexadecimal codes and color names for a selective sampling of over a hundred colors.

Specifying the Background Color

To specify a background color, add the BGCOLOR attribute to the BODY and enter the red, green, and blue color settings (rrggbb) in hexadecimal format. The syntax for specifying the background color is:

```
<BODY BGCOLOR="#rrggbb">Body text</BODY>
```

The following example displays a light blue background:

```
<BODY BGCOLOR="# ">Body text</BODY>
```

The Color Browser, explained in the next section, lets you easily select a color from a color matrix and display the hexadecimal value for the selected color. Table 6-5 in the previous section lists hexadecimal settings for a hundred colors.

Using the Color Browser to Specify a Background Color

Several utilities let you choose from the 16.7 million colors available and calculate the hexadecimal values for the RGB colors. One of the best programs for choosing colors is the ColorCenter from hIdaho Design at http://www.hidaho.com/colorcenter/cc.html. This online color picker is written in JavaScript, so it will run using a JavaScript-enabled browser such as Internet Explorer 4 or Netscape Navigator 4. You can choose to adjust the color by using hexadecimal, decimal (RGB 0-255), or percentages or by clicking on a color in the matrix of colors shown at the bottom of the window. You can also manually fine-tune your RGB color selections by using increment and decrement buttons. The page automatically updates to show you a sample of the colors you're using for backgrounds, links, and text. You can also test to see how a background would appear. The ColorCenter is shown in Figure 6-17. The site also includes a drop-down list of links to sites containing textured backgrounds and icons.

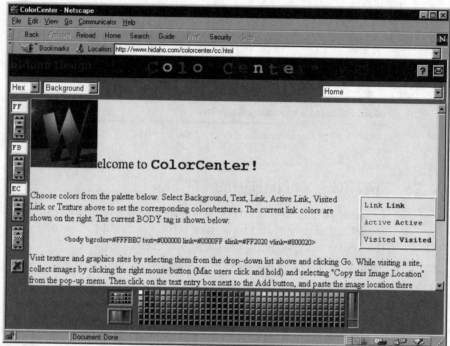

Figure 6-17: The ColorCenter lets you pick a color from a matrix of colors and save the color's hexadecimal value.

The page automatically displays the code for adding the background or link colors. To select the code and copy it, drag your mouse pointer over the hexadecimal color or the text you want to select and press Ctrl+C. The tag and values for the hexadecimal color settings are stored on the clipboard. Press Ctrl+V to paste the number from the clipboard directly into your HTML document.

Using an Image for the Background

The <BODY> tag's BACKGROUND attribute lets you specify a file to tile in order to create a background for your page. Although it is not recommended, it is possible to use the BACKGROUND attribute to specify a URL pointing to an image that is tiled to create a background. The syntax for using the BACKGROUND attribute is:

```
<BODY BACKGROUND="path/image.gif">Body text</BODY>
```

The URL can point to any location. In most cases, you will want to use a local file for your background. If you use a link to a file at another site and it changes, you will lose the background. It's possible that if you use a background image at another site, the person could change the image and even replace the image you're using with something you may not want to display. Because the image is tiled, you can create a small file and the image will repeat itself. For example, Figure 6-18 shows a tiled image that displays a page that looks similar to a notepad. Here is the code:

```
<BODY BACKGROUND="notepad.gif"></BODY>
```

TIP *One of the biggest problems with working with tiled background images is that the ragged or irregular edges of the image are often quite visible. The next chapter explains how you can create background images and smooth the edges for tiled backgrounds.*

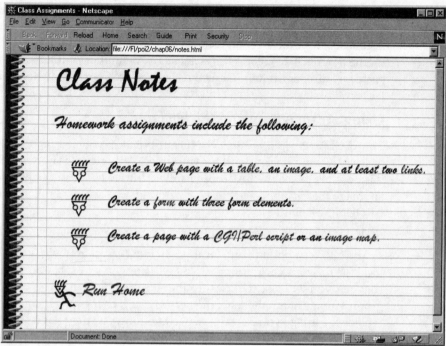

Figure 6-18: A background displayed by tiling an image.

Changing the Foreground: Text & Links

In addition to changing the background colors, you can also specify the color of text and links in a Web page. The TEXT attribute lets you specify the color of all the text other than links. The syntax for the TEXT attribute is:

```
<BODY TEXT="rrggbb">Body Text</BODY>
```

Like the background color, you specify the text color in hexadecimal. You must enter the red, green, blue color settings (rrggbb) in hexadecimal format. To enter a color, use the color-safe table or the colors listed in Table 6-5. Remember that you can also use the ColorCenter at http://www.hidaho.com/colorcenter/cc.html to find the color you want to use for your background, text, and links.

Three attributes let you specify the color of links: LINK, VLINK, and ALINK. LINK refers to the links as they first appear on the page. The default color for links is blue. The V in VLINK stands for *visited*. VLINK changes the color of links that the user has chosen. The default color for visited links is purple. The A in ALINK stands for *active*. ALINK changes the color when the hyperlink is chosen. The default for active links is red. The following is an example that includes a dark cyan color for the background, white for text, yellow for links, medium gray for visited links, and magenta for active links:

```
<BODY BGCOLOR="#000080" TEXT="#FFFFFF" LINK="#FFFF00" VLINK="#A0A0A0"
ALINK="#FF00FF">Body Text goes here</BODY>
```

Moving On

This chapter explained the Web graphic file formats and showed you how to use existing images to convey information about you and your company. In most cases, you will want to create your own graphics to make your site unique. The next chapter builds on the concepts introduced in this chapter and shows you how to use image editor and optimization tools to create and edit your own images, buttons, and backgrounds that download fast.

chapter 7

Editing & Optimizing Images

Image editing and optimization tools abound to help you create and present eye-catching images. Even though you are constrained in many ways when designing Web graphics, you can usually more than compensate for these limitations by careful application of a number of tried-and-tested image editing tools and techniques. This chapter introduces you to image editing tools and techniques that you can use to create memorable Web graphics that take advantage of features such as transparent backgrounds and interlacing and are optimized to download fast. This chapter also covers another important aspect of graphics on the Web: the ability to create interactive graphic images with image maps.

The Web Is a Bitmap World

There are two types of images: vector and bitmap. Bitmap graphics are composed of small dots, which are called pixels. Bitmap graphics contain information about each pixel displayed onscreen. As we mentioned in the section on bit-depth in the previous chapter, one or more bits represent each pixel that specifies the color and intensity in a bitmap image. A bitmap graphic is stored at a fixed resolution that is determined by the number and layout of the pixels. You can easily edit an image at that fixed resolution, but if you enlarge a bitmap graphic, you distort it and lose image quality.

Vector graphics are made up of a set of drawing instructions that describe the dimension and shape of every line, circle, arc, or rectangle. A vector image is resolution independent, meaning the resolution of your output device determines the quality of a vector image's appearance. You can enlarge, reduce, and edit vector graphics without affecting the resolution or image quality. Vector graphics are best for line art. They are stored as commands that create images. Sometimes vector graphics take longer to render (to convert from vector outlines to fully formed graphics) because your processor must draw them, whereas bitmap images are simply loaded directly into memory. Figure 7-1 shows an example of the difference between vector images and bitmap images.

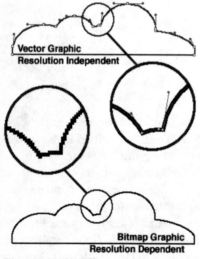

Figure 7-1: The difference between vector and bitmap images.

The Web is a bitmap world. You can start with many different graphic file formats, but to work on the Web, they must be converted into bitmap files in either GIF or JPEG, (possibly PNG) format with a resolution of 72 dpi. One common technique used to create very sharp crisp images is to use a drawing program like Adobe Illustrator or CorelDRAW to produce vector art and then import the vector art into a bitmap editor such as Adobe Photoshop. The import process will convert the vector art into a bitmap (this is called *rasterizing*). The resulting image will look very clean and crisp, especially if you choose to anti-alias as well. The graphic in Figure 7-2 was created using this technique.

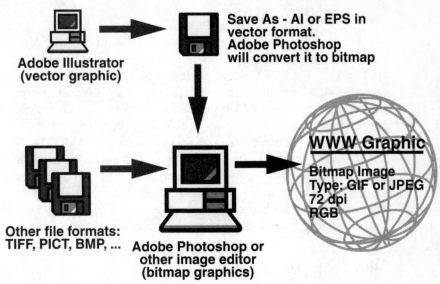

Figure 7-2: A common process is to import vector art into a bitmap editor and save it as a GIF image.

NOTE *When using a vector-based program, you should resize the image before converting the image into a bitmap. Resizing images is explained later in this chapter.*

Image Editors

Editing image files can be a tricky proposition. It's important to choose an image editor that matches the tasks you want to accomplish. Several shareware and commercial graphic editors let you convert images to GIF and JPEG formats and create and edit GIF and JPEG images. Be aware that while graphic editors let you convert, trim, apply filters, adjust the number of colors, and so on, mastering bitmap editing programs can be a time-consuming task. The following sections give you a quick overview of some of the best image editors for different types of users and image editing.

Adobe Photoshop

Anyone planning on working with graphics should consider purchasing Adobe Photoshop. This is the best image editor we've ever used, and it is the image editor of choice for most professional designers. The program is expensive, around $400, but it includes just about every feature you could want in an image editor. Version 4 lets you work with layers and add lighting effects. The layers feature alone makes Adobe Photoshop stand out among other image editors. You can make one layer invisible and work safely on a different layer. This is a great way to make rollovers and animated GIFs. Another advantage is the amount of third-party support for plug-in filters for adding special effects to an image. Some of the most impressive filter plug-ins are covered later in this chapter. Once you've spent some time getting familiar with Photoshop, it's hard to go back to another image editor.

Paint Shop Pro

One of the most popular shareware editors is Paint Shop Pro. Paint Shop Pro is a product of JASC. Version 4 is included on the Companion CD-ROM. Figure 7-3 shows the Paint Shop Pro image editor. You can visit JASC's Web site to check for newer editions of Paint Shop Pro at http://www.jasc.com/. If you are just getting started, try Paint Shop Pro. This package is so powerful that you may never need another image editor. Because it is available to all users as shareware, it was used for many examples in this chapter.

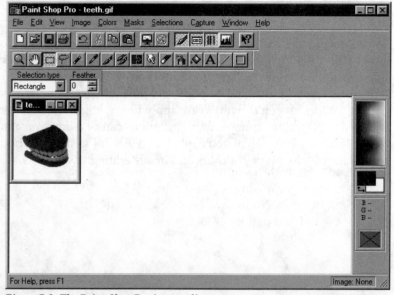

Figure 7-3: The Paint Shop Pro image editor.

PhotoImpact

In the commercial low-to-mid price range, we recommend PhotoImpact from Ulead. This package lets you convert almost any graphics format into a GIF or JPEG format. It comes with Web extensions (tools for creating and optimizing Web images) that are quite impressive. Many of these extensions are also available as Photoshop plug-ins. PhotoImpact also comes with an animation tool that is the best around. Ulead is constantly upgrading and offering new extensions free to owners of PhotoImpact. PhotoImpact is great for converting images from different formats. We were able to load and convert images that no other image editors could load. This image editor, along with its Web extensions, is a great value and we highly recommend it.

Fractal Design Painter

Numerous graphic applications and utilities exist that go beyond simple graphic editing. One impressive graphics application is Fractal Design Painter. Painter 5 lets you create images using tools that emulate traditional artist's tools, such as water colors, oil-based paints, charcoal, pastels, and so on. Painter includes several other features for creating and editing animations and videos. It also includes several Web-publishing-related features and is the only editor we know of that displays the hexadecimal settings for colors. And it includes built-in support for creating image maps (clickable images).

3D Tools

You'll find that 3D rendering applications, such as 3-D Studio, trueSpace and Ray Dream Studio, are quite a bit more complex than graphic editors are. These applications let you work with three-dimensional images to create eye-catching graphics that simulate and apply materials and textures; you can also change the lighting to create objects that reflect light and cast shadows. Most 3D rendering applications are also capable of creating and editing animations. Some 3D tools don't let you simply save files in GIF or JPEG formats. In most cases, you will need to export the file to a common 3D format and then open and save the file in an image editor. You should also be aware that most 3D images are very high-resolution and color-intensive images, so you will not be able to get near the quality if you export and save the file as a GIF image. The Authors home page, shown in Figure 7-4, was created using a 3D tool and Photoshop and saved in the JPEG format.

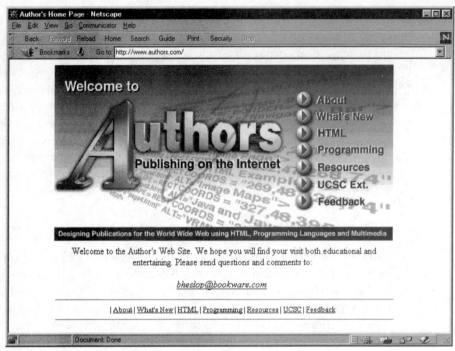

Figure 7-4: The Authors home page was created using a 3D tool.

The Electronic Canvas

As we pointed out in the last chapter, working in the print world is dramatically different than working in the screen-based world. To create effective Web graphics, you need to decide which image file format to use and then create as high a quality image as you can with as small a file size as possible for fast downloading. In the last chapter, we explained the different types of image file formats for the Web. Before you can effectively use a graphic editor and other graphic-related applications and tools, it's important to understand the basic components of an image and the factors that affect the image's output when it is published on different platforms. The following sections explain some of the essentials for creating and editing screen-based graphics.

Resolution

It's helpful to understand how resolution affects your image. First, it's important that you don't confuse the two types of resolution: image resolution and monitor resolution. *Image resolution* refers to the spacing of pixels in the image and is measured in pixels per inch (ppi). If the image has a resolution of 96 ppi, it contains 9,216 pixels per square inch (96 x 96 = 9,216). *Monitor resolution* is the number of dots per inch that your monitor uses to display an image. It determines how large and or how small images appear onscreen. Most monitors have a maximum resolution of 72 dpi for displaying graphics. Whenever you save an image that will be published on the Web, you will want to make sure you save it as 72 dpi.

RGB, CMYK & Index Modes

The color mode you work with on the Web is RGB and Indexed. RGB stands for red, green, and blue and relates to the colors your monitor creates by emitting different intensities of the red, green, and blue light. The numbers for selecting red, green, and blue colors range from 0 to 255. By using a value from 0 to 255 for each color, you can display up to 16.7 million colors. RGB colors are additive, so mixing colors creates white.

The print world works with CMYK color. CMY stands for cyan, magenta, and yellow, and the K stands for a percentage of black. CMYK is used to simulate inks used in print. Unlike RGB colors CMYK colors are subtractive, so mixing CMYK colors creates black.

Your image editor includes options for changing image modes. If the original image you are working with is in CMYK color mode and you try to save your file, you will notice that not all the file types are available. In order to make the file types appear, you will need to change image modes. In most cases, you want to work in RGB mode when you are making changes. For example, if you are working with line art or flat colors, you'll want to work in RGB mode, and when you are finished creating or editing the image, you'll want to choose the Indexed mode and save the file in the GIF file format.

TIP *Some RGB colors are not matched exactly with CMYK colors. Books that contain color charts of RGB colors show approximations of the screen-based colors. Pantone, a company known throughout the print industry for color matching, has published a color swatch guide named ColorWeb, which contains a swatch book of approximations of browser RGB colors and a system color picker for choosing browser-safe colors for the Macintosh.*

Gamma

A problem that has plagued Web designers for some time is that graphics appear darker when displayed on PCs than when displayed on Macintosh, Sun, and Silicon Graphics computer monitors. The reason for this is something called gamma. To understand what gamma is, you need to know a little bit about the physics of cathode ray tubes (CRTs). Don't panic, you don't have to be a scientist to understand, but knowing a little about the reasoning behind gamma correction, as it's called, will help you create graphics that look good on all platforms.

Before we begin the explanation, you should realize that when we describe how best to manipulate your images to take into account gamma differences, we are only talking about JPEG photographic images. GIF images are indexed, and you should use a browser-safe palette of colors. Unfortunately, selecting a so-called browser-safe color simply means it won't dither on different platforms. It does not mean your colors will look identical on each platform. For example, the same color tends to look darker on a PC compared to, say, a Mac.

Almost every computer display has one thing in common: the relationship between the brightness of display and how much voltage input is required. The formula looks something like the following:

```
brightness = voltage2.5
```

This is referred to as an exponential equation. What it means is that each time you input a voltage of X, the corresponding brightness on the CRT will be X raised to the power of 2.5. The range of voltage sent to a monitor can be from 0 percent to 100 percent. This means that the intensity or brightness will always be less than the input. Table 7-1 shows how different settings change the brightness. If you were to plot the results of the calculations in Table 7-1, you would produce a curve like the one shown in Figure 7-5.

Brightness Knob Position (input voltage)	Calculation	Brightness (output)
zero	0^2.5 = 0	zero (black display)
25%	0.25^2.5 = 0.31	3.1% (25% voltage but only 3.1% brightness)
50%	0.5^2.5 = 0.176	17.6% (only 17.7% voltage but 50% brightness)
75%	0.75^2.5 = 0.487	48.7% (75% voltage input, 48.7% brightness output. Brightness is catching up!)
100%	1^2.5 = 1	100% (100% voltage input and equal 100% brightness)

Table 7-1: How different gamma settings change brightness.

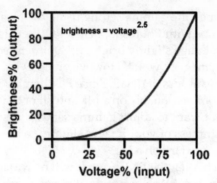

Figure 7-5: A gamma curve showing the results of the calculations in Table 7-1.

As you can see, as a user ups the brightness knob on his or her display, the brightness changes but not proportionally to the brightness knob position. Assuming you begin with a dark display, at first there is very little change to brightness as you twist the brightness knob; then suddenly a small twist of the dial produces a big change in brightness. This annoying problem of input voltage not being proportional to brightness produced is referred to as the *gamma effect*. Some computer manufacturers have attempted to correct this disproportionate response by adjusting the gamma with special electronic circuits. The aim is to produce a gamma curve as close to a straight line as possible. This means that the adjusted brightness is more linearly proportional to input voltage. When this is implemented, it's referred to as *gamma correction*. That's the good news. The bad news is that most PC computers and displays are not "gamma-corrected." Uncorrected computer displays are said to have a gamma of 2.5. Apple Mac computers are gamma-corrected. They have a gamma of 1.8. Notice the gamma value is lower than 2.5, meaning a brighter display compared with 2.5 the standard unadjusted gamma value. SGI computers have a gamma of 1.4.

So what does all this mean and how does it affect the brightness of your Web pages? A PC's gamma is greater than a Mac's or SGI's gamma, so images created on a Mac or SGI computer will look darker when displayed on a PC monitor. The safest way to make sure your images can be seen well on all platforms is to review your images on different monitors and computers and make adjustments. You can also change the gamma settings on your monitor to reflect an average gamma setting, say, 2.2. This means that if your images look fine on your monitor with a 2.2 gamma, they will probably look acceptable on a PC with a 2.5 gamma and an SGI computer with a 1.4 gamma.

On a Mac, you can easily change the gamma setting using the Gamma control panel from Knoll that ships with Photoshop. On a PC, there is no need to adjust gamma. Displaying an image slightly brighter than intended usually results in a slightly washed-out image at worst. However, displaying an image darker than expected usually means loss of detail. Since PCs display images the darkest, chances are it will look reasonable on a Macintosh or Silicon Graphics I computer. If you don't want to adjust gamma settings, just use your image editor to increase the brightness of your images slightly so they still look fine on a Mac but won't be too dark on a PC.

As we mentioned in the last chapter, the PNG format will be widely accepted and fully implemented by most Web browsers in the near future. One of the most exciting features of this new format is that it contains embedded within its file structure the gamma settings of the computer that created it. This means that browsers will have an opportunity to adjust the brightness of the image by comparing the gamma of the image with the gamma of the displaying computer and making the necessary adjustments automatically.

Dithering

After you've resized your image and reduced the color depth to 8 bits (256 colors), the next step is to select a dither type. *Dithering* is a process where the color value of a pixel is changed to the closest matching color value in the palette. Dithering reduces the number of colors needed to display an image by simulating colors. It places dots of color closer together, giving the appearance of more colors in an image than there really are. Another benefit of dithering is that it places similarly colored dots together so they appear to blend. This creates a smooth transition between two different colors. Figure 7-6 shows an example of how dithering is used to simulate a color. The magnifying glass shows a closeup of the different colors used to simulate a solid color.

Most image editing programs include dithering options. You can use various dithers to improve the range of perceived colors. For example, diffusion dithering is a popular option available in most image editors; it randomly positions pixels instead of using a set pattern. Choosing the Error Diffusion Dither option in Paint Shop Pro can have a dramatic effect on how images appear when published.

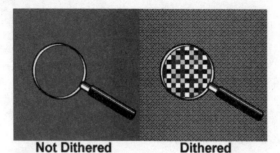

Not Dithered   **Dithered**

Figure 7-6: Dithering is used to simulate an unavailable color.

Anti-Aliasing

When you add text to images, the pixels can create text with jagged edges. These jagged edges are sometimes referred to as stairsteps or the jaggies. If you want to add text when using a graphic editor, make sure you choose the anti-aliasing option. The anti-aliasing option helps eliminate the jaggies by making the edges of text appear smooth, as if they blend into the background. This is also true for importing vector images into your image editor. To make the edges of the image appear smooth, choose the anti-aliasing option when importing the image. Figure 7-7 shows an example of aliased and anti-aliased text.

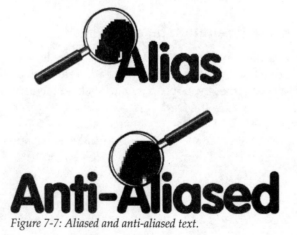

Figure 7-7: Aliased and anti-aliased text.

Editing Existing Image Files _____

Editing images can be frustrating for the beginner. To help ease the way, the following sections explain the fundamentals of working with Web graphics and making them compatible for different platforms and monitors and points out common image editing faux pas.

Start Big & Use a Lossless Format _____

One of the biggest mistakes beginners make when editing images is to work with a small lossy image in a low resolution. Don't think you can take a JPEG image and just start editing it. Always work in a lossless format, such as Photoshop's PSD format or the tagged image file format (TIFF). These formats store all your colors and don't lose colors when saved. Each time you edit and save a JPEG image, the compression scheme causes you to lose some parts of the picture. Just as photocopying a copy degrades the copy, each time you save an image in a lossy format, quality is lost.

TRAP *Photoshop does not show the effects of compression loss on the screen when you save a file in the JPEG format. The image in Photoshop doesn't change. In order to see the loss in quality, close the file and then load it again.*

How to Change the Resolution Setting _____

You can change the resolution setting of your monitor to see how pages will display on lower-resolution monitors. In Windows 95, right-click on the desktop and choose Properties from the pop-up menu. Click on the Settings tab (see Figure 7-8). You can change the Desktop Area slider to 640 X 480 to see how your page and images will appear at a lower resolution. You can also use the Color Palette drop-down menu to see how your images will appear on screens set to different color bit-depths.

Figure 7-8: By changing your display properties, you can see how your Web pages and images will appear on lower-resolution monitors.

If you're using a Mac, open the Apple menu, choose Control Panels, and select Monitors. You can click on the Options button to change to different monitor settings.

Using the Web-Safe Palette

Lynda Weinman, who discovered the Web-safe palette, has copies of it you can use with Photoshop, Paint Shop Pro, Painter, and other image editors. You can download the palette from her site at http://www.lynda.com/files/CLUTS/. To ensure that you are only using the browser-safe colors, replace the palette in Photoshop instead of loading it. To replace the existing palette with the Web-safe palette, follow these steps:

1. Download the Web-safe palette file named bclut2.aco from http://www.lynda.com/files/CLUTS/PHTOSHOP/. Save the file in the palette folder, which is a subdirectory of your Photoshop directory.

2. Start Photoshop. If the Swatches window isn't displayed, choose Windows | Show Swatches. The Swatches window appears.

3. Right-click on the right arrow in the upper right portion of the Swatches window. The Swatches menu appears.

4. Choose Replace Swatches. When the dialog box appears, navigate to the directory where you stored the bclut2.aco file.

5. Select the bclut2.aco file and click on the Open button. The swatch is replaced with the browser-safe palette.

If you're using Paint Shop Pro, you can download the Web palette at the JASC Web site at http://www.jasc.com or from Lynda Weinman's site. The palette file is stored as a ZIP file. When you unzip the file, choose to store the palette in the same directory as Paint Shop Pro. To load the palette, start Paint Shop Pro and choose Colors | Load Palette. A dialog box appears and asks you which palette to load. Choose the Netscape palette; you can see the available colors by clicking on either the foreground color swatch or the background color swatch. The Edit Palette dialog box appears, as shown in Figure 7-9.

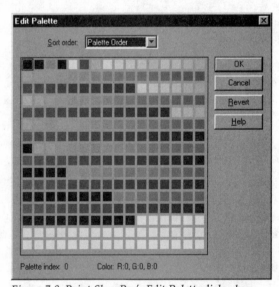

Figure 7-9: Paint Shop Pro's Edit Palette dialog box.

If you have an existing image open and you load the browser-safe palette, the image will dither all the colors to the ones available in the browser-safe palette. You can then replace the non-browser-safe colors with colors from the browser-safe palette.

Creating Your Own Palette & Using an Adaptive Palette

The browser-safe palette is not going to cut it for all your images. It is quite limiting. If you're just choosing flat colors for illustrations, it's the safest way to go. But in some cases, you will want to use a different palette or create your own palette. You should still use as few colors as possible. When multiple images share a single palette, the palette is sometimes called a *super palette*. One way to create a super palette (to make sure that more than one image shares the same colors) is to open the image, change the canvas size, paste in the other image, and crop both images. Some optimization programs, such as Equilibrium's Debabelizer, can automatically create super palettes for you. By using a super palette, you ensure that multiple images use the same palette.

Say, for example, you want to include an image with numerous gradations in color. Saving the file with the browser-safe palette may cause extensive dithering. Selecting colors from the more commonly used colors that appear in the image creates an adaptive palette. If you have an RGB image that has predominately brown colors, the resulting palette is made up primarily of shades of brown.

An adaptive palette gives precedence to the colors that are most prominent in the image. To control the colors that the adaptive palette will use, first select a part of the image that contains the colors you want to use in the adaptive palette. Photoshop gives precedence to the colors in the selection when building the palette. Figure 7-10 shows the Mona Lisa saved using both the browser-safe palette and the adaptive palette.

Adaptive Palette **Browser-safe Palette**

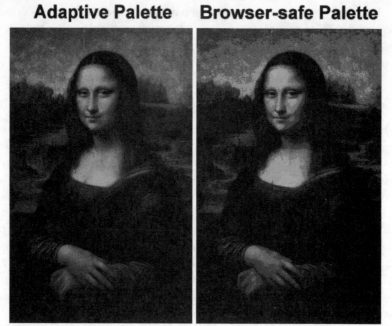

Figure 7-10: An image saved with the browser-safe palette and an adaptive palette.

Cropping & Resizing an Image

To give your page a uniform and consistent feel, it's important to keep images such as icons and buttons the same size. You may want to crop your graphic images to include only the image you want to show.

Images can be distorted when you resize them or change the resolution. As we mentioned earlier, most clip art comes in high-resolution format. It is best to edit, resize, and crop an image in its original high-resolution format before you convert the image to GIF format. You should also make sure the pixels per inch don't change when saving a high-resolution image to a different format, otherwise the image will be saved with different dimensions. If you have a small bitmap image that you want to resize to make larger, you're likely to be disappointed in the results. Enlarging images in GIF or JPEG format usually ends up giving your image the jaggies.

As we mentioned earlier in the chapter, you want to work with as large an image as possible. The loss of quality when resizing an image to make it smaller is not as dramatic as it is when you make an image larger. To resize an image in Photoshop, change the canvas size.

The canvas size is the amount of space the image takes. In some cases, you may want to add to an image, for example, to add a border or to make room for another image that you want to use to change the palette (as mentioned in the preceding section). To change the canvas size using Photoshop, choose Image | Canvas Size from the menu bar.

TIP *Because resizing bitmaps causes so much degradation of image quality, most professional designers like to work with vector files, such as Encapsulated PostScript, and convert the files to bitmap for publishing on the Web. Although vector files are usually limited to line art, they don't degrade when resized.*

Displaying Type as an Image

While dynamic HTML promises to bring nonresident fonts to Web documents, the font support is still in a developmental phase. If you want to present text in a decorative font that will display on all browsers, you need to display the type as images. Some graphics editors, such as Adobe Photoshop and Paint Shop Pro, include the capability to add text and save the files as GIF or JPEG graphic images.

Many drawing and paint graphics programs let you add special effects to text. For example, Adobe Photoshop lets you create layered, shadowed, recessed, embossed, glowing, and translucent text. Several high-end 2D and 3D products, such as trueSpace 2 and Ray Dream Studio, exist to let you render text in different textures. Figure 7-11 shows a sample of text in the GIF format created with Adobe Photoshop.

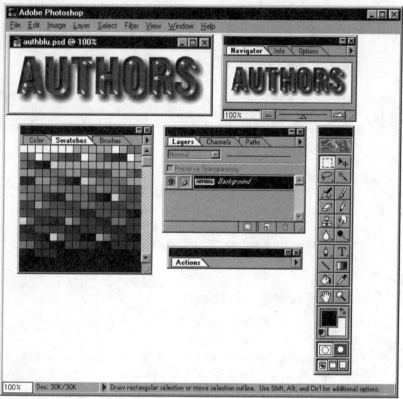

Figure 7-11: Text created with Adobe Photoshop.

Creating Interlaced GIF Images With a Transparent Background

There are several methods you can use to create an image with a transparent background, which will appear to float on the page. Figure 7-12 shows such an image.

Figure 7-12: An image with a transparent background.

As we mentioned in the previous chapter, interlaced images let readers start viewing your page without having to wait for the entire image to be displayed. When you save your image, the image editor lets you save GIF graphic files in the interlaced format. In this section, we'll explain how to create a transparent background and save files in a GIF89a interlaced format.

One of the first image editors that let users define a transparent background color and save the file as an interlaced image was Paint Shop Pro (which is included on this book's Companion CD-ROM). To use Paint Shop Pro to determine the background color, create a transparent background, and save files in a GIF89a interlaced format, follow these steps:

1. Start Paint Shop Pro and display the image for which you want to create a transparent background and save as an interlaced GIF image.

2. Click the color picker (the dropper in the toolbar). The cursor changes to a dropper icon. Move the dropper on the background color. The index color appears next to the letter *I* directly under the RGB (red, green, blue) values, as shown in Figure 7-13. Make a note of the number of the index color.

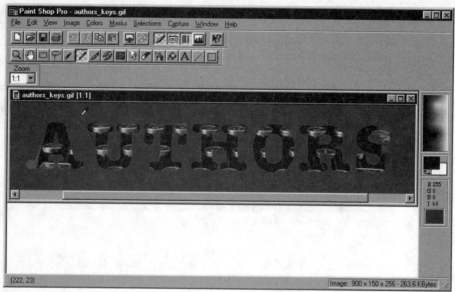

Figure 7-13: Paint Shop Pro displays the selected RGB (red, green, and blue) color values, the index color value, and the selected color.

TIP

If the background of an image is not a solid color and you want to specify a transparent background, you will need to double-click on the Magic Wand to specify the tolerance setting to select the background colors, so you can change it to a solid color. The tolerance setting determines how closely the color of the pixels it selects must be to the color of the selected pixel. Once the background is selected, you can use the flood fill tool (the paint bucket) to fill the background with a solid color. To prevent halos from appearing around anti-aliased images, choose a solid color that is close to the background color of your page.

3. To set the transparent color for the background, choose to save the image as a GIF-CompuServe image.

4. Choose Version 89a-Interlaced from the Sub type drop-down list, as shown in Figure 7-14.

Figure 7-14: Version 89a-Interlaced appears in the Sub type drop-down list.

5. Click on the Options button. The File Preferences dialog box appears, which displays the GIF transparency options, as shown in Figure 7-15.

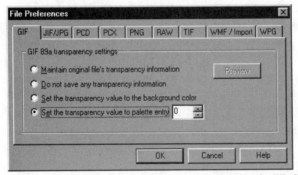

Figure 7-15: The GIF transparency options appear in the File Preferences dialog box.

TIP *If you edit the image later, make sure you choose the Maintain Original File's Transparency Information option so the current transparency information is retained.*

6. Click in the Set the Transparency Value to Palette Entry radio button.

7. Enter the index number in the text box you found in step 2 or use up or down arrows next to the text box to set the transparency color to the palette index number.

TIP   *A common mistake is to believe that one color will have the same index number in other images. It is true that several images may have the same setting for black and white, but the indexed colors in different palettes may vary. Just because one palette lists white as index 0 doesn't mean that index 0 will be white in another image. It is possible that another palette will specify a different index number for white.*

GIF & JPEG Compression

The simple fact of life when producing Web graphics is that you are seeking the best compromise between image quality and file size (compression). High quality usually means low compression. This is especially true for JPEG images. Low quality usually means high compression. High compression means smaller file sizes. Figure 7-16 shows the balancing act of choosing quality over compression or choosing compression over quality. Notice how file size and image quality is inversely proportional to each other. The following two sections explain how to find the size of a file and how GIF and JPEG files are compressed. Knowing how compression works can help you make intelligent decisions as to the type of image you want to use and the type of edits you want to make to an image.

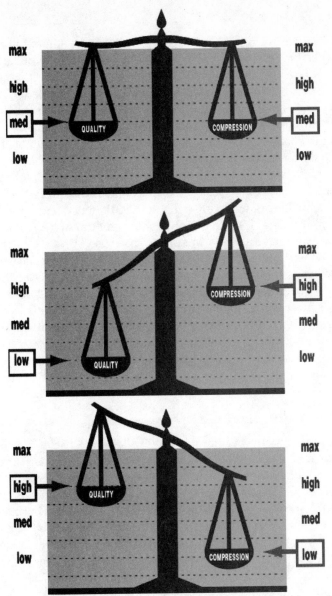

Figure 7-16: The balancing act of choosing between compression and quality.

Determining the File Size

The word *bit* stands for binary digit. A bit is the smallest unit of information in your computer. One bit is one electronic pulse of high or low voltage. It might be helpful to think of a bit as being a light that is either on or off. Eight bits make up one byte. One byte of information can store a single letter. A kilobyte is 1024 bytes and is usually referred to as 1K. Web images are measured in kilobytes. In most cases, you will want to keep your images small and try not to exceed a total of 30K for all the images on your page. It may not always be possible, but it's a goal worth striving for.

A common mistake when using Photoshop is to assume that the status bar in the lower left corner of the window displays the file size. These numbers actually relate to the amount of space for storing flattened and unflattened versions of your image. They can also show the amount of RAM Photoshop is allocating to your image and the amount of space used by the scratch disk for storing data when you are out of RAM. To see the size of your file on the PC, open My Computer or Windows Explorer and select the file. The actual size appears in the status bar at the bottom of the window. If you choose View | Details, the file size appears rounded up to the nearest kilobyte size. You can use the DOS DIR command to display the file size a little more precisely, but it's unlikely you'll need to go to that level.

On a Mac, you can find the byte size of a file by highlighting the file in the Finder and choosing File | Get Info. A dialog box appears listing the actual file size.

GIF Compression

The GIF file format works best for line art (like logos, icons, and cartoons) that contain no more than 256 colors, which is an 8-bit image. The GIF format is called an *index* format because the colors are numbered or indexed. GIF files compress well when the image contains large areas of flat colors. This is because the GIF compression algorithm counts (line-by-line and horizontally) the number of pixels that are the same color and next to each other and stores the result. Graphics with less color changes in the horizontal direction get compressed the most. An effective way to compress GIF images is to reduce the number of colors and horizontal color changes. Figure 7-17 shows an example of how color changes affect the file size of a GIF image.

399 bytes   **570 bytes**   **1633 bytes**

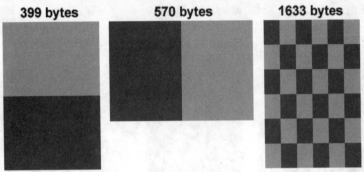

Figure 7-17: The less color changes in the horizontal direction, the better the compression.

JPEG Compression

The JPEG format has a variable compression algorithm. The more compression you use, however, the lower the quality of your images and the more artifacts are introduced. The most important point to remember when creating JPEG graphics is to experiment. Remember that the goal is to produce good-quality graphics that download quickly.

Creating effective JPEG graphics is all about finding a suitable compromise between file size and image quality. The only way to do this is to experiment. When you create JPEG files, start with the highest compression settings first. If the image quality isn't quite good enough, reduce the compression settings and try again. Always work from the original (non-JPEG) image. Remember, each time you create a JPEG file, some image data is lost. Figure 7-18 shows the effects different compression settings have on the same image. If you take the compression too far, artifacts will start to appear. Figure 7-19 shows an enlargement of an area showing some artifacts.

Maximum Quality
Low Compression
Size: 63 Kb

Medium Quality
Medium Compression
Size: 24 Kb

Low Quality
High Compression
Size: 21 Kb

Figure 7-18: An image with different JPEG compression settings.

Figure 7-19: Saving a JPEG image at a low-quality setting can cause artifacts to appear in the image.

Although the JPEG compression algorithm can compress up to 100:1, it does have some limitations. It discards some image information during the compression process (resulting in image quality reduction). In addition, the algorithm is optimized for photograph-like images containing soft edges and continuous-tone blends. For this reason, JPEGs are very good for organic images like landscapes, portraits, and so on, but they're not very good for line art or large areas of flat color. Also, JPEGs produce artifacts (unwanted pixels left over after the compression has finished). Usually these artifacts are only noticeable near sharp-edged graphic elements where pixels transition from a photographic blend to an area of flat color, like text for example.

It's unfortunate for artifacts to appear near the edges of text because it is very common for graphic designers to overlay text (a geometric form) on top of a photograph-like background (organic form). This is done because the sharp edges of the text contrast the smooth background image, so the text stands out. Take a look at the title graphics at the top of each main page at the Authors site (http://www.authors.com/) for an example of this technique. With experimentation, you can usually find a suitable compromise that will make your image's text look sharp with few surrounding artifacts but keep the file size relatively small. Figure 7-20 shows what happens when you mix geometric graphic elements with organic elements and save the result as a JPEG file. Notice the artifacts around the border of the letter.

Figure 7-20: Geometric graphic elements in a JPEG image cause artifacts to appear around the edges.

Image Optimization Tools

Numerous tools exist that can help you optimize your images. Using a good optimization tool can save you hundreds of hours. In fact, once you have seen how much time you'll save, it is unlikely you will want to be without one. There are several excellent tools to choose from. The following sections take a look at the best we have found for optimizing GIF and JPEG images.

Ulead's SmartSaver

Ulead's SmartSaver work as a stand-alone or plug-in for PhotoImpact, Adobe Photoshop, and FrontPage 97. It reduces file size of GIF images. This tool lets you view the effects your compression settings have on an image and the file size before you save it. The feature we love the most is the batch test command that allows you to quickly experiment with multiple test samples at various compression settings and see the file size and image quality of the samples.

SmartSaver also allows you to control interlacing, transparency, and built-in color reduction options. You can get a 14-day demo of Ulead's SmartSaver at http://www.ulead.com/. SmartSaver also includes a JPEG tool for optimizing JPEG images. Figure 7-21 shows the SmartSaver program displaying a GIF image after using the batch mode.

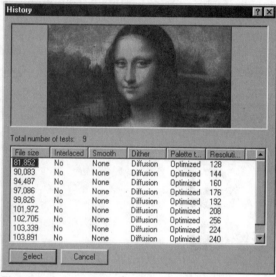

Figure 7-21: SmartSaver batch mode lets you choose from a batch of images with reduced colors.

Digital Frontiers's HVS JPEG & WebFocus

Digital Frontiers's HVS JPEG 2.0 plug-in is amazing. The JPEGs we created were around 50 percent smaller without losing noticeable image quality. When we demonstrate optimization tools in classes and seminars, the HVS JPEG filter draws the most attention. HVS JPEG is around $100 and is worth every penny. It also includes batch processing with Photoshop 4. HVS JPEG is available for the Macintosh and Windows. Digital Frontiers also sells the HVS Color plug-in, which is a GIF optimization tool for reducing 24-bit images to nondithered 8-bit images. A bundled version of HVS Color 2.0 and HVS JPEG 2.0, called WebFocus, sells for around $150. You can download a demo of HVS JPEG and HVS Color Filter plug-in at http://www.digfrontiers.com/demos.html. Figure 7-22 shows the HVS JPEG plug-in.

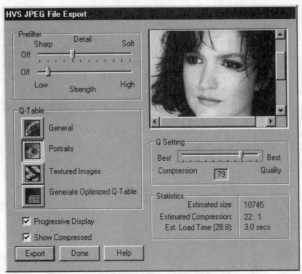

Figure 7-22: The HVS JPEG plug-in is great at optimizing JPEG image files.

WebVise Totality

The newest entry into image compression utilities is WebVise Totality from Auto F/X. WebVise is actually a collection of graphic optimization plug-ins and an animation tool. The optimization tools include a GIF compression program, a JPEG compression program, a digital watermarking tool, a tool for choosing Web-safe colors, and a tool for dithering colors. One unique aspect of the JPEG optimization tool is that you can select part of an image and use a shield tool to protect the selected portion when you optimize the image. The GIF and JPEG tools let you create image maps. The Hybrid Web Safe Colors tool lets you convert colors to Web-safe colors. The animator program lets you display and play animations as you work in Photoshop. Figure 7-23 shows the WebVise Totality JPEG Compression Engine plug-in.

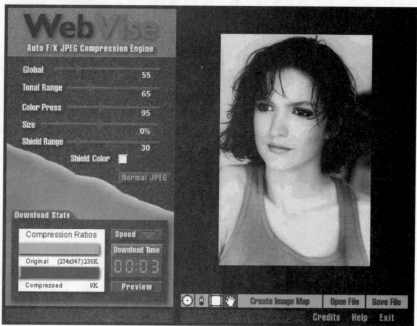

Figure 7-23: The WebVise Totality JPEG Engine.

GIF Wizard

If you don't want to shell out any cash for an optimization tool, you can use the GIF Wizard free. GIF Wizard performs a detailed analysis of your GIF and outputs optimized versions of it. You can find the GIF wizard at http://www.webreference.com/services/gw/.

TCP/IP Packets & Images

When the Web server sends your Web page data, the data is split up into small chunks called packets. Packets can be sent along several different routes and reassembled when they reach the client that requested the page. As the file is reassembled, the packets are checked for errors. If a packet has been corrupted, it is resent. Because packets may take different routes, two large graphics of the same size might not display at the same rate because the browser may be waiting for packets that make up one of the images. While image files are broken down into small packets, sent, and reassembled, other data is being processed that can also slow down the process of displaying an image.

Browsers can receive graphics in any order. Small images typically begin displaying before larger images. If you scroll down the page as images are loading, you may notice that a small image displays at the bottom of a page before a larger image displays at the top of a page.

In addition to being sent and reassembled from packets, some images require additional processing before they display in the browser. For example, the author may have used the HEIGHT and WIDTH attributes to scale an image, or if the image is in the JPEG format, it must be decompressed.

Once the HTML tags needed to display the page are received, the browser looks for the HEIGHT and WIDTH attributes in the <IMG> tag. If these attributes are set, the browser creates bounding boxes for the images and begins displaying the page. If the HEIGHT and WIDTH attributes are not set, the browser must determine the height and width of the graphics before displaying the page.

After an image has been received, it is stored in a memory cache and in a disk cache. The browser checks to see if the image is already cached. If the same image appears more than once on a page and it has been downloaded successfully, it is loaded from the cache. If you reuse graphics on your pages, they will load much faster than pages with different images do.

One trick used by Web designers is to split up images into a table to make several images instead of one large one. This causes the smaller images to start to appear a little faster than one larger image would. The navigation bar at the Authors site is an example of chopping up an image into a table, as shown in Figure 7-24.

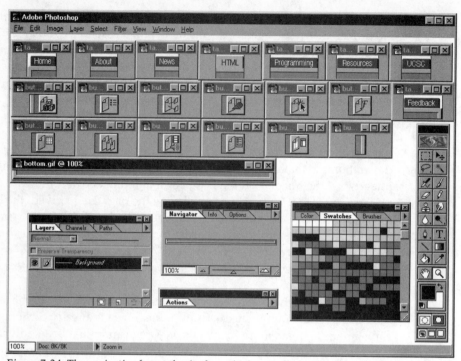

Figure 7-24: The navigation bar at the Authors site is actually a collection of individual images broken into table cells.

Creating Seamless Background Tiles & Borders

If you use an image to create a tiled background, you may see the edges of the image around each tile. Paint Shop Pro includes an option for creating a seamless background tile. Figure 7-25 shows a tiled background created using Paint Shop Pro. The following steps explain how to modify an existing image to create a seamless background tile image using Paint Shop Pro:

1. Open the image file you want to use as a tile for your background. Make sure it's not too dark.

2. Choose Colors I Increase Color Depth I 16 Million Colors (24 bit).

3. Select the center portion of the picture using the rectangular selection tool.

4. Choose Image | Special Effects | Create Seamless Pattern. If an error message appears stating that your selection is too close to the edge of the image, choose OK and reselect a smaller portion closer to the center of your image.

5. Choose File | Save and save the image in the same directory as your HTML document. A dialog box appears stating that the file format requires images to have a maximum of 256 colors.

6. Choose Yes.

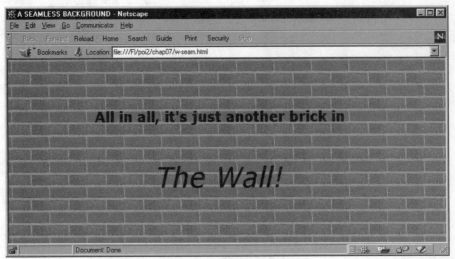

Figure 7-25: A tiled background created with Paint Shop Pro.

Borders are quite simple to create. Because background images are tiled, you can create a border by simply creating an image that is only a few pixels high. Figure 7-26 shows Photoshop displaying the border image used for the Authors site.

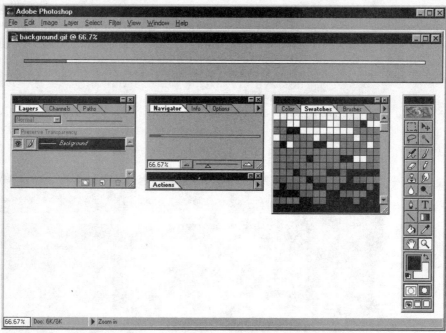

Figure 7-26: A background border image loaded in Photoshop. Because backgrounds are tiled, a border image only needs to be a few pixels high.

GIF Compression Using CRLI

As we mentioned earlier, the GIF compression algorithm scans images line-by-line looking for consecutive pixels of the same color. The more pixels found that are the same color as the ones next to them, the better the algorithm can compress the image, which results in a smaller file size. This type of compression scheme is often referred to as Consecutive Run-Length Insertion (CRLI), or *curly*.

The more you can increase the consecutive run-length of pixels of the same color in an image, the more the image will be compressed. One way of increasing the consecutive run-lengths in a GIF image (without destroying it) is to replace every other horizontal line with a line of solid color, usually white. The resulting image's contrast is reduced and the image is lighter. Figure 7-27 shows an image before and Figure 7-28 shows an image after applying the curly effect. The image is now much better organized for GIF compression. The CRLI technique is best used for images that don't require high contrast. It's especially useful for background images. Notice the difference in file sizes.

Figure 7-27: A GIF image before applying the CRLI effect (the file size of this image is 73K).

Figure 7-28: A GIF image after applying the CRLI effect (the file size of this image is 37K).

With Photoshop, it's easy to apply the CRLI technique. First you need to create a pattern. Create a new image in RGB mode that is 1 pixel wide and 2 pixels high with a transparent background. Zoom in to the highest magnification, and using the pencil tool and with the color white selected, make one of the pixels white or whichever color you prefer (leaving the other transparent). Choose Select | All to select the entire image and choose Define Pattern from the Edit menu. Next open the image you want to apply the CRLI technique to and then choose Fill from the Edit menu; you can do this on another layer if you prefer. Fill the image with the pattern you just created. Notice how the image has changed. You can now save the image in the Indexed mode.

JPEG Compression Using the Blur Technique

Images of lower contrast compress better than higher-contrast images with the JPEG compression scheme. You can use it to your advantage by selectively decreasing the contrast of parts or all of an image; you effectively are making an image that will compress easier. In Photoshop, this is easily done by selecting the parts of the image on which you want to reduce the contrast, feathering the selection (to soften the selection outline by making it harder to notice), and then blurring the selected area. To blur the selected area, try a gaussian blur of 1 pixel. Save your image as you would normally save a JPEG (choose a quality setting) and you'll notice the resulting compressed file will be smaller compared to the same image without the blurring applied. An example of an image before applying this technique is shown in Figure 7-29 and Figure 7-30 shows the same image with the mountain background blurred. In this example we have exaggerated the blurring of the background to make it more noticeable. Of course, you will probably want to be more subtle when blurring images you want to publish on the Web.

Figure 7-29: Before using the Blur technique.

Figure 7-30: The image in Figure 7-29 after using the Blur technique.

The JPEG Blur technique can be especially useful for minimizing the file size of large images like backgrounds or home page images by selectively blurring parts of the image that are less important or not usually seen on a 640 X 480 display.

A Checklist for Quality & Ensuring Fast Downloads _____

There are several factors to consider when working with graphics. To make things a little easier, we have included the following list and what's called a *mind map*, which ties all the related image editing issues together to make sure you are on the right path. The image editing mind map is shown in Figure 7-31.

To help ensure fast downloads, do the following:

■ Try to keep file sizes small, 30K or less if possible.

■ Crop or resize your images so they are physically smaller (remember the 600- X 300-pixel guideline).

■ Use thumbnails of larger images. Then when the user clicks on a thumbnail, the larger image is displayed on another page.

■ Try not to use too many graphics on a page. Instead, distribute them across multiple pages.

■ Reuse graphics like icons or navigational elements. Once an image is loaded into cache, it displays much faster.

■ If you use GIF files, minimize the number of colors used and interlace the image.

■ If you use JPEG, try highest compression and then reduce it to achieve a good compromise between file size and image quality.

■ Split large graphics into table cells; remember TCP/IP splits data into small packets so these smaller images will load a little faster.

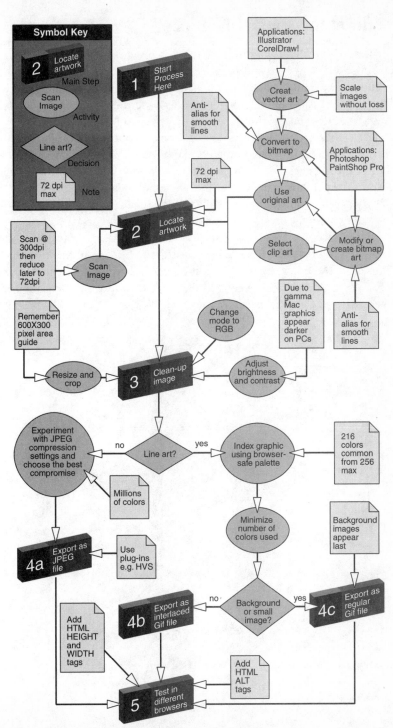

Figure 7-31: A mind map to use when creating images.

Using Filters for Special Effects

A filter is typically a plug-in used with an image editor to create unique special effects. Photoshop and Paint Shop Pro both come with a set of filters. Two of the most popular filter programs are Alien Skin's Eye Candy and Kai's Power Tools. Kai's Power Tools includes a seamless welder filter that lets you create seamless backgrounds.

Eye Candy from Alien Skin is our favorite collection of filters. Figure 7-32 shows a number of images created using Eye Candy. It is possible to create these type of special effects without using filters, but doing the job manually could take you hours instead of the seconds it takes with Eye Candy. Eye Candy saves you from having to learn advanced graphic techniques for working with channels, layers, and masks. The learning curve for these topics is a steep one. To use a filter, you usually select the image or portion of the image you want to apply the filter to and choose the filter from the Filter list on the Eye Candy menu. You can try a demo of Eye Candy and see just how easy it is. To get the demo, visit Alien Skin's Web site at http://www.alienskin.com/eyecandy/ec_demo.htm.

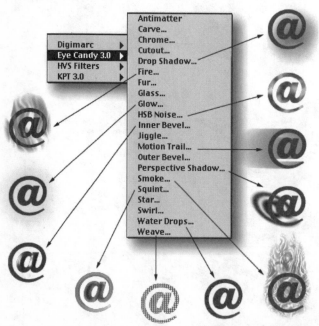

Figure 7-32: Alien Skin's Eye Candy applies stunning special effects in seconds.

Creating an Animated GIF

A GIF animation is a series of multiple GIF images stored in a single GIF file that displays as an animation. The GIF format has supported animation since 1989. The file format for creating animated GIFs is in fact GIF89a. Several tools exist to make creating an animated GIF fairly easy. Our favorite is GIF Animator from Ulead. You can download a demo of GIF animator from Ulead's home page at http://www.ulead.com. It is extremely easy to create animated GIFs using the GIF wizard. Figure 7-33 shows Ulead's GIF Animator.

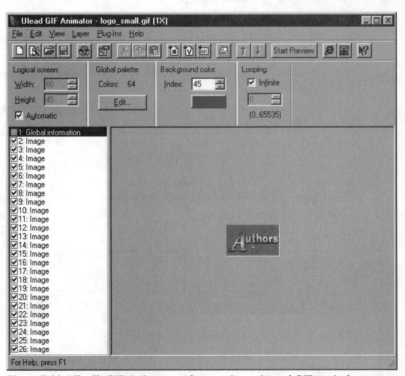

Figure 7-33: Ulead's GIF Animator makes creating animated GIFs a cinch.

Another popular program for creating animated GIFs is Alchemy Mindworks's GIF Construction Set. You can download the GIF Construction Set from http://www.mindworkshop.com/alchemy/gifcon.html.

Before you start working with the GIF Construction Set, you first need to create a series of images to be displayed one after the other. You can use any image editor, such as Paint Shop Pro or Photoshop, to create the images. There are two ways to create animated GIF images with the GIF Construction Set: using the Animation Wizard or manually specifying the settings for your animation.

The Animation Wizard is a quick and dirty way to create a GIF animation. If you have problems with how the animation Wizard creates your animated GIF, you may want to create and edit the animated GIF manually. To create an animated GIF using the Animation Wizard, first start the GIF Construction Set and choose File | Animation Wizard. The animation Wizard displays a series of dialog boxes for creating an animated GIF.

The following steps explain how to use the GIF Construction Set to manually create and edit a GIF animation:

1. Open the largest image you want to use in an image editor, such as Paint Shop Pro or Photoshop, and note the width and height of the image so you can enter these settings in the GIF Construction Set. Make sure you have specified the largest height and largest width of all the images. In Paint Shop Pro, the size of the image appears in the status bar at the bottom of the Paint Shop Pro window. To see the height and width of an image in Photoshop, choose Image | Image Size.

2. Start the GIF Construction Set.

3. Choose File | New. The HEADER GIF 89a Screen (640 X 480) appears as shown in Figure 7-34. The header is the first "block" in a GIF file. You will add an additional image block and control blocks for each image you add to your animation.

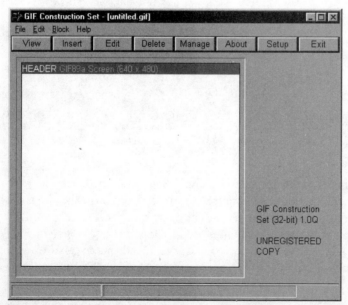

Figure 7-34: The HEADER GIF 89a Screen (640 X 480) appears in the GIF Construction Set.

4. Click the Edit button. The Edit Header dialog box appears as shown in Figure 7-35. Enter the width (screen width) and height (screen depth) of the largest image you want to use in the animation.

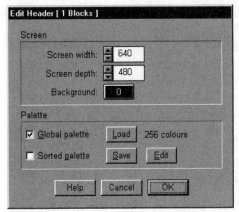

Figure 7-35: The Edit Header dialog box.

5. Click on the Background color setting and a color palette appears. Click on the background color of your image. Alternatively, you can enter the index color in the Background setting text box. Click OK.

TRAP   *Inserting an image larger than the specified screen size will cause a General Protection Fault (GPF) in Netscape Navigator.*

6. Click the Insert button. The Insert Object dialog box appears.

7. Click on the Loop button if you want the animation to loop continuously. This inserts a control block instructing the browser to restart the animation every time it finishes. Omit this step if you want to create an animation that plays once and then stops.

   If you don't loop your animation, the last image is the image that will remain in the window. If you loop your animation, the first image is the image browsers that can't play GIF animations display as the first image in the animation.

8. If you chose the Loop option, click on the Insert button to display the Insert Object dialog box. If you didn't choose Loop, the Insert Object dialog box is already open. If you want to create a transparent background for your animation or specify the amount of time to wait before

moving on to the next image, click the Control button. This inserts a control block for the image that you add in the next two steps. You must insert a control block for each image to specify a transparent color.

9. If the Insert Object dialog box isn't already open, click the Insert button. The Insert Object dialog box appears. Click on the Image button. The Open dialog box appears.

10. From the list box, select the image you want to start with and choose OK. If you insert an image that has a different palette than the current global palette of your GIF file, the Palette dialog box appears. The Palette dialog box lets you specify how to handle the new image's palette. If you are using a photograph image that isn't dithered, choose the Dither This Image to the Global Palette option. This option gives you color match with a slight loss in detail resolution. True color, 24-bit images are internally converted to 256 color images. When you have finished selecting the palette option, choose OK.

TIP *If the image is already dithered and you choose the Dither This Image to the Global Palette option, you will notice dots appearing in the image when the GIF animation is displayed. If you are experiencing a dithering problem, choose the Use a Local Palette for This Image option. Be aware that using the local palette increases the file size and may cause problems if you have other images using different palettes. It is still safer to use the local palette than the Use as Is option, which can cause colors to shift.*

11. If you chose to insert a control block in your animation to create a transparent background or specify the amount of time to wait before moving to the next image, select the Control Block header just above the image you just inserted and click the Edit button. The Edit Control Block dialog box appears. Click in the Transparent colour check box, and then either click on the color setting to choose the color from a palette or click on the color picker to select a color from the image itself.

TRAP *You also must select the Remove by Background option for every image unless you want a trail of previous images left on the screen.*

12. To specify an amount of time to delay before the next image, enter the interval to wait (measured in 1/100ths of a second) in the Delay text box. It is a good idea to use the same amount for each image or the animation may not play smoothly. When you have finished with the control block settings, choose OK and then click on the last image header.

TIP *If you don't change the timing for control blocks, you can copy and paste control blocks.*

13. Repeat steps 7 through 10 to add each control block and image you want to use in your animation. The Construction Set window will appear similar to the one shown in Figure 7-36.

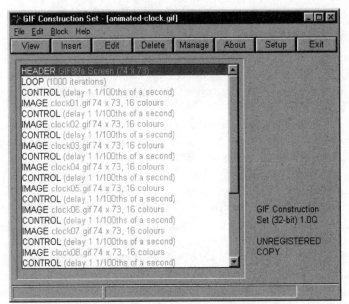

Figure 7-36: The Construction Set window after adding the control blocks and images.

14. Choose File | Save to save your animated GIF.

Creating Image Maps

The IMG element also lets you set up image maps. *Image maps* are graphic images that have defined *hot spots*. Each hot spot is a link. Clicking on the graphic is the same as clicking on a hyperlink. The image lets the user jump to the URL that is defined for that region of the graphic. Image maps bring new ways to publish interactive Web pages. For example, a graphic can be a series of labeled buttons with each button image set to a different location.

Remember, if you use an image map, no one using a text-based browser will be able to see the image. If you use image maps, be sure you create a text-only version of the links for text-based browsers.

In order to create an image map, you first need to create an image in which to include hot spots. You might want to use a motif or a metaphor for your images. For example, you could use an image of different buildings or an image of several planets, with each identifying a different link.

Specifying Hot Spots

There are different ways of identifying the parts of the image to specify a hot spot. You can manually enter the coordinates in a file and specify the URL you want to jump to, or you can use an image mapping program to create the file for you.

While it is possible to identify the areas by noting the coordinates of the region you want to include, using an image mapping program is much easier. One of the biggest time-savers for specifying hot spots is to use a program like LiveImage, formally called Map This, or Thomas Boutell's Mapedit. These utilities let you draw rectangles, circles, and arbitrary polygons and let you store the coordinates in a file. The Map This program is included on the Companion CD-ROM. You can check for updates at http://www.mediatec.com/. You can check for Mapedit at http://www.boutell.com/mapedit/.

Hot spots can be a variety of shapes, including a circle, rectangle, or polygon. The most upper left pixel is used as the beginning coordinate of an X- and Y-axis. This X-and Y-grid lets you identify collections of pixels, an area, you want to include as a hot spot. Most graphic editors use the same type of grid, allowing you to easily display specific coordinates. The next section explains how to use the Map This program to create a map file.

Creating Client Side Image Maps Using Map This

To map the hot spots in your image, you'll need to download an image mapping program like Map This. Map This is on this book's Companion CD-ROM. The new commercial version is called LiveImage and is available at http://www.mediatec.com/. Map This (version 1.3) is distributed as an executable file (.exe). Simply double-click the mpths13.exe file to install the Map This program. To help you visualize how an image map works, see Figure 7-37. The following steps explain how to use Map This to create a map of clickable coordinates for the image, modify your <IMG> tag to use the image map, and add the map coordinates to your HTML document.

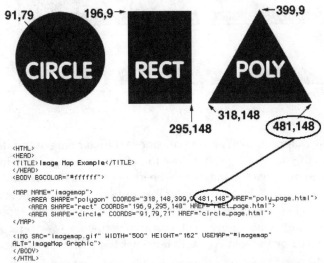

Figure 7-37: To create an image map, you create a map of clickable coordinates for the image, modify your <IMG> tag, and add the map coordinates to your HTML document.

1. Choose Map This 1.3 from the Windows 95 Start menu.

2. Choose File | New. The Make New Image Map dialog box appears.

3. Click the Okay button. The Open an Existing Image (GIF/JPEG) File dialog box appears.

4. Locate and select the GIF or JPEG image file you want to map and click the Open button. The image appears in the Map This window for you to begin editing, as shown in Figure 7-38.

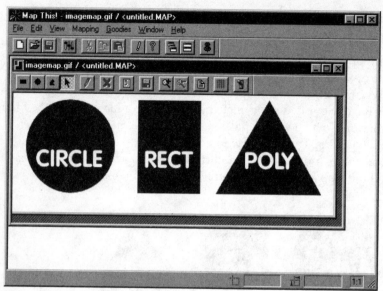

Figure 7-38: An image loaded in the Map This window.

5. Click the Mapping toolbar item or choose the Mapping menu item that specifies the shape you want to use to define a hot spot. If the image is small, you may need to maximize the image so you can see and use the Mapping toolbar. The Mapping toolbar buttons include the Rectangle, Circle, and Polygon. The following explains how to define different regions using the Mapping toolbar. If two defined areas overlap, the first matching shape in the map file determines the URL that will be returned.

- **Rectangle**. Click the left mouse button in one corner of the rectangle in the image and drag the mouse pointer to the opposite corner. The rectangle marquee outlines the rectangle. When you release the mouse button, the rectangle appears with crosshatch lines indicating the hot spot you just defined.

- **Circle**. Position the mouse pointer in an upper portion of the circle. Click the left mouse button and drag the mouse pointer to any point on the bottom edge of the desired circle. The circle appears with crosshatch lines indicating the hot spot you just defined. If the circle isn't centered correctly, you can click on the Select Arrow tool and drag the selected area to reposition the circle. You can also drag the selection handles to resize the circle.

- **Polygon**. Click the left mouse button on the edge of the area you want to begin mapping. Move the mouse pointer to outline the edge. Note that a line follows you from the point of the initial click. Click again at a second point that continues to outline the area you want to map. Continue clicking to create points until you have outlined all but the final connection back to the first point. Click the mouse button on the original point to finish defining the shape. The shape appears with crosshatch lines indicating the hot spot you just defined.

6. Click the Show/Hide Area List button. The Show/Hide Area list appears.

7. Select the first area from the list and click the Edit button, shown as a pencil in the area list. Alternatively, you can double-click inside of the first area. The Area #1 Settings dialog box appears. Enter the URL you want to link to. You can also add any comments in the Comments text box. Choose OK when you're finished.

8. Repeat step 7 for each hot spot you want to define. You can use full URLs or simply reference other local HTML documents.

9. Choose File|Save As. The Settings for This Map File dialog box appears.

10. Enter a name for your map information in the Title text box. For this example, we named the map Client Side Shapes.

11. If you want, you can enter your name in the Author text box and a description of the hot spot in the Description text box. Both of these text boxes are optional. The text you enter here will appear as comments in your HTML document.

12. Enter the document or URL you want to use if the person clicks outside one of hot spot areas in the default URL text box. For example, you may want to point to an HTML document that displays a message informing the reader that he or she needs to click an image.

13. Click the CSIM radio button (CSIM stands for client-side image map) and click the OK button. The Save the Image Map File dialog box appears.

14. Enter the name of a temporary HTML file you want to create in the File Name text box. You can name the file with an .htm or .html extension. The HTML file you created with Map This contains the map coordinates. Pay attention to the folder you're saving the temporary HTML document to because you'll need to retrieve the file later.

15. Click the Save button to save your map coordinates to a file.

16. Choose File | Exit to close Map This.

Adding the Image Map Coordinates

To use an image map, you need to add the USEMAP attribute to the <IMG> tag, assign the map name, and add the <MAP> tag and image map coordinates. The USEMAP attribute setting instructs the browser where to look for the <MAP> tag that contains the client-side image mapping information in the document. To add the image map information you generated using Map This to your HTML document, follow these steps:

1. Using a text editor such as the Windows Notepad, add the image (<IMG SRC="image.gif">) to your HTML document if it isn't already in your page.

2. Add the USEMAP attribute to your <IMG> tag. The map name is the same name you entered as the title in step 10 in the previous section. You can also specify that the image map doesn't appear with a border. For this example, you might enter

```
<IMG SRC="csshapes.gif" BORDER="0" USEMAP="#Client Side Shapes">
```

3. Using the Windows Notepad program, choose File | Open to open the HTML file you created with Map This.

4. The HTML source code containing your map coordinates appears.

5. Select and copy (Ctrl+C) the section starting with the <MAP> tag and ending with the </MAP> tag. The closing </MAP> tag is before the closing </BODY> tag in your HTML file.

6. Choose File | Open and open the HTML document to which you are adding the clickable image.

7. Paste (Ctrl+V) the section after the <IMG> tag. The following shows all the code for a client side image map:

```
<HTML>
<HEAD>
<TITLE>A Client Side Image Map Example</TITLE>
</HEAD>
<BODY>
<H1 ALIGN="CENTER">A Client Side Image Map Example</H1>
<IMG SRC="csshapes.gif" BORDER="0" USEMAP="#Client Side Shapes">
<MAP NAME="Client Side Shapes">
<!-- #$-:Image Map file created by Map THIS! -->
```

```
<!-- #$-:Map THIS! free image map editor by Todd C. Wilson -->
<!-- #$-:Please do not edit lines starting with "#$" -->
<!-- #$VERSION:1.30 -->
<!-- #$DESCRIPTION:A CSIM example -->
<!-- #$AUTHOR:Brent Heslop -->
<!-- #$DATE:Tue Oct 07 05:08:35 1997-->
<!-- #$PATH:C:\Class -->
<!-- #$GIF:csshapes.gif -->
<AREA SHAPE=POLY COORDS="103,29,13,207,192,208,103,29" HREF=http://
www.best.com ALT="Best Internet Communications">
<AREA SHAPE=CIRCLE COORDS="309,119,89" HREF=http://www.microsoft.com
ALT="Microsoft">
<AREA SHAPE=RECT COORDS="452,29,633,212" HREF=http://www.yahoo.com
ALT="Yahoo!">
<AREA SHAPE=default HREF=http://www.yahoo.com>
</MAP>
</BODY>
</HTML>
```

8. Choose File | Save to save your changes.

9. Start Netscape Navigator and choose File | Open File in Browser and load your file.

10. Move the mouse on the hot spots. Notice that when you move the mouse pointer over a hot spot, the status bar lists the location. Click the hot spot and you are transported to the new location.

Moving On

By now you should have a good idea of how images are compressed and how to work with and optimize both GIF and JPEG images. As you can see from this chapter, image editing is filled with complex issues, but by mastering the essentials you can beat the wait factor and increase the wow factor that images can bring to your site. The next chapter also increases the wow factor by explaining how to use style sheets to lay out your pages.

chapter 8
Style Sheets

The Web was created as a way for scientists to share information, and the quality of the information mattered more than the glitz of the presentation. Initially, the only presentation issues that the Web addressed were those that affected quick understanding and accurate delivery of information. However, as the Web grew in popularity and sophistication, Web page designers wanted to improve their presentations, both to stand out among the rapid proliferation of similar sites and to enhance the impact of their site's information. The result was the introduction of specialized HTML tags that offered more direct control over the display of text and images. However, this left some Web users, such as the visually impaired and those using graphically limited browsers, less able to gather information, thus limiting the Web's appeal and range.

For the Web to be truly "World Wide," it needs to have methods for presenting information that can be translated within the confines of a visually or graphically limited browser. On the other hand, years of experience in other media have shown that, because people are naturally visually oriented, they respond more positively and promptly to information that is presented with visual flair. This requires a robust set of tags that allow a page designer to control how the viewer will generally receive the page. The issue then becomes how to provide both flexibility and control within the confines of HTML tags.

Cascading Style Sheets (CSS) are the solution proposed by the Web community. They allow you to create complex layouts that will work for most of your readers, but readers with more limited capabilities can modify or even eliminate them. So you can specify fonts, set margins and indents, and create special effects with text and images without worry. Style sheets open up a full range of design possibilities while preserving the concepts of information access and exchange that mark the Web as a truly unique vehicle for presenting information.

The Elements of Styles

Style sheets are fundamentally easy to use, but it's helpful to understand some basic terminology before you start. To begin with, a *style sheet* is a collection of rules that determines how a browser displays HTML tags. Each *rule* in a style sheet is made up of two elements: a selector and a style. You construct a style rule as follows:

```
selector {property: value}
```

In the following example, *H1* is the *selector*. A selector is simply the HTML tag that the style will be used for (in this case, *heading 1*). The *style* itself is inside the curly braces. *Font-size* is the *property name*, and *24pt* is the *value*. The property name is listed first and is separated from the value by a colon and a space. A *property* is a stylistic parameter that can be set through a style sheet. Each property has a set of corresponding *value selections* that define how the property is applied:

```
H1 {font-size: 24pt}
```

If a style contains multiple property-value pairs, separate each pair with a semicolon. For example, the following code defines a style that sets a heading tag to display text in bold, large, red text:

```
H1 {font: bold 24pt; color: red}
```

In this example the selector is the heading tag <H1>, and the style consists of two property-value pairs. The first sets the font property to 24-point bold in the standard heading font, while the second sets the color property to red.

Contextual Selectors

Another method of specifying a style is to use a contextual selector. This lets you choose an element in a document based on the element's position in the document's structure. For example, you can specify that all the bold elements inside a paragraph appear in green by entering the following:

```
P B   {color: green}
```

TIP *Netscape Navigator version 4.0 does not yet support contextual selectors, but you can use contextual selectors with Microsoft Internet Explorer 4.0.*

Adding Comments

In addition to rules, you can also add comments to your styles. Comments in a style sheet are contained between the /* delimiter, which begins the comment, and the */ delimiter, which ends it. You can place text or white space characters between the two delimiters, which means that comments can consist of multiple lines. (Anyone familiar with the C programming language will immediately recognize this comment mechanism.) Anything between the comment delimiters is ignored by the browser. Note that the standard HTML comment delimiters, <!-- and -->, are not valid within a style sheet.

Specifying Styles & Linking to Style Sheets

Now that you know a bit about how to code style rules, you need to learn how to insert styles into your HTML code. This section shows you a variety of ways to specify styles and explains how styles interact within the document itself.

The three methods for inserting styles are *inline styles*, *internal styles*, and *external style sheets*. Each method is a powerful way to format one or multiple pages. Inline and internal styles allow you to insert individual style rules inside your documents. External style sheets let you use a single reference to specify formatting for multiple HTML pages. To insert the different style types:

- For an inline style, use the STYLE attribute to insert the style inline as formatting instructions in your HTML tags.

- For an internal style, use the <STYLE> tag to insert styles at the top of each page. This allows you to ensure that elements such as headers, paragraphs, and so on look the same on particular pages.

- For an external style sheet, you link to an external style sheet using the <LINK> tag. This lets you use one file to set up the formatting for an entire Web site.

TIP *The W3 Consortium has proposed another method for inserting styles into a document: using a new, @import attribute in the <STYLE> tag. With this method, you can add several interacting style sheets to your document and combine them with local styles defined with the <STYLE> tag. However, at present, no browser supports this tag. There is a more extensive discussion of importing style sheets later in this chapter.*

Adding Inline Styles

You can assign a style to a particular tag by using the method called *inline styles*. To create an inline style, add the STYLE attribute to a specific tag by inserting the style rule in quotes after the STYLE attribute. In this case, there is no selector, as the style rule only applies to the tag that contains the attribute. The following example adds the STYLE attribute to the <P> tag to specify that the paragraph text should appear in an 18-point font:

```
<P STYLE="font-size: 18pt">This paragraph text appears in an 18-point
font.</P>
```

This method of applying styles is limited as it changes only the text in the given paragraph; it doesn't affect any subsequent paragraphs. There are other methods of creating the same result using existing HTML tags such as the <FONT> tag. If this were all that styles did, they wouldn't be very interesting. However, when used in conjunction with other style specification methods, this limited application can be very helpful.

Applying Styles With SPAN

Another method of adding inline styles is to use the <SPAN> tag, which accepts the STYLE attribute described earlier. The <SPAN> tag surrounds, or *spans*, the text to which you want to add a particular style. The <SPAN> tag allows you to create or apply a style without attaching it to a structural HTML element. SPAN is a text-level element, so it can be used the same way that HTML elements such as EM and STRONG are used. The important distinction is that while EM and STRONG carry structural meaning, SPAN has no such meaning. It exists purely to apply a style and has no additional effect. For example, here's an illustration using the <SPAN> tag with the STYLE attribute to create a 1-inch margin:

```
<SPAN STYLE="margin-left: 1in"><H2>Special Spacing Example</H2><P>This
paragraph and its associated heading are 1 inch from the current left
margin.</SPAN>
```

Grouping Internal Styles

A more practical method of using styles is to insert the <STYLE> tag in the document's heading. The <STYLE> tag is inserted between the beginning and ending <HEAD> tags. For example, you might enter the code shown in Listing 8-1. The document defined in Listing 8-1 will display as shown in Figure 8-1.

Listing 8-1

```
<HTML>
<HEAD>
<TITLE>Style Example</TITLE>
<STYLE TYPE="text/css">
   BODY {background: white; color: black;}
   H1 {font: 24pt "Arial" bold}
   P {font: 12pt "Arial"; text-indent: 0.5in}
   A {text-decoration: none; color: blue}
</STYLE>
</HEAD>
<BODY>
<H1>The Heading 1 displays in 24-point Arial bold.</H1><P>The paragraph text
displays in 12 point Arial black on a white background.
The anchor <A HREF="http://www.w3.org/pub/HTML/">W3 Organization</A> appears
in blue, but it isn't underlined because the text-decoration for anchors is
set to "none".</P>
</BODY>
</HTML>
```

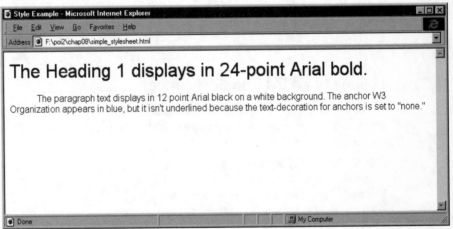

Figure 8-1: Even a simple style sheet can make a dramatic difference in how your pages display.

The <STYLE> tag shown here contains a series of four styles. The <STYLE> tag itself has a required TYPE attribute, which defines the style sheet language. At present, the only language that is supported by both Netscape and Microsoft browsers is "text/css," which stands for the text MIME type of Cascading Style Sheets. Netscape also supports the new "text/javascript" type that allows you to control and modify your styles with JavaScript.

The selector is given first, followed by a series of property-value pairs that define the style rules to be used for the specified tag. Note that the selectors cover different and overlapping sets of text. Everything within the <BODY> tag, for example, has a white background with black text. The <H1> headings, which are a part of the body, are displayed in 24-point Arial bold in black against the white background, combining both rules. If the rules for different tags conflict, then the more specific rule is applied. For example, if the header is specified as red, this is a more specific rule than the one covering the entire body text, so the heading text is displayed in red instead of black.

The style rules shown here are fairly self-explanatory. Don't worry at this point about how they are presented; the rest of this chapter shows you how to create specific style rules.

TIP
Use semicolons to separate each of the property value pairs in the style that you want to assign. For example, the following style sets the font of a page to 12-point Times New Roman font, the colors to black text on a white background, and both left and right margins to 1 1/2 inches:

```
<STYLE>
BODY {font: 12pt "Times New Roman"; color: black; background: white;
margin-left: 1.5in; margin-right: 1.5in}
</STYLE>
```

Linking to an External Style Sheet

To link to an external style sheet, first create a file that contains the styles you want to use. For example, you might create a file named styles.css with the following contents:

```
BODY {background: white; color: black}
H1 {font: 24pt "Arial" bold}
P {font: 12pt "Arial"; text-indent: 0.5in}
A {text-decoration: none; color: blue}
```

Note that you don't include the <STYLE> tag in this file. Once you have created this file, use the LINK tag to link the HTML page to the style sheet. The REL attribute, which defines the relationship between the linked file and the current document, must be STYLESHEET to indicate that this link points to an external style sheet. The HREF attribute points to the style sheet file itself, just as the SRC attribute points to the image file for an <IMG> tag. You also need to use the TYPE attribute to specify the Cascading Style Sheet MIME type. You add the <LINK> tag in between the opening <HEAD> and closing </HEAD> tags. The page shown in Listing 8-2 uses the Cascading Style Sheet named "styles.css," which is located in the same directory as the HTML file.

Listing 8-2

```
<HTML>
<HEAD>
<TITLE>External Style Example</TITLE>
<LINK REL=STYLESHEET HREF="styles.css" TYPE="text/css">
</HEAD>

<BODY>
<H1>The Heading 1 appears in 24-point Arial bold</H1>
<P>The paragraph text appears in 12-point Arial black on a white background.
The anchor <A HREF="http://www.w3.org/pub/HTML/">W3 Organization</A> appears
in blue, but it doesn't appear underlined because the text-decoration for
anchors is set to "none".</P>
<P>The styles used in this version are identical to those used in the
version with the &lt;STYLE&gt; tag.
</BODY>
</HTML>
```

This page is almost identical to the preceding example, with only minor changes—in the <TITLE> and in the body text—so that you can see that the page has changed when you load it into your browser.

TIP | *The file extension .css that is used for the style sheet here is not required. You can use any extension, or none at all. The style sheet itself is simply a text file and can be generated with any text editor, just like HTML files can. We have simply standardized the .css extension for style sheets as a convenient method of distinguishing these files from other files.*

Selecting a Style Specification Method

Each of the three methods of specifying styles has a useful place in your design repertoire, because each method has its own advantages and disadvantages. In general, external style sheets are the most flexible since they allow you to reuse a set of styles throughout a site, but inline and internal styles may be more appropriate in some cases. Here's a short comparison of how these methods stack up:

Inline STYLE attributes

■ Advantages:

  ■ Useful for setting styles for small sections of a document.

  ■ Can override all other style specification methods.

- Disadvantages:
  - Combine style information with content and structural information.
  - Cannot be used with other instances of the same tag within a document.
  - Cannot be used for multiple documents.

Internal <STYLE> tag

- Advantages:
  - Useful for setting styles for an entire document.
  - Can use classes to create styles for multiple types of tags.
  - Style information is included when the document downloads for fastest rendering.
- Disadvantages:
  - Cannot be used for multiple documents.

External style sheets

- Advantages:
  - Can be used to set styles for multiple documents on a site.
  - Can use classes to create styles for multiple types of tags.
  - Can be shared across sites as a standard template.
  - If used repeatedly, will be cached by browser for faster retrieval.
- Disadvantages:
  - Requires extra time to download a separate file.
  - Documents may not render correctly if style sheet fails to load or is delayed.
  - Too cumbersome for making small style settings in a document.

For our work in this chapter, we will use the <STYLE> tag primarily. This allows you to see both the styles and the content of a document in one listing. However, in real situations, you may want to use external style sheets for their convenience and ability to affect multiple pages at one time.

Creating Unique Styles With CLASS & ID

You can apply different styles to the same type of HTML tag in your documents by classifying them with the CLASS attribute or by creating a unique ID attribute and applying it to the tag. Since ID works very much like CLASS, let's first look at how you can create and use classified tags.

Defining Styles With CLASS

You've already seen how to add styles for a specific tag and how subsequent tags inherit these styles. "But," you may ask, "what if I want to have one paragraph be blue and the next red, or one italic and the next regular?" This is where the CLASS attribute comes to the rescue. Essentially, you create different style classes for each element that you wish to distinguish. Then, when you add the HTML tag for one of these elements, you add the CLASS attribute to specify which class that element belongs to. Look at the example shown in Listing 8-3, which produces the page displayed in Figure 8-2.

Listing 8-3

```
<HTML>
<HEAD>
<TITLE>Class Attribute Example</TITLE>
<STYLE TYPE="text/css">
   BODY {background: white; color: black; font-size: 14pt}
   P.large {font-size: 18pt}
   P.small {font-size: 10pt}
</STYLE>
</HEAD>

<BODY>
<H1>Using the CLASS Attribute</H1>
<P>This paragraph is unclassified. The text appears in the browser's default
font, set in 14 point type in black on a white background.</P>
<P CLASS="large">This paragraph is in CLASS large. The text appears in the
browser's default font in 18 point black type on a white background.</P>
<P CLASS="small">This paragraph is in CLASS small. The text appears in the
browser's default font in 10 point black type on a white background.</P>
</BODY>
</HTML>
```

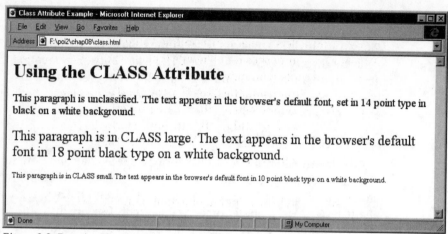

Figure 8-2: By using the CLASS attribute, you can vary the styles for a type of tag.

TIP

As a matter of convention, we've used uppercase letters exclusively for the tags and lowercase letters for the CLASS names. As you know, HTML tags are required to be insensitive to case; however, the CSS specification does not require that class names be case sensitive or case insensitive. At present, most browsers seem to be case insensitive, but this may change in the future. In particular, the Netscape-supported JavaScript style sheets (JSSS) do require you to match case, since JavaScript itself is case sensitive. The best practice, therefore, is to match the names exactly in both the style and the CLASS attribute as shown in the example code.

This code is fairly easy to follow. There are two classifications of the paragraph <P> tag created here: one called "large," which is set in 18-point type and one called "small," which is set in 10-point type. The style for the BODY sets the default text size to 14 points. As you can see, if you use the standard <P> tag, then the text is set in the default 14-point type. If you use the CLASS attribute, the paragraph is set in the class that you specify.

There's one other point that you should notice in Figure 8-2. The heading, which is the highest level <H1> tag, would normally be presented in 24-point bold text. Instead, it appears in 14-point type. Why? Because all the body text is set to 14-point type in the BODY style, and all headings inherit from that style. Notice that this example doesn't set the font to regular (instead of bold or italic), so the heading is still bold, as it would be normally; it's just the size, which you set explicitly, that is affected. This result is a direct effect of the cascading principle of style sheets (which you'll read more about in the next section). You should keep this effect in mind when creating styles; otherwise you may get results that surprise you.

Handling Exceptions With ID

The ID attribute lets you assign a unique value to an element. You can use the ID value to set properties for elements that are exceptions to existing assigned styles. For example, you may want to use the ID attribute to change one style of several styles set using the CLASS attribute. This way you don't have to create a new style for elements that share properties but have one or more different properties. To add the ID attribute, start with a pound sign and then specify the name you want to use for the style. The following example creates an ID named fire that specifies the color of text is red:

```
#fire color: red
```

If you had a style of 16-point, blue font named normal, adding the ID attribute named fire changes the text from blue to red:

```
<STYLE TYPE="text/css">
normal  {font-size: 16; color: blue}
#fire   {color: red}
</STYLE>
<P CLASS="normal">Normal text is 16-point blue.</P>
<P CLASS="normal" ID="fire">This text is 16-point red.</P>
```

Understanding Cascading & Inheritance

Cascading Style Sheets take the process of applying styles a step further. The styles defined by a series of style sheets *cascade* between multiple definitions within the same selector. If the rules don't conflict, the last definition of a style augments any previous style for that selector. If they do conflict, the last rule takes precedence.

Traditionally, a browser displays HTML tags according to a standard set of rules, with some features of the display set by the user. For example, a paragraph tag, <P>, tells the browser that the following text is a paragraph—it's been up to the browser to determine exactly what that means. Each browser may do a somewhat different display for this tag based on how the browser is designed and how the user has set various options. While the <P> tag determines the paragraph's position, the text that makes up the paragraph is displayed in the font and at the size specified in the browser's preferences, which are under the user's control. So the user decides whether to use a serif or sans-serif font, for example, and what color to use for the text. Style rules, whether embedded in style sheets or inserted into your HTML text, allow you, as the author of a Web page, to establish how your pages will look on the viewer's browser.

Inheriting Styles

Styles can be inherited throughout a document. Each tag in a document follows a chain of inheritance as part of the HTML structure. For example, the text in your document is formatted according to the style of the tag applied to it, like a <P> tag, but it also inherits any style that you provided in the <BODY> tag. In this way, you can set a global format for your documents once and then only override that standard in cases where you need to vary the style. Let's look at an example of how this might be coded:

```
<STYLE TYPE="text/css">
   BODY {background: white; color: black; font-size: 12pt}
   H1 {font-size: 24pt; color: green}
   UL {font-size: 10pt; font-style: italic}
</STYLE>
```

TIP *We noted earlier in the book that using RGB color values is more accurate than assigning colors by name and recommended that you use hexadecimal RGB settings whenever possible. The color specification here does allow you to use RGB color settings. However, to make these examples easier to follow, we have used the standard color names rather than hexadecimal RGB values. If these were pages for publication, we'd still recommend that you use RGB values for all the reasons we gave earlier.*

In this example, all the body text, such as the text within the <P> tags, will be in a 12-point regular face font and will be displayed in black against a white background. However, heading text inside a <H1> tag will be in green and 24 points but will still be regular font face against a white background, which is inherited from the BODY style. On the other hand, any text inside a <UL> tag will be black against a white background—inherited from the BODY style—but will be 10-point italic.

In the same way, if you set a style for a list in the <UL> tag, then that style applies to all the list elements used in the tag unless you specify another style. If you don't set a specific style for a tag, it will inherit its default style from its parent tag, if any, or from the <BODY> tag.

Importing Style Sheets

The @import option for importing style sheets has not, at this writing, been implemented in either Navigator 4 or Internet Explorer 4. However, by the time you read this, one or both of these browsers may have implemented some or all of the @import capabilities for handling style sheets. To keep you informed for future versions, we want to discuss importing style sheets and some of the important differences between importing and linking style sheets.

Like linking to a style sheet, importing a style sheet lets you change the styles in multiple Web pages. But unlike linking to a style sheet, where style sheets are linked from within the page, imported style sheets are included from within another external style sheet. You import a style sheet by referring to it within another style sheet.

To import a style sheet, you include @import url and enclose the name of the style sheet you want to import in parentheses. You can add the @import command as a document-level style definition, or you can nest it in an existing style sheet. The following example imports a Cascading Style Sheet named brochure.css into an HTML document linked to the style sheet named master.css:

```
<LINK REL=STYLESHEET HREF=master.css TYPE=text/css>
BODY {font-size: 14pt}
@import url(brochure.css)
```

You can import multiple style sheets by adding other import lines. There is a major difference in how imported style sheets and linked style sheets handle styles. If you use two or more <LINK> tags, the browser only pays attention to the style sheet referenced in the last <LINK> tag. (There's a good chance that later releases will provide a list of the linked style sheets, allowing the reader to choose which style sheet to use to format the page.) By using the @import command, you combine, rather than replace, styles. If you import more than one style sheet, all the unique styles are used to form a single set of styles for the page. If a style is defined in more than one style sheet, the definitions in the last imported style sheet take precedence.

Style Wars

Style sheets can be applied to a page from several sources. As you have already seen, there are several choices for adding style information to your Web documents. Moreover, you may have numerous styles applied to a document. In addition, the user or viewer can set style choices in their browser to affect how information is presented whether you have set a style or not. For example, someone with a visual disability may set the fonts in their browser to display at a large point size for easier reading. Finally, every browser has built into it a comprehensive set of style rules covering every tag, ensuring that every tag will have some default style so that it can be displayed. With all these methods of specifying styles, you may wonder how the browser chooses a style or styles to apply to a page.

In a word: cascading. All of the various styles that are provided for a document using all of these methods are sorted and combined by the browser to create a single, comprehensive, internal style sheet. When styles conflict, the browser uses any specific style sheet definitions and the inheritance mechanism outlined earlier and collects all the style rules that apply to a given tag. Then the rules are sorted according to a weight that is established by the importance of the rule. A rule's importance is based on the following factors:

- **An explicit weight to make it sort first.** The "!important" attribute gives a rule higher priority in the weighting mechanism.

- **Where did the rule originate?** The priority order for rules is as follows: designer's rules first, user's rules second, browser default rules last.

- **How specific the rule is.** As you read earlier, the more specific a rule, the higher its priority.

- **In what order the rules were presented.** The most recent rule has the highest priority. For priority purposes, any rules in an external style sheet are considered to come before any defined within a document.

After collection and sorting, the most important rule—the one with the highest priority—is applied. This process of collecting, sorting, and applying the rules is collectively known as *cascading*, since the rules cascade down, one after the other.

Understanding Style Properties

Once you have decided to use styles and how you want to implement them, you need to create some style rules. As you already learned, style rules consist of a property and a value. In this section, you will learn about the properties that you can use in creating styles and what values can be used with each property.

We won't cover all the possible combinations of properties here. We could easily spend several times the length of this chapter and still not cover all the intriguing or useful possibilities. Instead, we will cover what we feel are the most important and valuable properties—the ones you'll want to set time and time again. Appendix B gives you the complete set of Cascading Style Sheet properties. Once you've finished this chapter, you should be able to use that list to construct a style sheet for any type of page your design requires.

Setting Sizes in STYLE Properties

As you begin using the various style properties, you'll see that there are a number of them that allow you to specify various sizes. For convenience, we are going to discuss all of the various size measures.

By their nature, sizes are a combination of a numeric value and a unit designation. The number used can be a whole number or a decimal fraction; you can also use negative numbers where that makes sense—for example, you can use negative numbers for setting margins but not for font sizes. The unit designations are all two-letter abbreviations, with no period and no space between the numeric value and the unit abbreviation. For example, you could use any of the following to set a margin: 1.5in, 22.33mm, 12pt, -0.5cm, and so on. Table 8-1 shows you a list of the available measurement units you can use in style sheets.

Abbreviation	Measurement
in	inch
mm	millimeter
cm	centimeter
pt	point (72 points = 1 inch)
pc	pica (6 picas = 1 inch; 12 points = 1 pica)
em	the point size of the current font
ex	the x-height of the current font
px	pixel

Table 8-1: Units of measurement and their abbreviations used in style sheets.

Logically, these units can be grouped into the following three categories:

- Absolute measures—in, mm, cm, pt, and pc
- Relative measures—em and ex
- Device-dependent measure—px

Absolute measures are units that are independent of the computer system, the browser, and all the other elements on the page: one inch is one inch, regardless of what system you're running. *Relative measures* are units that are relative to the current font being used in the system. The *device-dependent measure* is a unit that depends on the resolution of the current display device: one pixel will vary in size depending on the system and the type of output device.

It's usually best to work with relative measures. With relative measures, you can ensure that your pages will display as you want them to even if the user has selected a very large or small font size and even if the browser's window is quite large or quite small. Using absolute units, which may seem more intuitive, can cause some problems. For example, someone displaying a page on a small notebook or palm-sized computer may not have enough room to display a complete page if you have set margins to 1.5 inches on both sides of your text. In such cases, the browser makes a "best-effort" to display your page correctly, but you can't be sure of the result. On the other hand, if you use relative units, the entire margin can be scaled to match the font size, which will probably give you a better-looking result.

The pixel measure can be ambiguous. For example, if the output is on a high-resolution device (a 600 dpi laser printer, for instance), the browser will scale a pixel measure so that a line specified as one pixel, for example, may display as four actual pixels. Generally, that's what you want, as one pixel on the screen is much larger than one pixel on the printer. However, it does mean that you can't be sure exactly what you'll get when you specify pixels as a measurement unit. The major advantage of using pixels for a measure is that you can be quite precise about the relative size of various items. For example, a four-pixel border will always be twice the size of a two-pixel border, while a four-point border may not be precisely twice the size of a two-point border. This occurs because the browser must round any other measurements into pixels for display, and four points may round to five pixels while two points comes out to two pixels.

All style sheet properties that accept a length value, such as font-size, accept any of these measurement units. Also, as mentioned earlier, most of them, where appropriate, allow you to use integer and decimal fractions and both positive and negative values for the numeric portion of the length. Many style sheet properties also provide two additional types of measurement: percentages and keywords. You have already seen an example of the keyword type of measurements in the use of "small," "medium," and "large" in the font-size property. Wherever a property accepts keywords, we will define what those are and what they mean.

The percentage values are a little harder to understand. When you specify a percentage value for a property, you are specifying that the property be that percentage of its parent's property. For example, if you specify that the font-size is 125%, you are saying that the font used for this style should be 25% larger than whatever font is being used currently. You can immediately see how useful this can be. If you have a style that you wish to apply to several different types of tags—a special emphasis, for example—set the font size relative to the other text, and it will work no matter what size the current text may be. The style will work exactly the same whether the current font is 10 points or 36 points. In most cases, all the properties that accept a length will also allow you to use a percentage. If a property does not accept percentages along with length values, we will tell you that explicitly.

In general, the use of relative measures—em and ex—and percentages will make the most flexible page formats because the styles will be able to match any browser settings. While setting relative sizes may not be easy at first, in the long run you will find that styles constructed using relative measures are safer for displaying your pages on screens with different resolution settings than styles constructed with absolute measures.

Borders, Padding & Bounding Boxes

Styles in CSS are built around the principle of the bounding box. Figure 8-3 shows you the major elements of a CSS positioning box around an HTML element. Figure 8-3 also shows a text element so you can see how the borders padding and bounding boxes are related to positioning elements on a page.

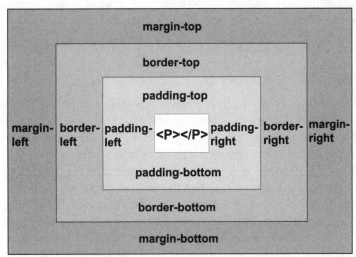

Figure 8-3: You can position an element using a style sheet by changing the borders, padding, and bounding box settings.

The element itself is enclosed in a bounding box, which is determined by the browser for the type of the element and the bounding box of its parent. Around that is a padding area, which you can set with a style. Around the padding is a border area, which you can make visible and set to display as various types of border. Finally, around the border is the margin, which defines how far away the element will be from the bounding box of its parent. Using these three properties, you can take fairly effective control of the positioning of any block-level element.

Selecting & Using Fonts

Surely the first and most important aspect that style sheets bring to the Web is the ability to set the appearance of the text on your pages. Although there have been some initial efforts to bring this feature to the Web before Cascading Style Sheets were available—like the <FONT> tag—CSS gives you more flexibility and options for controlling the type used by a browser than any previous method does. While CSS doesn't yet provide the complete control for setting type that print designers have come to expect, it is a long step in that direction and a major improvement in the design of Web documents.

Traditionally, a *font* is defined as a set of type—meaning alphabetic characters and variants, numbers, and punctuation symbols—in a single design, size, style, and weight. The advent of electronic fonts, however, has eliminated size as a constraint since electronic fonts can be readily scaled to any desired size, so that the definition of a font now covers only design, style, and weight. A font, therefore, gives specific form to each letter and character as it is displayed on a screen or printed on an output medium.

Fonts as Graphic Elements

Before we examine all the technical aspects of fonts and font selection in style sheets, let's discuss type as a graphic object. Many people, including the originators of the World Wide Web, have never thought of text as a graphic element; they naturally, but incorrectly, think of type as different from images or other artwork because type is used to convey words rather than pictures. Actually, the shape of letters is one of the most important graphic elements.

Originally, a font specified a size of type: for example, Times Roman 12 point and Times Roman 14 point were two different fonts. As a result, typesetters used *font* to refer to a single size of type and *typeface* to refer to a complete collection of fonts, all in one style and weight but in multiple sizes. Since electronic fonts have eliminated size as part of the definition of a font, a typeface is now, for all practical purposes, synonymous with a font.

The selection of a good typeface is an important part of page makeup and graphic design. The precise shape of each character in a well-designed typeface is a small work of art—an object of intricate graphic design. A good typeface must be clear and legible and often provides a certain stress or emphasis as well. Figure 8-4 shows how using a typeface with style sheets can make the page more visually appealing than pages using the default browser fonts.

Figure 8-4: Using fonts as a graphic element with style sheets can make a page more visually appealing than pages using the default browser fonts.

TIP

If you are not familiar with the world of printing and typesetting, it may surprise you to learn that fonts are not public property. Although the form of letters themselves cannot be owned by anyone, the precise electronic format and the name of a specific typeface can be, and usually is, owned by the designer. This is certainly appropriate because creating a typeface that is both beautiful and legible is a real design challenge and a work of significant artistic merit. However, the fact that typefaces are intellectual property complicates using them on the World Wide Web. We will discuss these complications when we discuss selecting fonts in style sheets later in this chapter. The important point to remember when we get into that discussion is that fonts are property, like images, and cannot be simply copied from one system to another without some controls.

What's a Glyph?

A font, as defined earlier, is a collection of shapes in a single design, style, and weight. To avoid confusion about the meaning of the word *character*, each element in a font is often referred to as a *glyph*. This covers alphabetic characters (a, b, c, and so on), numeric characters (1, 2, 3, and so on), punctuation marks (like commas and semicolons), and special characters (@ and $, for example). There are three reasons for using the word *glyph* rather than *character*. First, some fonts don't actually have any alphabetic or numeric characters; they are shapes or symbols used for purposes other than writing. For example, some fonts consist of shapes that are appropriate for setting musical scores. Second, some fonts include special characters, such as ligatures, which combine two letters into a single glyph. Finally, in some languages and in some types of font, the same character may require different glyphs depending on its position in a sentence or word.

Font Families

The most common way to classify fonts is by typeface design. A collection of fonts of the same typeface but representing different weights and styles is called a *font family*. Such font families have names, like Helvetica and Times Roman. Font families can be further organized into groups based on common design elements, like serif and sans-serif fonts. *Serifs* are small, thin lines that finish off the major parts of characters. The effect is similar to that of letters drawn with a calligraphic pen. These lines form a natural base and help the eye follow a line of text across a page; for that reason, serif fonts are usually preferred for setting large amounts of text. As you might guess, *sans-serif* means that the glyphs in the font don't have serifs. This gives a clean, strong look, which is suitable for headlines and short lines of text. Times Roman is a typical serif font, and Helvetica and Arial are typical sans-serif fonts. Figure 8-5 shows you the difference between serif and sans-serif fonts.

Times   Times New Roman

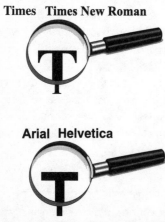

Arial   Helvetica

Figure 8-5: Times Roman is a serif font, while Helvetica and Arial are sans-serif fonts.

Monospaced vs. Proportional Fonts

Fonts vary in several characteristics within a family. The first and most important difference is variation in size. Glyphs in a font have both height and width. The width of a font is called the *pitch*. Fonts that have glyphs that are all the same width are called *monospaced* or *fixed pitch* fonts. In such a font, the letters *I* and *W*, for example, will take up the same space in a line of text. However, most quality fonts vary the width of glyphs based on the width of the character, so that *W* takes up more space on a line than *I*. These fonts are called *variable pitch* or *proportional* fonts. Figure 8-6 shows you a line of type displayed in both a monospaced and a proportional font.

Times New Roman is a proportional font.

`Courier New is a Monospaced font.`

Figure 8-6: Monospaced fonts require more room than proportional fonts for the same text.

Measuring Fonts

The height of a font is measured in points. A *point* is a traditional typesetter's measure and is approximately 1/72 of an inch. The point size is the distance required between two lines of type to keep the tops of the tallest letters (like *l*) on the bottom line from touching the bottoms of the letters on the upper line that descend below the line (like *p*). The *x-height* of a font is the size of the body of a lowercase letter (like *x*). Notice that the x-height of a font is not directly related to the point size; that is, you cannot simply measure the x-height and find out the size of the font. Because different typefaces have different x-heights, different typefaces at the same point size may appear smaller or larger than one another. The *leading* of a paragraph of text is the amount of space between the baselines of two successive lines of text. Normally, the leading will be at least the same as the font size.

Font Weight

The *weight* of a font is how heavy or light the strokes that make up the font's glyphs are. Besides heavy and light, weights have a variety of other names, like Bold and DemiBold. The essential ingredient is how dark or light the characters appear when they are displayed. In addition, many fonts come in different styles. Other than the normal, or *roman* style, the most common style is *italic*, where the strokes that make up the characters are slanted and curved to look like handwriting. Some font families do not have an italic style; instead, they have an *oblique* style. The difference is that an italic style is a different design for the type, while an oblique style is simply the roman style slanted. In Web browsers, bold weight fonts are traditionally used for the <STRONG> tag, while the italic or oblique style of a font is used for the <EM> tag. Finally, some fonts have only one style. For example, *cursive* fonts are designed to imitate handwriting exclusively and do not have a roman style. In the same way, many decorative, or *fantasy,* fonts only come in a single unusual style. Such fonts are only used for decorative or display purposes, like headlines, names, and so on. Figure 8-7 shows you examples of standard fonts in bold and regular weights and in italic and oblique styles.

Arial Regular
Arial Italic
Arial Bold
Arial Bold Italic

Helvetica Regular
Helvetica Oblique
Helvetica Bold
Helvetica Bold Oblique

Times New Roman Regular
Times New Roman Italic
Times New Roman Bold
Times New Roman Bold Italic

Times Roman
Times Italic
Times Bold
Times Bold Italic

Figure 8-7: Fonts usually offer different weights and styles within one family.

Specifying Fonts by Name & Type

You set fonts in a style sheet by setting the font-family property. The following line shows how to insert this into your style rules:

```
P {font-family: "Helvetica"}
```

You can specify a font either by specifying the font name or by using a generic font family keyword. The allowable generic keywords are shown in Table 8-2.

Keyword Value	Description
serif	Browser can choose any serif font available on the system.
sans-serif	Browser can choose any sans-serif font available on the system.
monospace	Browser can choose any monospace font available on the system.
cursive	Browser can choose any cursive font available on the system.
fantasy	Browser can choose any decorative font available on the system.

Table 8-2: The generic font families used for the font-family property.

If you use a generic keyword, the browser is allowed to select any font installed on the system that falls into the specified category. In general, browsers have a specific set of default fonts for each keyword and select one that is installed on the current system.

TIP *Although logically every font must fall into one of these five generic families, you don't want to rely too heavily on either you or the browser always being able to categorize all installed fonts into these categories. Our experience suggests that the browser is most likely to be able to find a serif or sans-serif font if one is installed and usually can find a monospace font as well. However, selecting a default cursive or fantasy font is much more unlikely. Even if fonts belonging to each of these families are installed, the browser may not be able to determine which of the available fonts fall into the requested category and so will fall back on using the default font—usually Times Roman or some variant.*

Note that we always use the quotation marks around font names in code. This isn't strictly necessary; as long as the font name doesn't have any spaces in it—as, for example, Times Roman does—then the browser should be able to tell the font name whether you use quotes or not. However, our experience is that some versions of some browsers seem to have difficulty with font names if they are not in quotes. Moreover, since some font names must be in quotes, it's best to make it a habit and put all font names in quotes for ease of use and recognition.

Another important issue here is that the browser will use exactly the name that you give it to match to the list of available fonts on the system. So, for example, if you specify "Times Roman" and the font is installed on your system as Times, the browser probably won't find the font. Even more important, the fonts Times and Times New Roman, although virtually identical in appearance, are not the same name and not the same font, and the browser that has one installed will not substitute it if you request the other.

TIP

If you have trouble figuring out exactly what name to use for a font that you have installed on your system, here's a quick trick to find out what it should be called. Most HTML editors, including FrontPage and Communicator, allow you to set fonts using a simple menu command. Although they use the <FONT FACE="name"> tag to set the font, the name used there is the same one that you need to insert in your style sheet. To find out a font name, follow these steps:

1. *Make a simple page with just one or two lines of text on it.*

2. *Select the text in your editor and set the font using the font menu.*

3. *Save the page.*

4. *Open the page in a text editor (or display the page as raw HTML if your editor offers that option) and see what name the editor used to apply the font.*

▼ **Fonts on the Web**

This naming confusion takes us directly to the heart of the problem of using fonts on the Web. Since fonts are intellectual property, you have to pay to get a copy of a font for your use. This won't come as a surprise to most designers, who have been purchasing fonts from vendors like Adobe and Bitstream for a long time. When you buy an electronic font, you usually get a license to use the font for any type of display: printing, screen display, or any other standard use. What you *cannot* do is reproduce the font and redistribute it to anyone else for their use. For most common use, this isn't a problem—the person reading a page can't copy the font and reuse it.

On the Web, however, this becomes a problem. If you want to use a specific font to display your text on a Web page, the reader, as well as the author, must have an electronic copy of the font for display. If you include the font in the document, then there is a possibility that the reader would be able to remove the font and reuse it. In fact, this is one of the problems of using images on the Web, because the same thing can happen. For font use, at the moment, the restriction is that the reader must have independently purchased and installed the font to use it. For this reason, most Web pages today stick to fonts that come bundled with common operating systems—fonts like Times Roman, Helvetica, Arial, Courier, and so on.

Netscape and Bitstream, a major font developer, have joined to create and promulgate the new, TrueDoc standard for fonts. Netscape has incorporated it into its latest browser, which allows you to create links to fonts for use in your

➡

documents. The linked fonts are loaded with the document and stored in the browser's cache, in a fashion similar to how images are handled. Since the fonts are not directly accessible, there is no concern about their misuse. However, you must purchase a special tool to create the necessary font files, and at present, the number of fonts available in this format is limited. Also, it requires additional download time to get the fonts loaded onto the client system, which may have a performance impact for some users.

As you might expect, Microsoft has approached the problem from a somewhat different viewpoint. Microsoft has joined forces with Adobe and is working on a format called OpenType. OpenType isn't yet implemented in Internet Explorer. In the meantime, Microsoft is giving away and installing a standard set of fonts whenever Internet Explorer is installed. These fonts include Arial Black, Comic Sans MS, Georgia, Impact, and Veranda. Two other fonts, Trebuchet and Webdings, are available for Windows at Microsoft's Web site. You can check for new fonts at http://www.microsoft.com/typography/fontpack/win.htm. In this way, you can easily create a page for viewing in Internet Explorer that contains only the standard fonts. As you can see, there are several approaches toward this issue in the works. If we want to progress beyond the current state of controlled anarchy, we need to have some way to transmit fonts with Web documents as required. Fortunately, the W3C and several major browser and font vendors, including Adobe, Bitstream, Microsoft, and Netscape, are all working on this issue. We can expect some definitive solution to emerge in the near future.

How Font Matching Works

Obviously, every font is not installed on every computer system. So the obvious question is how to specify your font requests in a way that makes it most likely that the browser will be able to satisfy you, at least to some extent. One way is to use generic font families in your font specifications.

If you use a generic font family designation, the browser may choose any font installed on the system that matches the designation. Therefore, generic fonts are an excellent fallback when a named font is not available. Helvetica is a common font that is installed on most computer systems; for example, it is standard on all Macintosh systems. When Helvetica isn't available, Arial, which is a similar, sans-serif font standard on all Windows systems, is usually installed. However, some platforms may not have either. So, one way to specify a font selection would be the following line of code:

```
P {font-family: "Helvetica", "Arial", sans-serif}
```

A list of multiple font choices like this is called a *font set*. The font set tells the browser that your first choice of fonts for the paragraph tag is Helvetica. If that isn't available, you'd like to use Arial. Finally, if neither is available, you'd like to use any sans-serif font that's installed on the system. If the browser still can't satisfy your request—if the output system were a Teletype, for example, that doesn't support multiple fonts—then the browser will use any available font. This strategy gives you the best chance that your pages will look more or less like you designed them.

TIP *If you want to apply this technique to unusual fonts, you may experience some problem in determining which family a font belongs to. It's pretty easy to tell if a font is monospace, but deciding whether a specific font falls into the fantasy font family or one of the other families, for example, is something of a guessing game. If you are unsure about a font's classification, the best way to distinguish whether it's a fantasy font is whether it has a distinct set of lowercase letters—regular fonts always will, while most fantasy fonts won't.*

There are some times, however, when you should use a generic family name by itself instead of a font set. For example, when designers specify the Courier font, it's usually because they want a monospaced font, and Courier is the most widely installed monospaced font. But often you don't care which font is used as long as it's monospaced. So if you use the generic family name "monospace" in your style sheet rather than calling out Courier explicitly, the browser can use whatever the default monospaced font is, which may display better on the target system than Courier even if Courier is installed. On a Macintosh, for example, Monaco is a monospaced font that is designed for best display on the screen. If Monaco was available, you'd prefer the browser to choose it if possible.

Setting the Font Size

You set the size of your font by using the font-size property as shown in the following example:

```
P {font-family: "Helvetica"; font-size: 12pt}
```

As you can see, you can set font sizes using standard point measurements. However, the font-size property also allows you to set sizes in several other ways. Setting physical sizes, like points, may not be the best way to display your pages because display on different browsers can cause your pages to look different and because different systems may not be able to render all point sizes of fonts clearly on the screen. In many cases, you will be better served by using keywords to specify absolute or relative sizes.

Absolute sizes are sizes fixed by the browser. The browser computes and maintains a table of font sizes. The absolute sizes are expressed in keywords, which represent an index into this table. The absolute size keywords are as follows:

- xx-small
- x-small
- small
- medium
- large
- x-large
- xx-large

Listing 8-4 shows you a set of the absolute sizes attached to the various heading tags, but in reverse order. The xx-small size is omitted because it's too small to display well onscreen. This page displays as shown in Figure 8-8.

Listing 8-4

```
<HTML>
<HEAD>
<TITLE>CSS Absolute Size Keywords</TITLE>
<STYLE TYPE="text/css">
    BODY {background: white; color: black}
    H1 {font-size: x-small}
    H2 {font-size: small}
    H3 {font-size: medium}
    H4 {font-size: large}
    H5 {font-size: x-large}
    H6 {font-size: xx-large}
</STYLE>
</HEAD>
<BODY>
<H1>Font size x-small</H1>
<H2>Font size small</H2>
<H3>Font size medium</H3>
<H4>Font size large</H4>
<H5>Font size x-large</H5>
<H6>Font size xx-large</H6>
</BODY>
</HTML>
```

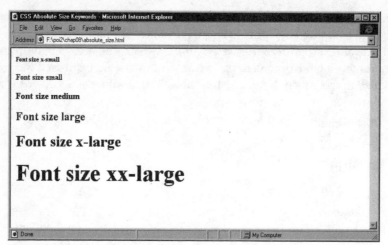

Figure 8-8: The absolute size keywords provide a regular progression of text sizes based on your browser.

The W3C specification recommends that each size be 1.5 times the next lower size; so, for example, x-large would be 1.5 times the size of large, and large would in turn be 1.5 times the size of medium, and so on. On that basis, x-large would be 2.25 times as large as medium (1.5 x 1.5). This is wonderfully mathematical, but totally impractical. In reality, that would mean that if the browser were using a 12-point font for medium, the x-large would be 27 points and xx-large would be 40.5 points. Since odd point sizes don't display well onscreen and fractional sizes are generally totally useless and impractical, the actual table created by your browser will probably not adhere to this rule. You should test any absolute sizes you use on several browsers and different systems to see how they display. What you can be sure of, however, is that the sizes will be correctly progressive in all systems, which may be all you need to ensure for certain types of information.

You can also set the font-size property using relative size keywords. There are two relative size keywords: larger and smaller. The keywords are interpreted by the browser relative to the table of font sizes used for the absolute sizes and the size of the parent element of the current text. For example, suppose you have the following styles set:

```
<STYLE>
   BODY {font-size: large}
   H2 {font-size: larger}
   UL {font-size: smaller}
</STYLE>
```

These styles tell the browser to display the body text in whatever point size is set for the *large* keyword. Headings with the <H2> tag will display larger than this—based on the previous discussion, you know that they will be x-large. In the same way, all the text in a <UL> tag will be set smaller than the body text— again, using the table, this will be medium. If you change the font size for the BODY style to medium, then all the other rules will automatically change; in this case, <H2> would become large and <UL> would become small.

Setting the Font Style

The font-style property is one of the easiest properties to understand and use. Here's a simple example of how to set the style:

```
H3 {font-style: italic}
```

Basically, there are three possible font styles: regular, oblique, and italic. As you read earlier, the difference between italic and oblique is that italic is a different design for a font, while oblique is simply the roman or normal version of the font slanted. However, most readers don't make these subtle distinctions, and most browsers don't either. If you want a slanted font, use "font-style: italic" and forget about oblique. The browser will give you an italic version of the font if there is one and will substitute the oblique version if no italic version exists. This is exactly what most word processing programs do if you select Italic from a Font menu.

Setting the Font Weight

Setting the font-weight can be a little more complex, but the simplest version is just as easy as the font-style, as you can see in this example:

```
H3 {font-weight: bold}
```

The complications come in because font-weight can be specified in two different ways: by using keywords like bold or by using absolute values ranging from 100 to 900. You can specify four different weights with the font-weight keyword:

- normal
- bold
- bolder
- lighter

As you would expect, *lighter* is lighter than *normal*, while *bold* is heavier, and *bolder* is the heaviest. Note that many font families either are not available in all weights or all the weights may not be installed on a system. As a result, you can only count on the "normal" and "bold" for most font families and using the other two keywords may simply get you the normal or bold version.

For similar reasons, the nine absolute values, ranging from 100 (the lightest) to 900 (the heaviest), are much less useful. In this range, 400 is equivalent to the *normal* keyword and 700 is equivalent to the *bold* keyword. If you use the other values, you are likely to get the same results if there aren't any fonts available to match these subtle changes in weight. If a family includes only normal and bold fonts, the range from 100 to 500 selects the normal font, while 600 and above selects the bold version.

TIP *Having made that point, we should also note that some systems, particularly designers' systems, might support all of these weights. The Adobe Type Manager (ATM) program is capable of synthesizing many more weights than this when coupled with a Multiple Master font. So, if you know or suspect that your audience is a sophisticated one, and that they have some specific Multiple Master font or fonts installed, then all these weights may be useful to you.*

Setting Text in Small Capital Letters

CSS also includes a font-variant property that has two keywords: *normal* and *small-caps*. If you set this property, you are requesting that the text be displayed in small capitals. Again, this can lead to a lot of complications. First of all, small capitals, like italic, are a variant of a font, not simply smaller capital letters. Only a few expert-quality fonts have this variant, and only a few systems are likely to have them installed. If the browser is clever, it may synthesize small capitals by displaying the existing font capitals at about 80 percent of the current point size—this is a good approximation of the small capitals for many serif fonts. However, at this time no browser supports small caps, and as a practical matter, use of this property is unlikely to work as you would want.

In fact, you don't need to set each of these properties individually. The font property allows you to set all of them in one style. For example, the following two lines of code are exactly identical—if one works, the other will too:

```
H3 {font-family: "Helvetica", sans-serif; font-style: italic; font-size:
24pt; font-weight: bold}
   H3 {font: bold italic 24pt "Helvetica", sans-serif}
```

As you can see, the second line is much easier to read and understand than the first. For practical purposes, using the font property in place of a series of the other properties is a good move.

Controlling Layout

The process of setting style elements other than fonts begins with an understanding of how an HTML page is laid out. All HTML tags define elements on the page that are divided into three categories: invisible, inline, and block-level. An *invisible* element is one defined by a tag like <BODY> or <HTML>; it is used by the browser, but it's not visible in the display of the page. An *inline* element is defined by a tag like <EM> or <A> and does not affect the structure of the page, although it may affect how the page is displayed. Finally, a *block-level* element is defined by a tag like <P>, <H1>, or <IMG> and represents a complete structural element on the page that the browser uses for both layout and display.

Basically, all block-level HTML tags use a bounding box to place the element. You may already be familiar with bounding boxes from various page layout programs or from working with images in HTML—the WIDTH and HEIGHT attributes define the bounding box of an image on an HTML page, for example. The bounding box for a block of text may be a little harder to visualize. Basically, a *bounding box* for any element is the imaginary rectangle drawn around the element that completely encloses all marks on the page made by that element. Figure 8-3, shown earlier in this chapter, shows a bounding box for a block of text.

Your browser positions elements on the page according to their bounding boxes. That's why, for example, you can speed up the display of your pages by using the WIDTH and HEIGHT attributes—they allow the browser to set up the necessary bounding box for the image before downloading it.

You can nest bounding boxes for HTML elements. For example, when you have a table, the table and table row definitions set up a series of cells, which are essentially bounding boxes, for the display of text and images. Then the bounding box of a block of text within a table row is confined by the dimensions of the bounding box of its individual cell.

In the absence of any other HTML element, the default bounding box for an HTML page is the size of the browser's display window. As you already know, images are displayed within the bounding box and defined by the WIDTH and HEIGHT attributes, if those have been set, or at the natural size of the image. Text, on the other hand, will expand to the size of the bounding box of its parent element; if there isn't any other boundary, it will expand to fill the browser's display area. Keep these ideas in mind as you plan your layout with CSS styles.

Controlling Margins

The four margin properties (margin-top, margin-bottom, margin-left, and margin-right) let you specify margin settings for your pages. You'll probably use the margin-left and margin-right properties more often than margin-top or margin-bottom. Listing 8-5 shows an example of left and right margin settings for a series of paragraphs. This page displays as shown in Figure 8-9. (The additional Latin text shown in Figure 8-9 and the remaining figures have been omitted from the listing to save space.)

Listing 8-5

```
<HTML>
<HEAD>
<HEAD>
<TITLE>Margin Style Example</TITLE>
<STYLE TYPE="text/css">
    BODY {background: white; color: black; margin-left: 15%}
    H1 {font: 24pt "Arial"}
    P.normal {font-size: 12pt}
    P.quote {font-size: 12pt; margin-left: 4em; margin-right: 4em}
    P.outdent {font-size: 12pt; margin-left: -2em}
</STYLE>
</HEAD>

<BODY>
<H1>A Margin Display</H1>
<P CLASS="normal">This paragraph has the normal margin settings. Lorem ipsum
dolor ...</P>
<P CLASS="quote">This paragraph has additional margins on both left and
right. Lorem ipsum dolor ...</P>
<P CLASS="outdent">This paragraph extends out to the left of the standard
text. Lorem ipsum dolor ...</P>
<IMG SRC="heather_small.jpg" ALT="Heather " ALIGN=LEFT WIDTH="96"
HEIGHT="115">
<P CLASS="normal">This paragraph has the normal margin settings and displays
next to an image. Lorem ipsum dolor ...</P>
</BODY>
</BODY>
</HTML>
```

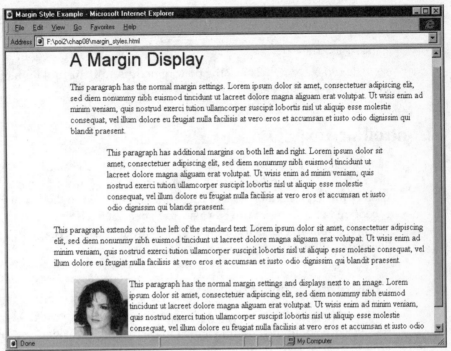

Figure 8-9: You can adjust both the left and right margins for your pages.

If you display this page in your browser, notice how the main margin, which is used for the heading and the normal paragraph text, expands and contracts as you resize the browser's display window. On the other hand, the internal offsets used for the other two paragraphs remain fixed; they are set relative to the font size, not to the browser window. Also, as you see, the margin settings are effective for both text and images. Because images have a fixed size, percentage margins are always best for setting margins for a page containing both text and graphics.

You can set all four margins at once using the margin property. The margin property takes four numbers, corresponding to the top, right, bottom, and left margins respectively. For example, the code:

```
P {margin: 2em 2em 1em 4em}
```

sets the top and right margins to 2 ems, the bottom margin to 1 em, and the left margin to 4 ems. You don't need to specify all of the margin values, either. If you use only one value, it's applied to all the margins. If you use two or three values, the missing value(s) are supplied by the opposite margin. For example, the code:

```
P {margin: 2em 4em}
```

sets the top and bottom margins to 2 ems and the right and left margins to 4 ems. And the code:

```
P {margin: 2em 4em 1em}
```

sets the top margin to 2 ems, the bottom margin to 1 em, and both the right and left margins to 4 ems.

Controlling Text

Margins control the outer space for the entire page. CSS also includes properties to indent the first line of text, change the leading (intra-line spacing), and change the alignment of lines of text, so text is aligned to the left or right or it is centered on the page. You can also add special effects to text, such as underlining it or placing lines through it. The following sections explain the most common properties for controlling text.

Controlling Indentation

Besides changing the margins of your pages, you can also use the text-indent property to indent the first line of text in each paragraph. Listing 8-6 shows how you can specify both regular and hanging indents. This page displays as shown in Figure 8-10.

Listing 8-6

```
<HTML>
<HEAD>
<TITLE>Indent Style Example</TITLE>
<STYLE TYPE="text/css">
   BODY {background: white; color: black; margin-left: 15%}
   H1 {font: 24pt "Arial"}
   P.indented {font-size: 12pt; text-indent: 4em}
   P.hanging {font-size: 12pt; text-indent: -2em}
</STYLE>
</HEAD>

<BODY>
<H1>Indentation Display</H1>
<P>The first line of this paragraph has no indentation. Lorem ipsum ...</P>
<P CLASS="indented">The first line of this paragraph is indented. Lorem
ipsum ...</P>
<P CLASS="hanging">The first line of this paragraph has a hanging indent, so
that it extends to the left of the rest of the text. Lorem ipsum ...</P>
</BODY>
</HTML>
```

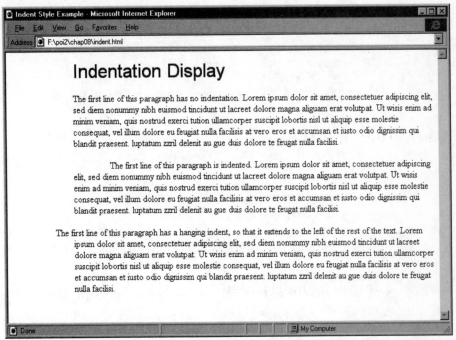

Figure 8-10: You can indent the first line of text in a paragraph or make it a hanging indent.

If you use a percentage value with the text-indent property, the percentage is relative to the paragraph's width. This means that the amount of indentation changes as the browser window is resized. This may not give the effect that you expected (for example, on a wide-screen display, the indentation might look disproportionately large).

The text-indent property is applied to the first line of a paragraph only. That means that, if you divide your text up using <BR> tags, the lines following the <BR> will not be indented even if the initial line of the paragraph is indented. Again, this may or may not be what you want. As always, check your code in several browsers and with several systems.

Controlling Spacing Between Lines

You can also control the spacing between lines of your text (which is called the leading) by using the line-height property. The spacing between the lines is defined as the distance from the baseline of one line of text to the baseline of the next line of text. Listing 8-7 shows how you can set line height for your text using em measurement units. This page displays as shown in Figure 8-11.

Listing 8-7

```
<HTML>
<HEAD>
<TITLE>Line Height Style Example</TITLE>
<STYLE TYPE="text/css">
   BODY {background: white; color: black; margin-left: 15%}
   H1 {font: 24pt "Arial"}
   P.normal {font-size: 12pt}
   P.farapart {font-size: 12pt; line-height: 2em}
   P.close {font-size: 12pt; line-height: 1em}
</STYLE>
</HEAD>
<BODY>
<H1>Line Height Display</H1>
<P CLASS="normal">The text of this paragraph has the normal, or default,
line spacing provided by the browser. Lorem ipsum ...</P>
<P CLASS="farapart">The text of this paragraph has double line spacing.
Lorem ipsum ...</P>
<P CLASS="close">The text of this paragraph has single line spacing. Lorem
ipsum ...</P>
</BODY>
</HTML>
```

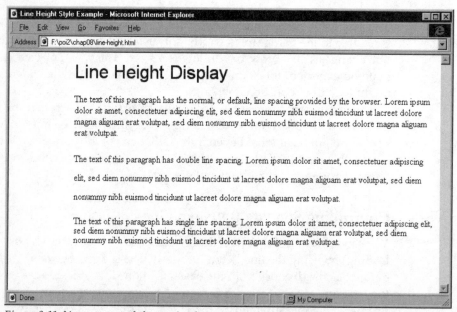

Figure 8-11: You can control the spacing between lines of your text by using the line-height property.

Besides using a length value, as shown in Listing 8-6, you can set the line-height as a percentage of the font size, which is the same as using em measurement units.

Aligning Text

You can control the alignment of text with the text-align property, which includes the following four keyword values: left, right, center, and justify. Listing 8-8 shows examples of these keywords. This page displays as shown in Figure 8-12.

Listing 8-8

```
<HTML>
<HEAD>
<TITLE>Text Alignment Style Example</TITLE>
<STYLE TYPE="text/css">
   BODY {background: white; color: black}
   H1 {font: 24pt "Arial"}
   P.lt {font-size: 12pt; margin-left: 6em; text-align: left}
   P.rt {font-size: 12pt; margin-left: 6em; text-align: right}
   P.cent {font-size: 12pt; margin: 0em 4em; text-align: center}
   P.just {font-size: 12pt; margin: 0em 6em; text-align: justify}
</STYLE>
</HEAD>
<BODY>
<H1>Alignment Display</H1>
<P>The text of this paragraph has the standard, default alignment set in the
browser (normally left). Lorem ipsum ...</P>
<P CLASS="lt">The text of this paragraph has the left alignment set
explicitly. Lorem ipsum ...</P>
<P CLASS="cent">The text of this paragraph is centered using the text-
alignment property. Lorem ipsum ...</P>
<P CLASS="rt">The text of this paragraph has right alignment set. Lorem
ipsum ...</P>
<P CLASS="just">The text of this paragraph is justified. Lorem ipsum ...</P>
</BODY>
</HTML>
```

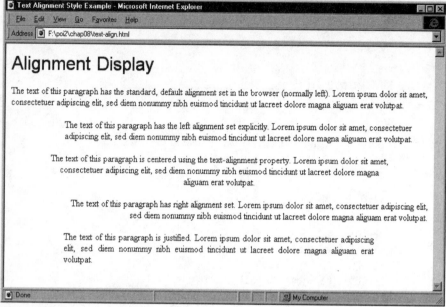

Figure 8-12: You can control text alignment by using the text-align property.

Notice how we used the margin properties to set off the various alignments of these paragraphs. We did this to illustrate how useful this property can be with a complex text page. When you combine the text-align property with other properties that you have learned, such as line-height and margin, you can use it to create just about any text structure you want.

Setting Special Text Effects

You can control special text effects in the browser using the text-decoration property, which supports five keyword values: none, underline, overline, line-through, and blink. Listing 8-9 shows examples of some of these keywords. This page displays as shown in Figure 8-13.

Listing 8-9

```
<HTML>
<HEAD>
<TITLE>Text Effects Style Example</TITLE>
<STYLE TYPE="text/css">
   BODY {background: white; color: black}
   H1 {font: 24pt "Arial"}
```

```
    A {color: red; text-decoration: none}
    SPAN.under {font-size: 12pt; text-decoration: underline}
    SPAN.strike {font-size: 12pt; text-decoration: line-through}
    SPAN.blink {font-size: 12pt; text-decoration: blink}
    SPAN.overline {font-size: 12pt; text-decoration: overline}
</STYLE>
</HEAD>
<BODY>
<H1>Text Decoration Display</H1>
<P>This is an example of <SPAN CLASS="under">text decoration using
underlining</SPAN> combined with the SPAN tag</P>
<P>This is an example of <SPAN CLASS="strike">text decoration using
strikeout</SPAN> combined with the SPAN tag</P>
<P>This example of <SPAN CLASS="blink">text decoration using blinking</SPAN>
combined with the SPAN tag will give readers a headache.</P>
<P>You can also use the text decoration property to remove the standard
underlining of anchors.
For example, this <A HREF="http://www.authors.com/" NAME="anchor">anchor</A>
will not be underlined.</P>
<P>This example of <SPAN CLASS="overline">text decoration using overline</
SPAN> currently only works with Microsoft Internet Explorer.</P>
</BODY>
</HTML>
```

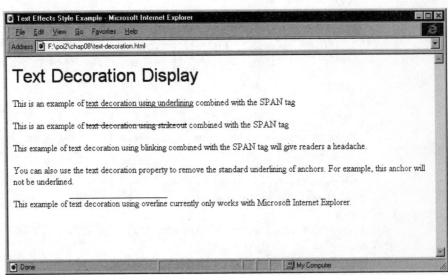

Figure 8-13: You can spice up or tone down the text display by using the text-decoration property.

Notice how we used the new <SPAN> tag to set these text decorations. This is generally how you would want to set such properties rather than redefining an existing tag like <B> or <EM>. However, if you want to suppress the normal features of a tag, as shown in Listing 8-8 for the <A> tag, then you want to set the text-decoration property for that tag explicitly.

TIP *At the time of this writing, only the Internet Explorer 4.0 browser supported the overline text decoration keyword option.*

Controlling Lists

You can control how a list is displayed on your pages using the list-style properties. Listing 8-10 shows an example of the list-style-type property. This page displays as shown in Figure 8-14.

Listing 8-10

```html
<HTML>
<HEAD>
<TITLE>List Style Example</TITLE>
<STYLE TYPE="text/css">
   BODY {background: white; color: black}
   H1 {font: 24pt "Arial"}
   UL.sq {font-size: 12pt; list-style-type: square}
   OL.roman {font-size: 12pt; list-style-type: upper-roman}
</STYLE>
</HEAD>
<BODY>
<H1>List Styles Display</H1>
<P>This is an example using a simple unordered list with no decoration.
<UL>
<LI>Item one: The First Item
<LI>Item two: The Second Item
<LI>Item three: The Third Item
</UL></P>
<P>This is an example using an unordered list with square bullets.
<UL CLASS="sq">
<LI>Item one: The First Item
<LI>Item two: The Second Item
```

```
<LI>Item three: The Third Item
</UL></P>
<P>This is an example using a simple ordered list with no decoration.
<OL>
<LI>Item one: The First Item
<LI>Item two: The Second Item
<LI>Item three: The Third Item
</OL></P>
<P>This is an example using an ordered list with upper-case Roman numerals.
<OL CLASS="roman">
<LI>Item one: The First Item
<LI>Item two: The Second Item
<LI>Item three: The Third Item
</OL></P>
</BODY>
</HTML>
```

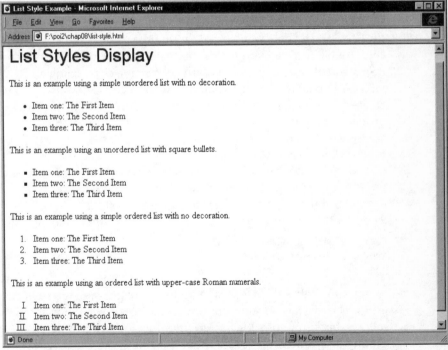

Figure 8-14: You can control how list items are displayed using the list-style properties.

You can use any of the following three individual list-style properties: list-style-type, shown in Listing 8-9; list-style-image, which allows you to use an image as a replacement for a bullet; and list-style-position, which allows you to position the list label—a bullet or a number, depending on which type of list you're using—inside or outside the text box that contains the list item text. In addition to these properties, there is a simple list-style property, which is a way to set all the subordinate properties for a list at once. For example:

```
UL {list-style: square inside}
```

sets both the list-style-type and list-style-position properties at the same time.

Changing Background Images & Colors

The color and background properties are already old friends; we've used them in every example so far with the <BODY> tag to set the background color of the pages to white with black text. Let's look at these two stalwarts a little more closely.

You can apply the color property to almost any tag to set the color. Because the COLOR attribute is inherited, setting the color of the <BODY> tag sets the color for all tags contained in the body of a page. Colors in style sheets can be specified either by using a standard color name or by using an RGB color value. You read in Chapter 6 about how to calculate and use RGB values to create colors on the Web. Colors can be specified with RBG values in the color property using the keyword rgb followed by the three values for the color in parentheses, as this example shows:

```
BODY {color: rgb(#0000FF)}
```

You can specify an RGB color in three ways: using percentages, using decimal values from 0 to 255, and using hexadecimal values from 00 to FF. For example, you can generate the same lime-green color—using 88 percent red, 94 percent green, and 9 percent blue—with these three color specifications:

```
BODY {color: rgb(88%, 94%, 9%)}
BODY {color: rgb(197, 240, 23)}
BODY {color: rgb(#C5F017)}
```

You can control the background for your page using the background properties. The five background properties that you can set individually are as follows: background-color, background-image, background-repeat, background-attachment, and background-position.

As you have already seen in the other examples in this chapter, the background property is a shortcut that allows you to specify the background color for an entire page. The background-color property lets you specify the background color of a text element or a division of your document. Besides specifying a color, you can specify that the background is transparent for an element, so a background image can show behind an element. The following rules specify that a page appears with a white background except for heading 1 text, which displays with a blue background:

```
BODY background-color: white
H1 background-color: blue
```

Background Images

The background-image property lets you use an image as a background. You specify an image file with a URL. You can also specify that the background is set to none, which is useful if you don't want to include a background image behind an element that would display its own background image.

To add a background image, you use url followed by the URL for the image:

```
BODY background-image: url(http://www.authors.com/images/fashion.gif)
```

The URL can specify the relative path and filename; it doesn't have to be a full URL. If you use a relative path, remember that the URL is relative to the location of the style sheet document, not the location of the HTML document:

```
BODY background-image: url(images/fashion.gif)
```

If you don't keep your style sheets in the same directory as your HTML documents, you may need to move up a directory by including two dots before the images directory, as shown in the following example:

```
BODY background-image: url(../images/fashion.gif)
```

Instead of using background images that you add to the <BODY> tag with the BACKGROUND attribute, you can choose to have a background tile or just display once using style sheets. To have the image just display once, enter:

```
background-repeat: no
```

To have the background tile horizontally and vertically, enter:

```
background-repeat: repeat
```

Besides specifying whether an image repeats, you can also specify that an image only repeats horizontally or vertically. To repeat or tile the image horizontally, you use the background-repeat-x property. To have the image repeat vertically, you use the background-repeat-y property.

When you use background images with styles, you can specify whether or not a background image is fixed or "scrolls" with the text of the Web page. To include a background image that scrolls with the contents of the page, you would use the background-attachment property with the scroll setting, as shown in the following example:

```
background-attachment: scroll
```

To have the image appear stationary, so the background image appears in one place and doesn't scroll, use the fixed setting, as shown in the following example:

```
background-attachment: fixed
```

As is the case with many style sheet properties, there are a few ways that you can specify the position of background images. You can define the background position using any of the following:

- Percentages
- Length
- Keyword

In order to use percentages for background position, you need to include two percentage values. The first value refers to the horizontal position; the second declares the vertical position. You can use 0% to 100%. To have the image begin at the upper left corner, you would use 0% 0%. To center a single background image vertically and horizontally you could enter the following:

```
BODY background-image: url(fashion.gif); background-position: 50% 50%
```

When you use lengths, you also need to specify two values. The first identifies the horizontal distance from the top left, and the second value is the vertical distance from the top left:

```
BODY background-image: url(fashion.gif); background-position: 300px 105px
```

In this example, the image display starts at three hundred pixels across and 105 pixels down the window.

If you specify one length value, the browser applies the value to both horizontal and vertical offset.

The easiest method for positioning a background is to use the keyword method:

- top
- bottom
- right
- center

As with percentages and lengths, the first value specifies the horizontal placement and the second, the vertical placement. Figure 8-15 shows an image that doesn't repeat positioned at the bottom right of the window using the following style properties:

```
BODY background-image: url(fashion.gif); background-repeat: no; background-
position: bottom center
```

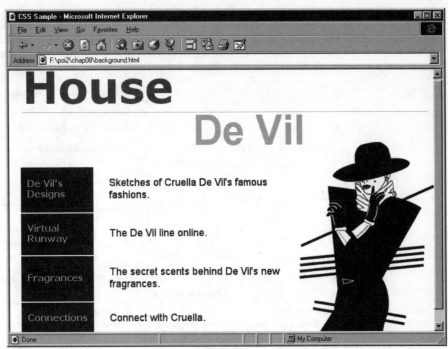

Figure 8-15: An image that doesn't repeat positioned at the bottom right of the window.

Borders

Several border properties exist, but only a few are supported by both Microsoft Internet Explorer 4 and Netscape Navigator. To add a solid border, you can use the border-style property with the solid setting. The CSS specification lets you set one style for all sides of the border or set each side individually. For example, you can use border-top to set only the top, or you can use border-right to set only the right border. You can use the border property to specify the appearance of all the borders. If you use border property by itself, the settings you use will apply to the entire border. Figure 8-16 shows paragraphs with double- and solid-color borders. Table 8-3 lists the border style settings and browser support for the style using Windows 95 and Netscape Navigator 4 and Microsoft Internet Explorer 4 browsers.

Style Setting	Description	Browser Support
dashed	A dashed line	Not supported by Microsoft Internet Explorer 4 or Netscape Navigator 4.
dotted	A dotted line	Not supported by Microsoft Internet Explorer 4 or Netscape Navigator 4.
double	Two lines	Supported by both Microsoft Internet Explorer 4 and Netscape Navigator 4.
groove	A 3D groove in colors based on the border-color setting	Supported by Netscape Navigator 4.
inset	A 3D inset in colors based on the border-color setting	Supported by Netscape Navigator 4.
none	No border	Supported by both.
outside	A 3D outset in colors based on the border-color setting	Supported by Netscape Navigator 4.
ridge	A 3D ridge in colors based on the border-color setting	Supported by Netscape Navigator 4.
solid	A solid line	Supported by both.

Table 8-3: Border style settings and browser support.

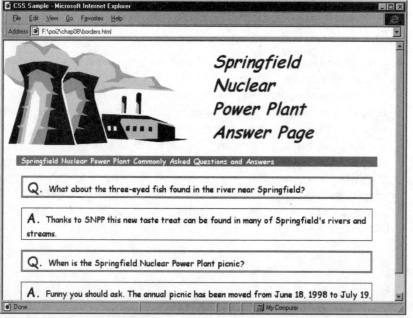

Figure 8-16: Question paragraphs appear with a red and a double border, and answer paragraphs appear with a solid blue border.

Creating Style Sheets for Style-Challenged Browsers _____

Since not all browsers support style sheets—and there will always be some older browser versions around—you should make it a practice to try to create pages that will display reasonably in any browser. With style sheets, this requires a little care.

The first problem, obviously, is how your pages will look in a browser that doesn't understand style sheets. For inline styles and external styles, this isn't a problem. The clueless browser simply overlooks these attributes because it doesn't recognize them and proceeds to render your page using the same techniques that you are familiar with. With the <STYLE> tag, however, things are a little more complex. The tag itself will be ignored because the browser doesn't understand that tag, and the default behavior of browsers toward unfamiliar tags is simply to ignore them. However, the style rules between the <STYLE> and </STYLE> tags will be displayed as standard text because the browser doesn't recognize the tags and therefore will take the rules to be simple text. That's certainly not what you want. The designers of the style sheet specification anticipated this dilemma, and they have a clever answer. You can simply insert HTML comment delimiters around your style rules, and any browser that doesn't understand the <STYLE> tag will then parse the rules as comments and will not display them. Here's an example of what we mean:

```
<STYLE TYPE="text/css">
<!--
   BODY {background: white; color: black;}
   H1 {font: 24pt "Arial" bold}
   P {font: 12pt "Helvetica"; text-indent: 0.5in}
   A {text-decoration: none; color: blue}
-->
</STYLE>
```

With this technique, a browser that understands style sheets will see this as a set of style rules, while a browser that doesn't will just see two tags that it doesn't understand with a bunch of comments in between. In general, if you're writing pages that may be displayed by browsers that don't understand style sheets and you're using the <STYLE> tag—as opposed to using external linked style sheets—then you should use this technique to protect your formatting.

TIP *You may wonder why this trick doesn't confuse a browser that understands style sheets. The answer is that HTML comments are not valid within the <STYLE> tag; only comments within the style sheet comment delimiters, /* and */ are valid. As a result, using the HTML comment delimiters within the <STYLE> tags has no effect on the rules, which will be accepted in the usual fashion by a style-sheet-enabled browser.*

You may also get some strange results if you make any errors in your style rules. Generally, if there are any mistakes in a style rule, or if the browser doesn't support a certain style property, the property that is incorrect or not understood is simply ignored, but any additional properties that are understood are parsed correctly. However, style sheets and their rules can be fairly complex, and some browsers will simply ignore all of a rule as soon as they find something they can't understand. In that case, you may have a rule that partially works on some browsers and won't work at all on others. As always, the best solution is to test your pages in several browsers and under several operating systems.

Moving On

Style sheets are the newest feature in Web design. In this chapter, you have learned a lot about how style sheets work and how they can be used. What you've seen here, however, is only the tip of the proverbial iceberg. As we mentioned earlier, Appendix B gives you a complete list of all the style sheet properties and how they are used. However, since they're so new, examples of great design using style sheets are still rare. We encourage you to experiment with style sheets properties as you use these techniques in your own page design. Based on the work we've done and what we've seen, we suspect that any design you create can be implemented more reliably and more efficiently using style sheets. The major factor holding back the widespread use of style sheets has been the browsers' lack of support for styles. However, the latest releases of Microsoft's Internet Explorer and Netscape's Navigator browsers now handle style sheets. So you can use styles for your Web pages to get the design features that you want without using many of the HTML tricks that have been required in the past. In the future, style sheets will become the most common way for designers to set up Web pages.

In the next chapter, you will learn how to add interactivity to your Web pages using forms that you can create with CGI and Perl.

## chapter 9

Getting Interactive With Forms, CGI & Perl

So far, you have learned how to create static Web pages. At this point, the only way you can really communicate with your reader is by adding an e-mail address to your page. But if you rely on e-mail for feedback, you may not get all the information you want or need from a reader.

By adding a form to your page, on the other hand, you can have two-way communication with your readers and prompt them for the information you want or need. For example, you can use *CGI (Common Gateway Interface)* and *Perl (Practical Extraction and Report Language)* to create an order form and be sure that you will get all the information you need to process the order.

In this chapter, we take a beginner's approach to show you how to use CGI and Perl to create forms. It includes step-by-step instructions for creating or modifying Perl CGI programs so you can interact with your readers and have information either sent to you via e-mail or appended to a file.

TIP *A little unclear of the relationship between Perl and CGI? CGI is the type of implementation we will be discussing for our form processing, and Perl is the programming language we will be using to create the CGI scripts. Not all CGI is done in Perl and Perl is not only used for CGI.*

Before we discuss the more complex details of using Perl for CGI programming, let's take a look at the general concepts of forms.

Forms

Forms allow a user to enter various information, they provide a method to supply information to a "back-end" CGI program, and they return results to a user via regular HTML page construction. Forms were not part of the original HTML 2 specification, but they are so useful that most (if not all) Web browsers now support them.

TIP | *You can find many examples of forms on the Web. And from these various examples, you can pick and choose the features you want to use in your Web pages.*

In the next few sections, you'll be introduced to the basics of form construction. You'll also learn more about how forms interact with the Common Gateway Interface (CGI). Enough talk—let's get into forms!

Understanding How Forms Are Submitted

Every form contains at least one element. If there is only a single text field on a form, the form is submitted when the user presses Enter.

On more complex forms, there is a button or bitmap that triggers a submit operation. When a form is submitted, all the information entered in the fields is sent via HTTP to the server application. The information is sent in plain ASCII text, in a *name=value* format, with the name of the field sent first, then an equal sign, and then the data that was entered in the field. Each *name=value* pair is separated with an ampersand (&). The way the information is sent to the server depends on the "method" used to send the form, which is described later in this chapter.

The server application processes the information in some appropriate way and then returns a "results" page to the viewer. The results page can be anything you want, ranging from a simple "OK" to a complete database query result with multimedia elements.

Now that we have taken a basic, arms-length look at how forms are submitted and processed, let's take a look at how to construct a form within the body of a Web page.

Constructing a Form

In this chapter, you'll be creating elements that could make up a Customer Comment form to link to the Canyon Software home page. Figure 9-1 shows a comment form that illustrates all the elements you'll be working with. Refer back to this figure to see how each element looks as rendered by Netscape's Navigator browser.

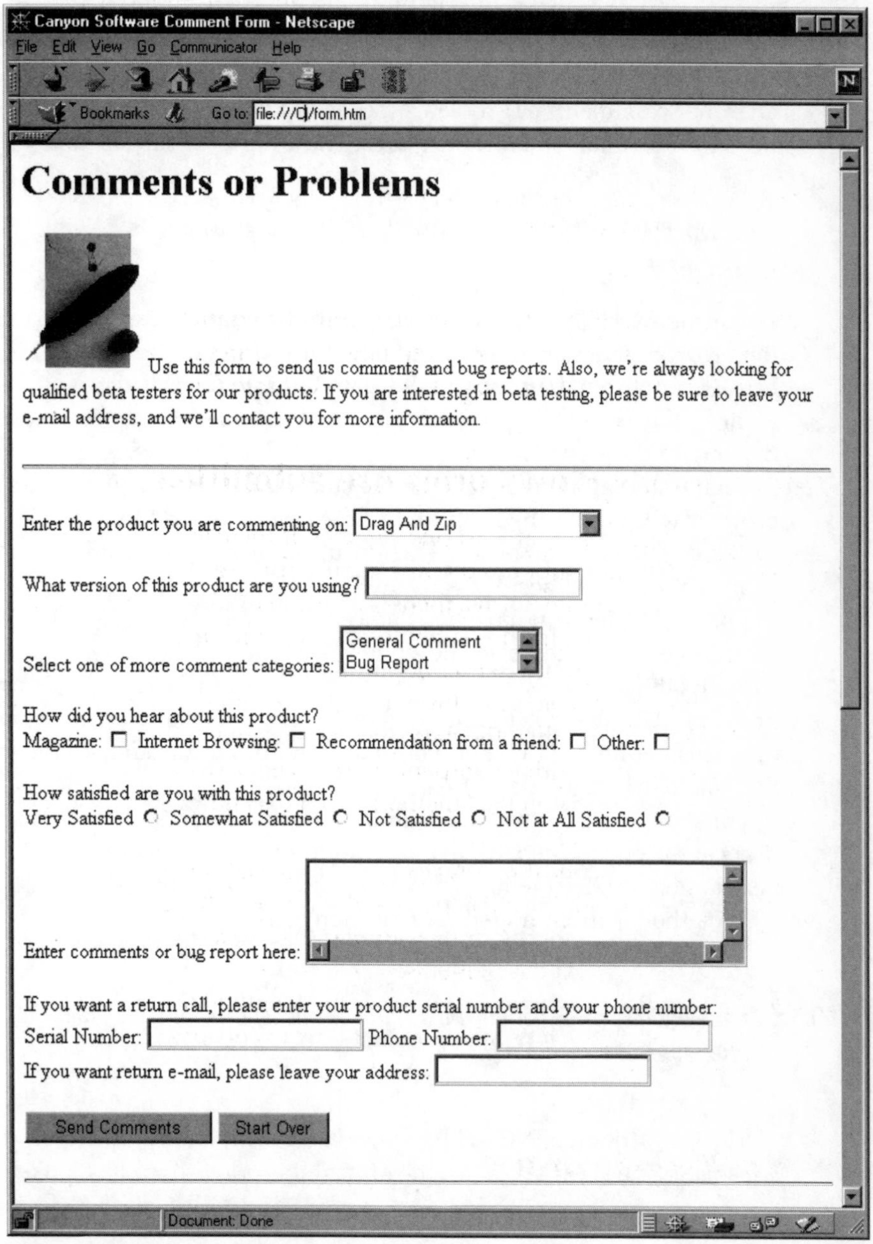

Figure 9-1: The Canyon Software comment form.

TIP   *Want to see the page loaded in your browser? Open the* form.htm *file that is located in the* resource/chap09/form *directory on the Companion CD-ROM.*

A form is started and ended with the <FORM> tag and can contain a variety of fields and buttons. To get started, insert a beginning and ending <FORM> tag after the "Comments or Problems" section of the page. Within the tag, you will need to enter data for a few attributes. These attributes are as follows:

- ACTION
- METHOD
- ENCTYPE

For the ACTION attribute, enter **/cgi-bin/comments.exe**. This is the name of the program that will be executed when the form is submitted, and in this case, the program *comments.exe* is located in a directory called *cgi-bin*. The name of the executable program directory you use for your own forms will depend on the server you are using. You could have entered a complete URL, hostname and all. If you leave off the starting part of the URL, your Web browser will submit the form to the host that supplied the form. Since the ACTION attribute can be any URL, you could actually create a form that is submitted to a host besides your own.

For METHOD, you have two choices: GET and POST. The METHOD you choose when you create your own forms will depend on how your server supports the protocols. Enter **POST** for now, since this is the recommended protocol. With the POST method, the information from the user is put into the data stream of the HTTP, and your back-end program can read the input via the "standard input" data stream.

For standard CGI, the GET method puts the information submitted by your users at the end of the URL that is submitted to your server. Since forms can be very large, the GET method can create URLs that are huge. For this reason, the GET method is discouraged for newly created forms.

TIP   *For Windows CGI, both methods put the information into disk files that your CGI program reads to obtain the data.*

The last attribute, ENCTYPE, is always set to *application/x-www-form-urlencoded*. The HTML code for the form at this point should look like Listing 9-1.

Listing 9-1

```
<HTML>
<HEAD>
    <TITLE>Canyon Software Comment Form</TITLE>
</HEAD>
<BODY>
<H1>Comments or Problems</H1>
<P><IMG SRC="envquill.gif">
Use this form to send us comments and bug reports. Also, we're always
looking for qualified beta testers for our products. If you are interested
in beta testing, please be sure to leave your e-mail address, and we'll
contact you for more information.</P>
<HR>
<FORM ACTION="/cgi-bin/comments.exe" METHOD="POST" ENCTYPE="application/x-
www-form-urlencoded"></FORM>
<HR>
</BODY>
</HTML>
```

Creating an Entry Field

Once the initial <FORM> tag is entered, you can start to enter the individual form elements. There are a variety of different form elements you can enter, including text fields, drop-down list boxes, scroll boxes, large text areas, buttons, and boxes.

When you create a form for submitting information, it is entirely up to you, the Web developer, to choose the method in which you wish your pages to interface with the users. But keep in mind that the more simple the design is, the more it helps to ensure that the pages will be easily understood by the users and that it will increase your chances of receiving correct information.

Creating a Drop-Down List Box

A drop-down list box presents choices to a user. You have undoubtedly seen one in many programs. The basic screen element is a box with a down-pointing arrow to the right of it. When the user selects the arrow, a list of choices is presented.

To include a drop-down list box in a form, follow these steps:

1. After your beginning <FORM> tag, insert a <P> (paragraph) tag followed by the text introducing the drop-down list box. For this example, enter the following text: **Enter the product you are commenting on:**.

2. Next, insert a <SELECT> tag at the point in your page you want to position the list box. For this example, insert the <SELECT> just after the text you just typed within the <P> tag.

3. After entering the <SELECT> tag, you will need to implement the NAME attribute. This attribute, which is within the body of the <SELECT> tag, is a unique name that will represent the list as a whole. For this example, type **prodname**. Every item on a form has a different name associated with it so that when the data is submitted, each piece of user data has a unique identifier. For your own forms, you can use any name you wish.

4. Now that you have the <SELECT> tag taken care of, you need to enter in the individual entries within the drop-down list. These are the entries that will appear when a user clicks on the down arrow to the right of the list.

   To implement these options, you must first enter in a beginning and ending <OPTION> tag. In between this beginning and ending tag, enter the text that you wish to display in the list. For this example, you will need to create six different options to appear with in the list:

   ■ Drag And Zip

   ■ Drag and View Gold

   ■ Drag and View Gold - DWG

   ■ Drag and File

   ■ Fileman Launcher

   ■ Unspecified

   The final HTML code for the <SELECT> tag looks like Listing 9-2.

Listing 9-2

```
<P>Enter the product you are commenting on:
<SELECT NAME="prodname">
<Computer Code> <OPTION>Drag And Zip</OPTION>
    <OPTION>Drag And View Gold</OPTION>
    <OPTION>Drag And View Gold - DWG</OPTION>
    <OPTION>Drag And File</OPTION>
    <OPTION>Fileman Launcher</OPTION>
    <OPTION>Unspecified</OPTION>
</SELECT>
</P>
```

The drop-down list box has now been created. If you take a look at Figure 9-1, you will notice that the next item we have to implement is a small "text area" that will be used to enter in the version number of the software the user is using. We will create this area in the following section.

Creating a TEXT Field

A TEXT field, which is what we will use to obtain the version number of our software from the user, gathers a single line of text and is one of the most common fields used on a form. A TEXT field is created by using an <INPUT> tag and applying one of its many options. To create this TEXT field, do the following:

1. Insert a <P> tag after the previous example's </P> (ending paragraph) tag and enter the text introducing the text area. For this example, type **What version of this product are you using?**

2. Insert an <INPUT> tag after the sentence you typed in step 1 to add the text field. Within the opening <INPUT> tag, you must use the NAME attribute again (as with the <SELECT> tag) to assign a name to this form element. For this example, type **"version"**.

3. After you have created the <INPUT> tag and entered the NAME attribute, you will need to also tell the form what type of information is contained in the text area. This is done using the TYPE attribute. For this example, set the value to **"text"**.

The HTML code you created for the text field should look like Listing 9-3.

Listing 9-3

```
<P>What version of this product are you using?
   <INPUT NAME="version" TYPE="text">
</P>
```

Even though we only used a simple implementation for the <INPUT> tag here, keep in mind that there are a number of other options for its fields that are discussed later in this chapter. The next element that we will implement within our form is a multiple selection list box.

Creating a Multiple Selection List Box

A multiple selection list box is a variant of the drop-down list box, but it allows the user to select more than one of the items on the list. This is very useful when you need the user to select two or three option you have listed. This functionality is similar to having multiple check boxes.

NOTE *The particular way a user selects the elements is dependent on the Web browser in use; however, most follow some form of* control-click.

To include a multiple selection drop-down list box in a form, follow these steps:

1. First, insert a <P> tag after the previous example's ending paragraph tag and enter the following text introducing the multiple selection list box: **Select one or more comment categories:**.

2. As you did with the drop-down list box, insert a <SELECT> tag after the text you just entered. This will create the actual element that you will be using for the multiple selection box.

3. Again, you must use the NAME attribute to signify the element in the form. For this example, type the name **type**.

4. In addition to the NAME attribute, you must also specify the SIZE attribute. This attribute tells the browser how many of the entries it should display by default. Any entries over and above this number will be accessed through the use of the scroll bars that will appear to the right-hand side of the list.

   For this example, set the SIZE attribute to 2.

5. There is one more attribute to implement within the <SELECT> tag: the MULTIPLE attribute. This is done by simply inserting **MULTIPLE="multiple"** within the <SELECT> tag.

6. Finally, use the <OPTION> tag to implement the various entries that will appear within the menu box. Seeing that we performed this same procedure just moments ago, we'll forgo the explanation of how to implement this tag and only tell you about the new attribute that we will be implementing: the VALUE attribute.

   VALUE instructs a Web browser simply to use the 1 as the value of the field when it is submitted to your server *instead* of the text between the opening and closing option tags.

   For this menu box, you need to set up options for the following entries. Don't forget to assign a value (1 for the first, 2 for the second, etc.) to each of the options.

   - General Comment
   - Bug Report
   - New Feature Request
   - Follow-up Comment

Once you have finished creating the HTML for this element, you should have something like Listing 9-4.

Listing 9-4

```
<P>Select one of more comment categories:
<SELECT NAME="type" SIZE="2" MULTIPLE="MULTIPLE">
    <OPTION VALUE="1">General Comment</OPTION>
    <OPTION VALUE="2">Bug Report</OPTION>
    <OPTION VALUE="3">New Feature Request</OPTION>
    <OPTION VALUE="4">Follow-up Comment</OPTION>
</SELECT>
</P>
```

While writing this HTML, you may have noticed a few new items in the SELECT element. In step 4, we entered a SIZE of 2 and in step 5 we specified the MULTIPLE option instead of leaving it as Unspecified. The SIZE indicates how many elements are to be expected in the list box. As stated in step 4 of the preceding example, if the actual number of elements exceeds the number specified, a scroll bar on the right of the list box becomes active so the user can scroll up and down to the desired entry. When there are the same number as or fewer elements than the SIZE parameter, the scroll bar is inactive.

The MULTIPLE attribute, on the other hand, specifies that more than one item in the list may be selected at a time. The user selects more than one element either by dragging with the mouse across multiple selections or by holding down the Ctrl key while selecting.

You also saw the use of the VALUE attribute within the body of the <OPTION> tag. You should understand from the example how this was implemented, but you may wonder exactly why you want to do this. For starters, it may be more complex for a CGI program to parse out long text strings than shorter ones. Or, if you are creating a form in multiple languages, the content of the list box may vary while the meanings do not. The VALUE attribute comes in handy in such cases.

We have now finished the first main section of our form. The next section, which is still part of our original form, will take us through the implementation of the check boxes, radio buttons, and a large text area. Up to this point, you should have the code in Listing 9-5, and the page should look something like Figure 9-2.

Listing 9-5

```
<HTML>
<HEAD>
    <TITLE>Canyon Software Comment Form</TITLE>
</HEAD>
<BODY>
<H1>Comments or Problems</H1>
<P><IMG SRC="envquill.gif">
<Use this form to send us comments and bug reports. Also, we're always
looking for qualified beta testers for our products. If you are interested
in beta testing, please be sure to leave your e-mail address, and we'll
contact you for more information.</P>
<HR>
<FORM ACTION="/cgi-bin/comments.exe" METHOD="POST">
<P>Enter the product you are commenting on:
    <SELECT NAME="prodname">
        <OPTION>Drag And Zip</OPTION>
        <OPTION>Drag And View Gold</OPTION>
        <OPTION>Drag And View Gold - DWG</OPTION>
        <OPTION>Drag And File</OPTION>
        <OPTION>Fileman Launcher</OPTION>
        <OPTION>Unspecified</OPTION>
    </SELECT>
</P>
<P>What version of this product are you using?
    <INPUT NAME="version" TYPE="text">
</P>
<P>Select one of more comment categories:
    <SELECT NAME="type" SIZE="2" MULTIPLE>
        <OPTION VALUE="1">General Comment</OPTION>
        <OPTION VALUE="2">Bug Report</OPTION>
        <OPTION VALUE="3">New Feature Request</OPTION>
        <OPTION VALUE="4">Follow-up Comment</OPTION>
    </SELECT>
</P>
</FORM>
<HR>
</BODY>
</HTML>
```

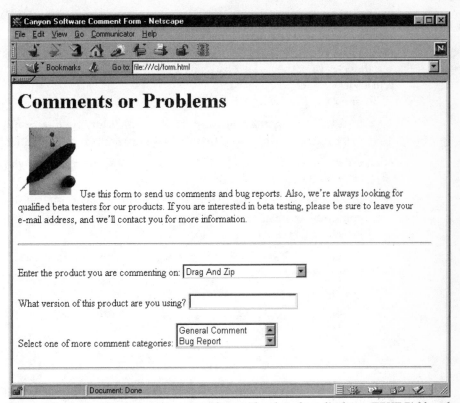

Figure 9-2: The Canyon Software comment form with a drop-down list box, a TEXT Field, and a multiple selection list box.

Creating Check Boxes & Radio Buttons

Check boxes and radio buttons are an alternative way to collect one or more choices from a list of options. When *check boxes* are used, the user can select any, all, or none of the choices you have provided.

With *radio buttons*, however, only one of the choices in a group can be selected, and one is always selected. (Some of us can actually remember car radios with mechanical push buttons!) Radio buttons are *grouped together* by using the same NAME for each button. The VALUE of the button is sent to the server to distinguish it from the others.

Check Boxes

In this example, we will be using check boxes to allow the user to select how they heard about the product they selected from our drop-down list box. As we stated earlier, the check box element will allow the user to select multiple entries if we so choose.

To enter the check boxes in our form, do the following:

1. Insert a <P> tag after the previous example's ending paragraph tag and enter the following text: **How did you hear about this product?**

2. Enter a line break with the <BR> tag; then type **Magazine**, which will identify the first check box.

3. Insert an INPUT element after the text entered in step 2. Within this tag, enter **magazine** as the NAME attribute. Set the value of the TYPE attribute to CHECKBOX.

4. Repeat steps 2 and 3 for each check box. For this example, add the following three check boxes:

   - Internet Browsing

   - Recommendation from a friend

   - Other

NOTE *For check boxes, the VALUE attribute specifies the text that should be sent to the server when the box is checked. If you leave the VALUE blank as we did in this example, the default is the text "on," which is usually okay. Unchecked check boxes send no data to the server instead of a value of "no" or "off."*

Once you have finished with this element, you should have HTML for the CHECKBOXes that looks like Listing 9-6.

Listing 9-6

```
<P>How did you hear about this product?
<BR>
Magazine:
    <INPUT TYPE="CHECKBOX" NAME="magazine">
Internet Browsing:
    <INPUT TYPE="CHECKBOX" NAME="Internet">
Recommendation from a friend:
    <INPUT TYPE="CHECKBOX" NAME="recommendation">
Other:
    <INPUT TYPE="CHECKBOX" NAME="other">
</P>
```

As you can see, it is quite simple to implement the CHECKBOX element in a form—in fact, it is one of the simplest elements you can implement. It is this ease that also allows a CHECKBOX to be easily added to a page.

Now let's take a look into another easy element to implement: the radio button.

Radio Buttons

The implementation of radio buttons is very similar that of to check boxes, except each button in a group has the same name, instead of unique names. What this does in the terms of functionality is that it forces only one of the buttons to be selected at a time. This is used when you want the user to select only one option from an entire group rather selecting multiple options.

Here's how to include a set of radio buttons in a form:

1. Insert a <P> tag after the previous example's ending paragraph tag and enter the text **How satisfied are you with this product?** followed by a <BR> tag.

2. After the <BR> tag, enter the text that will be beside the radio button. Type the text **Very Satisfied** to represent the identity of the first radio button.

3. Next, create a beginning and ending <INPUT> tag entry. Within the beginning tag, assign the TYPE attribute to RADIO to signify that this is to be a radio button.

4. After you have designated the TYPE, assign the radio button to the group of buttons it will interact with. This is done by assigning the NAME attribute within the body of the beginning <INPUT> tag. For this example, assign **howsat** to the NAME attribute.

5. Continue to add identifying radio buttons to the group until you have created all the following buttons:

   - Somewhat Satisfied
   - Not Satisfied
   - Not at All Satisfied

TIP *You can have more than one radio button grouping on a form by using different names for the different groups. Groups of radio buttons are defined by every button in the group using the same name.*

The HTML text for this radio button group you just created should look like Listing 9-7.

Listing 9-7

```
<P>How satisfied are you with this product?
<BR>
Very Satisfied
    <INPUT TYPE="RADIO" NAME="howsat">
Somewhat Satisfied
    <INPUT TYPE="RADIO" NAME="howsat">
Not Satisfied
    <INPUT TYPE="RADIO" NAME="howsat">
Not at All Satisfied
    <INPUT TYPE="RADIO" NAME="howsat">
</P>
```

Creating Text Areas

Text areas are large "scratchpad" areas designed for free text entry that exceeds a single line. As the form's designer, you have the ability to choose the size of the text area by specifying the number of columns (of an average character width) and rows (lines).

To create the text area needed for our form, which will be used to allow users to enter in comments, follow these steps:

1. Insert a <P> tag after the previous example's ending paragraph tag and enter the text **Enter comments or bug report here**.

2. Insert a beginning and ending <TEXTAREA> tag after the paragraph tag you just entered.

3. Within the body of the beginning <TEXTAREA> tag, create and assign three attributes. These attributes should be assigned as follows:
   - NAME="textcomment"
   - ROWS="3"
   - COLUMNS="40"

Because some Web browsers use variable pitch fonts in TEXTAREA fields, the number of COLUMNS is just an estimate of how many characters will fit across the field. To really see this in action, open your document in Navigator and in Internet Explorer at the same time. The differences in how the browsers interpret the COLUMNS attribute are quite apparent.

Notice that once you have loaded the page, the text field has both vertical and horizontal scroll bars. This is so the user can actually enter any amount of text (up to the internal limits set by the Web browser) in this kind of field.

The HTML code for a TEXTAREA should look like Listing 9-8.

Listing 9-8

```
<P>Enter comments or bug report here:
    <TEXTAREA NAME="textcomment" ROWS="3" COLS="40"></TEXTAREA>
</P>
```

Using Other INPUT Field Attributes

There are a few other attribute choices for an INPUT field in addition to the ones you have seen so far.

On the sample form in Figure 9-1, there is a PASSWORD field for a serial number and a *hidden field* that reports the revision level of the form. There is also an INPUT field used to create the required SUBMIT button at the bottom of the page plus a RESET button that lets the browser clear the fields in a form without reloading the form.

▼ **Images as Part of an INPUT Field**

You can use images as input fields as well. When you specify an IMAGE as the TYPE for an INPUT field, you also specify an image file in the SRC field. The image is what will be displayed to the user instead of a box or button. When the user clicks on the image, the form is *submitted*, and the coordinates of the mouse pointer are sent in the form "*name*.x" and "*name*.y" where *name* is the NAME of the image field.

Note that if there is also a SUBMIT button on the form and the user selects it, *no* information about the image is submitted.

You can use an image field, for example, to display a number of different models of some widget so the user can select the model of widget they are commenting on or requesting information about.

Before we get into the hidden fields and buttons, let's first take a look at a PASSWORD field that we will be implementing.

TIP

To create spacing on a form, use the transparent IMAGE file, spacer.gif, in the resource/chap09/misc directory on the Companion CD-ROM, to provide white space between the buttons. Without white space, they would normally be right next to each other. You can also accomplish this task with the use of tables if you are more comfortable doing so.

PASSWORD Fields

Use a PASSWORD field for text input areas that should be kept private. This is useful only for protection from "shoulder snoopers" and offers no real transmission security. On the Web browser's screen, asterisks appear instead of the text, which keeps wandering eyes from glimpsing your private information.

To create a PASSWORD field for our form, follow these steps:

1. Insert a <P> tag after the previous example's ending paragraph tag and enter the text **If you want a return call, please enter your product serial number and your phone number**. After this text, insert a <BR> tag.

2. Enter **Serial Number** followed by an INPUT field with the TYPE attribute set to PASSWORD. This will ensure that no one will be able to read your serial number by simply looking at your screen.

3. Next enter **Phone Number** and an INPUT field with the TYPE attribute set to TEXT.

4. Finally, enter **If you want return e-mail, please leave your address** followed by an INPUT field with the TYPE attribute set to TEXT.

Once you have finished the HTML code for this section, you should have something like Listing 9-9.

Listing 9-9

```
<P>If you want a return call, please enter your product serial number and
your phone number:
<BR>
Serial Number:
    <INPUT TYPE="PASSWORD" SIZE="20" MAXLENGTH="16">
Phone Number:
    <INPUT SIZE="20">
<BR>
If you want return e-mail, please leave your address:
    <INPUT SIZE="20">
</P>
```

HIDDEN Fields

The HIDDEN type is useful for when you want to preload information in a field that will be sent to a server, but you would rather the user not see it.

For example, if you have two forms identical in meaning but written in different languages, you may want to identify the language to the server when the form is sent. You could enter the language name (or some other identifier) in a HIDDEN field on the form so the user is not distracted by it. Then when the form is sent to your server, the server program can identify the language of the form and possibly change how the form is processed.

On the sample comment form, the HIDDEN field type is used to create a revision number field. This revision number will be sent to the server so that the revision number of the input form can be tracked. To create a HIDDEN field, add a paragraph tag and insert an INPUT field with the TYPE attribute set to HIDDEN. Enter **revision** for the NAME attribute and set the VALUE to 1.0. This value setting is sent to the server when the form is submitted.

The HTML code, once you have entered it, looks like Listing 9-10.

Listing 9-10

```
<P>
    <INPUT TYPE="HIDDEN" NAME="revision" VALUE="1.0">
</P>
```

SUBMIT & RESET

Although we cover them last in this section, the final two possibilities for the TYPE attribute of an INPUT field are very important: SUBMIT and RESET.

Every form that has more than one field *must* have a SUBMIT button. The default text for a SUBMIT button is "Submit Query." You can specify your own text for a SUBMIT button in the VALUE attribute. The resulting field on a form is a *push button* that is sized to the text you have specified. There is no NAME needed for a SUBMIT button, and when the SUBMIT button is selected, the contents of the form are transmitted to your server.

To add the SUBMIT button, enter an INPUT field with TYPE set to SUBMIT and the VALUE set to Send Comments. The code for this button should look like the following:

```
<INPUT TYPE="SUBMIT" VALUE="Send Comments">
```

The RESET button, on the other hand, has a default text of "Reset," and selecting it will clear all the fields on the local form. The form is not submitted when this action is performed, but all entries in the page are cleared.

You add the RESET button the same way you added the SUBMIT button except that two of the values of the attributes will change.

First enter an INPUT field with TYPE set to RESET and then set the VALUE to "Start Over." And there you have it—your RESET button. The HTML code for submit and reset buttons looks like this:

```
<INPUT TYPE="RESET" VALUE="Start Over">
```

TIP

You can have more than one RESET and SUBMIT button on a form, but remember that in many cases, the user will not see the entire form at one time. To avoid confusion, place only a single SUBMIT button at the bottom of the form to ensure that a user scrolls all the way to the end of a form before sending it to the server.

Wrapping Up

That completes our form creation. If you have done everything correctly, your code should look like Listing 9-11 and when loaded into a browser, your page should look like Figure 9-1.

Listing 9-11

```
<HTML>
<HEAD>
    <TITLE>Canyon Software Comment Form</TITLE>
</HEAD>
<BODY>
<H1>Comments or Problems</H1>
<P><IMG SRC="envquill.gif">
Use this form to send us comments and bug reports. Also, we're always
looking for qualified beta testers for our products. If you are interested
in beta testing, please be sure to leave your e-mail address, and we'll
contact you for more information.</P>
<HR>
<FORM ACTION="/cgi-bin/comments.exe" METHOD="POST">
<P>Enter the product you are commenting on:
    <SELECT NAME="prodname">
        <OPTION>Drag And Zip</OPTION>
        <OPTION>Drag And View Gold</OPTION>
        <OPTION>Drag And View Gold - DWG</OPTION>
        <OPTION>Drag And File</OPTION>
        <OPTION>Fileman Launcher</OPTION>
        <OPTION>Unspecified</OPTION>
    </SELECT>
</P>
<P>What version of this product are you using?
    <INPUT NAME="version" TYPE="text">
```

```
</P>
<P>Select one of more comment categories:
    <SELECT NAME="type" SIZE="2" MULTIPLE>
        <OPTION VALUE="1">General Comment</OPTION>
        <OPTION VALUE="2">Bug Report</OPTION>
        <OPTION VALUE="3">New Feature Request</OPTION>
        <OPTION VALUE="4">Follow-up Comment</OPTION>
    </SELECT>
</P>
<P>How did you hear about this product?
<BR>
Magazine:
    <INPUT TYPE="CHECKBOX" NAME="magazine">
Internet Browsing:
    <INPUT TYPE="CHECKBOX" NAME="Internet">
Recommendation from a friend:
    <INPUT TYPE="CHECKBOX" NAME="recommendation">
Other:
    <INPUT TYPE="CHECKBOX" NAME="other">
</P>
<P>How satisfied are you with this product?
<BR>
Very Satisfied
    <INPUT TYPE="RADIO" NAME="howsat">
Somewhat Satisfied
    <INPUT TYPE="RADIO" NAME="howsat">
Not Satisfied
    <INPUT TYPE="RADIO" NAME="howsat">
Not at All Satisfied
    <INPUT TYPE="RADIO" NAME="howsat">
</P>
<P>Enter comments or bug report here:
    <TEXTAREA NAME="textcomment" ROWS="3" COLS="40"></TEXTAREA>
</P>
<P>If you want a return call, please enter your product serial number and
your phone number:
<BR>
Serial Number:
    <INPUT TYPE="PASSWORD" SIZE="20" MAXLENGTH="16">
Phone Number:
    <INPUT SIZE="20">
<BR>
If you want return e-mail, please leave your address:
    <INPUT SIZE="20">
</P>
```

```
<P>
    <INPUT TYPE="HIDDEN" NAME="revision" VALUE="1.0">
</P>
<INPUT TYPE="SUBMIT" VALUE="Send Comments">
<INPUT TYPE="RESET" VALUE="Start Over">
</FORM>
<HR>
</BODY>
</HTML>
```

So far you have seen all the elements you can use when creating a form. It's likely that the forms you create for your Web pages will not include every form element like the form in Figure 9-1 does. This form looks busy and complicated and is likely to discourage people from actually filling it out, so be sure to put some thought into your design before implementing every possible feature.

In the following sections, we'll begin to discuss the Common Gateway Interface (CGI) and really get into the nitty-gritty of form submission and parsing.

What Is CGI?

Before we begin to implement it, let's talk a bit more about the Common Gateway Interface (CGI) and the impact it has on Web publishing.

TIP *A CGI program is any program that runs on the same system the Web server is running on and conforms to the CGI standard.*

CGI is a standard for interfacing external programs with an HTTP server. The word *gateway* is a broad term that refers to the common variables and conventions used to pass this information to and from a server. CGI lets you use custom programs to define the format and process of output when working with browsers.

For example, CGI lets you convert data input and format the data so the browser can display the results. Although people generally refer to these external programs as CGI programs, CGI is not a language, it is a standard. One of the most popular uses of CGI programs is to publish and process forms so that readers can submit comments, order a product, or search for information from a Web page.

Each time a reader activates a URL corresponding to a CGI program, the Web server invokes the CGI program with the information it has gathered from the browser. The CGI program processes this information and, in most cases, sends the response to the server. You can also send a response to the browser directly using a *No-Parse Header*.

TIP *Not sure what No-Parse Header (NPH) programs are? Don't worry, they are explained in "Controlling Server Responses With the Status Codes" later in this chapter.*

Using CGI With Your Web Page

Most HTML authoring is independent of the operating system running on the server. Once you venture into the realm of CGI and back-end processing, however, everything changes. Virtually anything you do relies heavily on the operating system and the HTTP server you are running.

NOTE *In this book, the discussion of forms is common across all operating systems. The CGI examples will focus on specific Windows or Windows NT HTTP servers, as indicated with each example. If you're using a UNIX-based server, the examples will illustrate the techniques you need to use, but the code will not be very portable.*

Unlike most other examples presented in this book, the examples in this chapter using CGI require you to be running server software. To allow you to try to implement these CGI programs, we have included a Windows 95/NT server program on the Companion CD-ROM. The server, WebSite, is from O'Reilly & Associates (http://website.ora.com).

TIP *For more information on servers in general, see Chapter 13.*

One of the interesting capabilities of the Windows-hosted servers is the addition of a Windows-based CGI extension, which was defined by Robert Denny. Because DOS and NT have such poor built-in batch-scripting capabilities, it's very difficult to write simple examples for CGI using batch programs, making the Windows CGI an appealing alternative.

The more complex examples in this chapter use this extended CGI. Since these extensions to CGI are not run by the browser itself, they only affect the creators of the server program; users are completely unaware that the CGI back end is different than the machine they are requesting the information from.

There's a lot of discussion in the Web community about the precise syntax and extensions of the forms under HTML, so some things may change. The syntax is certainly going to change in future versions of HTML, so stay tuned.

CGI Programming Options

CGI programs can be written in any programming language as long as the program is on the system running the Web server. Some common choices are UNIX shell scripting languages (such as the Bourne shell, the C shell, or the Korn shell) and programming languages (such as C, C++, Perl, Java, and TCL). If you are using a Windows Web server, such as WebSite, you can use a Windows-specific language, such as Visual Basic or Borland's Delphi, for these scripts.

CGI programs typically reside in a specific directory that the Web server uses to execute the program. For example, if you are using the NCSA server on a UNIX system, CGI programs are typically stored in a directory named */cgi-bin*. Most UNIX-based Web servers are configured to recognize the .cgi extension as a CGI program, so you can store CGI programs in a directory that you have created for your CGI programs.

On the other hand, if you are using Windows 95 or NT with the WebSite server, Perl programs are typically stored in the */cgi-shl* directory and set up to recognize the .pl extension as being a CGI program.

NOTE *Because CGI programs are stored in a directory named /cgi-bin on most UNIX-based systems, most service providers ask that you use a different name for the directory storing your CGI files. Some will require that you store CGI programs in a particular directory or that you use the .cgi extension rather than .pl extension for your CGI programs.*

So what language should you use to create you CGI scripts? Even though this is left entirely up to you, the most commonly used language is Perl.

Why Perl?

Perl was created by Larry Wall to be very adept at handling text. It is a multiplatform language, so you can easily transport it from one operating system to another. This is important because most service providers run UNIX Web servers. So if you are creating HTML pages on the Windows platform, but publishing the pages on a UNIX system, you can run Perl programs on both systems.

Reason number two is that Perl is free. Most Internet service providers have Perl installed on their systems and it's easy to find Perl scripts, modules, and libraries that will save you hours of development time. And if they don't have it, or you are planning on running your own server, then you can download the latest source code and binary ports from the Perl Home Page at http://www.perl.com.

NOTE *Perl users should be aware that there is a port for Perl to NT, which offers a great deal of scripting power. So, if you currently use Perl on UNIX but want the simplicity of an NT-based HTTP server, you should get a copy of Perl for your CGI back ends.*

Last, but not least, Perl has the benefits of parsing the program before executing it, so Perl scripts are easier to debug, modify, and maintain than typical compiled programming languages such as C and C++.

Getting & Setting Up Perl

In this chapter, we'll show you how to create your CGI scripts locally on a PC running Windows 95 or Windows NT, test them, and then transfer them to your service provider's UNIX-based Web server. To get Perl and set it up for Windows 95, follow these steps:

1. Download the Win32 port of Perl from http://www.activestate.com/software/ into a temporary directory.

2. Double-click on the file to open a dialog like the one shown in Figure 9-3. Click on the Unzip button to extract the necessary files and set up the Perl interpreter.

After you have clicked on the Unzip button, the files are placed on your hard drive and you are told when the process has completed successfully.

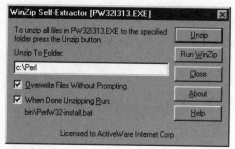

Figure 9-3: The first step in installing Perl for Win32.

3. Next the install script displays an MS-DOS window asking if you have unpacked Perl for Win32 into the final intended destination directory. Enter **Y** and press the Enter key to confirm.

   After processing a few lines of installation data, you are asked if the installer can modify your path statement in your autoexec.bat file. Enter **Y** here. This ensures that you will be able to run scripts from any location on your machine without explicitly declaring the path to your Perl executable.

4. When the installer has finished modifying your path statement, the release notes are launched in Notepad to inform you of any relevant information for this build of the interpreter. Please take the time to look over the contents of this file; then close the window.

5. Finally, go back to the MS-DOS box and you will see that the install is waiting for you to press any key to continue. Go ahead and do so, which will finish the installation. You can close the MS-DOS window once this has been done.

In order for your Perl programs to run from Windows 95, you will first need to restart you machine. This will ensure that the new path statement is in working condition.

Anatomy of a Perl CGI Program

The most common way to incorporate Perl programs in an HTML document is by using the <FORM> tag's *ACTION* attribute. When you use the FORM's ACTION attribute, the program runs when a user submits the form. This type of implementation looks like this:

```
<FORM METHOD=POST ACTION="/cgi-bin/process.pl">
```

▼ **Running a Perl Script From the Command Line**

It's also possible to run a Perl program from the UNIX or MS-DOS command line. For example, you can create a text file named *hello.pl* with the contents:

```
print "Hello World Wide Web!\n";
```

If you are using Windows 95 or Windows NT, open an MS-DOS window and change to the directory where you saved the *hello.pl* file. At the command-line prompt, type **perl hello.pl**. The output will display *"Hello World Wide Web!"* on a new line.

Keep in mind that Perl CGI programs typically are not run from the command line but instead are added as a FORM ACTION that is passed to the HTTP server and executed. The output of these scripts are then sent to the reader's browser.

If you write Perl scripts for use with the WebSite server, you need to store the script in the */cgi-shl* directory. The */cgi-shl* directory is created when you install WebSite, so don't worry about placing it in the correct location. If you follow the instructions in the previous section to associate Perl programs to run under Windows 95, the WebSite server automatically executes CGI program files that end with the .pl extension and are stored in the /cgi-shl directory.

Things are a bit different when executing a Perl program on a UNIX system. Most service providers currently run UNIX, so it is most likely the operating system on which your script will ultimately be run. Perl scripts on these systems are typically given the file extension .cgi. By using the .cgi extension, the server can associate any programming language file as being a CGI program.

A Perl CGI script stored on a UNIX system needs to begin with a line that includes the path to the Perl interpreter on the UNIX system; the line typically appears as:

```
#!/usr/local/bin/perl
```

To understand a simple Perl CGI program that generates HTML text for the user's browser, take a look at Listing 9-12.

Listing 9-12

```perl
#!/usr/local/bin/perl

print "Content-type:text/html\n\n";
print "<HTML>";
print "<HEAD>";
print "<TITLE>A Sample Perl program</TITLE>";
print "</HEAD>";
```

```
print "<BODY> ";
print "<H1>A Perl program that returns HTML</H1>";
print "<P>This is an HTML document created with Perl.</P>";"</BODY>";
print "</HTML>";
```

NOTE

The first line (#!/usr/ local /bin /perl) is not needed when you use WebSite, but it is required when you run Perl programs on a UNIX system.

Perl is made up of library functions, which you might find easier to think of as commands. For example, the *print* library function sends output to the server. In order to communicate with the browser, a special header, called the *Content-type header*, informs the browser what type of data to expect. The next section explains how to use different types of Content-type headers.

Perl Syntax

Notice that in Listing 9-12 the \n\n at the end of the Content-type header. Each \n sends a newline character. The two newline characters are essential to create a blank line to ensure that the server knows where to start processing the data. Notice also that each line of a Perl script ends with a semicolon (;). This character, called a *token*, is used to complete a statement, just as a period is used in English to complete a sentence.

You can save yourself the time of entering the print function, enclosing each line within quotations, and ending each line with a token by using print<<"_END_" to specify where to begin and end printing. The "_END_" reference is an arbitrary string of characters that you use to specify the ending point of the print function.

Using Listing 9-12 with print<<"_END_", the program looks like Listing 9-13:

Listing 9-13

```
#!/usr/local/bin/perl
print "Content-type:text/html\n\n";
print<<"_END_";
<HTML>
<HEAD>
<TITLE>A Perl Program that Returns HTML"</TITLE>
</HEAD>
<BODY>
<H1>A Perl Program that Returns HTML</H1>
```

```
<P>This is an HTML document created with Perl.</P>
</BODY>
</HTML>
_END_
```

Note: If you are using WebSite, don't add a space between the print statement and the angle brackets (print<<"_END_";). With WebSite, you also need a new line after the _END_ reference.

Besides using the print function with the << redirection symbols, you can also redirect the output from a form to a file, or you can have the output sent to you using a mail program. For example, to have the results of a form mailed to you, replace the line print<<"_END_"; with the following two lines:

```
open (MAIL,"|/usr/lib/sendmail yourname\@domain.com ");
print MAIL<<"_END_";
```

In order for this example to work, you need to replace *yourname@yourdomain.com* with your e-mail address.

Once you save your Perl program, you can start a Web (HTTP) server and test the program, but remember that you must have an active connection and a Web server running or your Perl CGI program will not run correctly! In other words, you cannot load and run a CGI program as a local file.

If you saved the Perl program in Listing 9-12 as html.pl and you are using the WebSite server, you run the program by first starting WebSite. Then start Netscape and enter the URL that contains your domain name or IP address, the directory containing the document, and the program name html.pl, as shown in the following line:

```
http://www.yourdomain.com/cgi-shl/html.pl
```

Of course, you will need to replace the domain name *www.yourdomain.com* with your domain name or your IP address.

TIP   *Although you need a Web server running to test CGI programs, there is a way to test the program without connecting to your service provider. To use a local connection, replace your domain or IP address with localhost. For example, using WebSite to run the Perl program named myprogram.pl, enter the following:*

http://localhost/cgi-shl/myprogram.pl

This runs the CGI program as a local connection and saves you from having to connect to a service provider to make sure your program works.

If you want to run the program at your service provider's on a UNIX-based Web server, you need to FTP the file to your service provider in ASCII mode. You may also need to change the filename extension (usually to .cgi). Additionally, you will need to use your Telnet tool to run the *chmod* command to change the permissions for the directory containing your CGI scripts (chmod 755 cgi), the cgi-lib.pl library file (chmod 644 cgi-lib.pl), and your program file so it can be executed (chmod 755 html.cgi). Some service providers running UNIX do not allow you to use Telnet but will allow you to create CGI scripts. You still need to change the permissions. To do this, you can use an FTP tool that has added a change permission mode option, such as the newest version of Drag and File, which is available at http://www.canyonsw.com.

Changing Permission Modes Using Numeric Notation

By adding the *-l* (long) option to the *ls* (list) command on a UNIX system, you can list permissions information about files. The first character in the permissions list that appears in the leftmost column indicates the file type (regular, directory, or device). The remaining nine characters in the series specify the permission modes for the three types of users: yourself (user), group, and the world (others).

There are three characters for each user type. To assign permissions using numeric notation, you enter numbers to specify the permissions you want. If you enter only one number after *chmod*, that permission will apply to the world. If you enter two numbers, the first number will specify permissions for the group and the second will set the permissions for the world. If you enter three numbers, the first number will set the owner's permissions, the second number will set group permissions, and the third number will apply to all others. The following table lists the numeric values that can be used to change permissions.

Values	Permissions	Definition
7	rwx	read, write, execute
6	rw-	read, write
5	r-x	read, execute
4	r—	read only
3	-wx	write and execute
2	-w-	write only
1	—x	execute only
0	—	no access

To change modes using numeric notation, enter the *chmod* command followed by the numbers indicating the mode you want to assign to each class of user. For example, entering the following:

```
chmod 750 script.cgi
```

indicates that the file named script.cgi can be read, written to, and executed by the owner. This is because the first number indicates that the owner's permission mode is equal to 7. The next number, 5, indicates that the file can be read and executed by a member of the owner's group. The last number, 0, indicates that there are no permissions for others on the system.

In some rare cases, your service provider may require your permissions to be set differently as well. For example, it's possible that the 755 setting will need to be set to 750. When you run the program, it displays the HTML document shown in Figure 9-4.

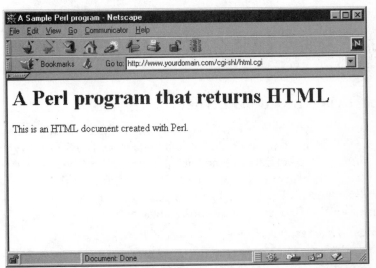

Figure 9-4: A simple HTML document created by executing a Perl CGI program.

TIP *To get more information on creating CGI programs with Perl, you can get on a mailing list for CGI Programming in Perl. To subscribe to the mailing list, send an e-mail message containing the word* subscribe *in the body to CGI-perl-request@webstorm.com. You can also check the comp.lang.perl newsgroup that covers Perl topics. The Resources section of this book lists links to some popular Perl-related Web pages.*

Controlling Output From a Perl CGI Program _____

CGI programs can return one of many data types back to the client's browser. For example, the program can send back an HTML document, an image, plain ASCII text, a video, or even an audio clip. But there is one catch: your CGI program must inform the server of the specific type of data you are sending back.

You can inform the server of the type of data you will be sending by placing a header before your output. The first output line of a CGI script includes a header that instructs the server how to handle the output of the script. The header is usually one of three types:

- Content-type

- Location

- Status

Remember that the header must be followed by $\backslash n \backslash n$ to indicate a blank line so the server will know where the header ends and the document or file data begins.

> **TIP** *A common error in beginner's CGI programs is the omission of a blank line using* \n\n *that allows the server to decipher the output.*

Specifying the Content Type _____

The Content-type header lets you specify any MIME (which was originally designed for handling multimedia mail) data type. The Content-type header specifies the type of data to send back to the browser. The first part of the Content-type header is the top-level MIME type, followed by a forward slash, and then the MIME subtype. For example, in the previous section, we returned an HTML document by adding the Content-type header:

```
Content-type:text/html
```

The text/html MIME type informs the server that you are sending text in the HTML format. Another common MIME type is text/plain for ASCII text. Valid MIME types must be supported by the browser and the server.

> **TIP** *If you don't specify the type of data being returned, the server sends a "500 Server Error" message to the reader.*

Using Location Header to Load a Document

Another header that you can use in a CGI script is the Location header. By using the Location header, you can redirect the browser to the location of a document.

From the server side, the script that uses the Location header requested by the browser is executed, which produces an HTML document. This document is then sent to the server. The server, in turn, sends the document back to the browser.

On the client end, when the browser sees the Location header, it requests the document represented by the URL of the location. The server at that location, as we just saw, services that request. The server then returns the document as if that particular document was requested by the browser.

All of this happens without the user being aware of it. The Location header can reference either the URL of the file you want to be returned or the full path of that file. The following is an example of using the Location header and a full URL:

```
#!/usr/local/bin/perl
print "Location:http://www.bookware.com/moved.html\n\n";
```

Or you can use a relative URL, such as:

```
#!/usr/local/bin/perl
print "Location:/pub/docs/index.html\n\n";
```

When this program is executed, the server will request the document http://www.bookware.com/moved.html and send it to the requesting browser.

TIP *Even though there aren't any lines that follow the location directive, you still need to end the directive with a blank line (\n\n).*

Just about all browsers today support the Location header. Most servers, such as the NCSA server, will display a default message to older browsers that don't support the Location header. If you want, you can include your own HTML code with links to the new location to address older browsers.

Controlling Server Responses With the Status Codes

When a CGI script runs, it provides the Content-type header field, and the server supplements it with a status code, the date, the server information, and other elements of the HTTP header. If you want a CGI script to send a status code directly to the browser, create it as a No-Parse Header script (by prefacing its name with *nph~*).

The status header consists of a three-digit status code followed by a response that is a string of characters representing the code. For example:

```
print "Content-type:text/plain","\n";
print "Status:204 No Response",\n\n;
```

In this example, the script instructs the browser to stay on the same page and not expect any input back from the server. A header set to "Status: 204 No Response" means the program was executed for its side effects and not for a response.

It is possible, however, that you want your program to force a different status code from the server. For example, if a person enters information incorrectly when filling out a form field, you can instruct the browser not to load the next page until the information is entered correctly.

In order to send a status code, you need to know the status codes and responses as defined by the HTTP specification. Table 9-1 lists and describes the possible status codes and responses.

Category	Code	Response	Description
Success	200	OK	Transaction succeeded.
	201	Created	Response indicates the *URI* (*Universal Resource Identifier*) by which the new document should be known.
	202	Accepted	Accepted for processing but processing hasn't completed.
	203	Partial Information	Information returned is not definitive or complete.
	204	No Content	Request was received but there is nothing to return.
Redirection	300	Multiple Choices	Resource requested is available at multiple locations.
	301	Moved	Data requested has been moved.
	302	Found	Data requested has been found at the other locations.
	303	Method	Recommends the client try different URL or access method.
	304	Not Modified	Client has performed a GET but the document hasn't been changed.

➡

Category	Code	Response	Description
Client Errors	400	Bad Request	Incorrect request, such as incorrect syntax.
	401	Unauthorized	Authentication request failed.
	402	Payment Required	Reserved for response with valid ChargeTo header.
	403	Forbidden	Request cannot be granted.
	404	Not Found	The document, query, or URL could not be found.
Server Errors	500	Internal Server Error	Server experienced an internal error.
	501	Not Implemented	The server doesn't support the function requested.
	502	Bad Gateway	Server is temporarily unavailable. Sometimes sent to prevent system overload.
	503	GatewayTimeout	Gateway is overloaded; server is using another gateway, or service took longer to respond than the client was configured to wait.

Table 9-1: HTTP status codes.

How the Server Gets & Passes Data to CGI Scripts

In order to create interactive, dynamic documents, you need to get data from the client and pass the data to the gateway program through the HTTP server. There are different ways in which input is passed to the gateway, including the forms-based GET and POST methods and the ISINDEX method. No matter which input method you use, the client passes data to the gateway program using environment variables or as standard input to the program. In most cases, you will use the <FORM> tag to create a form within an HTML document to get input from a user.

The following sections explain methods used by a CGI program to process data sent from the server.

CGI Environment Variables

In order to interact with your reader, you need to acquire information via the server. This information about the client/server environment is stored in *CGI environment variables*.

When the HTTP server receives a request for a CGI program, it creates a set of environment variables that contain information about the server, the browser, and the current request. The server then executes the script, captures the output of the script, and forwards it to the browser. Different servers can have different variables, or different names for variables. In this chapter, we use the standard CGI environment variables from the NCSA server and the Windows WebSite server.

Table 9-2 lists CGI environment variables common to the NCSA and WebSite server.

Environment Variable	Description
AUTH_TYPE	Method of authentication used to validate the user.
CONTENT_LENGTH	Size of the content file.
CONTENT_TYPE	Content type of POST data.
GATEWAY_INTERFACE	CGI version to which this server compiles.
HTTP_ACCEPT	MIME content types the client will accept.
HTTP_USER_AGENT	Name of browser software.
PATH_INFO	Extra path information, also called the logical path.
PATH_TRANSLATED	Translated PATH_INFO, also called the physical path.
QUERY_STRING	GET data (the text after the ? in the request URL).
REMOTE IDENT	Name of the remote user. (WebSite equivalent is REMOTE_USER.)
REMOTE_ADDR	IP address of the remote host making the request.
REMOTE_HOST	Hostname making the request.
REMOTE_IDENT	Name of the remote user. (WebSite equivalents REMOTE_USER.)
REQUEST_METHOD	Method used to request data.
SCRIPT-NAME	Path to the script being executed.
SERVER_NAME	Hostname of the server.
SERVER_PORT	Port number the server runs on.
SERVER_PROTOCOL	Protocol name and revision that accompanies the request.
SERVER_SOFTWARE	Name and version of the server software. *cont.*

WebSite-Specific Environment Variables	Description
AUTH_NAME	Authorized realm.
AUTH_USER	Authorized user.
CONTENT_FILE	File to write data into.
DEBUG_MODE	True when CGI debugging is turned on.
GMT_OFFSET	Number of hours from Greenwich Mean Time.
HTTP_REFERER	Referring document.
OUTPUT_FILE	File containing POST data.
SERVER_ADMIN	E-mail address of server's systems administrator.
USER_AGENT	Browser the client is using to send the request.

Table 9-2: Common NCSA and WebSite CGI environment variables.

To help you understand how these variables are retrieved, let's take a look at Listing 9-14. It is a Perl program that lets you display the CGI environment variables.

Listing 9-14

```
#!/usr/local/bin/perl
print "Content-type:text/plain\n\n";
foreach $variable (sort keys %ENV){
print "$variable:$ENV{$variable}\n";
}
```

If you just want to display one environment variable, use $ENV followed by the CGI environment variable enclosed in curly braces. For instance, a Perl program that displays the browser the reader is using to view your page would look like the following:

Listing 9-15

```
#!/usr/local/bin/perl

print "Content-type:text/plain\n\n";
$client=$ENV{HTTP_USER_AGENT};
print "You are using the $client browser.";
```

URL Encoding

When a reader submits the information from a form, the data is *URL-encoded* and transferred to a CGI program. URL encoding is the format the browser uses to identify the input to the form when it sends it to the server. The browser gets all the names and values from the form input and encodes them as name=value pairs, with each pair separated by the ampersand (&).

TIP *Having troubles visualizing this format? Well, the result of a form is stored into a text string with the format* name1=value1&name2=value2&name3=value3.

The browser also converts blank spaces to plus signs (+) and translates any other special characters. Special characters appear as hexadecimal ASCII escape sequences. The escape sequences appear as %*nn*, where *nn* is the hexadecimal number. For example, a plus sign is %2B, and an apostrophe is %27.

In order to use the results, you need to parse and decode the input (which is explained in "Parsing URL-Encoded Data" later in this chapter) and present it in a more readable format. Now, let's take a look at using GET.

Using GET to Pass Data

There are two methods of passing data using forms: GET and POST. To specify the GET method, you use the <FORM> tag's METHOD attribute. For example, you might include a line similar to the following in your HTML page:

```
<FORM METHOD=GET ACTION="/cgi-bin/script.pl">
```

GET is the default method for processing the contents of a fill-out form. Although it's the default method, there is a definite drawback to using GET. The GET method causes the user's keystrokes or the form's contents to be appended to the URL in the form of a query string. The problem is that the data may make the URL so long that it exceeds the available environment space, causing the server to truncate the URL, which will result in an incorrect submission.

If you decide that there will be no troubles using GET, then keep in mind that the output is stored in URL-encoded form in the environment variable QUERY_STRING. Each piece of data is sent in a *name=value* format. For example, if the reader selects a radio button with the name *mailing_list*, the QUERY_STRING environment variable appears as *mailing_list=on*.

TIP   *Still not sure if GET is for your implementation? In short, if the form you are presenting to the user contains a lot of information to be delivered to your CGI script, then GET is probably not for you. Use GET when you are only requesting a limited amount of information, like a username, in your form.*

Using POST to Pass Data

POST is the most common method used to submit fill-out forms to the server. It is more robust than the GET method because it doesn't limit the amount of data that can be passed to the gateway program.

In the same manner that you assigned the GET functionality, you specify the POST method by using the <FORM> tag's METHOD attribute. For example, to use the POST method with a form, you might include a line similar to the following:

```
<FORM METHOD=POST ACTION="/cgi-bin/script.pl">
```

The POST method sends the form input to the server as data rather than as part of the URL; in other words, the POST method passes data to a gateway program's standard input (STDIN in Perl). The data is then read by your script from this standard input.

To read and process the submitted data to the server, you first need to determine its length by using the CONTENT_LENGTH environment variable and read the exact number of bytes into a variable. The string will be URL-encoded, so you will have to parse it and decode the escape characters. Listing 9-16 is an example of a fill-out form that uses the POST method.

Listing 9-16

```
<HTML>
<HEAD>
    <TITLE>Guest Book</TITLE>
</HEAD>
<BODY>
<FORM ACTION="cgi-bin/guestbk.pl" METHOD="POST">
<P>Please enter your first name:</P>
    <INPUT NAME="fname">
<P>Please enter your last name:</P>
    <INPUT NAME="lname">
<P>Enter your phone number:</P>
    <INPUT NAME="phone">
<P>Enter your e-mail address:</P>
    <INPUT NAME="e-mail">
<INPUT TYPE="SUBMIT">
```

```
</FORM>
</BODY>
</HTML>
```

Say, for example, a user enters Brent in the text field named *fname*, Heslop in the field named *lname*, 233-555-1234 in the field named *phone*, and bheslop@bookware.com in the field named *e-mail*. When the user clicks on the submit button, the browser stores the input data into in the query string in the same order as it was entered in the form. You can then create the following Perl program to read and display the standard input:

Listing 9-17

```
#!/usr/local/bin/perl

read(STDIN, $query, $ENV{CONTENT_LENGTH});
print "Content-type:text/plain\n\n";
print "You entered $query into the input boxes.\n\n";
exit;
```

The *$query* is a variable that you create for the purpose of storing the data input from the user. When you execute this Perl program, the variable *$query* will contain this information, which will be similar to the following:

```
You entered fname=Brent&lname=Heslop&phone=233-555-1234&e-
mail=bheslop@bookware.com into the input boxes.
```

If the person had entered a special character, such as an apostrophe, the character would appear preceded by a percent sign and a number indicating the character's hexadecimal equivalent.

▼ **More GET & POST Information**

CGI lets you combine different methods to pass data to the gateway program. A form using the POST method, for instance, can make use of the environment variable as well as standard input (remember this is STDIN in Perl).

Whether you use GET or POST, if additional path information was present in the script's URL, that information will be available in the PATH_INFO and PATH_TRANSLATED environment variables. For example, to send data into both standard input and the PATH_INFO variable, you could specify data in the URL by entering:

```
<FORM METHOD=POST ACTION=cgi-bin/name.pl /
e-mail=bheslop@bookware.com>
```

The POST method passes this data to a gateway program's standard input, but the additional path information (e-mail=bheslop@bookware.com) is set as though you used the GET method.

Parsing URL-Encoded Data

In order to process a form, the client needs to package and format the data to a string of text that can be processed by the server. Using the previous section's example, the data from a form that adds a user's name and phone number to a guest book looks like this:

```
fname=Brent&lname=Helop&number=233-555-1234&e-mail=bheslop@bookware.com
```

The information is there, but it's a little too cryptic to be easily read. In order to process the form data and make it more readable, you need to use a program to parse out URL-encoded form entries.

TIP *A parsing program decodes and translates the URL-encoded information to return it to its original state so it is easier to read.*

For example, you need to separate the names from the values (separated by = sign) and remove the ampersands (&). You will also need to convert the plus signs (+) back to spaces and decode hexadecimal characters (%*nn*) to their ASCII equivalents. But guess what? You don't have to write a Perl program to parse form data. Several programs already exist that do it for you.

Parsing Data With CGI-LIB.PL

Cgi-lib.pl, written by Steve Brenner, is a popular library of Perl subroutines that includes a subroutine for parsing URL-encoded data. You can retrieve the file from http http://cgi-lib.stanford.edu/cgi-lib/. The file is named with a .txt extension. You will need to rename the file to remove the .txt extension and put cgi-lib.pl file in your perl\lib directory or store the file in the directory with your CGI programs.

TIP *Want more information on CGI and Perl parsing with cgi-lib.pl? Steve Brenner has written an excellent book on the subject, which is listed Appendix C.*

Script Setup

In order to use the subroutines contained in the cgi-lib.pl library once you have it installed, you need to include the following line in your Perl program:

```
require ('cgi-lib.pl');
```

If you use the cgi-lib.pl library at your service provider, you do not need to download the file and store it in the directory where you store your CGI files. You will, however, need to reference the server's /cgi-bin directory by adding the following line:

```
push (@INC,'/cgi-bin');
```

In this line, the @INC is a predefined Perl variable that in this example is added so the Perl interpreter can locate Perl programs found in the /cgi-bin directory on your service provider's server.

Using the Script

The ReadParse subroutine in cgi-lib.pl reads either GET or POST input and stores the variables in a Perl associative array (%in, for example). It's usually called in your Perl script as:

```
&ReadParse;
```

If you want to parse a specific array, you need to add the name of the array. For example, if the name of the array is *myarray*, you would enter:

```
&ReadParse (myarray);
```

After the form input is decoded, you can then read and process the variables by accessing the array in your Perl program. The following example prints out the value of the variable *fname*:

```
print $in{"fname"};
```

Listing 9-18 is an HTML form for user input, and Listing 9-19 is a Perl program that uses the cgi-lib.pl library to read and parse the HTML form and display a page with the form's input.

Listing 9-18

```
<!--HTML Guestbook guestbk.htm document-->
<HTML>
<HEAD>
    <TITLE>Guest Book</TITLE>
</HEAD>
<BODY>
<FORM ACTION="http://www.authors.com/cgi-bin/guestbk.pl METHOD="POST">
<P>Please enter your first name:</P>
    <INPUT NAME="fname">
<P>Please enter your last name:</P>
    <INPUT NAME="lname">
<P>Enter your phone number:</P>
    <INPUT NAME="phone">
```

```
<P>Enter your e-mail address:</P>
    <INPUT NAME="e-mail">
<INPUT TYPE= "SUBMIT">
</FORM>
</BODY>
</HTML>
```

Listing 9-19

```
#!/usr/local/bin/perl
# guestbk.pl Perl Guestbook program
#        that uses cgi-lib.pl

require ('cgi-lib.pl');

&Read Parse;
print "Content-type:text/html\n\n";
print<<"_END_";
<HTML>
<HEAD>
    <TITLE>Form Results</TITLE>
</HEAD>
<BODY>
<H1>Guest Book Entry Information</H1>
<P>Hello $in{"fname"} $in{"lname"}\n</P>
<P>Your e-mail address is $in{"e-mail"}\n</P>
<P>Your phone number is $in{"phone"}\n</P>
</BODY></HTML>
_END_
;
```

Using the Script to Send E-Mail

If you want to send the output of a form as e-mail, you need to add a couple of lines to open a mail program, send yourself mail, and then close the mail program. You can do this by using Perl's *open* and *close* functions, a pipe symbol (|), and the UNIX *sendmail* command.

The open and close functions, which are explained in "File Handling" later in this chapter, are basically used to "open" a connection to the specified file for processing and "close" it after you are finished. The pipe symbol is used to feed the output from one program to another program's input. The lines used to accomplish this task will be similar to the following:

```
open (MAIL,"|/usr/lib/sendmail yourname\@domain.com");
close (MAIL);
```

Assuming the *sendmail* program resided in your */user/lib* directory, you would only need to replace the *yourname\@domain.com* reference with your e-mail address. The mail message appears with the Web server's user ID, which is typically *nobody*.

To help you understand this sometimes trivial application, let's look at Listing 9-20, which sends a mail message and also displays the form output in the person's (who filled out the form) browser.

TRAP *Don't use an e-mail address to send mail based on user input! It is possible that a user could add a command to the end (or instead of) their e-mail address that would be run when the* sendmail *program is executed.*

Listing 9-20

```
#!/usr/local/bin/perl
# guestbk.pl Perl Guestbook program
#        that uses cgi-lib.pl

require ('cgi-lib.pl');

&ReadParse;
print "Content-type:text/html\n\n";
open (MAIL,"|/usr/lib/sendmail yourname\@domain.com");

print MAIL<<"_MAILEND_";
Guest Book Entry Information\n
Hello $in{'fname'} $in{'lname'}\n
Your e-mail address is $in{'e-mail'}\n
Your phone number is $in{'phone'}\n
_MAILEND_
;

close(MAIL);

print<<"_ENDMSG_";
<HTML><HEAD>
    <TITLE>Form Results</TITLE>
</HEAD>
<BODY>
<H1> Guest Book Entry Information</H1>
<P>Hello $in{"fname"} $in{"lname"}\n</P>
```

```
<P>Your e-mail address is $in{"e-mail"}\n</P>
<P>Your phone number is $in{"phone"}\n</P>
</BODY>
</HTML>
_ENDMSG_
;
```

NOTE *Want to make changes to the cgi-lib.pl library? In the copyright notice, you will see that Steven Brenner grants permission for modifying the library as long as the copyright is maintained, modifications are documented, and credit is given for any use of the library.*

Functions & Subroutines

Functions and *subroutines* are self-contained sections of code that perform a specific task. A function is executed by including its name in your Perl program. Perl includes numerous predefine functions, called *library functions*, that can be used in addition to any functions you may write.

The *print* function, for instance, is one of the many Perl functions you can use. It is used to display a string or a comma-separated list of strings.

TIP *As with all Perl functions, counting is initialized at 0, not 1. In other words, the first element is in the 0 position, the second element is in position 1, and so on.*

In order to include a subroutine from a library, you need to reference it in your script. For example, to include the cgi-lib.pl subroutines, you needed to add the line:

```
require ('cgi-lib.pl');
```

Subroutines can be stored anywhere in a script or can even be in another file. You can call a subroutine in a program by either prefacing the name of the subroutine with an ampersand (&) or by using the do function:

```
&sub1;
```

or:

```
do sub1();
```

The cgi-lib includes subroutines that can save you time by referencing them rather than entering one long line or multiple lines of common code. For example, instead of entering a Content-type header that includes two newline statements (\n\n), you could use the PrintHeader subroutine from Steven Brenner's cgi-lib.pl script. The code for the PrintHeader subroutine in the cgi-lib.pl script is:

```
sub PrintHeader{
    return "Content type:text/html\n\n;"
}
```

To include the subroutine PrintHeader in your Perl script, you would add the line:

```
print &PrintHeader
```

The ampersand indicates that the PrintHeader is a subroutine. To save you from entering the HTML code to begin and end an HTML document, cgi-lib.pl also includes the HtmlTop and HtmlBot subroutines.

Subroutines can also have arguments and return values. The arguments are passed to the subroutine by using the @_ array variable. You can access a value in the array by using standard array indexing; for example, @_[0] refers to the first value.

In addition to having the ability to access and execute subroutines, Perl also has the ability to manipulate entire files. As we hinted earlier, you will have the option of opening, closing, and writing to files.

File Handling

Perl accesses (reads and writes) files by way of *filehandles*. Filehandles are names in a Perl program that represent actual files that are used for input and output. STDIN, STDOUT, and STDERR are all examples of predefined filehandle names that Perl uses to handle input and output.

Filehandle names, as a general programming practice, are specified in uppercase letters. This makes it easy to find and locate specific instances quickly within the body of your script.

To open a file, for instance, you use the *open* function. This function is passed two arguments to perform this task: a filehandle and a filename. Essentially, what happens here is that the filehandle is assigned to represent the file. Now this may not seem like a big deal when the file is in the same directory as the script you are calling it from, but if you have to declare a long path to the file, then you will be able to save a lot of extra typing by referencing the file by the handle. Your only other alternative is to call the file by the actual path. Think of it as a shortcut, or link, to the file.

Once the file is opened for reading or writing, then the input can be read one line at a time by including the handle inside angled brackets (<MYFILE>). Listing 9-21 shows how you would open, read, and close a file (password.txt) with a filehandle (PW).

Listing 9-21

```
open (PW,'password.txt');
print "The password.txt file contains the following:\n\n";
while ($line=<PW>){
    print $line;
}
close (PW);
```

Do note that in this implementation, the file actually resided in the same directory as the script. If, for instance, the file was in the */user/info* directory, then you would have to reference it like: open (PW, '/user/info/password.txt'); To open a file for writing, however, you need to use a special prefix. In this type of implementation, you place a greater-than (>) sign before the file you plan to open. This basically says that the file is being opened to receive information. The syntax for opening a file for writing looks like the following:

```
open (OUTPUT,">output.txt");
```

TIP *If you open a file for writing and it already exists, it will be completely overwritten. In other words, any information that may currently be in that file will no longer be there as soon as the file is opened. See the next paragraph to learn how to append text to an existing file.*

Instead of opening the file for just writing (using the > symbol), you may wish to leave text in the file. For example, if you are making a log of everyone who logs on to your site, you will need to *append* each new entry to the end of the file. But to open a file and append text to the end, you must use two greater-than signs before the filename. This looks like the following:

```
open (DATABASE,">>database.txt");
```

Remember, in order to open a file, it must exist and the permissions to the file must allow access. If the file doesn't exist when you try to write, don't worry—one will be created for you. You must have permission to create and write to the file just as you must have permission to open a file.

When you are finished with a filehandle, you should close it using the *close* function. Exiting the program or opening a new file under the same filehandle automatically closes the previously opened file, but it is a good programming technique to close the file when you are finished with it. To close a file, you simply place the filehandler within the parentheses of the *close* function, as shown here:

```
close (DATABASE);
```

In addition to opening and closing a file, you may want to get information before working with it. For example, you may want to test to make sure a file doesn't exist so you don't overwrite an existing file. You may also want to check for access permissions.

Table 9-3 list numerous file tests you can use in Perl programs. An underscore character (_) represents the name of the file if the same file is tested more than once. The following example shows how to perform a file test to check for an existing file named password.txt:

Listing 9-22

```
$pwfile="password.txt";
if (-e$pwfile){
    print "The $pwfile exists!
}else{
    print "The $pwfile does not exit!\n"}
}
```

File Test	Description
-A	Days since the file was last accessed.
-B	File is binary.
-b	File is a block-special file (such as a mountable disk).
-C	Days since the Inode was last modified.
-c	File is a character-special file (such as an 1/0 device).
-d	File is a directory.
-e	File or directory exists.
-f	File is a plain file.
-g	File or directory is setgid.
-k	File or directory has the sticky bit set.
-l	File is a symbolic link.
-M	Days since the file was last modified.
-O	File or directory is owned by real user, not effective user.
-o	File or directory is owned by user.
-p	File is a named pipe or a FIFO.
-r	File or directory is readable.
-R	File or directory is readable by real user, not effective user.
-S	File is a socket.

➡

File Test	Description
-s	File or directory exists and has nonzero size (returns the size in bytes).
-T	File is text.
-t	Determines if the expression passed represents a terminal.
-u	File or directory is setuid.
-w	File or directory is writable.
-W	File or directory is writable by real user, not effective user.
-x	File or directory is executable.
-X	File or directory is executable by real user, not effective user.
-z	File exists and has zero size.

Table 9-3: File tests you can use in Perl programs.

Now that you know how to write effective CGI programs in Perl, let's take a look at the not-so-pleasant job of debugging faulty Perl programs.

Debugging Perl Programs

One of the best methods of testing and debugging a Perl program is to run it from the command line. When the Perl interpreter encounters an error, it displays an error message listing the line where it detected the problem. The interpreter, of course, will not be able to display the text as it will be formatted in a browser, but you will be able to see if the Content-type line and HTML code can be displayed.

Most of the error messages that Netscape Navigator, for instance, displays are generic. Two of the most common (and unhelpful) generic error messages that it displays when it cannot process a script are "Document contains no data" and "500 Server Error." To track down the real error that is keeping your script from running, enter the code in Listing 9-23 after the #!/usr/local/bin/perl line in your Perl program and test it again. This will print the entire error to your browser so you can see what the problem is.

Listing 9-23

```
open (STDERR,">&STDOUT");
select (STDERR);
$|=0;
print "Content-type:text/html\n\n";
print "<HTML>\n<head></head><body>\n";
```

Another common problem when working with CGI programs is caused by an unflushed buffer. The operating system typically holds on to received data in a buffer (a data-holding tank) until it reaches a certain point. When the point is reached, the data is sent and the buffer is cleared. Storing data in a buffer can cause a problem when the buffer is holding on to data you want processed.

Perl includes a special variable, $ | , to flush the buffer and make sure the data stream isn't stored in the buffer. To ensure that the buffer is flushed, set the variable to 1 or a nonzero value at the beginning of the program, as shown in the following example:

```
#!/usr/local/bin/perl
$|=1;
```

In addition to the problems we have just discussed, there are also several other problems you might encounter when writing Perl programs. The following is a list of some of the common Perl and HTML problems that can keep a CGI program from working correctly and how you can solve them:

- Make sure the access file permissions are set correctly for the directories and the files your program uses. It is important that the server be able to execute your program if you wish it to work.

- CGI programs usually run with a user ID of *nobody*, so the ID needs to be set to have read and execute permissions to the directory where you are storing your CGI programs.

- If you are publishing at a service provider running a UNIX-based system, make sure that the path to the Perl program is correct because the first line (#!/usr/local/bin/Perl) is set to its location.

- To check the location of the Perl interpreter type **which Perl** from a command line of a session (which can be initiated in Telnet) of your service provider's server.

- Make sure you have entered a content-type line and included the newline characters, /n/n, to create a blank line.

- Make sure each program statement line ends with a semicolon(;).

- Check for mismatched quote ("") or tick ('') marks in your Perl and HTML code.

- Check for mismatched curly braces ({}).

- Check for mismatched starting and ending brackets (<> and </>) in your HTML code.

- Make sure to use a trailing slash in links in your HTML code.

After the debugging process is complete, you are ready to test out your script. So, do you think you have a handle on this CGI programming and form processing? To help you, I have included a brief example with step-by-step instructions for creating and testing your first CGI program.

Example: Setting Up a Perl Script for an HTML Form _____

This example, even though a simple one, lays the foundation for your future CGI programming experiences. It will step you through the process of the requesting information from the user and generating a result page based on this input. It will even e-mail you the results of the entry.

The set-by-step approach should help in the understanding of the process as well as give you a more defined set of tasks you should perform when programming CGI scripts. Enough talk, let's get started!

Part 1: Creating the Form _____

As we saw earlier in this chapter, for you, the developer, to gain information from your readers, you must create an interface in which to do so. This, of course, is done by creating a form.

TIP *Don't want to type all of this in? Look on the Companion CD-ROM in the re-source/chap09/example directory for the files.*

The first step in our process is to create an HTML form named *guestbkm.htm* and set the ACTION statement to the directory of your CGI scripts. Going on the assumption that this is located in the */cgi-bin* directory, then your ACTION statement should reference */cgi-bin/guestbkm.cgi,* where *guestbkm.cgi* is the script that we will be creating shortly. Listing 9-24 is a variation of the HTML that you should be using for this form.

Listing 9-24

```
<HTML>
<!--HTML doc named guestbkm.htm that sends form input as e-mail-->
<HEAD>
    <TITLE>Guest Book</TITLE>
</HEAD>
<BODY>
<FORM ACTION="/cgi/guestbkm.cgi" METHOD="POST">
```

```
<P>Please enter your first name:
    <BR>
    <INPUT TYPE="TEXT" NAME="fname">
</P>
<P>Please enter your last name:
    <BR>
    <INPUT TYPE="TEXT" NAME="lname">
</P>
<P> Enter your phone number:
    <BR>
    <INPUT TYPE="TEXT" NAME="phone">
</P>
<P>Please enter your e-mail address:
    <BR>
    <INPUT TYPE="TEXT" NAME="e-mail">
</P>
<P>Please enter any comments you may have:
    <BR>
    <TEXTAREA NAME="comments">Enter comments here.</TEXTAREA>
</P>
    <INPUT TYPE="SUBMIT">
    <INPUT TYPE="RESET">
</FORM>
</BODY>
</HTML>
```

Part 2: Creating the CGI Script

Create a file named *guestbkm.cgi* for your script. Within this script we will enter all the information necessary to process the data we will be receiving off the form.

Listing 9-25 contains the text for our program. Do note that there will have to be a few changes for your implementation. You will have to replace the *youremailname* and *youremaildomain* with your specific information. You will also have to verify that there is a "sendmail" program in your */usr/lib* directory.

TIP | *Make sure you save this file in ASCII text file format.*

Listing 9-25

```perl
#!/usr/local/bin/perl

# CGI Perl program named guestbkm.cgi that uses cgi-lib.pl
require ('cgi-lib.pl');
&ReadParse;

print "Content-type:text/html\n\n";
open (MAIL,"|/usr/lib/sendmail youremailname\@youremaildomain.com");
print MAIL<<"_MAILEND_";
Guest Book Entry Information\n
The name of the person entering the form:\n
$in{'fname'} $in{'lname'}\n
The person's e-mail address is:\n
$in{'e-mail'}\n
The person's phone number is:\n
$in{'phone'}\n
The person made the following comments:\n
$in{'comments'}\n
_MAILEND_
close(MAIL);
print<<"_ENDMSG_";
<!--This begins the HTML document that is displayed after the CGI/Perl
script is run.-->
<HTML>
<HEAD>
    <TITLE>Form Results</TITLE>
</HEAD>
<BODY>
<H1>Guest Book Entry Information</H1>
<P>Hello $in{'fname'} $in{'lname'}</P>
<P>Thank you for filling out the form!</P>
<P>According to your input your e-mail address is $in{'e-mail'} and your
phone number is $in{'phone'}</P>
<P>Back to the <A HREF="http://www.yourdomain.com">Home page</A>.</P>
</BODY>
</HTML>
_ENDMSG_
```

Part 3: Transferring Your Files to the Server

If you haven't already done so, download the *cgi-lib.pl* file and copy it, your form, and the *guestbkm.cgi* file to your Web site in the appropriate directories (copy the Perl scripts to the */cgi-bin* directory and the form to your preferred location).

This example uses FTP from the command line in an MS-DOS window to move the files. The instructions should also apply to the command-line version of FTP on UNIX machines. If you have a graphical application that allows you to FTP the files, then feel free to use it. To transfer the files to the server, follow these steps:

1. Open an MS-DOS window and change directories to the directory where you stored *guestbkm.cgi*, your form, and the *cgi-lib.pl* file.

2. Enter **ftp** followed by your service provider's domain name or the domain name that your ISP specifies to use to transfer your HTML files; for example:
   ```
   ftp ftp.best.com.
   ```

3. Enter your login name and password at the prompts that appear.

4. Enter **ascii** to let the program know that you want to transfer the files in ASCII format. This will ensure that all the proper adjustments to formatting are made. When you have done this, the message "Type set to A" appears.

5. Change to the directory that your service provider has created for your HTML documents. For example, enter **cd public_html** if *public_html* is the directory used to store your HTML files. The message "CWD command successful" appears if you have made a successful change of directories.

6. Enter **put guestbkm.htm** to copy your HTML document to your Web site. A message appears telling you that the Port command was successful and the transfer was complete. You have now FTPed your form to your server.

7. Now change directories to the */cgi-bin* so that you can FTP your scripts over. Enter **cd /cgi-bin** if the */cgi-bin* is the location to which you are to FTP the files. The message "CWD command successful" appears.

8. Enter **put cgi-lib.pl** to copy the *cgi-lib.pl* file to your cgi-bin directory.

9. Enter **put guestbkm.cgi** to copy the *guestbkm.cgi* script to your cgi-bin directory.

10. Once these transactions have completed successfully, enter **quit** to exit your FTP session.

And that's it. The files we created in Parts 1 and 2 should now be on your system. Next we will have to set the appropriate permissions for access to your new files.

Part 4: Setting the Permissions

If you will be implementing your scripts on a UNIX server, then you will need to change the permission modes of the directory and CGI script. The following takes you step-by-step through the process of making these changes. Again, these steps are done on a Windows machine, but their application should apply across both UNIX and Macintosh. To set the permission modes, follow these steps:

TIP *If you have troubles with this section, you may need to contact your service provider for more information. It is possible that they are the only ones who can make these changes.*

1. At the DOS prompt, enter **telnet**. The Telnet window opens.

2. Choose Remote System from the Connect menu. A dialog box appears for you to enter your hostname, port, and term type. Enter your service provider's domain name in the Host Name field. This may be the domain name of the server that you entered earlier to FTP files on your site.

3. Choose the Connect button. Once you are prompted, enter your login name and password.

4. Change directories to the directory where you placed your HTML file. For example, enter **cd public_html** if your HTML file is stored in the *public_html* directory.

5. Enter **chmod 755 guestbkm.htm** to change the permissions for the file. In some cases, your service provider may require you to set the last number to 0. Check with them if your script doesn't run to make sure you have the permission set correctly.

6. To set the permissions for your CGI scripts, enter **cd /cgi-bin** to change to your *cgi-bin* directory.

7. Enter **chmod 644 cgi-lib.pl** to change the permissions for the CGI library program. Again, in some rare cases, your service provider may require you to set the last number to 0. Check with your service provider if your script doesn't run to make sure you have the permission set correctly.

It is also possible that if your service provider had you place the files in a common area with CGI scripts from other people, then you may not have to make these changes—they may be done for you automatically.

8. Next enter **chmod 755 guestbkm.cgi** to change the permissions for your CGI/Perl script. The same notes (about what your service provider allows) that are discussed in step 7 apply here as well.

9. Choose Connect | Exit to end the Telnet session.

And your permissions are set. Only one thing is left now: testing your implementation.

Part 5: Test Your Form & Scripts

In this step, you will test your newly created form and scripts. Use your browser to navigate to your page and fill in the form. After you have clicked the Submit button, wait a little while and check your e-mail. To test your forms and scripts, follow these steps:

NOTE *Problems? If your service provider automates the process of setting the permissions, then it is possible that it is done according to a schedule (e.g., every 15 minutes). If this is the case, then wait a while before testing again.*

1. Start your browser and enter the URL to your form. For example:
   `http://www.yourdomain.com/~yourlogin/guestbkm.htm`

2. Fill in the form and click the Submit button.

3. Check your e-mail.

And that's it! You should have just completed your first successful form processing on the Web.

In addition to the script used in Step 2, I have included two other scripts that will process this type of data as well. They do essentially the same thing, but were designed specifically for the system in which you will be running the script. If you plan to implement your script on a UNIX machine, then you should use the first one (Listing 9-26). If you have installed the WebSite server and plan to use it to server your pages, then see the second script (Listing 9-27).

As for the basic functionality, these scripts store form input into a log file rather than sending you an e-mail.

Listing 9-26: UNIX Web Servers

```
#!/usr/local/bin/perl

# guestf.cgi is a Perl Guestbook program
# that creates a log file of form input.

require ('cgi-lib.pl');
&ReadParse;

print "Content-type:text/html\n\n";

# If the Browser says, "Document contains
# no data" it means that the following line
# executed the "die" part -- in other words
# the program quit. To rectify this problem,
# create a file named guest.log in the current
# directory and change the permissions by
# entering chmod 666 guest.log

open (MYLOG,">>guest.log")||die"dead!";
flock(MYLOG,2);
print MYLOG<<"_LOGEND_";
Guest Book Entry Information\n
The name of the person entering the form:\n
$in{'fname'} $in{'lname'}\n
The person's e-mail address is:\n
$in{'e-mail'}\n
The person's phone number is:\n
$in{'phone'}\n
The person made the following comments:\n
$in{'comments'}\n
---------------------------------------------
_LOGEND_
flock(MYLOG,8);
close(MYLOG);
print<<"_ENDMSG_";
<!--This begins the HTML document that is displayed after the CGI/Perl
script is run.-->
<HTML>
<HEAD>
<TITLE>Form Results</TITLE>
</HEAD>
```

```
<BODY>
<H1>Guest Book Entry Information</H1>
<P>Hello $in{'fname'} $in{'lname'}</P>
<P>Thank you for filling out the form!</P>
<P>According to your input your e-mail address is $in{'e-mail'} and your
phone number is $in{'phone'}</P>
<P>Back to the
<A HREF="http://www.authors.com/Navigator4/prog.html">Perl CGI tutorial</A>.
</P>
</BODY>
</HTML>
_ENDMSG_
```

Listing 9-27: WebSite Server

```
# A Perl Guestbook program named
#       guestbk.pl that uses cgi-lib.pl
require ('cgi-lib.pl');
&ReadParse;

# Make sure you create the
# comment file named comments.log
# in the temp directory before you
# test your program.

$commentfile="c:/temp/comments.log";

print "Content-type:text/html\n\n";

open(COMMENT,">>$commentfile")||die"dead!";
print COMMENT<<"_LOGEND_";
Guest Book Entry Information\n
The name of the person entering the form:\n
 $in{'fname'} $in{'lname'}\n
The person's e-mail address is:\n
$in{'e-mail'}\n
The person's phone number is:\n
$in{'phone'}\n
The person made the following comments:\n
$in{'comments'}\n
-----------------------------------------------
_LOGEND_
close(COMMENT);
print<<"_ENDMSG_";
```

```
<!--This begins the HTML document that is displayed after the CGI/Perl
script is run.-->
<HTML>
<HEAD>
<TITLE>Form Results</TITLE>
</HEAD>
<BODY>
<H1>Guest Book Entry Information</H1>
<P>Hello $in{'fname'} $in{'lname'}</P>
<P>Thank you for filling out the form!</P>
<P>According to your input your e-mail address is $in{'e-mail'} and your
phone number is $in{'phone'}</P>
<P>Back to the
<A HREF="http://www.authors.com/Navigator4/prog.html">Perl CGI
tutorial</A>.</P>
</BODY>
</HTML>
_ENDMSG_
```

Now that you have an understanding of the basics in CGI programming, let's move into a couple more advanced topics: NPH scripts and cookies.

NPH Scripts

Typically, scripts produce output that is parsed by the server and sent back to the client. But you don't have to have the server process a script. It is possible to create a script that bypasses the server and communicates directly with the client. This type of script is called an *NPH (No-Parse Header) script.*

TIP   *An NPH script's name needs to begin with* nph-.

The major advantage of an NPH script is that it is slightly more efficient because the processing load is taken off the server. If you don't want the server to parse the header though, you need to add your own header to your script so it will return a valid HTTP/ 1.0 response to the client. NPH scripts are helpful for creating server push programs to issue your own status message to a browser.

The most common use of NPH scripts is to return a 200 or 204 status code. The 200 code informs the browser that everything is okay, while 204 is the code indicating that there is no response from the script and the browser should stay on the same page. When implementing this type of functionality in your script, there should be a line that looks like the following:

```
print "HTTP/1.0200\n";
```

To get a better understanding of how this is used in the real world, let's take a look at an example. The NPH program in Listing 9-28 communicates with the browser directly and references the SERVER_PROTOCOL as HTTP/1.0.

Listing 9-28

```
#!/usr/local/bin/perl
print "HTTP/1.0200\n";
print "Content type:text/html\n\n";
print "<HTML>";
print "<HEAD>";
print "<TITLE>A NPH Header script";
print "</TITLE></HEAD>";
print "<BODY>":
print "<H1>A Non-Parsed script</H1>";
print "<P>This is the result of a simple NPH script.</P>";
print "</BODY>":
print "</HTML>";
```

Cookies

Did you know that many of the sites you visit "drop" information, called cookies, on your computer? This section shows how you can be alerted when this information is being written. More importantly, it shows you how to store information on a visitor's site and reference it anytime the person makes a return visit.

What Is a Cookie?

The CGI client/server connection is stateless, which means that every time the HTTP server sends you a document, all the information stored in memory is lost when the CGI program or connection is terminated. In order to provide a method of storing and retrieving information on the client side, Netscape created the Persistent Client State HTTP Cookies specification.

A cookie is data you specify that is sent to the client (browser) from an HTTP server. It lets you preserve the state of a transaction because the cookie is sent back and forth as an environment variable during additional client/server transactions. This allows you to monitor, in some form or another, the browser that is requesting data.

The most common uses for cookies are to store information about visitors so you can deliver new or customized information to them and to store items that the visitor wants to purchase. For example, you may check to see if the person is visiting your site for the first time, you can display a different advertisement each time a person visits, and you can create a virtual shopping cart to store one or more products that a person considers purchasing at a later time.

So, how do cookies work? Well, from a user's standpoint, you should know that cookie data is typically hidden from the reader. In fact, most are "dropped" without your knowing it. Netscape Navigator and Microsoft Internet Explorer can be set to inform you when cookies are sent to your computer, but by default, they do not.

TIP
If you're using Netscape Navigator 2 or 3, choose Options | Network Preferences and look for the check box labeled Show an Alert Before Accepting a Cookie. Navigator 4 users can access this information by clicking on the Advanced entry in the Edit | Preferences window. Microsoft Internet Explorer users can choose View | Options | Advanced and in the Warnings group of controls, look for the Warn Before Accepting Cookies check box.

For the developer, on the other hand, there are some additional considerations.

Generating & Modifying Cookies

When a browser receives a cookie, the data is stored in a file (cookies.txt) on the user's computer. It should be located in the directory where the browser is installed. New cookies are written to the hard disk when the user exits his or her browser, whereas a modified cookie is written immediately.

To modify a cookie, the domain, path, and name portion of the data must match. Otherwise, a new cookie is created. You can associate multiple cookies with a single document by separating each cookie by a semicolon and a space (;). Netscape Navigator can hold a maximum of 300 cookies and up to 20 cookies from the same path and domain. If additional cookies are added that exceed these limits, the oldest cookies in the cookies.txt file are deleted. To ensure that no one writes large amounts of data to your disk, an additional limitation on the size of the cookie data has been imposed—it can be no larger than 4K.

Cookies can be created in three different ways:

- By sending a Set-Cookie header line in the HTML document header.
- By including a <META> tag within an HTML document.
- By using JavaScript and manipulating the cookie string property of a document object.

Cookies are designed to be secure. For instance, one site cannot access cookie information that came from another site. If you are an extremely paranoid user, then you can make sure you never receive cookie information by changing the cookies.txt file to a read-only file. This can be done by accessing the Properties dialog box on a Windows machine, using *chmod* to set the properties on a UNIX machine, or accessing the File Info dialog box on a Macintosh.

Cookie Settings

A cookie is sent to the client by including a Set-Cookie header as part of an HTTP response that is usually generated by a CGI script. A Set-Cookie header is sent in the following format:

```
Set-Cookie: name=value; expires=date; path=dirpath; domain=domain; secure
```

The following list explains each setting in the order it appears:

- **name=value.** The name and value you assign to the cookie. For example, if you were using a cookie to store the number of times a person has visited your site, you could use the name Visits and a value that stores the number of hits, which could be incremented each time the user reloads your page. The name=value must be defined.

- **expires=date.** Specifies how long the cookie persists. The date setting takes the following format:
  ```
  Wdy, DD-Mon-YYYY HH:MM:SS GMT
  ```

  The GMT stands for Greenwich Mean Time. If the date is not included, the cookie lasts only until the reader exits his or her browser.

TIP *Internet Explorer requires the entire date string; Netscape Navigator can deal with cookies that use expiration date settings as short as 01-Jan-99 GMT.*

- **path=dirpath.** Specifies the path on the server for which the cookie applies. This is typically set to "/" (the root of a UNIX server), but if you are using another provider and running your site out of your own directories, you may wish to restrict the path to account for only your files.

  If not specified, path defaults to the path of the document that contains the cookie. If you don't specify a path of at least "/", the cookie will not be set.

- **domain=domain.** Specifies the domain for which the cookie will be returned. This setting needs to have at least two or three periods (.) in it, depending on the top-level domain. Domains that end in .com, .edu, .net, .org, .gov, .mil, or .int require only two periods, while all other domains require three. If a domain is not specified, the domain setting defaults to the hostname of the server that generated the Set-Cookie response.

- **secure.** Indicates that the cookie should be transmitted only if you are running a secure server. If the secure setting is absent, the cookie will be sent to HTTP and HTTPS servers.

  Use the secure setting to keep the cookie from being transmitted on a nonsecure port. If you're not running a secure server and you use the secure setting, the cookies will not be sent.

Now that you know what cookies are and how they work, let's look at a real example that will show you how you will be interacting with cookies and how they can make your life easier.

Setting a Cookie

The most common method of creating a cookie is to use a CGI script to send a Set-Cookie header:

```
Set-Cookie: authors_cookie=class9; expires=Sat, 18-July-1998 12:00:00 GMT;
path=/; domain=.authors.com;
```

To help you get a better understanding of this concept, here is an example of a Perl CGI script that sets a cookie named authors_cookie=class9. Listing 9-29 shows the source code used to set the cookie.

Listing 9-29

```
#!/usr/local/bin/perl
print<<"_END_";
Set-Cookie: authors_cookie=class9; expires=Sat, 18-July-1998
12:00:00 GMT; path=/; domain=.authors.com;
Content-type: text/html\n\n

<HTML>
<HEAD>
    <TITLE>Setting a Cookie</TITLE>
</HEAD>
<BODY>
<H1>Setting a Cookie</H1>
```

```
<P>A cookie with the name "authors_cookie=class9" has been set. When you
exit your browser, it will be written to the cookies.txt file.</P>
</BODY>
</HTML>
_END_
```

▼ The <META> Tag

You can also use the <META> tag to set a cookie. Only Netscape Navigator supports setting cookies via the <META> tag.

The <META> tag's usefulness for generating the document is limited. The cookie value is fixed, so you can not perform any calculations. This may work for some applications, such as a name setting for counters, but it doesn't help much for interactive documents. The following is the HTML source that sets the cookie using the <META> tag:

```
<META HTTP-EQUIV="Set-Cookie" Content= "authors=class9;
expires=18-Jul-1998 12:00:00 GMT; path=/; domain=.authors.com;">
```

Listing 9-30 is the code for a document that uses the <META> tag to set a cookie named authors_cookie=class9. It shows the HTML source code used to set the cookie.

Listing 9-30

```
<HTML>
<HEAD>
    <META HTTP-EQUIV="Set-Cookie" Content="authors=class9;
expires=18-Jul-1998 12:00:00 GMT; path=/;
domain=.authors.com;">
    <TITLE>Setting a Cookie Using the META Tag</TITLE>
</HEAD>
<BODY>
<H1>Setting a Cookie Using the META Tag</H1>
<P>This document sets a cookie named authors=class9
using the META tag.</P>
</BODY>
</HTML>
```

In addition to having to set the cookies on users' machines, you also have to be able to read information from it. What good does it do to drop something intentionally if you can't pick it up?

Retrieving Cookie Data

On UNIX-based systems, the environment variable used to read data from a cookie is HTTP_COOKIE. If you're using the WebSite server from O'Reilly & Associates, the environment variable is COOKIE. Reading a cookie from the environment variable retrieves all data, including data that was created for documents in directories above the particular document. So to reference a cookie in a Perl script on a UNIX-based system, you would use the following:

```
$ENV{'HTTP_COOKIE'}
```

Listing 9-31 is a CGI script that lists the cookies environment variable.

Listing 9-31

```
#!/usr/local/bin/perl
print<<"_END_";
Content-type: text/html\n\n
<HTML>
<HEAD>
    <TITLE>Cookies as seen by the server</TITLE>
</HEAD>
<BODY>
<H1>Cookies as seen by the server</H1>
<P>Here is your Cookie: $ENV{'HTTP_COOKIE'}</P>
</BODY>
</HTML>
_END_
```

The following code shows how you can create an array of cookie data and scan for a particular cookie. Each cookie is separated by a semicolon and a space, so you can create an array of cookie data and parse the data you want from the cookies.txt file:

Listing 9-32

```
#!/usr/local/bin/perl
if(defined $ENV{HTTP_COOKIE}) {
   @cookieArray = split(/; /,$ENV{HTTP_COOKIE})
}
```

Once you've created your cookie array, it's easy to scan for a specific cookie. Listing 9-33 uses the Perl *foreach* function to scan for a cookie.

Listing 9-33

```
#Cookie Array has been loaded previously
function GetCookie {
   $cookieName = ARGV[0];
   $cookieValue = null;
    foreach $cookie (@cookieArray) {
    if($cookie =~ /$cookieName/) {
    (cookieName, $cookieValue) = split (=/,$_)
      }
   $cookieValue;
}
```

Now that we've covered how to write a cookie and read from one, what do you think is next? You guessed it: deleting a cookie.

Deleting a Cookie

To delete a cookie, set the cookie and specify an expiration date. The following code sets the date for the cookie to expire on Wednesday, January 1, 1999:

```
Set-Cookie: authors_cookie=class9; expires=Wed, 1-Jan-1999 12:00:00 GMT;
path=/; domain=.authors.com;
```

Listing 9-34 shows the Perl source code used to delete the cookie.

Listing 9-34

```
#!/usr/local/bin/perl
print<<"_END_";
Set-Cookie: authors_cookie=class9; expires=Wed,
1-Jan-1997 12:00:00 GMT; path=/; domain=.authors.com;
Content-type: text/html\n\n
<HTML>
<HEAD>
    <TITLE>Deleting a Cookie</TITLE>
</HEAD>
```

```
<BODY>
<H1>Deleting a Cookie</H1>
<P>
The authors_cookie=class9 cookie for this domain will be deleted since the
expiration date has been set to a past date.
</P>
</BODY>
</HTML>
_END_
```

Moving On

In this chapter, we have briefly touched on many issues (to study them in detail is beyond the focus of this book). We have taken a look at the general concepts of CGI and Perl programs as well as HTML form creation and cookies.

The next chapter will affect the entertainment level of your pages rather than their functionality. You will learn about the various formats that are used for audio and video on the Web, the HTML syntax that it takes to implement these features, and how to maximize your multimedia delivery.

## chapter 10

Adding Scintillating Sound & Vivid Video

To show off your computer to your friends, you would likely pull up a sound or video file that takes full advantage of your computer's multimedia capabilities. So it's little wonder that many Web publishers are trying to impress their audiences by pushing multimedia to the extreme. Many record companies, movie studios, and bands have discovered the benefits of using the Web to gain exposure by including sound and video clips. The ability to include a variety of media on Web sites is one of the most exciting aspects of the World Wide Web. HTML and MIME typing has opened the doors to just about any kind of media files imaginable. To handle the abundance of multimedia file formats, an informal standard has evolved for multimedia file types on the Web.

Multimedia is an enticing way to get noticed, but it has its drawbacks. The biggest drawbacks are the bandwidth and the disk space required by multimedia files. Limited bandwidth is a major problem that cable and telephone companies are trying to overcome by offering high-speed alternatives to analog modems. Software publishers are investing lots of time and money to create powerful multimedia authoring tools. Many software publishers and hardware companies are creating and improving sound and video file formats so they can capture the multimedia publishing market. True multimedia on the Internet may be around the corner, but it's a big corner.

Even though current bandwidth limitations restrict many possible uses of audio and video applications over the Net, steady advances in compression and networking technologies are helping to remedy this situation. Some of these technologies have been around for only a couple of years, but they're already posing formidable challenges to traditional analog media distribution systems.

To better prepare yourself for the coming dominance of digital media distribution, it's a good idea to become familiar with many of the multimedia technologies in use on the Net today. This chapter introduces you to the multimedia file formats currently in use on the Internet as well as ways in which you can create high-quality files of your own with software included on this book's Companion CD-ROM.

Adding Sound & Video to Your Web Site

Deciding to use sound or video on your Web site involves more considerations than using simple text and graphic documents does. Both require installation of specific software (plug-ins or helper applications), and sound files additionally require audio hardware (such as a sound board). Also, both need a lot of bandwidth for their large file sizes. If you are trying to reach the widest audience, you might want to forgo the use of sound and video. Alternatively, structuring your site so that sound and video are optional or unobtrusive is advisable. Giving the viewer a choice is often the favored approach.

TIP *When giving the viewer a choice, be sure you offer the option before they begin loading any files. For example, nothing is more annoying to your viewer than to have to wait while a large audio file downloads when the computer system doesn't have a sound card.*

A very different approach to delivering sound is the use of plug-ins, which read the content of your site. Obviously, this can make your site accessible to the visually impaired. You might consider this if your site has significant verbal content. More information can be found on Netscape's section on In-line audio and video plug-ins (check out www.netscape.com/download/).

To include audio for the most recent releases of both Navigator and IE, different tags are used. Microsoft Internet Explorer supports the <BGSOUND> tag for playing background sound files. This may seem problematic, but since each browser ignores the other's tags, the solution is simply to include both, as shown in the following example:

```
<BODY BGCOLOR="#ffffff" BGSOUND SRC="soundfile">
<EMBED SRC="your sounds file name" AUTOSTART=TRUE HIDDEN=TRUE></EMBED>
```

The <EMBED> tag can be used to include video as well as a variety of audio formats on a Web page. There are many controls available for this tag; the complete syntax can be found in "HTML Syntax" later in this chapter.

TIP *One point to keep in mind about complete file downloads as opposed to streaming is that complete file downloads offer the best way to maintain quality in your sound or video presentations (see the next section, "Ending the Wait With Streaming Sound & Video"). You need to examine the trade-offs between giving your users an immediate experience and providing the highest quality.*

▼ Multimedia in HTML 4.0

The <EMBED> tag, which is mentioned here and described later in this chapter, is being phased out of HTML. With the advent of HTML 4.0, there will be a new <OBJECT> tag that provides the capability to insert a wide variety of multimedia objects, including images, applets, sound files, and video files, into your pages. The <OBJECT> tag has several important attributes that allow you to specify how the object is to be handled by the browser. The "data" attribute points to the actual file to be used as data for the object; for example, if you were playing a movie file, this would be the URL of the movie itself. The optional "codetype" attribute tells the browser what MIMETYPE the object is; this allows the page creator to set what application or helper is used to render the data file in the browser. At present, the browser has to figure that out from the file extension, which doesn't always work. The new "standby" attribute allows you to specify a message that will be displayed while the data is loading. And, finally, the "classid" attribute allows you to specify exactly where the browser can find the necessary program for handing the data if it can't process it internally. As you can see, these new features give you a lot more control over how multimedia information is handled.

In addition, the new <OBJECT> tag has an associated <PARAM> tag that you use to specify parameters for initialization of the object reference. One OBJECT may have multiple <PARAM> tags associated with it. The <PARAM> tags allow you to set a variety of initial parameters for the object being rendered. For example, you could set volume or sampling rate for a sound or speed of display for a video clip.

Ending the Wait With Streaming Sound & Video

Originally, delivering sound or video on the Web involved waiting for an entire file to download, and then a helper application would launch and play the file. The next advance involved Netscape's implementation of plug-ins that allowed the playback of multimedia files within the browser window. You still had to wait for the entire file to download before you could enjoy the experience, but you didn't have to use a separate player.

Streaming technology, originated by RealAudio by Progressive Networks, dramatically changed the way sound and video was handled on the Web. Streaming permits the audio (or video) to start playing before the entire file downloads; in fact, the sound will usually start within a few seconds. Figure 10-1 shows RealPlayer for playing streaming sound and video.

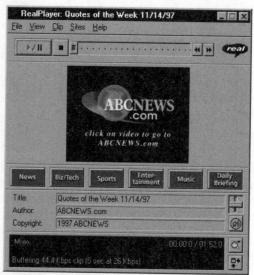

Figure 10-1: RealPlayer plays streaming sound and video.

While notable improvements have been made since the introduction of streaming technology, inherent limitations in the delivery of information over the Internet and the small bandwidth of modem connections limit the quality of sound and video transmissions. Additionally, voice-grade telephone lines were not designed to deliver the audio quality that would be considered an audiophile's delight.

RealAudio is the most popular format for delivering audio over the Web at this time. Progressive Networks provides a free application to convert sounds into RealAudio format and also sells a server application that enhances the delivery of RealAudio and enables simultaneous users. However, because the software is expensive, many ISPs and Web hosting services don't use it. Of those offering the service, most charge extra for its use.

While streaming technology has also been applied to video, even with a 56K modem, the motion can be quite jerky. Again, careful evaluation of your target audience and the quality needed should be foremost in deciding whether and how to use streaming video.

Best Supporting Multimedia Plug-ins

There are a variety of plug-ins for streaming multimedia, and many of them require their own proprietary compression programs to prepare files for delivery on the Web. Others use more standard formats, the foremost of which is QuickTime (discussed more fully later in this chapter). Many tools exist for preparing multimedia files with QuickTime. Both Fractal Design Painter and Adobe's Photoshop can make purely visual QuickTime movies from their own images. Adobe's Premier can produce QuickTime movies with both images and sound with a great variety of effects. Other applications can capture video from videotapes and make raw QuickTime movies if your computer has a video capture card. QuickTime movies can consist of only sound or MIDI (see next section).

A recent check of Netscape's site showed 35 plug-ins for audio and video and a similar number for 3D and animation, and a similar number of plug-ins are available for Microsoft's Internet Explorer at the Microsoft site. Both sites bring home the point that this arena is extremely active with a variety of approaches competing for this niche. This competitive environment demands that you should investigate the current situation at the time you plan to add these features to your site. Another complicating factor is that not all plug-ins are available for all platforms. When you want to reach the broadest possible audience, you need to use media formats supported by plug-ins available on all platforms. The following sections list and describe the most common multimedia plug-ins available for Web browsers.

Apple QuickTime & QuickTime VR

The Apple QuickTime plug-in lets you experience QuickTime animation, music, MIDI, audio, video, and VR panoramas and objects directly in a Web page. The Apple QuickTime Plug-in's "fast-start" feature allows you to experience QuickTime content while it's downloading. It works seamlessly within firewall environments and requires no special server software. A full discussion of QuickTime is provided later in the chapter. QuickTime is available for Macintosh 68K, Power Mac, Windows 3.X, Windows 95, and Windows NT. The official QuickTime site is http://www.quicktime.apple.com/sw/.

Bamba & Bamba for Java

Bamba is an audio-video streaming tool from IBM that supports high-quality audio-video streaming for low-bandwidth connections. It contains algorithms that determine connection bandwidth and file size and then makes adjustments to maximize the transmission of audio-video data. As a result, a typical PC user with a 14.4 or 28.8 Kbps modem can easily download and view large audio-video files. With Bamba, audio-video clips arrive in streams, so users can begin to view or hear the clip before the download is complete. A version of Bamba written in Java is available; it's called Bamba for Java. You simply embed the Bamba for Java applet in your HTML page. The applet then downloads and begins playing the specified Bamba audio or video clip. Bamba for Java is a cross-platform solution that will run on most computers with a browser running a Java Virtual Machine. Bamba is available for Windows 95, Windows NT, and OS/2. The official site for Bamba and Bamba for Java is http://www.alphaWorks.ibm.com/Home/.

Crescendo

LiveUpdate's version 3 of the Crescendo music plug-in delivers higher-quality stereo MIDI music to the Web. The free Crescendo plug-in has a CD-like control panel and digital counter. The Crescendo PLUS plug-in adds live and real-time streaming as well as "sticky" client-side preferences. Crescendo is available for Macintosh 68K, Windows 3.X, Windows 95, and Windows NT. The official site for Crescendo is http://www.liveupdate.com/midi.html.

MIDPLUG

MIDPLUG by Yamaha offers sound and music accompaniment for your Web pages using MIDI technology. Compact MIDI data means maximum speed and efficiency on the Internet with no extra equipment required. MIDPLUG features a built-in Soft Synthesizer with 128 GM-compatible voices, 8 drum kits, and even reverb. External MIDI playback equipment such as an XG sound module or daughter card can be connected if desired. MIDPLUG is available for Macintosh Power Mac, Windows 3.X, and Windows 95. The official site for MIDPLUG is http://www.ysba.com/midplug_index.html.

RealPlayer

RealPlayer by Progressive Networks provides live and on-demand real-time RealAudio and RealVideo streaming content on the Web. The RealAudio technology delivers AM-radio-quality sound at 14.4 Kbps, and progressively improved quality at higher speeds. RealVideo delivers newscast-quality video at 28.8 Kbps and full-motion at faster connections. The RealPlayer 5.0, which plays all RealAudio and RealVideo programming on the Web, introduces RealFlash animation synchronized with RealAudio. RealFlash incorporates Flash technology from Macromedia that lets you view streaming animations. Version 5 also lets you display video in a larger window than previous versions. RealPlayer is available for Macintosh 68K, Power Mac, Windows 3.X, Windows 95, Windows NT, OS/2, IRIX, Sun OS, and LINUX. The official site for RealPlayer is http://www.real.com.

Shockwave & Flash

Shockwave—a product of Macromedia (www.macromedia.com)—is a Netscape plug-in that permits the inline delivery of interactive multimedia. Shockwave was one of the first 2D animation plug-ins and remains one of the best. Numerous Web sites present games, animated interfaces, interactive ads and demos, and audio. The latest version of the Shockwave plug-in supports streaming audio and video. We'll cover how to create a shocked site later in this chapter. The Shockwave plug-in is included with Netscape Navigator and Microsoft Internet Explorer. Shockwave is compatible with Windows 3.1, Windows 95, Windows NT, Macintosh, and Power Macintosh.

Flash is a vector-based animation program from Macromedia. Using the Flash plug-in, you can display interactive animations with sound. This lets designers include Web interfaces such as buttons, banners, and image maps. Because Flash uses vector graphics, you can resize animations and graphics with no loss of quality. Flash also supports anti-alias fonts on the fly, so there are no jagged edges on Flash outline fonts. A combined Shockwave and Flash plug-in is available for Windows 3.1, 95, and NT, Macintosh, and Power Macintosh. A Microsoft Internet Explorer ActiveX control for Windows 95 is also available. The official site for Shockwave and Flash is http://www.macromedia.com.

TIP *Macromedia recently announced the Flash Player Java Edition, which makes it possible for your Flash movies to play on any Java-enabled browser; no plug-in is required.*

Publishing Sound Files

The surge in multimedia-compatible computers has made the addition of sounds to Web documents commonplace. Thanks to MIME typing, you can easily include in your Web documents sound files that can be played by Web browsers with the appropriate helper applications specified. However, down-loading and playing large sound files can be a time-consuming and processor-intensive operation. Sound files can easily exceed one megabyte for each minute of playing time. If you include hyperlinks to sound files on your pages, be sure the sound clips are relevant to your mission. You may be asking readers to devote a lot of time and hard disk space to get the sound, so don't disappoint them.

Digital Audio Basics: Sample Depth & Sampling Rates

You need to become familiar with a couple of fundamental digital audio concepts before you start digitizing your own audio clips. These concepts will give you the foundation for understanding how digital audio works and a working knowledge that will help you select the file formats most appropriate for your site.

The first concept, *sample depth*, refers to the number of discrete levels pro-vided for each "sample," or output, from an analog-to-digital (A/D) converter. Represented in bits, the sample depth determines the overall dynamic range, or span, between the quietest and loudest points of an audio sample. For instance, an 8-bit sample has 256 steps within the signal, while a 16-bit sample has 65,536. Obviously, the higher the sample depth, the greater the sound quality. Each bit contributes approximately 6 decibels (a measure of the ear's response to sound pressure levels, abbreviated dB) of dynamic range to the recording. Eight-bit audio files are therefore able to reproduce a dynamic range of 48dB, roughly that of an analog cassette deck, while 16-bit audio files are capable of yielding the 96dB of dynamic range found on CDs.

The second concept you should understand is *sampling rate*, the frequency at which the A/D converter samples an incoming audio signal. The sampling rate is the highest frequency that can be recorded or played back, so the higher the sampling rate, the closer the audio file's fidelity is to the original sound. The *hertz* (Hz), or *cycles per second*, is the unit of measurement for a sampling rate. Therefore, an audio file with a sampling rate of 22 kHz has been sampled 22,000 times every second. That means that the highest frequency stored in the file is 11 kHz because the highest possible sampled frequency is always one-half the sampling rate.

When preparing audio clips for use on the Web, keep in mind that you don't always have to use the highest possible sample depths and sampling rates. Higher sample depths and rates require more storage and throughput. You need to decide whether or not you can sacrifice disk space and bandwidth for high-quality audio files. While one minute of an 8-bit mono file sampled at 8 kHz is approximately 150K in size, a 16-bit stereo file sampled at 44.1 kHz can take up 10MB. Since most people have a hearing range of 20 Hz to 20 kHz, it's rarely necessary to use sampling rates higher than the 44.1 kHz CD standard, and that rate should be used only for the highest-quality samples. If an audio file consists solely of speech, an 8-bit, 8 kHz file will usually suffice. If it's absolutely necessary for you to provide CD-quality audio samples, take advantage of the various compression schemes discussed later in this chapter.

Sound File Formats

One of the issues surrounding any emerging technology is the flood of competing file formats that appear. Seemingly, every hardware manufacturer has developed its own way to record and play sound files, and each of them needs its own software program to deliver the sound to the speaker. Fortunately, you don't need to become a master of formats to place sound files in your documents. As previously mentioned, MIME typing allows you to transmit any file format between a client and a server, but fortunately a handful of audio formats have come to prominence on the Net. You already know about the RealAudio streaming format, which has become the most common standard for audio and video on the Web. The following sections explain other standard sound file formats in use on the Web, including μ-law (AU), used by Sun and NeXt workstations; AIFF, used by Macintosh computers; Microsoft's Wave (WAV) format, used by most PCs; and the increasingly popular MPEG compression format. We also briefly discuss ways to convert between formats.

While reviewing the following formats, keep in mind that some file format names are often used interchangeably with the compression/decompression algorithms, or *codecs*, on which they're based. For quick reference, we have included the appropriate MIME types for the formats before the descriptions.

TIP *If you're interested in learning more about sound file formats and compression schemes and getting sound-related technical information, check out ftp://ftp.cwi.nl/ pub/audio/ and get the FAQs titled Audio Formats.part1 and Audio Formats.part2. You can find the same information in a more browser-friendly format at http:// www.cs.ruu.nl/wais/html/na-dir/audio-fmts/.html.*

MIDI Files

MIDI stands for Musical Instrument Digital Interface. It's a protocol that enables computers and digital synthesizers to communicate. A MIDI file essentially contains the score of a piece of music. A fairly long and complex piece of music can be stored in a file of only a few thousand bytes. This makes MIDI files by far the most bandwidth-efficient way to include music on a Web page. For the Web, a user does not need a synthesizer to listen to the sounds on a site. What is needed is a MIDI file, a tag in your HTML, and a MIDI plug-in for the browser your site visitor is using. Browser users will also need sound hardware. The plug-in generates the notes of the score for the instruments specified using software techniques to produce the audio waves played by the speakers.

This leaves the question of how to obtain a MIDI file for your site. One possibility for the musically inclined is to use a synthesizer and associated software to generate a unique MIDI file. An easier way is to search the Web for public domain compositions. Be careful not to use copyrighted music without permission.

μ-law: The Sun/NeXT Audio File Format

audio/basic au snd

One of the most popular sound formats on the Web is the μ-law (pronounced mu-law) format. Often referred to as the Sun/NeXT audio format, the files are usually identified by the .au extension but occasionally end with the .snd extension. This can be rather confusing since Macintosh System sounds are also frequently identified by the .snd extension.

The μ-law format allows for various sample depths and sampling rates, but most of the ones found on the Net are 8-bit, 8 kHz monophonic files. Eight-bit sound files are the norm because they produce an acceptable audio quality for users wanting to get an idea of what a sample sounds like and save bandwidth and disk space—important factors for publishing multimedia files on the Net. Most commercial Windows sound editors don't directly support the μ-law format, but many shareware sound editors do. GoldWave, which is included on the Companion CD-ROM, can play and edit files in the μ-law format. Most audio editing applications for the Mac don't directly support the μ-law format either, but there are ways to convert standard Mac file formats to and from μ-law. This conversion process is discussed in detail later in this chapter.

The Waveform (WAV) Sound Format

audio/x-wav wav

Waveform is a proprietary format sponsored by Microsoft and IBM that was introduced in Microsoft Windows 3.1. The format is actually a subset of Microsoft's Resource Interchange File Format (RIFF). This is why the Waveform Audio Format (WAV) is grouped with the RIFF file format option in some sound editors. Waveform files can be saved as stereo or mono in 8-bit or 16-bit audio files. If you publish files in the Waveform (WAV) format, it is likely that Windows users will be the only people listening. In most cases, you'll want to save or convert the file to the AU format (see "Converting Sound Files," later in this chapter for more information).

The Audio Interchange File Format (AIFF)

audio/x-aiff aif aiff aifc

Developed by Apple, the Audio Interchange File Format (AIFF) and AIFC (AIF-Compressed) formats are primarily used on Macintosh and Silicon Graphics workstations. Since AIFF files allow for the storage of monaural and multichannel audio data at a variety of sampling rates and sample depths, they are the default file type for most Macintosh audio editors. AIFC files are usually compatible with AIFF editing and playback software, yet they can be compressed at ratios as high as 6:1 (at the expense of the file's signal quality).

The MPEG Audio Format

audio/x-mpeg mp2

MPEG is the acronym for Motion Picture Experts Group (http://www.crs4.it/~luigi/MPEG/), which is the organization responsible for development for the MPEG codec. The name refers to the file formats that use the codec. MPEG is a constantly evolving standard, and it's sure to play an increasingly important role in multimedia file distribution over computer networks.

Four versions of the MPEG codec (MPEG-1 through MPEG-4) are available. MPEG-1 is the version most commonly used on the Internet, even though MPEG-2 (and higher) compressed files are sure to be introduced as communication technologies evolve. MPEG audio compression specifies three layers, each of which specifies its own format. The more complex layers take longer to encode but produce higher compression ratios while keeping much of an audio file's original fidelity. Layer I takes the least amount of time to compress, but layer III yields higher compression ratios for comparable-quality audio files. MPEG layer II (MP2 or .mp2) has become a standard format for audio files. This is rapidly changing with the introduction of MPEG layer III (MP3 or .mp3) compression. Both layer II and layer III are based on psycho-acoustic models that attempt to determine which frequencies within the signal can be discarded without sacrificing original audio fidelity. The quality of an MPEG layer II- and layer III-compressed audio file remains similar to the original uncompressed file at ratios from 6:1 to 12:1.

Currently there are no plug-ins for playing MPEG layer III audio files, but there are some excellent MPEG layer III audio players. The best MPEG layer III audio player for Windows 95/NT is called WinAmp; it's available at http://winamp.lh.net/. A Macintosh version called MacAmp is available at http://macamp.lh.net/. You can create MPEG-compressed audio files with MPEG/CD, a software package discussed later in this chapter. Figure 10-2 shows the WinAmp player.

Figure 10-2: WinAmp lets you play high-quality MPEG layer III audio files.

TIP *The high compression and superior sound quality of MPEG layer III audio files have caused quite a stir on the Web. Circles of users have formed Web rings to share music in the MPEG layer III file format. Music companies seeking to protect their interest have sent cease and desist letters to numerous sites offering illegal archives of music files in the MPEG layer III format.*

Including Sound Files in a Web Page

To include a reference to a sound, use the same format you would use with any hyperlink text or image. You might want to include the size of the file since most audio files are quite large and letting users know the size will help them judge the download times. For example, a link to a sound file might be listed as follows:

```
Check out <A HREF=" file://sunsite.unc.edu/pub/multimedia/sun-sounds/
cartoons/speed_racer-complete-theme.au">Go Speed Racer</A> (498 Kb).
```

It's best to publish low-quality sound files in the μ-law format since most browsers are already configured to play back this format. Some browsers even include embedded sound players that are launched when μ-law files are downloaded.

You may want to point to a sound file that is published at some other site because of space limitations on your host or other reasons. A little caution should be exercised if you do that because external files may be changed without your knowledge. If you include the link, check occasionally to make sure the sound file is still available.

If you want to create an archive of sound files, be sure to identify the sound file with an icon that denotes a sound file, such as a speaker, a note, or an ear. The following is an example of a local sound file in a directory named sounds identified by an icon named speaker.gif in the icons directory:

```
<IMG SRC="/icons/speaker.gif" ALT="[Sound]"> <A HREF="/sounds/
splat.au">Splat!</A>
```

TIP *Make sure your intended audience has the necessary players. If there's a question as to whether or not your audience can listen to your sound files, refer them to the location of a player.*

Introducing the LiveAudio Player

Since Navigator 3.0, Netscape Navigator includes native support for standard sound formats such as AIFF, AU, MIDI, and WAV. Windows and Macintosh users can use the built-in LiveAudio player to play and hear sound files embedded in HTML documents. For these sound formats, you no longer have to download and install an additional plug-in or helper application.

LiveAudio plays audio files in WAV, AIFF, AU, and MIDI formats. Audio controls appear according to the size specified in the WIDTH and HEIGHT parameters in the <EMBED> tag. You can create an audio console with any of the following six views:

- The Console view consists of Play, Pause, Stop buttons and a volume control lever.

- The SmallConsole view consists of Play and Stop buttons and a volume control lever (upon invoking this view of the applet class, a sound will "autostart" by default). This view will have smaller buttons than the standard Console buttons.

- The PlayButton view presents a button that starts the sound playing.

- The PauseButton view presents a button that pauses the sound while it is playing without unloading the sound file from memory.

- The StopButton view presents a button that ends the playing of sound and removes it from memory.

- The VolumeLever view presents a lever that adjusts the volume level for playback of the sound (and adjusts the system's volume level).

Each view may be used many times on one Web page, with all the view instances controlling one sound file or many sound files, depending on how the file is called in the HTML or JavaScript. It is also important to remember that these controls can be called by other applets to do things like control the system's universal volume.

Using LiveAudio requires some special HTML coding. Here's a description of the code required to make this work for Netscape Navigator 3.0 or higher on both Windows and the Macintosh.

LiveAudio Syntax

To use LiveAudio, you need to embed the necessary controls into your pages using the HTML <EMBED> command. You can also use JavaScript functions and various built-in functions to control the exact play of your sound file.

HTML Syntax

```
<EMBED SRC= [URL] AUTOSTART=[TRUE|FALSE]
LOOP=[TRUE|FALSE|INTEGER]
STARTTIME=[MINUTES:SECONDS]
ENDTIME=[MINUTES|SECONDS] VOLUME=[0-100] WIDTH=[#
PIXELS] HEIGHT=[# PIXELS]
ALIGN=[TOP|BOTTOM|CENTER|BASELINE|LEFT|RIGHT
|TEXTTOP|MIDDLE|ABSMIDDLE|ABSBOTTOM]
CONTROLS=[CONSOLE|SMALL
CONSOLE|PLAYBUTTON|PAUSEBUTTON|STOPBUTTON|VOLUMELEVER]
HIDDEN=[TRUE] MASTERSOUND NAME=[UNIQUE NAME TO GROUP
CONTROLS TOGETHER SO THAT THEY CONTROL ONE
SOUND]...>
```

SRC=[URL] The URL of the source sound file.

AUTOSTART=[TRUE|FALSE] Setting the value to TRUE allows the sound, music, or voice to begin playing automatically when the Web page is loaded. The default is FALSE.

LOOP=[TRUE I FALSE I INTEGER]   Setting the value to TRUE allows the sound to play continuously until the Stop button is clicked on the console or the user goes to another page. If an INTEGER value is used, the sound repeats the number of times indicated by the integer.

STARTTIME=[MINUTES:SECONDS]   Use STARTTIME to designate where in the sound file you would like playback to begin. If you want to begin the sound at 30 seconds, you set the value to 00:30 (implemented only on Windows 95, NT, and Macintosh).

ENDTIME=[MINUTES:SECONDS]   Use ENDTIME to designate where in the sound file you would like playback to end. If you want to stop the sound at 1.5 minutes, you set the value to 01:30 (implemented only on Windows 95, NT, and Macintosh).

VOLUME=[0-100]   This value must be a number from 0 to 100 to represent 0 to 100 percent. This attribute sets the volume for the sound that is playing—unless the MASTERVOLUME (see NAME attribute later in this list) is used, then this value sets the sound for the entire system. The default volume level is the current system volume.

WIDTH=[# PIXELS]   This attribute is used to display the width of the console or console element. For the CONSOLE and SMALLCONSOLE, the default is WIDTH=144. For the VOLUMELEVER, the default is WIDTH=74. For a button, the default is WIDTH=37.

HEIGHT=[# PIXELS]   This attribute is used to display the height of the console. For the CONSOLE, the default is HEIGHT=60. For the SMALLCONSOLE, the default is HEIGHT=15. For the VOLUMELEVER, the default is HEIGHT=20. For a button, the default is HEIGHT=22.

ALIGN=[TOP I BOTTOM I CENTER I BASELINE I LEFT I RIGHT I TEXTTOP I MIDDLE I ABSMIDDLE I ABSBOTTOM]   This attribute tells Netscape Navigator how you want to align text as it flows around the consoles. Its action is similar to that of the <IMG> tag.

CONTROLS=[CONSOLE I SMALLCONSOLE I PLAYBUTTON I PAUSEBUTTON I STOPBUTTON I VOLUMELEVER]   This attribute defines which control a content creator wishes to use. The default for this field is CONSOLE.

HIDDEN=[TRUE]   The value for this attribute should be TRUE or it should not be included in the <EMBED> tag. If it is specified as TRUE, no controls will load and the sound will act as a background sound.

MASTERSOUND   This value must be used when grouping sounds together in a NAME group. This attribute takes no value (it must merely be present in the <EMBED> tag) but tells LiveAudio which file is a genuine sound file and allows it to ignore any stub files. Stub files have a minimum length necessary to activate LiveAudio.

NAME=[UNIQUE NAME TO GROUP CONTROLS TOGETHER SO THAT THEY CONTROL ONE SOUND] This attribute sets a unique ID for a group of CONTROLS elements so they all act on the same sound as it plays. For example, if you want to have one sound controlled by two embedded objects (a PLAYBUTTON and a STOPBUTTON), you must use this attribute to group the CONTROLS together. In this case, the <MASTERSOUND> tag is necessary to flag LiveAudio and let it know which of the two <EMBED> tags actually has the sound file you wish to control. LiveAudio ignores any <EMBED> tag(s) with no <MASTERSOUND> tag.

If you want one VOLUMELEVER to control multiple NAMEs (or the system volume), create an EMBED using the VOLUMELEVER CONTROL. Then set NAME to MASTERVOLUME.

Calling LiveAudio From JavaScript Functions

LiveAudio includes the ability to defer loading a sound file until the Play button is pushed. This enables a Web page designer to comfortably embed several sounds on one page without worrying about page load time.

To implement this feature, the Web designer must create a file like the following:

```
<SCRIPT LANGUAGE=SoundScript>
    OnPlay(http://YourURL/YourSound.aif);
</SCRIPT>
```

This file should be saved and named as a sound file (such as script1.aif). When the Play button is pushed, the URL you defined for the OnPlay function is loaded.

LiveAudio Examples

To play a sound as a background sound for a Web page:

```
<EMBED SRC="mysound.aif" HIDDEN=TRUE>
```

To have several CONTROLS controlling one sound file:

```
<EMBED SRC="mysound.aif" HEIGHT=22 WIDTH=37
CONTROLS=PLAYBUTTON NAME="MyConsole" MASTERSOUND>

<EMBED SRC="stub1.aif" HEIGHT=22 WIDTH=37
CONTROLS=PAUSEBUTTON NAME="MyConsole">

<EMBED SRC="stub2.aif" HEIGHT=22 WIDTH=37
CONTROLS=STOPBUTTON NAME="MyConsole">

<EMBED SRC="stub3.aif" HEIGHT=20 WIDTH=74
CONTROLS=VOLUMELEVER NAME="MyConsole">
```

To use a SMALLCONSOLE:

```
<EMBED SRC="mysound.aif" HEIGHT=15 WIDTH=144
MASTERSOUND CONTROLS=SMALLCONSOLE>
```

LiveAudio Control From LiveConnect

LiveAudio is LiveConnect enabled; LiveConnect is a series of functions and indicators you can use from JavaScript to control the behavior of your LiveAudio sound file. The following functions will work in JavaScript to control a loaded LiveAudio plug-in:

- Controlling functions (all Boolean, 0 or 1):
  ```
  play('TRUE/FALSE or int','URL of sound')
  stop()
  pause()
  start_time(int seconds)
  end_time(int seconds)
  setvol(int percent)
  fade_to(int to_percent)
  fade_from_to(int from_percent,int
  to_percent)
  start_at_beginning() = Override a
  start_time()
  stop_at_end() = Override an end_time()
  ```

- State indicators (all Boolean, except *, which is an integer):
  ```
  IsReady() = Returns TRUE if the plug-in
  instance has completed loading
  IsPlaying() = Returns TRUE if the sound is
  currently playing
  IsPaused() = Returns TRUE if the sound is
  currently paused
  GetVolume() = Returns the current volume as a percentage *
  ```

Acquiring Sound Files

Many sites on the Web include sound files. The problem is that many of these files are poor quality clips, and it's hard to tell which ones break copyright laws—use audio files from the Internet at your own risk. Of course, you can always create a link to a sound in an archive. Table 10-1 lists sites on the Web that include sound clips. Just because the sites are listed, however, doesn't mean you can publish the sound clips on your Web site. But you may want to experiment with the sound files, even if you don't add any of them to your Web pages.

URL	Description
http://www.acm.uiuc.edu/rml/Sounds/	A large collection of μ-law sounds, many from movies and cartoons such as *Roger Rabbit, Ren and Stimpy,* and *Beavis and Butthead.* The site includes other clips, such as computer sounds, dinosaur noises, Monty Python routines, music, quotes, Christmas sounds, and other sound effects.
http://sunsite.unc.edu/pub/multimedia/sun-sounds/	The University of North Carolina at Chapel Hill's SunSITE collection of sound files in the μ-law format. Some of the sounds include bird calls, cartoons, comedy, commercials, computer sounds, Monty Python routines, movies, clips from *Star Trek* and *Star Trek: The Next Generation,* sayings, screams, sound tracks, TV clips, whales, and other sound effects. Some sounds in the Waveform format are stored in a directory named PC Sounds.
http://www.cmf.nrl.navy.mil/radio/byte_RTFM.html	A short sound bite is added to this site just about every day. Most are single words or short phrases. Many are computer related.
http://web.msu.edu/ vincent/general.html	The MSU Vincent Voice Library collection of μ-law sound bites of famous people, such as Isaac Asimov, George Washington Carver, Amelia Earhart, Betty Ford, Will Rogers, and Babe Ruth.
http://www.eecs.nwu.edu/μ-law~jmyers/sun_sounds/	Miscellaneous sound files in the ? format, such as a bark, bong, bubbles, birds chirping, cowbell, crash, cuckoo, doorbell, drip, flush, gong, laugh, ring, rooster, space music, splat, and several telephone sounds.
http://155.187.10.12:80/sounds/	Assorted bird calls; includes, for instance, a cockatoo and a spinebill.

Table 10-1: URLs for sound files.

You can also find sound files in a few newsgroups, such as *alt.binaries.sounds.music* and *alt.binaries.sound.misc.* The sound files are posted in ASCII format and must be decoded with a program like uuUndo before the clip can be played on a computer. The sound files posted in newsgroups change daily. Most of the postings are multipart files that have to be assembled before decoding. If you have a newsreader that can put the parts together for you, such as NewsWatcher, this is a simple operation. If you're not using one of these programs, prepare yourself for some aggravation and read the newsgroup's FAQ (Frequently Asked Questions) file.

Sound in Windows

Most of today's PCs come with sound cards and speakers as standard equipment, or you can buy add-on kits from such vendors as Creative Labs, Diamond Multimedia, and Turtle Beach. Windows 95's plug-and-play features make installing a sound card a relatively painless process. Windows 95 includes built-in support for sound that includes system-level tools and applets for basic sound capabilities. Windows 95/NT ships with a sound recorder that is fairly limited, but there are some excellent commercial and shareware sound editing programs that we will cover a little later in this chapter.

If you don't have a sound card, it is possible to use the speaker in your PC, but you will definitely be disappointed with the quality. Microsoft includes a PC-Speaker driver, speaker.drv. There are several limitations to using this driver with Windows 95. For example, the PC speaker driver plays only WAV files. It does not play MIDI or AVI files. The version of Media Player included with Windows 95 does not play WAV files with the PC speaker driver. To play WAV files, you have to use Sound Recorder. The built-in Windows 95 Volume and Mixer tools will not control the PC speaker driver. Information on downloading and setting up the driver is available at http://support.microsoft.com/support/kb/articles/Q138/8/57.asp. You can download the speaker driver directly from http://premium.microsoft.com/download/support/mslfiles/SPEAK.EXE. You cannot use a PC speaker driver with Windows NT.

Sound on the Macintosh

All new Macs come equipped with the hardware and software necessary to play digital audio files, and many have hardware for recording high-quality audio samples. If there's a particular audio file format that your Mac can't play, there are publicly available software packages that will enable you to listen to it. We've included some of these audio editing and playback packages with the Companion CD-ROM, including SoundEffects, MPEG/CD, SoundHack, and Brian's Sound Tool, all of which will be discussed shortly.

The first step in making sure your Mac is well equipped to handle audio is to obtain the latest version of Apple's Sound Manager. First introduced in 1987, the Sound Manager allows any application to play and record sounds using built-in hardware. Support for 16-bit audio was added with the release of version 3.0 in 1993, and the newest version, 3.1, adds support for the IMA and μ-law audio codecs. It has also been streamlined for use with Power Macs, making audio handling much more efficient on the newest line of Power PC-based Macs. Sound Manager 3.1 (including a new version of the Sound control panel) can be downloaded for free from ftp://ftp.info.apple.com/ Apple.Support.Area/Apple.Software.Updates/US/Macintosh/System/ Other_System/Sound_Manager_3.1.sea.hqx.

TIP | *For the complete lowdown on Macintosh audio/video hardware and everything relating to Macintosh-based multimedia, see http://www.csua.berkeley.edu/ ~jwang/AV/.*

Sound Editors & Tools

Sound editors represent sound graphically, so you can cut and paste portions of the visual representation of the sound or insert silence or other effects into your sound file. Just as you can use filters in graphics editing packages to achieve different results, there are sound filters that let you control sound output. Editing software uses digital signal processing (DSP) algorithms to present tools and filters for controlling sounds with effects such as fades, delays, and reverb and for blending and equalizing sounds and adding distortion and other special effects.

Creating Sound Files

The ability to create a sound file, and the quality of that file once created, depends on the capabilities of your equipment. The sound file is recorded on a platform such as a PC using a sound board and one or more input devices, such as a microphone, tape deck, or keyboard. It's safest to record the sound and use the Export or Save As feature to save the file in the Sun Audio (.au) format. Depending on your audience, you may want to use Microsoft's Waveform format, Apple's AIFF format, or the MPEG audio (.mp2) format. The following sections explain how you can use some sound editors to create your sound files.

Sound Quality

As mentioned previously, most sound cards today are 16-bit or higher, but there is a huge installed base of 8-bit sound cards. The more bits, the better the audio quality. Eight-bit sampling lets you define 256 steps in the signal. Sixteen-bit sampling provides 65,536 steps. Some sites post sound files in two different formats (levels of quality), leaving the choice up to the user. If the user wants a high-quality sample, such as a 16-bit stereo file, it can be downloaded. If the user does not have the time or the equipment to benefit from this quality, a much smaller rendering of the same file is often offered in a more compact format, such as an 8-bit mono sound file.

Be careful when including sound files in your Web pages. If you record a file in stereo at a high sampling rate, the file can grow to an immense size, which will frustrate your readers when they download it. This is especially bad form if the sound file is not of a type that demands a high-quality recording, like a voice transcription. However, the converse can be true as well. If you are in the sound business, a poor-quality sound sample is a bad advertisement for your business.

Windows Sound Editing

Sampling and editing sound files is a fairly straightforward process. Most sound cards, such as the highly rated SoundBlaster 64 from Creative Labs and SoundBlaster-compatible sound cards, typically come with software for creating and editing sound files. The bottom line is, the better the sound card and editing software, the better the results. On the low end, Windows 95 comes with the Sound Recorder, which lets you create, mix, and edit sound files with special effects such as echo or reverse. The Sound Recorder only lets you record one minute at a time. You can cut and paste sound clips together, but you'll be much happier working with a high-end sound editor, such as Sound Forge from Sonic Foundry.

If you want to manipulate a sound file and don't have a sound editor, check out the GoldWave shareware sound editor on the Companion CD-ROM. Figure 10-3 shows the GoldWave sound editor with a sound file loaded. You can check for updates at http://www.goldwave.com/. Another excellent shareware sound editor is Cool Edit from Syntrillium. One nice feature of Cool Edit is that it can export to the RealAudio format. You can download Cool Edit from http://www.syntrillium.com/.

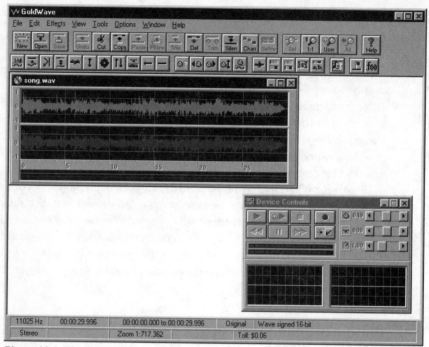

Figure 10-3: The GoldWave sound editor lets you create and edit sound files in both the AU and WAV formats.

It requires a great deal of precision to edit sound files. Some sound editors include a Society of Motion Picture and Television Engineers (SMPTE) time code. This is like the fast clocks that appear at the bottom of professional videos to help locate exact moments to cut. SMPTE time codes are extremely helpful when you are trying to synchronize two pieces of music.

You will most likely want additional features for working with sounds if you will be creating a video or animation. An advantage of some digital sound editors is that you can fade out or expand or compress the amount of time a sound file fills. This is a powerful feature when you have a video that is 15 seconds long and your audio is 20 seconds long. For example, Sound Forge, a commercial sound editor from Sonic Foundry, lets you mark a block of audio output and compress or expand the marked block. Figure 10-4 shows the time compression and expansion feature found in Sound Forge.

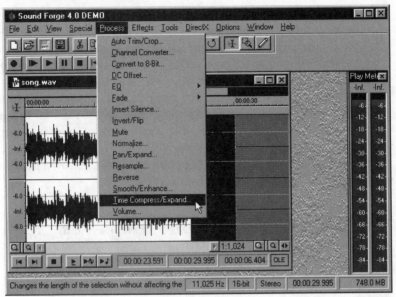

Figure 10-4: Sound Forge lets you compress or expand marked blocks of a sound file.

Macintosh Sound Editing

A number of high-quality commercial audio editors are available for the Mac, including Digidesign's Sound Designer II (which comes with Audiomedia II), Digidesign's Pro Tools and Sound Tools (http://www.digidesign.com), Alaska Software's Digitrax, OSC's Deck II, and Opcode Systems's DigiTrax (http://www.opcode.com). They are multitrack editors, meaning they allow you to overdub and mix down multiple audio tracks. They all provide onscreen mixers to control audio volume levels as well as numerous filters and effects for modifying individual waveforms.

TIP *Looking for a high-end audio card with digital input/output? Check out Digidesign's Audiomedia II, a NuBus card providing digital I/O as well as hardware-based DSP processing. You can read more about it at http://www.digidesign.com.*

If you just want to edit samples graphically and don't need a multitrack sound editor, consider Macromedia's SoundEdit 16 ($379, 800-326-2128). Better yet, try out SoundEffects, a feature-rich shareware audio editor that we've included on the Companion CD-ROM. It provides many of the same capabilities as commercially available packages and is ideal for users new to the world of digital audio editing. SoundEffects imports and exports audio files in both AIFF and native Macintosh SND format, comes with a number of special effects and filters, and supports multichannel sounds. One of the nicest things about the package is that its developer, Alberto Ricci, included a Developer's Kit in the distribution to encourage people to write their own plug-in effects for the editor.

TIP *You can keep up with the latest versions of SoundEffects at ftp://ftp.alpcom.it/ software/mac/Ricci.*

To familiarize you with the process of audio editing on the Mac, we're going to take you through the process of creating, editing, and formatting sound files using software on the Companion CD-ROM. We'll begin with the SoundEffects editor, but first make sure that your audio hardware is configured properly. To record a sample, you'll need to have an audio source plugged into the audio input jack (marked by a small microphone icon) on the back of your Mac. If your Mac doesn't have an audio input jack, you'll need to buy an audio input card mentioned in the previous section. Figure 10-5 shows the SoundEffects sound editor.

TIP *If you don't have an audio input card but you have an AppleCD 300CD-ROM drive, you can convert audio tracks from an audio CD with any QuickTime-aware application, such as SoundEffects or SimpleText. Simply choose Open from the File menu, find the file you want to convert, double-click the filename, and select where you want to save the converted file. If you use SimpleText, be aware that you will need a large amount of disk space and be prepared to wait a while for the file to be converted.*

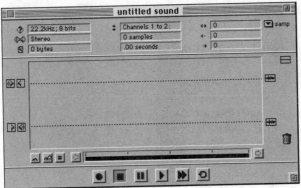

Figure 10-5: The SoundEffects sound editor lets you create and edit AIFF sound files and Macintosh System sounds.

Most Macs come with a microphone, so you can start by simply speaking into the microphone, or you can connect the output of a CD player or tape to the input. Once your hardware is configured, launch SoundEffects. When you're presented with the SoundEffects main window (Figure 10-5), click the Record button to pull up the Record dialog box (the Record button is the second button from the left at the bottom of the Record dialog box in Figure 10-6). Make sure that you've selected the correct sound input from the Sound control panel by opening the General Settings collapsible menu at the bottom of the Record dialog box. Click Device Settings to pull up the Input Source box and select External Audio and Playthrough (Figure 10-7). This lets you record and hear the signal coming in from your audio input jack.

Next, you can adjust the audio recording settings. Select Stereo, 44.1 kHz - CD, 16 bits, and a Play-Through Volume of 7. Make sure that the Auto Gain box is checked so the recorded signal won't be distorted. You're recording with these settings because you need a high-quality sample to convert to MPEG later.

Figure 10-6: The SoundEffects Record dialog box lets you easily adjust the recording settings.

Figure 10-7: The Device Settings button in the Record dialog box provides a shortcut to the Input Source dialog box.

The length of a sound clip you can record will be limited by the amount of memory you have allocated to SoundEffects, and since 16-bit, 44.1 kHz stereo samples require about 10 megabytes of space for every minute of audio, make sure you have made plenty of RAM available. If you have limited RAM, you can record in Mono mode or reduce the Sampling Rate and Sampling Size settings.

Now you're ready to record. When you click the Record button, the incoming waveform will turn red. Be sure to watch the continuous reading of the time left to record in the Available Seconds box. Click Save when you're done.

Now that you have a sample, you can manipulate it in a number of ways. You can select specific parts of the waveform by clicking and dragging over any area within the waveform display. The area you select will be the area affected by any special effects you apply to the sample. One of the nicest things about SoundEffects is that its author invites programmers to develop plug-in effects for the application. Included on the Companion CD-ROM is one group of such plug-ins from gopher://gopher.archive.umich.edu: 7055/ 00/mac/sound/soundutil/.

You can get help for individual effects at any time by holding down the Shift key and choosing the effect.

If you want the sound clip to fade in at the beginning, select the first few seconds of the sample and choose Effects | Fade In. Make sure you select both channels if you want the entire audio signal to fade smoothly. If you need a different view of the waveform, you can modify the display with the Zoom-In and Zoom-Out buttons, or you can look at the entire waveform with the Actual Size button. You can also adjust other aspects of the waveform display from the File | Preferences menu.

You can also add channels by dragging the New Channel icon to the right of the waveform, or you can delete channels by dragging the Waveform icon next to the channel to the SoundEffects trash can.

Converting Sound Files

Since most audio archives on the Net contain sound clips in the MPEG and μ-law formats, you should become familiar with the steps necessary for converting recorded audio clips to these formats. We will illustrate this process by discussing how to convert WAV files (from the PC) and AIFF files (from the Mac) into these two common formats.

Converting WAV to μ-law

In order to convert a WAV file to the standard AU format, the file can be "translated" into the language of another sound format by using one of the many widely available shareware programs such as GoldWave and WHAM. By saving or exporting the file in the AU format, you can be assured that everyone who has a computer with sound capability will be able to hear it. In most cases, you will want to use the sound editor's Export or Save As option to convert sound files from one format to another.

Creative Labs's SoundBlaster cards are the most popular sound cards for the PC. SoundBlaster has its own sound file format that ends with the extension .voc. If you have a SoundBlaster file you want to publish, you can convert it to the Sun AU format using a DOS-based program named sunvoc.exe. You can download the conversion program after accepting the licensing agreement from Creative Labs's FTP site by entering the following URL: http:// www.creaf.com/asp-scripts/download.asp?file=/creative/patches/ sunvoc.exe&Agrmt=slicense.html.

Shareware offerings change rapidly. To check for the latest shareware sound editor releases, use one of the following URLs. For Windows, check http:// www.tucows.com or http://www/windows95.com. For the Macintosh, check out http://hyperarchive.lcs.mit.edu/HyperArchive.html. For both Windows and Macintosh, check out C | Net's shareware site at http://www.shareware.com.

Converting AIFF to MPEG Layer II

We will illustrate this conversion by exporting the audio clip you prepared earlier with SoundEffects and converting it with two separate applications.

First, let's convert the 16-bit, 44.1 kHz stereo sample to an MPEG Layer II (.mp2) file. Start by saving (File | Save) the clip in SoundEffects as an AIFF file. Next, copy the MPEGAud application from the Companion CD-ROM to your hard drive and launch it. There are different versions of this program available for Macs with and without a floating point unit processor, so be sure to copy the one that's right for your machine. Open the AIFF file with MPEGAud (File | Encode) and click Save when you see the dialog box showing the filename with the .mp2 extension. At this point, you'll be given many options for how the sound file will be encoded (Figure 10-8). For now, leave the default settings as they are, and click OK. Be forewarned that the MPEG Encoding process with MPEGAud is not real-time, and on some computers it takes quite a while. You may want to make sure that the selected file is only a few seconds long, unless you have time to wait. As MPEGAud is encoding the file, it will provide a status window reporting on the progress of the encoding.

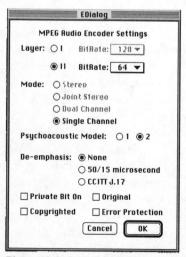

Figure 10-8: Once the MPEGAud application recognizes and opens the file to be encoded, it allows you multiple options for encoding.

When the MPEGAud is done, you can check to make sure it's encoded properly with the MPEG playback utility called MPEG/CD, which is also on the Companion CD-ROM. This program works with groups of MP2 files called *lists*. To create a new list, choose File I Add to List and select the file you just encoded. You could also select the demo file that comes with MPEG/CD if you think your file didn't encode correctly. To listen to the file, choose Audio I Decode List. It will attempt to play the file back in real-time, but if you don't have enough processing power, the audio signal may drop in and out. You can improve the playback by decoding only one channel at a time, which you can specify under Edit I Decoder Preferences. The MPEG/CD Manual offers a number of tips about how to improve playback performance.

The Decoder Preferences dialog box also gives you the option of decoding the audio clip to an AIFF file. This is handy if you're working on a lower-end Macintosh or if you want to edit the audio file. If you want to decode the file with full quality, duplicate the settings in Figure 10-9.

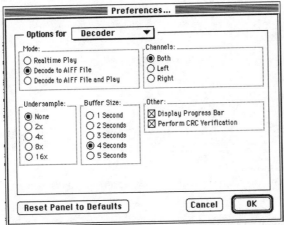

Figure 10-9: The correct MPEG/CD settings for converting an MPEG audio file to a high-quality AIFF file.

TIP *The makers of MPEG/CD, Kaua'i Media, sell a number of MPEG audio encoding/ decoding software solutions. You can check out their product specifications and compression statistics at http://www.kauai.com/~bbal/.*

Converting AIFF to μ-law

To create μ-law files for Web sites, you must convert the sample depth, sample rate, and number of channels so they are compatible with the existing standards on the Web. The conversion process will be different for every audio editor, but the process for SoundEffects described here should give you a pretty good idea of how to do it.

First, you need to convert the stereo file to mono. This isn't absolutely necessary, but since mono files are half the size of stereo files, and people who don't have a stereo playback system often use μ-law files, it's generally a good idea. From SoundEffects, choose Effects | Quick Mix. Adjust your settings to match those in Figure 10-10 and click OK. This will combine the stereo channels into a single channel so you can drag the waveform icon that is to the right of the empty channel to the trash can. This will leave you with a single-channel sample.

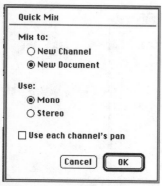

Figure 10-10: The proper Quick Mix filter settings to convert a stereo file to mono.

Next, you must change the sampling rate of the file by choosing Effects | Resampling | Resample Rate, manually entering 8000 Hz (since it's not a default option), and clicking OK. This is the standard sampling rate for μ-law files on the Net.

Finally, you need to downsample the sample depth by choosing Effects | Resample | Downsample Bits. Make sure the dialog box displays "Downsample to 8 bits" and click OK. As you might have guessed, 8 bits is the standard sample depth for μ-law files on the Net. Choose File | Save and save the modified file in the AIFF format.

To convert the 8-bit, 8 kHz mono AIFF to μ-law, you need to open it with SoundHack; this incredibly handy sound processing and conversion tool can be found on the Companion CD-ROM as well as at http://www.gmeb.fr/ SoftwareCompetition/SoundHack.html. SoundHack reads and writes to AIFF, AIFC, WAV, and AU sound files, as well as many others.

When you open the file with SoundHack, it displays the file's properties, similar to the properties shown in Figure 10-11. To convert the file, choose File | Save a Copy, set the File Type to NeXt • Sun and the Format to 8 Bit μ-law, and click OK. In the Save Soundfile As box, change the default .snd extension to .au so that browsers at your site won't be confused. The amount of time SoundHack needs to convert the file will depend on the size of the input file and the speed of your computer.

Voilà! You now have a Net-compatible Sun/NeXT μ-law file.

Figure 10-11: The SoundHack Soundfile Information dialog box.

If this conversion process seems rather laborious to you, don't worry. Since Sound Manager 3.1 supports μ-law compression, and more Mac users are encountering 8-bit, 8 kHz mono μ-law files, new conversion programs to automate the steps outlined here are sure to be introduced.

Converting to Other Formats

Since you may want to include other audio formats on your site, we've included a number of tools on the Companion CD-ROM that allow you to convert between numerous file types. Brian's Sound Tool is a handy utility that provides drag-and-drop conversion between Macintosh System sounds and Windows WAV files. It converts numerous non-Mac sound file formats (WAV, AU, VOC, and even AIFF) into Mac System sounds and converts just about any files with Mac SND resources in them to WAV files. Besides letting you convert between numerous file formats, Brian's Sound Tool allows you to apply gain changes, binaural filters, mutations, phase vocoders, and many other effects to audio files. Many of the settings on these effects are quite complex, but they can yield impressive results.

Publishing Video

Digital video has had an accelerated childhood and is quickly entering adolescence. In its current state, digital video is going through serious growing pains. It's awkward and unruly, but with a few preparatory measures, you'll see the promise of computer-based video editing and distribution. The following sections explore common digital video compression/decompression schemes and file format standards and explain what you need to create and publish video files at your Web site.

Video Codecs & File Format Standards

In discussions of digital video, you'll often come across references to "broadcast-quality" signals. This term refers to video signals that have been recorded using the National Television Standards Committee (NTSC) standard of 640 by 480 pixels at 30 frames per second (fps) in an interlaced fashion, with the odd and even horizontal lines alternating during each pass. The process divides each frame into two *fields*, thus producing 60 fields per second. Other video standards, such as PAL and SECAM, are used throughout the world, but NTSC is the most widely used.

As you enter the realm of digital video, you will undoubtedly encounter the term *codec*, which stands for a compression/decompression algorithm used to compress and decompress video files. For a video file to play smoothly, it needs to play back at a rate approaching 30 frames per second. A single frame of 24-bit video in its uncompressed state can require as much as a megabyte of disk space, *without* an audio track. This means that one second of uncompressed video is approximately 30MB and a minute is around 1.8GB. The most common solution to this heavy data load is to reduce the size of the images to a smaller than full-screen image. Other approaches include reducing the number of colors or even removing frames from the video, but all of these methods diminish the quality of the video signal. The need, then, is to find a standard codec that can compress the data to a manageable size so that it can be sent across the Internet without a noticeable loss in quality when decompressed and played back. Video files are the largest files you'll likely come across on the Internet. Some Web sites we've seen have published video files of over 12MB.

MPEG and QuickTime are the two video file format standards on the Internet. As more and more PCs enter the Internet scene, it is likely that the standard Windows AVI file format will also squeeze in between these formats. The following sections explain the most popular codecs and video file formats that have become Internet standards.

TIP *If you're interested in recording and working with broadcast-quality video, check out the Radius Digital Video Information Server. It includes information about audio, setting up high-speed disk arrays, and related Internet resources, among other topics. The DV Information server is at http://research.radius.com/dv/ maindv.html.*

Occasionally you'll run across some video and animation file formats on the Internet that are left over from days (and technologies) gone by. However, if you're working on a Mac, you'll be able to view them with the MacAnim Viewer on the Companion CD-ROM. It will play GL, FLI, FLC, FLX, and DL animations, as well as display GIF, JPEG, PCX/PIC, and raw PPM image files. MacAnim will even automatically unzip PC zipped files.

The MPEG Format

MPEG gets its name from the Motion Picture Experts Group. One confusing point about the term *MPEG* is that it refers to both the codec and the file format. Two types of MPEG codec standards exist: MPEG-1 and MPEG-2. MPEG-1 is the standard used on the Internet. MPEG-2 is a high-end broadcast-quality video standard. MPEG-1 videos use a resolution of 352 x 240 at 30 frames per second. In order to view an MPEG video at 30 frames per second, you must be using a video board that includes an MPEG decoder chip. MPEG decoder chips are quickly being added to graphic boards. An MPEG file typically ends with the filename extension .mpg. MPEG uses something called *predictive calculation* for compression. This method uses the current frame of video to predict what will be in the following frames. *This method of compression makes editing an MPEG video impossible.*

MPEG compresses and decompresses images and audio sounds at the same fast speed. It is the speed and ultra-high compression that has made MPEG the format of choice for video on the Internet. MPEG delivers decompressed data at 1.2 to 1.5MB per second and compresses at a ratio of 50:1 or higher before you start to notice a degradation in video playback. Compression ratios as high as 200:1 are possible, but at compression rates this high, images are typically degraded. MPEG has the highest level of compression and delivers the best quality video when decompressed. It sounds great, so far, but this is only one frame of the MPEG video picture. MPEG is typically hardware-based compression. The biggest drawback is that the compression hardware is expensive. The cost of creating a video in the MPEG format is covered later in this chapter.

Microsoft's Active Movie player, which ships with Internet Explorer, lets you play MPEG audio and movie files. You can also download the InterVu's

Multimedia Manager, EyeQ, which includes a free MPEG player, from http://www.intervu.com. Xing sells the XingMPEG player for under $30; you can download a demo version at http://www.xingtech.com/products/mpeg_player.html. If you're using a Macintosh, you can get Sparkle, a popular MPEG and QuickTime playback application that's also a QuickTime-to-MPEG converter, at http://www.cweb.net/~christer/mac-animation.html.

The QuickTime Format

Developed by Apple, QuickTime movies may contain any combination of video, sound, animation, audio, MIDI, text, and even interactive commands. QuickTime is sometimes referred to as the movie format. Appropriately, QuickTime movie files typically end with the filename extension .mov. Unlike files in the MPEG format, QuickTime files can be edited. QuickTime supports several codec schemes, including Photo (JPEG), Animation and Graphics, Apple Video, Cinepak, Indeo 3.2, MPEG, YUV, the Kodak Photo CD, and others. Each compressor is designed for a specific data type. Until recently, you had to use a Macintosh to create QuickTime files, but now you can use programs like Adobe Premiere for Windows (also available on the Mac) to create and edit video files in the QuickTime format. Autodesk Animator can also create QuickTime-compatible animations.

QuickTime is a Macintosh file format, which consists of a different structure than PC files. The main issue for QuickTime files is that there are two file forks, a resource fork and a data fork, that must be combined into one file in order to be displayed and edited on the PC platform. The process of converting QuickTime files so they can be used on other platforms is called *flattening*. A cross-platform QuickTime file is sometimes referred to as a flattened QuickTime file. Flattening a QuickTime file consolidates the video and audio into a single file.

The QuickTime Continuum, Apple's Web server devoted to QuickTime-related information, is located at http://quicktime.apple.com/. It is the best place to find all the latest news about QuickTime and related topics. The latest version of QuickTime is version 3.0. Apple has announced the QuickTime plug-in version 2.0 for Microsoft Internet Explorer and Netscape Navigator and Communicator. This new version brings the advanced digital media capabilities of QuickTime 3.0 to the Internet, including QuickTime VR 2.0 support, the ability to play alternate movie tracks, hot spots, and URL linking. The QuickTime plug-in supports most popular file formats so that users can have a wide and rich experience with digital media content on Internet Web sites. The QuickTime plug-in 2.0 will be available for Windows 95, Windows NT, and Mac OS. You can check for the latest version of the QuickTime plug-in at http://quicktime.apple.com/sw/. Figure 10-12 shows the QuickTime plug-in displaying a film clip in a Netscape Navigator window.

Figure 10-12: The QuickTime plug-in lets you automatically display a film clip inside a Netscape Navigator Window.

Using QuickTime requires some special HTML coding. Here's a description of the code required to make the QuickTime plug-in play QuickTime movies on both Windows and Macintosh.

QUICKTIME HTML SYNTAX:

```
<EMBED SRC=[URL] WIDTH=[# PIXELS] HEIGHT=[# PIXELS]
AUTOPLAY=[TRUE|FALSE] CONTROLLER=[TRUE|FALSE]
LOOP=[TRUE|FALSE|PALINDROME]
PLAYEVERYFRAME=[TRUE|FALSE] HREF=[URL]
TARGET=[FRAME] PLUGINSPAGE=[URL] PAN=[FIXED NUMBER]
TILT=[FIXED NUMBER] FOV=[FIXED NUMBER]
NODE=[INTEGER] CORRECTION=[NONE|PARTIAL|FULL]
HIDDEN...>
```

EMBED   This tag is used to put QuickTime movies in your document. When the document specified in the SRC parameter is a QuickTime movie, the QuickTime plug-in is used to display it. As with the rest of HTML, all of the following parameter keywords are case insensitive.

SRC=[URL]   The URL of the source document.

PLUGINSPAGE=[URL] - PLUGINSPAGE An optional parameter. The PLUGINSPAGE parameter allows you to specify a URL from which users can obtain the necessary plug-in if it is not installed. Navigator handles this parameter. If Navigator cannot find the plug-in when loading a page, it will warn users and allow them to go to the specified site to download the QuickTime plug-in. You need to set this parameter to http:// quicktime.apple.com, which will point to the most appropriate plug-in for various versions of Navigator and different operating systems. This parameter is appropriate for both QuickTime movies and QuickTime VR Objects and Panoramas.

WIDTH=[# PIXELS] The WIDTH attribute specifies the width of the embedded document in pixels. This option is appropriate for both QuickTime and QuickTime VR movies. The WIDTH parameter is required unless you use the HIDDEN parameter (described below). Never specify a width of less than 2, as this can cause problems with Navigator. If you don't know the width of the movie, open your movie with the MoviePlayer program (PLAYER.EXE or PLAY32.EXE on Windows 3.1) that comes with QuickTime and choose Get Info (Get Movie Info in Windows) from the Movie menu. If you supply a width that is smaller than the actual width of the movie, the movie is cropped to fit the specified width. If you supply a width that is greater than the width of the movie, the movie is centered within this width.

HEIGHT=[# PIXELS] The HEIGHT attribute specifies the height of the embedded document in pixels. This option is appropriate for both QuickTime and QuickTime VR movies. If you want to display the movie's controller, you will need to add 24 pixels to the height. The HEIGHT parameter is required unless you use the HIDDEN parameter (described below). Never specify a height of less than 2. If you don't know the height of the movie, open your movie with the MoviePlayer program that comes with QuickTime (PLAYEREXE or PLAY32.EXE on Windows 3.1) and choose GetInfo (Get Movie Info in Windows) from the Movie menu. If you supply a height that is smaller than the actual height of the movie (plus 24 if you are showing the controller), the movie is cropped to fit the height. If you supply a height that is greater than the height of the movie, the movie is centered within this height.

HIDDEN HIDDEN is an optional parameter. The HIDDEN parameter determines whether the movie is visible. There are no values to supply for this parameter. If you do not supply HIDDEN, the movie will be visible. If you supply HIDDEN, the movie is not visible on the page. This parameter is not appropriate for QuickTime VR objects or panoramas. You can use the HIDDEN setting to hide a sound-only movie.

When using the HIDDEN parameter, explicitly set CONTROLLER=FALSE. This is not necessary in the latest release available at http:// quicktime.apple.com/sw/sw.html.

AUTOPLAY=[TRUE I FALSE]   AUTOPLAY is an optional parameter. Acceptable values for this parameter are TRUE and FALSE.

AUTOPLAY=TRUE causes the movie to start playing as soon as the QuickTime plug-in estimates it will be able to play the entire movie without waiting for additional data. The default value of AUTOPLAY is FALSE. This parameter is not appropriate for QuickTime VR Objects or Panoramas.

CONTROLLER=[TRUE I FALSE]   CONTROLLER is an optional parameter.The CONTROLLER parameter determines whether the movie controller is visible. Acceptable values for this parameter are TRUE and FALSE. The default value of the CONTROLLER parameter is TRUE for non-VR movies. Remember to add 24 to the HEIGHT parameter of the movie if you display the controller. This parameter is not appropriate for QuickTime VR Objects or Panoramas.

LOOP=[TRUE I FALSE I PALINDROME]   LOOP is an optional parameter. When set, the LOOP parameter makes the movie play in a loop. Acceptable values for this parameter are TRUE, FALSE, and PALINDROME. Setting LOOP to PALINDROME causes the movie to play alternately forward and backward. The default value of LOOP is FALSE. This parameter is not appropriate for QuickTime VR Objects or Panoramas.

PLAYEVERYFRAME=[TRUE I FALSE]   PLAYEVERYFRAME is an optional parameter. When set, the PLAYEVERYFRAME parameter causes the movie to play every frame, even if it must play at a slower rate to do so. This parameter is particularly useful for playing simple animations and slide shows. Acceptable values for this parameter are TRUE and FALSE.

The default value of the PLAYEVERYFRAME parameter is FALSE. This parameter is not appropriate for QuickTime VR movies. Note that PLAYEVERYFRAME=TRUE should not be used with movies that have audio or MIDI tracks because PLAYEVERYFRAME=TRUE will turn the sound off.

HREF=[URL]   HREF is an optional parameter. When set, the HREF parameter provides a link to another page when the movie is clicked. This parameter is not appropriate for QuickTime VR Panoramas and Objects.

TARGET=[FRAME]   TARGET is an optional parameter. When set, the TARGET parameter is the name of a valid frame that will be the target of a link (including _SELF, _TOP, _PARENT, _BLANK, or an explicit frame name). This parameter is for use with the HREF parameter and is appropriate for QuickTime movies (accompanies HREF).

PAN=[FIXED NUMBER]   PAN is an optional parameter. The PAN parameter allows you to specify the initial pan angle, in degrees, for a QuickTime VR movie. The range of values for a typical movie is 0.0 to 360.0 degrees. This parameter has no meaning for a standard QuickTime movie.

TILT=[FIXED NUMBER]   TILT is an optional parameter. The TILT parameter allows you to specify the initial tilt angle, in degrees, for a QuickTime VR movie. The range of values for a typical movie is –42.5 to 42.5 degrees. This parameter has no meaning for a standard QuickTime movie.

FOV=[FIXED NUMBER]   FOV is an optional parameter. The FOV parameter allows you to specify the initial field of the view angle, in degrees, for a QuickTime VR movie. The range of values for a typical movie is 5.0 to 85.0 degrees. This parameter has no meaning for a standard QuickTime movie.

NODE=[INTEGER]   NODE is an optional parameter. The NODE parameter allows you to specify the initial node for a multinode QuickTime VR movie. This parameter has no meaning for a standard QuickTime movie.

CORRECTION=[NONE | PARTIAL | FULL]   Set CORRECTION to NONE, PARTIAL, or FULL. This parameter is only appropriate for QuickTime VR Objects and Panoramas.

The AVI Format

The Audio/Video Interleaved (AVI) format is Microsoft's format for video and audio. As the name of the format implies, the video data is interleaved with audio data within the same file, so the audio portion of the movie is synchronized with the video portion. AVI uses Intel's Indeo and the Cinepack codecs, which have been getting a lot of publicity lately. AVI files typically play at about 15 frames per second in a small window (320 x 240 pixels). With acceleration hardware or software, you can run AVI video sequences at 30 frames per second in a larger window or full screen. The AVI format accesses data from the hard disk without using great amounts of memory. It's quick loading and playing because only a few frames of video and a portion of audio are accessed at a time. AVI files are also compressed to boost the quality of your video sequences and reduce their size.

While AVI format is the standard Windows video file format, it is rare to find AVI files on the Internet. This is likely to change as the user base changes to reflect the huge number of Windows users jacking into the Internet.

Windows 95 ships with the Media Player for playing AVI and WAV files. To use the Media Player, click the Start button in the taskbar, click Programs, select Multimedia from the Accessories menu, then choose the Media Player from the Accessories menu.

For a QuickTime-to-AVI and AVI-to-QuickTime converter for the Mac, download the Video for Windows Macintosh Utilities at ftp://ftp.microsoft.com/developr/drg/Multimedia/VfW11-Mac/vfw11.sit.

How Much Is That MPEG in the Window? _____

If you're excited by the prospect of including MPEG video clips at your site, you might want to brace yourself before reading the following. In order for you to produce a top-quality MPEG video clip, you'll need a hardware encoder that runs at least $4,000. Currently, there is only one MPEG encoder board available for $4,000, the Producer, which was recently released by Sigma Designs. Sigma Designs also created the Reel Magic board, which was the first MPEG decoder board that can play back full-screen MPEG video. Sigma was one of the first companies to offer a video card, named Rave, that includes an MPEG decoder chip.

The Producer from Sigma Designs is more than an MPEG encoder. It takes a unique approach to make MPEG files editable. Sigma Designs worked with Microsoft to create an MPEG file format that can be edited with any AVI-compatible video editor. The Producer adds a header to an MPEG file so that it can be read and edited as an AVI file by a video editing program like Adobe Premiere. The AVI Editable MPEG format can be edited only at certain places in the video called I-frames. Producer is bundled with a software video tape recorder controller (VTR), Adobe Premiere, and the trueSpace 3D graphics and animation program. When you work with an AVI Editable MPEG file, it can only be compressed to a 50:1 ratio. Once the file is ready for publication, it can be compressed using MPEG compression up to a 200:1 ratio.

Other MPEG encoder boards are much more expensive. MPEG Lab Pro from Optibase, for example, is around $19,000, and Prime View from Future Tel is around $14,000. This is too expensive for most Web publishers. The following sections present a couple of solutions that are less expensive than purchasing an encoder board.

The Service Bureau Solution

Some service bureaus will take a VHS/Beta videotape or a file in a format such as AVI or QuickTime and convert it to MPEG format for you. This price can range from $30 to $300 a minute. Most service bureaus are used to working with videotape. Converting files to the MPEG format is relatively new, so don't be surprised if the service bureau requires you to use videotape. Some service bureaus require a minimum order, usually around three minutes. It pays to shop around. To find a service bureau, check the back of magazines like *DV Digital Video, PC Graphics and Video,* or *New Media.* There are always ads for service bureaus that can encode MPEG files. Appendix C lists a few MPEG encoder services.

The Software Solution

Another way to use MPEG video clips at your site is to use a software encoder. For example, a company called Xing makes Xing MPEG Encoder, a software encoder for Windows. Xing MPEG Encoder comes with an MPEG video and audio player. To use Xing MPEG Encoder, you need a video capture board. FAST's Movie Machine II and FPS 60, for example, are video capture boards that include a bundled version of Xing's MPEG Encoder.

After capturing your video, you can add effects with products such as Adobe Premiere or Ulead's MediaStudio Pro 5.0. You can also include still formats, such as BMP and TGA (Targa). Additionally, you can capture and edit audio in Waveform (WAV) or MPEG audio format. The Xing MPEG Encoder compresses the audio and video files and interleaves them to create an MPEG stream.

If you plan on using the Xing MPEG Encoder to convert an AVI file, be sure to save the file at 30 frames per second in a 24-bit format. This requires that you use at least a Pentium PC and a state-of-the-art video capture board, such as FAST's Movie Machine, FPS 60, or Intel's Smart Video Recorder III. You also need to make sure you have optimized your memory and defragmented your hard disk. If you don't have enough memory or your disk drive is fragmented, you may get a freeze in the video stream. Be aware that using Xing MPEG Encoder to encode a file to the MPEG format is a time-consuming process. An incredible amount of calculations have to be performed to compress the video. Xing MPEG Encoder can take over one and a half hours to encode one minute of MPEG output using a video in the AVI file format as the source.

Currently, there are no low-end MPEG interleaving packages available for the Mac, but numerous shareware and freeware QuickTime-to-MPEG, video-only encoding applications are available for both 680x0 and Power PC-based Macs. Most of them can be found on the MPEG server at ftp://ftp.crs4.it/mpeg/programs/.

Acquiring Video Files

The safest way to present a video file at your site is to create one yourself or use a royalty-free video clip. First Light Productions and Four Palms are two companies that sell royalty-free video clips. There is information about both of these companies in Appendix C. There are also lots of archives of videos on the Internet. As with audio files, some problems arise when using video files on the Internet. For one, many video files are of poor quality. Another problem is that it's hard to tell which videos break copyright laws. Use videos from the Internet at your own risk. Of course, you can always create a link to a video in an archive. Table 10-2 lists and describes sites that include video clip files on the Web. As we mentioned in the section on sounds, just because we have listed these sites doesn't mean that you can publish them on your Web site. However, you may want to experiment with videos even if you don't add any of them to your Web pages. Working with an existing QuickTime or AVI video is a way to save time when you are becoming familiar with a video-editing program.

Another approach to making your own video is to use a series of still images. This may not seem like a true "video" approach, but it can give you excellent results. This approach allows for greater compression and gives better results, particularly when using streaming video over modem-speed links. In fact, this is what Xing does for its 28.8 demos.

URL	Description
http://www.yahoo.com/ Computers_and_Internet/Multimedia/Archives	A listing of multimedia archives.
http://tsmileyland.home.ml.org/mmedia.html	Randolph Chung's archive of movie clips, including such copyright breakers as Disney's *Aladdin, The Lion King,* and *StarTrek.*
http://mambo.ucsc.edu/psl/thant/thant.html	Thant Nyo's huge list of links to computer-generated animations, visualizations, movies, and interactive images.
www.univ-rennes1.fr/ASTRO/anim-e.html	Astronomy clips, such as planets, eclipses, rocket launches, and astro nauts in orbit and clips from science fiction films.

Table 10-2: URLs for video files.

Including Video Files in a Web Page

To include a hyperlink to a video, use the same format you would use with a sound file. The only difference is the extension of the file you are pointing to. For example, a link to a video file uses the following syntax:

```
<A HREF = "URL/sample.mov">hyperlink</A>
```

The URL is the location of the file, including its full path. The sample.mov is the name of the video file.

Publish video files in the QuickTime or MPEG format so others can play the file directly from their browsers. If you use another file format, the file will have to be downloaded and loaded into an external helper application.

You may want to point to a video file that is published at some other site because of space limitations on your host or for other reasons. A little caution should be exercised if you decide to do this because external files may be changed without your knowledge. If you include the link, check regularly to make sure the video file is still available.

If you want to create an archive of video files, be sure to identify the video file with an icon that denotes what type of file it is, such as a camera, a film-strip, or an eye. The following is an example of a local video file named sample.mov in a directory named videos identified by an icon named camera.gif in the icons directory.

```
<IMG SRC="/icons/camera.gif" ALT="[Video Logo]"> <A HREF="/video/
sample.mov">A Sample of Video</A>
```

TIP *Make sure your intended audience has the necessary players. If there is a question as to whether or not your audience can view your video files, refer them to the location of a player.*

Video Editors

There are several programs that let you edit video. Windows 95 includes the Media Player, which lets you play AVI files. If you want to work with video files in the AVI format, you'll need to use a video editing program such as Ulead's MediaStudio Pro, Adobe Premiere, or Asymetrix Digital Video Producer. Remember, Macintosh users cannot view AVI files, so if possible, save your files in the QuickTime format.

If you want to work with QuickTime, and you should, check out Adobe Premiere. Adobe Premiere is an ideal solution for those who don't have thousands of dollars to invest in high-end digital video editing systems. Adobe Premiere presents a construction window, so you can easily edit multiple video tracks and add audio tracks. Working with multiple tracks can be helpful, especially when working with transitions between two video clips, which is commonly referred to as an *A/B roll*. Adobe Premiere lets you work with multiple AVI, QuickTime, video files, and other file formats. It also includes numerous special effects, such as blends and transitions from one scene to another, and it even includes *keying*, which lets you superimpose one video on top of another. Keying is the process used by your friendly TV weather reporter, who points out temperatures on a Chroma key weather map. Another powerful feature is *rotoscoping*, which lets you draw or paint on video frames to add animations to an existing video. You can also combine titles, sounds, and graphic images. We have worked with Premiere 4.2 under Windows NT without any problems. Figure 10-13 shows an Adobe Premiere window for creating a QuickTime video.

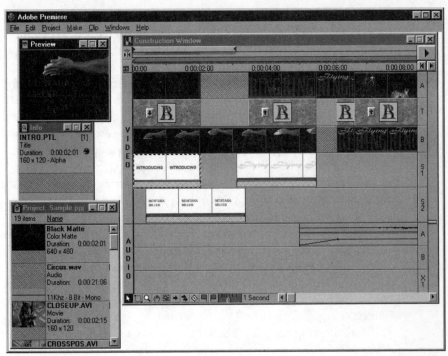

Figure 10-13: Adobe Premiere lets you work with different file formats and can save files in the QuickTime format.

Wondering about editing audio from within Premiere? A number of plug-ins bundled with Premiere 4.2 allow you to modify the audio track from within the application. Also, third-party plug-ins, such as Plugged-In Software's Noise Gate, are becoming increasingly commonplace. More plug-ins are sure to be introduced as desktop computers become better equipped for handling digital video and audio.

Capturing Video in Windows

The process of digitizing video signals, like the process of capturing audio, is called *sampling*. In order to sample a video, you will need a video capture board. It is almost impossible to buy a video capture board that doesn't come with video recording and editing software. There are lots of video capture boards and video editing packages on the market, but only a few produce quality results. Let us tell you up front that setting up a video capture board can be a daunting task. Many video capture boards require you to select one or more IRQ settings and unique memory addresses, which can be a time-consuming task.

The Movie Machine II and FPS 60 from FAST are two of the best video bundles you're likely to find. Both are priced under $500. They include a TV tuner and audio support and come bundled with Adobe Premiere and Xing MPEG Encoder. The FPS 60 includes White Pine's CU-SeeMe teleconferencing software and Visual Software's Simply 3D for creating animated objects to add to your video. Both bundles include FAST's own Movie Studio software for editing, adding effects, and titles. The FPS 60 digitizes 60 fields per second. Most capture cards digitize at only 30 fields per second. The FPS/60 lets you compress files using Motion JPEG—the digital video standard—or you can use the bundled Xing MPEG encoder. An optional plug-in M-JPEG board lets you view smooth MPEG clips that are scalable to full screen. The Movie Machine II and the FPS 60 let you connect to a VCR so you can grab frames and edit them to overlay images and titles.

Another state-of-the-art video capture board is Intel's Smart Video Recorder III. This low-cost board (under $200) excels at capturing video files in the AVI (Indeo and Cinepack codecs) format. It comes bundled with the Asymetrix Digital Video Producer (DVP) recording program and editing program and Asymetrix Web Publisher. DVP lets you add audio transitions and special effects.

The following are a few secrets to effective video capturing using Windows 95 or NT:

- When setting up your capture board, be sure to select the NTSC setting before capturing your video. NTSC stands for the National Television Standards Committee, which defines the TV video signal standard for the United States. NTSC videos consist of 30 frames per second. The UK standard is PAL (Phase Alternation Line), which is 25 frames per second.

- If you plan to edit the video file, capture the video without compression. Different cards have different names for this. Some call it raw while others call it uncompressed. Some boards, such as Intel's Smart Video Recorder, compress files automatically when they are captured, so this is not always a possible choice. After editing the file, you can save it using compression.

- Use at least a Pentium processor with at least 16MB of RAM. Capturing and editing video is memory intensive.

- Disconnect from any local area networks.

- Prepare to have a lot of hard disk space available to capture and edit your video clips. We would recommend having at least 50 to 100MB of free disk space.

- Remove any programs running in memory, such as a virus protection program or system monitoring or crash protection software such as Norton Utilities or Nuts & Bolts. Close all other programs.

■ Make sure that your hard drive has been optimized so the video stream can be written to a large, contiguous block of free space. It's a good idea to always defragment your hard disk before capturing video. To do so, choose Programs | Accessories | System Tools | Disk Defragmenter.

■ Use a high-quality VCR tape and high-quality cables.

Capturing Video on the Mac

With a properly equipped Mac and few preparatory steps, you can produce impressive digital video clips with fairly inexpensive hardware and software. This section provides you with some of the secrets for effective video capturing and editing on the Mac.

The process of digitizing video signals, like the process of capturing audio, is called *sampling*. To sample a video, you'll need a video capture board. Macs in the AV line (660/AV, 840/AV, and AV Power Macs) come equipped with the hardware necessary for capturing video, along with a copy of VideoFusion's Fusion Recorder. This software/hardware combination is sufficient for capturing medium-quality video files to put on your Web site. However, if you need high-quality video capture, check out Radius's SpigotPower AV ($999, 408-541-6100), which allows you to input and output broadcast-quality movies (640 x 480 pixel movies at 30 fps).

There are a few secrets to effective video capturing. These tips are applicable for just about any video recording hardware setup and video capturing program, including VideoFusion's Fusion Recorder and Adobe Premiere:

■ Run just the Finder and the video capture application. This will free all available memory for the capturing process. Make sure you have allocated as much memory as possible (all but 2MB or so) to the video capturing applications from within the Get Info dialog box.

■ Turn off AppleTalk and disable all nonessential extensions. Many times you can get away with running *only* the QuickTime extension and any enablers that might maximize the performance of your drive.

■ Make sure the Monitors control panel is set to 256 colors or fewer to help conserve system resources.

■ Set the Frames Per Second option within the Compression menu (which will differ between applications) to Best. This instructs the video capture hardware/software to save as many frames as possible.

■ Set the Sound Settings to 22.05 kHz, 8 bit, mono to help reduce the amount of storage space the movie will require.

■ Capture the video uncompressed. Video compression takes up unnecessary processor time that could be devoted to writing the incoming video stream to disk.

■ Use the Cinepak codec to post-compress the captured and edited video. Even though it takes quite a while to compress, the compression ratios and final quality are worth the wait. There's more information about various codecs in the FusionRecorder ReadMe file.

■ If you have enough memory, record directly to RAM. Otherwise, make sure that your hard drive has been optimized so the video stream can be written to a large, contiguous block of free space.

Using Conversion Programs

As you know by now, you won't find any options in video editing programs that allow you to save video files in the MPEG format. In most cases, you will capture the video in the AVI format and convert the file to a QuickTime format using a video editing program like Adobe Premiere. Another conversion program, available from Intel, is called SmartCap. The SmartCap conversion program translates an AVI video file into a flattened QuickTime file. Microsoft also has a developer tool that lets you convert AVI files to QuickTime.

If you want to convert a video file to MPEG, check with the service bureau to find out what format they recommend. Many service bureaus require that you deliver the video on tape, but this is changing with the advent of MPEG encoders that can process digital files, such as the Producer from Sigma Designs. When you use a service bureau to convert a video file to the MPEG format, you will most likely be asked to save the captured video file in the YUV format. When you save or capture a video using the YUV format, the file is actually split into three separate files: Y, U, and V. The MPEG encoder accepts the separate Y, U, and V files to produce the encoded MPEG file.

Creating a Shocked Site & Flash Animations _____

Macromedia provides three different authoring tools to generate content for Shockwave: Flash, Director, and Authorware. You can use Director to create streaming interactive multimedia with precise timing of events for Web-based entertainment; you can create games, product demonstrations, animated music sites, and Shocked CDs (hybrid Internet + CD/DVD applications). Web sites that include Shockwave files are commonly called Shocked sites. You can use Authorware to create streaming interactive multimedia learning applications, including intranet-based training, educational courseware, and content-rich CDs that connect to the Web for continuous updates.

Director is an animation and multimedia program that has been fawned over by Macintosh multimedia authors for some time. Director is not a video editor; instead, it's a multimedia-authoring package that lets you create stand-alone programs for multimedia presentations. It uses a metaphor of a stage, where you work with text, sound, graphics, and video clips. To add interactivity to a video, you use an English-like scripting language called Lingo. Director is a very powerful program, but it has a very steep learning curve. Figure 10-14 shows the Director program.

After creating the Shockwave file with any of the authoring tools, you can choose how to optimize the resulting file for Web delivery. Prior to version 6 of Director, you had to also compress the Director file with a special program called Afterburner in order to create the Shockwave file. A Shockwave file ends with a .dcr extension. Once you have created a Shockwave file, you can then incorporate the file in your site using the <EMBED> tag, as mentioned earlier in this chapter.

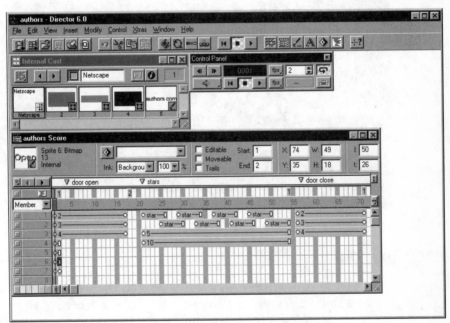

Figure 10-14: The Director program is used to create a Shocked site.

In order to create Flash animations, you need Macromedia's Flash 2.0, shown in Figure 10-15. This program includes several demos and tutorials to help you quickly begin creating streaming vector animations with sound. Using a sound and video/graphics timeline, you can integrate sounds, clip art, animations, fonts, and more. The program includes a set of drawing tools, or you can import and edit graphics from other vector-based drawing programs like Macromedia

Freehand, CorelDRAW, or Adobe Illustrator. Flash comes with ready-to-use buttons and actions that you can apply to your graphics or text. Several options exist for saving and optimizing Shockwave Flash movie files. Shockwave Flash movie files end with the extension .swf. As with other multimedia files, you use the <EMBED> tag to include the file in your Web page.

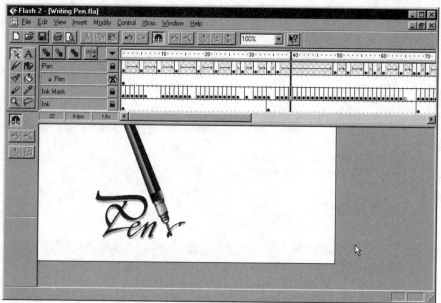

Figure 10-15: The Macromedia Flash 2 program is used to create a Shockwave Flash movie.

Moving On

Multimedia is a newly formed world filled with fascinating possibilities. Because multimedia is such a hotbed of activity, you'll need to keep up with the methods browsers use to add multimedia support and with new multimedia authoring techniques. Several magazines, such as *DV, New Media, PC Graphics and Video, MacWeek,* and *Macworld,* are great sources for keeping on top of new programs and following trends for publishing multimedia documents. Publishing multimedia files is a great way to entertain and involve the visitors to your site. The next chapter takes interactivity to another level by showing you how to create and publish interactive forms.

## chapter 11

Interactive Pages & Scripting

Only a few short years ago, it was fantastic enough that using this newly invented language of HTML, you could download and read a document from someone's computer halfway around the world. Soon, simply reading documents on the World Wide Web seemed like a humdrum activity. Web authors and users alike began to crave action, action, action. For a time, there were animated GIFs. Animated GIFs were fun while they lasted, but there had to be more.

Well, thanks to the creativity of programmers and the advent of some new simplified scripting languages, there is now lots more. There's little doubt that to make your pages truly interactive, you're going to have to open up the programmer's toolbox. That's becoming easier and easier to do these days as new Web authoring tools come along. This chapter is a guide to the world of interactive scripting on the Web and some of the things you can do with it.

Java

Java is actually two things: a full-fledged programming language and a platform that can be used on top of other platforms and on different hardware. It's the latter feature that has significance for Internet and intranet applications, because HTML is also designed to be a cross-platform language, and it's basically ignorant of what kind of machine it's running on. Java provides a way to embed mini-applications, appropriately called *applets*, into an HTML file so that different kinds of executable multimedia files, animations, or other applications can be brought to your desktop embedded in a Web document.

Java is a full-fledged programming language, but don't let that scare you. In order to use a Java applet in your page, you don't have to learn to program. It'll help, though, if you take the time to learn a few basics.

Java Basics

The Java language was designed to be as close to C++ as possible, but without many rarely used, poorly understood, and confusing features of C++. The key features of Java are:

■ Java is an *object-oriented* language. This means that every applet or application is itself an object that can be addressed by other objects. A complete functioning Java application is really a building block tower made of many independent building blocks, each of which contains reusable code. The key is that you can kick over the tower and scatter the pieces all over the place and they will still work.

■ Java is *distributed*. It's meant to function on networks. On the Web, this means you can open and access an object referred to by a URL on a remote site as easily as you can access a local file. On an intranet, this means that you don't need a single mainframe running the whole program. Instead, everyone can have just the pieces they need.

■ Java is *secure*. Even those among us who are not very conscious of security might tend to worry about importing a hunk of executable code that they don't personally understand. But since Java is intended to be used in network environments, a number of security mechanisms are built into the language. Applications do not have access to the underlying machine, so they can't do any real damage.

■ Java is an *architecture-neutral* language. Programs are compiled to a byte-code format that is independent of the machine on which it runs. There's one caveat: To use Java, the system on which it runs has to implement the Java Virtual Machine.

Java-enabled browsers include the Java Virtual Machine along with a series of predefined class definitions. These fundamental classes form the foundation on which you can build your own applications or applets. When you build a new application or applet, you are actually creating new class definitions that are added to existing ones and that call on the basic set for underlying operations. You can also use class definitions that have been created by other Java developers by referencing them.

The difference between a Java *application* and a Java *applet* is that an applet requires a network to run while an application does not. An applet is also restricted from having read or write access to any file system except the server from which it came, which is why applets are useful on the Web. Java programs written to run within the context of a Web browser are always applets, while stand-alone Java programs are applications.

Using a Java Applet

To get an idea of how you can use and adapt existing applets for your own use, let's take a simple Java script called CrazyText by Patrick Taylor. CrazyText's purpose is to animate a short text message. The letters of the message dance and change into a rainbow of colors on your screen. You can find it and download it at http://nicom.com/~taylor. To add this applet to your page, this is all you need to add to your HTML code:

```
<APPLET CODE="CrazyText.class" WIDTH=150 HEIGHT=50>
<PARAM name=text value="Java">
</APPLET>
```

The action is obviously all contained between the tags <APPLET> and </APPLET>. The file that contains the binary code for the applet is called CrazyText.class, therefore CODE="CrazyText.class." The size of the window in which the applet will be displayed is defined with the WIDTH and HEIGHT attributes. The second line of the applet information defines what kind of message will be displayed (in this case, text rather than an image or something else) and what the text of that message is (the word *Java*).

Take this file just as it is and load it into your browser; chances are it'll do nothing at all. Hmmm . . . What's missing? Well, first of all, this is not the code; it's just the file that *loads* the code. So unless you have the file called CrazyText.class for it to find, the browser can't do anything with it.

There are actually three class files that are necessary to make this run: CrazyText.class, CrazyLabel.class, and BorderPanel.class. If you download this applet yourself, you can copy the appropriate class files to the java/classes subdirectory of your Netscape program directory. Now, load the file into your browser and voilà, it finds the files it needs to run the applet (see Figure 11-1).

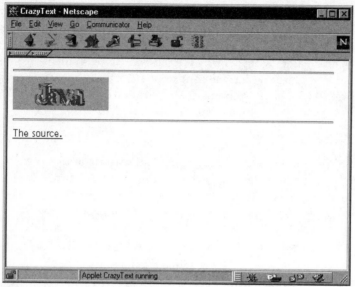

Figure 11-1: The CrazyText applet running in Netscape.

TIP *If you intend to post Java files on your Web site, first check to see if the server is Java-enabled. The administrator will have had to set up the basic configuration and Java protocol on the host machine. Once the server is configured, you can post the .java and .class files, along with the HTML file in which they're embedded, to your online directory. It's a good idea to make a separate java subdirectory to hold the java .class files you'll use.*

It only takes a little sporting sense to wonder if you can change the message text. Try changing "Java" to something like "Happy Birthday." The result (which is actually quite colorful) is in Figure 11-2. This is the code, altered just a little:

```
<TITLE>Happy Birthday</TITLE>
<HR>
<APPLET CODE="CrazyText.class"
        WIDTH=250 HEIGHT=50>
<PARAM NAME=text value="Happy Birthday">
</APPLET>
<HR>
<A HREF="CrazyText.java">The source.</A>
```

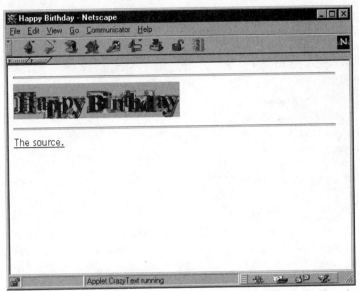

Figure 11-2: We've changed the message on the CrazyText applet by changing the text parameter.

Besides changing the "value" of the text message, the width of the message was changed to account for the fact that "Happy Birthday" is a bit longer than "Java." The Java source code is exactly the same. In other words, it's using the same original binary code file, just substituting a couple of different parameters.

If you look at the source code that creates this applet (the file called CrazyText.java), you'll see some other parameters you can change. Here's the relevant section:

```
// parameters
String text = "Java"; // string to be displayed
int delay = 100; // # of milliseconds between updates
int delta = 5; // "craziness" factor: max pixel offset
boolean clear = false; // should background be cleared on update
String fontName = "TimesRoman";
int fontSize = 36;
boolean fontBold = true;
boolean fontItalic = false;
    :
}
```

You'll see that there are parameters for defining the font name, the font size, the frequency of the action, and the offset in pixels of the text as it changes location on the screen. Each parameter has a default value. All of the parameters can be changed in the same way the text message was changed. Here's one variation:

```
<APPLET CODE="CrazyText.class"
        WIDTH=250 HEIGHT=50>
<PARAM name=text value="Happy Birthday">
<PARAM name=fontName value="Arial">
<PARAM name=fontSize value="48">
<PARAM name=delay value="200">
<PARAM name=delta value="10">
</APPLET>
```

This variation, seen in Figure 11-3, uses Arial 48-point font. The "frenzy level" of the applet was slowed down by doubling the default delay value of 100. And just to see what happens, the "craziness factor" was adjusted from the default 5 to 10.

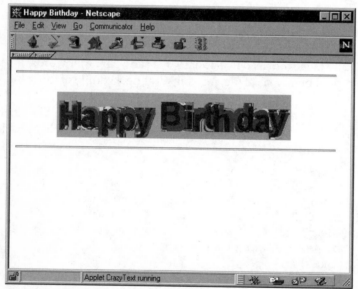

Figure 11-3: The Happy Birthday applet customized with several new parameters.

Note that you don't need to know how to write the Java code yourself in order to use this applet. You only have to interpret a couple of instructions in the code and understand what it needs to operate. You can use this same technique with any publicly available Java applet when the source code is available, and it's a very good place to start if you want to learn a little about it.

Remember that if you want to use an applet, you'll need the .class file for the applet for it to work and the .java file if you want to inspect it for change-able parameters. However, if you change anything in the .java file, it must be compiled again to create a new binary .class file to reflect your changes. For that, and to develop your own Java applets, you'll need the complete Java Development ment Kit, which contains the compiler, or the browser-based Java Workshop tool. Both are available from Sun Microsystems at http://javasoft.com/.

Addressing Non-Java-Enabled Browsers

A browser that can't execute Java applets will generally ignore the <APPLET> and <PARAM> tags, but it will display any regular HTML that occurs be-tween the <APPLET> tags. To display a message for non-Java-enabled brows-ers, you can add HTML tags and text after any <PARAM> tags and before the closing <APPLET> tag, as shown here:

```
<APPLET CODE="CrazyText.class" WIDTH=250 HEIGHT=50>
<PARAM name=text value="Happy Birthday">
<P>Unfortunately, you are not using a Java-enabled browser. If you were, you
would see a colorful birthday message. Have a happy birthday anyway!
</APPLET>
```

Java Resources

If you have a need for a particular kind of Java applet, a good place to start is with one of the online Java resource libraries. Some good Web sites for Java applets are:

- **Gamelan.** http://www.gamelan.com/index.shtml
- **The Java Boutique.** http://www.j-g.com/java/index.html
- **The Java Gallery.** http://www.charm.net/~web/Multimedia/Java/

If you decide to develop your own Java applets, a number of Java tools are available for nonprogrammers. All that's necessary is an understanding of multimedia formats and an idea of what you want to do. Some easy beginner packages are:

- **Jamba by Aimtech Corporation.** http://www.aimtech.com/jamba/index.html
- **AppletAce by Macromedia.** http://www.macromedia.com/
- **Activator Pro by Network Oriented Software.** http://www.noware.com/

For programmers or those who understand a bit more about the Java programming constructs or want to learn, there are some more sophisticated Java development tools, such as Symantec's Visual Café Pro. Visual Café Pro includes Netscape's FastTrack Server and dbAnywhere, a program that lets applets communicate with databases such as the Sybase SQLAnywhere database. Find out more about Visual Café Pro at http://cafe.symantec.com/.

Another excellent client-server Java development package that is designed especially to work with SQL Server database applications is the Apptivity Developer and Server. Look into this at http://www.apptivity.com.

The Browser Scripting Sandbox

Plug-ins and Java applets, as useful as they are, are often overkill for many of the common things most Web designers would like to do to add interactivity to their pages. Who needs Java if all you want to do is pop up a message or two with a form submission, display the date on your page, or do some quick, clever image switching? For precisely this reason, modified scripting languages designed for embedding directly in the HTML page have appeared in the last few years. In addition to the convenience these scripting languages provide for programmers, they allow nonprogrammers an entry into this world.

A scripting language is a simplified programming language that is used to manipulate, customize, and automate features of an existing system, in this case a Web browser. The browser provides a host environment of objects and facilities on which the scripting language operates—for instance, objects can represent windows, menus, pop-ups, dialog boxes, text areas, anchors, frames, history, and cookies. The scripting language can also act upon events such as page loading, mouseover, and form submission. Scripting languages are less rigid and more informal that regular programming languages because the environment is limited and they're intended for use by both professional and nonprofessional programmers.

Browser scripting languages are still evolving right now, and the next few years should see some welcome standardization coming along, but here's the state of the art right now.

JavaScript, JScript & ECMAScript

JavaScript, created and owned by Netscape, was the first of the scripting languages designed especially for Web browsers. JavaScript is based on Java, but it's simplified. While JavaScript 1.1 had support in both Netscape Navigator and Microsoft Internet Explorer 3.0, the latest version, JavaScript 1.2, has extended features that are only supported in Netscape Navigator 4.0.

JScript is Microsoft's answer to JavaScript. It contains most of the same features as JavaScript but has some extra Microsoft enhancements that include Component Object Model (COM) support. JScript 3.0 is built into Microsoft Internet Explorer 4.0 in all platforms (Windows, Mac, and UNIX). Documentation and tutorials on JScript, onscreen and downloadable, can be found at http://www.microsoft.com/scripting/. VBScript is yet another scripting language that has some utility for programmers who are comfortable with Visual Basic and who can confine themselves to working in an all-Windows environment.

Because of the desire to standardize scripting capabilities on the Web, the European Computer Manufacturers Association (ECMA) stepped in to mediate the standards for the development of a cross-platform, non-browser-specific scripting language. Both Netscape and Microsoft participated cooperatively in the discussions to formulate this language. A proposal has been put forward that frames the outlines of this language, called rather diplomatically ECMAScript. This does not necessarily mean that JavaScript and JScript will go away—more likely, they will become more and more like one another to the point that scripts written in one language will be recognizable by the other. At the moment, Microsoft's JScript is closer to the ECMA-compliant model, but it has not yet gained enough of a foothold for most Web authors to commit themselves to developing exclusively for it.

This being an imperfect world, and for the widest applicability, we'll confine our examples for the rest of this chapter to JavaScript. But anything you can do in JavaScript, you should also be able to do in JScript, or ECMAScript eventually.

A Crash Course in JavaScript

Of all the languages that have arisen as helpers to HTML, Java has the most secure future. Its value as a platform-independent programming language guarantees its longevity regardless of its application to Web publishing. JavaScript, JScript, and VBScript, however, will probably be redundant once support for true ECMAScript is well established and a library of useful routines has been built up. The pace of development on this cutting edge of the Web publisher's art is such that some or all of those scripting languages may fall into disuse within the lifetime of this book.

It's often said that there's no "right time to buy" computer hardware because there's always something really amazing just around the corner that you should be waiting for. It might seem that, similarly, there's no "right scripting language" to learn while standards are still fluid. But just as on the hardware side it simply isn't practical to occupy your desktop with a sign reading SITE

OF PROPOSED WONDER-COMPUTER, today a Webmaster or wannabe Webmaster *must* become fluent in a scripting language or risk getting flattened beneath the wheels of the chariots of progress. The trick is to learn one that's widely supported, flexible, and as close as possible to where we all think the technology is headed. For right now, the choice is JavaScript.

Embedding Your Script

In principle, JavaScript fragments may be placed anywhere within the overall <HTML> . . . </HTML> wrapper of an HTML file, and there may be as many separate fragments as necessary, each set off within a <SCRIPT> . . . </SCRIPT> container.

Most often, however, there is one section of script only, and it's placed in the HEAD of the document following the TITLE—or following the style sheet section if there is one. The language of the script is defined by the attribute LANGUAGE. Also, it's considered polite to corral off all script within an HTML comment wrapper for the benefit of browsers that don't support any kind of scripting and would otherwise simply display the raw script as though it were part of the page text. Here, then, is the standard JavaScript setup:

```
<SCRIPT LANGUAGE="Javascript">
<!--

//-->
</SCRIPT>
```

The double forward slash preceding the HTML "end-of-comment" is JavaScript's own comment marker.

JavaScript Sourcing

JavaScript—at least, client-side JavaScript (server-side JavaScript is a different kettle of fish)—is extremely powerful at handling user interaction with Web pages, but it's very limited in the amount of data it can handle and essentially incapable of reading in and using an external database. Nevertheless, JavaScript data arrays can and do grow to respectable proportions, and for these and other reasons, it's legitimate to banish all or part of a JavaScript code to a separate file. The auxiliary file is given the extension *.js* and referenced by a SRC attribute. The data used by an interactive staff-benefits Web site, for example, might be split off like this:

```
<SCRIPT LANGUAGE="Javascript" SRC="bensdat.js">
<!--
//JavaScript functions begin here...

//-->
</SCRIPT>
```

TIP *It's safest to stick to the .js file extension for external JavaScript fragments since the Web server needs to recognize them for what they are. The suffix may need to be mapped by the server to the MIME type "application/x-javascript," which the server sends back in the HTTP GET reply's Content-type: header.*

The only other attribute of the <SCRIPT> tag is ARCHIVE, which is used to reference JAR files in object signing, a process that is beyond the scope of this book.

JavaScript Objects & Properties

Most of the objects that JavaScript acts upon (mentioned briefly in Chapter 1) are nothing other than the elements of HTML—the document, the frame, the form, and so on. They're arranged in a hierarchy with *Window* at the top and things like an individual radio button down at the bottom. In addition, there's a suite of useful built-in objects such as *Math*, *Navigator*, and *Screen* to help JavaScript detect and sometimes modify the world around it.

Each object has a set of properties. To take an example that will be immediately recognizable to any HTML author, the *Document* object has properties *bgColor, fgColor, linkColor, vlinkColor,* and *alinkColor,* which correspond exactly to the HTML BODY attributes BGCOLOR, TEXT, LINK, VLINK, and ALINK. If they were all that simple, this crash course would be easy, but unfortunately the hierarchical nature of JavaScript objects requires that some properties also be objects, and vice versa. *Document* behaves as a top-level object, but technically it's a property of *Window*. *Form* is a property of *Document*, but it's also an object with a whole set of properties of its own, most of which also have properties and thus often need to be seen as objects.

But to stick with the simple example, the following set of JavaScript statements sets up the color rendering of a document exactly as the attributes of <BODY> do:

```
document.bgColor = "#668b8b";
document.fgColor = "red";
document.linkColor = "blue";
document.vlinkColor = "#808080";
document.alinkColor = "#668b8b";
```

Interestingly enough, these color values will override any that may be specified as BODY attributes in the document. Of those five properties, only the background color can be changed once the document has been composed (laid out) on the user's screen. We'll be showing how shortly.

JavaScript Style Sheets

The set of color values makes JavaScript declarations of this type look a lot like style sheets. Indeed, for a short while, JavaScript style sheets were an official Netscape technology. JavaScript has a special keyword *with*, which sets up the default object for a whole string of statements bracketed together. Rewriting color declarations using this convention is equally valid and makes them look even more style-sheet-like:

```
with (document) {
bgColor = "#668b8b";
fgColor = "red";
linkColor = "blue";
vlinkColor = "#808080";
alinkColor = "#668b8b";
}
```

JavaScript style sheets (JSS) are not covered in this book; however, because the Cascading Style Sheets (CSS) that were the subject of Chapter 8 have so much wider support, JSSes appear to be doomed.

JavaScript Functions

JavaScript is built around *functions* that accept parenthetical *parameters* (generally from some user activity) and use them as variables. Here's a simple function, complete with its wrapper:

```
<SCRIPT LANGUAGE="JavaScript">
<!--
function setColor(colorstr) {
  document.bgColor = colorstr;
}
//-->
</SCRIPT>
```

This function, *setColor*, accepts the *parameter* colorstr and sets the *property* bgColor of the *object* document to the *value* colorstr. So there's something dynamic right away—a function that changes the background color of the entire document to which it belongs. As to where *setColor* gets its parameter from, we'll get to that in a minute, but first we'll take a quick look at JavaScript conditional structures. Suppose we wanted to make quite sure that *document.bgColor* never got set to pure white. JavaScript accepts either "white" or "#ffffff" as white, so we have to test the incoming parameter and avoid the routine if it's either of them. Here's how:

```
function setColor(colorstr) {
  if (colorstr != "white" && colorstr != "#ffffff") {
    document.bgColor = colorstr;
  }
}
```

Note the != for "not equal to" and the && for "logical and." JavaScript allows cascades of conditional statements of the general form:

```
function someFunc() {
  if (condition1) {
    ....[thing1]....
  }
```

```
else if (condition2) {
  ....[thing2]....

}
else if (condition3) {
  ....[thing3]....
}
else {
  ....[the default thing]....
}
}
```

JavaScript Event Handlers

Let's juice up the *setColor* function we introduced in the previous section and make it do something that is under control of the user. We can do this in many ways—here are three.

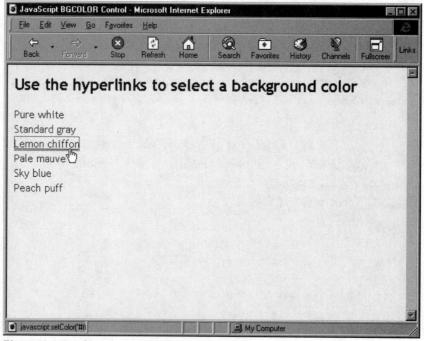

Figure 11-4: Invoking the setColor function from links.

It stands to reason that, if we want to give our users control of JavaScript functions such as *setColor*, we have to provide some way for them to express their desire to see something—such as a change in background color—happen.

Figure 11-4 illustrates the simplest of strategies—a set of hyperlinks to a range of colors. The JavaScript function is the version of *setColor* that allows all colors (including white) and the hyperlinks all use the pseudo-protocol *javascript:* to achieve the connection from the user's mouse finger through the HTML to the heart of the matter:

```
<A HREF="javascript:setColor('#ffffff')">Pure white</A><BR>
<A HREF="javascript:setColor('#c0c0c0')">Standard gray</A><BR>
<A HREF="javascript:setColor('#fff8b9')">Lemon chiffon</A><BR>
<A HREF="javascript:setColor('#c0c0f0')">Pale mauve</A><BR>
<A HREF="javascript:setColor('#64bae2')">Sky blue</A><BR>
<A HREF="javascript:setColor('#ffcb9f')">Peach puff</A><BR>
```

Just to belabor the point, the first line, when activated, passes the *value* #ffffff to the *parameter* colorstr of the *function* setColor, which then sets the *property* bgColor of the *object* document. Eureka!

Hyperlinks are not usually considered to be the best way to connect users to JavaScript functions, however. JavaScript can set up the connection more generally by capturing some action on the part of the user, such as moving/ clicking the mouse, depressing a keyboard key, or interrupting page loading. The action taken by the user is called an *event,* and the trigger that connects that event to the JavaScript function is called the *event handler.* The script for each of the links in Figure 11-4 could be rewritten to capture the click this way:

```
<A HREF="" onClick="setColor('#ffffff')">Pure white </A><BR>
```

Now the event handler called *onClick* has been moved inside the hyperlink tag to do its thing, leaving the A HREF="" free for a more conventional hyperlinking function. The trouble is, in this case we don't have any need for it—and leaving it null like that is extremely bad practice because it's liable to end up displaying the entire listing of the directory the HTML file resides in. Showing our users our directory listing is a gaffe akin to displaying racy underwear at a debutante's cotillion. If you ever do need to create an absolutely null hyperlink in order to pull off some JavaScript effect, here's the way to write it:

```
<A HREF="javascript:void(0)"
```

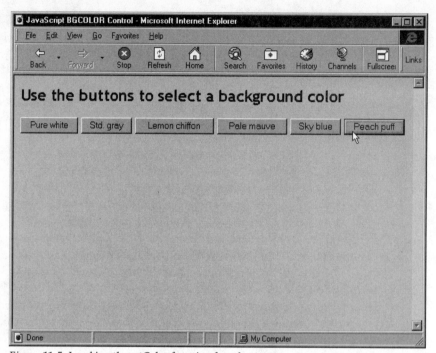

Figure 11-5: Invoking the setColor function from buttons.

Figure 11-5 shows the way most JavaScript programmers prefer to invite user interaction. Form submit buttons look smart, and people are used to clicking on them and expecting some action. For use in JavaScript, a special form input type, simply called *button*, is used, and although a form has to be created (and it's sometimes convenient to give it its own name), it's kind of a fake form in that it doesn't actually submit any data and so needs no ACTION or METHOD. Here's the meat of the JavaScript that makes the page in Figure 11-5 do its thing, showing how the onClick event handler sits inside the button tag:

```
<FORM>
<INPUT TYPE="button" VALUE="Pure white" onClick="setColor('#ffffff')">
<INPUT TYPE="button" VALUE="Std. gray" onClick="setColor('#c0c0c0')">
<INPUT TYPE="button" VALUE="Lemon chiffon" onClick="setColor('#fff8b9')">
<INPUT TYPE="button" VALUE="Pale mauve" onClick="setColor('#c0c0f0')">
<INPUT TYPE="button" VALUE="Sky blue" onClick="setColor('#64bae2')">
<INPUT TYPE="button" VALUE="Peach puff" onClick="setColor('#ffcb9f')"><BR>
</FORM>
```

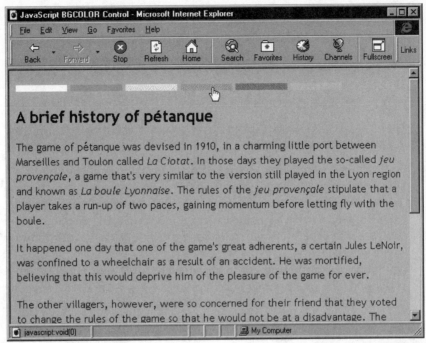

Figure 11-6: Invoking the setColor function with color swatches, and no need to click!

Clicking on a submit button is pretty convenient—but in this age, when expecting someone to get up off the couch to change the TV channel is regarded as an outrageous intrusion on the right to relax, couldn't we demand less of our users? How about if the mere act of waving the mouse pointer over something triggered a JavaScript function? Yes indeed—that's where the *onMouseover* event handler comes in, and we've used that for our final idea in dynamic background color control, illustrated in Figure 11-6. To save our users from the agony of imagining what "peach puff" and "lemon chiffon" might look like, we've actually shown previews of the colors in the form of little 80 X 10 GIFs that make up, in effect, a color chart across the top of the page. We've also added some whimsical text just so the effect of the color changes can be judged behind standard black text. Unfortunately, an image by itself cannot carry a JavaScript event handler, so we've reverted to the null hyperlink technique to make the following code, which is maximally kind to our users' carpal tunnels and quite an attractive presentation:

```
<A HREF="javascript:void(0)"  onMouseover="setColor('#ffffff')">
<IMG SRC="ffffff.gif" BORDER=0></A>
```

```
<A HREF="javascript:void(0)"  onMouseover="setColor('#c0c0c0')">
<IMG SRC="c0c0c0.gif" BORDER=0></A>

<A HREF="javascript:void(0)"  onMouseover="setColor('#fff8b9')">
<IMG SRC="fff8b9.gif" BORDER=0></A>

//...and so on for the other three
```

JavaScript Variables

No programming language could do a sensible job of controlling a computer without using *variables*. The variables are the *x*s, *y*s, and *z*s of classroom algebra, and they become much more interesting than the chalk scratches on the blackboard when they come to life on the Web as the price of a concert ticket, an RGB color string, or an interesting phrase such as "Sorry, that item is presently out of stock."

Some programming languages are very fussy about how variables are defined. The programmer needs to declare in advance what type of variable *x* is (integer, fraction, or string) and, in some cases, what the lower and upper limits are to legitimate values of *x*. One way in which JavaScript has simplified the business of programming is to do without variable typing. Technically, it's called a *loosely typed* language, but it might be called "untyped" given that a variable can have the value 44, 1.11875 and "Pink Floyd" at different moments *in the same script!*

There are, however, *some* rules about JavaScript variables, and here's a summary:

- The *scope* of a JavaScript variable may be either *global* (defined outside all functions and accessible to all functions) or *local* (defined inside a function and meaningful only to that function).

- Only the characters a-z, A-Z, 0-9, and underscore may be used in variable names. (JScript also allows the $ sign.)

- Variable names are case sensitive; *this_var* is not the same variable as *This_Var*.

Concatenation of string variables is done very simply with the + sign, being careful to quote immediate text. A generic "out of stock" alert message might be made more informative by filling in the item description and size, like this:

```
function stockout(itemdesc,itemsz) {
  alert("Sorry, " + itemdesc + "s of size " + itemsz + " are presently out
of stock.<BR>");
}
```

If called as "stockout('unisex boot',7)", this function would display:

```
Sorry, unisex boots of size 7 are presently out of stock.<BR>
```

By way of a very quick exercise in string variable declaration, using the keyword *var* to emphasize the local scope of variables, the stockout function would be equally successful if written:

```
function stockout(itemdesc,itemsz) {
  var str1 = "Sorry, ";
  var str2 = "s of size ";
  var str3 = " are presently out of stock.<BR>";
  alert(str1 + itemdesc + str2 + itemsz + str3);
}
```

JavaScript Tools

Demand for GUI-based JavaScripting applications has not been overwhelming. Many JavaScript programmers have come to the language from a background in other abstract languages, such as C++, and regard JavaScript itself as relatively trivial to code. However, the extension of JavaScript to the server side, plus the realization on the part of more "right-brained" Web authors that they can't afford to neglect scripting, has brought some user-friendly applications onto the market. You need a pretty capable computer to get the best out of them.

One very full-featured application, incorporating drag-and-drop Java, JavaScript and Active-X components, a clip art library, and a very full set of templates is Drumbeat, by Elemental Software. You can get information about Drumbeat at http://www.elementalsoftware.com/.

Visual JavaScript

Netscape has come up with *Visual JavaScript*, which is still in prerelease as this book goes to press but is obviously going to fill a niche with the nonprogramming population. The application extends JavaScript into the server side in order to relate to proprietary database applications. So to get the best out of it, you really need to install Netscape Enterprise Web Server (which has built-in support for server-side JavaScript) in addition to Communicator 4.02 or better. Actually, they recommend *two* Enterprise servers—one just for testing!

With Visual JavaScript, you can, however, add JavaScript components to an existing Web page; you can even compose pages from scratch with its built-in HTML editor or an external editor. The resulting scripts may be run locally in what's called preview mode. A frames editor and an active image editor are available as "accessories" that you can choose at install time. Even without these optional extras, Visual JavaScript wants around 15MB of your hard disk to romp around in and 32MB of RAM is *absolutely* essential.

Active page components can be positioned on a page by dragging and dropping them from a palette—Figure 11-7 shows a button just after positioning—and then modified by an Inspector window that in turn launches a script builder. Right-brainers please note: Some knowledge of JavaScript is definitely required.

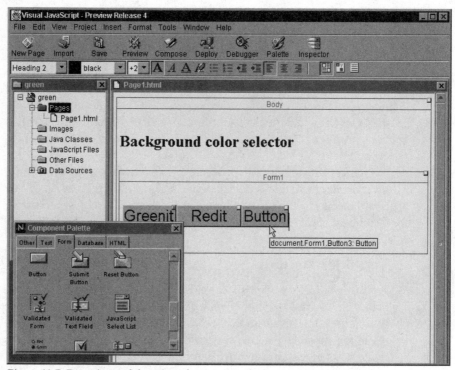

Figure 11-7: Dragging and dropping of active page elements in Visual JavaScript.

JavaScript Debugging

Even those JavaScript programmers who eschew the drag-and-drop way of life can hardly fail to recognize that some help is needed to make the task of JavaScripting efficient. JavaScript's own error reporting is cryptic, to put it mildly, and this means that progress in development can be held up out of all proportion to whatever minor scripting error may be preventing a routine from operating as required (see Figure 11-8).

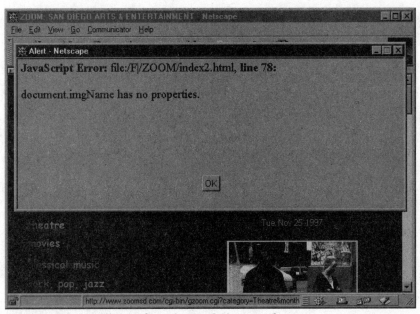

Figure 11-8: A typically uninformative JavaScript error alert.

The debugger that's built into Visual JavaScript is available as a stand-alone package from the Netscape Developer's Web site. When it's installed, it's a relatively compact 400KB (compared with over 13MB for the full Visual JavaScript package). It runs on top of Netscape Navigator and captures some of the browser's functions. As you load it, you will get an incidental look at what's meant by a *signed object*, as you're asked to give permission for some procedures that are considered a security risk. You can even see an actual security certificate by clicking on the Certificate button in the alert window.

To debug JavaScript, you simply open the troublesome document in Netscape Navigator. When a bug stops the show, the script automatically appears in the debugger's Source View window. Other panes are the Call Stack and the Console; the Console allows you to manually enter any JavaScript expression for evaluation. Alternatively, you may simply select an expression in the source and right-click on it for instant analysis. Other typical debug functions include a watch window and step in/step out/step over toolbar buttons. Figure 11-9 shows the debugger in action.

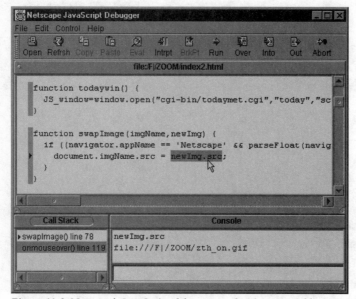

Figure 11-9: Netscape's JavaScript debugger evaluating a variable at a set breakpoint.

Useful JavaScript Routines

Like all the scripting languages mentioned in this chapter, JavaScript can get pretty complex, and a visual tool can be helpful if you have the computing power to use one. But many day-to-day JavaScript routines are really quite simple and not worth the bother of loading the GUI application. Here are some.

Determining the Browser

Even primitive versions of JavaScript allow for several properties of the navigator object, which are useful for determining which make, version, and language of browser is in use. Later versions add properties that detect plug-ins and MIME types. A fairly complete set of nav properties is depicted in Figure 11-10.

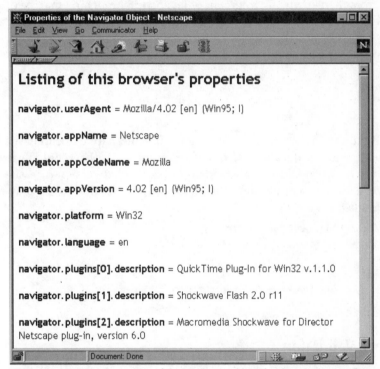

Figure 11-10: Some properties of the navigator object that JavaScript can detect and use.

The point of detecting these properties is, of course, to offer alternative pages or page elements to users according to which browser type, version, and language they have. Code that is only interpretable by Netscape, for example, might be included like this:

```
if (navigator.appName == "Netscape") {
  //....Netscape-only code
}
```

A fairly frequent requirement—for determining whether style sheets are supported, for instance—is to detect whether the browser is EITHER Netscape OR MSIE, AND ALSO version 4 or more. A JavaScript variable, *modernBrowser*, can be set to Boolean true or false by this test as follows:

```
modernBrowser = ((navigator.appName == "Netscape" || navigator.appName ==
"Microsoft Internet Explorer")
   && parseFloat(navigator.appVersion) >= 4);
```

From then on, in any fragment of JavaScript, branching may be done as follows:

```
if (modernBrowser) {
   //....advanced feature
}
else {
   //....primitive feature
}
```

If browser detection warrants it, an entire alternative document may be loaded by using the *window.location.href* = statement. This could be used to branch between CSS-enabled and non-CSS-enabled versions of a site. It might also be used on a multilingual site to determine whether to serve up a French or English page:

```
if (navigator.language == "fr") {
  window.location.href = "frvern.html";
}
else {
  window.location.href = "envern.html";
}
```

Form Validation

No part of your HTML documents is more exposed to JavaScript than their form elements. JavaScript knows everything about the state of every input field, check box, option list, and radio button in your forms and can change the state of many of them. JavaScript could write the string "rattlesnake" into a text input box named "biota" like this:

```
document.forms[0].biota.value = "rattlesnake";
```

Figure 11-11 shows a very simple form validation procedure in which a JavaScript function refuses to allow a form to be submitted if an e-mail address appears to be malformed.

Figure 11-11: Verifying form input with JavaScript.

The function and the markup are as follows:

```
<!DOCTYPE HTML public "-//Netscape Comm. Corp.//DTD HTML//EN">
<HTML>
<HEAD>
<TITLE>Required Form Field Demo</TITLE>
<SCRIPT LANGUAGE="Javascript">
<!--
function checkit(form) {
  if (form.Email.value == "") {
    alert ("You must provide an e-mail address")
    form.Email.focus()
    return false
  }
  else if (form.Email.value.indexOf("@") == -1 ||
form.Email.value.indexOf(".") == -1) {
    alert ("Invalid e-mail address")
    form.Email.focus()
    return false
  }

  else {
    form.submit()
    return true
  }
}
```

```
//-->
</SCRIPT>

</HEAD>
<BODY>
<FORM METHOD="get" ACTION="bjj.htm">
E-mail:<INPUT TYPE="text" NAME="Email" SIZE="25"
MAXLENGTH="50">
<INPUT TYPE="button" VALUE="Ready"
onClick="checkit(this.form)">
</FORM>

</BODY>
</HTML>
```

Note that the simple event handler *onClick* is used in conjunction with an input type of "button." If the e-mail address appears to be okay, the form is then submitted by a JavaScript statement. An alternative would be to have a conventional "submit" button and use the *onSubmit* event handler in the FORM element. Then form submit would be permitted by the JavaScript function returning true and inhibited by *return false*.

Real-Time Document Creation

For convenience, the entire document that created Figure 11-10 was written by JavaScript. The file had no <BODY> at all. The code was, in part:

```
document.writeln("<H2>Listing of this browser's properties</H2>");
document.writeln("<P><STRONG>navigator.userAgent = </STRONG>" +
navigator.userAgent);
document.writeln("<P><STRONG>navigator.appName = </STRONG>" +
navigator.appName);
```

It's no problem to write out a document from scratch using JavaScript's *document.writeln* statement. You can even mix n' match like this:

```
<P>Paragraph One
<SCRIPT>
document.writeln("<P>Paragraph Two");
</SCRIPT>
<P>Paragraph Three
```

By the way, that may not be as perverse as it looks. The content of paragraph two may be exactly the kind of thing that needs to be adjusted according to what browser or language the user has, as we just saw.

What you *can't* do—at least not until the document object model is fully implemented—is selectively rewrite a document after it has been displayed and all the layout calculations have been done. However, the page can be completely remade, including whatever modification is appropriate to the occasion, using *document.open()*. JavaScript's *document.open()* method was primarily invented for opening a fresh document in a newly created window, and it can also be used for writing to an applet. Technically, the method is known as *opening a stream* to a document/window/applet. Figure 11-12 shows a page that was not only written entirely by JavaScript, but had a rewrite function embedded in it. Here's the code:

```
<SCRIPT LANGUAGE="JavaScript">
<!--

Doctype = '<!DOCTYPE HTML public "-//Netscape Comm. Corp.//DTD HTML//EN">';
topText = "<HTML>\n<HEAD>\n<TITLE>Writing to a Document with JavaScript</
TITLE>";
hedText = "<H1>This is not HTML</H1>"
paraText = "<P>JavaScript did it all"

document.writeln(Doctype);
document.writeln(topText);
document.writeln('</HEAD>\n<BODY BGCOLOR="#c0c0f0">');
document.writeln(hedText);
document.writeln(paraText);
document.writeln('<P><A HREF="javascript:addline()">Add a line</A>');
document.writeln("</BODY>\n</HTML>");

function addline() {
    var Doctype = '<!DOCTYPE HTML public "-//Netscape Comm. Corp.//DTD HTML//
EN">';
    var topText = "<HTML>\n<HEAD>\n<TITLE>Writing to a Document with
JavaScript</TITLE>";
    var hedText = "<H1>This is not HTML</H1>";
    var paraText = "<P>JavaScript did it all";
    var newText = "<P><FONT SIZE=4 COLOR='red' FACE='arial'>...and JavaScript
added this too.</FONT>";
    document.open("text/html");
    document.writeln(Doctype);
    document.writeln(topText);
    document.writeln('</HEAD>\n<BODY BGCOLOR="#c0c0f0">');
    document.writeln(hedText);
    document.writeln(paraText);
    document.writeln(newText);
    document.writeln("</BODY>\n</HTML>");
    document.close();
}

//-->
</SCRIPT>
```

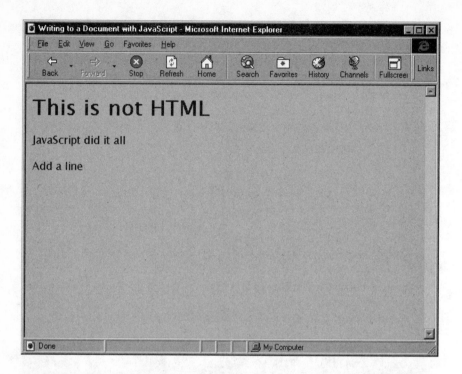

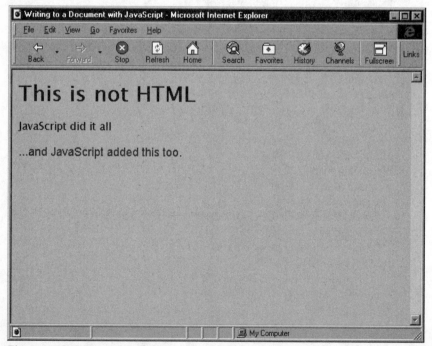

Figure 11-12: A Dynamic page entirely created by JavaScript.

Sources for Ready-Made JavaScript Routines

The Official Netscape JavaScript 1.2 Book (Ventana, 1997) is a very useful source of JavaScript snippets. The authors, Peter and John Kent, had a little more space than we have to devote to JavaScript here (550 pages as compared to around 40), so they were able to include an entire chapter on ready-mades, plus an appendix. Here's a short selection of Web sites:

- **Gamelan JavaScript Developer.** http://javascript.developer.com/
- **Cut and Paste JavaScript.** http://www.infohiway.com/ javascript.indexf.htm
- **JavaScript 411 (by Andy Augustine).** http://www.freqgrafx.com/411/
- **JavaScript Library (by Andrew Wooldridge).** http:// www.sapphire.co.uk/javascript/lib/
- **JavaScript Archive (by Michael P. Scholtis).** http:// planetx.bloomu.edu/~mpscho/jsarchive/
- **Timothy's JavaScript Page (by Timothy Wallace).** http:// www.essex1.com/people/timothy/js-intro.htm

The address of the "official" JavaScript site is http://developer.netscape.com/ one/javascript/index.html. The equivalent onscreen JScript site is http:// www.microsoft.com/JScript/us/Jstutor/Jstutor.htm. All of the usual search engines can come up with additional lists of JavaScript and JScript resources. Yahoo has a nice collection, listed under "computers and internet/programming languages."

Entering the Third Dimension With VRML

If you've ever played an arcade game or redesigned your kitchen with the aid of computer simulation, you know what virtual reality is. Thanks to a spin-off project of HTML called the Virtual Reality Modeling Language (VRML), you can now add virtual reality to the suite of things you can do in your Web pages. With VRML, you can turn the flat plane of your computer monitor into a three-dimensional space, allowing users to "walk" or "fly" around an object and observe it from all sides.

Netscape's VRML plug-in is called Live3D (developed by Paper Software, it was originally called WebFX). If you don't already have Live3D, you can download it for free from Netscape's plug-in site. Microsoft offers an add-on component to Microsoft Internet Explorer for navigating VRML worlds—it's called VRML 2.0. Several stand-alone VRML browsers are also available on the Web.

A VRML scene is called a *world*. There are three basic ways of viewing a VRML world; they basically represent the stages in the construction of each *object*. VRML objects (or nodes) start out life as *point clouds*, which look like miniature galaxies being born. A point cloud is simply a set of points that define an object's size and position in space. Connect the dots and you get a *wireframe*, which looks rather like a Tinkertoy construction. Wrap a surface around it and you get a *solid*. It takes less computer time to interpret and display a point cloud than a wireframe, and a wireframe is correspondingly faster to display than a solid. Therefore, VRML browsers usually allow you to speed things up (or just have a look at the inner workings) by choosing to display point clouds or wireframes.

Embedding a VRML World

When you're jumping from an ordinary Web page to a VRML site, you create the link with the anchor tag just as you would any other link, like so:

```
<A HREF="solarysys.wrl">Enter my solar system.</A> (A virtual reality
world!)
```

It's polite, of course, to let people know this is a link to a virtual reality site so they'll know if they're equipped to handle it.

Once you've created your VRML world, you can also embed it directly into your Web page using the <EMBED> tag. To insert the object, use the <IMG> tag just as you would to place a two-dimensional image. Naturally SRC is required, as is a WIDTH and HEIGHT, and you can align text and add a border if you wish.

Objects in the VRML world can also be hyperlinked to other worlds, HTML files, graphics, multimedia files—in short, anything you can normally link to in HTML. A sun over a beach scene, for instance, could be linked to a local weather information page. A boom box next to a beach towel could be linked to a music file, and clicking a surfer on the water could launch a QuickTime movie on surfing. In Figure 11-13, you can see the hyperlink revealed on an object in an architectural model done in VRML.

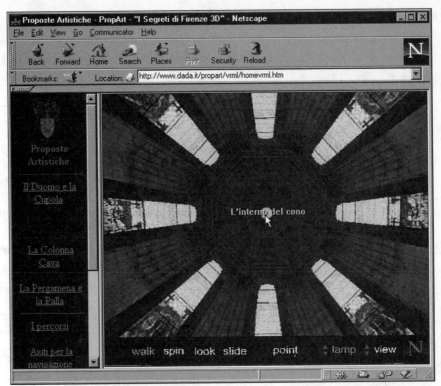

Figure 11-13: Giovanni De Stefano did this VRML model of the Cupola of Brunelleschi in Florence. The link leads to an internal view where you can examine the murals painted on the ceiling.

Custom Java and JavaScript functions are defined to help you control the behavior of your world. The functions in Table 11-1 can be used with Java or JavaScript to control the behavior of a VRML world.

Java and JavaScript Functions	What It Does
LoadScene(SceneURL, Frame)	Loads a new scene in the specified frame. If the frame is NULL, the URL is loaded into the current frame.
SetBackgroundImage (BackgroundImage)	Specifies the background image for the current scene. Supported formats include PNG, RGB, GIF, JPEG, BMP, and RAS.
GotoViewPoint(ViewPoint, nAnimationSteps)	Animates the camera to the named viewpoint over nAnimationSteps.
SpinObject(Object, Pitch, Yaw, Roll, nLocal)	Spins the named object around the specified axes. If nLocal is FALSE, rotations occur in World Coordinate Space. Otherwise, rotation occurs around the object's geometric center point.
AnimateObject(Object, URL)	Animates an object. The animation file is specified in the URL. Supported animation files include Autodesk's VUEformat.
Morph Object(Object, num_vertices, fCoords, nFrames, nMorphType)	Morphs the specified object. Morphing occurs over nFrames with interpolation between the object's original vertices to the target fCoords. nMorphType can be LOOP, ONCE, or BACKFORTH.
HideObject(Object)	Hides an object from visibility.
ShowObject(Object)	Makes an object visible.
DeleteObject(Object)	Deletes an object from the scene graph.
SetObjectAnchor(Object, Anchor)	Changes the anchor for the named object. The anchor may be a relative URL.

Java and JavaScript Callbacks	Used When:
onAnchorClick()	An anchor has been clicked.
onMouseMove()	The mouse moves over the plug-in window.

Table 11-1: Java and JavaScript functions for VRML.

VRML Tools & Resources

If you're interested in VRML, a good place to start (in fact, the *only* place to start) is the VRML Repository at the San Diego Supercomputer Center at http://www.sdsc.edu/vrml/. You'll find a comprehensive list of software there to help you create virtual reality worlds. These 3D drawing applications are generally called *geometry modelers* or *world builders*. A number of cross-platform modelers are available, as well as platform-specific ones. The address is http://www.sdsc.edu/vrml/gmmodelers.html.

Those who are already familiar with 3D modeling software will probably be interested in one of the several conversion programs that are available; these programs convert existing 3D worlds created in programs such as AutoDesk 3D Studio into VRML. Another comprehensive list of conversion software for various applications and multiple platforms can be found in the same directory under the filename gmtranslators.html.

You can also create and edit a VRML text file by hand if your needs are special. It's easy to define shapes like spheres, cubes, cones, and so on. You can imagine, however, that more complicated shapes (like the Sphinx) would be a bit more difficult to construct. But there's no reason to reinvent the wheel every time you want some new shape. Fortunately, cooperation is the name of the game, and there are libraries of VRML objects that you can access to find constructs that fit your needs or that you can build on (again, you'll find links to them at the VRML Repository). The details of the VRML language itself are archived at http://www.w3.org/hypertext/WWW/MarkUp/VRML.

Moving On

This chapter has just begun to tickle the surface of the things you can do to add interactivity to your Web pages with embedded applets, VRML worlds, or JavaScript functions. In the next chapter, we'll take you into the world of Dynamic HTML, where scripting languages can help you put some really powerful features into effect. The best thing about it is that it can be done with minimal drain on bandwidth and your users' computer resources.

chapter 12

Dynamic HTML

The very essence of the Web, ever since it first saw the light of those text-only, UNIX-only, HTTP clients, was instant change. See something you like in a list of hyperlinks? Wham! Go there. Filled out your form requesting data update? Wham! Submit it. Up comes the result.

So why should everybody be getting excited about something "new" called Dynamic HTML? The answer is that, under the original rules of the game, every request for a hyperlink and every form submission had to be routed back to the server for a fresh request, and all of the handshaking that introduces client software to server software had to be gone through all over again. That may have been a small penalty when the total population of the Web was a few thousand scientists and it was all text anyway. Now that you're competing with tens of millions of Web surfers for far more complex pages, "Wham!" has too often become "Wait!" Dynamic HTML is the way for Web authors to make their sites get a move on by providing a range of content that can be browsed without having to go back to the server.

What It Is & What It Isn't

Under the old rules, a Web page, no matter how complex, was just a page. The user downloaded it, scrolled through it, perhaps read it, and moved on. User influence over it was limited to the imposition of personal font and color preferences—to the annoyance of some Web authors. An overall Web *site* could have dynamic elements, but the rules said that once a page had been laid out in the browser, it couldn't be changed. Even when images began to animate, they did so within predefined parameters and not under user control.

Dynamic HTML is making some of the old rules about what can and can not be changed after a document has loaded obsolete. In its purest sense, Dynamic HTML allows for the download of a "kit of parts" capable of making up the page in many—possibly infinite—configurations and letting the user manipulate the page elements *without further reference to the server*. Images and blocks of type can appear and disappear; paragraphs can unfold or reduce themselves to summaries; styles can be changed on the fly; pages can be literally recomposed by the user.

Specifically, the technologies that this chapter will cover are:

- Cascading Style Sheets
- Dynamic style sheet control
- Positioning of page elements with precision
- Layering of elements in the third dimension
- Advanced event capture
- Animations and transitions under user control
- Dynamic fonts

Microsoft, but not Netscape, adds to that list a technique known as *Data Binding*, which allows for the download of a whole small database into the user's cache. Another element of Dynamic HTML is *canvas mode*, a technique that allows the author to be free of the usual constraints of the browser window and take control of the entire screen. However, this is an advanced technique that ultimately requires acquiring security certificates, so it won't be covered here.

Dynamic HTML can produce some stunning effects, but it can't work miracles. The time taken to download a page is the aggregate time needed for all of its elements, whether immediately seen or not. It's after everything's downloaded that the dynamic aspects can move like lightning.

The Document Object Model & CSS Extensions _____

As it is evolving now on the Web, Dynamic HTML is based on two important standards: extensions to the Cascading Style Sheet level-one standard (CSS-1) and the Document Object Model (DOM). CSS-1 is an accepted standard that has been used by Netscape and Microsoft in incorporating style sheet support in the 4.0 versions of their browsers. This was discussed in Chapter 8, "Style Sheets." The DOM is still a work in progress by the W3C, although it's existed since the spring of 1997 "by definition." At that time, the DOM working group declared that DOM Level Zero was "whatever you can do now with Netscape and Microsoft 4.0 browsers."

CSS-1 has already gone through one major revision to include new properties for positioning elements. These extensions are often referred to as CSS-P (or CSS Positioning). Using positioning coordinates, you can not only place elements exactly where you want them on the page, but you can also move them about and make them visible or invisible according to user actions. Both Netscape Navigator 4.0 and Microsoft Internet Explorer 4.0 recognize the CSSP extensions. The difference between them, however, lies in which scripting languages they respond to when you want to manipulate positioned elements.

The Document Object Model (DOM) is the other important standard, which lags well behind CSS in formulation and acceptance. The DOM has as its ultimate aim putting everything about an HTML document's format up for grabs at any time. The DOM proposes to do this by making every HTML element accessible to and changeable by scripting functions. The DOM is still far from full implementation as this is being written, but the mechanics and the underlying philosophy are already fairly clear.

The very phrase *object model*—a phrase on loan from the world of high-level computer programming—is an indication that the DOM experts would like to see HTML growing up into a real language, or at least put some kind of language wrapper around it that will make an HTML file behave more like the source code of a modern object-oriented language. This has very important benefits.

The public DOM Level 1 specification appeared on the Web in October 1997. As expected, it described a "core functionality" only and left implementation details to be thrashed out by the industry. The various components of a Web site are formalized as a hierarchy, with nodes descending through levels of *document, element, attribute, text, comment, and processing instruction (PI)*. Ways in which embedded languages such as JavaScript read/write to this hierarchy are reasonably familiar to the JavaScript or JScript programmer, who will be comfortable with the concept of objects and methods. However, the Level 1 spec owes more to Java, with its strong object orientation, than JavaScript, which is more process oriented.

Positioning Extensions to CSS

CSS-P adds to the first-level CSS syntax specific properties for positioning elements on the page. Both Netscape and Microsoft have incorporated some of the more stable features of CSS positioning into their 4.0 browsers. For the latest standards on CSS Positioning, check the W3C site at http://www.w3.org/.

What makes positioning a vital part of Dynamic HTML is that once an element is positioned, scripting can change element properties, including position, in response to user actions.

There are two types of positioning:

- **Absolute positioning.** Elements are given exact X- or Y-coordinates on the screen.

- **Relative positioning.** Elements are placed where they would appear in the natural flow of the document or displaced in relation to that point.

You can define positioning for elements using the CLASS and ID attributes with the <DIV> and <SPAN> tags. For example:

```
<DIV class="illus">
<IMG SRC="casablanca.jpg" WIDTH=400 HEIGHT=250>
<P class="caption">Casablanca, with its port, beaches and night life, is a
popular tourist destination for travellers in Morocco.
</DIV>
```

The style sheet positioning for this <DIV> might be written like this:

```
<STYLE TYPE="text/css"
<!--
#illus {
    position: absolute; top: 40px; left: 100px;
}
.caption {
    font: bold 12pt Helvetica;
    color: blue;
}
!-->
</STYLE>
```

You can also specify positioning properties with the STYLE attribute on the <SPAN> tag inline on most elements. For example:

```
<SPAN STYLE="position: absolute; top: 40px; left: 100px;"><IMG
SRC="casablanca.jpg"></SPAN>
```

The list of CSS positioning properties is rather short, but you can do a lot with them (see Table 12-1).

Property	Definition/Values
position	Specifies the type of positioning to be used to place the element. Values are *absolute, relative, static.*
left, top	The left, top (x, y) values specify the position of the element in relation to either the body (with absolute positioning) or another parent element (with relative positioning). Value can be a length, a percentage, or the default auto.
width	Specifies the width of the element. Value can be a length, a percentage, or the default auto. Percentage values are computed relative to the width of the parent element.
height	Specifies the height of the element. Value can be a length, a percentage, or the default auto. Percentage values are relative to the parent element. (If parent element's height is *auto,* the behavior is undefined.)
clip	Defines the visible part of the element (the *clipping rectangle*). Value is *rect (top right bottom left)* with top, right, bottom, and left coordinates in that order (clockwise from top). Values are separated only by spaces, *not* commas.
overflow	Specifies the behavior when the contents of absolutely positioned elements exceed the declared bounds. Values are *visible, hidden, scroll,* or *auto.*
z-index	Determines the stacking order of elements. Values are numerical, with higher numbers on top. Value may be negative.
visibility	Determines whether or not an element is initially displayed. Values are *inherit, visible,* or *hidden.* The default value is *inherit*, which means the element inherits its visibility from the parent element.

Table 12-1: CSS positioning properties.

Absolute Positioning With CSS

When you define absolute positioning for an element, you are defining a rectangular block into which your content will flow. An element with absolute positioning is laid out independently of any parent element or any other absolutely positioned element. For that reason, elements may overlay one another, and the element with the higher Z-order may obscure the contents of one with a lower Z-order.

To position an element exactly where you want it in the browser window, it's important to understand exactly where the 0,0 reference point is for X,Y. When you designate positioning coordinates, the 0,0 reference point is the upper left corner of your screen, without any reference to default page margins. If you do not specify positioning coordinates, the element's position includes the browser's default margins. Default margins may vary slightly in different browsers (from 5 to 10 pixels).

Besides the X,Y position, you may define a specific height and width for an absolutely positioned element. If width is not specified, the block will extend to immediately inside the right outer edge of the parent element. Height, if not specified, will adjust for the contents of the block.

Creating columns is a classic layout problem that Web hackers have been solving with tables up until now. CSS positioning can be used to accomplish the same thing and, in the end, with greater precision. A typical page with a banner and a table of contents with two columns next to it will be used as an example.

First, the positioning properties can be used to place the banner and the table of contents that makes the left column on the page. The dimensions of the banner (580 X 100) will be used for the total page width in order to place the columns evenly below it. The table of contents column needs to be about 175 pixels wide to accommodate the text. Allowing for a 10-pixel top margin and 10 pixels below the banner, the column should be positioned 120 pixels from the top and 10 pixels in from the left. This is the style sheet positioning syntax for the two items:

```
img.banner {
    position: absolute;
    top: 10;
    left: 10;
}
.col1 {
    width: 175px;
    position: absolute; top: 120px; left: 0px;
    background-color: red;
    padding-left: 10px;
    border: 1px;
}
```

As a matter of fact, if the banner and the column had no positioning declaration and were given default margins of 10 pixels, they might fall in exactly the same place. So why use absolute positioning? One good reason: Different browsers have different default margins. Giving absolute positions to both items assures that they will always "line up" to the same margin.

Note that a little padding was added to the column so the GIFs and text won't start right up against the edge of the red background. A border of 1 pixel also helps as a workaround to the problem that, in this version of Netscape, only the text elements themselves would inherit the background color, so adding the border makes the rest of the background area "fill in" with color. This is not a problem in Microsoft Internet Explorer, but the addition of a 1-pixel border does no harm.

The results so far are seen in Figure 12-1.

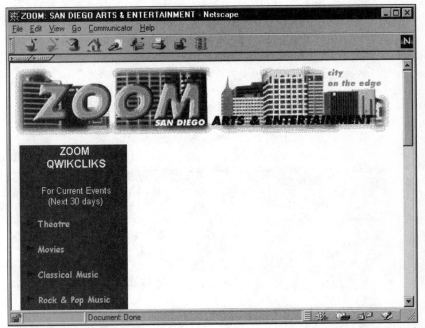

Figure 12-1: The table of contents column and the banner are made to line up with absolute positioning dictated in the style sheet.

The next thing to do is position the two text columns. A little trick here can help: Giving them a temporary background color will help you determine where the "corners" are so you can get a fix on the *x,y* positioning.

To figure out the positioning, the banner at the top can be used as a guide. In this case, it's the full width of the page, or 580 pixels. Subtracting the width of the first column, plus enough for margins between the columns, leaves a width of 185 pixels each for the text columns.

Finding the position of the first column is simply a matter of adding the 10px margin, the width of the first column, and an extra 15 pixels for spacing, so we arrive at a position of top 120, left 200. A little more basic math results in a position for the second column at 240, 410. Here's the style sheet statement with the proper positioning:

```
#col2 {
    position: absolute; top: 120px; left: 200px;
    width: 185px;
    background-color: yellow;
    border: 1px;
}
#col3 {
    position: absolute; top: 120px; left: 410px;
    width: 185px;
    background-color: yellow;
    border: 1px;
}
```

You can see the final result in Figure 12-2.

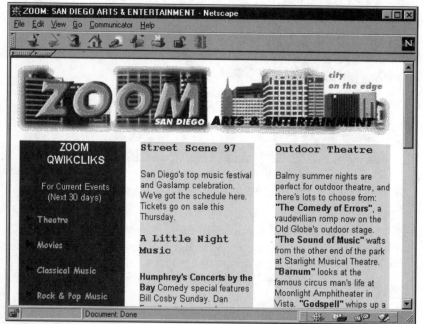

Figure 12-2: All of the elements on this page, including the banner and three columns, are positioned with CSS positioning. A background color has been temporarily added to the columns to show the positioning.

An added bonus to using DIV blocks and positioning is that it's possible to have the source of the page content come from an entirely different file. A simple, bare-bones text file elsewhere can contain the text for the columns, which need regular updating. Once the page is set up like this, the content can be completely divorced from the code, and the person responsible for updating that information need never deal with the master HTML page with all its complicated style declarations and forms. To include the source file, just add one more property-value statement to the style declaration for the column:

```
include-source: url("column2.html");
```

Remove the content of the second column and put it into a separate HTML file and save it as *column2.html*. What's left behind is this in the style sheet:

```
#col2 {
    position: absolute; top: 120px; left: 200px;
    width: 185px;
    background-color: yellow;
    border: 1px;
    include-source: url("column1.html");
}
```

and just this in the document:

```
<div id="col2">
</div>
```

It's easy to see that that could be extremely useful for automating updates to a Web page. However, this is getting a little ahead of the standards. As a matter of fact, this trick happens to work in Netscape Communicator 4.0, but it won't work in other browsers just yet. Check for this feature in the future, though, as it will obviously come in very handy.

Relative Positioning

Unlike those with absolute positioning, elements given relative positioning do not create a new independent box for their content. Rather they inherit their position from the parent element. Their position is dictated by the natural flow of the document. The real usefulness in relative positioning lies in the way it allows you to manipulate the positioned elements. You can:

■ Offset the element from its original position.

■ Adjust the Z-order relative to other elements.

■ Dynamically move, hide, or change the element by using scripting.

A Web page for a pie-in-the-sky business selling discount software (Figure 12-3) illustrates the difference between relative and absolute positioning and how relative positioning can be used with scripting.

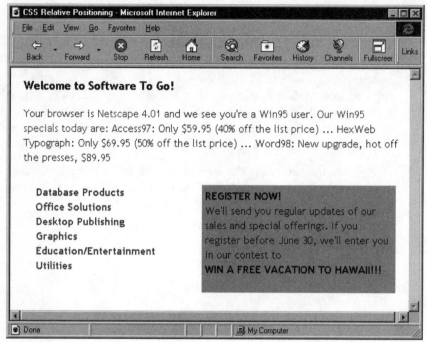

Figure 12-3: A combination of relative and absolute positioning with some clever JavaScript interpretation is used to present a specially tailored page to potential customers on this fictional Web site.

Two major elements on this page are the contest announcement and a table of contents. They're given absolute positions in these style sheet declarations:

```
#contents {
    position: absolute; top: 175px; left: 40px;
    color: green;
    font-weight: bold;
}
#register {
    position: absolute; top: 175px; left: 300px;
    width: 300px;
    background-color: orange;
    border: 1px;
    padding: 5px;
    color: black;
}
```

Within the document, the HTML for these components is set up like this:

```
<DIV id="contents">
<P>
Database Products<br>
Office Solutions<br>
Desktop Publishing<br>
Graphics<br>
Education/Entertainment<br>
Utilities
</DIV>

<DIV ID="register">
<P>
<a href="">REGISTER NOW!</a><br>
We'll send you regular updates of our sales
and special offerings. If you register
before June 30, we'll enter you in our contest to<br>
<a href="">WIN A FREE VACATION TO HAWAII!!!</a>
</DIV>
```

For something really special here, JavaScript will be used to interpret the browser and operating system and offer specials tailored to the visitor's own system. No sense wasting our valuable space trying to sell Windows specials to Mac customers and vice versa. Since these specials are going to be subject to change according to the trade winds and what's on the fictional shelves, the sales spiel is going to have to be adjustable. Relative positioning allows for all the variables necessary within the flow of the copy.

The copy for the different "specials" will come from any of several completely separate documents that will be referenced by JavaScript like this:

```
var wos = navigator.appVersion.match(/Win95/);
var mos = navigator.appVersion.match(/Mac/);

function fillSpan() {
  if (wos == "Win95") {
    document.specials.src = „winspec.html";
  }
  else if (mos == "Mac") {
    document.specials.src = "macspec.html";
  }
  else {
    document.specials.src = "generic.html";
  }
}
```

To insert the specials, this code is used in the style sheet:

```
#specials {
    position: relative;
}
```

In the document itself, the <SPAN> tag is used at the point the text is inserted, like this:

```
<SPAN ID="specials"></SPAN>
```

Offsetting Relatively Positioned Elements

A relatively positioned element takes as its 0,0 point the position in which it would naturally flow into the document relative to any parent element. You can offset the element from this position by using the position properties *top, right, bottom, left.* You can use negative values for top or left to make the element appear higher or to the left of its position. This can be used to create interesting overlay effects.

A simple version of this technique is used to create the "crooked man" text shown in Figure 12-4. Here's how it's done:

```
There was a c<SPAN STYLE="position: relative; top: -5">r</SPAN><SPAN
STYLE="position: relative; top: -10">o</SPAN>o<SPAN STYLE="position:
relative; top: 5">k</SPAN>ed man<br>
<SPAN STYLE="text-indent: 15px">who walked a
c<SPAN STYLE="position: relative; top: -5">r</SPAN><SPAN STYLE="position:
relative; top: -10">o</SPAN>o<SPAN STYLE="position: relative; top: 5">k</
SPAN>ed mile.</SPAN><br>
```

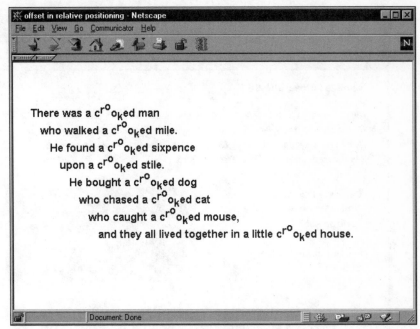

Figure 12-4: Relative positioning is used to offset the letters in this text.

In Flow Elements

Another useful thing you can do with relatively positioned elements is make them "float" according to the layout. Say you want to place a little red arrow in front of every line that contains a certain code word in a document. The code word will be part of the flow of the text, so it's hard to predict where it will fall. The arrow can be made to "float" along with the word by using relative positioning, as shown in Figure 12-5. The anchor word *specials* appears in red. Here's the code:

```
<P><SPAN STYLE="position: relative; left: 20px;">
Your browser is Netscape 4.01
and we see you're a Win95 user.
Our Win95
<SPAN STYLE="position: absolute; left: -12px;">
<IMG SRC="redtrism.gif">
</SPAN><font color="red">
specials</font></SPAN>
<SPAN STYLE="position: relative; left: 22px;"> today are:
Access97: Only $59.95 (40% off
the list price) ...
HexWeb Typograph: Only $69.95 (50% off the list price) ...
Word98: New upgrade, hot off the presses, $89.95
</SPAN>
```

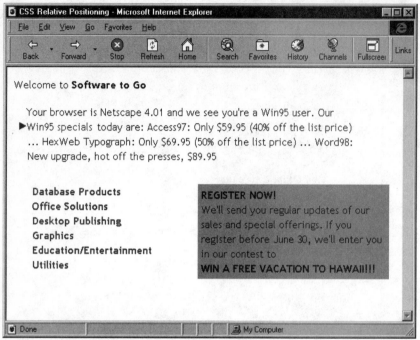

Figure 12-5: The arrow in the margin on this page will naturally "float" to the beginning of the line containing the code word.

It took three steps and three <SPAN> tags to accomplish this:

1. The first <SPAN> tag defines a left margin for this section of text. The close of this <SPAN> tag is found right after the anchor word.

2. The <IMG> tag is inserted right before the word to which the triangle will be anchored. The <IMG> tag is enclosed in its own <SPAN> tag with a left margin of –12px (the size of our GIF).

3. Then to bring the text that follows the anchor back to its normal position, a new left margin of 22px is defined for the rest of the paragraph.

Clipping Text & Images

Every page element—a picture, a text header, or a paragraph, or an entire external HTML document—has a clipping rectangle that defines the portion of it that is actually visible. By default, this portion is the same as the total dimensions of the object, but the clipping rectangle can be used to crop an element on all four sides either statically or dynamically by using the clipping coordinates. Although the clipping rectangle can be used with any HTML element, it is obviously most useful when applied to images.

For consistency's sake, CSS-P uses the same order as that for setting margins, padding, and borders, which is top, right, bottom, left (clockwise from the top).

A clipping property-value statement looks like this:

```
clip: rect (top right bottom left)
```

All measurements are in pixels *from top left*, so an image 200 X 100 pixels would be completely visible if clipped (0 200 100 0). The value *rect* is the shape of the clipped object. At the moment, the only possible shape is a rectangle, but the syntax allows for the possibility of other shapes at a later date.

TIP *Since the only possible shape at the moment is a rectangle, you may, in fact, omit the shape declaration* rect *in the clip definition. If you do, you should also omit the parentheses around the clip coordinates, and your statement should look like this:*

```
clip: 110 135 130 100;
```

To illustrate the use of the clipping rectangle, the Mona Lisa has been cropped right down to her enigmatic smile in Figure 12-6. This illustration actually contains three versions of the original: the full original, the dulled-out version, and the original (which is superimposed on the dulled-out version) with a clipping rectangle defined.

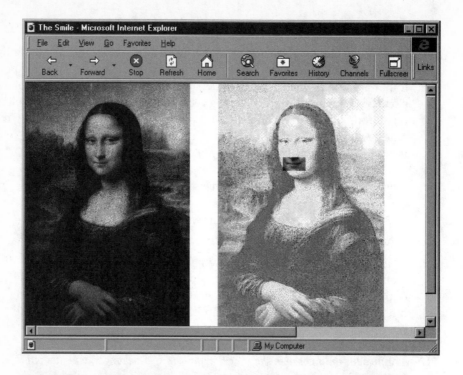

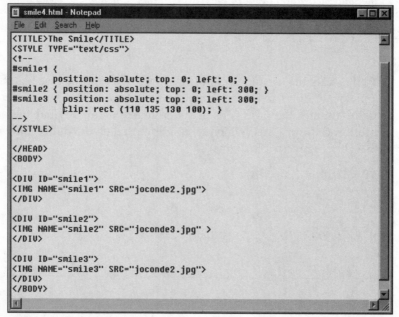

Figure 12-6: The Mona Lisa is cropped down to her enigmatic smile by using the clipping rectangle. (The grayed-out background is a separate image that shows the real dimensions of the superimposed cropped one.)

The style sheet contains an ID definition for each of the three versions of the Mona Lisa:

```
#smile1 { position: absolute; top: 0; left: 0; }
#smile2 { position: absolute; top: 0; left: 300; }
#smile3 { position: absolute; top: 0; left: 300; clip: rect (110 135 130
100); }
```

Within the page, each image tag is wrapped within a DIV containing the appropriate ID, like so:

```
<DIV ID="smile1">
<IMG NAME="smile1" SRC="joconde2.jpg">
</DIV>

<DIV ID="smile2">
<IMG NAME="smile2" SRC="joconde3.jpg" >
</DIV>

<DIV ID="smile3">
<IMG NAME="smile3" SRC="joconde2.jpg">
</DIV>
```

You can also use the STYLE attribute instead of a style sheet to position or clip images, like so:

```
<DIV STYLE="position: absolute; top: 0; left: 300; clip: rect (110 135 130
100)">
```

The STYLE attribute does not work with the image tag in Netscape Navigator 4.0, however, so it's safest to use the style sheet definition.

Another variation: Netscape supports the official CSS notation, allowing cropping at all four edges, and also a simplified version that assumes the top, left corner stays where it is and simply sets the width and height of the clipping rectangle. MSIE does not recognize this "shorthand," however.

The clipping rectangle can also be used to create effects like zooming in or out on an image, scrolling through the window, apparent movement of elements, and transitional effects. Two examples are worked through at the end of this chapter in the "Wish You Were Here" and "Venetian Blind" demos.

Layering Elements

In your daily computer life, you've probably become accustomed to having several applications open at once on your desktop. At any one time while you work, one application is "on top," the one you're working with, while others remain hidden or only partially visible. What keeps the order as you work is something both imaginary and real in computer terms, the *z-index*. Every one of the possible windows on your desktop has not only an X- and Y-coordinate, but also a Z-coordinate, indicating where it lies in a random priority you've established by cruising around your system from program to program. The X,Y position stays relatively fixed, changing only when you manually move or resize a window. The z-index, however, changes constantly, responding to your navigational whims as you bring different programs to the foreground.

In Figure 12-6 the mere order of the images in the file dictated which would appear on top (the clipped image of the smile over the dulled-out version). Figure 12-7 illustrates the use of the property *z-index* to overlay three elements on a page. A caption appears over the picture of a Moroccan desert Casbah. On top of that image is a second image that practically overlaps the first. The "Blue Man" has a transparent background that allows part of the Casbah image to show through. This type of "layering" should be familiar to those who use Adobe Photoshop to make composite images. In this case, however, CSS positioning did the whole thing and the three elements remain intact and separate.

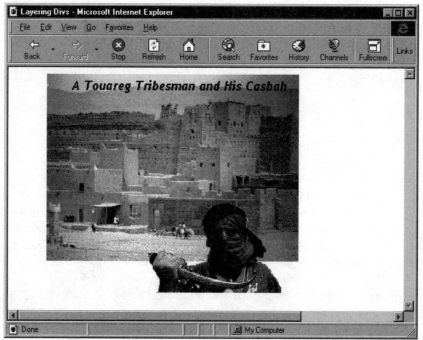

Figure 12-7: A Touareg tribesman and his Casbah illustrates transparency in layers. The top image has a transparent background, which allows the image in the lower layer to show through.

By using ID definitions, the style sheet defines the position and z-index of each of the three elements. This is it:

```
#caption {
    position: absolute; left: 100px; top: 15px;
    font: bold italic 14pt Trebuchet;
    z-index: 3;
}
#touareg {
    position: absolute; left: 220px; top: 200px;
    z-index: 2;
}
#casbah {
    position: absolute; left: 60px; top: 10px;
    border-color: blue;
    border-width: 2px;
    z-index: 1;
}
```

The HTML file contains these three DIV blocks for the content:

```
<DIV ID="caption">
<P>A Touareg Tribesman and His Casbah
</DIV>

<DIV ID="touareg">
<IMG SRC="touareg3.gif">
</DIV>

<DIV ID="casbah">
<IMG SRC="casbah2.jpg">
</DIV>
```

Higher z-index numbers appear over lower ones. So in this case, regardless of the fact that the Casbah image appears last in the file, the other two elements will appear over it, as their z-indices are higher.

Specifying Visibility & Layering Elements

By using CSS-P and scripting, you can manipulate the z-index of elements on your Web page, hiding them, changing the order, and making elements pop to the fore at will.

An active table of contents with various elements that pop up according to the MouseOver action of the user is shown in Figure 12-8. As you "mouse over" sections of the table of contents, different parts of the contents are highlighted by reversing the colors.

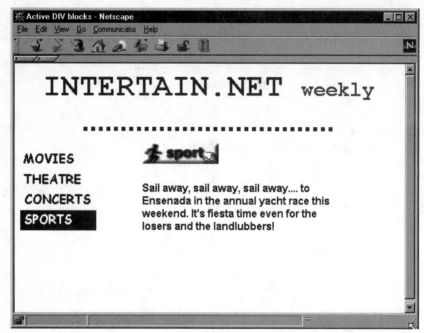

Figure 12-8: This table of contents for an entertainment calendar is an active image that changes as the mouse is moved down over each item. Different text also pops up in a layer to the right of the contents depending on what item in the contents is "selected."

This kind of "active" table of contents is actually becoming quite popular on the Web. There are several ways you can go about creating it. The way we've chosen is to make five different versions of our table of contents GIF— one for each area in which the area is shown turned "on" or highlighted and an "all off" version to start with. The actual image shown at any time is determined by a JavaScript "mouse over" action, but all five GIFs reference the same map file for the coordinates of the active sections.

An extra twist has been added to demonstrate that we can also control content in other parts of the screen. Here, different "highlight" text also pops up in a rectangular area of the screen to the right according to which item is "on." These are the steps it took to accomplish this sleight of hand:

1. First, five different text files were created (one for each selected item, plus an initial item for the all-off condition). Each file contains an image and the text to display for one selected item.

2. Then five DIV blocks were defined in the main file. Each was given an appropriate ID so it could be referenced.

3. A style sheet class was created for each DIV block. They were given absolute positioning with identical X-,Y-coordinates and identical widths of 300px (the height is not specified so that it will adjust to accommodate the text). The include-source property was also added with the appropriate file referenced for each instance.

It's easy to designate the layer that should be "on top" (the default intro text), but in this case that's not sufficient. To keep all the layers from showing at once and looking like alphabet soup, there's one more thing to do. Four of them must be initially hidden with the visibility property. Here's what the complete style sheet definition for the DIVs looks like:

```
#intro {
    position: absolute; top: 120px; left: 200px;
    width: 300px;
    visibility: show;
    include-source: url("intro.html");
}
#mpop {
    position: absolute; top: 120px; left: 200px;
    width: 300px;
    visibility: hide;
    include-source: url("mpop.html");
}
#tpop {
    position: absolute; top: 120px; left: 200px;
    width: 300px;
    visibility: hide;
    include-source: url("tpop.html");
}
#cpop {
    position: absolute; top: 120px; left: 200px;
    width: 300px;
    visibility: hide;
    include-source: url("cpop.html");
}
#spop {
    position: absolute; top: 120px; left: 200px;
    width: 300px;
    visibility: hide;
    include-source: url("spop.html");
}
```

Now, here's where JavaScript comes in for a little *presto-chango* routine. What the JavaScript will do is change the visibility value according to the "mouse over" action. Here's the JavaScript code that is added to the HEAD of the document:

```
<SCRIPT LANGUAGE="JavaScript">
<!--
Imageset = new Array();

for(j=1; j<5; j++) {
  Imageset[j] = new Image();
  Imageset[j].src = "pop" + j + ".gif";
}

function ChangeMenu(imnum,divname) {
  document.popmenu.src = Imageset[imnum].src;
  document.intro.visibility = "hide";
  document.mpop.visibility = "hide";
  document.tpop.visibility = "hide";
  document.cpop.visibility = "hide";
  document.spop.visibility = "hide";
  this.document.divname = divname;
  document.divname.visibility = "show";
}

//-->
</SCRIPT>
```

The function ChangeMenu is called up by the onMouseOver action in the map file like so:

```
<MAP NAME="menmap">
<AREA SHAPE="rect" COORDS="0,0,120,30" HREF="mpop.htm"
onMouseOver="ChangeMenu(1,mpop)">
<AREA SHAPE="rect" COORDS="0,30,120,60" HREF="theatre.htm"
onMouseOver="ChangeMenu(2,tpop)">
<AREA SHAPE="rect" COORDS="0,60,120,90" HREF="concerts.htm"
onMouseOver="ChangeMenu(3,cpop)">
<AREA SHAPE="rect" COORDS="0,90,120,120" HREF="sports.htm"
onMouseOver="ChangeMenu(4,spop)">
</MAP>
```

A thoughtful refinement that could be added to this example would be to let the JavaScript also determine the browser and present users with less-capable browsers an alternative static image and default text.

Netscape's Layer Tag

Before the CSS-P standard was agreed upon, Netscape had already implemented its own version of 3D positioning with the <LAYER> tag. Subsequently, Netscape has added support for the CSS-P extensions, as well. The <LAYER> tag is a little more intuitive and perhaps easier for nonprogrammers to understand, although support for this approach is not likely to expand.

The position of layers is dictated by the attributes LEFT and TOP, which indicate the X-,Y-coordinates of the top, left corner of the layer. The dimensions of the layer can be controlled with the WIDTH and HEIGHT attributes in the same way they are used with images and other elements. The full set of attributes for the <LAYER> and <ILAYER> tags is shown in Table 12-2. The <NOLAYER> tag can be used to provide alternate content for browsers without layer support (its use is identical to the <NOFRAMES> tag).

Attribute	Description
ID="name"	Specifies the name of the layer so that other layers and JavaScript functions can refer to them. (The original terminology, NAME, has been changed to ID to conform to CSS-P, although NAME still works as an attribute.)
LEFT=x, TOP=y	Specifies the absolute position of a layer (in pixels) defined with <LAYER> or the relative position for layers defined with <ILAYER>. Together, the two attributes define the top, left corner of the layer. The position is in relation to the parent element.
PAGEX=x, PAGEY=y	Specifies the absolute position of a layer in relation to the page (as opposed to the parent element). These can only be used with the <LAYER> tag, as <ILAYER> is inherently relative.
SRC="file"	Specifies the file that contains HTML-formatted content for the layer.
Z-INDEX, ABOVE, and BELOW	These three parameters specify the stacking order of the layer. Only one can be used at a time.
WIDTH=w	Specifies the width of the layer's content and controls the right margin for wrapping purposes.

➨

HEIGHT=h	Specifies the height of the layer's content. By default, the height will adjust to fit the contents. The main purpose of the HEIGHT parameter is to act as a reference for child layers.
CLIP=x_1,y_1,x_2,y_2	Specifies the clipping rectangle or boundaries of the viewable area of the layer. This can be less than the width and height of the content of the layer. The order of the values is left (x_1), top(y_1), right(x_2), bottom(y_2). (This order is different than the order in style sheet positioning, which is top, right, bottom, left.)
VISIBILITY=*show/hide/inherit*	Specifies whether the layer is visible or not.
BGCOLOR="*#rrggbb*"	Specifies the background color of the layer.
BACKGROUND="bg.gif"	Specifies the image to use as the background of the layer.

Table 12-2: Attributes for the <LAYER> and <ILAYER> tags.

Positioning Layers

Layers defined with <LAYER> can be positioned absolutely with the LEFT and TOP attributes. If you do not set these attributes, the default values of 0,0 are used, which places the layer at the top, left corner of the document.

Layers defined with <ILAYER> have relative positions and will appear wherever they naturally fall in the flow of the document. If not preceded by a line break or <DIV> tag, they will appear on the same line as preceding elements. The left, top corner (0,0 position) can be assumed to be the point at which the next inline element would naturally occur. An <ILAYER> may then be offset from this zero position with LEFT and TOP attributes.

Stacking Layers

Using the positioning attributes LEFT and TOP, you can give two independent layers the same or overlapping coordinates. That's what was done in Figure 12-9 to make a caption appear over the photo image.

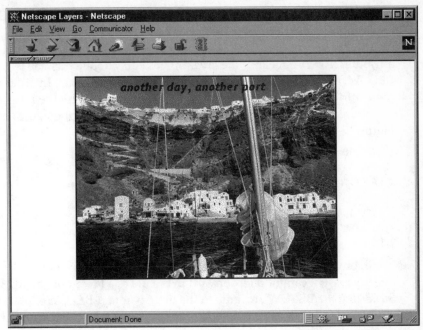

Figure 12-9: A layer containing text is placed over a layer with an image, creating a superimposed caption.

In this example, the order in which the layers appear in the file determines which will be on top. The layer of text is treated as transparent, so the image is visible beneath it. If the image were the top layer, it would completely hide the text. You can also specify the "stacking order" of the layers with the attribute Z-INDEX. Higher Z-INDEX numbers are stacked above lower ones. To designate the stacking order of the layers in Figure 12-9 with Z-INDEX, you could write:

```
<LAYER LEFT=170 top=25 Z-INDEX=2>
<B><I>another day, another port</I></B>
</LAYER>

<LAYER LEFT=100 top=20 Z-INDEX=1>
<IMG SRC="greece1.jpg">
</LAYER>
```

Now, even though the image layer appears last in the file, the text will be superimposed over the image since its Z-INDEX number is higher.

Another way to designate stacking order is to use the ABOVE and BELOW attributes. ABOVE means "the layer immediately above this one is...," and BELOW means "the layer immediately below this one is...." In order to use these attributes, the layers must have names assigned with the ID attribute so the desired layer can be addressed. With the ABOVE attribute, the code for Figure 12-9 would look like this:

```
<LAYER ID="text" LEFT=170 TOP=25>
<B><I>another day, another port</I></B>
</LAYER>

<LAYER ID="photo" LEFT=100 TOP=20 ABOVE="text">
<IMG SRC="greece1.jpg">
</LAYER>
```

In order to use the ABOVE and BELOW attributes, the named layer must already exist; it cannot refer forward in the file to a layer not already known. So adding the BELOW attribute to the first layer tag (BELOW="photo") in this example would not have worked because "photo" was not a known layer at that point in the file.

You can designate a background color for a layer with BGCOLOR. However, if you designate a background color for a higher-level layer, it will not be transparent. A background color added to the text layer in our example produces the effect seen in Figure 12-10.

This shows an important thing about layers: when no size is indicated, layers will have a variable rectangular dimension according to their content. The actual 0,0 reference point is easy to see with the background color added in this figure.

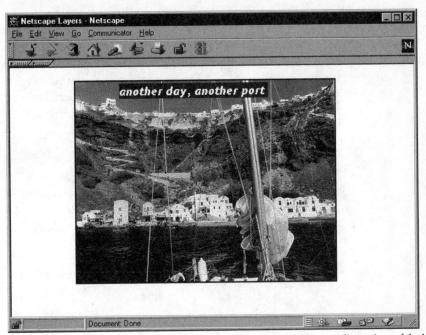

Figure 12-10: A background color added to the text layer reveals the true dimensions of the layer.

TIP
When you work with multiple layers, it is often helpful to add a temporary background color to a layer in order to get your bearings. The background color will reveal the "true" dimensions of the layer and help you to determine the correct positioning.

Likewise, you can designate a background image for a layer. Again, the layer will not be transparent unless there are transparent color sections in the image itself. In that case, the lower layer will shine through in the areas of the transparent color.

Using External Files in Layers

Since text layers are by nature transparent (unless the layer has a designated background color), one stylish thing you can do with layers is overlay several different bits of text. Figure 12-11 shows a whimsical example that uses both <LAYER> and <ILAYER> for illustration. For convenience, the overlay text is contained in separate files and referenced with the SRC attribute.

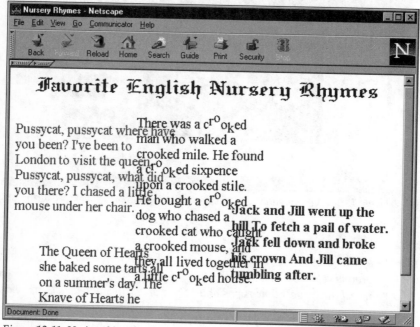

Figure 12-11: Various bits of text can be overlaid on one another in stylish or whimsical ways with layers. This example uses defined widths; the text of each layer is called in from other files with the SRC attribute.

By using the SRC attribute to call in external text, you can make it easier to control what users whose browsers do not recognize the <LAYER> tag will see. Because those browsers will simply ignore the <LAYER> tag (and its subsequent source file), the main file can include only the information that we want these users to see. The tag for one of the layers looks like this:

```
<LAYER ID="crooked" SRC="crooked.html" LEFT=200 TOP=45 WIDTH=200>
</LAYER>
```

Note the way we used the WIDTH attribute to control the area that each piece of our text would fill. The width calculation begins at the LEFT, or *X-coordinate,* value. The height will adjust naturally to the required size for the content unless the CLIP attribute is used to define a precise viewable area. You might want to define only part of an image as viewable, for instance, and you could do so by denoting the left, top (x_1,y_1) values followed by the right, bottom (x_2,y_2) values.

The "crooked" text in the Crooked Man rhyme was done with <ILAYER>. This is the markup:

```
<P>There was a c<ILAYER TOP=-5>r</ILAYER><ILAYER TOP=-10>o</ILAYER>o<ILAYER
TOP=5>k</ILAYER>ed man who walked a crooked mile
```

Note that in order to raise the text above the baseline, a minus value was used for TOP. A positive value lowers the text from the baseline.

Clipping Layers

The CLIP attribute allows you to designate the portion of an element that is displayed by effectively cropping the content. The clipping rectangle with the <LAYER> tag is defined by the X-,Y-coordinates of the *left, top* corner and the *right, bottom* corner of the item to be clipped, in that order (the order is important). This can be used with a text layer, but it's most natural to think of doing it with an image. Figure 12-12 shows the reproduction of the Mona Lisa used in the CSS-P clipping example, this time using the <LAYER> tag. This is the code:

```
<LAYER ID="smile3" LEFT=300 TOP=0 CLIP="100,110,135,130">
<IMG SRC="joconde2.jpg">
</LAYER>
```

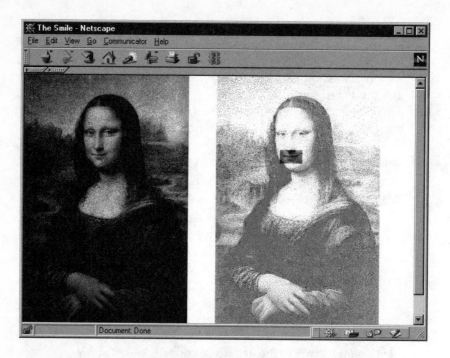

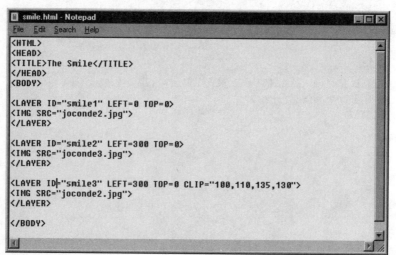

Figure 12-12 : The Mona Lisa is reduced to her famous smile by using the CLIP attribute with the <LAYER> tag. To show the actual dimensions of the hidden image, we used another layer beneath the cropped image for the grayed-out version of the picture.

TIP | *When you use the clipping rectangle with the <LAYER> tag, the order of the coordinates is different from the order used with CSS-P positioning. With the LAYER tag, the order is left, top, right, bottom. The order for style sheet positioning is clockwise from top (top, right, bottom, left). See "Clipping Text & Images" earlier in this chapter.*

Specifying Visibility & Changing Layer Order

The VISIBILITY attribute allows you to hide some layers while others remain visible. Using JavaScript, you can then "reshuffle" the layers to change which one appears by manipulating the visibility value.

The same kind of active table of contents shown in Figure 12-8 can be created with Netscape layers. This time, the position and display of the layers is controlled with the attributes of the <LAYER> tag. Here's the HTML that produces the identical result with layers:

```
<LAYER ID="intro" LEFT=200 TOP=120
WIDTH=300 SRC="intro.html" VISIBILITY=show>
</LAYER>

<LAYER ID="mpop" LEFT=200 TOP=120
WIDTH=300 SRC="mpop.html" VISIBILITY=hide>
</LAYER>

<LAYER ID="tpop" TOP=120 LEFT=200
WIDTH=300 SRC="tpop.html" VISIBILITY=hide>
</LAYER>

<LAYER ID="cpop" LEFT=200 TOP=120
WIDTH=300 SRC="cpop.html" VISIBILITY=hide>
</LAYER>

<LAYER ID="spop" LEFT=200 TOP=120
WIDTH=300 SRC="spop.html" VISIBILITY=hide>
</LAYER>
```

The JavaScript that affects the mouse-over changes is slightly different. Here it is:

```
<SCRIPT LANGUAGE="JavaScript">
<!--
Imageset = new Array();
```

```
for(j=1; j<5; j++) {
  Imageset[j] = new Image();
  Imageset[j].src = "pop" + j + ".gif";
}

function ChangeMenu(imnum) {
  document.popmenu.src = Imageset[imnum].src;
  for (j=0; j<5; j++) {
  document.layers[j].visibility = "hide"
  }
  document.layers[imnum].visibility = "show"
}
//-->
</SCRIPT>
```

The function ChangeMenu is called up by the onMouseOver action in the map file, which looks like this:

```
<MAP NAME="menmap">
<AREA SHAPE="rect" COORDS="0,0,120,30" HREF="mpop.htm"
onMouseOver="ChangeMenu(1)">
<AREA SHAPE="rect" COORDS="0,30,120,60" HREF="theatre.htm"
onMouseOver="ChangeMenu(2)">
<AREA SHAPE="rect" COORDS="0,60,120,90" HREF="concerts.htm"
onMouseOver="ChangeMenu(3)">
<AREA SHAPE="rect" COORDS="0,90,120,120" HREF="sports.htm"
onMouseOver="ChangeMenu(4)">
</MAP>
```

Advanced Event Capture

When Dynamic HTML came along in 1997, several upgrades seemed appropriate—and one important area of improvement was event capture. Up to then, a fairly full range of events (such as mouse clicks and filling out forms) had been capturable, but *only in relation to very specific elements* such as hyperlinks or form fields. If you wanted to capture a click over an image, you were out of luck (unless it was an active image, at least). Dynamic HTML pretty much required that events should be capturable anywhere in the window and that the script should figure out what the event was and where it happened and proceed accordingly. Obviously, then, some sort of list of event properties had to be passed to the event handler—and as usual, at that point Netscape and Microsoft diverged.

Document-Level Event Capture in Netscape _____

In Netscape 4.x, either a document object or a window object can be set up to capture events—and they are synonymous for most purposes. To set up a window to capture events, you need to do three separate things:

1. Declare the event(s) that the window will capture.
2. Declare the name(s) of the JavaScript function(s) that will handle the event(s).
3. Write and debug the event-handling function(s).

You might declare that you want to capture both mouseDown and mouseUp events as follows:

```
window.captureEvents(Event.MOUSEUP|Event.MOUSEDOWN);
```

(Any number of events may be listed like this, separated by the vertical bar.) Now you declare functions—*mouse_start* and *mouse_stop*, let's say—to handle these events:

```
window.onMouseDown = mouse_start;
window.onMouseUp = mouse_stop;
```

Note that, unlike more conventional JavaScript event handlers, whether the functions are passing parameters or not, they do not have to be followed by parentheses. The event itself is the only parameter, often symbolized as *ev*. We can get information about the event as a series of properties of the event object. The *mouse_start(ev)* function could, for example, retrieve the X- and Y-coordinates of the click event as *ev.pageX* and *ev.pageY* and then initialize some variables depending on whether the click event happened within a given area of the screen.

One very attention-getting feature that window-level event capture enables is actual dragging and dropping of page elements by the user. If, let's say, the *mouse_start(ev)* function calculated that the mousedown event happened within the perimeter of a draggable page object called *portable* (this would be a DIV block or a Netscape LAYER), it could trigger the capture of the MOUSEMOVE event and make it work like this:

```
document.captureEvents(Event.MOUSEMOVE);
document.onMouseMove = Drag;

function Drag(ev) {
  document.portable.moveTo(ev.pageX, ev.pageY);
}
```

That's the drag part of the drag and drop. The drop part is taken care of by the *mouse_stop(ev)* function, which disables capture of the MOUSEMOVE event when the user releases the button, as follows:

```
document.releaseEvents(Event.MOUSEMOVE);
```

There are some spectacular examples of Netscape event capture on the Web. The Netscape developer site has some of its own in the dynamic HTML section, and the Macromedia "Superfly" demo site at http://www.dhtmlzone.com/tutorials/index.html includes a "dressing room" page; the user can try out a range of clothes items on a mannequin by drag and drop.

Event Bubbling in MSIE

Microsoft's approach is to let every HTML element automatically sense all events; if no specific event handler is provided in a particular element, that element tries to find an appropriate event handler by "bubbling up" to its parent element, then to its parent's parent, and so on. The element continues until it finds one or until the topmost element, the document itself, is reached and still no handler is found. In practice, this means that most events can be handled at the document level. The capture statement is simplified:

```
document.onmousedown = mouse_start;
```

Parameters of the event are passed as properties of the *window.event.srcElement* object. In particular, the event handler can detect which actual element triggered the event by reading its ID. Consider this code fragment:

```
<DIV ID="ratdiv" onmouseover="whatrat()">
<P>The brown rat is ubiquitous in the Paris Metro
<IMG ID="bratpic" SRC="brownie.jpg ALIGN=right>
</DIV>
```

Either the text or the image can trigger the *whatrat()* function. The code can tell which because, if the user moused over the text, then *window.event.srcElement.id* will have the value *ratdiv,* whereas mousing over the image passes control to the same function but with *window.event.srcElement.id* having the value *bratpic.*

Sometimes it's too much of a good thing to have every single element of a complex page go looking for an event handler every time a user waves a mouse pointer over it. To exclude an image, say, from a window-level event handler, Microsoft allows for what you might call an event "unhandler," like this:

```
<IMG SRC="desrat.jpg" onmouseover = "window.event.cancelBubble = true;">
```

Dynamic Fonts

Web authors and designers who come to the Web from the world of print are often frustrated by their inability to use fonts in the way they are accustomed to using them when designing a magazine layout or an advertising brochure, for instance. Even amateur publishers who are accustomed to the modern wizardry of desktop publishing are often puzzled by the seeming lack of sophistication and inflexibility of the average Web page. The problem is that a computer screen is not as precise a medium on which to execute one's artwork as a canvas or a piece of paper. Font appearance is highly variable from system to system, and rendering varies greatly according to different resolutions.

Discussions are underway to resolve some standards for the Web that will result in better and more reliable font rendering. A proposal for extending CSS to include more precise font descriptions is in the working draft stage at the W3C. Until these discussions and the technologies that will be based on them proceed further, a couple of different approaches to this design problem exist.

Basically, there are three ways to embed fonts in Web pages: (1) send only the characters necessary to do the job, (2) send the entire font as read only, or (3) send the entire font and let the user keep it. Microsoft's approach has been a combination of the latter two. Netscape has combined forces with some professional font companies to work on the first approach—sending only the characters necessary to do the job.

Microsoft's Font Embedding

Logically enough, as owners of the most widely used operating system on the planet, Microsoft already has a fair share of font resources at their command. Microsoft ships a selection of common fonts know as "core Windows fonts" with its operating system. Web designers can have some assurance that these core fonts will be available at least on any current Windows operating system. Microsoft is now enlarging the set of core fonts to include online and Web-related fonts, and a number of them are available for free download from the Microsoft Web site. This includes versions for Mac systems. This generosity goes some way toward providing some variety for Web authors, but not quite far enough for designers with special demands.

Microsoft's proposed solution is *font embedding*, which is a method of including fonts with the documents in which they are used. Through standards that have been set up in consultations between Microsoft and TrueType, font designers have the option of setting different types of permissions on their fonts. These TrueType permissions include:

- *Fully installable* fonts may be installed on the recipient's machine without restriction.

- *Editable* fonts allow the user to make changes to the document using the font, but do not allow it to be used in other documents or applications.

- *Print preview* allows the document to be viewed and printed with the font, but the font cannot be used in other applications or in editing the document.

- *Do not embed* is used by font designers who do not wish to have the font travel with the document under any circumstances.

In order to use font embedding, the application that creates and reads the document must support it. Font embedding is available via a simple check box when you save a document in some of the more recent Windows applications. In the File Save box, simply check the Embed TrueType check box. The application will determine which fonts are used in the document and include an encrypted version with the document. Of course, this limits you to those fonts that support the latest TrueType embedding standard.

Embedded fonts can add considerably to the size of your file and, consequently, the time it takes to download, but there are ways that this can be overcome. Subsetting a font—that is, selecting for only the characters used in a text to be sent with the document—can reduce the file to a manageable size, but it does make the font no longer editable. And that is where the Netscape dynamic font approach comes in.

Netscape's Dynamic Fonts

With dynamic fonts, you can theoretically design your page with any of the fonts available to you on your system. When you're done, you use a font recorder to create the PFR files that will be posted along with your document. Your fonts can thus be faithfully reproduced on the user's system regardless of whether the user has the specified font.

Dynamic fonts differ from downloadable fonts in that the Portable Font Resource (PFR) file accompanying the document is not a full font set (which can be cumbersome to download); it is instead a limited font description relevant only to the current document. The PFR files are relatively small, easy to download, and need only be downloaded once per document. The "document lock" feature ensures that they cannot be pirated and reused, thus avoiding the hotly contested copyright issues over font design and ownership.

A page using dynamic fonts initially loads just like any other Web page. After the PFR file is fully downloaded, the screen is redrawn to show the document with the designated font, which is then used throughout as you scroll through the document. The PFR file should be used only if the designated font is not present on the system (although this seems variable in practice). If the user's browser does not include dynamic font support, it will use a designated alternate font or the closest approximation to the designated font it finds on the user's system.

There are still a couple of problems with this technology. The constant redrawing of the page during the scrolling process can be irritating to readers. And the aliasing procedure on many fonts renders their dynamic versions less than ideal. Both of these problems may be overcome as the technology moves on and more fonts designed especially for computer screen use are made available.

A plug-in to Netscape Composer that allows you to create dynamic fonts is available from the Netscape site. Several popular HTML editors will also be incorporating the font recorder in their software. If you have a favorite HTML editor, you should look for an update that includes a font recorder. A stand-alone application for Windows 95 and Mac, HexWeb Typograph, is also available. A version of this called HexWeb XT is available as an extension to QuarkXPress. Get current information at http://www.hexmac.com/.

A wide selection of popular fonts, digitized and optimized for the Web, can be purchased online from Bitstream at http://www.bitstream.com/.

Creating a Page With Dynamic Fonts

At the moment, the easiest way to experiment with dynamic fonts is to use the font recorder plug-in for Netscape Composer. Using dynamic fonts requires very little more than creating an ordinary HTML page—and if you use style sheets, quite a lot less. To use dynamic fonts, first create your page the way you want it to look using any fonts you have installed on your system. Use the font tag or a style sheet to specify the fonts within your document.

Next, use the Composer plug-in to create the PFR file to accompany your document. When installed, the Composer plug-in will create a new item called Fonts/Font Recorder on the Tools menus of Netscape Composer. Bring your document up in Composer and select the Font Recorder. It will search your document for any font tags and compile a list of fonts, as seen in Figure 12-13. (This early version of the plug-in does not recognize style sheet font designations and works only with the font tags.) If you're satisfied with the list, press Record Fonts and the PFR file will be created. If this is your first use of the font recorder, you will likely see an alarming warning panel pop up (see Figure 12-14). Just a reminder that this webmeistering business is not for the faint of heart! Not to worry—your computer won't self-destruct if you continue. This is actually a Security Certificate informing you that the maker of the application is a bona fide company that has jumped over the requisite number of hurdles to obtain this certification.

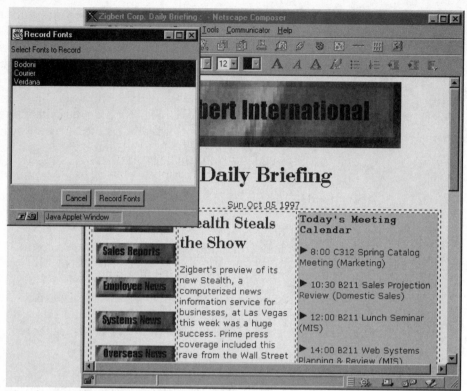

Figure 12-13: The Font Recorder plug-in for Netscape Composer is ready to record a list of fonts found in the document.

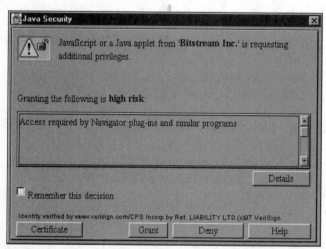

Figure 12-14: This warning box is a Security Certificate from Bitstream, just another hurdle you have to leap to create dynamic fonts.

If you continue, Composer will do two things: (1) create the PFR file, and (2) insert a link to the PFR file into the head of your document. You can see the format of the link tag by choosing View/Page Source. You'll see a tag like this in your document:

```
<LINK REL="fontdef" SRC="myfont.pfr">
```

The PFR file has already been created, so you needn't overwrite your document by saving it in Composer at this time. In fact, it's recommended that you don't. If you're fussy about your code, you'll be alarmed by all the extra tags that Composer will throw in when you save your document in the editor. Also, if you use JavaScript or other scripts in your page, you may want to exercise extreme caution because the program code may be misinterpreted by the editor. Just copy the <LINK> tag from the source code, paste it into your document in a separate file, and wish Composer good-bye and a better life in future.

The PFR file that has been created will have the same name as your document and the .pfr extension. Post the PFR file on the server along with the HTML file. That's all you need. However, note the tip about Web server configuration.

TIP *In order for your users to download and view TrueDoc PFRs from their Web browsers, the Web server on which the document resides must be configured to recognize the PFR MIME type. The MIME type is application/font-tdpfr. The file extension is pfr. Depending on the Web server, the extension may have to be entered in upper- or lowercase or both and may require a period before the extension. An additional MIME type, /font/truedoc, may also be necessary.*

Using Dynamic Fonts With Style Sheets

At the time this book was written, style sheet support was not yet officially in effect with dynamic fonts. However, this may well be overcome in the near future. If you use style sheets with dynamic fonts, you will need to include a reference to the PFR file within your style sheet. The syntax for this is still evolving within the CSS standards committee of the W3 Consortium, so the method we include here should be rechecked before you attempt it. However, this is the way it is currently expected to work.

Let's say you're using Lucida Sans Unicode for your level 1 heads and Palatino as your body text style. This is a sample style sheet statement that includes the PFR reference:

```
<STYLE TYPE="text/css">
<!--
@font-face {
    font-family: Lucida Sans Bold;
    src: url(http://domain/path/myfile.pfr);
}
@font-face {
    font-family: Helvetica;
    src: url(http://domain/path/myfile.pfr);
    font-weight: normal;
}
@font-face {
    font-family: Trebuchet MS;
    src: url(http://domain/path/myfile.pfr);
    font-weight: normal;
}
H1 {
    font-family: Lucida Sans Unicode, Helvetica, sans-serif;
    font-size: 16pt;
}
BODY {
    font-family: Trebuchet MS, Helvetica, sans-serif;
    font-size: 12pt;
    line-height: 16pt;
}
-->
</STYLE>
```

By the style sheet rules, the browser will use Lucida Sans Unicode as the first choice font for the heads, which will match the first @font-face. If the font resides on the user's system, then it will be used in the document; if not, a TrueDoc-enabled browser will access the PFR file for this font. If the browser is not TrueDoc enabled and the preferred font is not available, it will use Helvetica or another sans-serif font since these are the second and third choices in the font preferences list. The body text will be in Trebuchet MS, which matches the second @font-face. If the browser is not TrueDoc enabled and Trebuchet MS is not available, the text will be in Helvetica or another sans-serif font. Note that all three fonts are contained in the same PFR file, but a separate style sheet statement is required for each font that needs to reference the file.

Microsoft's Data Binding

It hardly needs stating that two-way communications between Web pages and relational databases are considered the future of the Web, especially by those institutions and corporations that already have large databases and want to put them pretty much straight up on the Net. At least 20 companies have major interfacing products designed to facilitate this—all of the major players, such as Oracle, Informix, and Foxbase, plus a raft of "niche market" software companies, all of whom figure they have the best ideas.

Very little, if any, of this activity comes legitimately under the heading of Dynamic HTML. The heavyweight corporate stuff involves a Web server talking through some intermediate API server to a Database Manager, and it often involves more bells and whistles, too—the very antithesis of Dynamic HTML, which is supposed to download everything and let the user play around without further reference to the server side.

Microsoft has, however, come up with a lightweight database interface scheme that qualifies in theory because a module called a Data Source Object (DSO) is related to a part of an HTML page (such as a table, the Data Consumer) through a Data Binding Agent. The whole kit comes down to the user's cache, and once downloaded, the contents of the Data Consumer reflect the content of the DSO as ordered and formatted by certain Microsoft tags. A very simple tabulation of merchandise, for example, might declare its data source like this:

```
<TABLE DATASRC=#dsoKayaks>
```

Data fields would then be inserted into cells of the table with the <DATAFLD> tag:

```
<TR>
    <TD><DIV DATAFLD=manufacturer></DIV></TD>
    <TD><DIV DATAFLD=style></DIV></TD>
    <TD><DIV DATAFLD=name></DIV></TD>
    <TD><DIV DATAFLD=length></DIV></TD>
    <TD><DIV DATAFLD=width></DIV></TD>
</TR>
```

DSOs can be constructed in Java, C++, or Visual Basic. They can be much more complicated than that simple example, supporting full SQL statements and extractions from data tables other than simple delimited ASCII. Microsoft has a DSO "gallery" at http://www.microsoft.com/gallery/files/datasrc/ datasrc-intro.htm from which some samples may be downloaded. Unfortunately, the gallery was still incomplete as this book went to press. Although there is clearly a need for some such lightweight solution to database/Web linking, there is no sign of Microsoft's data binding ideas being adopted by the standards bodies.

Dynamic HTML Tools

Virtually every manufacturer of HTML editing software is racing to catch up with Dynamic HTML, Cascading Style Sheets (CSS), and CSS positioning. By the time this book is on the shelves, there will undoubtedly be a range of tools to choose from—right now, two that have already solved the problems very nicely are WebberActive, from Expertelligence Inc., and Macromedia's Dreamweaver.

Expertelligence is also one of the firms making a living from Web/database interactivity—they market Webbase, a combined Web server and database management system (DBMS) that will talk to any ODBC-compliant database and is an ideal all-in-one package for a corporate intranet. WebberActive supports all the latest HTML tags and inline styles, but works with MSIE only.

Macromedia's Dreamweaver is the top of the line—it can work out your style sheets for you and "translate" between Netscape and Microsoft conventions. It has some powerful site management features as well. Figure 12-15 shows Dreamweaver in the process of editing an internal style sheet. On the left is the object palette, which facilitates the insertion of objects such as images, tables, and layers. At the bottom is the property inspector, allowing an absolutely complete range of attribute adjustments for any legitimate HTML object. The style sheet editor was initiated by a button on the launcher toolbar, seen at top right.

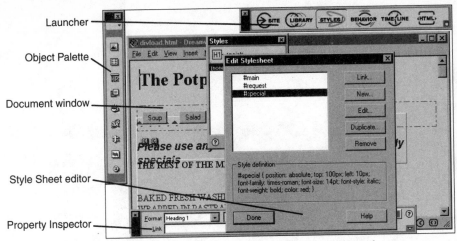

Figure 12-15: Macromedia Dreamweaver in Style Sheet Edit mode.

Dynamic HTML Examples

A Simple Animation

So long as DIV blocks are given an absolute position on the screen, it's extremely simple to make them move, or animate, by using a combination of the JavaScript methods *MoveBy(x,y)* and *setInterval(func,time)*. *MoveBy(x,y)* moves the DIV by *x* pixels horizontally to the right and *y* pixels vertically down; *setInterval(func,time)* starts the separate JavaScript function *func* executing every *time* milliseconds. If *func* includes *MoveBy*, you've got an animation. The only loose end to tidy up is to figure a way to stop *func* when the animation has gone as far as you want. Figure 12-16 depicts a sailboat that's made to move by the function *away_we_go()*. Here is the code:

```
function away_we_go() {
  goship = setInterval(sailaway,1);
}
```

```
function sailaway() {
  document.sailboat.moveBy(4,0);
  if (document.sailboat.pageX > 500) {
  clearInterval(goship);
  }
}
```

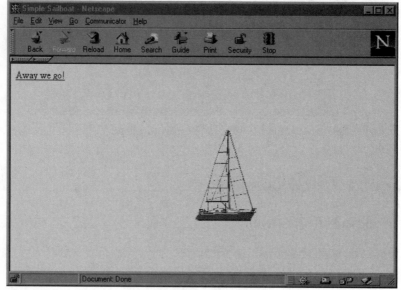

Figure 12-16: An extremely simple left-to-right animation under user control.

Before you scoff that animated images are nothing new, remember that it's the user who sets this in motion—and it would be a trivial matter to allow the user to control the speed and direction of the animation, too.

A Venetian Blind Transition

Web designers with knowledge of video effects have long been dying to make their Web pages behave more like their television screens (or more like their video mixing desks, to be more professional about it). The kind of professional effects that Dynamic HTML makes available includes not only the ability to manipulate text and move objects about the screen, but also the ability to apply sophisticated wipes and dissolves.

Figure 12-17 shows three stages of an eight-panel "venetian blind" wipe between two images of the same size.

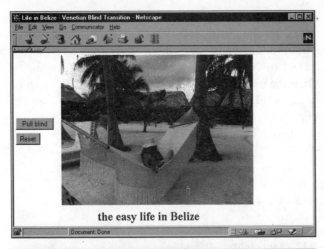

Figure 12-17: An eight-fold horizontal wipe creates the effect of vertical blinds opening to reveal a new image.

Implementing wipe effects of this type is really simple. You simply set up the background image in a positioned DIV block (*panel0*) and then overlay it with the foreground image eight times in eight separate DIV blocks (*panel1 - panel8*). Fortunately, this does not mean the image needs to be downloaded eight times! When the user says go, the clipping rectangle of each of the eight foreground images is set so that each of them becomes only one vertical "slat"; then all eight clipping rectangles are animated using the *setInterva()l* method to make the wipe effect. Here are the JavaScript functions:

```
wspeed = 10;

function vvb() {
  document.panel1.clip.right = 50;

  document.panel2.clip.left = 50;
  document.panel2.clip.right = 100;

  document.panel3.clip.left = 100;
  document.panel3.clip.right = 150;

  document.panel4.clip.left = 150;
  document.panel4.clip.right = 200;

  document.panel5.clip.left = 200;
  document.panel5.clip.right = 250;

  document.panel6.clip.left = 250;
  document.panel6.clip.right = 300;

  document.panel7.clip.left = 300;
  document.panel7.clip.right = 350;

  document.panel8.clip.left = 350;

  wipe = setInterval(vvba,1);
}

function vvba() {
  document.panel1.clip.left += wspeed/2;
  document.panel2.clip.left += wspeed/2;
  document.panel3.clip.left += wspeed/2;
  document.panel4.clip.left += wspeed/2;
```

```
    document.panel5.clip.left += wspeed/2;
    document.panel6.clip.left += wspeed/2;
    document.panel7.clip.left += wspeed/2;
    document.panel8.clip.left += wspeed/2;
    if (document.panel1.clip.left == 50) {
      clearInterval(wipe);
    }
  }
}
```

Wish You Were Here

Figure 12-18 shows three stages of development of a whimsical holiday wish
that must have been created by an HTML author who just couldn't stay away
from his work. This is done entirely by CSS positioning and clipping.

There are three DIV blocks involved: #*hotel* is the full-size image of the
luxury hotel (the Hotel Casa Maya in Cancún, if you must know), and
#*herebutton* and #*arrow* are what they sound like. When the action begins, the
#*hotel* block is iteratively resized by unequal steps until the clipping rectangle
has zoomed in on the desired hotel room window. At that point, the resizing
function is stopped, #*arrow* is made visible, and #*herebutton* is made invisible.
Here's the code:

```
<STYLE TYPE="text/css">
BODY {
  background: f0f0f0;
}
#hotel {
  position: absolute; top:45px; left:140px;
}
#arrow {
  position: absolute; top:126px; left:142px;
  visibility: hidden;
}
#herebutton {
  position: absolute; top:22px; left:180px;
}
</STYLE>

<SCRIPT LANGUAGE="JavaScript">
<!--
clipbase = 205;
```

```
function resizeit() {
  squeeze = setInterval(shrinkit,1);
}
function shrinkit() {
  if (document.hotel.clip.left > 42) {
    clearInterval(squeeze);
    document.arrow.visibility = "visible";
    document.herebutton.visibility = "hidden";
    return;
  }
  document.hotel.clip.left += 1;
  if (document.hotel.clip.left < 36) {
    document.hotel.clip.right -= 7;
  }
  if (document.hotel.clip.left < 32) {
    document.hotel.clip.top += 2;
  }
  if (document.hotel.clip.left < 34) {
    document.hotel.clip.bottom -= 4;
  }
}
//-->
</SCRIPT>
</HEAD>
<BODY>
<H2>Wish you were</H2>

<DIV ID="herebutton">
<H2>
<FORM>
<INPUT TYPE="button" VALUE="HERE" onClick="resizeit()">
</FORM>
</H2>
</DIV>

<DIV ID="arrow">
<IMG SRC="here.gif">
</DIV>

<DIV ID="hotel">
<IMG SRC="csamaya.jpg">
</DIV>
```

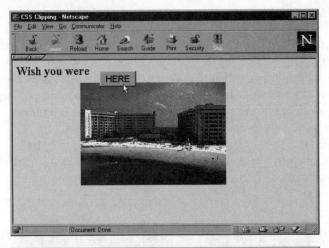

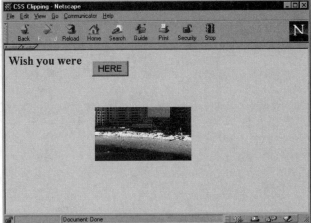

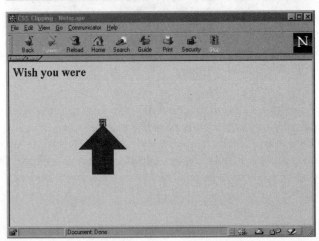

Figure 12-18: A Dynamic "Wish-You-Were-Here" postcard, seen at three stages.

A Simple Pop-Up

Footnoting of HTML pages has been a bone of contention in the standards committees for years. A special HTML tag, <FN>, was close to acceptance for HTML Level 2 but never made it. Footnotes don't have enough sex appeal for the major browser manufacturers to preempt the situation, either. The Document Object Model at last allows Web authors to provide instant pop-up extras for their users. Pop-ups can be used just like footnotes or Windows help definitions, or an entire up-front document may be reduced to its headers, allowing users to pop into reading position only those paragraphs that tickle their fancy—an extremely compact and pleasant way of presenting certain types of material.

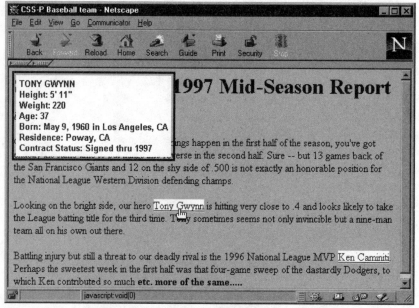

Figure 12-19: Supplementary information made available in a pop-up.

Figure 12-19 shows an extremely convenient arrangement whereby pop-ups are presented whenever users merely pass the mouse over keywords or phrases, which are identified by a special style. The pop-up stays up only so long as the mouse pointer is over the key phrase, which is set apart from normal text by a <SPAN> style imposition. Here's a compressed version of the code and markup:

```
<STYLE TYPE="text/css">
<!--
#player1bio {
  position: absolute; top: 5px; left: 5px; visibility: hidden;
  border-width: 3px;
  padding: 5px;
  color: red;
  background: white;
  font-family: Arial, Sans-serif;
  font-weight: bold;
  font-size: 10pt;
}
#tgwynn {
  color: red;
  background: white;
}
-->
</STYLE>
<SCRIPT LANGUAGE="JavaScript">
<!--
function showp(pb) {
  this.document.bio = pb;
  document.bio.visibility = "visible";
}
function unshowp() {
  document.bio.visibility = "hidden";
}
//-->
</SCRIPT>
</HEAD>
<BODY>
<P>Leading the San Diego Padres in hits this season is outfielder

<A HREF="javascript:void(0)" onMouseOver="showp(player1bio)"
onMouseOut="unshowp()">
<SPAN ID="tgwynn">Tony Gwynn</SPAN></A>,
who looks likely to take the League batting title for the third time.
```

```
<DIV ID="player1bio">
<P>
TONY GWYNN<BR>
Height: 5' 11"        <BR>
Weight: 220<BR>
Age: 37<BR>
Born: May 9, 1960 in Los Angeles, CA<BR>
Residence: Poway, CA<BR>
Contract Status: Signed thru 1997<BR>
</DIV>
```

It's unfortunate that the <SPAN> section has to be made into a null hyperlink in order to get it to capture the JavaScript functions, but the fact is that JavaScript event handlers don't (at the moment) work inside <SPAN> ... </SPAN>.

One of the reasons the <FN> tag fell afoul of the W3C committee was that an argument broke out about what they called "pop-up persistence." How long should a pop-up stay popped up? As long as the mouse pointer is over the triggering object? Until the user clicks again, as for Windows help screens? For a certain time period? This example is of the first type, but similar techniques of Dynamic HTML can achieve many pop-up conditions.

Changing DIV Content

Individual DIV blocks within a document may be reloaded with fresh content on the fly so long as they are positioned by a style sheet statement. The incoming file needs to be HTML formatted and have a .htm or .html extension, but it need not be a full-fledged HTML document with HEAD, TITLE, and so on.

There are several obvious uses for this—a section of a diplomatic document might be loadable in several languages, or a TV schedule might have a variable section for several time zones. Figure 12-20 shows a restaurant menu into which the user can load any of several daily specials. The menu itself is a properly done HTML document, but the daily special files are so simple that even a lowly *sous-chef* might be trusted to make the files, if not the dishes themselves.

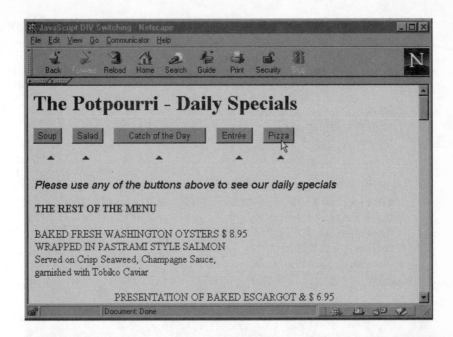

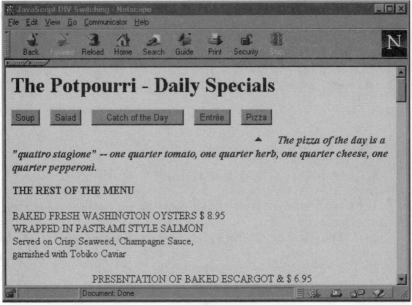

Figure 12-20: Daily Specials in this online menu are contained in positioned DIVs, which can be easily changed by someone with no knowledge of HTML.

The section of the document for the daily specials was labeled <DIV ID="special">, and the switcheroo was achieved by capturing mouse clicks on a series of buttons. The operative parts of the file are these:

```html
<STYLE TYPE="text/css">
<!--
#request {
  font-family: arial;
  font-weight: bold;
  color: blue;
}
#special {
  position: absolute; top: 100px; left: 10px;
  font-family: times-roman;
  font-size: 14pt;
  font-style: italic;
  font-weight: bold;
  color: red;
}
#main {
  position: absolute; top: 175px; left: 10px;
}
//-->
</STYLE>
<SCRIPT LANGUAGE="javascript">
<!--
function changemenu(newdish) {
  document.special.src = newdish;
}
//-->
</SCRIPT>
</HEAD>
<BODY BGCOLOR="#f0f0c0">
<H1>The Potpourri - Daily Specials</H1>
<FORM>
<INPUT TYPE="button" VALUE="Soup" onClick="changemenu('ssoup.html')">
  
<INPUT TYPE="button" VALUE="Salad" onClick="changemenu('ssalad.html')">
  
<INPUT TYPE="button" VALUE="Catch of the Day"
onClick="changemenu('sfish.html')">
  
<INPUT TYPE="button" VALUE="Entr&eacute;e"
onClick="changemenu('sentree.html')">
  
```

```
<INPUT TYPE="button" VALUE="Pizza" onClick="changemenu(,spizza.html')">
</FORM>
</DIV>
<DIV ID="special">
<SPACER TYPE="horizontal" SIZE=20>
<IMG SRC="redup.gif">
<SPACER TYPE="horizontal" SIZE=40>
<IMG SRC="redup.gif">
<SPACER TYPE="horizontal" SIZE=100>
<IMG SRC="redup.gif">
<SPACER TYPE="horizontal" SIZE=110>
<IMG SRC="redup.gif">
<SPACER TYPE="horizontal" SIZE=50>
<IMG SRC="redup.gif">
<P ID="request">Please use any of the buttons above to see our daily
specials
</DIV>
<DIV ID="main">
<!--etc...(rest of markup) -->
```

Unfortunately, the incoming "stub files" don't successfully inherit the imposed styles (as they do in Netscape layers), so the style has to be repeated inline. Here's the pizza special, for example:

```
<SPACER TYPE="horizontal" SIZE=380><IMG SRC="redup.gif"><SPACER
TYPE="horizontal" SIZE=20>
<SPAN STYLE="color:red; font: italic bold 14pt times-roman">
The pizza of the day is a "quattro stagione" -- one quarter tomato, one
quarter herb, one quarter cheese, one quarter pepperoni.
</SPAN>
```

Moving On

Until now, this book has stayed mostly on the user's desktop, with the client software (a.k.a. the browser) only venturing onto the server side when needed to explore the mysteries of form data handling (in Chapter 9).

The emphasis on the client side is deliberate and appropriate because that's where the fruits of the Web author's labors are seen and that's where 90 percent of Web development is done and checked. But sooner or later, if a Web site is to be *published*, it has to find its way onto a server in order to be accessible to the big wide world of Web surfers. A prudent Web publisher knows the ins and outs of Web servers, and perhaps even installs one—a process that's not at all daunting, as you are about to discover.

chapter 13

Web Servers at Your Service

Now that you've created your HTML-based Web masterpiece, the only remaining question is how to bring your work to the international Internet. For some, this may not be an issue—particularly if you're developing an internal corporate server and already have a network set up. For many, however, the issue of getting a server onto the Internet is a big decision: Should I run my own server and have my own connection to the Internet, or should I rent space on someone else's server and just look like I have a direct connection?

This chapter provides the information you need to weigh the option of sharing space on a Web server against the option of setting up and running your own server. Some Web hosting options include virtual domain service (including a unique domain name and access to a Web server and FTP servers), virtual storefronts (dedicated to commercial trade), and co-locating (renting space for your Web server at an appropriate facility). Web hosting companies sometimes provide dial-up Internet access in addition to Web services. Companies that offer dial-up access (whatever other services they provide) are also called Internet service providers, or ISPs. Whatever option you choose for your Web site depends to a large degree on what you're trying to accomplish.

Understanding the Services Available

Before you choose your commercial service provider, you need to define the services you want to provide to the readers of your Web pages. A broad range of services is available. The most basic Web server might just deliver your

HTML pages with no additional services, no CGI (Common Gateway Interface), and no dynamic page support. On the other hand, the most sophisticated Internet shopping center server might support secure transactions, credit cards, and advertising and perhaps provide you with your own unique domain name. Although the range of options is fairly continuous from the simple to the sophisticated, there are three basic types of commercial services: sharing a server, using the services of a virtual storefront, or sharing a server without appearing to. A fourth option is to store the server on-site—in your home or office—and connect it to the Internet from there. This is only cost effective if you already have a reliable, high-speed Internet connection installed.

The first option is to share domain space at a Web hosting company. Here, your Web address may look like http://www.*serviceprovider*.com/~*yourname*/ index.html. This is the most appropriate choice for a casual Web publisher or for someone who had information to share but doesn't need a high profile or have a great interest in developing a unique identity.

A second option is to use the services of a virtual storefront, or mall. Typically, these services cater to the needs of a business that has a product or service to sell and wants a way to sell it on the Internet. These services may also provide you with advertising and are more aggressive in promoting you and other companies on their server.

Third, you can *appear* to have your own server and identity without actually purchasing the hardware or the connection. With this kind of service, the fact that you share your service is not apparent, which allows you the freedom to develop your own home page with its own unique look and feel. This option is the most like having your own server.

As you search for a Web site solution, you need to consider any additional Internet service you may want to provide to your customers or readers. For example, you may want to distribute information electronically to your users and therefore need an anonymous FTP capability. Or perhaps you want to allow text searching of your pages. Also, almost every form or other CGI interface requires adjustments and configuration on the Web server. Is your service provider willing to do this for you? We include a list of questions you may want to ask your service provider when shopping for a server to publish your Web pages. As you read through the chapter, decide which features are important to you so that when you start researching service providers, you're armed with a ready list of requirements.

Going It Alone

Without a doubt, you can get the most control over your World Wide Web pages and other Internet services if you run your own server. For most individuals and many companies, however, this option is an economic or technical impossibility. Although providing your own Web server is covered in detail later in this chapter, this is a good time to stop and examine your options.

Connections to the Internet at this time are the single biggest cash expense when you consider ongoing maintenance of a directly connected Web site. For decent commercial-grade performance, you'll want at least a 56,000 bits-per-second link (56 Kbps); you'll also want a full-time link so people can reach you any time of the night or day. While the cost of a link like this from your business or home to the closest Internet service provider varies widely, you should figure that you won't get away for less than $200–$400 dollars per month. It doesn't take much more calculation than that to realize a private Internet connection is out of the question for most people. And, unfortunately, even though you pay for this line 24 hours a day, the actual amount of time you have data going over the line is far, far less—unless, of course, you have a very popular site or have more activity than just your Web server. By using the services of a commercial Internet service provider, the costs of the lines to the Internet are spread out over many, many users. Remember, although you are sharing your Internet connection, the average load on the service provider's Internet line still permits your customers to retrieve information from your pages very rapidly. Most of the time Internet service providers have line speeds of a T1 (1.544 megabits per second) or greater. Of course, if the service provider has *too* many customers, the average link load goes up—and your individual performance goes down. One big advantage to having your Web pages on a commercial service is that it doesn't matter where the service provider is located. You can be in California, but you could use a service provider in Chicago if it has the price and services you want. So you have at least a nationwide market for services, which keeps prices down and service quality up.

In addition to the cash expense is the technical overhead. Running your own server, even the simplest Windows NT or Macintosh server, requires a fair amount of technical expertise. Many of the server packages detailed in this chapter come with extensive explanations and helpful documentation. Nevertheless, to get the most out of it, you'll need to understand quite a bit about how the Internet and the World Wide Web work, how your software packages work, and how your operating system works. If you're not familiar with these topics, you may find that the real cost of running your own server escalates sharply as you take time away from your business or leisure to service your computer system.

Sharing Space

Many companies and individuals get by just fine with the simplest of options. The idea of sharing space on a provider's computer is very simple. You have your own "home" directory, and you put your HTML pages in that directory or in subdirectories of your home directory. The most rudimentary service of this type is found on many UNIX-based systems, where there are many individuals who have accounts on the system, and any of the users can add Web pages directly in their own account's space. Each user can have an HTML link to the master home page of the service provider simply by putting an HTML file with a specific name, such as index.html, in his or her home directory. The service provider then scans the users' home pages on a regular basis and creates a list of everyone who has an HTML page in his or her home directory.

How Much Does It Cost?

Sharing space on a service is about the cheapest option for having a Web presence. Many Internet service providers offer this service as part of their basic service plans or at a small ($5 to $10 a month) additional charge. Sonoma Interconnect, for example (http://www.sonic.net) provides 25 megabytes of storage for Web pages as a part of its basic service, along with simple scripting options. The average HTML document is less than 10K, with anywhere from 1 to 10 graphics between 1 to 30K in size. One megabyte (MB) is equal to about 1000K. You can fit a *lot* of Web pages into 25 megabytes of disk. Most online business card/brochure types of sites (purely informational in nature) will do fine with less than 10MB of space.

What Does My Address Look Like?

In most cases, when you share space, the URL to your HTML page would look something like this:

```
http://www.yourisp.net/~yourlogin/index.html
```

The important issues to remember about this URL are that (1) the name of the system is *your service provider's name,* and (2) people reach you through a reference to your login: *~yourlogin.* If you just want to get information to the Internet community, this may be the fastest and cheapest way to do it. The drawbacks for a company, however, are that a casual browser is unlikely to stumble across your latest sales brochure and someone who knows your company's name wouldn't think to look on the system owned by your service provider.

On the other hand, there are many Web searching programs and indexes available to the Internet community, and these programs will eventually find you and your home page. If you've chosen the words used in page titles and text carefully, you can ensure that people who are interested in the product you're selling or service you're providing can find you.

There are also ways to "seed" search databases with your URL and inform the Internet community about your site. Almost all the popular search engines and directories have this option, although many do not automatically accept everyone who applies. Nevertheless, it's always worth a try. For example, the Lycos search engine at http://www.lycos.com/ has a form you can fill out that lets their search engine know about your site. The Yahoo! directory will accept candidates to be included in its list, which is arranged by category. This directory is indexed as well. Go to http://www.yahoo.com/yahoo/bin/add/ to fill out a form requesting placement on their lists. For general advertising to the Internet community, you can also send information about new sites to the moderated Usenet newsgroup comp.internet.net-happenings.

TIP *If you want to find out exactly how these search services work, or you'd like more specific and practical guidance on how to get your pages listed, go to the Search Engine Watch at http://searchenginewatch.com/. This site, created and maintained by Danny Sullivan, provides a comprehensive explanation of how to interact with the various search services and how each one finds, maintains, and displays listings. You can also subscribe to his very informative newsletter (which also gives you access to some additional, private areas on the Web site) that will keep you up-to-date on all the changes and news regarding search services on the Web.*

What Other Services Can I Get?

You may be interested in Internet services other than a basic Web server, such as anonymous FTP and Usenet news. If you develop or sell software, for example, you could use anonymous FTP as a way to distribute shareware or software updates. In some cases, you might want customers to upload files to you. You should ask your service provider if it can make an anonymous FTP service available to your customers.

Having the ability to access Usenet newsgroups is very common and can be a great benefit if you want to scan the newsgroups for topics that concern your business or interest. Often, you can find people who are inquiring about some product or service you offer, and you can reply to them via e-mail. Most service providers also provide some selection of Usenet groups to subscribers to their services whether or not they post Web pages.

Can I Add CGI Scripts?

When you share a server, you also share the HTTP server and its associated services. If you want to use a form, for example, or Java-enabled pages, or just about any type of "active" or dynamic pages, you'll need to add information about those pages to the shared server. For example, forms require the use of server-side CGI programs. Find out if your service provider will allow you to create your own CGI programs or if they must be installed in a protected area that only the service provider can access. Many service providers offer consulting and programming services to help with the creation of CGI programs, so even if you are allowed to write your own programs, you may not want to.

Also note that using creation tools like Microsoft's FrontPage may require special software to be installed on the server. To take advantage of FrontPage forms, for example, special server extensions must be installed on the server. If you intend to use forms and other interactive elements provided by these tools, be sure your service provider has, or is willing to install, the required server support features.

Virtual Servers: Having Your Own Server Without Your Own Server

Virtual servers are fairly common on the Internet today and are perfect for the company or person who wants an identity on the Internet but doesn't want to go through the expense and bother of running a site. A Virtual Web Hosting company owns a server (hardware and software) and leases it out to several client companies, each with its own domain name. When customers look at the Web sites, there is no way to tell that the server is not located at and owned by the company they're viewing.

How Much Does It Cost?

The cost for a virtual server service is comparable to that of standard hosting of your Web pages; typical charges might be $100 to set up and $75 monthly for the first 10MB of disk storage. This compares favorably with the cost of a 56 Kbps private line, which *starts* at over $100 month and can be many times more expensive, depending on how far you live from the telephone company's switching office and what your local telephone company charges for private lines. Additional storage is available for a small additional charge, and the account will include the ability to post pages, scripts, and other related files and to retrieve log information, so you have complete control of your own "server." Moreover, your Web hosting company will most likely have some staff or affiliated consulting services that are familiar with the Internet and can help you get up and running quickly.

TIP *Be careful when shopping for a service provider. Although this has become much less common, some service providers charge you based on how many bytes are transmitted for you over the Internet, which in turn depends on how complicated your pages are and how many people access them. Since the number of accesses cannot be predicted, you leave yourself open for a huge end-of-the-month bill!*

What Does My Address Look Like?

With a virtual server, a common system is shared among many users, but through some clever programming of the HTTP server, the service provider can actually support multiple IP addresses on one host. In this way, you get your own unique IP address and name, such as www.*mycompany*.com, but when people connect to this computer, they are actually connecting to a computer that has many identities on the Internet. In this way, your small company can have the same Internet name stature as AT&T, DEC, or IBM without actually having its own computer on the Web!

Many Web users commonly try to locate a company they're interested in by creating a URL that starts with "www," putting the company's name or initials in the middle, and ending it with ".com." When you establish your service, pick a name that people would think of when trying to find you. The name must then be registered with the coordinating body known as the InterNIC that keeps the master list of Internet address. You may find that your perfect name is already taken, so be prepared with a few additional options. There is a small charge for this service—$100 to register a name for the first two years and $50 per year thereafter. Your Web hosting company will probably help you with this process, although some charge an additional fee.

An excellent example of a service provider that can support multiple IP addresses (and multiple domain names) on a single host is Best Internet Communications (http://www.best.com), located in Mountain View, California. Best uses a virtual service program called WWWDirect to provide individual accounts with IP addresses and names. For example, the Authors pages, the main example in this book, is one of numerous accounts located on a computer at Best, but it has the unique domain name authors.com and the IP address 204.156.147.35.

Another prime example of a virtual server is Macro Computer Solutions, a commercial provider located in Chicago (http://www.mcs.com/vserv.html). Their service is called VSERVE for Virtual Service, and they currently host New Office Temps (http://www.newoffice.com/), the *Chicago Reader* (http://www.chireader.com/), *Pause Magazine* (http://www.pause.com/), and Advanced Network Products, Inc. (http://www.advance-net.com/).

There's no way for anyone to tell if these four companies are on four different systems or all on the same system. With a shared service such as this, you're still left with the problems of setting up your own way of selling products and conducting secure transactions. If you aren't trying to conduct actual business transactions over the Internet just yet, the Virtual Presence solution may be perfect for you.

One particular benefit of this approach is that your clients access you by your company name, or some appropriate variant, which is registered on the Internet for you alone. Therefore, when and if you are ever ready to go to your own dedicated server, your customers never have to change their Net address for you. Although the Internet is electronic, changing addresses can be as much trouble here as it is in the real world, so this can be important to you if you plan to grow in the future.

Cybermalls

Being part of a collection of companies on a commercial system, often called a *cybermall*, is another way to bring your pages to the Internet. In this model, you are one of many companies that share space on a Web server that is specifically set up to house online stores. In this storefront (or mall) system, a person interested in buying something or learning about your product would first enter the stores by going to the main home page for the cybermall company. From that point, the browser is led to your page by lists or a directory of stores on the server. Once at your home page, the user can look at whatever materials you've put on display. Very often, the service provider for the mall will also provide a way for people to pay for merchandise you have for sale.

This is a great way for a small business to get started. The service provider takes care of setting up the server, creates a front end that will attract people to the mall, and provides you with a way to actually make sales over the Internet. Since the service provider is responsible for the security and authentication of the consumer, you're off the hook when it comes to taking credit card numbers or setting up customer accounts. Some of the Web servers now on the market offer encrypted transaction protocols and a secure way to conduct business on the Internet. Security on the Web is a tricky business—especially when financial transactions are involved—and your customers will always expect you to bear the ultimate responsibility for the privacy of their information. You should always be familiar with the security techniques used by your provider. The available security schemes are discussed later in this chapter.

Some cybermall operators will also provide access to credit card acceptance and authorization services. This can be an important issue since most transactions on the Web are done by credit card and getting a bank to give you credit card services can be difficult if you don't have an actual store or place of business. For a variety of reasons, banks are reluctant to provide credit card merchant accounts (as they are called) for businesses that don't have a physical location—and a lot of Internet-based businesses don't. Having your mall operator provide the merchant account can be a vital issue to doing business online.

Just as in the previous example of sharing space on a commercial Web site, the various Web indexes will eventually pick up trails to your pages; it's also likely that your mall service provider will make an effort to link its storefront to as many other Web pages as possible. Also, security remains the job of the service provider, but in this case, since the entire mission of the service provider is commercial, it is likely that it will be running with a high degree of emphasis placed on privacy and security.

Co-Locating

A co-located machine is a system in which the hardware is owned by you but is stored and connected to the Internet by somebody else. In this situation, you have complete control over everything on the computer. You'll have to decide what kind of Web server to install, and you'll be responsible for maintaining the server by reading the log files and fixing any errors that come up. However, it may be inconvenient to access the computer directly because you'll have to travel to the Web co-location facility to make adjustments or repairs to the hardware itself. In this situation, a loose cable is no longer merely a minor problem.

The benefit of co-locating is that you will probably get a less expensive or faster Internet connection this way, and the facility that co-locates your server will probably be especially well designed for computer storage. You won't have control over the network connection, so if the connection to the Internet goes down, the co-location company is responsible. Make sure your co-location company monitors the network connection 24 hours a day. In any Web hosting or co-location arrangement, excellent customer service is a must.

Server Services & Web Pages

Although this book is mostly about creating your own HTML pages, you may decide that you don't want to go it completely alone. Many server services have close relationships with consultants willing to help with almost any aspect of Web site creation. For example, if you're not artistically inclined, a server service can direct you to a graphic designer. Most service providers can also hook you up with local programming talent if you don't want to create your own HTML pages or need help with a CGI program.

Going Shopping

Now that you've read about the different options available when choosing a provider, here's a list of questions to ask when shopping for a service provider or server service. Many Web hosting companies answer these questions on their Web pages for you.

The Basics

- Do you offer a Web server, and can I control my own Web pages? How do people find me on your server?

- What is the cost of this account? Is there a time limit or bandwidth limit that I have to watch out for? If so, how do I know what I've already used?

- What services do you offer to the public? Can I have anonymous FTP space that anyone can read from? Is there a place for "incoming" files, and is it visible or hidden? Do you limit the size of files placed in an "incoming" anonymous directory?

- Are there any limits on what type of material I can put on the site? Is commercial use allowed? Can I resell the Web space? Will my site be blocked by parental-control software (such as SurfWatch)?

- Can I also send and receive electronic mail? What about Usenet newsgroups? Can you alias my e-mail account to use a more personal system name?

- How fast is your link to the Internet? How fast is your equipment? Do you measure the load on your links, and when do you add capacity?

■ How do you handle disk storage? What's my limit, and is it advisory or enforced?

■ How much experience does your systems administration staff have, and how do I reach you?

■ How secure is my data? What's your policy on backups?

TIP *Even though your data may be backed up by your service provider, you should always keep a copy of your Web pages on your own computer and on your own backup media. This way, you can be sure the pages will never be destroyed.*

■ How often do system outages or partial outages occur? Do you have records, and can I look at them? What is your policy on repairing the system during off-hours? Can I report system problems 24 hours a day?

■ What billing methods do you support? Can I use a credit card? Will you bill me?

■ Do you keep credit card numbers on the computers that are connected to the Internet?

■ Can I create and manage my own image maps? How quickly can I make changes if I need to ask you to update your server?

■ Can I create CGI programs and control them myself?

■ What kind of Web server hardware and software are you using? (If you plan on writing your own CGI scripts, this can be very important!)

Shopping for a Virtual Server

■ Do I get to pick my own domain name? Will I use a standard IP port number for my Web server?

■ Do I share hardware with others, or is this my own machine? If I share space, can others measure the volume of information being offered by my Web server?

■ Do you charge me a flat rate? Or do you measure the amount of information sent over the Internet?

Shopping for Virtual Storefronts

- What methods are available for collecting money from my customers? Credit cards? Individual accounts?

- What is your charge for purchase transactions?

- What is your security scheme? Do clients need a special Web browser to conduct secure transactions?

- Do you provide an alternate way to accept orders if a customer doesn't want to leave a credit card number?

- Do you keep my customers' credit card numbers on an Internet-connected system, or do you transmit them to a protected system?

Understanding Web (HTTP) Servers

HTTP stands for HyperText Transfer Protocol. If a Web browser and a Web server are going to share information, they need to speak the same language. HTTP is the "language" of the World Wide Web, and Web servers must speak this language.

The word *server* means many different things. A file server or network server is usually a combination of hardware and software, such as a Windows NT computer. It has some method of connecting to other computers, such as an ethernet card or a routing hub. A Web server, on the other hand, is a program. It is loaded onto a file server and allows Web browsers to retrieve Web pages from the system.

Server-Side Services

A server-side service is anything related to your Web page that requires the server's intervention. In a typical Web transaction, the Web browser requests an HTML page (and any included graphics) from the server and displays it for the user. The server only has to do one thing: get the HTML and graphics files and send them to the browser.

However, server-side services require the server to run programs, rewrite HTML files, and produce on-the-fly documents and graphics. All these features have the potential to bog down your Web server, making it run more slowly. However, the benefits in interactivity and functionality may be well worth the drop in performance.

Server-Side Image Maps

Server-side image maps (or SSIMs) were the first type of image map available on the Web. They come in two varieties: CERN and NCSA. CERN is the European Laboratory for Particle Physics where Tim Berners-Lee originated the concept of the World Wide Web in 1989. NCSA stands for the National Center for Supercomputing Applications, which is located at the University of Illinois at Urbana-Champaign. The first Web browser and the NCSA HTTPd Web server were developed there.

Server-side image maps are used in a Web site the same way a standard hyperlink is used. After creating the graphic to be mapped, you create an image map file to map it. This file is usually of the form *filename*.map and can be created using one of the many image map creation programs available. Some graphic design programs also have an image map feature, although these image maps are usually client-side image maps (or CSIM). After creating both files, put them in the same directory (such as your images directory) and provide a link to them. A simple example is shown here:

```
<A HREF="images/map.map"><IMG SRC="images/map.gif" ISMAP></A>
```

This places the map graphic into the Web page and connects it to the image map file. Server-side image maps don't allow you to have independent URLs for each area on the map that appears in the browser's status bar. For those, you must use a client-side image map, which is an HTML file and is often included in the Web page's source code. Client-side image maps are discussed in detail in Chapter 7.

Server Side Includes

Server Side Includes (SSIs) are special comments in HTML that give the Web server special instructions. Not all SSIs work on all servers, and some Web servers require a special file extension, such as .shtml, .shtm, or .sht, to tell the Web server that there's an SSI inside the file. The syntax for a Server Side Include is:

```
<!--#directive variable_name="variable_value" -->
```

You might recognize that the opening and closing <!-- --> usually go around comments in HTML, so they will be ignored by the browser. That's fine—the server is what reads the tag to produce the input. As you can probably guess, the server needs a way to tell the difference between a server-side include and an ordinary comment. That's what the # sign is there for. <!--# opens a server-side include, and the Web server should recognize that as a command, also called a directive.

The "directive" part of the include is a specific command. For example, the server-side include might be a simple HTML or text file that you want to include on every page at your Web site (like a common header or footer). In this case, you'd use the SSI directive "include" to include the file. Your code would look like:

```
<!--#include file="path/filename.html" -->
```

Another example might be an included counter. This would use the exec directive, and look like:

```
<!--#exec counter="path/countername.cgi" -->
```

You can name the variable anything. In the previous two examples, We called them file and counter, because those are easy to remember. If you are using a pre-installed program on an exec (program) include, you will probably have to use a specific type of variable, which your Web administrator will provide. Table 13-1 shows a list of some commonly used Server Side Include directives. All these directives are used in the syntax <!-- #directive variable="path/filename.cgi" --> where #directive is the name of the directive. Some of these directives may not be available on your Web server, while there may be additional ones not listed here. Check your server documentation for the available Server Side Include directives.

SSI Directive	Usage
#exec	Runs a program on the server, such as a CGI script.
#include	Places a simple file, such as another Web page, into the Web page.
#flastmod	Shows the date the current file was last modified.
#fsize	Shows the size of the current file.
#config	Lets you use specific variables to format the Web page.
#email	Sends an e-mail to the specified address whenever the page is accessed.
#echo	Puts data from a form or other variable into the Web page.
#if	Lets you execute more than one SSI, on a conditional basis.
#goto	Lets you jump to a label without displaying the HTML or executing SSIs in between the #goto and the #label directives.
#label	Gives the goto a place to jump to.
#break	Stops reading and displaying the Web page.
#timefmt	Lets you specify a format to use when printing dates. Table 13-2 describes the different formats you can assign using #timefmt.
#fsize	Prints the size of the file.
#sizefmt	Lets you specify the format to use when printing the size of a file. The format can be set to *bytes*, which displays the size in bytes or *abbrev* to display the size as kilobytes or megabytes.

Table 13-1: Server Side Include directives.

Timefmt code	Displays
%a	Abbreviated form of the weekday name
%A	Full weekday name
%b	Abbreviated form of the month name
%B	Full month name
%c	Date and time representation for location
%d	Day of month as decimal number (01-31)
%H	Hour in 24-hour format (00-23)
%I	Hour in 12-hour format (01- 12)
%I	Day of year as decimal number (001-366)
%m	Month as decimal number (01- 12)
%M	Minute as decimal number (00-59)
%p	Current location's A.M./P.M. indicator for a twelve-hour clock
%S	Seconds as decimal number (00-59)
%U	Week of year as decimal number, with Sunday as first day of week (00-51)
%w	Weekday as decimal number, with Sunday as the first day of week (0-6)
%W	Week of year as decimal number, with Monday as first day of week (00-51)
%x	Date representation for current location
%X	Time representation for current location
%y	Year without century, as decimal number (00-99)
%Y	Year with century, as decimal number
%z,%Z	Time zone name or abbreviation; doesn't display if time zone is unknown
%%	Percent sign

Table 13-2: Timefmt codes.

TIP A thorough introduction to Server Side Includes can be found at the Server Side Includes Tutorial at http://www.carleton.ca/~dmcfet/html/ssi3.html.

Server-Side Scripting

There are several types of server-side scripting, but all of them have something in common. They are all programs or scripts that run on the server when a particular Web page is requested.

CGI programs can be written in any language. They transfer information from the Web browser to the server and back, and use particular headers to help format information. A CGI program can use an uncompiled language, such as Perl, or a compiled language like C. The benefit of using an uncompiled language is portability—an uncompiled program can be easily adapted to several different platforms. For example, you can share Perl programs with other Web server types (and vice versa). Compiled programs, on the other hand, process complicated instructions more quickly. CGI programs are the most common method of handling forms, as well as of generating HTML on the fly.

Although the Java applets are very popular, Java can also run on a server. In fact, it is extremely powerful when used this way, as many Web servers now implement the Java API, allowing them to run Java programs on busy servers with little loss in performance. Java also comes with the Java Database Connectivity (JDBC), allowing easy connections between your database program and your Web server. Server-side JavaScript was implemented as LiveWire, long before JavaScript was around. As in server-side include files, server-side JavaScript files usually have a different file extension, such as .web, which are used to identify the server-side JavaScript file to the server. The Web server scans the file for the JavaScript, and executes it before the page goes to the user's Web browser.

The HTTP Protocol

HyperText Transfer Protocol (HTTP) is the underlying protocol used by Web browsers and Web servers. A protocol is the method used by two different pieces of technology to "talk" to one another. Just as human beings must share a language to be able to communicate, so, too, do pieces of hardware and different software programs need to speak the same language. In HTTP, the communication is occurring between two pieces of software—the browser software and the Web server software. Other protocol types communicate directly from software to hardware, such as a dial-up software program communicating with a telephone/modem connection.

HTTP is governed by the World Wide Web Consortium (W3C), a standards body for the Web. The original protocol, HTTP 1.0, was so terrific that, despite years of Web usage, they've only needed to improve it once. HTTP had two methods of transmitting data (Get and Post) as well as support for application programming interfaces (APIs).

HTTP 1.1 has three methods for sending and receiving data; Get, Post, and Put (optional). If you write CGI programs, you'll need to know how to use each method to your advantage. In short, the Get method requests information such as a Web page from the Web server. Post sends information to the Web server, such as user information entered in some forms. Finally, Put uploads a file to the Web server. Put is not supported by all HTTP Web servers.

Application Programming Interfaces (APIs)

HTTP also has several application programming interfaces, or APIs, to help developers make the most of their Web servers and improve performance. Here's how it works.

In a typical CGI program, the Web server runs the CGI as a separate program. The server has to perform several independent tasks to start, run, and stop the CGI program. This makes the server run less efficiently. When there is only one CGI running, the loss in performance is almost imperceptible. However, a given Web page could have several CGIs running for counters, user feedback, and chat sites, for example. Multiply those CGIs by the number of users on the site at any given time, and the server quickly bogs down. An API lets you write programs that will run directly on the server, thus extending the server's capabilities. This is more efficient than simple CGI programs because there is no overhead in the creation of new processes for the CGI programs. Instead, the API programs are part of the Web server's own process. They effectively become part of the Web server.

NSAPI, developed for the Netscape servers, and ISAPI, developed for Microsoft, are the two most common APIs available. There are several third-party programs that use the various APIs to run their programs. These programs are usually written to be compliant with more than one API, which allows the program to run on several different Web servers. An example of an API application can be found in Microsoft's FrontPage Extensions, which must be installed onto a Web server in order to take advantage of all of FrontPage's features.

TIP *If you aren't managing your own Web server, you may need to know what programs and APIs are already installed on the Web server you use. Even if you are allowed to install CGI programs, it is unlikely that you will be given permission to add an API program to your hosting company's Web server.*

"Keep-Alive"

A new and important feature of HTTP 1.1 is its ability to keep a connection open during file transfer. This is especially useful for the World Wide Web, where one HTML file may contain several graphic files. Rather than close the connection between each file—which would require it to be reopened at a cost of time and efficiency—HTTP supports a "keep-alive" technology where the connection is not closed automatically. Instead, the connection remains up until one side terminates it.

Multi-Homing

Multi-homing is another recent addition to HTTP 1.1, and it's one of the most important ones for businesses. With multi-homing, the same Web server could house several different domains. This led to a proliferation of domain-grabbing (registering several similar domains to one company) as well as to the success of Web hosting companies (which could now offer virtual domain hosting).

Security Issues

Since the World Wide Web was first opened to commercial enterprises, businesses and individuals have been asking, "Is it safe to order online yet?" Businesses in particular eagerly anticipated the days when online transactions would be easy, fast, and safe, allowing them to put together cheap, virtual storefronts. In addition, people have wanted to be able to share information with just a few friends or colleagues without having everyone in the world stop by.

Authentication

User authentication is the simplest form of security. With it, you can restrict access to files and directories on your Web or FTP site. A user must have a valid username and password to be able to read and use files protected this way. However, the information is not encrypted when it is transferred from your host computer (where the pages are stored) to the user's Web browser. In addition, authentication doesn't mean anonymous access. Users must preregister to access the pages, although certain CGI scripts can help you create user registration pages.

User registration pages allow an individual user to sign up for access to a Web page (such as an online forum or magazine) with a username and password. The user can be instantly granted access or may be required to confirm the registration by e-mail. Meanwhile, the CGI script takes the user registration information—which can be as simple as a name and password or can include personal preferences and contact information—and stores it in a database of users. The user's name and password are added to the list of accepted users for the protected pages, and the user may now access those pages.

User authentication is good for restricting access to a specific group of users, for keeping track of regular users of your Web site, and for restricting access to downloadable files until users have registered. For example, if you have classroom materials that you want to make available to your students, you can control access to the information by putting them on a restricted Web page. In some cases, this will help protect copyrights (although it is no substitution for an author's permission).

Because files and information are not encrypted during transmission, authentication is not a good option for sensitive or highly confidential material. Credit card numbers, medical records, and other sensitive information should have additional security for transmission (though access should be restricted as well).

Secure Sockets Layer (SSL)

Secure Sockets Layer, or SSL, is one form of additional security. There are several levels of SSL encryption available, although only one (40-bit encryption) may be exported from the United States. More information on SSL and Web security in general can be found in the Web security FAQ at http://www.w3.org/Security/Faq/.

▼ Hacker Challenges

Several individuals and organizations have taken up challenges to "crack" the various encryption algorithms available. These hacker challenges take an encrypted message and systematically try to decrypt it, often using several high-speed computers to do so.

The 40-bit encryption scheme that can be exported from the United States was first cracked by Damien Doligez, who did it in 8 days using 120 computers and 2 supercomputers. Mr. Doligez has a Web site devoted to his triumph at http://pauillac.inria.fr/~doligez/ssl/.

The 128-bit encryption scheme, which is not usable outside the United States, was cracked (not for the first time) in August 1997 by a ring of Web hackers called cypherpunks. It took this ring less than 32 hours to crack the encryption scheme; 174 people (and their computers) contributed to the result.

The highest level of encryption is called "strong encryption," and uses a 158-bit key. At the time this book was written, 158-bit encryption has not been cracked. Due to legislative concerns, it has also not been widely used in the industry.

"If it can be cracked, then why should I use it?" Good question. The answer is that no security scheme is 100 percent perfect. If it were, there'd be no further need to improve security and encryption, and the only people who would still worry about it are congressmen.

There are two sides to the SSL transaction, the client side and the server side. On the client side, a user needs an SSL-enabled Web browser. When a user requests a secured document (such as an order form), the Web browser is able to decrypt the document and display it for the user. Then the user can safely type in his or her personal information and credit card number and submit the form. The browser encrypts the data and sends the encrypted information to the Web server.

The second part of the SSL transaction is the server side. An SSL Web server can encrypt and decrypt data from SSL browsers. Thus, when the user enters a secure area, the server sends an encrypted Web page to the user's browser. With an order form, for example, the server receives the encrypted information, decrypts it, and saves it in a highly protected area of the server. Some Web servers do not decrypt the information until it has been retrieved by an authorized user or administrator.

S-HTTP, another form of encryption technology, stands for Secure HTTP. S-HTTP has had a convoluted and unpromising history. S-HTTP extends HTTP to allow secure transactions without compromising HTTP's normal transaction methods.

Digital Certificates

Digital certificates are yet another way to ensure security on the Web. In the digital certificate scheme, a third party ensures that the Web site (or Web user, depending on whose certificate is being read) is who they say they are. It's sort of like showing your driver's license or business license to prove your identity before making a transaction. Digital certificates are issued by a number of companies, although one of the more popular ones is VeriSign (http://www.verisign.com).

Digital certificates aren't really required for standard Web browsing, but they're nice if you want your users to make purchases over the Web or to download and install software from your site. With the proliferation of viruses on the Web, site certificates can be very useful in getting people to "trust" your site to provide what you claim to provide. A digital certificate will let your customers know who you really are.

Choosing a Web Server

As mentioned earlier, a Web server is a software program that runs on a networked computer. Whether you're running your own server or using a server that belongs to a Web hosting company, you should know some of the features and strengths of the Web servers that are available.

Your Web server should be appropriate for your purposes and your abilities. For example, don't use a Web server that only runs on UNIX if the rest of your Web strategy calls for Windows NT. Similarly, don't choose your Web server based on its popularity with other users. Although the server's reputation is important, reliability, stability, and usability should be the lessons of the day. If any of the features discussed in this chapter are "must haves" for your system, make certain that the Web server can support them. If you especially admire a particular site, you can usually contact the Webmaster for information about the site's servers and setup.

If it finally does come down to a popularity contest, there are several Web sites that keep track of which servers are used and how much. Of course, the results differ from site to site, but they can be useful if you want some additional information on your Web server of choice. One such site is Netcraft, available at **http://www.netcraft.com/cgi-bin/Survey/whats**. Netcraft offers two services: one tells you what Web server is used on a given site, and the other provides reports on what Web servers are being used most often. In the following sections, you'll find brief descriptions (including general features and security features) of some of the most popular Web servers.

Apache (UNIX, Windows 95/NT, OS/2)

The Apache server is free and is available on UNIX and Windows 95 and NT platforms. It's at http://www.apache.org, with lots of helpful information for Apache users. Apache is also one of the most popular Web servers currently running, especially among low-cost hosting companies.

Features

One of the most important features of the Apache server is that its source code is completely available. In fact, the normal way to install the Apache server is to compile the source code on the server machine or an identical development machine. This makes it extraordinarily easy to modify and customize. In addition, since it has been open to the scrutiny of thousands of programmers already, it's less likely to contain bugs. Apache also has server-side includes and multi-homing available.

Finally, Apache has a module language, which lets you further customize the server. As part of that customization, you can have specific responses appear instead of the common error pages. For example, "Error 404: File Not Found" is a common error on the World Wide Web. With Apache, the standard "Error 404: File Not Found" page can be replaced with one that helps trouble-shoot the problem, which could be common spelling errors and syntax mistakes, outdated hyperlinks, and closed accounts.

Security Features

Apache offers basic user authentication. The secure version of Apache is called Stronghold, by C2Net Software. Stronghold is $995 and includes a Thawte Server Certification. It's only available for the UNIX platforms, but it will soon be available for Windows NT. Stronghold supports the current implementation of SSL (3.0), but not S-HTTP.

NCSA HTTPd (UNIX)

One of the oldest Web server programs available, NCSA HTTPd is only available for some UNIX platforms. HTTPd, on the other hand, has been ported to several other operating systems, including Windows NT. More information on NCSA HTTPd can be found at http://hoohoo.ncsa.uiuc.edu/.

Features

NCSA has a large variety of features, but its main strength is in its long-term reliability and use of open standards. Its features include server-side scripts, server-side includes, and multi-homed domains.

Security Features

NCSA security is fairly simple, and there's nothing available in SSL or S-HTTP. However, you can keep unauthorized users out of your files with NCSA HTTPd, and basic user authentication is available. NCSA HTTPd also lets you restrict access to certain machines or domains through host filtering. For example, you could limit access to only the computers on your local intranet. Or you could restrict access from certain domains, such as those of your competitors, the government, notorious spammers, or whomever.

O'Reilly's WebSite Server

O'Reilly & Associates produce the WebSite Server, a fully functional Web server for Windows 95/NT. One of the key features of WebSite is its own API, which can be used to develop applications to run directly on the server. WebSite also comes with SSL and preinstalled merchant applications like shopping carts. WebSite is available at http://website.ora.com.

Features

WebSite Pro is feature intensive, with several additions to the standard Web server model. It supports both ISAPI and the WebSite API, as well as the JavaAPI. In addition, WebSite has introduced iHTML, an extended HTML framework to provide dynamic pages and Web applications.

Finally, WebSite Pro supports the WinCGI interface, a method of creating CGI programs quickly and easily.

Security Features

WebSite Pro comes with SSL security, user authentication, and a built-in merchant application. This online store template lets you quickly create your Web store and shopping basket.

Netscape's FastTrack Server (UNIX, Windows 95/NT)

The FastTrack Server is Netscape's least-expensive server. A bare-bones solution for anyone trying to put together a Web site, it includes Java and JavaScript for server-side programming.

Features

FastTrack Server supports the Netscape Server application programming interface (NSAPI), the WinCGI Interface, and LiveWire. Also known as server-side JavaScript, LiveWire lets you implement scripts before your Web pages are sent to the Web browser. Pages that use LiveWire must use the file extension .web.

Security Features

FastTrack uses basic authentication, user certificates, and Secure Sockets Layer (SSL) 3.0 to create a secure online environment for your Web site.

Netscape's Standard SuiteSpot Server & Professional SuiteSpot Server (UNIX/Windows NT) _____

The SuiteSpot Server is Netscape's primary Web server, available for both UNIX and Windows NT. It's an integrated Web server, which complements Netscape's integrated Web client, Communicator 4.0.

Features

SuiteSpot comes with several features and programs. The Calendar Server lets you coordinate schedules via the World Wide Web. With the Collabra Server, users join together with virtual meeting rooms and newsgroups. Directory Server lets you maintain lists of users (for your Web server as well as for your company directory) from all over the world. Enterprise Server is the main Web server application of SuiteSpot. It delivers the HTTP services to your Web site. LiveWire is a database connectivity tool and comes with one of several popular database programs. SuiteSpot also includes an e-mail (SMTP and POP) server; e-mail servers are usually a separate program that must be installed on the server (e-mail uses a different protocol than Web servers).

Finally, Compass Server lets users of the Professional SuiteSpot system store personal and corporate information in a personalized, searchable index. This index can be updated automatically with user profiles and interest lists.

Security Features

User authentication is found on both versions of SuiteSpot. Professional SuiteSpot uses certificates to verify user and server identification. It also includes a proxy server for managing network traffic between your company and the Internet.

Microsoft Personal Web Server (Windows 95/NT) _____

Microsoft Personal Web Server is a simple, easy-to-use Web server that can run on Windows 95. Because Windows 95 lacks advanced network management, the Personal Web Server can bog down rapidly. However, it is a free Web server, perfect for Web site development.

Features

Active Server Pages, Microsoft's hot integration technology, lets you combine several types of Web technologies, including scripting languages and ActiveX, to produce dynamic HTML pages.

In addition, the Personal Web Manager administration tools let you manage the Personal Web Server without learning complicated command languages.

Security Features

Although Windows 95 doesn't require user login, Personal Web Server can restrict user access to pages and directories. This feature works particularly well with Microsoft's FrontPage.

Microsoft Internet Information Server (Windows NT) _____

Internet Information Server (IIS) is a free Windows NT Web server from Microsoft. Although fully functional, IIS does not have any advanced security features, so it is a questionable choice for online stores and commercial sites.

Features

Active Server Pages are also implemented on Windows NT, for which they were originally developed. IIS supports the Internet Server application programming interface (ISAPI), which is Microsoft's Web server API. The Index Server creates a fully featured search capability for the Internet Information Server. Crystal Reports creates interactive, online reports and presentations (including Web logs) for your Web site.

Security Features

IIS supports the Windows NT Challenge/Response (NTLM) Authentication, another form of user authentication discussed earlier in this chapter.

Microsoft Site Server, Enterprise Edition (Windows NT) _____

Microsoft Site Server, Enterprise Edition is the commercial version of Site Server and one of the only Microsoft servers to offer advanced security options.

Features

Site Server's features include a Personalization System, which allows users to store individual profiles and dynamically generate user pages based on personal preferences. Its Usage Analyst lets you easily read and understand usage logs. Site Server also supports the Visual InterDev application environment for developing Site Server applications.

Security Features

Site Server is an SSL-enabled commercial server, which uses templates to generate dynamic order forms. These forms help you take orders, calculate sales tax, and verify information in an order.

StarNine WebSTAR Server (Macintosh)

Although Macintosh is not the first name in Web servers, it can be used as a Web server platform if desired. Macintosh's built-in networking (through AppleTalk) makes it a functional file server as well. StarNine's WebSTAR makes the Macintosh Internet-ready with a fully functional HTTP 1.1 server.

Features

WebSTAR's features include HTTP 1.1 with Keep-Alive; extended server-side includes file uploading with the PUT method, remote administration, and support for the WebSTAR API SDK.

Security Features

In addition to user authentication, WebSTAR supports the WebSTAR/SSL, providing SSL security to the Macintosh Web server.

Setting Up & Configuring an HTTP Server

An HTTP Web server is usually set up on a specific port of the file server. The default port is 80. Many operating systems (including UNIX) require you to be a privileged user in order to install anything on ports below 1024.

TIP *A* port *is like a channel on your network server. The standard Web port is 80; that's used for HTTP (Web) requests. Other ports are dedicated to FTP, Gopher, e-mail, and so forth. You can set ports above 1024 to act as site mirrors or development stations.*

After you install the Web server, you'll need to configure the document root, which is the default location for your Web documents. If you have multiple domains, the document root will be different for each domain.

Some files types, such as Shockwave and RealAudio, require you to configure the server to recognize special MIME types. MIME types are basically recognized file types, and there are several ones automatically set up in most Web servers. For example, you won't have to configure a MIME type for files with the .html, .htm, .gif, or .jpg file extensions. However, depending on your Web server, you may have to configure it for other types of files, such as .wav or .zip files (even though these are common file types on the Web).

Finally, you need to set up your permissions correctly. Part of Web security is in the permissions, and improper permission settings can be worse than no security at all. In brief, the Web server program must be able to read the Web documents. In Windows NT, the Web server is usually called INET_USER, while it's often called nobody in UNIX (Macintosh and Windows 95 do not have special file permissions).

If you set your permissions incorrectly (or not at all), you invite disaster. Permissions are used extensively in computer systems to determine who (or what) has access to files, directories, and programs. Imagine for a moment that you decide not to set up permissions. Ideally, your Web server will have certain "default" permissions that will prevent catastrophe. However, if it doesn't, you could be faced with one of the following scenarios:

- None of your Web pages can be seen—the anonymous Web user doesn't have access to them.

- None of your CGI scripts run—the anonymous Web user doesn't have access to them, either.

- Your guestbook script runs, but the guestbook is empty—the CGI script (or anonymous Web user) doesn't have write access to the file.

- You (or anyone at all) can browse your e-mail, FTP directories, and private files over the World Wide Web—you've given read permissions to the world, making your "private" files very, very public.

- You no longer can log on to your system—someone saw that your permissions were set up incorrectly, logged on, and changed your password, your permissions, and your Web site!

Whatever Web server you use, carefully read about and set the permissions. Take time to learn it right the first time; you don't want to have to fix it later.

Databases & Servers

Right after security, databases are the next hot topic on the Web. After all, security is great, but how can you keep track of all those orders? In truth, databases serve many different functions beyond the commercial, so connecting a database to your Web site may be really important to you.

There are three basic components of a database-to-Web setup. The first is the database program itself. On Windows NT, the database program is usually Oracle, Sybase, MS Access, or SQL. On UNIX, common databases are Oracle,

Sybase, and Informix. Finally, the Macintosh has Filemaker Pro and 4th Dimension (4D) as its high-end databases. Whatever database you use, it should be adequate for your needs. Don't expect a simple database program to have all the programmable features of Sybase, for example. When you shop for databases, look for flexibility, ease of use, and stability.

The second part of a database-to-Web setup is the Web server. You already know what to look for in a Web server. Remember that a database may get a lot of use. You can optimize your system by putting the database and the Web server on different computers. This will increase performance because your Web server won't get bogged down with database processes.

You may wonder how you'll get the database and the Web server to "talk" if they're on separate computers. That's where the third part of the system comes in. It's usually called *middleware*, or *database connectivity software*. Despite the buzzwords, this part of the system is fairly simple. It forms the connection between your Web server and your database. Microsoft's Internet Data Connector (included in Internet Information Server), Allaire Cold Fusion, Borland's IntraBuilder, and Java are all examples of database connectivity software. As we mentioned before, Java comes with the JDBC, a database connector that uses Java to access the database. Whatever program you use as middleware, make sure it's capable of handling all the traffic your database is going to generate.

Managing Your Web Site

Managing a Web site can either be a chore or a breeze, depending on how much you automate with programs and scripts. There are several aspects to managing your site. They include updating your Web pages and hyperlinks, reading your log files, and verifying your HTML with current and newer browsers.

Updating Your Pages

When you launch your Web site, chances are that the hyperlinks will all be current and your site will have up-to-date information on it. As time passes, however, changes may occur, and you will quickly find yourself with one of the many obsolete Web sites on the Internet. Either the information is outdated, or your external hyperlinks no longer work.

To keep your Web site from becoming obsolete, update information on your site no less than once per month (more often for heavily trafficked sites). The update process can be as simple as going through your pages and checking for references to old events. Or it can be as complex as publishing a new issue of a newsletter. Make sure each Web page includes the date of its last modification so you'll know how long it's been since you checked it for accuracy. Since a file may be opened and saved without being updated, you can't always rely on the last save date for this information. To add this information, you can use a comment tag:

```
<!-- Last updated on 10/31/97 -->
```

You can also use a meta tag:

```
<META NAME="UpdatedOn" VALUE="10/31/97">
```

Either method will put the date into the HTML file without making it appear onscreen. Later, you can search for either the comment or the meta tag to find the date. Don't forget to update the tags whenever you change the file.

Verify your hyperlinks every time you update your Web site. Some Web authoring programs come with an automatic link verification tool, and other such tools abound on the Web. Use a link verifier to make sure your hyperlinks are current, or go through and manually check each link. Nothing will turn your users away quicker than an obsolete list of "cool links." Chapter 4 discusses link verification in detail.

Reading Log Files

Ah, log files. Finally, a way to figure out what's important to your audience. Who goes where? Who does what? What kind of problems are you having?

A log file is a file (or series of files) that describes requests and accesses on your Web site (also known as *hits*). In HTTP, certain information is automatically reported, such as the name and IP address of the client computer. In addition, log analysis and monitoring software will help you gather more information about your users and organize it into useful reports. Most Web hosting companies offer some form of log analysis to their customers.

Your log files may be the only reliable form of customer feedback you have. They provide you with a wealth of information about who visits and when and why, but you may not be able to decipher them easily.

The standard HTTP log file has seven parts: client IP address, user authorization (if required), time, date, method (Get, Post, or Put), URI (or URL), error or response code, and number of bytes. Some Web servers also generate more detailed logs that include the domain names that most commonly access the site, what times of day are higher in traffic, which pages are used most, and the response codes found. You can also buy third-party software, which will log your Web site and analyze your logs into convenient reports. Some Web servers come with their own log analysis tools, such as WebSite's QuickStats.

Some Web servers support an extended log file in which more information is provided about your site's visitors. Although the information in an extended log file depends on your Web server, it often includes the previous URL for the browser, the Web browser software being used, and the length of time spent on each page.

The response codes are divided into 5 types, going up in code number from 100. The 100s are informational codes; they are usually not logged because they do not provide any useful information. The 200s are successful responses—the data transferred as requested with no problems. The 300s include all redirections. They include temporarily or permanently moved files as well as unmodified files.

The 400s are client errors, including incorrectly formatted URLs, "File not Found (404)" errors, and unauthorized user or forbidden access. Keep an eye out for excessive "File not Found" errors—they may indicate an incorrect hyperlink in your own pages or an outdated one from outside your Web site.

Finally, you should especially watch out for the 500 series of response codes. These are server-side errors. They indicate that your server may be bogging down from too much activity, may be running inefficiently, or may be configured improperly. Be diligent about these errors—if they get out of control, they can add up to some serious problems for your Web server!

Since reading a log file is time-consuming and difficult, some very wise programmers have developed many log analysis tools to help you out. Some of the more popular ones are the free wwwstat (http://www.ics.uci.edu/pub/websoft/wwwstat), which uses Perl to analyze a common log file. Naturally, some of these programs are commercially available with additional features. WebTrends (http://www.webtrends.com), wusage (http://www.boutell.com/wusage), and SurfReport (http://software.bienlogic.com/SurfReport/surfhome.html) are all commercial log analysis programs. When combined with an extended log file, some log analysis programs can provide some very powerful reports. A report can tell you where your visitors are located and the cities from which most visitors browse your site. You can track ad views and clicks, which is critical for generating revenue based on Web advertising. You can find out how long people spend on your pages, which versions of the Web browsers are being used, and the referring URL that people use most often. All of this information should be important if you plan to keep your site updated and to respond to the interests and needs of your Web users. Even an online business card, resume, or brochure can benefit from careful log analysis; it's as important for you to learn about your visitors as it is for them to learn about you.

HTML Validation

You may or may not know about HTML validation. It's an inexpensive, quick way to find out if your Web pages will show up correctly on different browsers. Several validation tools are available on the World Wide Web, either as CGI forms or as downloadable programs. Validate your HTML every time you publish something on the Web. Validation will find errors you didn't know you made as well as point out the places where you used proprietary tags or HTML extensions. It's also a good idea to revalidate your HTML every six months or so. Pretty much everything on the Web changes every six months. If you haven't checked your HTML lately, it's time to do so now. You can find more information about validation in Chapter 3.

Moving On

Now that you've learned about Web servers, you can make an informed decision about which one to use. You can evaluate your own Web server needs and budget and decide if the cost of housing and maintaining a server is worth it to you.

In the next chapter, you'll learn about the future of HTML, XML, and SGML. Because existing software and hardware may not support some of the newer technologies yet, you may find that they don't always work on your Web server. If you plan to use experimental Web technologies, make sure you have a Web server that is not only flexible, but is in a constant state of development as well. The Web servers discussed in this chapter are all being actively developed by programmers. Above all, take the time to learn how to use whatever Web server you choose. You'll feel more confident experimenting with new technologies if you already know what you're doing.

## chapter 14

XML & Metadata: The Future of Web Publishing

B y now, you're a dedicated Web publisher. And having created a great site with good traffic and support, you naturally wonder where the Web is headed and when you'll need to revamp your pages entirely. The idea of "Web years," which are much shorter than chronological years, has become commonplace among Web publishers and designers. So the obvious question is, "Where do we go from here?"

This chapter provides a brief look into the crystal ball and discusses two of the most interesting and compelling new features of the Web that are being discussed and worked on by various groups: Extensible Markup Language (otherwise known as XML) and Metadata tagging. Don't make any mistake, however; like any attempt to forecast the development of the Web, we're going out on a limb somewhat; no one can predict exactly what the hot Web topic will be next year—not even us! We'll try to give you some insight into what these technologies are, why they're being looked at with such favor, and how they may affect your site in the future. Keep in mind that all the information here, although we have researched it as thoroughly as we can, is subject to change as implementation of these features comes closer to reality. As always, we'll also provide you with some pointers to sites where you can follow these developments for yourself.

Extensible Markup Language (XML) & SGML

The World Wide Web has grown explosively in its short life. To large corporations, small start-up companies, and a multitude of individuals all around the world, the Web has become the medium of choice for distributing information, communicating with colleagues, and sharing insights and ideas. HTML documents, with their various multimedia attachments, are the common elements we all use to perform this magic. However, documents have become more complex with the growth of the Web, and users are now working on more complex tasks than simple information presentation. As this happens, Web developers have come to find that HTML has some inherent limitations that hinder, or even prevent, sharing information in the best and easiest ways. In particular, HTML does not allow document markup to be extended in order to add additional information in a common format, nor does it provide structural and data tagging information that would allow Web client software to perform additional processing tasks. With the advent of Java as a cross-platform language, properly structured Web documents have the potential to become even more useful than they are now if these features were added to them.

The World Wide Web Consortium (W3C) has recognized this fact and is currently working on Extensible Markup Language (XML) as a solution. Like HTML, XML is a relatively simple markup mechanism that allows content providers to present information over the Web. Unlike HTML, however, XML allows users to extend markup tags by defining new tags within the document. Joined with appropriate processing tools, XML allows content developers to present and process information over the Web in ways that were not possible before.

HTML Limitations

To understand how this works, you need to step back for a moment and look at how HTML developed. HTML is a simple markup mechanism that facilitates presentation of small and relatively standard documents that may include hypertext links, multimedia, and other formats within the document. HTML is based on SGML (Standard Generalized Markup Language), which is an international standard for creating and using document formats. SGML is a well-known tool for creating large, complex documents—volumes like government regulations, for example, or repair manuals for complex aircraft. However, SGML requires a lot of expertise to use and a lot of processing power to implement. HTML, as a very simple subset of SGML, can be implemented in small, fast applications, and can be used by almost anyone with a small amount of training. However, HTML achieves its simplicity by eliminating three key elements in SGML: extensibility, document structure, and validation processing.

There is no provision in HTML to allow users to define their own tags. The issue of creating new tags has been one of the most controversial on the Web. Individual browser manufacturers have repeatedly come up with specialized tags to perform common functions, like <BLINK>. Often, these conflicting tags have had to be sorted out, either by the marketplace or by the W3C—or both. If HTML were extensible like SGML, then manufacturers or users could define their own tags without causing incompatibility problems.

With the use of the <HEAD> and <BODY> tags, HTML documents have a very rudimentary structure. This basic structure, however, is not complex or robust enough to allow HTML documents to be printed or merged into a database, for example, without some extensive parsing code, the addition of nonstandard structure elements (usually), and the use of comments (often), which break an HTML document into more distinct and useful parts.

Finally, HTML documents do not have enough information in them to allow a browser to validate a document. For example, it's virtually impossible for a browser to parse a page and discover whether an element is missing or incomplete. In the few cases where HTML markup fails a simple syntax check, the browser normally ignores the markup elements and proceeds with processing the remainder of a page. This behavior can be used, as you have seen earlier, as a means to load a document into a variety of browsers. Nevertheless, it would be nice if the browser would notify the user in some way that elements of the document were not understood or were missing. In some cases, such validation is essential: for example, you'd be very unhappy if your medical records were being reviewed by a new doctor and a vital portion of them were missing and no one noticed.

SGML Features

In contrast to HTML, SGML offers all these features. SGML allows a user to define any number of tags with any desired meaning and to create a complex structure with these arbitrary tags. SGML documents have proven their worth in presenting large amounts of dynamic information to users in flexible and tailored formats. Further, SGML is an international standard with quite an extensive library of software and document-handling utilities behind it.

However, SGML is very complex. The very flexibility of SGML makes it almost impossible to learn quickly, and the tools to create and manage SGML documents are generally both slow and difficult to use, particularly if you don't understand SGML syntax and handling. In general, full SGML offers too many options and requires too many resources—both human and automated—to work well as a widely used medium for communications. It was recognition of these limitations that led the original designers of the Web to create HTML as a very simple SGML subset.

Comparing HTML & XML

XML is the next step forward in this process of extending Web document formats. Like HTML, XML is a simplified version of SGML designed for wide and easy use. However, like SGML, XML allows extensibility in several important but restricted ways. This new markup language allows for the use of new tags to extend documents, provides additional structure to a document, and offers parsers the ability to validate the markup. While retaining these advantages, XML is also designed to be easy to learn, more expressive than HTML, and simple to implement.

XML is not backward compatible with HTML; that is, existing HTML documents do not meet the XML standard and would not be understood by XML parsers. However, the design of XML allows users to convert documents from HTML to XML very easily, assuming that the original documents meet the HTML 3.2 specification (just one of the many reasons to be sure that your documents use clean HTML coding). By the same token, XML is designed so that any existing SGML document can also be easily converted to XML and so displayed and processed using the Web. Since many SGML documents are generated from information databases, this will lead to a large increase (if you can imagine that!) in the amount and quality of information presented via the Web.

XML enhances HTML in four major areas. It will allow a Web client, like your browser, to navigate and coordinate information from multiple databases at one time. It will help applications move processing requirements from the server to the client, thus balancing the processing load and making the Web more responsive to users' needs. It will allow you to design sites that present different views of the same information to different users. Finally, it will allow site design that tailors the available information to the user's current needs and requirements.

XML isn't the only means to accomplish these ends, of course. But the alternatives are to create private networks using shared data and tools or to use the Web as an interchange medium but create new proprietary code, either as independent applets or as plug-ins for a user's browser, that understand and can process the required information. In either case, maintaining the data structures and application code would be an expensive and difficult task. Add the requirement to share data among many users in different companies and the task becomes almost impossible.

Uses for XML Documents

Let's consider a theoretical example of how XML might improve document utility for users. Suppose you are an engineer with a consumer electronics firm and you're designing a new product with tight time and budget constraints. In the old (pre-Web) days, you would rough out a circuit and then pull together a variety of printed materials—gathered from printed catalogs, specification sheets, and so on and provided at irregular intervals—from various manufacturers about the circuit's components. Once you had settled on a particular set of components, you would contact sales representatives to get the latest specifications for the components you wanted. Often, of course, the specifications would have changed since the last printed catalog, so you would have to reengineer the product to take this into account. Then you would get detailed engineering data and use the available tools to model your product to ensure that all the elements worked correctly together, a process that would possibly require another round of changes in components to make it all work to specification.

Enter the Web. Now you can go online and review current specifications from the manufacturers. You can look up components based on your product requirements and get the latest version of each device that meets your specifications. But you still have to review each item separately and work out how all the items work together. The process of integration still requires that you visit multiple Web sites and review a variety of documents in different formats. You would probably download a variety of documents for printing so you can look at the specifications side by side. And since HTML doesn't import very well into your modeling tools, you would also download multiple files for use in designing your product. A real improvement, but still a lot of extra work. Not to mention that availability, price, and scheduling of the various components are all still handled by contacting a sales representative directly.

Now consider the same material presented in XML documents on the Web. First of all, XML would allow you to specify the parameters of a component, for example, and review documents meeting your specifications from multiple sites at one time. Moreover, you could do a quick, high-level review of comparable components from various manufacturers. When you had selected, say, five possible items from three different manufacturers, you could then expand the display to see the detailed specifications side by side. You could also import the modeling information directly into your design tools and play with the design to see how each component would work. Finally, since XML allows data to be easily exchanged with existing databases, you would be able to check price, availability, and scheduling online by inquiry made directly to the manufacturer's current online order tracking systems. The new XML documents make it much easier for you to meet time and budget constraints for your new product because they bring all the information you need to your desktop at one time.

Extending Linking With XML

You may have noticed that the scenario just described requires some pretty fancy linking of various types of information from different sites and in different formats. This extended linking is an integral part of XML and is one of its most important features.

Although HTML stands for HyperText Markup Language, it actually only supports very simple hypertext links. Basically, in HTML you can only link in one direction: to a specific, hard-coded URL. This simple mechanism, however, is the source of much of the utility of the Web and most of the headaches in Web maintenance. Broken links are the bane of Webmasters everywhere and a constant frustration to Web users.

XML, however, provides for more sophisticated linking, which should help solve the broken link problem and will additionally enable you to create more complex links. XML allows links that are not hard-coded, so you can use location-independent names for links. You can also specify links outside the document itself, so you could have a single source for a variety of links. This would allow you to manage a single set of links in one place and use them seamlessly in a variety of documents. You can create bidirectional links, thus simplifying page navigation. In fact, you can create multiple related links and have, for example, a series of documents that each point to the next in a ring. You can include one document inside another seamlessly even though the included document resides on a separate site—a process called *transclusion*. Finally, you can link different types of information into your documents and provide attributes on the links that allow the user to manipulate the information.

TIP *In the next few sections of this chapter, we're going to describe some of the characteristics of XML documents. As we have already discussed, this specification is a work in progress by the W3C and is subject to change. Access to the latest version of the working draft for the XML specification, along with other W3C technical reference materials, can be found at http://www.w3.org/TR. The work on XML is part of the W3C SGML Activity. You can find out the current status of all the SGML work underway at http://www.w3.org/MarkUp/SGML/Activity.*

XML Document Structure

XML documents have both a logical and a physical structure. To understand how XML documents work, it's important to understand each of these concepts and how they work together.

Physical Structure

The *physical* structure of an XML document comprises a series of units called entities. Each *entity* is a virtual storage unit with a name and contents. An XML document must have at least one document entity—which may comprise the entire document—that is the starting point for all XML processing, but a document may contain multiple entities.

Entities may be either binary or text. A text entity, naturally, contains text data. This data is an integral part of the document. XML text consists of intermingled character data and markup. Markup takes the form of start tags, end tags, empty elements, entity references, character references, comments, CDATA sections, document type declarations, and processing instructions. (These types are briefly described in "Data Types & Declarations" later in this chapter.) All text that is not markup constitutes the character data of the document.

A binary entity contains binary data with some associated notation. For processing purposes, references to complete internal entities may only point to text entities; only the names of binary entities may be used directly within a document. For example, if you are referring to a Java applet, which would be a binary entity (since it's a set of compiled code elements), you can only refer to the applet by name, and it would have to be loaded by the client. You cannot put the code for the applet inside the document itself. Essentially, this is the same as inserting an <APPLET> tag inside a current HTML document. However, XML places no constraints on the contents or use of binary entities. Although an entity is labeled as binary data, it might in fact be textual; its identification as binary simply means that an XML processor need not be concerned with its content.

Logical Structure

The *logical* structure of an XML document comprises declarations, elements, comments, character references, and processing instructions. Each must be indicated in the document by explicit markup using tags.

Although an XML document may contain all of the types mentioned, each XML document must contain one or more *elements*. Elements are either delimited by start tags and end tags or, for empty elements, by a specific empty-element tag. Each element has a type, is identified by a name, and may have a set of attributes. If present, each attribute has a name and a value.

XML tags look very much like HTML tags. The element start tag begins with the character < followed by a name and possibly a series of attributes and values and finishes with a >; the end tag must start with the characters </ followed by the same name as the matching start tag and finish with a >. So, for example, <BODY> and </BODY> are matching start and end tags that are valid in XML as they are in HTML. Attributes are written much as they are in HTML—an attribute name followed by an = sign and then the value, which may be enclosed in quotes or not, as required. So <BODY BGCOLOR="white"> is an acceptable XML start tag. Like HTML, XML allows you to use either double quotes (") or single quotes (') to delimit values.

Empty tags, however, are a little different. An *empty tag* is a markup element that does not enclose any content and that therefore does not allow an end tag; in HTML, for example, the <BR> tag is an empty tag. XML also allows empty tags, but the syntax of an empty tag is slightly different than it is for start and end tags. In XML, an empty tag must end with the characters />. So the empty <BR> tag becomes <BR/> in XML.

You should also notice another subtle difference between HTML tags and XML tags. In HTML, some tags have attributes that do not have values; for example, many of the list tags, such as <UL>, accept a COMPACT attribute—<UL COMPACT>. In XML, attributes without values are not allowed, so the format for the <UL> tag would have to be something like <UL FORMAT="compact"> or <UL COMPACT='yes'>.

Why do we say "something like . . ."? Because, as you will read later in this chapter, unlike HTML, XML allows you to determine both the valid attributes for a tag and the valid values for those attributes. As a result, either of the preceding examples might be valid for different XML documents, depending on how the document defined the <UL> tag.

Relationship of Logical & Physical Structures

As you have just read, the physical structure of an XML document consists of entities, while the logical structure consists of elements. These two structures (elements and entities) in an XML document must be *synchronous*. This means that tags and elements must each begin and end in the same entity, although they may refer to other entities within their content—the way an anchor tag refers to an external document, for example. All other types of data must also be contained entirely within a single entity. Entities must each contain an integral number of elements, comments, processing instructions, and references. Entities may contain character data not contained within any element in the entity—text for display, for example—or else they must contain nontextual (binary) data, which by definition contains no elements.

Creating Well-Formed XML Documents

The first requirement for an XML document is that it must be well formed. An XML document is *well formed* if it meets the following criteria:

- The document must have a DTD defined, or if there is no DTD in use, the document must start with a Required Markup Declaration (RMD) saying so:

  ```
  <?XML version="1.0" RMD="NONE"?>
  ```

- All tags in the document must be balanced; that is, all elements that may contain character data must have both start and end tags present (omission is not allowed except for empty elements, see below).

- All attribute values must be in quotes. Either the single quote or the double quote may be used. The single-quote character must be used if the value contains a double-quote character and vice versa.

- Any empty element tags (for example, those with no end tag like HTML's <IMG>, <HR>, and <BR> and others) must either end with the string /> or you have to make them non-empty by adding a real end tag;

  ```
  Example: <HR> would become either <HR/> or <HR></HR>.
  ```

- There must not be any isolated markup characters (< or &) in your text data (i.e., they must be escaped as < and &), and the sequence]]> (which is used as an ending for CDATA sections, as explained later) must be escaped as]]> if it does not occur as the end of a CDATA marked section. Well-formed XML files with no DTD are considered to have "<", ">", "'", """, and "&" predefined and thus available for use even without a DTD. Valid XML files must declare them explicitly if they use them.

- Elements must nest inside each other properly. That is, there must be no overlapping markup.

  Example: `<P> This is <EM>an illegal</P>construction</EM>`

- Well-formed files with no DTD may use attributes on any element, but the attributes must all be of type CDATA by default.

Note that setting the value of the RMD attribute to "NONE" indicates that an XML processor can parse the document correctly without first reading any part of the DTD so it can also be used if you do supply a DTD but don't want it used on this occasion.

Creating Valid XML Documents

To be useful, an XML document must also be valid. This involves more than just being well formed, although all valid XML document will be well formed by definition.

Over and above the criteria for being well formed, a valid XML document requires two specific sections. First, it must contain a *prolog*. The prolog gives specific information about the document's markup. Second, the document must contain a well-formed document element as described earlier.

The function of the markup in an XML document is to describe its storage and logical structures and associate attribute-value pairs with the logical structure. XML provides a mechanism, the *document type declaration,* or DTD, to define constraints on that logical structure and to support the use of pre-defined storage units. An XML document is said to be *valid* if there is an associated document type declaration specified in the prolog and if the document complies with the constraints expressed in it.

In order to understand the DTD, an XML document must also have a Required Markup Declaration (RMD) attribute. The RMD can take three values: "NONE," "INTERNAL," and "ALL."

- "NONE," which we discussed in the previous section, tells the XML parser that the document can be parsed without using a DTD. This option is required for well-formed documents that do not have a DTD associated with them via the DOCTYPE tag.

- "INTERNAL" indicates that the XML processor is required to read and process at least the internal subset of the DTD, if provided, to parse the document correctly.

- "ALL" is the default, used when the RMD attribute is not present or when no XML tag is present and indicates that the DTD and the internal subset must both be read in order to parse the document correctly.

The document prolog may, and should, begin with an XML declaration that specifies the version of XML being used, the Required Markup Declaration (RMD), and the encoding used in the document. If these are omitted, the parser will use the default values: "1.0" for version, "ALL" for the RMD, and "UTF-8" for the encoding. The prolog also must contain a document type declaration. The document type declaration must appear before the first start tag in the document element.

So, to sum up, here's an example of a well-formed and valid XML document:

```
<?XML VERSION="1.0" RMD="ALL" ?>
<!DOCTYPE HTML PUBLIC "-//W3C//DTD HTML 3.2//EN">
<HTML>
<HEAD><TITLE>A Sample Page</TITLE></HEAD>
<BODY><H1>Hello XML World!</H1></BODY>
</HTML>
```

As you can see, the XML declaration that starts the document begins with <?XML, carries the version information and RMD information as attribute-value pairs, and ends with ?>. The document type declaration is given by the <!DOCTYPE> tag, which we will discuss further in the next section. Finally, the entire document is included within the start tag <HTML> and the end tag </HTML>, as required by the well-formed document principles outlined earlier. Perhaps not too surprisingly, a valid XML document can look a lot like a well-coded HTML document.

Although this looks like a typical HTML document, there are a few points to note. First, an HTML document should have the enclosing <HTML> and </HTML> tags but will display correctly in most current browsers whether they are present or not. In XML, missing these elements would violate the well-formed document principle that the document must have a single root element containing all other elements, and so you would be unable to display the document. Second, many valid HTML documents today do not start with a <!DOCTYPE> tag—in fact, many Web coders feel that this type of tag is really unnecessary—not, however, in XML. Without the <!DOCTYPE> tag, the document would be well formed but not valid, since it would be missing an essential element of the prolog and so would generate an error in an XML browser. Finally, the specification states that the prolog of an XML document "may and should" begin with the XML declaration; however, the document will be valid even if it is missing. As a result, a well-coded HTML document— that is, one that includes the <HTML> start and end tags and a valid <!DOCTYPE> tag—could be displayed or processed by an XML parser with no further modifications.

Accessing the DTD

Let's look a little harder at the DTD and its associated <!DOCTYPE> tag. As you have just seen, the tag begins with the characters <!DOCTYPE. This is followed by a name, which must exactly match (and this match is case sensitive) the root element of the document. In our example, the name was "HTML" and the root element start and end tags must be, therefore, <HTML> and </HTML>. The name element must be followed by either a pointer to an external DTD or by an internal DTD or a combination of both. In the example, we have used a reference to an external, public DTD—the one published by the W3C for HTML 3.2. The tag then closes with the > character.

In general, external DTD references consist of a keyword, either "SYSTEM" or "PUBLIC," and a URL that points to the DTD itself. An XML version of the specified DTD must be accessible to the XML processor, either by being available locally (for example, a copy on disk) or by being retrievable via the network. You can either supply the complete URL for the DTD in a SYSTEM identifier or supply the formal PUBLIC identifier, as shown in the preceding code, and provide a catalog file that equates these with their URL equivalents.

Internal DTD references must be enclosed within left and right brackets: [and]. The various elements that are allowed in the document are defined within these brackets using the <!ELEMENT> tag. For example, the simple document given earlier could also be coded in XML as follows:

```
<?XML VERSION="1.0"?>
<!DOCTYPE HTML
    [
        <!ELEMENT HEAD (TITLE)>
        <!ELEMENT TITLE (#PCDATA)>
        <!ELEMENT BODY (#PCDATA | H1)>
        <!ELEMENT H1 (#PCDATA)>
    ]>
<HTML>
<HEAD><TITLE>A Sample Page</TITLE></HEAD>
<BODY><H1>Hello XML World!</H1></BODY>
</HTML>
```

Let's look at each of these <!ELEMENT> tags in turn. The first definition is <!ELEMENT HEAD (TITLE)>, which says that the HEAD tag must consist of a TITLE tag and nothing else. The second definition, <!ELEMENT TITLE (#PCDATA)>, says that the TITLE tag consists of character data—indicated by the keyword "PCDATA"—and nothing else. The third definition, <!ELEMENT BODY (#PCDATA | H1)>, is the most complex. This says that the BODY tag must contain either character data or an H1 tag, but not both. The | character between the two elements that make up the <BODY> tag shows that either one or the other, but not both, elements must be present. Finally, the last definition, <!ELEMENT H1 (#PCDATA)>, says that an H1 tag must contain only character data. Overall, this is a very simpleminded DTD, but it fits the document presented here.

Note that the DTD doesn't tell you how to use these tags. It simply tells the parser how the tag is named and what the content of the tag should be. In other words, this defines the syntax of the document, but not the meaning. In this example, we have used common HTML tags, but nothing here specifies what the program that gets the parsed data should do with these tags.

Data Types & Declarations

You can have a variety of types of data in a valid XML document. Acceptable types of data are character data, program data, markup information, and comments. Each type plays an important role in creating XML documents and DTDs. Don't be surprised if these types look pretty familiar; as you have already seen, XML and HTML look very much alike as far as markup and structure are concerned. Nevertheless, there are some subtle but important differences between data as presented in HTML pages and in XML pages.

As you have already seen, XML allows you to store information within the document in either text or binary form. If the data is stored in binary form, then it's simply passed directly through to the application without any parsing. If the data is text, then it will be a series of characters, as defined by the International Standards Organization (ISO) specification 10646, the Unicode standard for worldwide character encoding. (The standard Latin-1 encoding used in HTML is a subset of this encoding.) The encoding used in the document can be specified using the ENCODING attribute in the XML tag at the start of the document. The ability to use alternate encodings in your documents is an important advantage of XML over HTML.

XML text consists of intermingled character data and markup. Markup takes the form of start tags, end tags, empty elements, entity references, character references, comments, CDATA sections, document type declarations, and processing instructions. Markup is distinguished from character data by its use of certain reserved character codes. Specifically, the ampersand (&) and the left angle bracket (<) must only be used in text as markup delimiters; to include these codes in character data, they must be escaped using either numeric character references or the strings "&" and "<".

The most basic type of text data is character data. All text in a document that is not markup constitutes the character data of the document. Character data is called out in DTD elements as PCDATA.

Comments are also an accepted part of XML notation. XML comments look and are processed exactly like HTML comments: they begin with <!-- and end with -->. Comments must not occur within declarations or tags and are not part of the document's character data. Note that an XML parser may, but need not, make it possible for an application to retrieve the text of comments.

Some information within the document, like attributes and script objects, is not considered text, as it is neither character data nor markup. Instead, such information is considered program code, or CDATA. CDATA sections can occur anywhere character data may occur; they define blocks of text containing characters that would otherwise be interpreted as markup. CDATA sections begin with the string "<![CDATA[" and end with the string "]]>". Within a CDATA section, only the "]]>" string is recognized, so left angle brackets and ampersands may occur in their literal form; in fact, they should always be presented as characters and never be escaped using the < and & format. A CDATA section is called out in DTD elements as CDATA.

XML documents may also contain processing instructions that are passed on to the processing application. Processing instructions begin with the characters <? and end with ?>. As you can tell from this, the required XML declaration is a processing instruction.

XML Tools & Browsers

Given the interest in XML, it's not surprising that a number of commercial vendors are preparing XML software tools. In addition, because of XML's relationship to SGML, which is fairly well studied and widely used, many individuals and academic institutions are undertaking XML efforts for various research and validation purposes. The W3C has a good list of the work being done on XML at http://www.w3.org/XML/.

At the time of this writing, the leading examples of XML tools available for free noncommercial use include the following:

- A validating XML parser written in Java by Microsoft and widely available with the Internet Explorer 4.0 release. The latest version of this parser is available at http://www.microsoft.com/standards/xml/xmlparse.htm.

- NXP is a validating XML parser written in Java by Norbert Mikula and available at http://www.edu.uni-klu.ac.at/~nmikula/NXP.

- Lark is a nonvalidating XML processor written in Java by Tim Bray and available at http://www.textuality.com/Lark/.

- TclXML is a validating XML parser written in Tcl by Steve Ball and available at "http://tcltk.anu.edu.au/XML/".

- <A href="http://www.ltg.ed.ac.uk/software/xml/">LT XML</A> is an XML developers' toolkit from the Language Technology Group at the University of Edinburgh.

- <A href="http://www.venus.co.uk/~pmr/README">JUMBO</A> is a Java-based XML browser designed for the <A href="http://www.venus.co.uk/omf/cml/">Chemical Markup Language</A>, an XML application developed by Peter Murray-Rust.

If you're interested in how XML can be used, check these applications and their related documentation.

What Is Metadata?

Literally, *metadata* means "beyond data"—and that's exactly what metadata on the Web is: information stored in a document about the structure and content of the data contained in the document.

HTML documents have always provided for some types of metadata. The <META> tag allows you to put any type of metadata you want within the tag. In fact, many sites use these tags as ways to insert search keywords, special structural information, and other site-specific information. In addition, as you read in earlier chapters, you can use the <META> tag to insert specific HTTP information for use by the browser.

However, the data available in a <META> tag is limited by the two available attributes, NAME and CONTENT. Also, you can't have information spanning more than one tag. As a result, the information provided is pretty basic.

Using XML, however, you can easily construct a general metadata scheme that gets around these limitations. Since XML allows you to define what tags are valid, how they interact, and what their content is, you can use an XML DTD to define a set of metadata tags that allow a wide variety of related information to be stored in a document.

Categorizing & Indexing Information With Metadata

There are a variety of initiatives to add metadata information to Web pages. They all use similar techniques, allowing XML parsers included with browser technology to analyze the content of the document and present the information to the browser for appropriate action. Of these approaches, two stand out: Microsoft's use of metadata for its Channel Definition Format (CDF) that adds data channels to the latest version of Internet Explorer and the PICS initiative that allows Web sites to provide rating information on content so that anyone with a suitable browser can prevent unauthorized viewing of inappropriate content. The next section examines the CDF format to show you how XML and metadata work together to make a more interactive Web.

A Metadata Example: Microsoft's Channel Definition Format (CDF)

Microsoft has included a new technology, called Channels, in Internet Explorer. The technology allows you to "subscribe" to defined "channels" on the Web. As content is published for these channels, you receive it automatically for viewing on your browser. This provides automatic delivery of up-to-date, personalized information. However, developing a format for publishing content that can be delivered to end users by several different mechanisms (pull, push, streaming) and that can scale to meet various device limits, network sizes, and bandwidth constraints is quite a task.

Microsoft has created the Channel Definition Format (CDF), which provides Web publishers with the ability to author content a single time and publish it via many different avenues without fracturing network resources. A Channel is defined as a set of documents or a grouping of content that can be pushed, pulled, or operated on as a unit. Currently, the types of operations on a channel primarily involve automatic scheduled downloads or multicast delivery for later viewing offline.

Here's an example of how channel information might be coded:

```
<CHANNEL>
    <ITEM HREF="http://www.mycompany.com/intro.html" level="2"
precache="NO">
        <A HREF="http://www.mycompany.com/page1.html">A link to the first
page.</A>
        <TITLE>Welcome to The Company!</TITLE>
        <ABSTRACT>Company articles, news, events, and promotional offers</
ABSTRACT>
    </ITEM>
    <SCHEDULE STARTDATE="1997-11-05" ENDDATE="1998-11-04">
        <INTERVALTIME DAY="1"/>
        <EARLIESTTIME HOUR="12"/>
        <LATESTTIME HOUR="18"/>
    </SCHEDULE>
</CHANNEL>
```

First of all, you can see here how the XML works to create the CDF tags. These tags are not standard HTML; instead they are special tags that must be parsed and passed to the browser application so that the appropriate download of the channel information can take place.

By having a sophisticated tag structure, CDF allows a browser to handle a channel in several different ways. At the simplest level, the browser could just look at the first item URL and then use Web-crawler technology to pull all the associated pages and check whether any were changed. If so, then the changes would be downloaded for display when requested. In this way, the site seen by the "channel" subscriber will always be up-to-date.

However, the browser could be a bit smarter and use the additional information provided to program the scheduler so that it will pull only the content that is necessary to present to the user as part of a "channel" experience. Regular HTTP polling determines when new content is available and pulls it automatically for presentation to the user. In these more advanced clients, an external application-specific file optimizes the "smart pull" mechanism, providing content publishers a mechanism that specifies the schedule and exact set of resources that need to be pulled. The Channel Definition Format, as shown here, allows for the use of a standardized file for this external information.

Moving On

As you can see, the Web continues to evolve at a rapid rate. Whether XML and Metadata tagging come to pass or not, you can be sure that the Web of the future will provide more information with more interactivity than the current generation of Web documents. The Web represents the sum of the hard work of an enormous group of people, scattered across the globe but united by their desire to bring the information they care about to colleagues and customers everywhere. The use of XML and Metadata tagging—or some other, similar technologies—will allow users to manage this flood of information and tailor both its selection and presentation to their precise needs.

Although we've finished our discussion of publishing on the Internet, this is in no way the last word on Web publishing. As you continue to traverse the Web, you are bound to come upon many exciting, new Web publishing features and vehicles. The more you continue to explore the possibilities of Internet publishing, the greater the rewards. The next move is up to you, but fortunately you have the Web publishing world at your fingertips and the next step is only a hyperlink away.

Appendix A

About the Companion CD-ROM

The CD-ROM included with your copy of *HTML Publishing on the Internet, 2nd Edition* includes valuable software and author example files.

Navigating the CD-ROM

To find out more about the CD-ROM and its contents, please open the "README.HTM" file in your favorite browser. You will see a small menu offering several links.

Software

The software provided on the Companion CD-ROM is described below in Table A-1.

Adobe Acrobat Reader	The Adobe Acrobat Reader allows you to view, navigate, and print PDF files across all major computing platforms. Acrobat Reader is the free viewing companion to Adobe Acrobat 3.0 and to Acrobat Capture software. For more information, visit http://www.adobe.com.
Bandwidth Buster	Bandwidth Buster is the latest Internet tool from Sausage Software that will minimize the size of your Web site files, and insert tags and features that will speed the rate at which users are able to view your site.

➡

Caligari Pioneer Pro	Caligari Pioneer Pro is a VRML tool that a professional Web site developer can use to author and browse commercial-quality 3D "Home Worlds" on the Internet. The product seamlessly integrates professional level 3D modeling ("Home World" building) with complete VRML browsing in a powerful, direct manipulation-based interface. While Pioneer Pro shares many of the same features as its entry-level brother, Pioneer, there are a number of unique features that make it the perfect VRML authoring solution for professional site developers. Check it out at http://www.caligari.com.
cgi-lib.pl	A library of Perl code to parse and manage data from the Common Gateway Interface. This library is useful for processing forms submitted over the World Wide Web. Valuable library features include: simple and easy to use; designed for operation under Perl5 and Perl4; compatibility with all CGI interactions, including File Upload; debugging facilities; and convenient utility functions. The cgi-lib.pl is an excellent starting point for migration to more sophisticated libraries. Visit http://www.bio.cam.ac.uk/cgi-lib/.
Clikette	Clikette allows you to create pictorial 3D buttons that can be linked to multiple URL destinations. In short, this means that you can now make The Button That Launched A Thousand Links! Well, maybe not a thousand, but 50 at a time is probably enough to keep you and your Web page readers cruising the Internet in finest style.
CMX Viewer Trial Version	The Corel CMX viewer marks a technological advancement for graphics on the Internet. The viewer, now available in beta, makes it possible for Internet users to view Corel CMX files (vector format) online as opposed to the traditional GIF or JPEG files (raster format) currently being used.
Corel WEB.DATA Trial Version	PC format. Corel WEB.DATA is the power solution for publishing your data directly to the Internet. It interacts with a variety of data sources to quickly and easily create static or dynamic information-rich Web pages. If you want full control over how your database information looks when it is published to the Web, this is the tool that will give you the results you want.
Corel WEB.DESIGNER	With this version you will have access to 5 of the 120+ professionally designed templates. Note that version 1.2.18 of Corel WEB.DESIGNER does not support frames and that this trial version of Corel WEB.DESIGNER does not include Corel WEB.Transit and Corel WEB.GALLERY. If you are interested in purchasing a copy of the complete Corel WEB.DESIGNER box, please call Customer Service in Canada 1-613-728-3733 or 1-800-394-3729, and in the U.S. 1-800-772-6735.

➡

Crystal 3d Impact! for the Web	Within minutes, Crystal 3D Impact! allows you to very easily animate photorealistic text, logos, objects, and photographs in 3D, quickly and affordably. For more info about this and other Crystal Graphics products, visit http://www.crystalgraphics.com/ on the World Wide Web.
Crystal Flying Fonts LE	This is a light edition of Crystal Flying Fonts Pro, the world's easiest-to-use 3D animation software for creating and animating broadcast-quality titles and logos. Crystal Flying Fonts will enhance your Web sites, videos, presentations, and print work. Awarded as one of Videomaker's Best Products of the Year, Crystal Flying Fonts uses the same broadcast-renderer as CrystalTOPAS, the animation tool used by professionals to create TV commercials. Visit http://www.crystalgraphics.com.
CuteFTP	CuteFTP is a Windows-based Internet application that allows novice users to utilize the capabilities of FTP without having to know all the details of the protocol itself. It simplifies FTP by offering a user-friendly, graphical interface instead of cumbersome command-line utility. Visit http://www.cuteftp.com.
DeBabelizer Lite LE	With over 55 graphics readers and writers, DeBabelizer Lite is perfect for simple image translation and slideshow functions. Its compatibility with Photoshop Filter, Acquire, and Export plug-ins also provides an extremely cost-effective filtering solution. For bitmap, scan, or paint files, DeBabelizer Lite offers nearly the same translation capabilities as DeBabelizer Toolbox without the internal scripting, image processing, or palette manipulation. Slideshow creates onscreen thumbnails of a folder full of images which can all be translated automatically. DeBabelizer Lite intelligently maintains maximum color integrity and quality to and from each format and platform. Scan or digitize images with Photoshop (and third party) acquired plug-ins. Visit http://www.equilibrium.com.
DeBabelizer Pro demo	A projector demo of Debabelizer Pro, a comprehensive automated application for anyone working with graphics, animations, and digital video in multimedia, Web, and desktop productions.
DeBabelizer Toolbox	An essential tool for anyone working with computer graphics. This award-winning product combines graphics processing, palette optimization, and translation in one program. With easy "Watch Me" scripting and batch features, thousands of images can be processed automatically to specifications. A true production powerhouse, DeBabelizer Toolbox translates between 70+ bit-mapped graphics, animation, and digital video formats, including DOS/Windows, Amiga, Sun, XWindows, Alias, Electric Image, SoftImage formats, and more. DeBabelizer Toolbox supports

➡

	Photoshop and third-party Acquire, Filter, and Export plug-ins, as well as AppleScript. It includes dozens of image-editing and palette-manipulation tools, including SuperPalette, which automatically creates the best palette for a series of images. DeBabelizer Toolbox complements all paint, scan, and image processing programs. Visit http://www.equilibrium.com.
Drag and File Gold	A shareware application offering all the features of Drag and File and Drag and Zip under Windows 95 and Windows NT. Drag and File Gold features include: ability to copy, move, delete, and view files and directories, launch bars that enable users to streamline the desktop with buttons to access drives, commands, programs, URLs etc., directory synchronization, filter sets, and more.
Drag and Zip	Canyon Software's full 32-bit application running under Windows 95 and Windows NT. Drag and Zip will create and extract files with long filenames and long directory names, make self-extracting Windows-based executable files, and zip, unzip, and extract Zip, GZ, and TAR formats. Other Drag and Zip features include: built-in zipping to multiple floppy disks; zipping and unzipping files with a right mouse button click, and much more.
Egor	Egor is the world's first commercial Java animator application. Egor's simple frame-by-frame assembler lets you create your own Java animations, add sounds, and associate URLs with each frame or with the whole animation. Egor is the simplest and most effective way to get your page moving and shaking with Java. For more information, visit http://www.sausage.com.
Enliven Viewer	Narrative Communications Corp.'s Enliven Viewer gives the user fast multimedia delivery over low bandwidth connections. This highly interactive Web solution eliminates file size limitations, and takes advantage of low bandwidth connections to enable development of informative, entertaining, and interactive Web applications.
Envoy 7	The Envoy 7 Viewer and plug-ins are free applications which allow you to view Envoy documents created on any platform, regardless of which fonts and applications are present on your system. The Envoy 7 Viewer can be distributed to anyone who wants to read an Envoy document. The free Envoy Viewer, plug-in, and ActiveX are available at http://www.tumbleweed.com/download.htm.
Eye Candy	A demo of the new set of Photoshop plug-ins from Alien Skin Software. Eye Candy 3.0 (formerly known as The Black Box) is the answer to serious Photoshop users' prayers. These filters create special effects in seconds that would normally require hours of hand tweaking. You have probably heard experts explain complex 12-step processes for creating 3D bevels or flames. Now you can

➡

stop trying to follow those frustrating recipes and simply use Eye Candy. Version 3.0 makes professional effects even easier by giving you flexible previews and a thumbnail for rapidly navigating your image. Visit http://www.alienskin.com.

Flash	Sausage Software's Flash is a user-friendly little tool that allows you to display scrolling text on a browser's status line—sort of like tickertape. In this latest version of Flash, you can pause the scrolling to display status bar URLs. It's a great way to pass subtle bits of info to your viewers! Check out http://www.sausage.com.
Fractal Design Detailer	Fractal Design Detailer is an amazing graphics program that lets you paint directly onto the surface of 3D models. It's the closest thing to actually holding an object in your hand and painting it! If you're a 3D artist, Detailer is a one-stop shop for creating texture, bump, and other surface maps for your 3D models. You'll enjoy substantial time savings, increased accuracy, greater control, and real-time results. If you're a 2D artist, Detailer provides the enormous flexibility of 3D with the compositional simplicity of 2D. With Detailer, you can easily create rendered 3D objects which become elements of your image-editing designs. The Detailer demo is a save-disabled version of this award-winning application for Mac OS. It will show you all the capabilities but without the ability to save, print, export, or copy objects to another application.
Fractal Design Expression	Fractal Design Expression combines the stylistic expressiveness of traditional artist's tools with the flexibility, speed, editability, and resolution independence of a vector-based drawing application. If you're a graphic designer or illustrator, Fractal Design Expression will change the way you think about vector-based illustration and the way you work as a computer artist. Expression's power and agility come from its exclusive Skeletal Strokes technology. For the first time ever, artists can use a single vector path to draw sophisticated, multi-element strokes or even complete illustrations. Simply select a drawing tool and a stroke style, and begin drawing.
Fractal Design Painter	Fractal Design Painter 4 is the world's leading paint program. With more than 150 unique brushes, Painter's rich set of painting tools and special effects empower your creativity. Painter 4 mixes raster and vector artwork, offers exciting Web features, and supports collaborative painting across a network. Painter's astounding Natural-Media features simulate the tools and textures of traditional artists' materials. From crayons to calligraphy, oils to airbrushes, pencils to watercolor, Painter turns your computer into an artist's studio. Whether you are an experienced Painter user or you've never seen its extensive capabilities, you'll see how easily version 4 can transform the way you create!

➡

FrameGang	FrameGang is the hot new Web design tool from Sausage Software that brings frames to your Web pages. With some basic knowledge of HTML frames and your trusty mouse, you can point and click your way through frame generation for your Web page(s). FrameGang allows you to display multiple HTML documents on one Web page, and allows hyperlinks in one frame to interact with another frame, opening up exciting possibilities.
Gatling	Gatling is Sausage Software's latest FTP tool, designed to simplify life for novice and expert Net users alike. Gatling, as its name suggests, allows the rapid-fire, repeated transmission of a file by the FTP protocol. It solves the common problem of getting files on remote servers to regularly update as content changes. How do you do this? Specify the local file and the remote host, then choose the interval you want in seconds, minutes, hours, or days. Click the Upload button and Gatling takes over, firing the file at the server for as long as you want.
GIF/JPEG SmartSaver	A non-destructive WYSIWYG image optimization utility, GIF/JPEG SmartSaver features side-by-side image previews and file size comparisons. Allows you to reduce colors in GIF images, using Netscape Navigator and Internet Explorer "safe palettes." Lets you quickly reduce colors in GIF images to ensure the ideal compression/quality ratio for JPEG images. Batch processing of images at different color and compression ranges offers fast fine-tuning for perfectly optimized images.
Goldwave	Chris Craig's Goldwave is a digital audio player, editor, recorder, and converter, complete with Java and Web audio format support. The application has full editing features, such as copy, cut, paste, trim, and mix as well as a large selection of effects, including echo, flange, doppler, and parametric EQ.
Graphic Converter	This application will convert files between most formats. It can also be used to read, save, and prepare graphic files for distribution over the Web. Detailed user instructions for Graphic Converter are available on the Web at http://www.pen.k12.va.us/Anthology/Help/Mac/graphic.converter.html.
HotDog Professional Trial Version	HotDog for Windows 95 is out, and it's more powerful and more full-featured than ever before! HotDog from Sausage Software is a fast, flexible, and user-friendly way of creating HTML documents for publishing on the World Wide Web. HotDog is one of the most highly rated Web editors in the world for professional Web designers and hobbyists alike, thanks to its powerful features, ease of use, and support for all HTML features—official and otherwise.

➡

HoTMetaL Light	This simple yet powerful tool allows Web users of all levels to create Web pages quickly. HoTMetaL Light complies to HTML 3.2 industry standards, provides WYSIWYG Web page authoring, and offers a drag and drop environment. Visit http://www.softquad.com for more information about this and other SoftQuad products.
HVS Color	A demo of HVS Color, the award-winning color-reduction Export plug-in for Photoshop 3 and 4. This demo will give you an idea of the color reduction quality, but it's not unlockable, and it inserts a watermark in the center of images. An unlockable demo of the next generation HVS ColorGIF 2.0 will be available soon. Visit http://www.digfrontiers.com for more information.
HVS ColorGIF	HVS ColorGIF is a successor to award-winning HVS Color. Now available as Filters, HVS allows Web developers to maintain 24-bit image quality at 8 bits or less (256 colors) that look as good as 24-bit original and download up to 70% faster.
HVS JPEG	A plug-in filter that exports superior-quality, progressive JPEGs for use on the Web and in multimedia. HVS JPEG provides the smallest size while maintaining superior graphic image quality via proprietary optimization techniques. This unlockable demo allows customers to use the full-featured product free for seven days, and may be purchased thereafter via a convenient online module. Visit http://www.digfrontiers.com to learn more.
HyperWire	The first visual, object-oriented programming tool from Kinetix is the fastest, easiest way to create sophisticated interactive 3D applications and Java applets without programming or script coding. Designed for corporate intranet and interactive graphics content creators, HyperWire builds sophisticated 2D and 3D interactive Web content, Java applets, and connected CD-ROM titles.
ImageWiz Plus	Sausage Software's ImageWiz Plus does for images what Swami does for text effects. Rather than animating complex sequences of frames, ImageWiz allows you to specify 40 effects for your images.
InfoLink Link Checker	BiggByte Software's InfoLink Link Checker is an Internet utility that verifies links in HTML documents. Packed with verification features, InfoLink Link Checker returns all test results in HTML format in the built-in InfoLink Browser. This tool also offers visual frame support for verification of frame-enhanced pages. Check out BiggByte's site at http://www.biggbyte.com.

Jackhammer	Next time you hit road work on the information superhighway, Sausage Software's Jackhammer will help you dig yourself out of the hole. Whenever you find a site that's too busy to get onto, or an FTP server that's always full, paste the URL into Jackhammer. Set it hammering and it will try the sites until it can get on. Then Jackhammer will launch a new browser window for you or automatically download the file!
Jamba	If you design or develop Web pages, Jamba is the fastest and most productive way to add the excitement and the power of multimedia and interactivity to static HTML pages. Combining an intuitive, award-winning user interface with Java's cross-platform delivery, Jamba eliminates the need for plug-ins while providing an open environment for applet development. Visit http://www.aimtech.com for more information.
Kai's PowerTools	A demonstration version of MetaTools, Inc.'s Kai's PowerTools 3.0. KPT 3.0 is available as a 32-bit native application extension for the Intel-based Windows 95/NT platforms, as well as for the Apple Macintosh/Power Macintosh platforms. Kai's PowerTools 3.0 is a unique and powerful collection of extensions that expand the power of image-editing applications which support the Adobe plug-in specifications. Visit http://www.metatools.com.
LiveImage	The heir to MapThis!, LiveImage is a client-side, user-friendly image mapping program for Windows 95 and Windows NT 4.0. With LiveImage, you can create your first client-side image map with embedded hyperlinks in under five minutes. Features include: zoom-in up to 8x magnification; cut, copy, and paste; GIF, JPG, and PNG file format support; doesn't require a TrueColor video board—can operate from 16 colors to 16 million colors; supports dragging links from Netscape into a map; the Image Wizard allows you to create common navigation bars; product menus, and item grids; the Image Map Wizard simplifies creating a new image map; full support for HTML 3.0 image maps—can edit existing map or add a new map to an existing html file, and much more. For more information about Mediatech's LiveImage, and to secure the required files, OLEAUT32.DLL and OLEPRO32.DLL, visit http://www.mediatec.com.
Macromedia Flash!	With its advanced vector-based technology, Flash! breaks the bandwidth barrier by enabling you to create interactive Web animations, interfaces, buttons, drawings, cartoons, and more—now with sound! Visit http://www.macromedia.com. Copyright Macromedia, Inc. 1996-1997. All Rights Reserved.

➡

Mailto Converter	Mailto Converter makes it possible to use forms on your Web pages without any access to a CGI-script. It can read a single file, a folder of files, the clipboard, or Netscape and Eudora mailboxes. Files can be dropped onto the application to convert text and save it into files or in the clipboard. With only one click, or just a drag-and-drop action, all your form results can be saved into a single file, ready to import into your favorite database. Mailto Converter supports both the standard BinHex conversion method and ISO Latin-1, used in Western Europe. One of the first programs of its kind for the Mac! Visit http://www.calles.pp.se/nisseb to learn more about this and other Nisseb products.
MapEdit	Boutell.Com, Inc.'s graphical editor for World Wide Web image maps (clickable imagemaps). With MapEdit and the latest Web browsers, you can use client-side imagemaps, which reside in your HTML page and are very easy to create. MapEdit will also create server-side maps for backward compatibility with old browsers.
Mapper	Mapper is the easiest way to create imagemaps (for the World Wide Web in CERN, NCSA, and client side formats. It combines an easy-to-use WYSIWYG interface with powerful tools which will be useful even for the most experienced user. Just open the image, place the objects, and save! Mapper can open and save in all formats. Requires: System 6.0.7, QuickTime to open GIF and JPEG files. Visit http://www.calles.pp.se/nisseb.
MapThis!	The last version of MapThis!, the award-winning image map editor for Win32, corrects any UI issues, deals with zooming and panning, remembers the last used directory for both images and maps, and solves the problem of garbage on the end of Windows 95 HTML files. Highlights of the 1.31 version include: true dockable, resizable area listbox which allows you to reorder areas and edit URLs on the fly; AreaTips that show the URL as you move the cursor over your areas; area grab handles that can be doubled in size or turned off completely, and much more.
MetaPhotos	MetaPhotos is a breathtaking collection of high-resolution, royalty-free drum scanned images that make standard stock photography obsolete. This demo version of MetaPhotos comes with 240 art-directed photo poses of 20 different characters and props. To ensure consistent quality, all files have been thoroughly cleaned and color corrected by the same digital imaging experts. Go to http://www.metatools.com.

➡

missinglink	missinglink (ml for short) is a program, written in Perl, that is designed to help a Webmaster debug his or her Web site. ml searches through HTML files and checks each hyperlink to make sure the file it references really does exist. ml can check links to files on the server, links that point to files on other HTTP servers, and links within imagemaps. ml will report any problems it finds to the user. Visit http://www.rsol.com for more information.
Mousetrap	Mousetrap brings true user interactivity to your Web pages. Armed with only the barest essentials of HTML, you can create Java-enhanced Web pages that play sounds and change pictures or text, depending only on where the surfer moves the mouse.
MPEG Plugin	The InterVU MPEG plug-in works with Netscape Navigator version 2.0 and greater to allow the user to view MPEG-1 video files within the browser, either alone (e.g., as the only thing in the browser window), or embedded within a Web page. Once installed, the use of the MPEG plug-in is automatic—if you visit a Web page that has an embedded MPEG video, it will launch the plug-in. You can also play local MPEG video files (i.e., those on your hard drive or a CD-ROM). To do so, simply open them in the browser (or drag and drop them onto the browser window). For more information about InterVU, go to http://www.intervu.com on the World Wide Web.
NetObjects Fusion	NetObjects Fusion 2.0 for Macintosh is the next generation of site-oriented applications from NetObjects. It combines automatic site-building, professional-quality design, and data publishing features. NetObjects Fusion provides unique, complete visual control over the design and production of your Web site. Visit NetObjects at http://www.netobjects.com.
NetObjects Fusion for Windows	NetObjects Fusion 2.0 for Windows is the next generation of site-oriented applications from NetObjects. It combines automatic site-building, professional-quality design, and data publishing features. NetObjects Fusion provides unique, complete visual control over the design and production of your Web site. Visit NetObjects at http://www.netobjects.com.
Paint Shop Pro	A powerful and easy-to-use image viewing, editing, and conversion program that supports over 30 image formats. With numerous drawing and painting tools, this may be the only graphics program you will ever need! Visit http://www.jasc.com for more information about this and other Jasc products.
PageSpinner	PageSpinner is an HTML editor for MacOS. It supports HTML 2.0, HTML 3.2, plus additional Netscape extensions and is useful for both the beginner and the more advanced Web author. PageSpinner is shareware. You are permitted to use the application on a trial basis for up to 30 days. If you wish to continue using the product beyond that period, you must register by paying a fee of $25.00 in

➡

	U.S. currency or remove it from your computer storage medium. This fee entitles you to a single user license of PageSpinner 2.x and any future updates to the 2.x version of PageSpinner and the included extensions and helper applications. For more info, please go to http://www.algonet.se/~optima/ps_registration.html on the World Wide Web.
Perl for Win32	ActiveWare Tool Corp.'s Perl for Win32 Intel/x86 binary is a port of most of the functionality in Perl, with extra Win32 API calls that allow you to take advantage of native Windows functionality. Perl for Win32 runs on Windows 95 and Windows NT 3.5 and later. The Perl for Win32 package contains perl.exe, perlx00.dll, supporting documents, and extensions that allow you to call Win32 functionality. For more information, visit ActiveWare's homepage at http://www.activeware.com.
PhotoImpact GIF Animator	An award-winning 32-bit GIF animation composition tool that provides an intuitive workspace for producing compact GIF89a animations. PhotoImpact GIF Animator features advanced color palette and optimization controls, powerful design features, and special effects. GIF Animator offers nine transition effects, including blind, split, and spiral, which give you variations for starting and closing your animations. An Add Banner text dialog box lets you create scrolling text banners anywhere within your animation. Smart frame comparison chooses the best options for reducing frame sizes, and auto palette optimization converts any local palettes and reduces the global palette to only the needed colors. Visit http://www.ulead.com.
PhotoImpact GIF Optimizer	A Web imaging tool, PhotoImpact GIF Optimizer batch optimizes GIF files to produce savable reports listing before/after file sizes for each file optimized, plus the total savings per folder. Eliminates duplicate colors, pixels, and non-essential elements to ensure foolproof optimization of the exact same image quality. Only redundant pixels and colors are deleted. No need for an image editing application, GIF Optimizer automatically goes through an entire list of GIF files at the click of a button. Works on single files, folders, or entire Web sites to reduce bandwidth, lower storage, and improve Web site performance. Visit http://www.ulead.com.
RTFtoHTML	RTFtoHTML is designed to translate existing RTF documents into HTML, the format of the World Wide Web. By converting RTF documents to HTML, RTFtoHTML allows you to publish Microsoft Word, WordPerfect, FrameMaker, Claris Works, and other word processing documents on the WWW. RTFtoHTML can also be used to author new documents specifically for the WWW. To find out more about this product, check out http://www.sunpack.com/RTF.

➡

SiteFX	SiteFX is a collection of compact Java-based applications, each of which performs its "specialty" very well. Thanks to the intuitive interface and superb built-in Help files, SiteFX is very user-friendly. In one handy bundle, SiteFX provides efficient tools that are all you need to bring your Web pages to life. Go to http://www.sausage.com.
SoundApp	SoundApp will play or convert sound files dropped onto it. Using QuickTime 1.6 or later, SoundApp can also convert audi CD tracks. It requires at least System 7.0, Apple's Sound Manager 3.1 or greater, the Drag Manager (a.k.a. Macintosh Drag and Drop part of System 7.5 and at least a Macintosh with 68020 or a Power Macintosh).
SoundEffects	SoundEffects is a powerful sound editor for the Mac. Its strength resides in the capability of applying many digital effects to recorded sounds, and since the effects are plug-in modules, you can enhance the program at any time by just adding any new modules as they become available. SoundEffects is shareware. You can find more info about registering at ftp://ftp.alpcom.it/software/mac/Ricci/html/sfx.html.
SoundMaker	This demonstration version of SoundMaker is save-disabled, but otherwise fully functional. SoundMaker gives you all the tools you need to create and modify digital sound. You can import sounds at any sampling rate from clip sound disks or audio CDs, or record straight from your Mac's microphone. SoundMaker then lets you modify sounds any way you desire and provides you with multiple tracks so you can work on individual pieces. For more information go to http://www.allegiant.com/soundmaker/prod_desc.html on the World Wide Web.
Swami	Swami is a snaglet designed to take a text string and animate it in any one of twelve different ways. The fabulous Swami will help you make your message jump, ripple, expand, slide around, and generally create arresting and unusual effects on your Web page.
ThumbsPlus	The most effective, elegant, and inexpensive way to locate, view, edit, print, and organize your image, metafile, font, and multimedia files on Windows 95/NT/3.1. Visit http://www.cerious.com for more information.
trueSpace3	Like its predecessor, Caligari Corp.'s trueSpace3 is a fully integrated, intuitive, modeless interface that makes it easier to learn and become proficient in 3D graphics and animation. This new version of trueSpace includes an exciting array of new animation, rendering, human engineering, and Internet tools. Visit http://www.caligari.com.

➡

VDOLive Player Plugin	The VDOLive Player enables you to see VDOLive clips and movies. For more information, go to VDO's Web site, at http://www.vdo.net.
VivoActive Player	VivoActive software enables production and viewing of streaming video and audio from Web sites over low-bandwidth connections, using existing Web infrastructure (HTTP, TCP/IP). No special server hardware or software or modifications to firewalls is required.
V-Realm Builder	V-Realm Builder is an authoring tool that allows professionals to create 3D objects and worlds that completely support the new VRML 2.0 standard. V-Realm Builder is the only VRML authoring package that outputs files in native VRML code, allowing direct editing of VRML nodes. The authoring tool also features translators for most popular 3D modeling packages and has extensive libraries that provide for storage and reuse of VRML objects, textures, and materials. V-Realm Builder's user-friendly interface greatly reduces the learning curve for novice VRML worldbuilders.
WebMania!	WebMania! is a full-featured HTML editor that includes unparalleled support for frames, forms, and client-side image maps. It also includes 60 user-programmable toolbar buttons which allow you to add new HTML tags as you learn them, or as HTML standards evolve. WebMania! will never become obsolete. New features in this version include: SpellChecker, CGI forms and Perl script generation, mailto forms, and open and edit multiple documents. Go to http://www.q-d.com on the Web.
WebImage	WebImage is an image manipulation program used to enhance, optimize, and create graphics for the World Wide Web. For more information about this and other Group 42 software, go to http://www.group42.com on the Web.
WebLint	WebLint is a syntax and minimal style checker for HTML: a Perl script which picks fluff off html pages, much in the same way traditional lint picks fluff off C programs. The following checks and warnings are currently performed: basic structure and syntax checks; warnings for use of unknown elements and element attributes; checks for html portability across all browsers, and more. All warnings can be enabled or disabled, using a configuration file, $HOME/.weblintrc. A sample configuration file, weblintrc, is included in the distribution. WebLint also supports a site-wide configuration file, which lets a group of people share a common configuration.
WS_FTP32 LE	A Limited Edition of WS_FTP32, a file transfer client with a highly intuitive graphical user interface. For more information, visit http://www.ipswitch.com on the Web.

➡

| Wusage | Wusage is a statistics system that helps you determine the true impact of your Web server. By measuring the popularity of your documents, as well as identifying the sites that access your server most often, Wusage provides valuable marketing information. Practically all organizations, whether commercial or educational or nonprofit, need solid numbers to make credible claims about the World Wide Web. Wusage fills that need. Visit http://www.boutell.com/. |

Table A-1: Software on the Companion CD-ROM.

Limits of Liability & Disclaimer of Warranty

The authors and publisher of this book have used their best efforts in preparing the CD-ROM and the programs contained in it. These efforts include the development, research, and testing of the theories and programs to determine their effectiveness. The authors and publisher make no warranty of any kind expressed or implied, with regard to these programs or the documentation contained in this book.

The authors and publisher shall not be liable in the event of incidental or consequential damages in connection with, or arising out of, the furnishing, performance, or use of the programs, associated instructions, and/or claims of productivity gains.

If there is software on this CD-ROM, then it may be shareware. There may be additional charges (owed to the software authors/makers) incurred for their registration and continued use. See individual program's README files for more information.

Appendix B

An HTML & Style Sheet Reference

This appendix is a concise reference guide to HTML; it lists almost all of the elements, with a brief description and illustration of each one.

HTML is an evolving language, and different World Wide Web browsers may recognize slightly different sets of HTML elements. This appendix covers HTML version 3.2, the most current version supported by a majority of browsers. But, as we discussed in the text, HTML 4.0 is coming soon and includes even more advanced features. This appendix also covers the HTML tags and characteristics for Cascading Style Sheets (CSS). These topics were covered in detail in this book, but you can use this appendix as a quick and complete reference for markup information.

HTML markup elements fall into two classes: *markup tags* and *character entities*. Markup tags define elements of the document that require special display or presentation. Character entities define special characters that are used within the document. The list here is divided into four sections. The first section covers all the standard document markup tags and extended tags. The second section covers the special markup tags that are used in HTML forms. The third section presents the CSS properties and values, and the fourth lists all the character entities. Within each section, the items are listed alphabetically by tag or property for easy reference. So, for example, the anchor tag <A> comes before the address tag <ADDRESS>.

Uniform Resource Locator

The URL (Uniform Resource Locator) is not a tag; it is a standard method for inserting document linking information into an HTML document. The structure of a URL is expressed as resource_type://host.domain:port/pathname. The possible resource types include file, http, news, gopher, telnet, ftp, and wais. Each resource type interprets the pathname in its own way, and note that each resource type relates to a specific server type. The domain name may be optionally followed by a colon and an integer TCP port number, which is used when a server is listening on a nonstandard port. If the port number is absent, the standard port number is used. The standard port for WWW servers is :80. Most URLs don't require a port number.

For example, the following link refers to a page showing all the current work being done by the World Wide Web Consortium (W3C), which is the organization responsible for coordinating and defining Net protocols and languages like HTTP and HTML:

```
http://www.w3.org/pub/WWW/TR/Overview.html
```

You would use the following URL to point to a local home page on the C drive in the http directory:

```
file:///HardDisk/http/home.html
```

Notice that the URL section containing the host and domain name is missing in this reference since this file is located on the local host. In this case, the two forward slashes separating the host and domain name section from the pathname are directly before the single forward slash marking the beginning of the pathname.

Section I: Markup Tags

An HTML markup tag may include a name, some attributes, and some text or hypertext. Each markup tag has a specific name and is bracketed by the < (less than) and > (greater than) symbols. Tag names are not case sensitive, so the tag <DL COMPACT>, for example, is exactly the same as <dl compact>. For easier reading, we display all tags in uppercase letters.

Depending on the type of tag, it will use one of three formats:

- `<tag_name>`
- `<tag_name>...</tag_name>`
- `<tag_name attribute_name="argument">...</tag_name>`

The first type indicates a tag that stands alone and affects the information that follows in some way. For example, the <DD> tag marks the following item in the document as a definition description.

The second type of tag encloses some portion of the document, which may consist of text, graphics, or other HTML commands—or all of these. For example:

```
<TITLE>My Home Page</TITLE>
```

creates a title element in a document. Both the beginning and ending tags are required to specify which text is affected by the tag.

The last type of tag also uses beginning and ending tags to enclose some portion of the document, but in addition, attribute information can be inserted within the tag itself. Attributes can be used in either of two formats. The first format is simply the attribute name itself, like this:

```
<tag_name attribute_name>
```

For example, the tag <DL COMPACT> defines a definition list that is presented in a compacted form, as indicated by the attribute COMPACT.

In the second format, the attribute has an argument associated with it, like this:

```
<tag_name attribute_name="argument">
```

For example, the anchor tag <A NAME="Tag1"> is an anchor tag that marks a location named "Tag1." Arguments that are text information usually must be enclosed in double quotation marks; attributes that are numbers usually can be inserted without quotations. However, most browsers will accept quotation marks around any argument, so inserting them, even if they are not required, is usually acceptable.

Because HTML is an evolving standard, not all documents use all these tags or follow all these rules. In a similar way, not all browsers or servers will understand and present information with all of these tags. The listings here will give you a way to determine the use and visual presentation of most standard HTML tags for your documents. In particular, to allow older HTML documents to remain readable, the <HTML>, <HEAD>, and <BODY> tags are optional within HTML documents.

NOTE *We noted in the main part of this book that using RGB color values is more accurate than using color names when assigning colors, and we recommended that you use hexadecimal RGB settings whenever possible. When describing tags in this section, we will use the keyword "color" where appropriate to show that you may use either color names or RGB color values in setting the colors. However, to make the examples easier to follow, we have used the standard color names rather than hexadecimal RGB values. If these were pages for publication, we'd still recommend that you use RGB values for all the reasons we gave earlier.*

Anchor

<A> . . . </A>

Defines an anchor tag. An anchor is either the origin or destination of a hyperlink within the document.

Syntax
```
<A NAME="Anchor_Name" | HREF="URL|#Anchor_Name |
URL?search_word+search_word"  REL="relationship" |REV="relationship" |
TITLE="HREF_document_name"  >Hypertext</A>
```

Attributes & Their Arguments

The anchor tag has two attributes: HREF and NAME. An anchor must include either a NAME or an HREF attribute and may include both.

NAME="anchor_name"
The "anchor_name" defines a target location in a document. This target location can be referenced by other anchors in the document by using the "anchor_name" as part of an HREF attribute within another anchor tag.

HREF="#anchor_name"
Links to a location in the same document.

HREF="URL"
Links to another file or resource.

HREF="URL#anchor_name"
Links to a target location in another document.

HREF="URL?search_word+search_word"
Sends a search string to a server. Different servers may interpret the search string differently. In the case of word-oriented search engines, multiple search words might be specified by separating individual words with a plus sign (+).

In addition to these, there are three optional attributes: REV, REL, and TITLE. However, these attributes are not widely used in the anchor tag.

REL="relationship"
Defines the relative relationship between the anchor document and the link URL given in the HREF attribute.

REV="relationship"
Defines the reverse relative relationship between the link URL given in the HREF attribute and the anchor document. This is the reverse of the specification provided by the REL attribute.

TITLE="HREF_document_name"
Indicates the document title of the document pointed to by HREF. This is not used much by current browsers. It might be useful when the link is to a document that doesn't have an internal name, such as a Gopher menu. You can use this attribute to display a title along with the menu.

Examples   **A link to a page at another location**
The following includes an HREF that links to The Coriolis Group's home page:

`<A HREF="http://www.coriolis.com/">The Coriolis Group</A>`

A local link to a file
This HREF points to the local file product.zip in the files directory:

`<A HREF="/files/product.zip">Our Product listing</A>`

A link within a page
The following example uses the HREF attribute to specify the destination anchor named *end*:

`<A HREF="#end">Jump to Conclusions</A>`
In order to move to the destination labeled *end*, the document must also include an anchor with the NAME attribute set to *end* (as shown below) at the end of the document:

`<A NAME="end"></A>`

A link to a target location in another document
Similar to a link within a page, this link must include the HREF attribute to specify the document (order.html) as well as the destination anchor within the document(feedback):

`<A HREF="order.html#feedback">Place an order</A>`
In order to move to the destination, the document order.html must exist and must include an anchor with the NAME attribute set to *feedback*, like this:

`<A NAME="feedback"></A>`

See Also   LINK, URL, IMG, and FORM

Address   `<ADDRESS> . . . </ADDRESS>`

Purpose Defines a signature or address. This tag is normally used at the bottom or top
of a page to provide address, signature, or other author information.

Syntax `<ADDRESS>Signature</ADDRESS>`

Attributes & Their Arguments

None.

Example The following inserts the author's name and e-mail address on two separate
lines. Note that the <ADDRESS> tag forces a paragraph break:

`<ADDRESS> Brent Heslop <BR> bheslop@bookware.com </ADDRESS>`

See Also BLOCKQUOTE, BODY, BR, and FORM

Applet   `<APPLET> . . . </APPLET>`

Purpose Embeds a Java applet in the document.

Syntax `<APPLET CODE="class_name" HEIGHT=x WIDTH=y [ALIGN="keyword" ALT="textstring"`
`CODEBASE="URL" HSPACE=h VSPACE=v NAME="namestring"] >`

Attributes & Their Arguments

The applet tag has three required attributes: CODE, WIDTH, and HEIGHT; it
also has several optional attributes: ALT, ALIGN, CODEBASE, HSPACE,
VSPACE, and NAME.

CODE="class_name"
Specifies the name of the Java class that is to be run. This is always a relative
name; if you need to specify the path information for this name, you must use
the CODEBASE attribute.

HEIGHT=x
Specifies the intended height of the applet window in pixels. When this attribute is used with WIDTH, the browser reserves screen space for the display
before the applet begins running, thus speeding up display of the page.

WIDTH=y
Specifies the intended width of the applet window in pixels. When this attribute is used with HEIGHT, the browser reserves screen space for the display before the applet begins running, thus speeding up display of the page.

ALIGN="keyword"
Specifies a position relative to surrounding text. Possible keyword entries are: "left" | "right" | "top" | "texttop" | "middle" | "absmiddle" | "baseline" | "bottom" | "absbottom." The meaning and use of these keywords is the same as for the <IMG> tag.

ALT="textstring"
Allows a text string to be displayed in place of the applet in browsers that recognize the <APPLET> tag but cannot run Java code.

CODEBASE="URL"
If CODEBASE is present, it is used as the base URL for finding the applet code. If this attribute is not specified, then the document's base URL is used.

HSPACE=h
This attribute sets white space (in pixels) to the immediate left and right of the image. By default, HSPACE is a small nonzero number.

VSPACE=v
This attribute sets white space (in pixels) immediately above and below the image. By default, VSPACE is a small nonzero number.

NAME="namestring"
This optional attribute specifies a name for this instance of the applet. This makes it possible to distinguish between multiple occurrences of the same applet code on one page and for applets on the same page to find (and communicate with) each other.

Associated Tag: Parameter <PARAM>

Purpose   Defines any parameters that must be passed to the applet. The only way to specify applet-specific parameters is to use PARAM elements. Applets read user-specified values for parameters with the getParameter() method.

Syntax   `<APPLET CODE="class_name" WIDTH=x HEIGHT=y>`
`<PARAM NAME="namestring" VALUE="parameters"> ...</APPLET>`

Attributes & Their Arguments

The NAME attribute specifies the parameter name, while the VALUE attribute specifies the parameter values.

Examples **A simple applet**

The following might be used to execute an applet from a navigation bar:

```
<APPLET CODE="NavBar.class" WIDTH=80 HEIGHT=400 ALT="Nav Bar -- Requires
Java"> Java-enabled Navigation</APPLET>
```

An applet with parameters

The following might be used to display an animation on a page:

```
<APPLET CODE="JumpAround.class" WIDTH=400 HEIGHT=68 ALT="Jumping Man
display"> <PARAM NAME="useGif" VALUE="Man01.gif">Java Applet to display a
jumping man.</APPLET>
```

See Also SCRIPT

Bold   `<B> . . . </B>`

Purpose Displays the text between the tags in boldface type. The strong tag is more general.

Syntax `<B>Text</B>`

Attributes & Their Arguments

None.

Example The following markup defines the enclosed text to be displayed in a bold font:

```
<B>The Coriolis Group</B>
```

See Also EM, I, STRONG, and TT

Base Tag <BASE>

Purpose Specifies the pathname to be used to resolve relative addresses within the document. This is useful when link references within the document do not include full pathnames (i.e., are relative pathnames).

Syntax `<BASE HREF="URL">`

Attributes & Their Arguments

The base tag has one required HREF attribute.

HREF="URL"
Can link to a location on the site, or may link to another server or system.

Examples **A pointer to a remote server or system**
Generally, all pointers used in a document for local links use relative addressing. This means that the links within the document will work even when the document and its associated files are moved to a different location. However, if the server cannot find a link, the base tag provides a pointer to the original location of the links. For example, this HREF points to the files directory on The Coriolis Group's server:

`<BASE HREF="http://www.coriolis.com/files">`
All relative anchor references in the document would use this as a base when accessing relative file information if a reference could not be found on the local server. For example, an HREF that points to the local file product.zip would be inserted into the document as:

`<A HREF="product.zip">Our Product listing</A>`
The server would first look for this file in the current directory that holds the document; if it was not found there, the server would concatenate the anchor tag and the base information to access the following reference:

`http://www.coriolis.com/files/product.zip`

See Also A and HEAD

Basefont

<BASEFONT>

Purpose Sets the base font size. The base font size applies to the normal and preformatted text but not to headings, except where they are modified by using the FONT element with a relative font size.

Syntax `<BASEFONT SIZE=number>`

Attributes & Their Arguments

The basefont tag has one required SIZE attribute.

SIZE=number
Establishes the desired size for the text between the <FONT> tags. The number argument may be an integer from 1 to 7 that sets the font to the new size. The default basefont size is 3.

Example You can set the base font to a smaller size if you wish to display more text on a standard browser page. For example, this code will set the displayed font to one size smaller than normal:

`<BASEFONT SIZE=2>`

See Also FONT and STYLE

Block Quote

<BLOCKQUOTE> . . . </BLOCKQUOTE>

Purpose Formats a section of quoted text.

Syntax `<BLOCKQUOTE>Block of text</BLOCKQUOTE>`

Attributes & Their Arguments

None.

Examples The following block quote displays as an indented, single-spaced block of text, which is separated from the body text by a paragraph break:

```
<BODY>A recent press release from Canyon software tells you about their new
software.
<BLOCKQUOTE><I>Drag And Zip</I>, Drag And File's built-in Zip Manager, links
directly to Internet World Wide Web browsers including Mosaic and Netscape.
Drag And Zip also supports files compressed with PKZIP, LHA and GZIP
programs and has a built-in virus scanner.
</BLOCKQUOTE></BODY>
```

See Also   BODY, P, and PRE

Body

`<BODY>` . . . `</BODY>`

Purpose   Defines the beginning and ending of the actual document contents. Distinguished from the Head section of the document.

Syntax   `<BODY [BACKGROUND="image_URL" BGCOLOR="color" TEXT="color" LINK="color"`
`VLINK="color" ALINK="color"] >`

Attributes & Their Arguments

BACKGROUND="image_URL"
Specifies a URL that points to an image to be used as background for the body of the document. The image is tiled to fill the background viewing area.

BGCOLOR="color"
Specifies a background color for the body of the document. The argument "color" is either a standard color name or a set of three hexadecimal numbers in the format #rrggbb that specifies the color you wish to be displayed.

TEXT="color"
Specifies the color of all text in the document that is not specially colored to indicate a link or other special attribute. The argument "color" is either a standard color name or a set of three hexadecimal numbers in the format #rrggbb that specifies the color you wish to be displayed.

LINK="color"
Specifies a color for body text that gives link information. The argument "color" is either a standard color name or a set of three hexadecimal numbers in the format #rrggbb that specifies the color you wish to be displayed. The default color is blue (#0000FF).

VLINK="color"
Specifies a color for body text showing a link that has already been visited. The argument "color" is either a standard color name or a set of three hexadecimal numbers in the format #rrggbb that specifies the color you wish to be displayed. The default color is purple (#FF00FF).

ALINK="color"
Specifies a color for body text showing a link that is currently activated. The argument "color" is either a standard color name or a set of three hexadecimal numbers in the format #rrggbb that specifies the color you wish to be displayed. The default color is red (#FF0000).

Examples When the body tag is used without any attributes, as shown below, everything inside the body tags (unless otherwise specified) is displayed using the browser's defaults:

```
<BODY>This text will display as a single paragraph
</BODY>
```

You can gain more control by using attributes with the body tag. For example, the following displays white text on a black background with links displayed in red.

```
<BODY BGCOLOR="black" TEXT="white" LINK="red">This text will display as a
single paragraph of white text on a black background. This <A
HREF="test.html">link</A> will display in red.
</BODY>
```

See Also HEAD and HTML

Break

Purpose Forces a line break without beginning a new paragraph so text retains whatever styles are specified for the paragraph.

Syntax `<BR CLEAR="keyword" >`

Attributes & Their Arguments

CLEAR="keyword"

The CLEAR attribute specifies whether to take floating images into account when producing a break. Possible keywords are "left," "right," and "all."

- CLEAR="left" inserts a line break in the text and moves vertically down until the left margin is clear.
- CLEAR="right" inserts a line break in the text and moves vertically down until the right margin is clear.
- CLEAR="all" inserts a line break in the text and moves vertically down until both margins are clear.

Example The following inserts the author's name and e-mail address on two separate lines. The break tag forces a new line immediately after the name but retains the address tag style for the e-mail address:

```
<ADDRESS> Brent Heslop <BR>bheslop@bookware.com
</ADDRESS>
```

See Also P and PRE

Center <CENTER> . . . </CENTER>

Purpose Centers the enclosed text. This is an obsolete tag that has been replaced by the more flexible <DIV> tag. It is retained for compatibility with older documents, but it should not be used in new documents.

Syntax `<CENTER>Text</CENTER>`

Attributes & Their Arguments

None.

Example The following shows an example of centered text:

```
<CENTER>This text will be centered on the line.</CENTER>
```

See Also DIV, IMG, and TABLE

Citation `<CITE> . . . </CITE>`

Purpose Style tag for display of a citation. Text is typically displayed in italics or underlined.

Syntax `<CITE>Citation text</CITE>`

Attributes & Their Arguments

None.

Example The following shows how a typical citation might appear in a document:

```
<CITE>Caesar: The Gallic War; English Translation by H. J. Edwards, C.B.;
Loeb Classical Library, Cambridge, MCMLXXIX </CITE>
```

See Also B, EM, STRONG, and TT

Code `<CODE> . . . </CODE>`

Purpose Defines a text element to be rendered in a format suitable for computer program text. Text is usually rendered in a monospaced font.

Syntax `<CODE>code_text</CODE>`

Attributes & Their Arguments

None.

Example The following is a sample of computer code rendered in a code tag:

```
<CODE>class CErectorView : public CView</CODE>
```

See Also PRE and TT

Definition

`<DFN> . . . </DFN>`

Purpose Displays a term (usually a definition) using emphasized text (generally bold or italic). Similar to the strong tag. This is an HTML 3.2 tag and may not yet be supported by all browsers.

Syntax `<DFN>Text</DFN>`

Attributes & Their Arguments

None.

Example The following includes a definition item within a normal text paragraph:

```
<P>In Windows, <DFN>resources</DFN> are user-interface items (like menus,
icons, and dialog boxes)that are used to interact with the user. </P>
```

See Also VAR, STRONG, DL, B, I, and U

Directory List

`<DIR> . . . </DIR>`

Purpose Defines a list of directory items. A directory list is an unordered list consisting of one or more List Item tags. List items in this type of list should be less than 24 characters long. The intention is to generate a short, concise list. This limit is not generally enforced by browsers. If you exceed this limit, however, the displayed list may not look as you intended. Note that directory lists should not be nested.

Syntax `<DIR [COMPACT]>`

Attributes & Their Arguments

The definition list tag has one optional attribute.

COMPACT
This attribute requests the browser to display the list using a minimum amount of indentation and white space.

Associated Tag: List element   `<LI> . . .`

Purpose   Defines an element in a list. Note that this tag should never be used outside of a list definition tag as it may not be correctly displayed by a browser. Also notice that this tag does not have a matching termination.

Syntax   `<DIR><LI> List_element</DIR>`

Attributes & Their Arguments

None.

Example   The following displays a directory list with three entries:

`<DIR> <LI>First Directory Entry <LI>Second Directory Entry <LI>And so on...`
`</DIR>`

See Also   DL, MENU, OL, and UL

Division   `<DIV> . . . </DIV>`

Purpose   Provides alignment specification for any enclosed elements, including text and images. Note that <DIV> behaves like a new paragraph and will terminate a preceding <P> tag.

Syntax   `<DIV ALIGN="keyword">...</DIV>`

Attributes & Their Arguments

`ALIGN="keyword"`
Specifies how to align the elements within the browser's display. Possible keyword entries are "center," "left," and "right."

- ALIGN="center" aligns the enclosed elements in the center of the browser's display area.

- ALIGN="left" aligns the enclosed elements flush left in the browser's display area.

■ ALIGN="right" aligns the enclosed elements flush right in the browser's display area.

Example   The following shows an example of centered text:

```
<DIV ALIGN=center">This text will be centered in the browser window.</DIV>
```

See Also   CENTER, IMG, and TABLE

Definition List   <DL> . . . </DL>

Purpose   Presents a list of items and their definitions; it may also be used for a glossary. A definition list is an unordered list consisting of one or more definition term tags and an associated definition description tag. These tags always occur together in the list, and each list element is composed of one set of tags.

Associated Tag: Definition Term   <DT> . . .

Purpose   Marks a term to be defined within a Definition List. Note that this tag should never be used outside of a definition list tag as it may not be correctly displayed by the browser. Also notice that this tag does not have a matching termination. It must be followed by a definition description tag.

Associated Tag: Definition Description   <DD> . . .

Purpose   Provides the definition text for the associated definition term tag within a definition list. Note that this tag should never be used outside of a definition list tag as it may not be correctly displayed by the browser. Also notice that this tag does not have a matching termination. It must be preceded by a definition term tag.

Syntax   `<DL [COMPACT]> <DT>Defintion_term <DD>Definition_text </DL>`

Attributes & Their Arguments

The definition list tag has one optional attribute.

COMPACT

This attribute saves display space by requesting that the browser display shorter terms and their descriptions on the same line whenever possible.

Example   The following displays a definition list with two entries:

```
<DL> <DT>First Term <DD>Definition of First Term <DT>Second Term
<DD>Definition of Second Term </DL>
```

See Also   DIR, MENU, OL, and UL

Emphasis   `<EM> . . . </EM>`

Purpose   Displays the text within the tags in emphasized format (usually italic). The important point is that the emphasized text is noticeably different from the surrounding normal text.

Syntax   `<EM>Text</EM>`

Attributes & Their Arguments

None.

Example   The following markup creates a text element that is emphasized (usually in italic font):

```
<EM>coriolis</EM>
```

See Also   B, I, STRONG, and TT

Font <FONT> . . . </ FONT>

Purpose Changes the size and color of the enclosed text from the size set by the basefont tag (or from the default size if no basefont tag has been set). Where possible, using an appropriate STYLE element is preferable to using the <FONT> tag.

Syntax `<FONT COLOR="color" SIZE=number>Text</FONT>`

Attributes & Their Arguments

COLOR="color"
Specifies the color of the text between the <FONT> tags. The argument "color" is either a standard color name or a set of three hexadecimal numbers in the format #rrggbb that specifies the color you wish to be displayed.

SIZE=number
Establishes the desired size for the text between the <FONT> tags. The number argument may be an integer from 1 to 7 that sets the font to the new size. The number may be preceded by + or – to indicate a relative change to the basefont size. The default basefont size is 3.

Examples The following defines the font for the enclosed text to be larger than the current basefont size:

```
<FONT SIZE=+2><P>This is larger type for easier reading.
</P></FONT>
```

The following defines the color for the enclosed text to be red rather than the default color:

```
<FONT COLOR="red"><P>Please note the following items.
</P></FONT>
```

See Also BASEFONT and STYLE

Header Tags

`<H1> . . . </H1>` Most prominent header

```
<H2>...</H2>
<H3>...</H3>
<H4>...</H4>
<H5>...</H5>
<H6>...</H6> Least prominent header
```

Purpose Defines the data contained between the tags as a text header. There are six descending categories of headers. The first header tag, <H1>, is the most prominent, and each successive level is less prominent but still distinct from the normal text and from the others. Headings are generally distinguished by size and bold type, but a browser may use another method of display if required.

Syntax `<Hn [ALIGN="keyword"]>Header_text</Hn>`

Attributes & Their Arguments

The header tag has one optional attribute: ALIGN. If the ALIGN attribute is not specified, the heading uses a default alignment supplied by the browser.

ALIGN="keyword"
Specifies a position relative to surrounding text. Possible keyword entries are "center" | "left" | "right."

- ALIGN="center" aligns the heading in the center of the text area in the browser window.

- ALIGN="left" aligns the heading flush left.

- ALIGN="right" aligns the heading flush right.

Examples The following shows a series of headers:

```
<H1>Major Heading</H1>
<H2 ALIGN="center">First sub-heading, centered</H2>
<H3>Minor heading</H3>
<H3>Another minor heading</H3>
<H2 ALIGN="left">Final sub-heading, displayed flush left</H2>
```

See Also BODY and HEAD

Head `<HEAD> . . . </HEAD>`

Purpose Defines the part of the document that contains general data about the page. Distinguished from the Body section of the document. Data between the `<HEAD>` tags is not displayed in the browser. If you include title information, however, it will be displayed in the browser's title bar.

Syntax `<HEAD>Header information</HEAD>`

Attributes & Their Arguments

None.

Examples The head tag defines the page description and information elements of the document. They are placed ahead of the body of the document. For example:

```
<HEAD><TITLE>Minimum Page</TITLE></HEAD> <BODY>This is a minimum of text to
be inserted into the body of a document. It will display as a single
paragraph
</BODY>
```

See Also BODY and HTML

Horizontal Rule `<HR>`

Purpose Draws a horizontal rule across the width of the document. The browser controls the size and presentation of the line, and some browsers may render a line of fixed length.

Syntax `<HR ALIGN="keyword" NOSHADE SIZE=number WIDTH=value >`

Attributes & Their Arguments

`ALIGN="keyword"`
For rules that are not the full document width, the ALIGN attribute specifies where the rule is to be placed. Possible keyword entries are ["left" | "right" | "center"].

NOSHADE

Specifies that you want a solid rule instead of the default horizontal rule, which is a shaded, engraved line.

SIZE=number

Defines the vertical size of the rule in pixels.

WIDTH=value

Specifies the width of the rule. The default rule is automatically the width of the page. The value argument is [number | percent], which allows you to specify the width of the rule in pixels or as a percentage of the document width.

Example   The following inserts a centered horizontal line half the width of the browser window between the two paragraphs of text:

```
<P> This is two paragraphs of text divided by a single, horizontal line.</P>
<HR ALIGN="center" WIDTH="50%"> </P> This is the second paragraph of text.
</P>
```

See Also   BR and P

HTML   <HTML> . . . </HTML>

Purpose   Specifies that the data contained between the tags be in HTML format.

Syntax   `<HTML>Document_data</HTML>`

Attributes & Their Arguments

None.

Example   The HTML tag defines the entire document. They are placed around the contents of the document. For example:

```
<HTML>
<HEAD><TITLE>Minimum Page</TITLE></HEAD> <BODY>This is a minimum of text to
be inserted into the body of a document. It will display as a single
paragraph
</BODY>
</HTML>
```

See Also   BODY and HEAD

Italic   `<I> . . . </I>`

Purpose   Presents the text within the tags in italic type.

Syntax   `<I>Text</I>`

Attributes & Their Arguments

None.

Examples   The following markup displays the enclosed text in an italic font:

`<I>Looking Good in Print, R. Parker, Ventana Press</I>`

See Also   B, EM, STRONG, and TT

Image   `<IMG> . . . </IMG>`

Purpose   Embeds a graphic image in the document.

Syntax   `<IMG SRC="URL" [ALT="textstring" ALIGN="keyword" HEIGHT=x WIDTH=y BORDER=n HSPACE=h VSPACE=v USEMAP="URL" ISMAP] >`

Attributes & Their Arguments

The image tag has one required attribute: SRC; it has several optional attributes: ALT, ALIGN HEIGHT, WIDTH, BORDER, HSPACE, VSPACE, USEMAP, and ISMAP.

SRC="URL"
Specifies the location of the image that is to be rendered by the browser in the document at the point where the image tag is located.

ALT="textstring"
Allows a text string to be put in place of the image in browsers that cannot display images.

ALIGN="keyword"
Specifies a position relationship to surrounding text. Possible keyword entries are "left" | "right" | "top" | "texttop" | "middle" | "absmiddle" | "baseline" | "bottom" | "absbottom."

- ALIGN="left" defines a floating image. The image is rendered at the left margin and subsequent lines of text are wrapped around the right side of the image.

- ALIGN="right" defines a floating image. The image is rendered at the right margin and subsequent lines of text are wrapped around the left side of the image.

- ALIGN="top" aligns the top of the image with the top of the tallest element in the line of surrounding text. This is the same as the standard behavior.

- ALIGN="textop" aligns the top of the image with the top of the tallest text in the line of surrounding text. This is usually, but not always, the same as ALIGN="top."

- ALIGN="middle" aligns the center of the image with the baseline of the line of surrounding text. This is the same as the standard behavior.

- ALIGN="absmiddle" aligns the center of the image with the center of the surrounding text line.

- ALIGN="baseline" aligns the base of the image with the baseline of the surrounding text line. This is the same as ALIGN="bottom."

- ALIGN="bottom" aligns the base of the image with the baseline of the surrounding text line. This is the same as the standard behavior.

- ALIGN="absbottom" aligns the base of the image with the bottom of the surrounding text.

WIDTH=y

Specifies the intended width of the image in pixels. When given with the height, this attribute allows the browser to reserve screen space for the image before the image data has arrived over the network, thus speeding up display of the page.

HEIGHT=x

Specifies the intended height of the image in pixels. When given with the width, this attribute allows the browser to reserve screen space for the image before the image data has arrived over the network, thus speeding up display of the page.

BORDER=n

When the IMG tag is used as part of a hypertext link, the integer value argument defines the thickness of the border around the image. The integer argument may be 0, indicating no border. Note that BORDER=0 on images that are part of a link may confuse users who are accustomed to seeing a colored border around active images.

HSPACE=h

Sets white space to the immediate left and right of the image. The HSPACE attribute sets the width of the white space in pixels. By default, HSPACE is a small nonzero number.

VSPACE=v

Sets white space to the immediate top and bottom of the image. The VSPACE attribute sets the height of the white space in pixels. By default, VSPACE is a small nonzero number.

USEMAP="URL"

If USEMAP is present and the image tag is within an anchor, the image will become a "clickable image." The URL specified must be a client-side image map identified by the <MAP> element.

ISMAP

If ISMAP is present and the image tag is within an anchor, the image will become a "clickable image." The pixel coordinates of the cursor will be appended to the URL specified in the anchor if the user clicks within the ISMAP image. The resulting URL will take the form "URL?m,n", where m and n are integer coordinates.

Examples   **A simple image**

The following is a typical image tag that might be used to display a picture of the author of a page:

```
<H3> <IMG HREF="author.gif" ALIGN="top" WIDTH=50 HEIGHT=80 ALT="Brent
Heslop"> My Picture </H3>
```

An image within an anchor tag

A better way to use the image might be to link the image tag to an anchor tag that references a resumé, for example:

```
<A HREF="bio.html"> <IMG HREF="author.gif" ALIGN="top" WIDTH=50 HEIGHT=80
BORDER=0 ALT="Brent Heslop"> My Resum$eacute; </A>
```

See Also   A and FORM

Indexed Tag

<ISINDEX>

Purpose   Specifies that the current document describes a database that can be searched using the index search method appropriate for whatever client is being used to read the document. This tag occurs in the Head section of the document. It is meaningful only if the document resides on a server that provides indexing services. For this reason, you should be careful about adding this tag manually. Most servers that support searching will add this element automatically to the document when they send it.

Syntax   `<ISINDEX [PROMPT="text"] >`

Attributes & Their Arguments

PROMPT="keyword"

Specifies the message that should appear in front of the search window. The default message (used by the standard search tag) is "This is a searchable index. Enter search keywords:"

Example   The following markup defines an indexable document:

```
<HEAD> <TITLE>An Indexable Document</TITLE> <ISINDEX></HEAD>
```

See Also   HEAD and TITLE

Keyboard Input Tag <KBD> . . . </KBD>

Purpose   Defines a text element that defines a sequence of characters to be entered by the user from a keyboard. This is intended for use in instructional or other text as a distinctive graphic element to show users what to enter. This is not a fill-out section of a form. Text is usually rendered in a monospaced font.

Syntax   `<KBD>user_entry_text</KBD>`

Attributes & Their Arguments

None.

Example   The following is a sample of keyboard code rendered in a keyboard input tag:

```
<P>When requested, enter your user name at the login: prompt, like this
<KBD>login: dh</KBD></P>
```

See Also   FORM and PRE

Link Tag <LINK>

Purpose   Defines a link with another document. The link tag allows you to define relationships between the document containing the link tag and the document specified in the HREF attribute. A link tag must contain an HREF attribute.

Syntax   `<LINK HREF="URL" [ REL="relationship" |REV="relationship" | TITLE="HREF_document_name" ] >`

Attributes & Their Arguments

The link tag has one required attribute: HREF; it has three optional attributes: REL, REV, and TITLE.

HREF="URL"
Defines the link between this document and another entity, which is usually specified by the REL or REV attributes.

REL="relationship"
Defines the relationship between this document and the link URL given in the HREF attribute.

REV="relationship"
Defines the relationship between the link URL given in the HREF attribute and this document. This is the reverse of the specification provided by the REL attribute.

TITLE="HREF_document_name"
Indicates the title of the document pointed to by the HREF attribute. This is not used much by current browsers. It is most useful when the link is to a document that does not have an internal name, such as a Gopher menu. This lets you display the menu with a name in the browser window.

Examples
A simple link
The following includes an HREF that points to Ventana's home page and indicates that Ventana Media was the maker of this document:

```
<LINK HREF="http://www.vmedia.com/" REL="made">
```

A link within a series
The following example shows links for a document that represents Chapter 2 (chapt2.html) in a series of chapters:

```
<HEAD> <TITLE>Chapter 2: How I grew up</TITLE> <LINK HREF="http://
www.myserver.com/Bio/chap3.html" REL="precedes" <LINK HREF="http://
www.myserver.com/Bio/chap1.html" REV="supercedes" </HEAD>
```

See Also A and FORM

Listing Tag   `<LISTING> . . . </LISTING>`

Purpose Displays example computer listing; similar to the preformatted text tag except that no embedded tags will be recognized. To preserve formatting, the text is displayed in a monospaced font. This is an obsolete tag; the preformatted text tag is preferred.

Syntax `<LISTING>Text</LISTING >`

Attributes & Their Arguments

None.

Example   The following shows how you may use text in a listing text block:

`<LISTING>This is sample listing text</LISTING>`

See Also   XMP and PRE

Map Tag   `<MAP> . . . </MAP>`

Purpose   Defines a client-side image map, which differs from the server-side image map
in that the processing for the map is done in the browser rather than being
sent back to the server. This increases speed and minimizes handling. Generally, you will prefer to use client-side image maps when the browser supports
them.

Syntax   `<MAP [NAME="namestring"]>`

Attributes & Their Arguments

`NAME="namestring"`
Associates a name with a map. This attribute is then used by the USEMAP
attribute on the IMG element to reference the map. Note that the value of the
NAME attribute is case sensitive.

Associated Tag: AREA Tag   `<AREA>`

Purpose   Defines an active area in the associated image map. Note that this tag should
never be used outside of an image map as it may not be correctly interpreted
by a browser. Also notice that this tag does not have a matching termination.

Syntax   `<MAP><AREA HREF="URL"|NOHREF ALT="text" SHAPE="keyword" COORDS="c1, c2,`
`c3...."></MAP>`

Attributes & Their Arguments

HREF="URL" | NOHREF

Defines the target of the hypertext link pointed to by the area. The NOHREF attribute can be used to define an area on the image map that is inactive. This is particularly useful if you wish to define an inactive area inside an active area.

ALT="text"

Allows a text string to be displayed in the status line as the mouse moves over the active area in the image map.

SHAPE="keyword" COORDS="c1, c2, c3..."

These two keywords together define an active area on the image map. The coordinate values required depend on the SHAPE keyword. Coordinates are given in pixels from the top, left corner of the image used as the map. Possible combinations are as follows:

```
SHAPE=rect COORDS="left-x, top-y, right-x, bottom-y"

SHAPE=circle COORDS="center-x, center-y, radius"

SHAPE=poly COORDS="x1,y1, x2,y2, x3,y3, ..."
```

Example   The following displays a navigation bar with two rectangular active areas and one circular one:

```
<MAP NAME="NavMap">
<AREA HREF="search.html" ALT="Search by keyword" SHAPE=rect
COORDS="0,0,80,40">
<AREA HREF="news.html" ALT="News & Events" SHAPE=rect COORDS="0,50,80,90">
<AREA HREF="feedback.html" ALT="Let us know what you think" SHAPE=circle
COORDS="40,130,30"> </MAP>
```

See Also   IMG

Menu Tag   `<MENU> . . . </MENU>`

Purpose   Defines a list of menu items. A menu list is an unordered list consisting of one or more list item tags. Each item in this type of list should be a single line. The list generated on a browser may be rendered more compactly than an Unordered List. Note that menu lists should not be nested.

Syntax   `<MENU [COMPACT]>`

Attributes & Their Arguments

The definition list tag has one optional attribute.

COMPACT
Requests that the browser display the list using a minimum amount of indentation and white space.

Associated Tag: List Item Tag <LI>

Purpose   Defines an element in a list. Note that this tag should never be used outside of a list definition tag as it may not be correctly displayed by a browser. Also notice that this tag does not have a matching termination.

Syntax   `<MENU><LI> List_element</MENU>`

Attributes & Their Arguments

None.

Example   The following displays a menu list with three entries:

`<MENU> <LI>First Menu Item <LI>Second Menu Item <LI>Third Menu Item </MENU>`

See Also   UL, OL, DL, and DIR

Meta Tag <META>

Purpose   The META element can be used to include arbitrary name/value pairs describing properties of the document, such as author, a list of key words, and so on.

Syntax   `<META NAME="name"|HTTP-EQUIV="keyword" CONTENT="value" >`

Attributes & Their Arguments

The NAME attribute specifies the property name while the CONTENT attribute specifies the property value.

A special version of the <META> tag allows you to influence how the client treats the page. The HTTP-EQUIV attribute can be used in place of the NAME attribute and has a special significance when documents are retrieved via the HyperText Transfer Protocol (HTTP), as most Web documents are. HTTP servers may use the property name specified by the HTTP-EQUIV attribute to create a header in the HTTP response, which sets certain values that are used by the client. For example, inserting the following META data tag:

```
<META HTTP-EQUIV="Expires" CONTENT="Tue, 20 Aug 1996 14:25:27 GMT">
```

will result in the following HTTP header being sent by the server to the client:

```
    Expires: Tue, 20 Aug 1996 14:25:27 GMT
```

This can be used by caches to determine when to fetch a fresh copy of the associated document. If you intend to use this feature, see the HTTP specification and your server documentation for complete details.

Example The following shows how you might use meta data in a document to specify a publication number for the document:

```
<META NAME="PubNo" CONTENT="5145-9168 (3/97)">
```

See Also HEAD

Nobreak Tag (Netscape Extension)   `<NOBR> . . . </NOBR>`

Purpose Forces enclosed text to stay together without any line breaks.

Syntax `<NOBR>Text</NOBR>`

Attributes & Their Arguments

None.

Example The following shows a single line of text that will be kept together on one line by the nobreak tag:

```
<NOBR>This text must stay together on one line. </NOBR>
```

See Also BR and WBR

Ordered List Tag

<OL> . . . </OL>

Purpose   Defines an ordered (numbered) list consisting of one or more list item tags.

Syntax   `<OL [TYPE="style" START=n COMPACT]>...</OL>`

Attributes & Their Arguments

There are three optional attributes: TYPE, START, and COMPACT. The COM-PACT attribute asks the browser to display the list in a more compact format; however, many browsers ignore this.

TYPE="style"
Allows you to specify how you want list items marked. Use of the TYPE attribute in the list tag affects the entire list; use of the attribute in a list item tag affects that tag and all subsequent tags. Possible style keyword entries are as shown in the following table:

Type Keyword	Numbering Style	Numbering Sequence
1	Arabic numbers	1, 2, 3, ...
a	lower alpha	a, b, c, ...
A	upper alpha	A, B, C, ...
i	lower Roman	i, ii, iii, ...
I	upper Roman	I, II, III, ...

START="n"
Allows you to specify the starting position in the list numbering scheme. Note that this is always a Roman numeral, even if the list type does not use numbers. For example, START=3 for TYPE="a" will set the list to start with "c":

Associated Tag: List Item Tag <LI>

Purpose Defines an element in a list. Note that this tag should never be used outside of a list definition tag as it may not be correctly displayed by a browser. Also notice that this tag does not have a matching termination.

Syntax `<OL><LI [TYPE="style" START=n]> List_element</OL>`

Attributes & Their Arguments

The optional TYPE and START attributes may be specified for individual list elements. If used, they will override any other specification.

Examples **A simple ordered list**
The following displays an ordered list with three entries:

`<OL> <LI>First List Item <LI>Second List Item <LI>And so on... </OL>`

An ordered list nested with other lists
The following list has three items; the first item is a sublist with two items. The numbers start over for each nested list:

```
<OL> <LI>First List Item <OL> <LI>First Sub-Entry Item <LI>second Sub-Entry
Item </OL> <LI>Second List Item. This is a long entry to show how the
browser handles list elements that are longer than a single line. In fact, a
list element may be a significant block of text. <LI>And so on... </OL>
```

See Also UL, DL, DIR, and MENU

Paragraph Tag <P> . . . </P>

Purpose Presents the text within the tags as a single paragraph. The ending tag is not required as the browser will automatically end the paragraph when another paragraph-level tag occurs; however, preferred usage is to include the paragraph text within starting and ending tags.

Syntax `<P [ALIGN="keyword"]>Text</P>`

Attributes & Their Arguments

The optional ALIGN attribute specifies the text placement. If the ALIGN attribute is not specified, the heading has a default alignment supplied by the browser, usually left for most languages.

ALIGN="keyword"
Specifies a position relationship to surrounding text. Possible keyword entries are "center" | "left" | "right."

> ALIGN="center" aligns the heading in the center of the text area in the browser window.

> ALIGN="left" aligns the heading flush left.

> ALIGN="right" aligns the heading flush right.

Examples The following displays two separate paragraphs of text divided by a horizontal rule:

```
<P ALIGN="left"> This is two paragraphs of text divided by a single,
horizontal line. This paragraph is aligned flush left. </P> <HR> <P
ALIGN="right"> This is the second paragraph of text. It is aligned flush
right</P>
```

See Also BR and PRE

Preformatted Text Tag   `<PRE> . . . </PRE>`

Purpose Identifies text that has already been formatted (preformatted) by some other system and must be displayed as is. Preformatted text may include embedded tags that will be interpreted for rendering, but not all tag types are permitted. The preformatted text tag can be used to include tables in documents. To preserve formatting, the text is displayed in a monospaced font. The preformatted text tag is preferred to the obsolete listing <LISTING> and example <XMP> tags.

Syntax `<PRE>Text</PRE>`

Attributes & Their Arguments

The preformatted text tag has one optional attribute.

WIDTH="value"
Tells a browser the maximum width to expect in the block of preformatted text. This allows the browser to adjust the window, and perhaps the font and size of the displayed text, to improve rendering.

Examples   The following shows how you may use text in a preformatted text block:

```
<PRE>
    Act Three, Scene Two
<I>Antony:</I> Friends, Romans, countrymen, lend me your ears
                I come to bury Caesar, not to praise him.
                The evil that men do lives after them,
                the good is oft interred with their bones.
</PRE>
```

See Also   BR, P, CODE, LISTING, and XMP

Sample Tag   `<SAMP> . . . </SAMP>`

Purpose   Defines a text element that represents a series of literal characters. Text is usually rendered in a monospaced font.

Syntax   `<SAMP>sample_text</SAMP>`

Attributes & Their Arguments

None.

Example   The following is a sample of sample text:

```
<SAMP>This is a sequence of sampled characters</SAMP>
```

See Also   CODE, KBD, and PRE

Script Tag <SCRIPT> . . . </SCRIPT>

Purpose Allows you to add script functions to your document; the script functions are processed by the client software.

Syntax `<SCRIPT LANGUAGE="name">`

Attributes & Their Arguments

The required LANGUAGE attribute specifies the scripting language used in the script that follows. Valid language names depend on the browser's support for the language.

Example The following shows how you can insert a script into your document. This script does nothing and consists only of a comment:

```
<SCRIPT LANGUAGE="JavaScript">
// This is a script comment
</SCRIPT>
```

See Also HEAD

Strikeout Tag <STRIKE> . . . </STRIKE>

Purpose Presents the text within the tags in strike-out format (with a line through the text). This is a common style used in legal documents and in revisions and editing of text. This is a new tag and not supported by all browsers. If a browser does not support this tag, the text is generally rendered just like normal text.

Syntax `<STRIKE>Text</STRIKE>`

Attributes & Their Arguments

None.

Example   The following markup creates a display in which the text enclosed by the tags has a line through it:

```
<P>You can use type-specific tags to show edits by <STRIKE>striking out
</STRIKE> text rather than removal.</P>
```

See Also   EM, STRONG, I, and B

Strong Tag   `<STRONG> . . . </STRONG>`

Purpose   Presents the text within the tags with a stronger emphasis than the emphasis tag presents it. The text is usually displayed in bold. This tag is preferred to the bold tag.

Syntax   `<STRONG>Text</STRONG>`

Attributes & Their Arguments

None.

Example   The following markup displays the enclosed text in a very different manner than it displays the body text (usually in bold font):

```
<STRONG>Pay Attention. This is important.</STRONG>
```

See Also   B, EM, I, and TT

Style Tag   `<STYLE> . . . </STYLE>`

Purpose   Defines a set of styles to be applied to your document. This is only one of three methods of adding styles to a document; see Chapter 8 for a complete discussion of how to insert and use styles.

Syntax   `<STYLE TYPE="type_value">`

Attributes & Their Arguments

The required TYPE attribute defines the style sheet language. At present, the only language that is supported by both Netscape and Microsoft browsers is "text/css," which stands for the text MIME type of Cascading Style Sheets. Netscape also supports the new "text/javascript" type, which allows you to control and modify your styles with JavaScript.

Example The following shows how you can insert a style into your document using the STYLE tag. This style sets the text of the document to black on a white background and makes all anchors blue and not underlined:

```
<STYLE TYPE="text/css">
    BODY {background: white; color: black;}
    A {text-decoration: none; color: blue}
</STYLE>
```

See Also HEAD

Subscript Tag   `<SUB> . . . </SUB>`

Purpose Renders the enclosed text as a subscript.

Syntax `<SUB>subscript</SUB>`

Attributes & Their Arguments

None.

Example The following markup displays a value in italic text with a subscript:

```
<P>The distance recorded for the time interval <I>t</I> is shown by the
value <I>D<SUB>t</SUB></I>.
```

See Also SUP and PRE

Superscript Tag `<SUP> . . . </SUP>`

Purpose   Renders the enclosed text as a superscript.

Syntax   `<SUP>superscript</SUP>`

Attributes & Their Arguments

None.

Example   The following markup displays the reference values as superscripts in the text:

```
<P>The local newspaper articles<SUP>1,2</SUP> detailed the story of the
accident.
```

See Also   SUB and PRE

Table Tag `<TABLE> . . . </TABLE>`

Purpose   Defines a table. A table is an ordered set of data presented in rows and columns. Tables may be nested.

Associated Tag: Table Row Tag `<TR> . . . </TR>`

Purpose   Defines a row of a table. This tag should never be used outside of a table definition tag. The number of rows in a table is equal to the number of table row tags that it contains.

Associated Tag: Table Data Tag `<TD> . . . </TD>`

Purpose   Defines a data cell in a table. Table data must appear within a table row. Each row need not have the same number of data cells; short rows are padded with empty cells to the right.

Associated Tag: Table Header Tag   `<TH> . . . </TH>`

Purpose   Defines a header cell in a table. Header cells are identical to data cells except that text or data in header cells is presented in a bold font. Table headers must appear within a table row.

Associated Tag: Caption Tag   `<CAPTION> . . . </CAPTION>`

Purpose   Defines the caption for the table. Caption tags are optional. If used, they must appear between the table tags but outside of table rows or cells. Captions are horizontally centered with respect to the table.

Syntax
```
<TABLE BORDER | BORDER=value | CELLSPACING=value | CELLPADDING=value |
WIDTH=value>
<CAPTION ALIGN="keyword"> Caption_text </CAPTION>
<TR ALIGN="keyword" | VALIGN="keyword">
<TH | ALIGN="keyword" | VALIGN="keyword" | NOWRAP | COLSPAN=value |
ROWSPAN=value | WIDTH=value> Table_heading_text </TH>
</TR>
<TR ALIGN="keyword" | VALIGN="keyword">
<TD | ALIGN="keyword" | VALIGN="keyword" | NOWRAP | COLSPAN=value |
ROWSPAN=value | WIDTH=value> Table_element </TD>
</TR>
</TABLE>
```

Attributes & Their Arguments

Many attributes are available in several different tags used in tables. Each attribute listed here describes any special effects that depend on the tag it is associated with. The general rule is that attributes at a lower level override any previous attribute settings. For example, the default alignment of a table is ALIGN=:"left." This is overridden for any given row by specifying the ALIGN attribute for that row. Within a row, the ALIGN attribute specified for a cell or header overrides the alignment for that row.

ALIGN="keyword"
Sets the alignment of the data controlled by the tag. For the <CAPTION> tag, the ALIGN attribute specifies where the caption text is to be placed. Possible keyword entries are "top" | "bottom." The default setting is ALIGN="top."

For the <TR>, <TH>, or <TD> tags, the ALIGN attribute specifies where the data is to be placed. Possible keyword entries are "left" | "right" | "center." The default setting is ALIGN="left."

BORDER=value

Specifies that you want a border around the table and all table cells. If this attribute is absent, the table is drawn without borders, but space is allocated for the border by default. This means that a table without the BORDER attribute will occupy the same space as one with the BORDER attribute but without a value argument. The optional value argument allows you to specify the size of the border. If a value of 0 is used, the table will not have a border and no space will be saved for the border, making the table more compact than simply eliminating the BORDER attribute will.

CELLPADDING=value

Controls the padding around the data in a cell. The cell padding is the space between the borders of the cell and the contents of the cell. The default CELLPADDING is 1. Note that using CELLPADDING=0 in a table with visible borders is not recommended because the data in the cells may touch the border.

CELLSPACING=value

Controls the spacing between cells of the table. The default CELLSPACING is 2.

COLSPAN=value

Specifies how many columns of the table this cell should span. The default COLSPAN is 1.

NOWRAP

Prevents the data within the cell from being broken to fit the width of the cell. The resulting cell may be larger than a standard cell to accommodate the data.

ROWSPAN=value

Specifies how many rows of the table this cell should span. The default ROWSPAN is 1. The rows spanned must be defined by table row tags. An attempt to extend a cell into a row not specified with a <TR> tag will be truncated.

VALIGN="keyword"

Sets the alignment in the vertical direction within the cell for the data controlled by the tag. Possible keyword entries are "top" | "middle" | "bottom" | "baseline." The default setting is VALIGN="middle."

WIDTH=value

Specifies the width of the overall table or of a specific cell within a table. The default width for tables and cells is determined by complex algorithms within the browser. The value argument is number | "percent," which allows you to specify the width of the element in either pixels or as a percentage of either the document width (for a table) or the table width (for cells).

Example   The following displays a three-column table with two rows and a caption:

```
<TABLE BORDER>
<CAPTION>A Table</CAPTION>
<TR><TH> Heading 1 </TH> <TH COLSPAN=2> Heading 2
</TH></TR>
<TR><TD>Item Name</TD> <TD ALIGN="center"> 100
</TD> <TD ALIGN="center"> 200 </TD> </TR> </TABLE>
```

See Also   OL, UL, and PRE

Title Tag   `<TITLE> . . . </TITLE>`

Purpose   Specifies a title for an HTML document. This tag occurs in the Head section of the document and is required by HTML standards. Note that the title will not appear directly on the document as is customary on printed documents; instead, it will usually appear in a window bar where the document information that identifies the contents of the window is displayed. HTML header tags perform the functions usually reserved for titles in printed documents.

Syntax   `<TITLE>Text</TITLE>`

Attributes & Their Arguments

None.

Example   The following markup defines a title for an HTML document:

`<TITLE>Sample Document</TITLE>`

See Also   HEAD and BODY

Typewriter Tag   `<TT> . . . </TT>`

Purpose Presents the text within the tags in a monospaced font (usually Courier) that looks like a typewritten text.

Syntax `<TT>Text</TT>`

Attributes & Their Arguments

None.

Example The following markup displays the enclosed text in a monospaced font (usually Courier or a variant of that font):

`<TT>This is simple, monospaced text that looks like a typewriter.</TT>`

See Also B, EM, I, and STRONG

Underline Tag   `<U> . . . </U>`

Purpose Presents underlined text within the tags.

Syntax `<U>Text</U>`

Attributes & Their Arguments

None.

Example The following markup defines the enclosed text to be displayed underlined:

`<P>You can use type-specific tags to force <U>underlining</U> when you require that and nothing else.</P>`

See Also B, I, EM, and STRONG

Unordered List Tag <UL> . . . </UL>

Purpose   Defines an unordered (bulleted) list consisting of one or more list item tags.

Syntax   `<UL [TYPE="style" COMPACT]>`

Attributes & Their Arguments

There are two optional attributes: TYPE and COMPACT. The COMPACT attribute asks the browser to display the list in a more compact format; however, many browsers ignore this.

TYPE="style"
Allows you to specify how you want list items marked. Use of the TYPE attribute in the list tag affects the entire list; use of the attribute in a list item tag affects that tag and all subsequent tags. Possible style keyword entries are "disc" | "circle" | "square."

> TYPE="disc" uses the default solid round bullet for list elements.
>
> TYPE="circle" uses an open circle bullet for list elements.
>
> TYPE="square" uses a square bullet for list elements.

Associated Tag: List Item Tag <LI>

Purpose   Defines an element in a list. Note that this tag should never be used outside of a list definition tag as it may not be correctly displayed by a browser. Also notice that this tag does not have a matching termination.

Syntax   `<UL><LI [TYPE="style"]> List_element</UL>`

Attributes & Their Arguments

The optional TYPE attribute may be specified for individual list elements. If used, it will override any other TYPE specification.

Examples **A simple unordered list**

The following displays an unordered list with three entries:

```
<UL> <LI>First List Item <LI>Second List Item <LI>And so on... </UL>
```

An unordered list nested with other lists

The following list has three items; the first item is a sublist with two items. Many browsers will show different bullet types to indicate the level of indentation within an unordered list:

```
<UL> <LI>First List Item <UL> <LI>First Sub-Entry Item <LI>second Sub-Entry
Item </UL> <LI>Second List Item. This is a long entry to show how the
browser handles list elements that are longer than a single line. In fact, a
list element may be a significant block of text. <LI>And so on... </UL>
```

See Also UL, DL, DIR, and MENU

Variable Tag   `<VAR> . . . </VAR>`

Purpose Provides a variable term or phrase within a text block. Similar to the emphasis tag.

Syntax `<VAR>Variable_text</VAR>`

Attributes & Their Arguments

None.

Example The following includes a variable item within a normal text paragraph. The variable term is displayed with emphasis within the text:

```
<P>In C++, <VAR>variables</VAR> may be private, public, or protected. </P>
```

See Also DFN, STRONG, DL, B, I, and U

Word Break Tag (Netscape Extension)   `<WBR>`

Purpose   Allows Netscape to break a word or text block at the tag if necessary.

Syntax   `<NOBR>Text el<WBR>ement</NOBR>`

Attributes & Their Arguments

None.

Example   The following shows a single line of text that will be kept together on one line
by the use of the nobreak tag but may be broken at the word break tag if
necessary:

```
<NOBR>This text must stay together <WBR>
on one line if possible.</NOBR>
```

See Also BR and NOBR

Example Text Tag   `<XMP> . . . </XMP>`

Purpose   Similar to the preformatted text tag except that no embedded tags will be
recognized. To preserve formatting, the text is displayed in a monospaced
font. This is an obsolete tag; the preformatted text tag is preferred.

Syntax   `<XMP>Text</XMP>`

Attributes & Their Arguments

None.

Example   The following shows how you may use text in an example text block:

```
<XMP>This is sample example text</XMP>
```

See Also LISTING and PRE

Comment Tag   `<!-- . . . -->`

Purpose Allows you to insert comment data into the HTML document without displaying it on the screen. Often used to provide information about the author, revision data, and so on. Some browsers have problems with comments that are longer than a single line. For best compatibility, you should make multiline comments into several comment lines.

Syntax `<!-- Comment text -->`

Attributes & Their Arguments

None.

Examples The following shows a typical use of comments. Note that the comment has been broken into several different lines, and each line is an individual comment:

```
<!-- Created by: David Holzgang -->
<!-- using HoTMetaL Pro 4.0 -->
<!-- on 23 February 1997 11:22 -->
<!-- Revised: dh 1 Sep 97 16:35 -->
```

See Also HEAD and TITLE

Section II: HTML Forms

The HTML forms interface allows document creators to define HTML documents that contain information to be filled out by users. When a user fills out the form and presses a button indicating the form should be "submitted," the information on the form is sent to a server for processing. The server will usually prepare an HTML document using the information supplied by the user and return it to the browser client for display.

A form may contain any of the standard HTML tags. In addition, forms have certain special tags that are only used, and recognized, within a form document. The following tags define and implement the forms interface:

```
<FORM>...
<INPUT>
<SELECT>...</SELECT>
<OPTION>
<TEXTAREA>...</TEXTAREA> </FORM>
```

The last four tags are only valid within a form tag.

Form Tag   `<FORM> . . . </FORM>`

Purpose Defines a form within an HTML document. A document may contain multiple form tags, but form tags may not be nested. Note that non-Form tags can be used within a form tag.

Syntax `<FORM ACTION="URL" METHOD=[GET|POST]>` Text of form, including additional standard HTML tags and form tags if desired `</FORM>`

Attributes & Their Arguments

Forms have two required arguments.

ACTION="URL"
The URL location of the program that will process the form.

METHOD=method
The method may be either GET or POST. This is the method chosen to exchange data between the client and the program that is started to process the form.

This is an example of how a form tag might be used to define a registration form for a university:

```
<FORM ACTION="http://kuhttp.cc.ukans.edu/cgi-bin/register" METHOD=POST>...
</FORM>
```

See Also   BODY

Input Tag   `<INPUT>`

Purpose   Defines an input field where the user may enter information on the form. Each input field assigns a value to a variable that has a specified name and a specified data type.

Syntax   `<INPUT TYPE="keyword" NAME="textstring"`
`|VALUE="textstring"|CHECKED|SIZE=number| MAXLENGTH=number">`

Attributes & Their Arguments

TYPE="keyword"
Specifies the data type for the variable. Possible values for keyword are ["text" | "password" | "checkbox" | "radio" | "submit" | "reset"].

> TYPE="text" and TYPE="password" accept character data.
>
> TYPE="checkbox" is either selected or not.
>
> TYPE="radio" allows selection of only one of several radio fields (if they all have the same variable name).
>
> TYPE="submit" is an action button that sends the completed form to the query server.
>
> TYPE="reset" is a button that resets the form variables to their default values.

NAME="textstring"

Where textstring is a symbolic name (not displayed) identifying the input variable.

VALUE="textstring"

Where the function of textstring depends on the argument for type as follows:

- TYPE="text" or TYPE="password" —textstring is the default value for the input variable.
- TYPE="checkbox" or TYPE="radio" —textstring is the value of the input variable when it is "checked."
- TYPE="reset" or TYPE="submit" —textstring is a label that will appear on the submit or reset button in place of the words *submit* and *reset*.

CHECKED

No arguments. For TYPE="checkbox" or TYPE="radio," if CHECKED is present, the input field is "checked" by default.

SIZE=number

Where number is an integer value representing the number of characters allowed for the TYPE="text" or TYPE="password" input fields.

MAXLENGTH=number

Where number is an integer value representing the number of characters accepted for TYPE="text" or TYPE="password." This attribute is valid only for single line "text" or "password" fields.

Examples **A simple text input area**

The following provides an input area for entering a user's name:

```
<P>Please enter your name:</P> <INPUT TYPE="text" NAME="username" SIZE=30 >
```

Using input for submission of data

These two input tags add the necessary buttons to submit data accumulated in the form or to cancel it:

```
<INPUT TYPE="submit" VALUE="Send Form">
<INPUT TYPE="reset" VALUE="Clear Form">
```

Using radio buttons as input

The following example defines four radio buttons. The third button is checked by default when the form is first displayed:

```
<P> Please select one of these destinations:
<INPUT TYPE="radio" NAME="S1" VALUE="CANADA"> Canada
<INPUT TYPE="radio" NAME="S1" VALUE="GB"> Great Britain
<INPUT TYPE="radio" NAME="S1" VALUE="USA" CHECKED> United States of America
<INPUT TYPE="radio" NAME="S1" VALUE="AUS"> Australia</P>
```

See Also   FORM

Select Tag   `<SELECT> . . . </SELECT>`

Purpose   Defines and displays a set of optional list items from which the user can select one or more items. This element requires an <OPTION> element for each item in the list.

Associated Tag: Option Item Tag   `<OPTION>`

Purpose   Defines an element in a selection list. Within the select tag, the option tags are used to define the possible values for the select field. Note that this tag should never be used outside of a select tag as it may not be correctly displayed by a browser. Also notice that this tag does not have a matching termination.

Syntax   `<SELECT NAME="textstring" [SIZE=value MULTIPLE] <OPTION [SELECTED]>Option_item </SELECT>...`

Attributes & Their Arguments

NAME="textstring"

Where textstring is a symbolic name (not displayed) identifying the input variable.

SIZE=value

The argument for SIZE is an integer value representing the number of <OPTION> items that will be displayed at one time.

MULTIPLE
If present, the MULTIPLE attribute allows selection of more than one
<OPTION> value.

SELECTED
If this attribute is present, the option value is selected by default.

Example In the following example, all three options may be chosen, but bananas are
selected by default:

```
<SELECT MULTIPLE>
<OPTION>Apples
<OPTION SELECTED>Bananas
<OPTION>Cherries
</SELECT>
```

See Also FORM

Textarea Tag   <TEXTAREA> . . . </TEXTAREA>

Purpose Defines a rectangular field where the user may enter text data. If a default text
element is present, it will be displayed when the field appears. Otherwise the
field will be blank.

Syntax `<TEXTAREA NAME="textstring" ROWS=value COLUMNS=value >default_text</TEXTAREA>`

Attributes & Their Arguments

NAME="textstring"
Where textstring is a symbolic name (not displayed) identifying the input
variable.

ROWS=value COLS=value
Both attributes take an integer value that represents the lines and number of
characters per line in the text area to be displayed.

Example The following demonstrates the use of a textarea tag:

```
<P>Please enter your comments below:<BR> <TEXTAREA NAME="tree_data" ROWS=5
COLUMNS=40>I like trees because...</TEXTAREA></P>
```

See Also FORM

Section III: Cascading Style Sheets

Style sheets allow a Web page designer to set margins, text features, and other important layout items as desired while letting users who cannot or do not wish to use these features modify or even eliminate them to suit their individual tastes and circumstances. Style sheets allow a full range of design possibilities while preserving the concepts of information access and exchange that mark the Web as a truly unique vehicle for presenting information.

A *style sheet* is a collection of rules that determine how a browser displays HTML tags. Each *rule* in a style sheet is made up of two elements: a selector and a style. Style rules are formed as follows:

```
selector { property: value }
```

The *selector* defines the HTML tag that the style will be used for. The *style* itself follows the selector and is contained within braces. It describes how the selector should be presented and consists of property and value pairs. The property name is listed first and is separated from the value by a colon. A *property* is the name of a stylistic parameter that can be set through a style sheet. Each property has a set of corresponding *value selections*, which define how the property is applied. If a style contains multiple property-value pairs, they are separated by a semicolon. For example, you could use the following code to define a style that can be used to set a heading tag to display text in large, bold, red letters:

```
H1 {font: bold 24pt; color: red}
```

In this case the selector is the heading tag <H1>, and the style consists of two property-value pairs. The first sets the "font" property to bold and displays at 24 points in the standard heading font, while the second sets the "color" property of the text to "red."

This appendix presents the properties and allowed values for all the elements in a Cascading Style Sheet. Properties shown in quotes are specific keywords that must be entered as shown. For a compete description of how to insert styles into your Web pages and how to use style sheets, see Chapter 8.

Sizes

Many properties allow the use of various numeric sizes, most of which require some type of units. The following types of measurements are in common use throughout style sheet properties. Each measurement described here is given a keyword. When the keyword appears as a property, you may enter the measurement as described.

Length Measurements

keyword: "length"

Lengths are a combination of a numeric value and a unit designation. The number used may be a whole number or a decimal fraction; you may also use negative numbers where it makes some sense—for example, you can use negative numbers for setting margins but not for setting font sizes. The unit designations are all two-letter abbreviations with no period and no space between the numeric value and the unit abbreviation. The possible abbreviations are as follows:

```
in   inch
mm   millimeter
cm   centimeter
pt   point (72 points = 1 inch)
pc   pica (6 picas = 1 inch; 12 points = 1 pica)
em   the point size of the current font
ex   the x-height of the current font
px   pixel
```

Percentage Measurements

keyword: "percent"

Percentage measurements are a combination of a numeric value and a percent sign. The number used may be a whole number or a decimal fraction; you may also use negative numbers. By specifying a percentage value for a property, you set the property to be that percentage of its parent's property. For example, if you specify **font-size: 125%**, then you are saying that the font used for this style should be 25 percent larger than whatever font is being used currently.

Font Properties

The font properties allow you to set selections for font use within your document. Because there is no accepted universal taxonomy of font properties, you must match properties to font faces carefully. The font properties are matched in a well-defined order to ensure that the results of the matching process are as consistent as possible across browsers and platforms so that font property requests will be answered in the same way, assuming that the same library of font faces is present. See Chapter 8 for details on how font properties are matched.

font-family

Defines the font family that you want to use for the text. Multiple entries are separated by commas. Font names containing white space should be quoted.

Allowed Values

`family-name | generic-family-name`
Where the family name is the name of the font you wish to use; the generic family name may have one of the following allowed values:

> `"serif" (e.g., Times)`
>
> `"sans-serif" (e.g., Helvetica)`
>
> `"cursive" (e.g., Zapf-Chancery)`
>
> `"fantasy" (e.g., Wingdings)`
>
> `"monospace" (e.g., Courier)`

font-style

Requests the style that you wish used on the text.

Allowed Values

`"normal" | "italic" | "oblique"`
Where "normal" is the default roman or upright version of the font and "italic" or "oblique" are alternative faces. Note that a font family will normally have only italic or oblique forms, but not both. If "italic" is requested, the browser will use an oblique form if that is available and italic is not.

font-variant

Requests a specific variant within a font family.

Allowed Values

`"normal" | "small-caps"`
If "small-caps" is requested, the browser may (but is not required to) substitute smaller size capital letters from the font for the small letters in the text.

font-weight

Requests the weight of the text for display.

Allowed Values

`"normal"` | `"bold"` | `"bolder"` | `"lighter"` | `100` | `200` | `300` | `400` | `500` | `600` | `700` | `800` | `900`

The values '100' to '900' form an ordered sequence, where each number indicates a weight that is at least as dark as its predecessor. The keyword "normal" is synonymous with "400," and "bold" is synonymous with "700." The "bolder" and "lighter" keywords select font weights that are relative to the weight inherited from the parent element.

font-size

Requests a **specific** font size.

Allowed Values

`absolute-size` | `relative-size` | `length` | `percent`

The length and percent values were described earlier. The other values are:

`absolute-size`

An absolute-size keyword is an index to a table of font sizes computed and kept by the browser. The table may be different from one font family to another. Possible values are:

- `"xx-small"`
- `"x-small"`
- `"small"`
- `"medium"`
- `"large"`
- `"x-large"`
- `"xx-large"`

relative-size

A <relative-size> keyword is interpreted as relative to the table of font sizes and the font size of the parent element. For example, if the parent element has a font size of "medium," a value of "larger" will make the font size of the current element be "large," and so on. If the parent element's size is not close to a table entry, the browser is free to interpolate between table entries or round off to the closest one. Possible values are:

`"smaller"`

`"larger"`

font

The font property is a shorthand property for specifying multiple font-related properties with a single entry. Note that you can also use the font property to set the line-height property, which is described later under "Text Properties."

Allowed Values

```
font-family  [font-style font-variant font-weight  font-size
line-height]
```
The font-family entry is required; all others are optional.

Color & Background Properties

Color and background properties describe the color, also called foreground color, and background of an element—that is, the surface onto which the content is displayed. You can set a background color and/or a background image; you can also set the position of the image (if/how it is repeated) and whether it is fixed or scrolled relative to the display window.

color

Sets the text color of the element.

Allowed Values

```
color
```
Allowed color values are the same as for HTML tags. See our earlier note on color specification.

background-color

Sets the text color of the element.

Allowed Values

```
color | "transparent"
```
Allowed color values are the same as for HTML tags. See our earlier note on color specification. The "transparent" keyword makes the background clear so that any elements behind will show through. This is the default setting.

background-image

Sets the specified image as a background.

Allowed Values

`URL | "none"`
The image loaded from the URL value is displayed as the background. When an image is displayed, it is placed over the background color, if specified. The "none" keyword is the default setting.

background-attachment

If a background image is specified, the value of "background-attachment" determines if it is fixed with regard to the display or if it scrolls along with the content.

Allowed Values

`"scroll" | "fixed"`
The "scroll" keyword is the default setting.

background-position

If a background image is specified, the value of "background-position" specifies its initial position. Two values are required to specify the horizontal and vertical position, respectively; if only one is given, it is used as the horizontal position and the vertical position defaults to 50%.

Allowed Values

`percent | length | [["left" | "center" | "right"] ["top" | "center" | "bottom"]]`
Note that keyword values cannot be combined with percentage or length values.

background

The background property is a shorthand property for specifying multiple background-related properties with a single entry.

Allowed Values

```
background-color background-image background-repeat
background-attachment background-position
```

Text Properties

These properties describe the text used on the page.

word-spacing

Sets the spacing between words of the text. The browser is free to select the exact spacing algorithm. The word spacing may also be influenced by justification, which is a value of the text-align property.

Allowed Values

```
length | "normal"
```
A length entry indicates an addition to the default space between words. Values can be negative, but there may be implementation-specific limits.

letter-spacing

Sets the spacing between letters of the text. The browser is free to select the exact spacing algorithm. The letter spacing may also be influenced by justification, which is a value of the text-align property.

Allowed Values

```
length | "normal"
```
A length entry indicates an addition to the default space between letters. Values can be negative, but there may be implementation-specific limits. Most browsers at this time do not support negative values.

text-decoration

The text-decoration property describes features that are added to the text of an element. If the element has no text (e.g., the 'IMG' element in HTML) or is an empty element (e.g., '<EM></EM>'), this property has no effect.

Allowed Values

`"none" | ["underline" "overline" "line-through" "blink" ]`
Browsers must recognize the keyword "blink," but are not required to support the blink effect.

vertical-align

The vertical-align property affects the vertical positioning of the element.

Allowed Values

`percent | "baseline" | "sub" | "super" | "top" | "text-top" |`
`"middle" | "bottom" | "text-bottom"`
Percentage values refer to the value of the line-height property of the element itself. They raise the baseline of the element (or the bottom, if it has no baseline) the specified amount above the baseline of the parent. Negative values are allowed. The other keywords have the following meanings:

`"baseline"`
Aligns the baseline of the element (or the bottom, if the element doesn't have a baseline) with the baseline of the parent element.

`"sub"`
Subscripts the element.

`"super"`
Superscripts the element.

`"top"`
Aligns the top of the element with the tallest element on the line.

`"text-top"`
Aligns the top of the element with the top of the parent element's font.

`"middle"`
Aligns the vertical midpoint of the element (typically an image) with the baseline plus half the x-height of the parent element.

"bottom"
Aligns the bottom of the element with the lowest element on the line.

"text-bottom"
Aligns the bottom of the element with the bottom of the parent element's font.

text-transform

The text-transform property affects the capitalization of the text of an element.

Allowed Values

"capitalize" | "uppercase" | "lowercase" | "none"
The keywords have the following meanings:

"capitalize"
Changes the first character of each word to a capital letter.

"uppercase"
Changes all letters of the element to uppercase.

"lowercase"
Changes all letters of the element to lowercase.

"none"
Removes the effect of any text transformations applied to a parent element.

text-align

The text-align property affects the alignment of the text of an element.

Allowed Values

"left" | "right" | "center" | "justify"
The keywords have the usual meanings:

text-indent

The text-indent property specifies the indentation that appears before the first formatted line. The value provided may be negative, but there may be implementation-specific limits.

Allowed Values

`length | percent`
Percentage values refer to the parent element's width.

line-height

The line-height property specifies the distance between the baselines of two succeeding lines of text. This is functionally the same as leading. Negative values are not allowed.

Allowed Values

`"normal" | length | percent | number`
Percentage values refer to the font size of the element itself.

number
When a numerical value is specified, the line height is calculated as the font size of the current element multiplied by the given number. Functionally, this is the same as a percentage, but it differs from a percentage value in the way it inherits. When a numerical value is specified, child elements will inherit the factor itself, not the resultant calculated value (as is the case with percentage and other units).

Box Properties

Box properties set the size, circumference, and position of the boxes that represent elements. See "Setting Formats" in Chapter 8 for a discussion of box properties. The following properties and values assume that you understand the structure and use of element boxes.

margin-top

Sets the top margin for the element.

Allowed Values

`"auto" | length | percent`
Percentage values refer to the parent element's width. A negative value is allowed, but there may be implementation-specific limits.

margin-right

Sets the right margin for the element.

Allowed Values

`"auto" | length | percent`
Percentage values refer to the parent element's width. A negative value is allowed, but there may be implementation-specific limits.

margin-bottom

Sets the bottom margin for the element.

Allowed Values

`"auto" | length | percent`
Percentage values refer to the parent element's width. A negative value is allowed, but there may be implementation-specific limits.

margin-left

Sets the left margin for the element.

Allowed Values

`"auto" | length | percent`
Percentage values refer to the parent element's width. A negative value is allowed, but there may be implementation-specific limits.

margin

The margin property is a shorthand property for specifying multiple margin-related properties with a single entry.

Allowed Values

`margin-top margin-right margin-bottom margin-left`
If four values are specified, they apply to top, right, bottom, and left respectively. If there is only one value, it applies to all sides; if there are two or three, the missing values are taken from the opposite side. At least one value is required.

padding-top

Sets the top padding for the element.

Allowed Values

`length | percent`
Percentage values refer to the parent element's width. Negative values are not allowed.

padding-right

Sets the right padding for the element.

Allowed Values

`length | percent`
Percentage values refer to the parent element's width. Negative values are not allowed.

padding-bottom

Sets the bottom padding for the element.

Allowed Values

`length | percent`
Percentage values refer to the parent element's width. Negative values are not allowed.

padding-left

Sets the left padding for the element.

Allowed Values

`length | percent`
Percentage values refer to the parent element's width. Negative values are not allowed.

padding

The padding property is a shorthand property for specifying multiple padding-related properties with a single entry.

Allowed Values

`padding-top padding-right padding-bottom padding-left`
If four values are specified, they apply to top, right, bottom, and left respectively. If there is only one value, it applies to all sides; if there are two or three, the missing values are taken from the opposite side. At least one value is required. Negative values are not allowed.

border-top-width

Sets the width of an element's top border.

Allowed Values

`length | "thin" | "medium" | "thick"`
The actual width of the keyword values depend on the browser, but the following relationships always hold: "thin" <= "medium" <= "thick." Negative values for length are not allowed.

border-right-width

Sets the width of an element's right border.

Allowed Values

`length | "thin" | "medium" | "thick"`
The actual width of the keyword values depend on the browser, but the following relationships always hold: "thin" <= "medium" <= "thick." Negative values for length are not allowed.

border-bottom-width

Sets the width of an element's bottom border.

Allowed Values

`length | "thin" | "medium" | "thick"`
The actual width of the keyword values depend on the browser, but the following relationships always hold: "thin" <= "medium" <= "thick." Negative values for length are not allowed.

border-left-width

Sets the width of an element's left border.

Allowed Values

`length | "thin" | "medium" | "thick"`
The actual width of the keyword values depend on the browser, but the following relationships always hold: "thin" <= "medium" <= "thick." Negative values for length are not allowed.

border-width

The border-width property is a shorthand property for setting all four border widths at once.

Allowed Values

`border-top-width border-right-width border-bottom-width border-left-width`
If four values are specified, they apply to top, right, bottom, and left respectively. If there is only one value, it applies to all sides; if there are two, top and bottom border widths are set to the first value, right and left are set to the second; if there are three values, top is set to the first, right and left to the second, and bottom to the third. At least one value is required. Negative values are not allowed.

border-color

Sets the border color for an element. From one to four colors may be entered and are applied to the different sides in the same way as border-width values are applied.

Allowed Values

`color`
Allowed color values are the same as for HTML tags. See our note on color specification in "Section I: Markup Tags" earlier in this appendix.

border-style

Sets the border style for an element. From one to four style keywords may be entered and are applied to the different sides in the same way as border-width values are applied.

Allowed Values

`"none"` | `"dotted"` | `"dashed"` | `"solid"` | `"double"` | `"groove"` | `"ridge"` | `"inset"` | `"outset"`
The keywords have the following meanings:

- "none"   No border is drawn even if the border-width value is present. This is the default.

- "dotted"   The border is a dotted line drawn on top of the element's background.

- "dashed"   The border is a dashed line drawn on top of the element's background.

- "solid"   The border is a solid line.

- "double"   The border is a double line drawn on top of the element's background. The sum of the two single lines and the space between equals the border-width value.

- "groove"   The border is a 3D groove drawn in colors based on the border-color value.

- "ridge"   The border is a 3D ridge drawn in colors based on the border-color value.

- ■ "inset" The border is a 3D inset drawn in colors based on the border-color value.
- ■ "outset" The border is a 3D outset drawn in colors based on the border-color value.

border-top

The border-top property is a shorthand property for setting the width, style, and color of an element's top border.

Allowed Values

```
border-top-width border-style border-color
```

border-right

The border-right property is a shorthand property for setting the width, style, and color of an element's right border.

Allowed Values

```
border-right-width border-style border-color
```

border-bottom

The border-bottom property is a shorthand property for setting the width, style, and color of an element's bottom border.

Allowed Values

```
border-bottom-width border-style border-color
```

border-left

The border-left property is a shorthand property for setting the width, style, and color of an element's left border.

Allowed Values

```
border-left-width border-style border-color
```

border

The border-bottom property is a shorthand property for setting the same width, color, and style on all four borders of an element. Unlike other shorthand properties, the border property cannot set different values on the four borders. You must use one or more of the other border properties to set individual border values.

Allowed Values

```
border-width border-style border-color
```

width

The width property sets the width of the element. Although this property can be applied to text elements, it is most useful with replaced elements such as images. The width is to be enforced by scaling the image if necessary. When the image is scaled, the aspect ratio of the image is preserved if the height property is "auto." If the width and height of a replaced element are both "auto," these properties will be set to the intrinsic dimensions of the element.

Allowed Values

```
"auto" | length | percent
```
Percentage values refer to the parent element's width. Negative values are not allowed.

height

The height property sets the height of the element. Although this property can be applied to text elements, it is most useful with replaced elements such as images. The height is to be enforced by scaling the image if necessary. When the image is scaled, the aspect ratio of the image is preserved if the width property is "auto." If the width and height of a replaced element are both "auto," these properties will be set to the intrinsic dimensions of the element.

Allowed Values

```
"auto" | length | percent
```
Percentage values refer to the parent element's width. Negative values are not allowed.

float

The float property affects where an element displays.

Allowed Values

`"left" | "right" | "none"`
With the value "none," the element will be displayed where it appears in the text. With a value of "left," the element will be moved to the left and the text will wrap on the right side of the element. With a value of "right," the element will be moved to the right and the text will wrap on the left side of the element. With a value of "left" or "right," the element is treated as block-level; that is, the display property (see "Classification Properties") is ignored.

clear

The clear property determines whether the element allows floating elements to display beside it.

Allowed Values

`"none" | "left" | "right" | "both"`
The value of this property lists the sides where floating elements are not accepted. For example, when the clear property is set to "left," the element will be moved below any floating element on the left side. When it is set to "none" (the default), floating elements are allowed on all sides.

Classification Properties

Classification properties classify elements into categories more than they set specific visual parameters. For example, the list-style properties describe how elements with a display value of "list-item" are formatted.

display

The display property describes whether an element is displayed and how it is displayed.

Allowed Values

`"block"` | `"inline"` | `"list-item"` | `"none"`
Each element in HTML has a standard display property. For example, a list item <LI> has a display property of "list-item." The keywords have the following meanings:

- ■ "block"   A display value of "block" opens a new box. The box is positioned relative to adjacent boxes according to the style sheet formatting model. Typically, elements like 'H1' and 'P' are of type 'block'.

- ■ "list-item"   A value of "list-item" is similar to "block" except that a list-item marker is added. In HTML, <LI> will typically have this value.

- ■ "inline"   An element with a display value of "inline" results in a new inline box on the same line as the previous content. The dimensions of the box are set according to the formatted size of the content. If the content is text, it may span several lines and there will be a box on each line. The margin, border, and padding properties apply to "inline" elements but will not have any effect at the line breaks.

- ■ "none"   A value of "none" turns off the display of the element, including children elements and the surrounding box.

white-space

The white-space property declares how white space characters inside the element are handled.

Allowed Values

`"normal"` | `"pre"` | `"nowrap"`
The initial value of white-space is "normal," but a browser will typically have default values for all HTML elements according to the suggested rendering of elements in the HTML specification. The keywords have the following meanings:

`"normal"`
White space in the element is collapsed—that is, multiple white space characters are rendered as one character.

`"pre"`
White space characters in the element are not collapsed—that is, multiple white space characters are rendered as indicated in the text. This is similar to how white space is handled within the <PRE> tag.

"nowrap"
White space characters in the element are not collapsed and text lines are not broken except at <BR> tags.

list-style-type

The list-style-type property is used to determine the appearance of the list-item marker if list-style-image is "none" or if the image pointed to by the image URL cannot be displayed. This property only applies to elements with a display property of "list-item."

Allowed Values

"disc" | "circle" | "square" | "decimal" | "lower–roman" | "upper–roman" | "lower–alpha" | "upper–alpha" | "none"
The keywords have the same meanings and results as the style settings for the appropriate list type.

list-style-image

The list-style-image property is used to determine the image that will be used as the list-item marker. This property only applies to elements with a display property of "list-item."

Allowed Values

URL | "none"
The image loaded from the URL value is displayed as the list-item marker. The "none" keyword is the default setting.

list-style-position

The list-style-position property is used to determine where the list-item marker is positioned. This property only applies to elements with a display property of "list-item."

Allowed Values

"inside" | "outside"
The keyword determines how the list-item marker is drawn with regard to the content. The "outside" keyword is the default setting.

list-style

The list-style property is a shorthand property for specifying multiple list-related properties with a single entry.

Allowed Values

`list-style-type list-style-image list-style-position`

Section IV: Character Entities

One problem that occurs when transmitting text across computer systems is the problem of how to represent punctuation marks, accented characters, and other characters that may be commonly used in one language or system and not in another. Each computer system has some method for handling these problems. For example, on the Macintosh, you can generate an *e* with an acute accent—the last é in the word *resumé*—by pressing the Option key and the "e" key, followed by the "e" key again. However, the character generated in this way cannot be displayed correctly on any system other than a Macintosh, so if you use this character within an HTML document, the recipient will probably not see the correct character. This is one type of character display problem.

Another problem is how to display certain punctuation marks. For example, the HTML language uses the characters <(the less than sign) and > (the greater than sign) to signal HTML commands within a document. For obvious reasons, you cannot insert these same characters in the text of the document without causing problems when the document is displayed. You need another method for displaying these characters in your text.

To solve this problem, the HTML language defines character entities that are used instead of these special characters. These may take one of two formats:

&keyword

Displays a particular character identified by a special keyword. For example the entity *&* displays the ampersand character (&), and the entity *<* displays the less than (<) character. Note that the semicolon following the keyword is required, and the keyword must be one from Table B-1. The definitive list of acceptable keywords is presented at http://info.cern.ch/hypertext/WWW/MarkUp/Entities.html.

`&#ascii_equivalent`

Uses a character from the ISO Added LATIN I character set identified by the decimal integer ascii_equivalent. Again, note that the semicolon following the ASCII numeric value is required. Table B-2 shows the characters and gives the ascii_equivalent value for all the characters in the ISO Added LATIN I character set that are not available from the keyboard and do not have a character keyword. Note that Table B-1 shows the integer ascii_equivalent for the characters as well as the keyword. You can use either method (keyword or ascii_equivalent) to insert these into your text; however, the keyword is considered the better alternative.

Mnemonic	As Displayed	Description	Decimal ASCII Equivalent
AElig	"Æ"	capital AE diphthong (ligature)	#198
Aacute	"Á"	capital A, acute accent	#193
Acirc	"Â"	capital A, circumflex accent	#194
Agrave	"À"	capital A, grave accent	#192
Aring	"Å"	capital A, ring	#197
Atilde	"Ã"	capital A, tilde	#195
Auml	"Ä"	capital A, dieresis or umlaut mark	#196
Ccedil	"Ç"	capital C, cedilla	#199
Eth	"_"	capital Eth, Icelandic	#208
Eacute	"É"	capital E, acute accent	#201
Ecirc	"Ê"	capital E, circumflex accent	#202
Egrave	"È"	capital E, grave accent	#200
Euml	"Ë"	capital E, dieresis or umlaut mark	#203
Iacute	"Í"	capital I, acute accent	#205
Icirc	"Î"	capital I, circumflex accent	#206
Igrave	"Ì"	capital I, grave accent	#204
Iuml	"Ï"	capital I, dieresis or umlaut mark	#207
Ntilde	"Ñ"	capital N, tilde	#209
Oacute	"Ó"	capital O, acute accent	#211
Ocirc	"Ô"	capital O, circumflex accent	#212

➡

Mnemonic	As Displayed	Description	Decimal ASCII Equivalent
Ograve	"Ò"	capital O, grave accent	#210
Oslash	"Ø"	capital O, slash	#216
Otilde	"Õ"	capital O, tilde	#213
Ouml	"Ö"	capital O, dieresis or umlaut mark	#214
Thorn	"_"	capital Thorn, Icelandic	#222
Uacute	"Ú"	capital U, acute accent	#218
Ucirc	"Û"	capital U, circumflex accent	#219
Ugrave	"Ù"	capital U, grave accent	#217
Uuml	"Ü"	capital U, dieresis or umlaut mark	#220
Yacute	"Y"	capital Y, acute accent	#221
aacute	"á"	small a, acute accent	#225
acirc	"â"	small a, circumflex accent	#226
aelig	"æ"	small ae diphthong (ligature)	#230
agrave	"à"	small a, grave accent	#224
amp	"&"	ampersand	#38
atilde	"ã"	small a, tilde	#227
auml	"ä"	small a, dieresis or umlaut mark	#228
ccedil	"ç"	small c, cedilla	#231
eacute	"é"	small e, acute accent	#233
ecirc	"ê"	small e, circumflex accent	#234
egrave	"è"	small e, grave accent	#232
eth	"?"	small eth, Icelandic	#240
euml	"ë"	small e, dieresis or umlaut mark	#235
gt	">"	greater than	#62
iacute	"í"	small i, acute accent	#237
icirc	"î"	small i, circumflex accent	#238
igrave	"ì"	small i, grave accent	#236
iuml	"ï"	small i, dieresis or umlaut mark	#239
lt	"<"	less than	#60
ntilde	"ñ"	small n, tilde	#241
oacute	"ó"	small o, acute accent	#243

➡

Mnemonic	As Displayed	Description	Decimal ASCII Equivalent
ocirc	"ô"	small o, circumflex accent	#244
ograve	"ò"	small o, grave accent	#242
oslash	"ø"	small o, slash	#248
otilde	"õ"	small o, tilde	#245
ouml	"ö"	small o, dieresis or umlaut mark	#246
quote	"'"	single quote	#62
szlig	"ß"	small sharp s, German (sz ligature)	#225
thorn	"_"	small thorn, Icelandic	#254
uacute	"ú"	small u, acute accent	#250
ucirc	"û"	small u, circumflex accent	#251
ugrave	"ù"	small u, grave accent	#249
uuml	"ü"	small u, dieresis or umlaut mark	#252
yacute	"y"	small y, acute accent	#253
yuml	"ÿ"	small y, dieresis or umlaut mark	#255

Table B-1: Character keywords in HTML.

Number	As Displayed	Description
#161	"¡"	inverted exclamation mark
#162	"¢"	cent sign
#163	"£"	pound sign
#164	"¤"	general currency sign
#165	"¥"	yen sign
#166	"¦"	broken (vertical) bar
#167	" "	section sign
#168	"¨"	umlaut
#169	"©"	copyright sign
#170	"ª"	ordinal indicator, feminine
#171	"«"	angle quotation mark, left
#174	"®"	circled R/registered sign
#175	"¯"	macron

➡

Number	As Displayed	Description
#176	"o"	degree sign
#177	"±"	/pm B: plus-or-minus sign
#178	"2"	superscript two
#179	"3"	superscript three
#180	"´"	acute accent
#181	"µ"	micro sign
#182	"¶"	pilcrow (paragraph sign)
#183	"·"	/centerdot B: middle dot
#184	"¸"	cedilla
#185	"1"	superscript one
#186	"o"	ordinal indicator, masculine
#187	"»"	angle quotation mark, right
#188	"1/4"	fraction one-quarter
#189	"1/2"	fraction one-half
#190	"3/4"	fraction three-quarters
#191	"¿"	inverted question mark

Table B-2: ISO Added LATIN 1 character entities with only a numeric representation.

Appendix C

Resources

The Web contains a wealth of information about all aspects of Web page creation and online publishing. This resource guide includes a list of books and magazines related to Web publishing that we think are worthy of note. The topics include TCP/IP software, Web browsers, HTML editors and converters, portable document viewers, graphic editors, 3D rendering applications, clip art, multimedia applications, Web servers, CGI programs, and utilities.

To maximize space, the resource listings only include the name and the URL. Magazines and books have additional information. Platform-dependent resources, such as software archives and programs, have been broken into Windows, Macintosh, and UNIX subheadings.

In addition, some great resources can be found at the WWW Virtual library (http://www.w3.org/hypertext/DataSources/bySubject/Overview.html) and at the HTML Writer's Guild (http://www.hwg.org).

WWW Search Engines

AltaVista
http://www.altavista.digital.com/

Excite
http://www.excite.com/

Wired HotBot
http://www.HotBot.com/

InfoSeek
http://www.infoseek.com/

Lycos
http://www.lycos.com/

OpenText
http://index.opentext.net/

TradeWave
http://www.einet.net/galaxy.html

WebCrawler
http://www.webcrawler.com/

Yahoo
http://www.yahoo.com/

The Search Everywhere Page
http://www.fwi.uva.nl/~mes/search.html

Webprowler
http://www.webprowler.com/

Going Online

TCP/IP Software

Windows

Chameleon
http://www.netmanage.com/

LAN WorkPlace for MS Windows or DOS
http://www.novell.com/

PathWay Access on DOS/Windows
http://www.twg.com/

PC-NFS
http://www.sun.com/

PC/TCP OnNet for DOS/Windows
http://www.ftp.com/

SuperTCP Suite
http://www.frontiertech.com/

TCP/Connect II
http://www.ascend.com/

Macintosh

AppleShare IP
http://appleshareip.apple.com/appleshareip/index.html

MacSLIP
http://www.zilker.net/~hydepark

Apple IP Gateway
http://www.claris.com/products/apple/applegateway/applegateway.html

PathWay Access on Macintosh
http://www.twg.com/

VersaTerm with VersaTilities
http://www.synergy.com/

Web Browsers

Macintosh

Cyberdog
http://www.cyberdog.apple.com/

NCSA Mosaic for Macintosh
http://www.ncsa.uiuc.edu/SDG/Software/MacMosaic/
MacMosaicHome.html

MacLynx
http://www.edprint.demon.co.uk/se/lynx.html

Microsoft Internet Explorer
http://www.microsoft.com/ie/

Netscape Commmunicator
http://home.netscape.com/

Windows

Ariadna
http://www.amsd.ru/eng/default.asp

Microsoft Internet Explorer
http://www.microsoft.com/ie/

Netscape Navigator
http://home.netscape.com/

Opera
http://operasoftware.com/

Trawler
http://dwave.net/~bitsafe/trawler/

UNIX

Lynx
ftp://ftp2.cc.ukans.edu/pub/WWW/lynx

Netscape Navigator
http://home.netscape.com/

Browser-Specific Information

Ask Dr. Internet
http://promo.net/drnet/

Unofficial Netscape FAQ
http://www.sousystems.com/faq/

BrowserCaps
http://www.browsercaps.com/picker.ptx

Browser Watch
http://browserwatch.internet.com/

Club IE
http://www.clubie.com/

Plug-ins for Web Browsers

Adobe Acrobat PDF Viewer
http://www.adobe.com/

GhostScript Viewer
http://www.cs.wisc.edu/~ghost/index.html

QuickView Plus plug-in
http://www.inso.com/

Macromedia (Shockwave)
http://www.macromedia.com/

Microsoft PowerPoint Viewer
http://www.microsoft.com/

Net Toob
http://www.duplexx.com/

QuickTime
http://quicktime.apple.com/

RealPlayer
http://www.real.com/products

Shockwave
http://www.macromedia.com/Tools/Shockwave/Gallery/

StreamWorks
http://www.xing.com/

ToolVox
http://www.voxware.com/

Windows 95.com Web Browser Plugins
http://www.windows95.com/apps/plugins.html

WordPower Viewer
http://www.spco.com/

Xing's OpenMOM
http://www.xing.com/

Portable Document & Other Document Viewers

Portable Documents are files and documents that can easily be read across platforms, similar to HTML files.

Adobe Acrobat Reader
http://www.adobe.com/prodindex/acrobat/readstep.html

Microsoft WordViewer
http://www.microsoft.com/msword/internet/viewer

Microsoft PowerPoint Viewer
http://www.microsoft.com/office/mspowerpoint/internet/viewer

Microsoft Excel Viewer
http://www.microsoft.com/office/msexcel/internet/viewer

Envoy
http://www.corel.com/

HTML Authoring

HTML Editors

Macintosh

BBEdit HTML Extensions
http://www.uji.es/bbedit-html-extensions.html

BBEdit HTML Tools
http://www.york.ac.uk/~ld11/BBEditTools.html

BeyondPress (QuarkXPress)
http://www.astrobyte.com/astrobyte/BeyondPressInfo.html

GT_HTML.DOT
http://www.gatech.edu/word_html/release.htm

HTML Editor for Macintosh
http://dragon.acadiau.ca/~giles/HTML_Editor/Documentation.html

HoTMetaL and HoTMetaL PRO
http://www.sq.com/

MSWToHTML (MS Word 6.0)
http://dreyer.ucsf.edu/mswtohtml.html

WebDoor
http://www.opendoor.com/WebDoor/WebDoor.html

WebWorks Publisher (FrameMaker)
http://www.quadralay.com/products/WebWorks/Publisher/index.html

Windows

AOL Press
http://www.navisoft.com/

GT_HTML.DOT
http://www.gatech.edu/word_html/release.htm

HotDog 32 Bit
http://www.sausage.com/hotdog32.htm

HoTMetaL and HoTMetaL PRO
http://www.sq.com/

HTML Assistant
http://www.brooknorth.com/products/products.html

Netscape Communicator
http://home.netscape.com/comprod/products/communicator/index.html

WebWorks Publisher (FrameMaker)
http://www.quadralay.com/products/WebWorks/Publisher/index.html

Microsoft FrontPage
http://www.microsoft.com/frontpage/

Microsoft Internet Assistant for Word
http://www.microsoft.com/pages/deskapps/word/ia/default.htm

HTML Reference

A Compendium of HTML Elements
http://www.htmlcompendium.org/index.htm

HTML 4 You Tag Index
http://www-ia.hiof.no/~linettev/html4U/tag-inx.htm#tag

Introducing HTML 3.2
http://www.w3c.org/pub/WWW/MarkUp/Wilbur

Project: Cougar (HTML 4.0)
http://www.w3.org/MarkUp/Cougar/

HTML Reference Manual
http://www.sandia.gov/sci_compute/html_ref.html

The HTML Station
http://www.december.com/html/

Style Guides

HTML Bad Style Page
http://www.earth.com/bad-style/

The HyperTerrorist Checklist of WWWeb Design Errors
http://www.mcs.net/~jorn/html/net/checklist.html

Netscape's Creating Net Sites
http://home.netscape.com/assist/net_sites/

Net Tips for Writers and Designers
http://www.dsiegel.com/tips/

Sun's Guide to Web Style
http://www.sun.com/styleguide/

The Ten Commandments of HTML FAQ
http://www.visdesigns.com/design/commandments.html

Thoughts on WWWeb Style
http://www.mcs.net/~jorn/html/net/style.html

Top Ten Ways to Tell If You Have a Sucky Home Page
http://www.glover.com/ss.html

Yale C/AIM WWW Style Manual
http://info.med.yale.edu/caim/manual/index.html

HTML Validation

Doctor HTML
http://www2.imagiware.com/RxHTML/

HTML Validation Tools (list)
http://www.khoros.unm.edu/staff/neilb/weblint/validation.html

htmlchek
http://uts.cc.utexas.edu/~churchh/htmlchek.html

Kinder, Gentler Validation
http://ugweb.cs.ualberta.ca/~gerald/validate/

Weblint
http://www.khoral.com/staff/neilb/weblint.html

WebTechs HTML Validation Service
http://www.webtechs.com/html-val-svc/

Why Validate Your HTML
http://www.earth.com/bad-style/why-validate.html

Online Marketing & Business

Online Marketing

Art of Business Web Site Promotion
http://deadlock.com/promote/

The Comprehensive Guide to Internet Marketing
http://web.nstar.net/~harshaw/marketing.html

Marketing Tips Page
http://www.onlineconsulting.com/tips.html

Virtual Promote
http://www.virtualpromote.com/

Gator's Byte
http://www.gators-byte.com/default.htm

Banners & Advertising

BannerCentral
http://www.bannercentral.org/

Link Buddies
http://www.linkbuddies.com/

The Link Exchange
http://www.linkexchange.com/

Net-On's Banner Exchange
http://www.net-on.se:81/banner/index.html

Search Engine Tools

123 Register Me
http://www.123registerme.com/

Acclaim Web Services
http://www.acclaimweb.com/

Submit It!
http://www.submit-it.com/

Position Agent
http://www.positionagent.com/

WebStep Top 100 Free Listings
http://www.mmgco.com/top100.html

Cutting-Edge Technologies

DHTML

Dynamic HTML at Microsoft
http://www.microsoft.com/workshop/author/dhtml/

Dynamic HTML Zone
http://www.dhtmlzone.com/

Inside Dynamic HTML
http://www.insideDHTML.com/dl/home.htm

Macromedia Dreamweaver
http://www.macromedia.com/

W3C Document Object Model
http://www.w3.org/DOM/

JavaScript

Gamelan JavaScript List
http://javascript.developer.com/

LiveSoftware's JavaScript Resource Center
http://jrc.livesoftware.com/

Netscape 3.0 JavaScript Documentation
http://home.netscape.com/eng/mozilla/3.0/handbook/javascript/

Netscape's JavaScript Newsgroup
http://developer.netscape.com/index.html

The JavaScript FAQ
http://www.freqgrafx.com/411/jsfaq.html

Java

Black Coffee (Applets and Source code)
http://www.km-cd.com/black_coffee/

EarthWeb's Gamelan
http://www.gamelan.com/

EGOR Animator
http://www.sausage.com/store/indexST1.htm

Java Animation Samples
http://java.sun.com/applets/applets/TumblingDuke/example1.html

Java Applet Rating Service
http://www.jars.com/

The Java Boutique
http://javaboutique.internet.com/

The Java Centre
http://www.java.co.uk/javacentre.html

Java Developers Kit (JDK)
http://www.javasoft.com/java.sun.com/products/JDK/index.html

JavaSoft Applets
http://java.sun.com/applets/

RadJa (create Java applets without programming)
http://www.radja.com/

Symantec's Java Central
http://www.symantec.com/javacentral/

VRML

blaxxun interactive's Passport
http://www2.blacksun.com/products/index.html

Live 3D
http://home.netscape.com/comprod/products/navigator/live3d/download_live3d.html

Caligari trueSpace
http://www.caligari.com/

Virtual Home Space Builder (VHSB)
http://cosmo.sgi.com/products/homespace/vhsb/

VRealm Builder
http://www.ligos.com/

VRML Repository at SDSC
http://www.sdsc.edu/vrml

VRMLUser at ZDNet
http://www.zdnet.com/products/vrmluser.html

VRScout viewer
http://www.chaco.com/cgi-bin/download.cgi?def-product=scout+plugin

WIRL Interactive 3D Browser
http://www.platinum.com/

XML (Extensible Markup Language)

Microsoft XML Parser in Java
http://www.microsoft.com/standards/xml/xmlparse.htm

W3C Extensible Markup Language
http://www.w3.org/XML/

What is XML?
http://www.gca.org/conf/xml/xml_what.htm

XML, Java, and the future of the Web
http://sunsite.unc.edu/pub/sun-info/standards/xml/why/xmlapps.html

Graphic Arts

Graphics, Backgrounds, Lines, Icons & More

The Color Machine (HTML Background Color Generator)
http://ucunix.san.uc.edu/~hamilte/colors.html

Iconolog 96: The Art of Virtual Litter
http://www.ozemail.com.au/~afactor/iconolog.html

Kira's Icon Library
http://www59.metronet.com/kicons/

Leo's Icon Archive
http://www.silverpoint.com/leo/lia/

Terry Gould's Home Page Graphics

http://netaccess.on.ca/~kestrel/list1.html
mirror site: http://www.vol.it/mirror/Graphics/list.html

Timid Textures
http://www.santarosa.edu/~tmurphy/texture.html

The Virtual Library
http://www.mindspring.com/~phaeton/Vsteve.html

Clip Art

ClickArt Studio Series
http://www.clickart.com/

Corel Professional Photos
http://www.corel.com/

Image Club Graphics Inc.
http://www.adobe.com/imageclub/

Artbeats WebTools
http://www.artbeatswebtools.com/

Graphic Applications & Utilities

Windows

CorelDRAW!
http://www.corel.com/

Fractal Design Painter
http://www.fractal.com/

Graphic Workshop for Windows and GIF Construction Set
http://www.mindworkshop.com/alchemy

Group 42 WebImage
http://www.group42.com/webimage.htm

Lview Pro
http://www.lview.com/

LiveImage
http://www.mediatec.com/

Map Edit (shareware image map editor)
http://www.boutell.com/

Microsoft Image Composer
http://www.microsoft.com/imagecomposer/

Kai's Power Tools
http://www.metatools.com/kpt/

Paint Shop Pro
http://www.jasc.com/

WinGIF
http://heart.engr.csulb.edu/~acm/swreviews/grafix/wingif.html

Macintosh

Adobe Dimensions, Illustrator, Photoshop
http://www.adobe.com/

clip2gif
ftp://ftp-2.amug.org/info-mac/gst/grf/

Fractal Design Painter
http://www.fractal.com/

Kai's Power Tools
http://www.metatools.com/kpt/

Macromedia Freehand
http://www.macromedia.com/Tools/Freehand/

Multimedia Applications & Utilities

Macintosh

Adobe Premiere
http://www.adobe.com/

Avid's VideoShop
http://www.avid.com/

Cambium Sound Choice
http://cambium.com/cambium

ClickArt
http://www.clickart.com/

Digidesign's Sound Designer II
http://www.digidesign.com/

Elastic Reality
http://www.avid.com/

flattenMoov
ftp://mirror.apple.com/mirrors/info-mac/_Graphic_&_Sound_Tool/
_Movie/flatmoov.hqx

InterActive

Kai's Power Tools
http://www.hsc.com/
Macromedia Director http://www.macromedia.com/

Maven QTR viewer
ftp://mirrors.aol.com/pub/info-mac/comm/_MacTCP/maven-20d37.hqx

MPEG/CD
http://www.kauai.com/~bbal/

Multimedia Utilities

CamraMan
http://www.mtw.com/

Opcode Systems audio products
http://www.opcode.com/

QuickEditor
ftp://mirror.apple.com/mirrors/info-mac/_Graphic_&_Sound_Tool/
_Movie/quick-editor-361.hqx

QuickTime for Windows & QuickTime Development Kit
http://www.apple.com/

Radius Spigot Power AV and Spigot Pro
http://www.radius.com/

SoundEdit 16
http://www.macromedia.com/

Sound Effects
ftp://ftp.alpcom.it/software/mac/Ricci

Sound Hack
ftp://music.calarts.edu/pub/SoundHack/

Sound Manager
ftp://ftp.info.apple.com/Apple.Support.Area/Apple.Software.Updates/US/
Macintosh/System/Other_System

SoundTrack
http://www.softek.com/mmworks.htm

Sparkle
ftp://mirror.apple.com/mirrors/info-mac/_Graphic_&_Sound_Tool/_Movie

Windows

Goldwave
http://www.goldwave.com/

Opcode Systems audio products
http://www.opcode.com/

Adobe Premiere
http://www.adobe.com/

Cambium Sound Choice
http://cambium.com/cambium

ClickArt Studio Series
http://www.clickart.com/

Macromedia Director for Windows
http://www.macromedia.com/

Intel Smart Video Recorder
http://www.intel.com/

MediaStudio
http://www.intel.com/

MPEGPlay
http://www.ncsa.uiuc.edu/SDG/Software/WinMosaic/

QuickTime for Windows & QuickTime Development Kit
http://www.apple.com/

SoundTrack
http://www.softek.com/mmworks.htm

Turtle Beach Systems
http://www.voyetra.com/tbwelcome.htm

WPLANY
http://www.ncsa.uiuc.edu/SDG/Software/WinMosaic/
http://www.govst.edu/users/xwww/ecn/software/win/wplany.html

XingCD
http://www.xing.com/

Software

Software Archives

Windows

Beverly Hills Software Windows NT Resource Center
http://www.bhs.com/

Comprehensive List of Freeware and Shareware Sites
http://pilot.msu.edu/user/heinric6/soft_win95.htm

c | net SHAREWARE.COM
http://www.SHAREWARE.COM/

Jumbo!
http://www.jumbo.com/

Microsoft's FREE Windows 95 Companion Software
http://www.microsoft.com/windows/software.htm

Nerd's Heaven
http://boole.stanford.edu/nerdsheaven.html

Tucows
http://www.tucows.com/

Windows95.com
http://www.windows95.com/

Spry, Inc.
http://www.spry.com/

Topsoft
http://topsoft.com/

Macintosh

Comprehensive List of Freeware and Shareware Sites
http://pilot.msu.edu/user/heinric6/soft_mac.htm

Info-Mac Archive
ftp://mirrors.aol.com/pub/info-mac/

Nerd's Heaven
http://boole.stanford.edu/nerdsheaven.html

Spry, Inc.
http://www.spry.com/

Topsoft
http://topsoft.com/

Tucows
http://www.tucows.com/

ZDNet Software Library
http://headlines.yahoo.com/zddownload/macintosh/

UNIX/Linux

Comprehensive List of Freeware and Shareware Sites
http://pilot.msu.edu/user/heinric6/soft_unix.htm

Topsoft
http://topsoft.com/

GNU Software Project
http://www.gnu.org/

Compression Utilities

Windows

Drag And Zip
http://www.acs.oakland.edu/oak/SimTel/win3/archiver.html

GnuZip
ftp://prep.ai.mit.edu/pub/gnu

PKZip
http://www.acs.oakland.edu/oak/SimTel/win3/archiver.html

WinZIP
http://www.winzip.com/

Macintosh

Compact Pro
ftp://ftp.uwtc.washington.edu/pub/Mac/CompEnc/

MacBinary II +
ftp://ftp.uwtc.washington.edu/pub/Mac/CompEnc/
StuffIt Deluxe, StuffIt Expander http://www.aladdinsys.com/

UNIX

GNU tar
http://www.ensta.fr/internet/unix/archive_compress/GNU-tar.html

MKS Toolkit
http://www.mks.com/solution/tk/

UUDeview
http://www.uni-frankfurt.de/~fp/uudeview/

Web Servers

Web Server Programs

Macintosh

Aretha/Frontier
http://www.scripting.com/gimme5/default.html

httpd4Mac
http://sodium.ch.man.ac.uk/pages/httpd4Mac/home.html

MacCommon LISP Server
ftp://ftp.ai.mit.edu/pub/users/jcma/cl-http/

MacTCP Switcher
ftp://ftp.acns.nwu.edu/pub/jlnstuff/mactcp-switcher/

Netscape Communications Server
http://home.netscape.com/

WebSTAR Server
http://www.starnine.com/webstar.html

Windows

HTTPD
http://tech.west.ora.com/win-httpd

EMWAC HTTPS and WAIS Toolkit
http://emwac.ed.ac.uk./html/internet_toolchest/top.html

Microsoft Internet Information Server (NT)
http://www.microsoft.com/iis

Microsoft Personal Web Server (95)
http://www.microsoft.com/

Netscape SuiteSpot Server
http://home.netscape.com/

Purveyor
http://www.process.com/

WebSite
http://website.ora.com/

UNIX

AOLServer
http://www.aolserver.com/index.html

Apache SSL Server
http://www.c2.net/products/stronghold/

Apache Week
http://www.apacheweek.com/

Common Lisp Hypermedia Server
http://www.ai.mit.edu/projects/iiip/doc/cl-http/home-page.html

NCSA httpd
http://hoohoo.ncsa.uiuc.edu/

OpenMarket Servers
http://www.openmarket.com/products/

W3C httpd (formerly CERN httpd)
http://www.w3.org/Daemon/

CGI (Common Gateway Interface) & Perl

Aretha/Frontier
http://www.scripting.com/gimme5/default.html

BIPED (BI-protocol Page EDitor)
http://www.eol.ists.ca/~dunlop/biped/

The cgi-lib.pl Home Page
http://www.bio.cam.ac.uk/web/form.html

CGI.pm—a Perl5 CGI Library
http://www-genome.wi.mit.edu/ftp/pub/software/WWW/cgi_docs.html

CGIHTML
http://www.eekim.com/software/cgihtml/

CSM Proxy
http://alibaba.ustria.eu.et

Fly
http://www.unimelb.edu.au/fly/fly.html

Forms in Perl
http://www.seas.upenn.edu/~mengwong/forms/

Matt's Script Archive
http://www.worldwidemart.com/scripts/

Perl for Win32
http://www.perl.hip.com/

Un-CGI
http://www.hyperion.com/~koreth/uncgi.html

O'Reilly's WebBoard, PolyForm, and Perl Resource Kit
http://software.ora.com/

Yahoo—Computers and Internet: Internet: World Web: Programming
http://www.yahoo.com/Computers_and_Internet/World_Wide_Web/
Programming

Log Analysis

Access Watch
http://accesswatch.com/

BrowserCounter
http://www.nihongo.org/snowhare/utilities/browsercounter.html

FTPWebLog
http://www.nihongo.org/snowhare/utilities/ftpweblog/

httpd_log 3.0
http://alumni.dgs.monash.edu.au/~richard/httpd_log/

MacHTTP Utilities
http://arpp.carleton.ca/mac/tool/logs.html

VBStats
http://tech.west.ora.com/win-httpd/

wusage 5
http://www.boutell.com/wusage/

Link Verification

Dr.Watson
http://www.addy.com/watson/

InfoLink
http://www.biggbyte.com/

Linkbot
http://www.linkbot.com/

lvfry
http://www.cs.dartmouth.edu/~crow/lvrfy.html

Net Mechanic
http://www.netmechanic.com/

Web Hosting Companies

American Information Systems Inc.
http://www.ais.net

Automatrix, Inc.
http://www.automatrix.com/

BBN Planet
http://www.bbnplanet.com/

Best Internet Communications Inc.
http://www.best.com/

BizNet Technologies
http://www.BizNet.com.blacksburg.va.us/index.html

BudgetWeb (Hosting Selection Service)
http://www.budgetweb.com/

Clark Internet Services, Inc.
http://www.clark.net

Computing Engineers
http://www.wwa.com/

CTS Network Services
http://www.cts.com/

GeoCities
http://www.geocities.com/

Infoboard
http://www.infoboard.com/infoboard

InterNex Information Services, Inc.
http://www.internex.net

Mnematics, Incorporated
http://www.mne.com/

Multispace
http://multispace.com/

Nets.com
http://www.nets.com/

Webcom
http://www.webcom.com/

UUNET Technologies, Inc.
http://www.uu.net

Print Resources _____

Magazines _____

Boardwatch Magazine
8500 W. Bowles Avenue, Suite 210
Littleton, CO 80123-9701
http://www.boardwatch.com/

BYTE
McGraw-Hill Companies, Inc.
P.O. Box 552
Hightstown, NJ 08520
http://www.byte.com/

Internet & Java Advisor
Advisor Publications Inc.
P.O. Box 469048
Escondido, CA 92046-9048
http://www.advisor.com/

Internet World
Mecklermedia Corporation
P.O. Box 7461
Red Oak, IA 51591-2461
http://www.iw.com/

Java Report
SIGS Publications
P.O. Box 5050
Brentwood, TN 37024-5050
http://www.sigs.com/

MacUser
Newsstand/Subscription
P.O. Box 56986
Boulder, CO 80322-6986
http://www.zdnet.com/macuser

Macworld
Newsstand/Subscription
501 Second Street
San Francisco, CA 94107
http://www.macworld.com/

The Net
Imagine Publishing, Inc.
150 North Hill Drive
Brisbane, CA 94005
http://www.thenet-usa.com/

NetGuide Magazine
CMP Media Inc.
P.O. Box 420235
Palm Coast, FL 32142-0235
http://www.netguide.com/

PC Magazine
Ziff-Davis Publishing Company
P.O. Box 54093
Boulder, CO 80322-4093
http://www.zdnet.com/pcmag/

PC World
P.O. Box 55029
Boulder, CO 80322-5029
http://www.pcworld.com/

The Perl Journal
P.O. Box 54
Boston, MA 02101
http://work.media.mit.edu/the_perl_journal/

The Red Herring
Herring Communications, Inc.
1550 Bryant Street, Suite 950
San Francisco, CA 94103-9574
http://www.herring.com/

WEB Developer
Mecklermedia Corporation
P.O. Box 7436
Red Oak, IA 51591-0463
http://www.webdeveloper.com/

Web Techniques
Miller Freeman, Inc.
P.O. Box 58730
Boulder, CO 80322-8730
http://www.web-techniques.com/

WebServer Magazine
Computer Publishing Group
320 Washington Street
Brookline, MA 02146
http://www.cpg.com/ws/

Windows Sources
Ziff-Davis Publishing Company
P.O. Box 59100
Boulder, CO 80322-9100
http://www.zdnet.com/wsources/

WIRED
Wired Ventures Inc.
P.O. Box 191826
San Francisco, CA 94119-9866
http://www.hotwired.com/

Yahoo! Internet Life
Ziff-Davis Publishing Company
P.O. Box 53380
Boulder, CO 80322-3380
http://www.zdnet.com/yil

Books

Designing Web Graphics 2
Lynda Weinman
New Riders
ISBN: 1-56205-715-4

The CGI Book
William E. Weinman
New Riders
ISBN: 1-56205-571-2

CGI Programming in C & Perl
Thomas Boutell
Addison-Wesley
ISBN: 0-201-42219-0

CGI Programming on the World Wide Web
Shishir Gundavaram
O'Reilly & Associates, Inc.
ISBN: 1-56592-168-2

Creating Killer Web Sites 2nd Edition
David Siegel
Hayden Books
ISBN: 1-56830-433-1

How to Set Up & Maintain a World Wide Web Site
Lincoln D. Stein
Addison-Wesley
ISBN: 0-201-63389-2

HTML: The Definitive Guide
Chuck Musciano and Bill Kennedy
O'Reilly & Associates, Inc.
ISBN: 1-56592-175-5

Introduction to CGI/Perl
Steven E. Brenner and Edwin Aoki
M&T Books
ISBN: 1-55851-478-3

Java Primer Plus
Paul M. Tyma, Gabriel Torok, and Troy Downing
Waite Group Press
ISBN: 1-57169-062-X

The Java Programming Language 2nd Edition
Ken Arnold
Addison-Wesley
ISBN: 0-20131-006-6

JavaScript & Netscape Wizardry
Dan Shafer
Coriolis Group Books
ISBN: 1-883577-86-1

Learning Perl
Randal L. Schwartz
O'Reilly & Associates, Inc.
ISBN: 1-56592-284-0

Official Netscape JavaScript Book
Peter Kent and John Kent
Netscape Press
ISBN: 1-56604-465-0

Perl by Example
Ellie Quigley
Prentice Hall
ISBN: 0-13-122839-0

Programming Perl
Larry Wall and Randal L. Schwartz
O'Reilly & Associates, Inc.
ISBN: 1-56592-149-6

Teach Yourself Java in 21 Days
Laura Lemay and Charles L. Perkins
Sams Net
ISBN: 1-57521-030-4

Teach Yourself JavaScript in a Week
Arman Danesh
Sams Net
ISBN: 1-57521-073-8

Teach Yourself Web Publishing With HTML 3.2 in 14 Days
Laura Lemay
Sams Net
ISBN: 1-57521-096-7

Web Catalog Cookbook
Cliff Allen, Deborah Kania
John Wiley & Sons
ISBN: 0-47118-331-8

Web Design Resources Directory : Tools & Techniques for Designing Your Web Pages
Ray Davis, Eileen Mullin
MacMillan Computer Publishing
ISBN: 0-78971-060-9

Appendix D

Sample Scripts That Store Form Input Into a Log File

UNIX Web Servers _____

```perl
#!/usr/local/bin/perl

# guestf.cgi is a Perl Guestbook program that
# creates a log file of form input.

require ('cgi-lib.pl');
&ReadParse;

print "Content-type:text/html\n\n";

# If the Browser says, "Document contains no data"
# it means that the following line executed the
# "die" part -- in other words the program quit.
# To rectify this problem, create a file named
# guest.log in the current directory and change
# the permissions by entering chmod 666 guest.log
```

```
open (MYLOG,">>guest.log")||die"dead!";
flock(MYLOG,2);
print MYLOG<<"_LOGEND_";
Guest Book Entry Information\n
The name of the person entering the form:\n
$in{'fname'} $in{'lname'}\n
The person's e-mail address is:\n
$in{'email'}\n
The person's phone number is:\n
$in{'phone'}\n
The person made the following comments:\n
$in{'comments'}\n
-------------------------------------------------

_LOGEND_
flock(MYLOG,8);
close(MYLOG);
print<<"_ENDMSG_";
<!--This begins the HTML document that is displayed after the CGI/Perl
script is run.-->
<HTML>
<HEAD>
<TITLE>Form Results</TITLE>
</HEAD>
<BODY>
<H1>Guest Book Entry Information</H1>
<P>Hello $in{'fname'} $in{'lname'}</P>
<P>Thank you for filling out the form!</P>
<P>According to your input your e-mail address is $in{'email'} and your
phone number is $in{'phone'}</P>
<P>Back to the
<A HREF="http://www.authors.com/Navigator4/prog.html">Perl CGI tutorial</
A>.</P>
</BODY>
</HTML>
_ENDMSG_
```

Web Site Server

```
# A Perl Guestbook program named
#       guestbk.pl that uses cgi-lib.pl
require ('cgi-lib.pl');
&ReadParse;
```

```perl
# Make sure you create the
# comment file named comments.log
# in the temp directory before you
# test your program.

$commentfile="c:/temp/comments.log";

print "Content-type:text/html\n\n";

open(COMMENT,">>$commentfile")||die"dead!";
print COMMENT<<"_LOGEND_";
Guest Book Entry Information\n
The name of the person entering the form:\n
 $in{'fname'} $in{'lname'}\n
The person's e-mail address is:\n
$in{'email'}\n
The person's phone number is:\n
$in{'phone'}\n
The person made the following comments:\n
$in{'comments'}\n
-----------------------------------------------
_LOGEND_
close(COMMENT);
print<<"_ENDMSG_";
<!--This begins the HTML document that is displayed after the CGI/Perl
script is run.-->
<HTML>
<HEAD>
<TITLE>Form Results</TITLE>
</HEAD>
<BODY>
<H1>Guest Book Entry Information</H1>
<P>Hello $in{'fname'} $in{'lname'}</P>
<P>Thank you for filling out the form!</P>
<P>According to your input your e-mail address is $in{'email'} and your
phone number is $in{'phone'}</P>
<P>Back to the
<A HREF="http://www.authors.com/Navigator4/prog.html">Perl CGI
tutorial</A>.</P>
</BODY>
</HTML>
_ENDMSG_
```

Index